INFORMATION UPDATE

Real Estate Education Company, 500 No.

W9-CRZ-879

☐ Please inform me of new real estate publications as soon as they are available.
☐ Please inform me of special offers on real estate publications.
I understand that these requests in no way obligate me.
I have already purchased _____

(name of books)

Name _____

Organization _____

Title _____

Address _____

City _____ State _____ Zip _____

Please send me:

Quantity

ORDER FORM QUANTITY DISCOUNT AVAILABLE FOR SCHOOL ORDERS

Title **Price**

Title	Price
Effective Real Estate Sales and Marketing	$19.95
Essentials of Real Estate Finance, 2nd ed.	$24.95
Essentials of Real Estate Investment	$24.95
Fundamentals of Real Estate Appraisal, 2nd ed.	$24.95
Guide to Passing the Real Estate Exam (ACT)	$14.95
Home Buying	$ 1.95
How About a Career in Real Estate?	$ 1.95
How to Fill Out the Freddie Mac—Fannie Mae Residential Appraisal Report	$ 9.95
How to Fill Out the Fannie Mae—Freddie Mac Appraisal Report/Small Residential Income Property	$ 9.95
How to Prepare for the Texas Real Estate Exam, 2nd ed.	$14.95
How to Save Tax Dollars When You Sell Your House, 4th ed.	$ 1.95
Introduction to Real Estate Law	$22.50
The Language of Real Estate 2nd ed.	$21.95
Mastering Real Estate Mathematics, 3rd ed.	$17.25
Modern Real Estate Practice, 9th ed.	$26.50
The Professional Guide to Real Estate Closing	$16.95
Profits from Real Estate Publicity	$21.95
Property Management	$24.95
Protecting Your Sales Commission: Professional Liability in Real Estate	$24.95
Questions and Answers to Help You Pass the Real Estate License Exam (ETS)	$14.95
Real Estate Fundamentals	$19.95
Real Estate: A Woman's World	$12.95
Real Estate Brokerage: A Success Guide	$29.95
Real Estate Brokerage in the '80s: Survival Among the Giants	$14.95
The Real Estate Education Company Real Estate Exam Manual, 2nd ed. (ETS)	$14.95
Real Estate Ethics	$ 9.25
Real Estate Investment Decisions: Taxation After ERTA	$69.95
Real Estate Revolution: Who Will Survive?	$12.95
Residential Construction	$19.95
Successful Industrial Real Estate Brokerage, 2nd ed.	$59.95
Successful Leasing and Selling of Office Property	$59.95
Successful Leasing and Selling of Retail Property	$59.95
Taxation of Real Estate in the United States	$59.95

The following supplements for MODERN REAL ESTATE PRACTICE are priced at $8.95 each:

__ Alabama	__ Illinois 6th ed.	__ Maryland 3rd ed.	__ Nevada	__ North Dakota	__ Tennessee
__ Arizona 3rd ed.	__ Indiana	__ Massachusetts 2nd ed.	__ New Hampshire 2nd ed.	__ Ohio 5th ed.	__ Virginia
__ Arkansas 2nd ed.	__ Iowa	__ Michigan 2nd ed.	__ New Jersey 3rd ed.	__ Oklahoma	__ Washington
__ Connecticut 2nd ed.	__ Kansas	__ Minnesota 3rd ed.	__ New York	__ South Carolina	__ Wisconsin 2nd ed.
__ Idaho 3rd ed.	__ Kentucky 2nd ed.	__ Missouri	__ North Carolina		

Other titles in the Modern Real Estate Practice series:

Title	Price
Modern Real Estate Practice Study Guide	$ 9.25
*Modern Real Estate Principles in California, 2nd ed.	$27.95
*Modern Real Estate Practice in Florida	$18.50
*Modern Real Estate Practice in Pennsylvania, 3rd ed.	$27.95
*Modern Real Estate Practice in Texas, 3rd ed.	$26.50

*MODERN REAL ESTATE PRACTICE and its supplement are combined.
Prices subject to change without notice. Turn card over to complete your order.

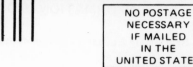

BUSINESS REPLY MAIL
FIRST CLASS PERMIT NO. 56502 CHICAGO, IL

POSTAGE WILL BE PAID BY:

REAL ESTATE EDUCATION COMPANY
500 NORTH DEARBORN STREET   DEPT. E
CHICAGO, ILLINOIS 60610 9987

ORDER CARD

PAYMENT MUST ACCOMPANY ALL ORDERS: (check one)
☐ check or money order enclosed (payable to Real Estate Education Company)
☐ charge to my credit card (circle one) VISA or MASTERCARD
    Account No._____ Exp. date_____
OR CALL OUR TOLL-FREE ORDERING HOTLINE (800) 621-9621 WITH YOUR CHARGE CARD (Illinois residents please
call (800) 572-9510).

Total cost of books ordered	$ _____
Add $2.50 or 7% for postage and handling, whichever is greater	$ _____
Add sales tax:	
Illinois residents please add 6%;	
	$ _____
TOTAL ENCLOSED	$ _____

BPNA-086

Prices subject to change without notice.
All orders will be shipped 4th class mail or equivalent, unless special handling is requested and paid for in advance.

Please ship books to:
Name _____
Organization _____
Address _____
City _____ State _____ Zip _____
Authorized Signature _____

Mail your payment and order form to: **Real Estate Education Company, Dept. E,** 500 North Dearborn, Chicago, IL 60610. 4/82

Turn card over to indicate your book selections.

The Language of Real Estate

2nd Edition

John W. Reilly

 REAL ESTATE EDUCATION COMPANY/ Chicago

To Kristine, Sean Patrick, and Jennifer, who tore, scribbled on, mutilated, crumpled, chewed—but, fortunately, did not swallow the manuscript.

ISBN: 0-88462-603-2

Copyright © 1982, 1977 by Development Systems Corporation

Published by Real Estate Education Company/Chicago, a subsidiary company of Longman Group Limited

82 83 84 10 9 8 7 6 5 4 3 2 1

Library of Congress Cataloging in Publication Data

Reilly, John W.
  The language of real estate.

  Includes index.
   1. Real property—United States—Dictionaries.
2. Real estate business—Law and legislation—
United States—Dictionaries. I. Title.
KF568.5.R44   1982   346.7304'3'0321   82-15026
ISBN 0-88462-603-2   347.306430321

preface

The Language of Real Estate is the result of many years of difficult and thorough work in researching the answers to everyday problems in real estate. Numerous books and articles on real estate taxes, condominiums, appraisal, finance, law, contracts, and the like, are good source materials for the real estate broker or salesperson, but their volume requires one to maintain an extensive and expensive real estate library. This book is designed to eliminate this problem. **The Language of Real Estate** is a totally functional real estate reference book—a comprehensive, single-volume, instant-answer book to just about any problem or question concerning real estate principles and practices in the United States.

The real estate industry has undergone considerable change since this book was first published in 1977. This second edition has been created to reflect those changes. Over 500 new terms have been added to the book, bringing the total number of definitions to more than 2200. Definitions that appeared in the first edition have been revised, and in many cases expanded, in order to provide the reader the most current and precise answers possible. Under each word is a basic definition, several applications, and cross-references to aid the reader in understanding related items.

The Language of Real Estate also contains several helpful special features:

A **complete subject classification of terms** to assist those who are concentrating their studies in specific areas.

A **list of over 300 abbreviations** and their meanings, frequently encountered in the real estate business, such as special words, concepts, and organizations.

The **REALTORS® Code of Ethics** of the NATIONAL ASSOCIATION OF REAL-TORS®, included in its entirety, as well as the complete **Standards of Practice** relating to the Code.

A **sample closing problem,** featuring prorations and computations common to most residential real estate transactions. The closing problem is illustrated on a settlement statement worksheet, as well as on a common closing statement and on a RESPA settlement statement.

acknowledgments

What started out ten years ago as a basic 40-page glossary has evolved into the comprehensive real estate reference book you are now reading. The book is designed to quickly resolve the many questions about real estate often posed to me as a real estate attorney, broker, instructor, and lecturer in real estate law and practice. Many people have helped along the way and to them I extend a warm "Mahalo."

Special thanks goes to **Ms. Jacqueline L.S. Earle,** a Honolulu attorney and REALTOR® who contributed a considerable amount of time, energy, and talent in the process of putting together the original version of the book.

I want to give special recognition to **Norwood Robb,** president, and **George Ratterman,** vice president, of the Jones Real Estate Schools, Inc., Denver, Colorado. The school has used the first edition with nearly 10,000 of its students, and Robby was thus able to give me invaluable insight into areas of improvement for this edition. Once again, Robby, thanks for your support and input.

I also wish to acknowledge the time and effort in reviewing the entire manuscript of two exceptional real estate attorneys in the state of Hawaii: **Thomas A. Bodden** and **Jeffrey S. Grad.** Thanks also goes to **Alan N. Tonnon** of Bellevue, Washington.

For their special assistance and patience in typing the manuscript, I thank **Yvonne Gates, Karen Hara,** and **Irene Honjo.**

Another special thanks goes to **Peter A. Clarke** and **Paul Cramer** of the San Francisco firm of Clarke and Cramer, Inc., for their expertise in developing the industrial and commercial real estate terms.

I would also like to thank **W. Dean Davis** of William Rainey Harper Junior College, Palatine, Illinois, **Melvyn Lissner** of the New Jersey Realty Institute, Garwood, New Jersey, **John L. Schlapman** of Wauwatosa Realty Company, Wauwatosa, Wisconsin, **Joseph E. Spalding,** J.E. Spalding Real Estate, Waukesha, Wisconsin, and **Ridgely P. Ware** of Rutgers University, Paterson, New Jersey, for their contributions to the edition.

It is indeed a rare occasion when an author can work with a publisher that is so well-versed in the subject. **Real Estate Education Company** retains a team of experts in all phases of real estate publication. They made my writing job a relatively simple one. It was a pleasure working with many members of their team, especially **Ingrid Ashcroft** who directed the organization and production of the final copy of the second edition.

And last, a very special word of appreciation to my wife, **Patty,** for all her support and encouragement throughout all stages of the book's production.

The author and the publisher welcome any comments, criticisms, or suggestions from readers that will help future revisions.

John W. Reilly
Honolulu, Hawaii

subject classification of terms

ACCOUNTING (SEE TAX)

ACCOUNT PAYABLE
ACCOUNT RECEIVABLE
ACCRUAL METHOD
ACCRUED
ACCRUED DEPRECIATION
ACQUISITION COST
ASSET
BALANCE SHEET
BOOK VALUE
CAPITALIZE
CASH METHOD
CREDIT
DEBIT
DEPRECIATION ALLOWANCE
DISBURSEMENT
LIABILITY
NET WORTH
PROFIT AND LOSS
  STATEMENT
PRO FORMA STATEMENT
QUICK ASSETS
WRITE-OFF

AGENCY (SEE BROKERAGE)

AGENCY
AGENCY COUPLED WITH AN
  INTEREST
AGENT
ATTORNEY-IN-FACT
BROKER
CODE OF ETHICS
COMMINGLING
DUAL AGENCY
EQUAL DIGNITIES RULE
ETHICS
FIDUCIARY
FULL DISCLOSURE
GENERAL AGENT
IMPLIED AGENCY
IMPUTED NOTICE

INSPECTION
LIMITED POWER OF
  ATTORNEY
OSTENSIBLE AGENCY
PARTIALLY DISCLOSED
  PRINCIPAL
POWER OF ATTORNEY
PRINCIPAL
RATIFICATION
RESPONDEAT SUPERIOR
SCOPE OF AUTHORITY
SPECIAL AGENT
SUBAGENT
TRUSTEE
UNDISCLOSED AGENCY

APPRAISAL

ABSTRACTION
ACQUISITION APPRAISAL
ADJUSTMENTS
AESTHETIC VALUE
AGE-LIFE DEPRECIATION
AMENITIES
APPOINTMENTS
APPRAISAL
APPRAISAL REPORT
APPRAISER
APPRECIATION
ASSEMBLAGE
ASSESSED VALUATION
AXIAL GROWTH
BALTIMORE METHOD
BAND OF INVESTMENT
BEFORE-AND-AFTER
  METHOD
BUILDING RESIDUAL
  TECHNIQUE
BUILT-UP METHOD
CAPITALIZATION
CAPITALIZATION RATE
COMPARABLES
COMPARATIVE UNIT
  METHOD

CONTRACT RENT
CONTRIBUTION
CORNER-LOT APPRAISAL
  METHODS
COST APPROACH
DEFERRED MAINTENANCE
DEMAND
DEMOGRAPHY
DEPRECIATION (APPRAISAL)
DEPTH TABLES
DIRECTIONAL GROWTH
DISCOUNTING
ECONOMIC-BASE ANALYSIS
ECONOMIC LIFE
ECONOMIC OBSOLESCENCE
ECONOMIC RENT
EFFECTIVE AGE
EFFECTIVE GROSS INCOME
ENGINEERING BREAKDOWN
  METHOD
FAIR MARKET VALUE
FEE APPRAISER
FILTERING DOWN PROCESS
FORECAST
FUNCTIONAL
  OBSOLESCENCE
FUNCTIONAL UTILITY
GOING CONCERN VALUE
GOOD WILL
GROSS INCOME MULTIPLIER
GROSS RENT MULTIPLIER
HIGHEST AND BEST USE
HOMOGENEOUS
INCOME APPROACH
INCURABLE DEPRECIATION
INFILTRATION
INTRINSIC VALUE
INWOOD TABLE
LAND ECONOMICS
LAND RESIDUAL TECHNIQUE
LETTER REPORT
MAI
MARKET-DATA APPROACH
MARKET VALUE
MISPLACED IMPROVEMENT

APPRAISAL (CONT.)

NARRATIVE REPORT
NET OPERATING INCOME
OBSERVED CONDITION
OBSOLESCENCE
OVERIMPROVEMENT
PHYSICAL DETERIORATION
PHYSICAL LIFE
PLOTTAGE VALUE
PRESENT VALUE OF ONE
  DOLLAR
PRICE
PROPERTY RESIDUAL
  TECHNIQUE
QUANTITY SURVEY
RECAPTURE RATE
RECONCILIATION
REGRESSION
REPRODUCTION COST
RESIDUAL PROCESS
REVERSIONARY FACTOR
REVERSIONARY VALUE
SCARCITY
SOCIETY OF REAL ESTATE
  APPRAISERS
SPECIAL-PURPOSE PROPERTY
SPLIT-RATE
SQUARE-FOOT METHOD
SUBJECTIVE VALUE
SUBSTITUTION
SUMMATION APPROACH
SUPPLY AND DEMAND
UNBALANCED
  IMPROVEMENT
UNDERIMPROVEMENT
UNEARNED INCREMENT
UNIFORMITY
UNIT-IN-PLACE METHOD
UNIT VALUE
USE VALUE
UTILITY VALUE
VALUE

BANKING

ACCOMMODATION PARTY
CASHIER'S CHECK
CERTIFIED CHECK
CHECK
ENDORSEMENT
HOLDER IN DUE COURSE
LETTER OF CREDIT
LINE OF CREDIT
MAKER
NEGOTIABLE INSTRUMENT
NOTICE OF DISHONOR
PAYEE

POSTDATED CHECK
SETOFF
WITHOUT RECOURSE

BROKERAGE (SEE AGENCY, LISTING)

ADVANCE FEE
ADVERTISING
AUCTION
BIRD DOG
BLIND AD
BLUE BOOK
BOILER ROOM
BRANCH OFFICE
BROKER
BROKERAGE
BROKERAGE COMMISSION
BROKER-IN-CHARGE
BUSINESS OPPORTUNITY
BUYER'S MARKET
CARAVAN
CLIENT
CLIENT TRUST ACCOUNT
COLD CANVASS
COMMISSION
COOPERATING BROKER
COUNSELING
COURTESY TO BROKERS
CUSTOMER
DEFERRED COMMISSION
DRAW
EMPTY NESTER
EXPOSURE
FALSE ADVERTISING
FARM AREA
FLOOR DUTY
FOR SALE BY OWNER
FRANCHISE
GUARANTEED SALE
  PROGRAM
INDEPENDENT CONTRACTOR
LIMITED SERVICE BROKER
LOCK BOXES
LOTTERY
ONE HUNDRED PERCENT
  COMMISSION
OPEN HOUSE
PARTICIPATING BROKER
PRINCIPAL BROKER
PROSPECT
PUFFING
READY, WILLING AND ABLE
REBATE
REFERRAL
RELOCATION COMPANY
RESIDUAL
SALES KIT

SALESPERSON
SHOPPING
  SIGNS
SITE OFFICE
SPLITTING FEES
STANDARDS OF PRACTICE
SUBMITTAL NOTICE
TRADE-IN
TRADE USAGE
TRUST FUND ACCOUNT
TURNOVER
UNETHICAL
WORKERS' COMPENSATION
  LAW

BUILDING TERMS (SEE CONSTRUCTION, DEVELOPMENT, SUBDIVISION)

ABUTMENT
ACCESSORY BUILDING
ANCHOR BOLT
APARTMENT BUILDING
ARCADE
ASH DUMP
ATTIC
BACKFILL
BALCONY
BALUSTER
BAND OR BOX SILL
BANK PARTITIONS
BASEBOARD
BASEMENT
BASE SHOE
BASE TOP MOLDING
BATTEN
BAY
BAY WINDOW
BEAM
BEARING WALL
BEDROCK
BLACKTOP
BOARD FOOT
BRACING
BRIDGING
BRITISH THERMAL UNIT
BUILDING PAPER
BUS DUCT
CANTILEVER
CASING
CATWALK
CAULKING
CHIMNEY
CHIMNEY CAP
CHIMNEY FLASHING
CHIMNEY POT

BUILDING TERMS (CONT.)

CINDER FILL
CLAPBOARD
CLEANOUT DOOR
CLEAR SPAN
COLLAR BEAM
COMBED PLYWOOD
CONDUIT
CORNICE
CORRIDOR
CURTILAGE
DAMPER
DAMPPROOFING
DEMISING WALL
DOORSTOP
DOUBLE CORNER STUD
DOUBLE-LOAD CORRIDOR
DOUBLE PLATE
DOUBLE WINDOW HEADER
DOWNSPOUT
DUCT
EAVE
EAVE TROUGH
FACADE
FELT JOINT COVER
FINISH FLOORING
FLASHING
FLOOR JOIST
FLUE
FOOTCANDLE
FOOTING
FORMICA
FOUNDATION DRAIN TILE
FOUNDATION WALL
FREE STANDING BUILDING
FRIEZE BOARD
FURRING
GIRDER
HEAD CASING
HEARTH
INDIRECT LIGHTING
INSULATION
INSULATION DISCLOSURE
JALOUSIE
JAMB
JOIST
LATH
LINTEL
LOUVER
LUMINOUS CEILING
MANTEL
MASTER SWITCH
MITER
MULLION
MUNTIN
NOSING
OVERHANG
PARAPET

PILASTER
PLATE
RAFTER
RETAINING WALL
RIDGEBOARD
ROOF BOARDS
ROOFING FELT
ROOFING SHINGLES
SHAKE
SHEAR WALL
SHOE MOLDING
SIDING
SILL
STRINGER
SUBFLOORING
TONGUE AND GROOVE
TREAD
TRIM
TRUSS
UNDER-FLOOR DUCTS
VENEER
VENT
WAINSCOTING
WALLBOARD
WALL SHEATHING
WALL STUD
WASTE LINE
WINDOW JAMB TRIM
WINDOW SASH
X-BRACING

CLOSING

ADJUSTMENTS
APPORTIONMENT
ARREARS
BACK-TO-BACK ESCROW
CLOSING
CLOSING COSTS
CLOSING STATEMENT
COLLECTION ACCOUNT
CREDIT
DOUBLE ENTRY
DOUBLE ESCROW
ESCROW
ESCROW INSTRUCTIONS
HOLDING ESCROW
IMPOUND ACCOUNT
PRECLOSING
PREPAID EXPENSES
PREPAID ITEMS
PROCEEDS-OF-LOAN
  ESCROW
PRORATE
REAL ESTATE SETTLEMENT
  PROCEDURES ACT
RELATION-BACK DOCTRINE

SETTLEMENT
UNIFORM SETTLEMENT
  STATEMENT

COMMERCIAL INVESTMENT PROPERTY (SEE LEASING)

ABSORPTION RATE
BREAK-EVEN POINT
BUILD-TO-SUIT
BULK TRANSFER
CASH FLOW
COMMERCIAL PROPERTY
COVENANT NOT TO
  COMPETE
DISCOUNTED CASH FLOW
DOWNSIDE RISK
DOWNSTROKE
GROSS AREA
GROSS INCOME
INCOME PROPERTY
INTERNAL RATE OF RETURN
LAND POOR
LEVERAGE
MAINTENANCE
NEGATIVE CASH FLOW
NEIGHBORHOOD SHOPPING
  CENTER
NET AFTER TAXES
NET INCOME
NET YIELD
NUT
OFFICE BUILDING
OVERALL RATE
PYRAMIDING
RATE OF RETURN
RESORT PROPERTY
REVERSE LEVERAGE
SHOPPING CENTER
VACANCY FACTOR
YIELD

CONDOMINIUM

APPURTENANT
ASSOCIATION OF UNIT
  OWNERS
BYLAWS
COMMON AREAS
COMMON ELEMENTS
COMMON EXPENSES
COMMON INTEREST
COMMON PROFITS
COMMON WALL

CONDOMINIUM (CONT.)

COMMUNITY ASSOCIATION
  INSTITUTE
CONDO
CONDOMINIUM MAP
CONDOMINIUM OWNER'S
  ASSOCIATION
CONDOMINIUM OWNERSHIP
CONVERSION
COOPERATIVE OWNERSHIP
DECLARATION
HIGH RISE
HOMEOWNER'S
  ASSOCIATION
HORIZONTAL PROPERTY
  ACTS
HOUSE RULES
LIMITED COMMON
  ELEMENTS
MAINTENANCE FEE
MASTER DEED
MIXED USE
PROPRIETARY LEASE
PROXY
UNIT

CONSTRUCTION (SEE BUILDING TERMS)

ADDITION
A-FRAME
ARCHITECTURAL DRAWINGS
ARCHITECTURE
AS-BUILT DRAWINGS
BID
BLUEPRINT
BROWNSTONE
BUILDING LINE
BUILDING PERMIT
BUILDING STANDARDS
BUNGALOW
CARPORT
CESSPOOL
CHALET
CHANGE ORDER
CISTERN
COMPACTION
COMPONENT BUILDING
CONCRETE BASEMENT
  FLOOR
CONTRACTOR
COST-PLUS CONTRACT
CUSHION
DECK
DISPOSAL FIELD
DORMER
DRAINAGE
DRY ROT

DRYWALL CONSTRUCTION
DUPLEX
DWELLING
EFFICIENCY UNIT
EFFLUENCE
ESCARPMENT
FIRE SPRINKLER SYSTEM
FIRE STOP
FIRE WALL
FIRE YARD
FLAT
FLOOR AREA RATIO
FLOOR PLAN
FROST LINE
GABLE
GAMBREL ROOF
GARDEN APARTMENT
GAZEBO
GENERAL CONTRACTOR
GRANNY FLATS
HABITABLE ROOM
HEIGHT, BUILDING
KILN
KITCHENETTE
KNOCKDOWN
LANAI
LEACHING CESSPOOL
LIVE LOAD
LOAD
LOBBY
LOFT
MALL
MARINA
MEZZANINE
MODULE
MOLD
MOTEL
MUD ROOM
MULTIPLE DWELLING
PARQUET FLOOR
PAVILLION
PAYMENT BOND
PENTHOUSE
PERFORMANCE BOND
PIER
PLASTER FINISH
PORTE COCHERE
PROCEED ORDER
PROGRESS PAYMENTS
PUNCH LIST
R-VALUE
RETAINAGE
ROOMING HOUSE
ROW HOUSE
SANITARY SEWER SYSTEM
SEMI-DETACHED DWELLING
SEPTIC TANK
SHORING
SINGLE-FAMILY RESIDENCE
SINGLE-LOAD CORRIDOR

SKYLIGHT
SLAB
SOLAR HEATING
SPECIFICATIONS
SPLIT-LEVEL
STAGING
STAGING AREA
STRUCTURE
STRUCTURAL
  ALTERATIONS
STRUCTURAL DEFECTS
STRUCTURAL DENSITY
STUCCO
STUD
STUDIO
SUBCONTRACTOR
SUMP
TERMITE SHIELD
TOPPING-OFF
TOWN HOUSE
TRACT HOUSE
TRIPLEX
UNIFORM BUILDING CODE
UTILITY ROOM
VESTIBULE
VOUCHER SYSTEM
WALK-UP
WALL-TO-WALL CARPETING
WAREHOUSE
WEEP HOLE
WET COLUMN
WORKING DRAWINGS

CONTRACTS

ACCEPTANCE
ACCORD AND SATISFACTION
ADDENDUM
ADHESION CONTRACT
ALEATORY CONTRACT
ANTENUPTIAL AGREEMENT
ANTICIPATORY BREACH
ARM'S LENGTH
  TRANSACTION
ASSIGNMENT
BENEFIT-OF-BARGAIN RULE
BILATERAL CONTRACT
BOILER PLATE
BREACH OF CONTRACT
CAPACITY OF PARTIES
CONSEQUENTIAL DAMAGES
CONSIDERATION
CONTRACT
COOLING-OFF PERIOD
COUNTEROFFER
COUNTERPART
DAMAGES
DATE
DEFAULT

CONTRACTS (CONT.)

DISCHARGE OF CONTRACT
DISCLAIMER
DUAL CONTRACT
DURESS
ELECTION OF REMEDIES
EXECUTORY CONTRACT
EXHIBIT
FORBEARANCE
FORCE MAJEURE
FORFEITURE
FORUM SHOPPING CLAUSE
FRAUD
GOOD CONSIDERATION
GRACE PERIOD
HOLD HARMLESS CLAUSE
IMPLIED CONTRACT
INCORPORATION BY
   REFERENCE
INSTRUMENT
IRONCLAD AGREEMENT
LATENT DEFECTS
LIQUIDATED DAMAGES
LOVE AND AFFECTION
MARK
MEASURE OF DAMAGES
MEETING OF THE MINDS
MINOR
MISREPRESENTATION
MISTAKE
MUTUALITY OF CONSENT
NATURAL AFFECTION
NONDISCLOSURE
NOTICE
OFFER
OFFER AND ACCEPTANCE
OPTION
ORAL CONTRACT
PARTY TO BE CHARGED
PLAIN LANGUAGE LAW
PRIVITY
QUALIFIED ACCEPTANCE
REFORMATION
RELEASE
RESCIND
RESCISSION
SHORT-FORM DOCUMENT
SIGNATURE
STATUTE OF FRAUDS
TENDER
THIRD PARTY
TIME IS OF THE ESSENCE
UNCONSCIONABILITY
UNDUE INFLUENCE
UNENFORCEABLE CONTRACT
UNIFORM VENDOR AND
   PURCHASER RISK ACT
UNILATERAL CONTRACT
UNJUST ENRICHMENT

UNREASONABLY WITHHOLD
   CONSENT
UPSET DATE
VALUABLE CONSIDERATION
VOID
VOIDABLE
WAIVER
WARRANTY
WITNESS
X

CONTRACTS OF SALE (SEE CONTRACTS, ESCROW)

ADDITIONAL DEPOSIT
AGREEMENT OF SALE
"AS IS"
BACKUP OFFER
BUY-BACK AGREEMENT
CONDITIONAL SALE
   CONTRACT
CONSUMMATE
CONTINGENCY
CONTRACT FOR DEED
CONTRACT OF SALE
COVENANTS AND
   CONDITIONS
DEPOSIT
DOWN PAYMENT
DUMMY
EARLY OCCUPANCY
EARNEST MONEY
EQUITABLE CONVERSION
ESCAPE CLAUSE
EXTENSION
NETTING OUT
NOMINEE
OCCUPANCY AGREEMENT
ON OR BEFORE
PROPOSITION
RECEIPT
RISK OF LOSS
ROOF INSPECTION CLAUSE
SALE BY THE ACRE
SALES CONTRACT
SPECIAL CONDITIONS
SPECIFIC PERFORMANCE
STRAW MAN
"SUBJECT TO" CLAUSE
TERMITE INSPECTION
TRADING ON THE EQUITY
UPGRADES

CONVEYANCE (SEE DEED)

ALIENATION
ASSIGNMENT OF LEASE
CONVEYANCE

CONVEYANCE TAX
COUNTERPART
DESCRIPTION
DOCUMENTARY TAX
   STAMPS
DOCUMENTS
EXCEPTION
EXECUTE
FEDERAL REVENUE STAMP
GOVERNMENT PATENT
GRANT
INITIALS
LOCUS SIGILLI
MASTER FORM INSTRUMENT
MESNE CONVEYANCE
MISNOMER
PATENT
RIGHT, TITLE, AND INTEREST
RULE AGAINST
   PERPETUITIES
SEALED AND DELIVERED
SUBSCRIBE
SUCCESSORS AND ASSIGNS
TESTIMONIUM CLAUSE
TRANSFER TAX
UNDERSIGNED
UNIFORM LAND
   TRANSACTIONS ACT

CORPORATION

ANNUAL MEETING
ANNUAL REPORT
ARTICLES OF
   INCORPORATION
ASSOCIATION
BOARD OF DIRECTORS
BUY-SELL AGREEMENT
CLOSE CORPORATION
COLLAPSIBLE CORPORATION
CORPORATE RESOLUTION
CORPORATION
DBA
DOUBLE TAXATION
ELEEMOSYNARY
   CORPORATION
FICTITIOUS COMPANY NAME
FISCAL YEAR
FOREIGN CORPORATION
HOLDING COMPANY
INCORPORATE
NAME, RESERVATION OF
NONPROFIT CORPORATIONS
PERSONAL PROPERTY
SEAL
SECTION 1244 CORPORATION
SPIN-OFF
SUBCHAPTER S
   CORPORATION

CORPORATION (CONT.)

THIN CAPITALIZATION
ULTRA VIRES
UNINCORPORATED
  ASSOCIATION

DEATH

ADMEASUREMENT OF
  DOWER
ADMINISTRATOR
CODICIL
COLLATERAL HEIRS
CURTESY
DESCENT
DEVISE
DOWER
ELECTIVE SHARE
ESCHEAT
EXECUTOR
HEIR
HEIRS AND ASSIGNS
HOLOGRAPHIC WILL
INHERITANCE TAX
INTESTATE
JOINTURE
LINEAL
NUNCUPATIVE WILL
PERSONAL REPRESENTATIVE
PER STIRPES
PROBATE
TESTATOR
WIDOW'S QUARANTINE
WILL
WORTHIER TITLE DOCTRINE

DEED

BARGAIN AND SALE DEED
CESSION DEED
CORRECTION DEED
COVENANT
COVENANTS RUNNING WITH
  THE LAND
DEED
DEED IN TRUST
DEED POLL
DELIVERY
ESTOPPEL BY DEED
GIFT DEED
GRANT DEED
GRANTEE
GRANTOR
HABENDUM CLAUSE
INDENTURE DEED
LEGACY

NOMINAL CONSIDERATION
PREMISES
QUITCLAIM DEED
REDDENDUM CLAUSE
RESERVATION
RESTRICTIVE COVENANT
SHERIFF'S DEED
SPECIAL WARRANTY DEED
SUPPORT DEED
TAX DEED
UNRECORDED DEED
WARRANTY DEED
WILD DEED

DEVELOPMENT (SEE SUBDIVISION, CONSTRUCTION)

BEDROOM COMMUNITY
CARRYING CHARGES
CLUSTER DEVELOPMENT
COMMERCIAL ACRE
COMMUNITY SHOPPING
  CENTER
COMPLETION BOND
COMPLIANCE INSPECTION
CONTRACT DOCUMENTS
DEVELOPER
DEVELOPMENT IMPACT FEE
DEVELOPMENT LOAN
DEVELOPMENT RIGHTS
ELEVATION SHEET
ENTREPRENEUR
ENVIRONMENTAL IMPACT
  STATEMENT
FEASIBILITY STUDY
FRONT-ENDING
FRONT MONEY
GUEST-CAR RATIO
HOMEOWNER'S WARRANTY
  PROGRAM
HOUSING FOR THE ELDERLY
HOUSING STARTS
HUNDRED-PERCENT
  LOCATION
IMPACT FEES
INCREMENTS
INDIRECT COSTS
JOINT VENTURE
LAND BROKER
LETTER OF INTENT
MASTER LEASE
MOBILE-HOME PARK
MODEL HOME
MODULAR HOUSING
NATIONAL HOUSING
  PARTNERSHIP
NET USABLE ACRE
OFFSITE COSTS

OFF-STREET PARKING
OPEN SPACE
PAD
PEDESTRIAN TRAFFIC
  COUNT
PERCOLATION TEST
PLANS AND SPECIFICATIONS
PLAZA
PRELIMINARY COSTS
PRE-SALE
REDEVELOPMENT AGENCY
RENDERING
RULE OF FIVE
SCHEMATICS
SOFT MONEY
SPECULATOR
STARTS
SUBSIDY
SUBSIDY RENT
SWEETHEART CONTRACTS
TRACK RECORD
TRAILER PARK
TRANSFER OF
  DEVELOPMENT RIGHTS
TURN-KEY PROJECT
UTILITIES
VENTURE CAPITAL

DISCRIMINATION

AFFIRMATIVE MARKETING
  PROGRAM
AGE
ANCESTOR
BLOCKBUSTING
CONCILIATION AGREEMENT
DISCRIMINATION
EQUAL CREDIT
  OPPORTUNITY ACT
ETHNIC GROUP
FEDERAL FAIR HOUSING
  LAW
GHETTO
OPEN HOUSING
PANIC PEDDLING
REDLINING
STEERING
TIPPING POINT

EASEMENT

ADVERSE USER
ANCIENT LIGHTS DOCTRINE
DECLARATION OF
  RESTRICTIONS
DOMINANT ESTATE
EASEMENT

EASEMENT (CONT.)

EASEMENT BY NECESSITY
EASEMENT BY
  PRESCRIPTION
EASEMENT IN GROSS
EAVE DRIP
EQUITABLE SERVITUDE
IMPLIED EASEMENT
LANDLOCKED
LINE-OF-SIGHT EASEMENT
NEGATIVE EASEMENT
PARTY DRIVEWAY
PARTY WALL
RECIPROCAL EASEMENTS
RIGHT-OF-WAY
RUN WITH THE LAND
SCENIC EASEMENT
SERVIENT ESTATE
SOLAR EASEMENT
SUBSURFACE EASEMENT
VISUAL RIGHTS

ESTATE (SEE TITLE)

AUTRE VIE
CONVENTIONAL ESTATE
CURTESY
DOWER
ESTATE
ESTATE AT WILL
ESTATE OF INHERITANCE
EXECUTORY INTEREST
FEE SIMPLE
FEE SIMPLE DEFEASIBLE
FEE TAIL
FREEHOLD
FREEHOLDER
FUTURE INTEREST
HEREDITAMENT
HOMESTEAD
INCHOATE
INCORPORAL RIGHTS
LAND, TENEMENTS, AND
  HEREDITAMENTS
LESS THAN FREEHOLD
  ESTATE
LIFE ESTATE
MERGER
POSSIBILITY OF REVERTER
PROFIT A PRENDRE
PUR AUTRE VIE
QUALIFIED FEE
QUANTUM
QUARTER SECTION
RE-ENTRY
REMAINDER ESTATE
REMAINDERMAN
REVERSION

RIGHT OF REENTRY
SEISIN
SERVITUDE
TENEMENT
TENURE
USUFRUCTUARY RIGHT
VESTED INTEREST

FEDERAL GOVERNMENT

AGRICULTURAL FOREIGN
  INVESTMENT DISCLOSURE
  ACT
ENVIRONMENTAL
  PROTECTION AGENCY
  (EPA)
FARM CREDIT SYSTEM
FEDERAL TRADE
  COMMISSION
FOREIGN INVESTMENT IN
  REAL PROPERTY TAX ACT
  OF 1980
HUD
OFFICE OF EQUAL
  OPPORTUNITY
OFFICE OF THE
  COMPTROLLER OF THE
  CURRENCY
OPERATION BREAKTHROUGH
SMALL BUSINESS
  ADMINISTRATION
SOIL BANK
STANDARD METROPOLITAN
  STATISTICAL AREA

FINANCING (SEE INTEREST, MORTGAGE)

ADD-BACK
ADJUSTABLE RATE LOAN
ADVANCE
ALLOTMENT
AMORTIZATION
AMORTIZED SCHEDULE
ANNUAL DEBT SERVICE
ANNUAL PERCENTAGE RATE
ANNUITY
ARRANGER OF CREDIT
ASSUMPTION OF MORTGAGE
BALLOON PAYMENT
BASIS POINT
BASKET PROVISION
BOND
BONUS CLAUSE
BRIDGE-LOAN
BUILDING AND LOAN
  ASSOCIATION

BUYDOWN
CARRYBACK FINANCING
CERTIFICATE OF CLAIM
CERTIFICATE OF ELIGIBILITY
CERTIFICATE OF
  REASONABLE VALUE
COLLATERAL
COLLECTION REPORT
COMMERCIAL BANK
COMMITMENT
COMPENSATING BALANCE
CONSTRUCTION LOAN
CONTRACT FOR DEED
CONVENTIONAL LOAN
CREATIVE FINANCING
CREDITOR
CREDIT RATING
CREDIT REPORT
CREDIT UNION
CURTAIL SCHEDULE
CUSTOMER TRUST FUND
DEBENTURE
DEBT COVERAGE RATIO
DEBT FINANCING
DEBTOR
DEBT SERVICE
DISCOUNT
DISCOUNT POINTS
DISCRETIONARY FUNDS
DISINTERMEDIATION
END LOAN
EQUITY BUILD-UP
EQUITY PARTICIPATION
EQUITY SHARING LOAN
FACE VALUE
FAIR CREDIT REPORTING
  ACT
FANNIE MAE
FARMER'S HOME
  ADMINISTRATION
FEDERAL DEPOSIT
  INSURANCE CORPORATION
FEDERAL HOME LOAN BANK
  SYSTEM
FEDERAL HOME LOAN
  MORTGAGE CORPORATION
FEDERAL HOUSING
  ADMINISTRATION
FEDERAL LAND BANK
FEDERAL NATIONAL
  MORTGAGE ASSOCIATION
FEDERAL RESERVE SYSTEM
FEDERAL SAVINGS AND
  LOAN ASSOCIATION
FINANCE CHARGE
FINANCE FEE
FINANCIAL INSTITUTION
FINANCIAL STATEMENT
FINANCING
FIRM COMMITMENT

FINANCING (CONT.)

FIXED RATE LOAN
FLOAT
FLOOR LOAN
FREDDIE MAC
GAP FINANCING
GAP GROUP
GOVERNMENT NATIONAL
  MORTGAGE ASSOCIATION
GUARANTEED MORTGAGE
  CERTIFICATE
HANGOUT
HOLDBACK
HOME LOAN
IN-SERVICE LOAN
INSTITUTIONAL LENDER
INTERIM FINANCING
KICKERS
LAND CONTRACT
LAND LEASEBACK
LATE CHARGE
LEAD LENDER
LIQUIDITY
LOAN COMMITMENT
LOAN CORRESPONDENT
LOAN SUBMISSION
LOAN-TO-VALUE RATIO
LUMP SUM PAYMENT
MAGGIE MAE
MINIMUM PROPERTY
  REQUIREMENTS
MONEY MARKET FUND
MORTGAGE GUARANTY
  INSURANCE CORPORATION
MORTGAGE SUBSIDIES
MUTUAL SAVINGS BANK
NEGATIVE AMORTIZATION
ORIGINATION FEE
PAPER
PAR
PARTIALLY AMORTIZED
PARTICIPATION SALE
  CERTIFICATE
PENSION FUND
PERMANENT FINANCING
PIGGYBACK LOAN
PLEDGE
POINTS
QUALIFICATION
RECASTING
REFINANCE
RESCISSION CLAUSE
RULE OF 78s
SALE-LEASEBACK
SATISFACTION
SAVINGS AND LOAN
  ASSOCIATIONS
SAVINGS AND LOAN
  SERVICE CORPORATION

SEASONED LOAN
SECONDARY FINANCING
SECONDARY MORTGAGE
  MARKET
SECURED PARTY
SERVICING
SET-ASIDE LETTER
SINKING FUND
SPLIT-FEE FINANCING
SPOT LOAN
STANDBY FEE
STANDBY LOAN
STANDING LOAN
SUBAGREEMENT OF SALE
SUBORDINATED
  SALE-LEASEBACK
SWEAT EQUITY
SWING LOAN
TAKE DOWN
TAKEOUT FINANCING
TANDEM PLAN
TIGHT MONEY MARKET
TIME-PRICE DIFFERENTIAL
TIME VALUE OF MONEY
TRUTH-IN-LENDING LAWS
UNDERLYING FINANCING
U.S. LEAGUE OF SAVINGS
  ASSOCIATIONS
USURY
VENDEE
VENDOR
VETERANS ADMINISTRATION
WAREHOUSING
YIELD TO MATURITY

GOVERNMENT (SEE ZONING)

APPROPRIATION
BETTERMENT
CERTIFICATE OF
  OCCUPANCY
CONDEMNATION
COUNTY
DEDICATION
EMINENT DOMAIN
EXCESS CONDEMNATION
GENERAL IMPROVEMENT
  DISTRICT
INVERSE CONDEMNATION
IRRIGATION DISTRICTS
JUST COMPENSATION
LAND GRANT
LARGER PARCEL
LETTER OF PATENT
LOCAL IMPROVEMENT
  DISTRICT
OCCUPANCY PERMIT

ORDINANCES
PARTIAL TAKING
POLICE POWER
SEVERANCE DAMAGES
SLUM CLEARANCE
SPECIAL BENEFIT
ZONE CONDEMNATION

INDUSTRIAL PROPERTY

BUMPER
CLEARANCE POINT
DOCK-HIGH BUILDING
DRILL TRACK
INDUSTRIAL PARK
LOADING DOCK
MAIN LINE
MINIWAREHOUSE
PIGGYBACK
POINT OF SWITCH
SPUR TRACK
TRUCK WELL
UP-RAMP

INSURANCE

ACTUARY
BINDER
BUILDER'S RISK INSURANCE
BUREAU RATE
BUSINESS LIFE INSURANCE
CERTIFICATE OF INSURANCE
COINSURANCE
COMMERCIAL LEASEHOLD
  INSURANCE
ERRORS AND OMISSIONS
  INSURANCE
FIRE INSURANCE
FLOOD INSURANCE
HAZARD INSURANCE
INSURABLE INTEREST
INSURANCE
KEYMAN INSURANCE
LOSS PAYEE
MORTGAGE INSURANCE
MUTUAL MORTGAGE
  INSURANCE FUND
PREMIUM
PRIVATE MORTGAGE
  INSURANCE
REINSURANCE
REISSUE RATE
RIDER
SHORT RATE
TSUNAMI DAMAGE
UNDERWRITER

INTEREST (SEE FINANCING, MORTGAGE)

ADD-BACK
ADD-ON INTEREST
AMORTIZATION
ARBITRAGE
BLOCK INTEREST
COMPOUND INTEREST
CONSTANT
EFFECTIVE INTEREST RATE
INTEREST
LAWFUL INTEREST
LEGAL RATE OF INTEREST
NOMINAL INTEREST RATE
PREPAID INTEREST
PREVAILING RATE
PRIME RATE
REDISCOUNT RATE
REGULATION Q
RULE OF 72
SIMPLE INTEREST
VARIABLE INTEREST RATE

LAND

ACCESS
ACRE
ACRE FOOT
AEOLIAN SOIL
AGREED BOUNDARIES
AIR RIGHTS
ALLUVION
AREA
BEACH
BOTTOMLAND
BOUNDARIES
CONTOUR MAP
FARMLAND
FILLED LAND
FLAG LOT
FLOOD PLAIN
FLOOD PRONE AREA
FORESHORE LAND
FRUCTUS NATURALES
IMPROVED LAND
LAND
LATERAL AND SUBJACENT
  SUPPORT
LIGHT AND AIR
LITTORAL LAND
LOT SPLIT
MARGINAL LAND
MINERAL RIGHTS
PARCEL
PUBLIC LAND
QUADRANGLE
RANGE

RAW LAND
REAL ESTATE
REAL PROPERTY
REALTY
RECLAMATION
SHORELINE
SITE
SPITE FENCE
SUBJACENT SUPPORT
TIDEWATER LAND
TOPOGRAPHY
TRACT
UNIMPROVED PROPERTY
WASTELAND
WATERFRONT PROPERTY
WETLANDS
YARD

LAND DESCRIPTION (SURVEYING)

ANGLE
AZIMUTH
BASE LINE
BEARING
BENCH MARK
BOUNDS
CALL
CHAIN
CLOSURE
COMPASS POINTS
CONNECTION LINE
CORNER STAKES
CORRECTION LINES
DEGREE
DESCRIPTION
FRONT FOOT
GEODETIC SURVEY SYSTEM
GOVERNMENT SURVEY
  METHOD
GUIDE MERIDIANS
HECTARE
HIGH-WATER MARK
LAND DESCRIPTION
LANDMARK
LEGAL DESCRIPTION
LINE STAKES
LOT, BLOCK, AND
  SUBDIVISION
MAPS AND PLATS
MEANDER LINE
MEASUREMENT TABLES
MERIDIAN
METES AND BOUNDS
MILE
MONUMENT
MORE OR LESS
PLAT MAP
PLOT PLAN

POINT OF BEGINNING
PRINCIPAL MERIDIAN
RANGE LINE
ROD
SECOND
SECTION
SPOT SURVEY
SQUARE
STAKING
STANDARD PARALLEL
SURVEY
TAX MAP
TIER
TOWNSHIP
U.S. GEOLOGICAL SURVEY

LEASING

AAA TENANT
ABANDONMENT
ADDITIONAL SPACE OPTION
ANCHOR TENANT
ATTORNMENT
ATTRACTION PRINCIPLE
BACK-TO-BACK LEASE
BASE PERIOD
BASE RENT
BUILDING LEASE
CANCELLATION CLAUSE
CHAIN STORE
CONCESSIONS
CONCURRENT LEASE
CONSTRUCTION
  ALLOWANCE
CONSTRUCTIVE EVICTION
CONSUMER PRICE INDEX
COST-OF-LIVING INDEX
DEMISE
DISPOSSESS PROCEEDINGS
DISTRAINT
EFFECTIVE RATE
ESTOVERS
EVICTION
EXCULPATORY CLAUSE
EXPANSION OPTION
FIRST REFUSAL
FIXTURING PERIOD
FLAT LEASE
GRADUATED RENTAL LEASE
GROSS LEASE
GROUND LEASE
HABITABLE
HOLDOVER TENANT
IMPLIED WARRANTY OF
  HABITABILITY
INDEX LEASE
LANDLORD
LEASE
LEASED FEE

LEASING (CONT.)

LEASEHOLD
LEASE OPTION
LESSEE
LESSOR
LOSS FACTOR
MASTER LEASE
MILITARY CLAUSE
MITIGATION OF DAMAGES
MONTH-TO-MONTH
 TENANCY
MOST FAVORED TENANT
 CLAUSE
NET LEASE
NONCOMPETITION CLAUSE
NORMAL WEAR AND TEAR
NOTICE TO QUIT
OFFSET STATEMENT
OIL AND GAS LEASE
OVERAGE
OVERRIDING ROYALTY
OWELTY
PERCENTAGE LEASE
PERIODIC TENANCY
PERMISSIVE WASTE
PRIME TENANT
QUIET ENJOYMENT
RECAPTURE CLAUSE
RECREATIONAL LEASE
RELOCATION CLAUSE
RENEGOTIATION OF LEASE
RENEWAL OPTION
RENT
RENTABLE AREA
RENTAL AGENCY
RENTAL AGREEMENT
RENT CONTROL
RENT-UP
RETALIATORY EVICTION
RIGHT OF FIRST REFUSAL
ROYALTY
SALE OF LEASED PROPERTY
SANDWICH LEASE
SATELLITE TENANT
SECURITY DEPOSIT
SELF-HELP
SHELL LEASE
SKY LEASE
SPACE PLAN
STEP-UP LEASE
SUBLEASE
SUMMARY POSSESSION
SURCHARGE
SURRENDER
TAX PARTICIPATION CLAUSE
TAX STOP CLAUSE
TENANT
TENANT CONTRIBUTIONS
TENANT MIX
TENANT UNION

TRIPLE "A" TENANT
TRIPLE NET LEASE
UNDERTENANT
UNFINISHED OFFICE SPACE
UNIFORM RESIDENTIAL
 LANDLORD AND TENANT
 ACT
UNLAWFUL DETAINER
 ACTION
USABLE AREA
VACATE
VETO CLAUSE
WASTE
WEAR AND TEAR
WORK LETTER
YEAR-TO-YEAR TENANCY

LEGAL TERMS

ABANDONMENT
ABATEMENT
ABSOLUTE
ACKNOWLEDGMENT
ACT OF GOD
ACTUAL NOTICE
AFFIDAVIT
AFFIRMATION
AGGRIEVED
ALLEGATION
ANTITRUST LAWS
ARBITRATION
ATTACHMENT
ATTESTATION
ATTORNEY'S FEES
ATTRACTIVE NUISANCE
BANKRUPTCY
BENCHMARK
BENEFICIARY
BLUE LAWS
BUSINESS DAY
BY OPERATION OF LAW
CAVEAT EMPTOR
CEASE AND DESIST ORDER
CERTIFIED COPY
CERTIFY
CERTIORARI
CHANGE OF NAME
COMMISSIONER
COMMON LAW
COMPLAINANT
CONFESSION OF JUDGMENT
CONFIRMATION OF SALE
CONSERVATOR
CONSTRUCTIVE
COURT
CRAM DOWN
DEFAULT JUDGMENT
DEFENDANT
DEPOSITION
DISCLOSURE STATEMENT

DOMICILE
EJECTMENT
ENABLING LEGISLATION
ENJOIN
EQUITY
ESTOPPEL
ET AL.
ET UX.
ET VIR.
EXECUTION
FAMILY
FELONY
GARNISHMENT
GUARDIAN
HEARING
HOLIDAY
INCOMPETENT
INJUNCTION
INTERLOCUTORY DECREE
INTERPLEADER
JOINT AND SEVERAL
 LIABILITY
JUDGMENT
JUDGMENT-PROOF
JURAT
JURISDICTION
LACHES
LAW
LEGAL AGE
LEGAL NAME
LEVY
LIABILITY
LIMITATIONS OF ACTIONS
LIS PENDENS
MAJORITY
MANDAMUS
MISDEMEANOR
NAME, CHANGE OF
NATURAL PERSON
NOTARY PUBLIC
NUISANCE
NULL AND VOID
OATH
OPERATION OF LAW
PAROL EVIDENCE RULE
PENALTY
PERSON
PETITION
PLAINTIFF
PRACTICE OF LAW
PREEMPTION
PRESUMPTION
PREVAILING PARTY
PRICE FIXING
PRIMA FACIE EVIDENCE
PRO FORMA
PUNITIVE DAMAGES
QUASI
QUORUM
REASONABLE TIME
RECEIVER

LEGAL TERMS (CONT.)

REFEREE
REGULATION
REPLEVIN
RESIDENCE
RESTRAINT OF TRADE
RESTRAINT ON ALIENATION
RESULTING TRUST
REVOCATION
RIGHT OF CONTRIBUTION
SEQUESTRATION ORDER
SERVICE OF PROCESS
SHALL
SHOULD
SMALL CLAIMS COURT
SPENDTHRIFT TRUST
STATUTE
STATUTE OF LIMITATIONS
SUBPOENA
SUBPOENA DUCES TECUM
SUBROGATION
SUMMONS
SURETY
TIE-IN CONTRACT
TOLLING
TORT
TREBLE DAMAGES
TRESPASS
TRUSTEE IN BANKRUPTCY
UNFAIR AND DECEPTIVE
  PRACTICES
UNIFORM AND MODEL ACTS
VALID
VENUE
VERIFY
VIOLATION
WRIT OF EXECUTION

LICENSING

ASSOCIATE BROKER
BROKER-IN-CHARGE
EXAMINATION, LICENSING
FORFEITURE
INACTIVE LICENSE
LICENSE
LICENSEE
LICENSE LAWS
MORAL TURPITUDE
NARELLO
POCKET LICENSE CARD
REAL ESTATE COMMISSION
RECIPROCITY
RECOVERY FUND
SUSPENSION
VOCATION

LIEN

AGRICULTURAL LIEN

COMMENCEMENT OF WORK
ENCUMBRANCE
EQUITABLE LIEN
FLOATING LIEN
GENERAL LIEN
JUDGMENT LIEN
LIEN
MATERIALMAN
MECHANIC'S LIEN
MORTGAGE LIEN
NOTICE OF COMPLETION
NOTICE OF LIEN
NOTICE OF
  NONRESPONSIBILITY
SPECIAL LIEN
SPREADING LIEN
TAX LIEN
VENDOR'S LIEN

LISTING

ABLE
ASKING PRICE
AUTHORIZATION TO SELL
CASH OUT
CONTINGENCY LISTING
EXCLUSIVE AGENCY
EXCLUSIVE LISTING
EXCLUSIVE RIGHT TO SELL
EXTENDER CLAUSE
IMPLIED LISTING
LISTING
LISTOR
MULTIPLE LISTING
NEGOTIATION
NET LISTING
NO DEAL, NO COMMISSION
  CLAUSE
OFFICE EXCLUSIVE
OPEN LISTING
OPTION LISTING
OVERRIDE
POCKET LISTING
PROCURING CAUSE
TERMINATION OF LISTING

MORTGAGE—DEED OF TRUST (SEE INTEREST, LIEN, FINANCING)

ACCELERATION CLAUSE
ADDITIONAL CHARGE
  MORTGAGE
ALIENATION CLAUSE
ALL-INCLUSIVE DEED OF
  TRUST
ALTERNATIVE MORTGAGE
  INSTRUMENT

ANACONDA MORTGAGE
ANNUAL MORTGAGOR
  STATEMENT
ASSIGNMENT OF RENTS
BENEFICIARY STATEMENT
BLANKET MORTGAGE
BUDGET MORTGAGE
CALL PROVISION
CALL REPORT
CERTIFICATE OF NO
  DEFENSE
COLLATERALIZED
  MORTGAGE
CROSS-DEFAULTING CLAUSE
DEED IN LIEU OF
  FORECLOSURE
DEED OF RECONVEYANCE
DEED OF TRUST
DEFEASANCE CLAUSE
DEFICIENCY JUDGMENT
DEFLATED MORTGAGE
DIRECT REDUCTION
  MORTGAGE
DRAGNET CLAUSE
DRY MORTGAGE
DUE-ON-SALE CLAUSE
EQUITY OF REDEMPTION
ESCALATOR CLAUSE
FIRST MORTGAGE
FLEXIBLE-PAYMENT
  MORTGAGE
FLIP®
FORECLOSURE
FULL RECONVEYANCE
FUTURE ADVANCES
GRADUATED PAYMENT
  MORTGAGE
GUARANTY
HARD MONEY MORTGAGE
HYPOTHECATE
INSTALLMENT NOTE
JUDICIAL FORECLOSURE
JUNIOR MORTGAGE
LAW DAY
LEASEHOLD MORTGAGE
LEVEL-PAYMENT MORTGAGE
LIEN STATEMENT
LIEN-THEORY STATES
LIFTING CLAUSE
LOCK-IN-CLAUSE
MAGIC-WRAP
MARGINAL RELEASE
MATURITY
MORTGAGE
MORTGAGE BANKER
MORTGAGE BROKER
MORTGAGEE
MORTGAGE LIEN
MORTGAGE SPREADING
  AGREEMENT
MORTGAGOR

MORTGAGE—DEED OF TRUST (CONT.)

NONDISTURBANCE
NONJUDICIAL FORECLOSURE
NONRECOURSE LOAN
NOTE
NOTICE OF DEFAULT
NOVATION
OBLIGATION BOND
OBLIGOR
OFFERING SHEET
OPEN-END MORTGAGE
OPEN MORTGAGE
"OR MORE" CLAUSE
OUTSTANDING BALANCE
PACKAGE MORTGAGE
PARAGRAPH 17
PARITY CLAUSE
PARTIAL RECONVEYANCE
PARTIAL RELEASE CLAUSE
PARTICIPATION MORTGAGE
PAYOFF
P.I.T.I.
PLACEMENT FEE
PLEDGED ACCOUNT
    MORTGAGE
POWER OF SALE
PREPAYMENT PENALTY
PREPAYMENT PRIVILEGE
PRIMARY MORTGAGE
    MARKET
PROMISSORY NOTE
PUBLIC SALE
PURCHASE MONEY
    MORTGAGE
REAL ESTATE MORTGAGE
    TRUST
RECOGNITION CLAUSE
RECONVEYANCE
RECOURSE NOTE
REDEMPTION, EQUITABLE
    RIGHT OF
REDEMPTION PERIOD
REDUCTION CERTIFICATE
REINSTATEMENT
RELEASE CLAUSE
RENEGOTIABLE RATE
    MORTGAGE
RESERVE FUND
REVERSE ANNUITY
    MORTGAGE
SATISFACTION OF
    MORTGAGE
SECOND MORTGAGE
SHARED APPRECIATION
SOLDIERS AND SAILORS
    CIVIL RELIEF ACT
STRAIGHT NOTE
"SUBJECT TO" MORTGAGE

SUBORDINATION
    AGREEMENT
SUBORDINATION CLAUSE
SUBSTITUTION OF
    COLLATERAL
SURMORTGAGE
TITLE-THEORY STATES
UNSECURED
UPSET PRICE
VARIABLE PAYMENT PLAN
VARIABLE RATE MORTGAGE
WORK-OUT PLAN
WRAPAROUND MORTGAGE

ORGANIZATIONS

BOARD
BUILDING OWNERS AND
    MANAGERS ASSOCIATION
    (BOMA)
FARM AND LAND INSTITUTE
FIABCI
GRI
NATIONAL ASSOCIATION OF
    REALTORS®
REALTIST
REALTOR®
REALTOR-ASSOCIATE®
URBAN LAND INSTITUTE
WOMEN'S COUNCIL OF
    REALTORS®

OWNERSHIP

ABSENTEE OWNER
ABUTTING OWNER
AIR RIGHTS
ALIEN
ALLODIAL SYSTEM
BUNDLE OF RIGHTS
COMMUNITY PROPERTY
CONDO
CONTRIBUTION, RIGHT OF
COOPERATIVE OWNERSHIP
CORPOREAL PROPERTY
COTENANCY
DISSEISIN
DIVIDED INTEREST
ENTITY, LEGAL
GENERAL PARTNER
GENERAL PARTNERSHIP
HOME OWNERSHIP
INTEREST IN PROPERTY
INTER VIVOS TRUST
JOINT TENANCY
LAND TRUST

LEASED FEE
LEASEHOLD
LIMITED PARTNERSHIP
OWNER/OCCUPANT
OWNERSHIP
PARTITION
PARTNERSHIP
PASSIVE INVESTOR
POSSESSION
PRESCRIPTION
PROPERTY
PROPRIETORSHIP
REAL ESTATE INVESTMENT
    TRUST
RIGHT OF SURVIVORSHIP
SEPARATE PROPERTY
SEVERALTY
SOLE PROPRIETORSHIP
SURVIVORSHIP
SYNDICATION
TACKING
TENANCY AT SUFFERANCE
TENANCY AT WILL
TENANCY BY THE ENTIRETY
TENANCY FOR LIFE
TENANCY FOR YEARS
TENANCY IN COMMON
TENANCY IN PARTNERSHIP
TENANCY IN SEVERALTY
TIME SHARE OWNERSHIP
    PLAN
TIMESHARING
TRUST
TRUST BENEFICIARY
UNDIVIDED INTEREST
UNIFORM SIMULTANEOUS
    DEATH ACT
UNITY

PERSONAL PROPERTY

ASSET
BAILMENT
BEQUEATH
BILL OF SALE
CAPITAL
CHATTEL
CHATTEL MORTGAGE
CLEARANCE LETTER
EMBLEMENT
FINANCING STATEMENT
INVENTORY
PERSONAL PROPERTY
SECURITY AGREEMENT
SEVERANCE
TERMINATION STATEMENT
TRADE FIXTURE
UNIFORM COMMERCIAL
    CODE

PROPERTY MANAGEMENT (SEE LEASING)

AREA MANAGEMENT
BROKER
BUDGET
CERTIFIED PROPERTY
  MANAGER
FIDELITY BOND
FIXED EXPENSES
MANAGEMENT AGREEMENT
MANAGEMENT SURVEY
OPERATING BUDGET
OPERATING EXPENSES
PROPERTY MANAGEMENT
RESERVE FOR
  REPLACEMENTS
RESIDENT MANAGER

RECORDING (SEE TITLE EVIDENCE)

BONA FIDE
CONSTRUCTIVE NOTICE
CONVEYANCE TAX
DEFECT OF RECORD
FILE
GOOD FAITH
GRANTOR-GRANTEE INDEX
INNOCENT PURCHASER FOR
  VALUE
INQUIRY NOTICE
LEGAL NOTICE
LIBER
PRIORITY
RECORDING
REGISTRAR
REGULAR SYSTEM
SUBSEQUENT BONA FIDE
  PURCHASER
TRACT INDEX

SECURITIES

ANTIFRAUD PROVISIONS
BLIND POOL
BLUE-SKY LAWS
DIRECT PARTICIPATION
  PROGRAM LICENSES
DUE DILIGENCE
INTRASTATE EXEMPTION
INVESTMENT CONTRACT
LEGEND STOCK
MORTGAGE-BACKED
  SECURITY
NO ACTION LETTER
OFFER TO SELL

PASS-THROUGH
PRIVATE OFFERING
PROSPECTUS
REAL PROPERTY SECURITIES
  REGISTRATION
RED HERRING
REGULATION A
REGULATION T
RENTAL POOL
RISK CAPITAL
RULE 10-B5
RULE 146
RULE 147
SECURITY
SUBSCRIPTION
UNIFORM LIMITED
  PARTNERSHIP ACT
UNIFORM PARTNERSHIP ACT

SUBDIVISIONS (AND ROADS)

ALIQUOT
AVENUE
BOULEVARD
CC&R'S
CIRCLE
CONSOLIDATE
CONTIGUOUS
CUL DE SAC
CURVILINEAR
DECLARATION OF
  RESTRICTIONS
DRIVE
EGRESS
FREEWAY
FRONTAGE
FRONTAGE STREET
GRADE
GRADIENT
GRIDIRON
HIGHWAY
INSIDE LOT
INTERSTATE LAND SALES
KEY LOT
LANE
LIMITED ACCESS HIGHWAY
LOOP
OFFICE OF INTERSTATE
  LAND SALES
  REGISTRATION
ORIENTATION
PARKWAY
PLACE
PLANNED UNIT
  DEVELOPMENT
PLAT BOOK
PROPERTY REPORT

PUBLIC OFFERING
  STATEMENT
RESTRICTION
RESUBDIVISION
STATEMENT OF RECORD
STREET
SUBDIVIDER
SUBDIVISION
SUBDIVISION REGISTRATION
  LAW
WAY

TAXATION

ACCELERATED COST
  RECOVERY SYSTEM
ACCELERATED
  DEPRECIATION
ADJUSTED BASIS
AD VALOREM
ANNUAL EXCLUSION FOR
  GIFT TAX
ASSESSED VALUATION
ASSESSMENT
ASSESSMENT ROLLS
ASSESSOR
ASSET DEPRECIATION
  RANGE SYSTEM
AT-RISK RULES
BARGAIN SALE
BASIS
BOOT
BUSINESS ENERGY
  PROPERTY TAX CREDIT
CAPITAL ASSETS
CAPITAL EXPENDITURE
CAPITAL GAIN
CAPITAL IMPROVEMENT
CAPITAL LOSS
CHURNING
COMPONENT DEPRECIATION
CONSTRUCTIVE RECEIPT
CONTRACT PRICE
COST RECOVERY
DEALER
DECLINING-BALANCE
  METHOD
DEFERRED-PAYMENT
  METHOD
DELAYED EXCHANGE
DEMOLITION LOSS
DEPLETION
DEPRECIABLE LIFE
DEPRECIABLE REAL
  PROPERTY
DEPRECIATION (TAX)
DONOR
EQUALIZATION BOARD
ESTATE TAX

TAXATION (CONT.)

EXCHANGE
EXCISE TAX
FARM ASSETS
FEDERAL TAX LIEN
FIRST USER
FIRST-YEAR DEPRECIATION
FIXING-UP EXPENSES
GAIN
GIFT CAUSA MORTIS
GIFT TAX
GRIEVANCE PERIOD
HISTORIC STRUCTURE
HOLDING PERIOD
IMPROVEMENTS
IMPUTED INTEREST
INCOME AVERAGING
INDIVIDUAL RETIREMENT
  ACCOUNT
INSTALLMENT SALE
INTERNAL REVENUE CODE
INVESTMENT CREDIT
INVESTMENT INTEREST
INVOLUNTARY CONVERSION
KEOGH PLAN
LANDSCAPING
LEASEHOLD IMPROVEMENTS
LIKE-KIND PROPERTY
MARITAL DEDUCTION
MILL
MULTIPLE ASSET EXCHANGE
NOTICE OF ASSESSMENT
ONCE IN A LIFETIME
  EXCLUSION
OPEN SPACE TAXATION LAW
ORDINARY AND NECESSARY
  BUSINESS EXPENSE
ORDINARY GAIN
ORGANIZATIONAL
  EXPENSES, PARTNERSHIP
PROPERTY TAX
RECAPTURE
RECOGNITION
REHABILITATE
RELATED PARTIES
REPAIRS
RESIDENCE, SALE OF
RESIDENTIAL ENERGY
  CREDIT
RESIDENTIAL INSULATION
  CREDIT
ROLL-OVER
SAFE HARBOR LEASE
  ELECTION
SAFE HARBOR RULE
SALE OF PERSONAL
  RESIDENCE, ELDERLY
SALES-ASSESSMENT RATIO
SALVAGE VALUE

SHORT-TERM CAPITAL GAIN
SPECIAL ASSESSMENT
STRAIGHT-LINE
  DEPRECIATION
SUBSTANTIAL
  IMPROVEMENT
SUM-OF-THE-YEARS'-DIGITS
  METHOD
TAX
TAX BASE
TAX BRACKET
TAX CLEARANCE
TAX-DEFERRED EXCHANGE
TAX PREFERENCE
TAX RATE
TAX ROLL
TAX SALE
TAX SHELTER
TRADING UP
UNDISTRIBUTED TAXABLE
  INCOME
UNEARNED INCOME
UP-LEG
USEFUL LIFE
USE TAX
VACATION HOME
WASTING ASSET

TITLE (SEE ESTATES)

ACCESSION
ACCRETION
ADVERSE POSSESSION
AFTER-ACQUIRED
ANNEXATION
APPURTENANCE
AVULSION
CLAIM OF RIGHT
CLEARING TITLE
CLEAR TITLE
CLOUD ON TITLE
COLOR OF TITLE
CONTINUATION
DILUVION
ENCROACHMENT
ENCUMBRANCE
EQUITABLE TITLE
EROSION
ESCHEAT
FIXTURE
FREE AND CLEAR TITLE
GAP IN TITLE
HOSTILE POSSESSION
LOST-GRANT DOCTRINE
MARKETABLE TITLE
MUNIMENT OF TITLE
OPEN AND NOTORIOUS
  POSSESSION
PERFECTING TITLE

QUIET TITLE ACTION
RECORD OWNER
RECORD TITLE
ROOT TITLE
SLANDER OF TITLE
TITLE
TITLE PARAMOUNT
UNENCUMBERED PROPERTY
UNMARKETABLE TITLE

TITLE EVIDENCE (SEE RECORDING)

ABSTRACT OF TITLE
AFFIDAVIT OF TITLE
AMERICAN LAND TITLE
  ASSOCIATION
BRING DOWN SEARCH
CADASTRAL MAP
CERTIFICATE OF TITLE
CHAIN OF TITLE
CLOSING PROTECTION
  LETTER
DERAIGN
EVIDENCE OF TITLE
EXTENDED COVERAGE
FORGERY
HIATUS
HIDDEN RISK
IDEM SONANS
INDORSEMENT
INSURABLE TITLE
LATE DATE ORDER
LETTER REPORT
OFF-RECORD TITLE DEFECT
OPINION OF TITLE
OWNER'S DUPLICATE
  CERTIFICATE
PLANT
PRELIMINARY REPORT
PURCHASER'S POLICY
REGISTERED LAND
STARTER
TAX AND LIEN SEARCH
TAX SEARCH
TITLE INSURANCE
TITLE PLANT
TITLE REPORT
TITLE SEARCH
TORRENS SYSTEM
TRANSFER CERTIFICATE OF
  TITLE

WATER

CORRELATIVE WATER RIGHT
DIFFUSED SURFACE WATERS

WATER (CONT.)

GROUNDWATER
MUTUAL WATER COMPANY
NAVIGABLE WATERS
OVERFLOW RIGHT
POTABLE WATER
PRIOR APPROPRIATION
RELICTION
RIPARIAN
SURFACE WATER
WATER
WATERCOURSE
WATERSHED
WATER TABLE

ZONING (SEE GOVERNMENT)

ACREAGE ZONING
AIRPORT ZONING
BLIGHTED AREA
BUFFER ZONE
BUILDING CODES

BUILDING PERMIT
BUILDING RESTRICTIONS
CEMETERY LOTS
CENTRAL BUSINESS
  DISTRICT
CLUSTER ZONING
COASTAL ZONE
  MANAGEMENT ACT
CONDITIONAL USE
  ZONING
CONSERVATION
DENSITY
DENSITY ZONING
DOWNZONING
DWELLING UNIT
EXCLUSIONARY ZONING
FLOATING ZONE
GENERAL PLAN
GRANDFATHER CLAUSE
HEAVY INDUSTRY
HOTEL
INCLUSIONARY ZONING
INNER CITY
LAND BANK
LAND-USE INTENSITY

LIGHT INDUSTRY
LIVABILITY SPACE RATIO
MASTER PLAN
MINIMUM LOT AREA
MORATORIUM
MUNICIPAL ORDINANCE
NEW TOWN
NONCONFORMING USE
PLANNING COMMISSION
PRESERVATION DISTRICT
RURAL
RURBAN
SATELLITE CITY
SETBACK
SPECIAL USE PERMIT
SPOT ZONING
UPZONING
URBAN ENTERPRISE
  ZONE
URBAN RENEWAL
URBAN SPRAWL
VARIANCE
ZERO LOT LINE
ZONING
ZONING ESTOPPEL

AAA TENANT   A triple-A tenant is a well-known business tenant with an exceptionally high credit rating, or one whose national or local name will lend prestige to a shopping center or office project.

ABANDONMENT   Abandonment occurs when someone voluntarily surrenders or relinquishes possession of real property without vesting this interest in any other person. A vested fee simple estate cannot be abandoned, although a leasehold estate can be. Each case of possible abandonment must be evaluated to determine whether the property has indeed been legally abandoned. Mere nonuse of the property is insufficient evidence that the possessor will not reclaim the property—a more overt act is usually needed to prove abandonment. For example, the owner of an easement footpath across a neighboring property might demonstrate the intent to abandon the easement by erecting a stone wall between the two properties. When a condemning authority abandons an easement, the fee owner (condemnee) regains exclusive ownership of the parcel. An owner's failure to pay real estate taxes is sometimes taken as evidence of an intent to abandon.

Abandonment can be distinguished from "surrender," which requires some form of agreement (as between lessor and lessee), and from "forfeiture," which occurs against the owner's wishes. Abandonment of use takes place when an owner terminates a permitted right of nonconforming use under the current zoning ordinance.

A tenant who vacates leased property, no longer intending to perform under the terms of the lease, is abandoning the property. The landlord then gains full possession and control, but the lessee remains liable for rent until the lease expires. If the landlord accepts the abandonment (agrees to terminate the tenancy), it is recognized as a surrender, and the tenant is not obligated to pay future rents under the terms of the lease. (See SURRENDER.)

The Uniform Residential Landlord and Tenant Act, adopted by many states, provides that the landlord must make "reasonable efforts" to relet abandoned property at a fair rental. The lessor may then deduct the cost of reletting (commissions, redecorating, and so on) from the rent to be collected for the remainder of the original lessee's term and apply the balance toward the original tenant's liability. In some states, reletting abandoned property automatically creates a surrender; in other states, the landlord may still hold the tenant responsible for future rents despite reletting.

In states that recognize homestead rights, a claimant may abandon a homestead by filing a declaration of abandonment in the public record. Merely leaving such premises will not officially constitute an abandonment of a person's homestead rights. (*See HOMESTEAD.*)

There is also an income tax consequence of an abandonment. The taxpayer-owner who abandons real estate may be able to treat the abandonment as a "sale" for which the taxpayer received no payment (other than relief from any mortgages or liens). In this case, the taxpayer may claim a loss to the extent of the adjusted basis in the property.

Most states have laws covering the rights and obligations of the government and various parties in cases of unclaimed or abandoned personal property. The owners of mini-warehouses, for example, should carefully examine the possible liabilities involved in disposing of unclaimed property at the termination of a rental. (*See ESCHEAT.*)

ABATEMENT A reduction or decrease in amount, degree, intensity, or worth. For example, a lessee usually is entitled to an abatement of rent during the time the premises are made uninhabitable by fire, flood, or other acts of God. Also, there may be an abatement of rent if the landlord fails to give tenant possession at the beginning of the agreed-upon lease term.

If a property owner is maintaining a nuisance such as a chemical plant emitting harmful fumes, an abutting owner may bring an action to abate the nuisance.

When a defect is discovered in a seller's title and the seller refuses to correct it before closing, the buyer can seek specific performance of the contract with an *abatement* from the purchase price because of the defect. For example, Gloria Russell enters into a contract to purchase Bill Park's $100,000 house. At the time of closing, a title search reveals that Park has not paid $5,000 in property taxes. Park refuses to pay the taxes and also changes his mind about selling the property to Ms. Russell. She could deposit $95,000 into court and force a sale of the property in an action for specific performance. Ms. Russell would then pay the state the $5,000 in unpaid taxes and obtain clear title to the property.

Tax abatement occurs when there is tax reduction or cessation of an initial assessed valuation, such as an error in the tax assessment.

A summary abatement is the court-ordered destruction of premises that are considered to be unsafe or partially destroyed.

ABLE In the phrase, "ready, willing, and able buyer," used to determine if a broker is entitled to a commission, "able" refers to financial ability. It does not mean the buyer must have all the cash for the purchase; it means the buyer must be able to qualify for and arrange the necessary financing within the time specified in the purchase agreement. (*See PROCURING CAUSE.*)

ABSENTEE OWNER A property owner who does not reside on the property and who usually relies on a property manager to manage the investment. A slum landlord is most often an absentee owner.

In recent years, the Securities and Exchange Commission (SEC) has closely scrutinized the sale of resort condominiums to nonresident investors. Of particular interest to the SEC are cases in which the developer or agents of the developer stress the economic and investment benefits of absentee ownership, and offer property management as part of the purchase transaction. In certain cases, the SEC characterizes the sale of the condominium (when coupled with a management program or rental pool sponsored by the developer) as an "investment contract" and therefore requires that the developer register the condominium security with the SEC prior to selling any of the units. This is a time-consuming and costly process.

There have been many recent changes in federal tax laws dealing with the ownership of depreciable real property when the owner is absent most of the year but occupies the property on vacations or at other times for part of the year. These changes are aimed at reducing the tax depreciation advantages when an absentee owner uses the property as a second home. In this area, tax advice from experienced counsel should be sought. (See *REAL PROPERTY SECURITIES REGISTRATION, VACATION HOME.*)

ABSOLUTE   Describes something that is unrestricted and without conditions or limitations, as in a fee simple absolute estate or an absolute conveyance.

ABSORPTION RATE   An estimate of the rate at which a particular classification of space—such as new office space, new housing, or new condominium units—will be sold or occupied each year. A prediction of this rate is often involved in a feasibility study or an appraisal in connection with a request for financing. (See *FEASIBILITY STUDY.*)

ABSTRACTION   The allocation of the appraised total value of the property between land and building. An appraisal method whereby an appraiser compares several improved properties by deducting or abstracting the value of any improvements to the land from the total cost of the real estate. The figures that remain represent the supposed cost of the land itself. The comparison is then made as if it were a raw land appraisal, and the abstracted value is adjusted depending on the kind and condition of the improvements.

ABSTRACT OF TITLE   A full summary of all consecutive grants, conveyances, wills, records, and judicial proceedings affecting title to a specific parcel of real estate, together with a statement of all recorded liens and encumbrances affecting the property and their present status. The person preparing the abstract of title, called an abstractor, searches the title as recorded or registered with the county recorder, county registrar, circuit court, and/or other official sources. He or she then summarizes the various instruments affecting the property and arranges them in the chronological order of recording, starting with the original grant of title. The abstract also includes a list of the public records searched and not searched in preparation of the report. In summarizing a deed in the chain of title, the abstractor might note the recorder's book and page number, the date of the deed, the recording date, the names of the grantor and grantee, a brief description of the property, the type of deed, and any conditions or restrictions contained in the deed.

The abstract of title does not guarantee or assure the validity of the title of the property. It is a condensed history that merely discloses those items about the property that are of public record, and thus does not reveal such things as encroachments and forgeries. The abstractor, therefore, is usually liable only for damages caused by his or her negligence in searching the public records. (*See CERTIFICATE OF TITLE, CHAIN OF TITLE, PRELIMINARY REPORT, TITLE INSURANCE, TITLE REPORT.*)

ABUTMENT   A specific part of a wall or pier on which an object presses, such as the supports at either end of a bridge.

ABUTTING OWNER   An owner whose land adjoins a public road or any contiguous property. The major problems between abutting owners occur regarding encroachments, party walls, light and air easements, and lateral support. Abutter's rights include the right to see and be seen from the street. (*See ACCESS, LATERAL AND SUBJACENT SUPPORT.*)

ACCELERATED COST RECOVERY SYSTEM   Under the Economic Recovery Tax Act of 1981, a new and simplified depreciation system was created to replace the former complicated acceler-ated depreciation rules. On all improved properties purchased after January 1, 1981, new depreciation schedules have been set up permitting a 175 percent of straight-line write-off over a 15-year period or a straight-line write-off using 15-, 35-, or 45-year recovery periods. This new method results in the fastest recovery of cost and also eliminates the prior IRS challenges over the appropriate useful life. In addition, there is no longer any question over salvage value since a qualified asset can be depreciated down to the last dollar of cost.

Under this new cost-recovery system, component cost allocation cannot be used to establish shorter lives for parts of a building. If the taxpayer makes any "substantial improvement" to the building, then that improvement is, in essence, deemed to be another building and the taxpayer can use a different recovery period for the improvement. Also, certain low-income housing can qualify for a special 200 percent declining balance method over a 15-year period.

A critical aspect of this new system is the recapture-of-depreciation rule. For residential real property, the recapture rule stays the same; that is, any excess depreciation taken over the straight-line amount will be recaptured as ordinary income when the property is transferred. However, if nonresidential property is depreciated using the accelerated 15-year method, then *all* depreciation taken (not just the excess) will be recaptured as ordinary income. Whereas if the taxpayer chooses the 15-year straight line or the 35-year or 45-year periods, then all gain will be recognized as long-term capital gain with no recapture.

Under the law, most real property is deemed to have a 15-year recovery period (mobile homes are 10 years) totally unrelated to the property's true economic life. However, the taxpayer may choose to use the 35- or 45-year periods.

Under the straight-line method, an owner can depreciate about $6\frac{2}{3}$ percent of the cost of the building each year. By contrast, under the 175 percent declining balance method, an owner can depreciate approximately 12 percent of the building cost in the first year; however, that percentage declines each year thereafter.

For real property, first year write-offs start to accrue on the first day of the month the property is purchased or converted to investment property. Set forth below is a chart for a calendar year taxpayer to use in the 15-year accelerated 175 percent method. Simply multiply the property cost by the appropriate percentage. For example, if a property costing $140,000 was placed in service during July 1982, the amount of the deduction would be $140,000 × 5.833 percent or $8,166.20.

Month	Percentage	Month	Percentage
January	11.667%	July	5.833%
February	10.695%	August	4.860%
March	9.723%	September	3.889%
April	8.750%	October	2.917%
May	7.779%	November	1.944%
June	6.805%	December	0.972%

(See ACCELERATED DEPRECIATION.)

ACCELERATED DEPRECIATION   A method of calculating, for tax purposes, the cost write-off (depreciation) of certain property and improvements to real property used in a trade or business, or held for the production of income, at a faster rate than would be achieved by using the straight-line method of depreciation. This method assumes that an asset deteriorates more rapidly in its early years.

Pursuant to the Internal Revenue Code, a taxpayer may use the following methods of accelerated depreciation for assets placed in service prior to 1981:

1. *125 percent declining balance* for used residential properties with a remaining useful life of 20 years or more.

2. *150 percent declining balance* for all new depreciable real estate. This is the fastest available method for new depreciable nonresidential real estate.

3. *sum of the years' digits* for new residential rental properties.

4. *200 percent declining balance* (double declining balance) for new residential rental properties. If a property combines residential and commercial uses, at least 80 percent of the property must be residential to qualify for 200 percent depreciation.

5. *straight-line method* using a 60-month useful life for rehabilitation expenditures on low- and moderate-income residential rental properties

The main tax advantage of accelerated depreciation methods is larger depreciation write-offs during the earlier years of ownership, when most investors are anxious to get the largest tax write-offs possible.

For depreciable property placed in service after 1980, accelerated depreciation methods have been replaced by the "Accelerated Cost Recovery System" (ACRS) by which personal property may be depreciated over 3, 5, or 10 years, and depreciable real property over 15 years at 175 percent. The IRS has prepared a chart showing the percentage of cost (with no deduction required for salvage value) that may be deducted each year.

It is important to consider the effects of the depreciation recapture rules on accelerated depreciation. For real property, any depreciation taken in excess of allowable straight-line depreciation with respect to residential depreciable real estate is subject to recapture as ordinary income to the extent of gain resulting from the sale. Note also that excess depreciation is a tax preference item subject to the minimum tax on tax preference income. (*See ACCELERATED COST RECOVERY SYSTEM, FIRST YEAR DEPRECIATION, RECAPTURE OF DEPRECIATION, STRAIGHT-LINE METHOD, TAX PREFERENCE.*)

ACCELERATION CLAUSE A clause in a mortgage, trust deed, promissory note, or contract for deed (agreement of sale) that gives the lender (payee) the right to call all sums due and payable in advance of the fixed payment date upon the occurrence of a specified event, such as default on an installment payment, or destruction (waste) of the premises, or placing an encumbrance on the property, or its sale or assignment. Usually the payee has the option to accelerate the note upon default of payment of any installment of interest or principal when due, provided he or she gives adequate notice and specifies a time within which the defaulting party may cure the default. In addition to nonpayment of an installment, the payee may also accelerate for other breaches of provisions in the contract, such as failure to pay taxes and assessments or to keep the property insured or in repair. Acceleration may also be exercised by a lender when it is discovered that the borrower (mortgagor) does not hold good title to the mortgaged property, contrary to his or her prior claims at the time the mortgage was created or upon condemnation of all or part of the premises.

The provision for acceleration must be expressly set forth in the mortgage or contract-for-deed document; otherwise the right does not exist. There should be a consistency between the acceleration provisions stated in the mortgage and those stated in the promissory note. An acceleration clause is also called a "due-on-sale" clause or call provision when it provides for acceleration upon the sale of the property. A court might hold an acceleration clause to be unenforceable if it is deemed to be an unreasonable restraint or restriction on alienation.

The seller under a contract for deed usually inserts an acceleration clause in order to declare the entire balance due and payable when the buyer fails to cure a default. Without this clause, the seller would have to sue the buyer as each installment payment became due. (*See ALIENATION CLAUSE, DUE-ON-SALE CLAUSE, MORTGAGE, PREPAYMENT PRIVILEGE.*)

ACCEPTANCE The expression of the intention of the person receiving an offer (offeree, usually the seller in a real estate transaction) to be bound by the terms of the offer. The acceptance must be communicated to the person making the offer (offeror, usually the buyer). It is not essential that the communication be in writing—it may be a mere nod of the head—but if the offer is in writing and pertains to real property, the acceptance also must be in writing. Silence is usually not a sufficient indication of an intent to accept. However, where a broker has handled many sales for a developer at a 4 percent commission and the developer offers another property that the broker sells, the broker may be held to have agreed to another 4 percent rate, even though a more reasonable rate in the community might be 6 percent.

The buyer has the right to revoke his or her offer at any time prior to receiving notice of the seller's acceptance. This is true even if the buyer has stated that he will keep the offer open for a certain time, so it is important for the broker to insert in the sales contract the exact time of the acceptance and to communicate such acceptance to the buyer or offeror as soon as practicable. Communication is particularly significant because the buyer might effectively revoke his or her offer to purchase at a time after the seller has accepted the offer but before such acceptance has been effectively communicated to the buyer.

Also, the acceptance must be made within the time limit stated in the offer. If no time limit is stated, then the acceptance is valid if made within a reasonable time of the offer. A late acceptance is, at most, a counteroffer.

If the offer prescribes a specific method of acceptance—for instance, by telegram—then the acceptance is not effective unless that method is used. On the other hand, if the offer does not specify any method of acceptance, then any reasonable and customary method may be used. For instance, acceptance of a mailed offer becomes an effective and binding contract when deposited in the mails. (The law presumes the buyer appointed the post office the agent to receive notification of acceptance.) Where the acceptance is communicated in an unusual manner (such as placing it in an ad in the newspaper), then the contract is not effective until and unless the acceptance is received by the buyer within a reasonable time. (What constitutes a reasonable time depends on the facts of each particular case and custom within the community.) To avoid the confusion that might be caused by the communication rule, some offers specify that the acceptance is not effective unless a signed copy is received by the offeror or broker within a certain time.

Voluntary and unconditional acceptance of a deed by the grantee is essential to a valid delivery of the deed—if the grantee does not want title to the property, he need not take it. Acceptance is often inferred from certain acts of the grantee, such as taking possession, recording the deed, paying the sales price, or obtaining a mortgage on the property. The courts will usually presume acceptance when the grantee is benefited by the transaction, but a court would probably not presume acceptance when, for example, Mr. Brown grants his $100,000 farm, heavily encumbered with $600,000 in debt and full of building code violations, to Mr. Smith, who dies without ever being aware the property was deeded to him. If, however, the property were free and clear of debt and code violations, the court would probably presume *acceptance* by the unaware decedent and the property would thus pass to his estate, provided there was a valid delivery. (*See CONTRACT, DELIVERY, OFFER AND ACCEPTANCE.*)

ACCESS   A means by which property is approached, or a method of entrance into or upon a property. Access is also a general or specific right of ingress and egress to a particular property. A property owner usually has the right to have access to and from the property to a public street or highway abutting thereon. This includes the right to the unrestricted flow of light and air from the street to the property. The term "access" also refers to the right of a riparian owner to pass to and from the waters upon which the property borders.

Many state laws maintain that a residential tenant shall not unreasonably withhold consent to his or her landlord to enter the dwelling unit in order to inspect the premises, make necessary or agreed repairs, decorations, alterations, or improvements, supply services as agreed, show the dwelling unit to prospective purchasers, mortgagees, or tenants, or demand rent. However, the landlord shall not abuse this right of access nor use it to harass the tenant. Except in cases of emergency or when impracticable to do so, the landlord should give the tenant notice of his or her intent to enter, and enter only during reasonable hours. As long as the request is not unreasonable, the tenant cannot refuse access to the landlord. The landlord is liable for any damages caused by an entry made without the consent of the tenant. However, for damages caused under emergency circumstances in which the landlord was not negligent, the tenant leaving the bathtub water running for instance, the landlord is not liable for damages. (*See LANDLOCKED, UNIFORM RESIDENTIAL LANDLORD AND TENANT ACT.*)

ACCESSION The acquisition by an owner of title to additions or improvements attaching to the property as a result of the annexation of fixtures, or as a result of alluvial deposits along the banks of streams by accretion. For example, if Ben Brown builds a fence on his neighbor's property without an agreement permitting Brown to remove it, ownership of the fence accedes to the neighbor, unless the neighbor requires that it be removed. (*See ALLUVION.*)

ACCESSORY BUILDING A building located on a lot and used for a purpose other than that of the principal building on the same lot. For example, a garage, pump house, or storage shed would be considered an accessory building if erected on the same parcel of land as the property's main building.

ACCOMMODATION PARTY A party who signs a negotiable instrument (such as a promissory note) as maker, acceptor, or endorser, without receiving any consideration, to accommodate another party and enhance the creditworthiness of the paper by lending his or her name as further security. For example, a brother who co-signs a bank note with his sister so that she can borrow money to buy a house would be an accommodation party to the lending contract. (*See GUARANTOR.*)

ACCORD AND SATISFACTION The settlement of an obligation. An accord is an agreement by a creditor to accept something different from or less than what the creditor feels he or she is entitled to. When the creditor accepts the consideration offered by the debtor for the accord, the acceptance constitutes a "satisfaction," and the obligation of the debtor is extinguished. For these rules to apply, it is essential that the obligation be in dispute (that is, an unliquidated debt). For example, if Gary Green clearly owes Bob Brown $100 and Green sends a $75 check marked "payment in full," Brown still has a claim against Green for the $25 balance. If, however, the amount owed is disputed, and Green offers a $75 check as payment in full, then the act of cashing the check would be an accord and satisfaction, and the obligation would be extinguished. (*See NOVATION.*)

ACCOUNT PAYABLE A liability (debt) representing an amount owed to a creditor, usually arising from the purchase of merchandise, supplies or services is an account payable. It is not necessarily due immediately.

ACCOUNT RECEIVABLE A claim against a debtor usually arising from sales or services rendered to the debtor is an account receivable, the opposite of an account payable. It is not necessarily due or past due at any specific time.

ACCRETION The gradual and imperceptible addition of land by alluvial deposits of soil through natural causes, such as shoreline movement caused by streams or rivers. This added land upon a bank or stream, navigable or not, becomes the property of the riparian or littoral owner, and also becomes subject to any existing mortgages. Conversely, the owner can lose title to land that is gradually washed away through erosion. (*See ALLUVION, AVULSION, RIPARIAN.*)

ACCRUAL METHOD   An accounting method of reporting income and expenses in which expenses incurred and income earned for a given period are reported, although such expenses and income actually may not have been paid or received yet. It is the right to receive, not the actual receipt, that determines the inclusion of the amount in gross income. Similarly, expenses are deducted when the taxpayer's liability becomes fixed and definite, not when he or she actually pays the expense. The accrual method is generally not available for use by individuals.

In the popular cash-basis method, income is reported only upon receipt and expenses reported only when they are actually paid.

ACCRUED   That which has accumulated over a period of time is accrued, such as accrued depreciation, accrued interest, or accrued expenses. Accrued expenses have been incurred but are not yet payable, such as real property taxes. In a closing statement, accrued expenses are credited to the purchaser, who will pay these expenses at a later date for the benefit of the seller.

ACCRUED DEPRECIATION   A bookkeeping account that shows the total amount of depreciation taken on an asset since it was acquired; also called accumulated depreciation. For appraisal purposes, it is often called diminished utility, which is the difference between the cost to replace the property (as of the appraisal date) and the property's current appraised value as judged by its "observed condition." (See *BOOK VALUE, DEPRECIATION [APPRAISAL]*.)

ACKNOWLEDGMENT   A formal declaration made before a duly authorized officer, usually a notary public, by a person who has signed a document, is an acknowledgment, as is the document itself. It is designed to prevent forged and fraudulently induced documents from taking effect. The officer confirms that the signing is the voluntary act and genuine signature of a person either who is known to the officer or who provides adequate identification. Though typical, it is not necessary that the person sign in the presence of the officer. The officer will be liable for damages caused by his or her negligent failure to identify the person correctly—for instance, if forgery occurs because the officer accepted a verification by telephone.

In most states, a document will not be accepted for recording unless it is acknowledged. A *foreign acknowledgment* (one that has taken place outside of the state in which it is to be recorded) is generally valid if it is valid where made. The signature of the foreign officer is sufficient evidence that the acknowledgment is taken in accordance with the laws of the place where made and of the authority of the officer to take the acknowledgment, thus entitling the acknowledged document to be recorded and, where appropriate, to be read into evidence in any judicial proceeding without further proof of its authenticity. However, for documents signed outside of the U.S., many states require that the acknowledgment be made by an official at a U.S. Consulate Office.

If there is any material crossed out, erased, or changed in the document, the officer should initial these changes if so approved by the parties, otherwise the document may not be acceptable for recordation. Because of modern methods of reproducing documents, it is generally recommended that signatures be made in black ink. (See *AFFIDAVIT, ATTESTATION, JURAT, NOTARY PUBLIC, RECORDING*.)

There are different types of acknowledgment forms for corporations, partnerships, trustee, and attorneys-in-fact.

A typical acknowledgment for an individual's signature is shown below.

```
┌─────────────────────────────────────────────────────────┐
│  STATE OF:                                                │
│                              SS:                          │
│  COUNTY OF:                                               │
│                                                           │
│    On this _____ day of _____, 19 ____,  │
│  before me personally appeared _____    │
│  _____,      │
│  to me known to be the person(s) described in and who     │
│  executed the foregoing instrument and acknowledged to    │
│  me that _____ executed the same as _____ free act        │
│  and deed.                                                │
│                                                           │
│                    _____   │
│                    Notary Public                          │
│  (NOTARY SEAL)                                            │
│                    My Commission Expires: _____       │
└─────────────────────────────────────────────────────────┘
```

ACQUISITION APPRAISAL   The appraisal for market value of a property to be acquired for a public use by governmental condemnation or negotiation. The purpose of the appraisal is to set the amount of just compensation to be offered the property owner. (*See CONDEMNATION.*)

ACQUISITION COST   The amount of money or other valuable consideration expended to obtain title to property, which includes, in addition to the purchase price, such items as closing costs, appraisal fees, mortgage origination fees, finance charges, and title insurance. (*See BASIS.*)

ACRE   A measure of land area equal to 43,560 square feet; which is equivalent to 208.71 feet by 208.71 feet, 4,840 square yards, 4,047 square meters, 160 square rods, or 0.4047 hectare. (*See MEASUREMENT TABLES.*)

ACREAGE ZONING   Zoning intended to reduce residential density by requiring large building lots. Also called *large-lot* zoning or "snob zoning." (*See DENSITY, ZONING.*)

ACRE FOOT   A volume of water, sand, or minerals, equal to an area of one acre with a depth of one foot (43,560 cubic feet). If a liquid, it equals 325,850 gallons.

ACT OF GOD   An act of nature beyond human control, such as a tidal wave, flood, volcanic eruption, or earthquake. Many contracts include a *force majeure* clause that temporarily or

permanently relieves the parties of performance of a contract where
has destroyed or damaged the subject matter or prevented performa
called a *destroyed or materially damaged clause*, which relieves th
real estate sales contract from performance when an act of God has
property's improvements prior to the transfer of title. (*See FORCE*

ACTUAL NOTICE   Express information or fact; that whic
actual knowledge. Constructive not
other hand, is knowledge that is implied by law—that which the law (
with knowing. Thus, for example, a person having either actual or c
notice of the prior rights of a third party to a property normally takes th
subject to that third party's rights. One cannot claim the benefits of the
law if he or she takes title to property with actual notice of a previously
but unrecorded instrument. There is also a third type of notice calle
notice, where circumstances, appearances, or rumors are such that one l
to inquire further in order to determine whether property ownership exi
person other than the one claiming that ownership. (*See CONSTI*
NOTICE, INQUIRY NOTICE, LEGAL NOTICE, RECORDING.)

ACTUARY   A person, usually associated with an in
company or savings and loan association,
in calculating the value of life interests, pension plans, and annuities. (*S*
ESTATE.)

ADD-BACK   This refers to the practice of deferrir
payment of a portion of interest due and a
this amount to the balloon payment due at the end of the loan. (*See NEG*
AMORTIZATION.)

ADDENDUM   Additional material attached to and made p
a document. There often is insufficient spa
write all the details of the transaction on the sales contract form, so the parties
attach an addendum or supplement to the document. The addendum shoul
incorporated by reference in the sales contract and should be dated and signe
initialed by all the parties. (*See RIDER*.)

ADDITION   Any construction that increases a building's s
or significantly adds to it. For example, co
struction of a second floor on top of a one-level structure would be an additio

ADDITIONAL   A mortgage-type instrument used to secure a
CHARGE MORTGAGE   additional advance of money from the holder o
the mortgage to the mortgagor subsequent to the
original loan transaction. (*See FUTURE ADVANCES*.)

ADDITIONAL   The additional earnest money given by the buyer
DEPOSIT   to the seller or to escrow under a purchase
agreement. The additional deposit is usually
tendered within a short period of time after acceptance of the offer. If a broker is
able to obtain only a small initial deposit, he or she should attempt to get an
additional deposit that brings the total deposit up to 5 to 10 percent of the
purchase price. Otherwise, there may not be enough money to pay some of the

costs (title policy, commission, escrow fees, attorney fees, and so on) in the event the buyer defaults. For example, Francine Buyer might deposit $1,000 with her offer to purchase Jim Seller's $50,000 condominium unit and agree to pay an additional deposit of $4,000 within five working days after the seller's acceptance. In the event the buyer breaches the contract, the seller may elect to keep all deposit money, including the additional deposit, as his damages.

If the buyer is late in making the additional deposit payment, the seller may be able to terminate the contract if a court holds that failure to make timely payment is a material breach. (See DEPOSIT.)

ADDITIONAL SPACE OPTION

A right within a lease giving a tenant the option to expand the tenant's leased space during the lease term as required and on terms specified in the lease.

ADD-ON INTEREST

A method of computing interest whereby interest is charged on the entire principal amount for the specified term, regardless of any repayments of principal that are made. The end result is an effective interest charge that is almost double the stated rate. The borrower is paying interest on the full principal sum for the entire loan period (and not on the declining balance), even though the principal is being reduced each month. (See BLOCK INTEREST, INTEREST.)

ADHESION CONTRACT

A contract that is very one sided, favoring the party who drafted the document. In fact, an adhesion contract can be so one sided that doubt arises as to its being a voluntary and uncoerced agreement because it implies a serious inequality of bargaining power. Courts will not enforce provisions in adhesion contracts that are unfair and oppressive to the party who did not prepare the contract. Contracts with a lot of fine print, such as franchise agreements, mortgages, and leases, are sometimes challenged as adhesion contracts on the basis that the nondrafting party did not have a chance to bargain on the various provisions of the agreement. Also called a "take it or leave it" contract.

An insurance contract (property, title, life) is sometimes challenged as being an adhesion contract. Courts have held that any ambiguity is to be construed in favor of the insured and any exclusion from coverage must be clearly and conspicuously stated. Courts will also apply the doctrine of unconscionability. (See BOILER PLATE, UNCONSCIONABILITY.)

ADJUSTABLE RATE LOAN

A broad term for all loans (mortgage or deed of trust) with rates and terms that can change. Both the Comptroller of the Currency, which regulates national banks, and the Federal Home Loan Bank, which governs federal savings and loan associations, issued guidelines in 1981 allowing the issuance of real estate loans having provisions that the rate of interest being charged the borrower could increase or decrease at certain time intervals (e.g., every 6 months) within a certain range (e.g., 1%). It can be anticipated the adjustable rate loan will become commonplace. It can also be anticipated that the allowable ranges as to time intervals, percent of increase or decrease, and total increases or decreases will change as market conditions change.

ADJUSTABLE RATE MORTGAGE (ARM)

See ADJUSTABLE RATE LOAN.

ADJUSTED BASIS   The original cost basis of a property reduced by certain deductions and increased by certain improvement costs. The original basis determined at the time of acquisition is reduced by the amount of allowable depreciation or depletion allowances taken by the taxpayer, and by the amount of any uncompensated property losses suffered by the taxpayer. It is then increased by the cost of capital improvements plus certain carrying costs and assessments. The amount of gain or loss recognized by the taxpayer upon sale of the property is determined by subtracting the adjusted basis on the date of sale from the adjusted sales price. (*See BASIS, BOOK VALUE, DEPRECIATION [TAX], GAIN.*)

ADJUSTMENTS   Adjustments are the increases or decreases of value that help to set the market price of a subject property by comparing its features or amenities to those of comparable properties sold recently in the same neighborhood. Each feature is assigned a relative worth, and the subject property's market value goes up or down for each feature that differs from the comparables. (*See COMPARABLES, MARKET-DATA APPROACH.*)

In real estate closings, adjustments refer to the credits and debits of a settlement statement such as real property tax, insurance, and rent prorations.

ADMEASUREMENT OF DOWER   Admeasurement means the determination and apportionment of shares. In the administration of an estate, the admeasurement of dower is an heir's judicial remedy when the widow has been assigned more than she was entitled to under her dower right. In valuing her dower interest, standard annuity tables of mortality are used to ascertain the actuarial value of the wife's future life interest, which is then applied to her proportionate share of the estate. (*See DOWER.*)

ADMINISTRATOR   A person appointed by the court to settle the estate of a person who has died intestate (leaving no will). Sometimes referred to as the personal representative. (*See EXECUTOR.*)

AD VALOREM   Latin for "according to valuation," usually referring to a type of tax or assessment. Real property tax is an ad valorem tax based on the assessed valuation of the property. Each property bears a tax burden proportionate to its value, as opposed to a specific tax per unit based on quantity, such as a tax per gallon of gasoline or package of cigarettes.

ADVANCE   The giving of consideration before it is due. Money is advanced by one party, such as a mortgagee or vendor, to cover carrying charges, such as taxes and insurance, on the property which were not properly paid by the other party in default. These amounts paid are credited to the account of the advancing party. For example, a second mortgagee might advance delinquent first-mortgage payments of the borrower in order to prevent a foreclosure of the secured property.

Also refers to additional funds disbursed under an open-end mortgage, or to advances made by a construction lender to a developer-borrower. (*See DRAW.*)

ADVANCE FEE An advance fee is paid before any services are rendered. Specifically, it is a practice of some brokers to obtain a nonrefundable fee from the seller in advance to cover the advertising of properties or businesses for sale, while giving no guarantee that a buyer will be found, which is often held to be improper conduct.

ADVERSE POSSESSION The acquiring of title to real property owned by someone else by means of open, notorious, and continuous possession for a statutory period of time. The burden to prove title is on the possessor. A possessor must show that: 1. he or she has been in possession under a claim of right or color of title (such as a defectively executed deed); 2. he or she was in actual, open, and notorious possession of the premises so as to constitute reasonable notice to the record owner; 3. possession was both exclusive and hostile to the title of the owner (that is, without the owner's permission and evidencing an intention to maintain the claim of ownership against all who may contest it); and 4. possession was uninterrupted and continuous for at least the prescriptive period stipulated by state law. In this regard, successive occupation of the premises by persons who are successors in interest (that is, by privity of contract or descent) can be added together to meet the continuous-use requirement. For example, a father adversely occupies a certain parcel of land for four years. Upon his death his son succeeds to his interest and "tacks on" to his father's four years' prior possession. The word "POACH" will help you remember that Possession is Open, Actual, Continuous, and Hostile.

The statutory period does not run against any individual under a legal disability (insanity) or until the individual has a legal cause of action to oust the possessor. For example, an adverse possessor could acquire title against a life tenant, but not against the remainderman who has no right to possession until the prior life estate is terminated.

The main purpose of adverse possession statutes is to insure the fullest and most productive use of privately-owned land. Land has been, is, and will continue to be in short supply, and if someone makes no attempt to use his or her real estate for a long period of time, it is deemed better for someone who intends to make good use of the property to take title.

Any person who takes title by inheritance or conveyance from the owner takes title subject to the claim of an adverse possessor, since the new titleholder is charged with knowledge of the rights of parties in possession of the property. This also applies to purchasers and donees. However, if the owner's interest was subject to liens and encumbrances at the time an adverse possessor entered into possession, then the adverse possessor is subject to them.

One who claims title to property by adverse possession does not have readily marketable title until he or she obtains and records a judicial decree "quieting" the title or obtains a quitclaim deed from the ousted owner. Once this is done, however, the title becomes of equal dignity with that of an owner who had acquired title by way of a deed.

When all requirements have been met, the owner's title is extinguished and a new title is created in favor of the adverse possessor. The effective date of the new title, as far as the original owner is concerned, is the first adverse entry. Thus, suits by the former owner based on trespass, profits, or rents during the adverse period are barred.

Some states have added a requirement that the adverse possession must be "in good faith." This means that at the time the claimant gained possession of the property the claimant must have honestly believed that he or she had some right to the land, and this belief must have been based on some fact, such as a deed that would have created good title for the claimant but for the fact that it was improperly executed.

In all but a few states, it is not usually a prerequisite that the claimant have paid taxes on the property for any certain period of time (although in some states a claimant's paying taxes may shorten the prescriptive period). However, a court might consider that a claimant's failure to pay taxes is evidence that he or she really did not claim ownership of the property.

Prudent owners of raw land held for future sale or development make periodic inspections of their property to check against adverse possessors. The mere posting of "no trespassing" signs may not be sufficient to prevent an adverse possessor from acquiring rights to the property. An owner must defend his or her ownership rights and do so within a certain period of time. An owner could stop the adverse possession by a re-entry, an action for ejectment, or an action to quiet the title.

The courts do not usually allow a claim of adverse possession where the owner and claimant have a close family relationship, such as father and son or husband and wife, because in these cases hostile claims are too difficult to prove. Cotenants normally cannot claim adverse possession against each other without an actual and clear ejectment of one cotenant by another.

Prescriptive rights in general are not usually favored by the law, insofar as they create forfeitures of the rights of others. There is often a presumption that, when a person has entered into possession of another's property, such possession was with the owner's permission and consistent with the true owner's title.

Generally, one cannot take title to state or federal lands by adverse possession. However, the federal Color of Title Act provides that a claimant who has met all the tests of adverse possession on public land may receive a patent to such land, provided the land does not exceed 160 acres and all taxes are paid. The United States, however, reserves the right to all coal and mineral rights to the property. In addition, title to Torrens-registered property usually cannot be taken by adverse possession. (See COLOR OF TITLE, OPEN AND NOTORIOUS POSSESSION, PRESCRIPTION, QUIET TITLE ACTION, TRESPASS.)

ADVERSE USER   The prescriptive acquisition of the right to a limited use of the land of another, such as a pathway easement across another's property. In order to acquire an easement by adverse user, the claimant must satisfy generally the same requirements as those for adverse possession, including the prescriptive period. While most easements cannot be lost by mere nonuse, an easement created by an adverse user can be terminated by nonuse for the prescriptive period of adverse possession. (See LOST-GRANT DOCTRINE.)

ADVERTISING   The public promotion of one's products and services. In real estate, advertising is governed by various rules and regulations established by federal, state, local, and private authorities.

A broker needs a client's written authorization to advertise a property, and in any offering the price quoted shall not be other than that agreed on with the owner as the offering price. (To quote another price involves a *dual price agreement*, which is a violation of the Realtors® Code of Ethics and many state license laws.) Generally, the broker pays for advertising listed property unless a prior agreement has been made with the seller to share the costs. Many state license laws prohibit the use of *blind ads*; that is, advertisements placed by a real estate licensee on behalf of the seller which do not include the name of the licensed real estate broker.

Under usual multiple-listing service (MLS) rules and regulations, advertisements must include the MLS number. The recommended format is to place the MLS number in parentheses.

Truth-in-Lending: Federal Truth-in-Lending laws require certain types of disclosure information if the ad includes specific financing terms or credit terms. (*See TRUTH-IN-LENDING LAWS.*)

Condominiums and Subdivisions: Many state condominium, timesharing, and subdivision laws control advertising relating to condominium and subdivision sales. These laws require that ads contain no false or misleading statements, and that no part of any material contained in a public report or public offering statement be used for advertising purposes unless the report is used in its entirety. In addition, some state agencies insist on reviewing all such ads before publication. In some states, strict disclosure laws have been passed that apply to real estate advertising. In many states, a developer's right to advertise new projects may be restricted until certain state registration requirements have been met.

Discrimination: Federal regulations prohibit advertisements for housing that discriminate on the basis of race, color, religion, sex, or national origin. State regulations may also include marital status, age, or physical handicap.

AEOLIAN SOIL   A type of soil that has been formed from windblown solid materials, such as sand dunes and volcanic ash deposits. Also, soil transported by the wind.

AESTHETIC VALUE   An appraisal term describing an intangible benefit of property that is exceptionally attractive or pleasing as opposed to purely utilitarian. Protecting the aesthetic value such as a hillside site overlooking the ocean, for example, by zoning ordinance is a permissible exercise of the government's police power.

AFFIDAVIT   A sworn statement written down and made under oath before a notary public or other official authorized by law to administer an oath. It literally means "has pledged his faith." The affiant (person making the oath and sometimes called the "deponent") must swear before the notary that the facts contained in the affidavit are true and correct.

An example of a simple affidavit format is shown on the facing page.

The purpose of an affidavit is to help establish or prove a fact. Affidavits may be used to prove, among other things, identity, age, residence, marital status, and possession of property.

An affidavit is a complete instrument within itself, whereas an acknowledgment is always part of or an appendage to another instrument. An affidavit is sworn to, but an acknowledgment is not. (*See AFFIRMATION.*)

```
STATE OF:
                        SS:
COUNTY OF:


_____ being duly sworn, deposes and says
      (he)
that  (she) is the _____ of _____,
                   Office Held      (Name of Company)
the applicant named in the foregoing application, and that
the statements made in the application are true and correct
              (his)
to the best of (her) knowledge and belief.


_____
      (signature)


Subscribed and sworn to before me this
_____ day of _____, 19 ___

_____
Notary Public
My Commission Expires: _____
```

AFFIDAVIT OF TITLE (AFFIDAVIT OF OWNERSHIP) A written statement made under oath by the seller or grantor and acknowledged before a notary public in which the grantor: (1) identifies him- or herself and indicates marital status; (2) certifies that since the examination of title on the date of the contract there are no judgments, bankruptcies, or divorces against him or her, no unrecorded deeds or contracts, no repairs or improvements that have not been paid for, and no known defects in the title; and (3) certifies that the grantor is in possession of the premises. Customarily used in several states (New York). (*See CONTINUATION.*)

AFFIRMATION A declaration as to the truth of a statement. An affirmation is used in lieu of an oath, especially when the affiant or deponent objects to taking an oath for personal or religious reasons.

AFFIRMATIVE MARKETING PROGRAM A program designed to inform all buyers in the minority community of homes for sale without discrimination and to provide Realtors® with procedures and educational materials to assist in compliance with the law. An active affirmative marketing program is currently being conducted by many Realtor® boards in conjunction with the federal Department of Housing and Urban Development (HUD). After a local Realtor® board adopts the affirmative program, the board is then responsible to HUD for compliance.

HUD also requires developers to submit affirmative fair housing marketing plans prior to HUD granting any feasibility or fund reservations. These plans are intended to encourage the integration of minority groups into housing. In addition, HUD has published specific advertising guidelines, some of which prohibit the selective use of advertising with a discriminatory effect.

A-FRAME CONSTRUCTION A type of residential construction in which the exterior design of the building resembles the letter A.

AFTER-ACQUIRED Something acquired after a certain event takes place. An after-acquired title is acquired by a grantor of property *after* the grantor has attempted to convey good title. Upon the grantor's obtaining good title, it will automatically pass by operation of law to the grantee. For example, Smith conveys his farm to Jones on January 1, 1982, by warranty deed. However, Smith did not have valid title on January 1 because he held title to the property under a forged deed. On March 5, 1982, Smith did receive good title under a properly executed deed, so Jones automatically acquires good title on March 5.

Note that an after-acquired title will not pass to a grantee under a quitclaim deed, since such an instrument only purports to transfer the grantor's current interest in the land, if any.

Fixtures that are bought, paid for, and installed by the property owner-mortgagor are subject to the lien of the mortgage. In addition, many mortgages provide that all fixtures found on the property *after* the mortgage has been made are subject to the mortgage. The Uniform Commercial Code (UCC) has established guidelines to settle conflicting claims between mortgagees and chattel security claimants involving prior rights to after-acquired property, such as appliances bought on time and installed on the mortgaged premises. Under the UCC, a debtor can grant a superior security interest in such after-acquired property to a chattel mortgagee. (*See FIXTURE.*)

AGE (1) As applied to a structure, the effective age is the years of age indicated by the condition and utility of the structure, as opposed to the actual or chronological age. (2) Some states extend the coverage of their antidiscrimination housing laws to age, although the Federal Fair Housing Act does not yet cover age. (3) The Federal Equal Credit Opportunity Act does prohibit discriminatory lending practices based on considerations of old age.

AGE-LIFE DEPRECIATION An appraiser's method for computing depreciation based on the life expectancy of a particular building, assuming the structure receives normal care and maintenance. Also refers to useful life for income tax purposes. (*See DEPRECIATION [APPRAISAL].*)

AGENCY A relationship created when one person, the *principal*, delegates to another, the *agent*, the right to act on his or her behalf in business transactions and to exercise some degree of discretion while so acting. There is a vast body of law, both common and statutory, controlling the rights and duties of principal and agent. In addition to this general law of agency, which is applicable to all business transactions, state real estate licensing laws also directly affect the agency relationship between real estate licensees, their clients, and the public. Although agency law is separate from contract law, the two frequently come together in interpreting relationships between real estate agents and their principals.

Note that a valuable consideration need not be involved in an agency relationship. One may gratuitously undertake to act as an agent and will be held to the standards of agency upon assumption of those duties.

An agency gives rise to a fiduciary relationship and imposes on the agent, as the fiduciary of the principal, certain duties, obligations, and high standards of good faith and loyalty. An agency may be a *general agency*, as when a principal gives a property manager the power to manage a real estate project on behalf of the principal on a continuing basis, or it may be a *special agency*, such as the standard listing contract wherein the broker is employed only to find a ready, willing, and able buyer and is not authorized to sell the property nor to bind his or her principal to any contract for the sale of the property.

A client and broker can create a principal/agent relationship with the consequent duties and responsibilities arising from this status, even though the broker does not have a written contract and thus cannot usually collect a commission. In other words, the creation of the fiduciary relationship may be implied from the acts of the parties and does not depend on the existence of a written contract. A licensee often represents the buyer in a transaction without having any written agreement. Once the agency relationship is created, certain rights and obligations attach to it and the broker is liable for any breaches of duty.

The real estate licensee is generally subject to two distinct areas of liability for breach of fiduciary duties to his or her principal: (1) the principal can bring civil action against the licensee-agent for money damages, and (2) the state licensing authority can bring disciplinary proceedings for violation of its regulations. The state is very protective of the consumer in this area since the principal is legally bound to the acts and representations of the agent done within the scope of authority.

Under common law principles, the agent owes the principal personal performance, loyalty, obedience, disclosure of material facts (such as a proposed new school, highway relocation, or new zoning ordinance that would tend to increase the property value over the agreed on listing price), to take reasonable care not to exceed the authority granted to the agent or to misrepresent material facts to the principal or to third parties, to keep proper accounts of all monies, and to place the principal's interests above those of the persons dealing with the principal. Note that an agent has expanded authority in an emergency, including the right to disobey instruction when it is clearly in the best interests of the principal to do so.

Without the principal's authorization, an agent cannot disclose to a third party confidential information or information that hurts the principal's bargaining position, such as the fact that the seller is forced to sell due to loss of job, poor health, or pending divorce, or that the seller will actually accept less than the listing price.

Confidential information learned during the course of the agency cannot be used at a later date against the principal, even after the transaction is closed. This includes financial information used in negotiations involving subsequently listed properties.

While agents are required by law to provide their principals with all material and pertinent facts, race, creed, color, religion, and sex are not material facts and should not be disclosed even at the principal's request.

Frequently, an agent may secure an offer to purchase from a buyer who agrees to list the buyer's own home with the same agent. A prudent broker will disclose this fact to the seller when submitting the offer; otherwise, the broker may be accused of receiving undisclosed profits.

Various state license laws require additional duties of the agent in a principal/ agent relationship. For instance, an agent must disclose in writing any interest the agent may have in the property, such as when one of his or her salespeople or a relative or related corporation offers to purchase the listed property; for example, an agent must disclose that his wife was submitting an offer using her maiden name. An agent may not act for both the seller and the buyer without their written consent, nor may the agent commingle the principal's money or other property with his or her own. A broker may not advertise property without the specific authorization of the owner. A broker must present all written offers to his or her principal.

In dealing with third persons, (for whom he is not the agent), an agent must be fair and honest and must exercise care and diligence because he or she is liable for any material misrepresentations or negligent acts. For this reason, it is a good idea for a broker to make his or her own inspection of the premises and not rely solely on information supplied by the seller. The principal is also liable to the third person for all acts the agent performs within the scope of his or her employment.

An agency may be terminated between a principal and an agent at any time, except if the agency is coupled with an interest. However, if the agency is terminated prior to the stated expiration date, there could be a claim for money damages. An agency is terminated by the death or incapacity of either party (notice of death is not necessary), destruction or condemnation of the property, expiration of the terms of the agency, mutual agreement, renunciation by the agent or revocation by the principal, bankruptcy of the principal (since the title of the property is transferred to a receiver), or completion of the agency. (See AGENCY COUPLED WITH AN INTEREST, DUAL AGENCY, LISTING, RESPONDEAT SUPERIOR, REVOCATION, SCOPE OF AUTHORITY, SUBAGENT, TERMINATION OF LISTING, UNDISCLOSED AGENCY.)

AGENCY COUPLED WITH AN INTEREST

An agency relationship in which the agent acquires an estate or interest in the subject of the agency (the property). Such an agency cannot be revoked by the principal nor is it terminated upon the death of the principal. For example, a broker may supply the financing for a condominium development provided the developer agrees to give the broker an exclusive listing to sell the furnished condominium units. The developer would not be able to revoke the listing after the broker had provided the financing.

AGENT

One who is authorized to represent and to act on behalf of another person (called the principal). Unlike an employee who merely works for a principal, an agent works in the place of a principal. A real estate broker is the agent of the client (seller or buyer) to whom he or she owes a fiduciary obligation. A salesperson, on the other hand, is the agent of his or her broker and does not have a direct personal contractual relationship with either the seller or the buyer. This fact is very relevant when a salesperson decides to change firms and becomes upset when the broker won't let the salesperson take his or her listings. Note that a minor cannot appoint an agent to execute his or her contracts, but an adult may designate a minor to act as an agent.

The main difference between an agent and an employee is that the agent may bind his or her principal by contract, if within the scope of authority, whereas an employee may not, unless given express authorization. (See AGENCY, DUAL AGENCY, FIDUCIARY.)

AGGRIEVED   Having suffered loss or injury from infringement
or denial of rights, such as one who has been the
victim of racial housing discrimination. The term also refers to an injured party or
a person who has lost some personal or property rights or has had an obligation or
burden imposed on him or her.

AGREED   A doctrine affecting rights of ownership to bound-
BOUNDARIES   aries. Where there is uncertainty as to the location
of the true boundary line between adjoining par-
cels of land, the landowners can mutually agree and establish a boundary line. If
the parties act in conformity with the agreed boundary, then the doctrine of agreed
boundaries holds that line to be the legal boundary line between the properties.

AGREEMENT   A contract between buyer and seller covering the
OF SALE   sale of specific real property. Some of the many
names for this contract are sales contract, pur-
chase agreement, deposit receipt, offer and acceptance, contract for sale, or purchase and sale agreement. In a few states, an agreement of sale refers to a land
contract or contract for deed. (*See* CONTRACT, CONTRACT FOR SALE.)

AGRICULTURAL LIEN   A statutory lien advanced to a farmer to secure
money or supplies for raising a crop. The lien
attaches only to the crop, not to the land.

AGRICULTURAL   A 1978 federal law requiring foreign persons who
FOREIGN   have an interest in U.S. agricultural land of more
INVESTMENT   than one acre to file disclosure information with
DISCLOSURE   the Secretary of Agriculture.
ACT (AFIDA)

AIRPORT ZONING   Regulations that aim to eliminate potential hazards to aircraft (including electronic interference)
by governing land uses, height of buildings, and natural growth in the areas surrounding an airport.

AIR RIGHTS   The rights to the use of the open space or vertical
plane above a property. Ownership of land in-
cludes the right to all air above the property. Until the advent of the airplane, this
right was unlimited, but now the courts permit reasonable interference with one's
air rights, such as is necessary for aircraft, so long as the owner's right to use and
occupy the land is not lessened. Thus, low-flying aircraft might be unreasonably
trespassing and their owners would be liable for any damages. Governments and
airport authorities often purchase air rights adjacent to an airport, called an
avigation easement, to provide glide patterns for air traffic.

The air itself is not real property; airspace, however, is real property when described in three dimensions with reference to a specific parcel of land, as in a
condominium unit.

A Maryland case has decided that where there are separate owners of the land and
the air rights, the air rights may be separately assessed for tax purposes. Air rights
may be sold or leased and buildings constructed thereon, such as was done with
the Pan Am Building constructed above Grand Central Station in New York City.

Air rights may also be transferred by way of easements, such as those used in constructing elevated highways or in acquiring scenic easements or easements of light and air. Because of the scarcity of land, many developers are examining the possibilities for developing properties in the airspace above prime properties owned by schools, churches, railways, and cemeteries.

ALEATORY CONTRACT   A contract that depends upon a contingency or uncertain event, such as a fire insurance contract or a lottery agreement.

ALIEN   A person born outside the jurisdiction of the United States who has not been naturalized under the Constitution and laws of this country and is not a citizen of the U.S. Aliens are allowed to acquire and hold an interest in lands in most states, although some states are limiting the ability of businesses and nonresident aliens to purchase and hold property. Some of the forms of restraint are limitations on the amount of holdings, restricted use for agricultural or industrial purposes, and identification requirements. There is a question as to the constitutionality of such legislation under the Constitution's equal protection provisions. State laws may also be challenged as an infringement on the federal government's constitutional authority over foreign commerce. (See *AGRICULTURAL FOREIGN INVESTMENT DISCLOSURE ACT*.)

ALIENATION   The act of transferring ownership, title, or an interest or estate in real property from one person to another. Property is usually sold or conveyed by voluntary alienation, as with a deed or an assignment of lease. Involuntary alienation takes place when property is sold against the owner's will, as in a foreclosure sale or a tax sale. Unreasonable restraints on alienation may be held void. (See *DEED, DUE-ON-SALE CLAUSE, FORECLOSURE, RESTRAINT ON ALIENATION*.)

ALIENATION CLAUSE   A clause sometimes found in a promissory note or mortgage that provides that the balance of the secured debt becomes immediately due and payable at the option of the mortgagee upon the alienation of the property by the mortgagor. Alienation is usually broadly defined to include any transfer of ownership, title, or an interest or estate in real property, including a sale by way of a contract for deed. Also called a *due-on-sale clause*. (See *ACCELERATION CLAUSE, ASSIGNMENT, DUE-ON-SALE CLAUSE*.)

ALIQUOT   It literally means "contained in something else an exact number of times"; aliquot is a number which when divided into another number leaves no remainder; as 6 is an aliquot part of 24. An aliquot parts subdivision is a term used in legally describing large parcels where parts are not less than 10 acres (popular in Alaska).

ALLEGATION   A statement by a party to a legal action of what he or she expects to prove. A declaration made as if under oath but prior to proof, such as an assertion made in a pleading or summons.

ALL-INCLUSIVE
DEED OF TRUST   A security device which is a purchase money deed of trust subordinate to, but still including, the original encumbrance or encumbrances. It is similar to a wraparound mortgage, except that a deed of trust is used rather than a mortgage. (See WRAPAROUND MORTGAGE.)

ALLODIAL SYSTEM   The free and full ownership of rights in land by individuals, which is the basis of real property law in the United States. By contrast, under the feudal system, ownership of the land was vested in the king or sovereign. The king then alloted select land to his noblemen, chiefs, and others. Such allotments were on a revocable basis and only represented the right to use the land.

ALLOTMENT   The funds allocated for the purchase of mortgages within a specified time by a permanent investor with whom a mortgage loan originator has a relationship but not a specific contract in the form of a commitment. The allotment may state the investor's requirements as to processing, loan terms, and/or underwriting standards. (See SECONDARY MORTGAGE MARKET.)

ALLUVION   The material that constitutes the increase of soil on a shore or riverbank, added by the process of accretion. Also called alluvium, it is the fine material, such as sand or mud, carried by water and deposited on land. The words alluvion and accretion are sometimes mistakenly used as synonyms. (See ACCRETION, EROSION.)

ALTERNATIVE
MORTGAGE
INSTRUMENT   A type of mortgage that differs from the standard mortgage in either the amount of principal, the interest, repayment terms, or the periodic payments. Some examples are the variable rate mortgage, graduated payment mortgage, renegotiable rate mortgage, the adjustable rate loan, the reverse annuity mortgage, and the shared appreciation mortgage.

AMENITIES   Features, both tangible and intangible, that enhance and add to the value or desirability of real estate. In a condominium, for example, common amenities include a swimming pool, clubhouse, and a good view. (See INTRINSIC VALUE.)

AMERICAN LAND
TITLE ASSOCIATION
(ALTA)   An association of more than 2,000 land title companies throughout the nation whose collective objectives are "to promote the safe and efficient transfer of ownership and interest in real property within the free enterprise system; to provide information and education to consumers, to those who regulate, supervise, or enact legislation affecting the land title evidencing industry, to its members, and to affiliated regional and state associations; to maintain liaison with users of the products and services provided by . . . members, and with government; and to maintain professional standards and ethics." (From the ALTA bylaws as amended in October, 1976.)

Some ALTA members provide abstracts only, others issue title insurance, while still others act as agents for title insurance underwriting companies. Many members are both abstractors and title insurance agents. ALTA members use uniform

ALTA title insurance forms, designed by the association to achieve a satisfactory measure of standardization within the industry. (*See TITLE INSURANCE.*)

AMORTIZATION   The gradual repayment or retiring of a debt by means of systematic payments of principal and/or interest over a set period so that at the end of the period there is a zero balance. The principal is thus directly reduced or amortized over the life of the loan (hence the term "direct reduction loan").

The amortized mortgage came into vogue as a result of the many realty foreclosures during the depression in the 1930s. Prior to that time, most mortgages were straight loans payable at interest only for five years, with the entire principal due at maturity. Savings and loan associations were the leaders in introducing amortized loans for residences. The standards set by the Federal Housing Administration were also influential in switching to the long-term amortized loan.

Most pre-1980 mortgages are fully amortized (i.e., self-liquidating) and are paid in equal monthly installments, which include interest and amortization of principal. The interest is set at a predetermined percentage rate and is charged only on the unpaid balance. As the payments are made, the amount allocated to interest decreases and that applied to reduction of principal increases.

For example, Mr. Shaw obtains a new mortgage of $40,000, amortized over a period of 25 years at an interest rate of 9 percent. Based on amortization table figures, the monthly payment on this mortgage is $335.68. If Mr. Shaw continues to make this monthly payment for 25 years, at the end of that period the mortgage will have been repaid in full, including interest. At the beginning of the loan period, the monthly payment will go primarily to the payment of interest and only a small amount will go toward the principal. The first monthly payment on the $40,000 loan includes $300 of interest and $35.68 of principal. As the principal amount is reduced, the interest is calculated on an increasingly lower amount, and the monthly payment of interest decreases while the balance credited toward principal increases. By the time the loan balance has been reduced to $20,000, the interest payment will be only $150, while the principal payment will have increased to $185.69. It may come as a surprise that, at the end of 25 years, Mr. Shaw will have paid a total of $100,704 to pay back his original $40,000 loan.

An *extended-term amortized loan,* or *balloon mortgage,* is often used in contracts for deed and in commercial and industrial real estate loans with very stable and secure tenants. The amortized payments are based on a payment schedule that is longer than the actual term of the loan.

Due to the effects of inflation, most lenders in the 1980s will be using alternative mortgage instruments to avoid getting locked into fixed rate amortized loans for long periods of time.

AMORTIZATION   A table showing the amounts of principal and in-
SCHEDULE   terest due at regular intervals and the unpaid balance of the loan after each payment is made. An example of a 9 percent amortization table is shown below.

MONTHLY AMORTIZED PAYMENTS

Term in Years

Amount	5	10	15	20	25	30	35
39,000	809.67	494.08	395.59	350.91	307.30	313.81	305.76
40,000	830.43	506.75	405.73	359.91	335.68	321.86	313.60
41,000	851.19	519.42	415.88	368.91	344.08	329.90	321.44

ANACONDA MORTGAGE   A mortgage containing a clause, sometimes called a *dragnet clause*, stating that the mortgage secures all debts of the mortgagor that shall at any time be due and owing to the mortgagee. Because the mortgagee could acquire all the debts the mortgagor owes to others at substantial discounts and then enforce them by threat of foreclosure, the courts regard such clauses with disfavor. The unsuspecting debtor becomes enwrapped in the folds of indebtedness—thus the name *anaconda*. Also called a "Mother Hubbard" clause.

Most courts require some relationship between the two debts as well as some specific reference in the second loan agreement to the earlier anaconda clause. Also, if the second debt is secured by its own collateral, the anaconda clause usually won't apply. (*See* MORTGAGE.)

ANCESTOR   A person from whom one lineally descends (such as a father or grandmother) and from whom land is lawfully inherited. Under some state discrimination laws, it is unlawful to discriminate on the grounds of a person's ancestry. Under the federal fair housing law, it is unlawful to discriminate on the basis of a person's national origin. (*See* COLLATERAL HEIRS, DESCENT.)

ANCHOR BOLT   A bolt that secures the sill of the house to the foundation wall.

ANCHOR TENANT   Major department or chain stores strategically located at shopping centers so as to give maximum exposure to smaller, satellite stores. In the usual strip shopping center, two anchor stores, also called magnet stores, such as a supermarket and a large drugstore, are located at opposite ends of a mall with smaller stores in between. This helps to generate maximum sales volume in the entire shopping center, and is of importance to the lessor, since most commercial lease rents are based on a percentage of gross sales.

In recent years the Federal Trade Commission has sought to limit the powers of the anchor tenant in controlling the selection of satellite tenants and their merchandise. (*See* PERCENTAGE LEASE, SHOPPING CENTER.)

ANCIENT LIGHTS DOCTRINE   This legal principle of early English common law prevented an adjoining owner from construction that would block off the light that is admitted into a neighbor's window. The insufficient interior lighting in those days was the rationale for this doctrine.

This doctrine has not been accepted by our modern courts although the courts are starting to refer to it as they develop new laws regarding solar easements.

ANGLE   A measure of rotation about a point, generally used in surveys to show the relationship of one line to another. Angles are usually measured in a clockwise direction and, in the United States, are normally measured in degrees—360 degrees to a full circle or one full rotation back to the point of beginning. Each degree is broken down into 60 minutes and each minute into 60 seconds. For example, the direction of a line may be written as North 42°20′15″ easterly. This line would be located using north as the line of reference and measuring an angle easterly which is 40 degrees, 20 minutes, and 15 seconds clockwise from north.

Reference lines can be north or south and angles can be east or west of the reference line. (*See AZIMUTH, DEGREE.*)

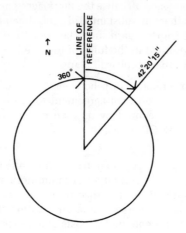

ANNEXATION   An addition to property by the act of joining or uniting one thing to another, as in attaching personal property to real property, thus creating a fixture. For example, a sink becomes a fixture when it is annexed to the plumbing outlet.

ANNUAL CONSTANT   *See CONSTANT.*

ANNUAL DEBT SERVICE   The amount of money on an annual basis required for payment of interest and principal on all security interests on the real property (for example, mortgages, deeds of trust, and contracts for deed); also called debt service coverage.

Note that many real estate lenders are more concerned with the ratio between net operating income and annual debt service than they are with the loan-to-value ratio. (*See AMORTIZATION SCHEDULE, CONSTANT.*)

ANNUAL EXCLUSION FOR GIFT TAX   Each person is entitled to an annual gift tax exclusion of $10,000 per donee per year. Thus, a mother could make six $10,000 gifts to six different children in one year (a total of $60,000), no part of which would be subject to the gift tax. She could repeat the process every year. Her husband could give an additional $10,000 per donee per year. (*See GIFT TAX.*)

ANNUAL MEETING   A yearly meeting of shareholders of a corporation or members of an association held for the purpose of permitting them to vote on the election of directors and various other matters of corporate or association business. Shareholders who will not be present may vote via proxy.

A condominium association usually has an annual meeting in addition to special meetings throughout the year.

ANNUAL MORTGAGOR STATEMENT A report by the lender or servicing agent to the mortgagor detailing what taxes and interest were paid during the year and how much principal balance remains.

ANNUAL PERCENTAGE RATE An expression of the relationship of the total finance charge to the total amount to be financed as required under the federal Truth-in-Lending Act. There are tables available from any Federal Reserve bank that may be used to facilitate computing the annual percentage rate, which must be calculated to the nearest one-eighth of one percent. Use of the annual percentage rate permits a standard expression of credit costs, which facilitates easy comparison of lenders. (See TRUTH-IN-LENDING LAWS.)

ANNUAL REPORT A statement of the financial status and progress of a corporation during its previous fiscal year, usually containing a balance sheet, operating statement, and auditor's report. It is presented to the corporate stockholders prior to the annual stockholders' meeting. If a security is registered with the Securities and Exchange Commission (SEC), an SEC annual report must be filed.

ANNUITY A sum of money received by the annuitant at fixed intervals as one of a series of periodic payments. Real property is sometimes traded or exchanged for a private annuity. The distinguishing characteristic of an annuity transaction is that the annuitant has an interest only in the payments themselves, not in any principal fund or source from which they may be derived. The buyer pays for the property by guaranteeing a monthly income to the seller for the seller's remaining life. The payments are determined by reference to standard annuity tables. Properly structured by a qualified person, a private annuity transaction involving the transfer of realty to another member of an annuitant's family can produce savings in estate, income, and gift taxes.

The proper use of annuity tables, such as the Inwood Table, will provide a factor to be multiplied by the desired yearly income to estimate the present worth of an investment (what amount the investor should pay to acquire the property).

ANTENUPTIAL AGREEMENT A contract entered into by two people contemplating marriage for the purpose of settling the property rights of both. It is advisable for each person to have his or her own legal counsel to negotiate such a contract. The enforceability of the agreement may depend upon the completeness of disclosure and the existence of independent counsel for each party. (See JOINTURE.)

ANTICIPATORY BREACH An anticipatory breach or repudiation of a real estate contract occurs when either buyer or seller, prior to closing, declares by words or acts an intention not to perform. At that time, the other party, not being in default, is entitled to enforce the contract in court without first having to offer or tender performance. (See TENDER.)

ANTIFRAUD PROVISIONS The provisions in both federal and state securities laws that make it unlawful for any person, in connection with the offer, sale, or purchase of any security, to directly or indirectly employ any device, scheme, or artifice to defraud; to make any untrue statement of a material fact or to omit to state a material fact, which omission makes a statement misleading; or to engage in any act, practice, or course of business which operates or would operate as a fraud or deceit upon any person. The federal antifraud provisions are covered under Rule 10(b)(5) of the Securities Act of 1934, and come into play when there is the minimal contact with interstate commerce in the offer of the security, such as when the United States mail is used. It is important to note that, even though the offer of a security may be exempt from the registration requirement under the private offering exemption, the intrastate offering exemption, or the Regulation A exemption of the federal laws, the offer is still subject to the antifraud provisions of the Securities Act of 1934 and the licensing requirements. In the event a purchaser of a security is injured by any violation of the antifraud provision, he or she may sue for rescission of the contract and recover the amount paid for the security, plus interest from the date the security was purchased. (*See INTRASTATE EXEMPTION, PRIVATE OFFERING, REGULATION A, RESCISSION, RULE 10-B5.*)

ANTITRUST LAWS State and federal laws designed to maintain and preserve business competition. The Sherman Antitrust Act (1890) is the principal federal statute covering competition, which is defined by most courts as "that economic condition in which prices are determined by market forces without interference from private concerns and there is reasonable freedom of entry into most businesses." Section I of the Sherman Antitrust Act provides that "every contract, combination in the form of trust or otherwise, or conspiracy in restraint of trade or commerce among the several states or with foreign nations is declared to be illegal." Antitrust situations include price fixing, certain types of boycotts, allocation of customers or markets, restrictions on competition in shopping center leases, and certain restraints placed on franchisees by franchisors. Also challenged are certain "tie-in" arrangements, such as a developer who conditions a sale by insisting that the buyer promise to list the property with the developer if the buyer wishes to resell, or a property manager who attempts to force a client's commitment to list with the manager in the event of sale.

In recent years, certain real estate brokerage activities have come under public scrutiny, such as the fixing of general commission rates by local boards or groups of brokers and the exclusion of brokers from membership in local boards or in multiple listing arrangements due to unreasonable membership requirements. As a result of court cases, local real estate boards no longer directly or indirectly influence fixed commission rates or commission splits between cooperating brokers. Moreover, in some states, clients must be specifically informed that commission rates are negotiable between client and broker.

APARTMENT BUILDING A building having separate units for permanent tenants who rent or lease them. Common facilities, such as lights, heat, elevator, and garbage disposal services, are provided and common entrance and hallways are maintained by the owner of the apartment house. (*See UNIT.*)

APPOINTMENTS Furnishings, fixtures, or equipment found in a home, office, or other building. These items may either enhance or detract from the intrinsic value of the property.

APPORTIONMENT   1. The division or partition of property into proportionate (though not necessarily equal) parts
(tenants in common seeking partition of a property). 2. The pro rata division of
real estate carrying charges between buyer and seller at closing. (*See CARRYING
CHARGES, PRORATE.*)

APPRAISAL   The process of formulating and supporting an
opinion of value. An appraisal is usually required
when real property is sold, financed, condemned, taxed, insured, or partitioned.
Note that an appraisal is an estimate, not a determination, of value. The appraiser
does not determine value; people make value. An appraisal may be in the form of
a lengthy written report, a completed form, a simple letter, or even an oral report.

The following are the three major approaches to estimating the market value of a
property.

The Market-Data Approach: A comparative analysis of current sales prices of
similar properties, after making necessary adjustments for any differences in the
properties. This approach, also called the *direct sales comparison approach*, is
used most frequently by real estate brokers in evaluating residences and is based
on the principle of substitution.

The Cost Approach: An estimated value based on the cost of reproduction or
replacement of the improvements, less depreciation, plus the value of the land
(land value being usually determined by the market-data approach). The cost approach is used primarily to determine the value of service-type properties, such as
churches and post offices.

The Income Approach: An estimated value based on the capitalization of income
and productivity; often referred to as the *income* (or economic) *approach to value.*
It is concerned with the present worth of future benefits of the property, and is
used mostly in connection with such income-producing properties as apartment
buildings.

In most appraisals, the appraiser reconciles (correlates) the information derived
from using all three approaches (where applicable) and considers the purpose of
the appraisal, the type of property, and the adequacy of the compiled data to
determine the relative weight to be given to each approach in reaching his or her
conclusion of value. Moreover, these three different appraisal methods serve as
checks on each other when all are used for the same property.

When an independent appraisal is required, most lending institutions require the
services of a professional, such as a member of the American Institute of Real
Estate Appraisers, the Society of Residential Appraisers, or the American Society
of Appraisers. Government agencies seem to employ a great number of appraisers,
as do lending institutions and trust companies. The cost of the appraisal is usually incurred by the person seeking the loan. The Realtors® Code of Ethics (Articles 11, 12, 17, and 18) contains strict rules regarding appraisals. (*See COST AP-
PROACH, INCOME APPROACH, MARKET-DATA APPROACH, REALTORS®
CODE OF ETHICS, VALUE.*)

**APPRAISAL
REPORT**   The formal appraisal report contains the estimate
of value, the date of the valuation, the certification and signature of the appraiser, the purpose,
the qualifying conditions, description of neighborhood, identification of the property and its ownership, the factual data, an analysis and interpretation of the data,

correlation and use of one or more of the three approaches to value, and supporting material such as maps and photos. The appraisal report is basically a business report.

APPRAISER   One who estimates value. One who possesses the necessary qualifications, ability, education, and experience to conduct the appraisal of real or personal property.

Appraisers may be independent contractors or employed by the government, lending institutions, or trust companies. An appraiser's fees are typically based on time and expenses; fees are never based on a percentage of the appraised value. Some of the professional designations an appraiser might possess are ASA, MAI, SRA, SREA and SRPA.

While mathematics is a helpful tool in making an appraisal, the final opinion of value is based primarily on the experience and logic of the particular appraiser.

APPRECIATION   A temporary or permanent increase in the worth or value of property due to economic or related causes; the opposite of depreciation.

APPROPRIATION   The act of selecting, devoting, or setting apart land for a particular public use or purpose, such as a public park or school; also called *dedication*. The taking of a *public* thing for a *private* use (just the opposite of condemnation); as in the taking of water from a natural stream for private use which, in some states, is sufficient to establish a prior right against other owners to the continued use of that water. (*See* EMINENT DOMAIN.)

APPURTENANCE   That which belongs to something, but not for all time; all those rights, privileges, and improvements which belong to and pass with the transfer of the property but are not necessarily a part of the actual property. Appurtenances to real property pass with the real property to which they are appurtenant unless a contrary intention is manifested. A deed normally describes the property granted and then states, "together with all appurtenances." Typical appurtenances are rights-of-way, easements, water rights, condominium parking stalls, and property improvements.

APPURTENANT   Belonging to; adjunct; appended or annexed to. For example, the garage is appurtenant to the house, and the common interest in the common elements of a condominium is appurtenant to each apartment. Appurtenant items pass with the land when the property is transferred. (*See* LIMITED COMMON ELEMENTS.)

ARBITRAGE   1. The spread, or difference, between interest rates; a common item in all-inclusive or wraparound mortgage financing. For example, Joe Smith sells his parcel to Mary Jones for $10,000 by way of a purchase money mortgage at 12 percent. Mary Jones then sells the parcel to Susan Brown under a wraparound mortgage at 12.5 percent. Mary Jones uses the monthly payments to pay her debt to Mr. Smith and the 0.5 percent arbitrage is income to Mary Jones. 2. Also, the simultaneous purchase and sale of mortgages or mortgage-backed securities in different markets to profit from price differentials. (*See* WRAPAROUND MORTGAGE.)

ARBITRATION   The nonjudicial submission of a controversy to selected third parties for their determination in a manner provided by agreement or by law. Disputes between listing Realtors® and cooperating Realtors® are often settled by arbitration, with both parties agreeing to comply with the final decision of the arbitrator. (*See Article 14 of the REALTORS® CODE OF ETHICS—APPENDIX B.*)

Many disputes involving construction contracts are settled according to detailed rules established by the *American Arbitration Association*. The prime feature of a binding arbitration is that it is fast and final, which can be good or bad depending on whether you win or lose!

Lease documents often specify a fixed rental for a certain period, with subsequent renegotiations based on appraised value. If the parties cannot agree on the appraisal value, the matter is resolved by a form of arbitration. Normally, the lessor and the lessee each select an appraiser, and those two appraisers agree on a third appraiser to help them determine the final appraised value. Combining mediation with arbitration is a less rigid form of settlement. Under this approach, an independent third party attempts at first to get the disputing parties to compromise and settle the controversy themselves. If such attempts at conciliation fail, the third party is empowered by the parties to make the final decision as in a straight arbitration proceeding.

ARCADE   A series of arches on the same plane, either open or closed. A walkway or passageway with an arched roof, frequently with shops along one or both sides. A passageway open on the street side, usually colonnaded. A colonnaded sidewalk.

ARCHITECTURAL DRAWINGS   Data prepared or assembled by an architect that form part of a proposal or part of contract documents. The data may include such things as plot plans, floor plans, elevations, or sections, but usually not mechanical, electrical, or structural plans or other specialized data furnished by consultants to the architect. (*See WORKING DRAWINGS.*)

ARCHITECTURE   1. The science and art of structural design. 2. The style in which a building is designed and built.

AREA   A parcel of land assumed to be level and at sea level. These assumptions are used to obtain consistent descriptions of land. Thus, the land surface of a ten-acre, sloping parcel will actually contain more usable square feet than a ten-acre level parcel, although the legal descriptions of both parcels will be the same.

AREA MANAGEMENT BROKER   Property managers who work directly for the Federal Housing Administration in the field of subsidized housing. Their principal duties include taking over the property, preparing repair specifications, soliciting repair bids from contractors, coordinating and inspecting repair work, supervising maintenance and security, and submitting financial reports. They are usually employed under a three-year contract.

ARM'S LENGTH TRANSACTION A transaction in which the parties are dealing from equal bargaining positions. Parties are said to deal "at arm's length" when each stands upon the strict letter of his or her rights and conducts the business in a formal manner without trusting the other's fairness or integrity and without being subject to the other's control or dominant influence (as is sometimes the case in transactions between related parties). The absence of an arm's length transaction may give rise to tax consequences when there is a transfer of property at less than fair market value. Whether there existed an arm's length transaction is also relevant to the "willing-buyer, willing-seller" concept in the estimation of fair market value.

ARRANGER OF CREDIT As defined under the federal Truth-in-Lending law, a person who regularly arranges for the extension of consumer credit by another person if a finance charge will be imposed, or if there are more than four installments, and the person extending the credit is not a creditor. At present, the term does not include a person such as a real estate broker who arranges seller financing of a dwelling or real property.

ARREARS The state of being delinquent in paying a debt. Also, in many cases mortgage interest and real estate taxes are paid in arrears; that is, at or after the end of the period or year for which they are due or levied; the opposite of *in advance*.

ARTICLES OF INCORPORATION The document that sets forth the purposes, powers, and basic rules of operation for a corporation. Also called *articles of association*. (*See CORPORATION.*)

AS-BUILT DRAWINGS Architectural drawings showing the precise method of construction and the location for the installation of equipment and utility lines. As-built drawings are usually prepared by an architect with the cooperation of the general contractor to the project.

ASH DUMP A container under a fireplace where ashes are temporarily deposited. Ashes can be removed later through a cleanout door.

"AS IS" Words in a contract intended to signify that no guaranties whatsoever are given regarding the subject property and that it is being purchased exactly as it is found. It is intended to be a disclaimer of warranties or representations. The recent trend in the courts to favor consumers tends to prevent sellers from using "as is" wording in a contract to shield themselves from possible fraud charges brought on by neglecting to disclose material defects in the property.

While an "as is" clause may give some protection to the seller from unknown defects, the clause is inoperative when the seller actively misrepresents the condition of the property. The seller does not make any repairs to the readily observable condition of the property, basically saying that "you take it as you *see* it". The idea is that the buyer takes the visible condition into account when making an offer and setting the purchase price. Therefore, if a buyer should be expected to discover a defect upon a reasonable inspection, the buyer will be charged with notice; otherwise, the broker and/or seller have the affirmative duty to inform the buyer of the defect, preferably in writing.

Sellers can protect themselves by being quite specific in the contract about, for example, recurring plumbing problems, cracked foundation, leaky roof, den built without a building permit, all in "as is" condition. If, for example, the roof defect was not obvious and the buyer did not know of this material defect, but the seller did know, then a general "as is" clause is probably worthless.

Even where an "as is" clause can protect a seller, many courts hold that a broker cannot use the "as is" clause to avoid liability for misrepresentation, since the broker is not a party to the contract in which the "as is" clause is contained. (*See* CAVEAT EMPTOR.)

ASKING PRICE

The listed price of a parcel of real estate—the price at which it is offered to the public by the seller or broker. An asking price differs from a *firm price* in that it implies some degree of flexibility in negotiation. For this reason, some sellers object to their listing brokers using the phrase "asking price" in their advertisements of the seller's property.

ASSEMBLAGE

The combining of two or more adjoining lots into one large tract. This is usually done to increase the value of the individual lots because a larger building capable of producing a larger net return may be erected on the larger parcel. The resulting added value is called *plottage*. The developer often makes use of option contracts to tie up the right to purchase the desired adjacent parcels. Care must also be taken through exact surveys to avoid the creation of gaps or strips between the acquired parcels through faulty legal descriptions.

ASSESSED VALUATION

The value of real property established for the purpose of computing real property taxes. In general, property is valued or assessed for tax purposes by county and township assessors. The land is usually appraised separately from the building, and the building value is usually determined from a manual or set of rules covering unit cost prices and rates of depreciation, although some states require assessments to be a certain percentage of true or market value (*assessment ratio*). State laws may provide for property to be reassessed periodically. Each taxing district has its own methods for constantly updating assessments, although most use a combination of building permit records, on-site inspections, and conveyance tax records. Generally, property owners claiming that errors were made in determining the assessed value of their property may present their objections to the local boards of appeal or boards of equalization. (*See* PROPERTY TAX, TAX RATE.)

ASSESSMENT

1. An official valuation of real property for tax purposes based on appraisals by local government officials; synonymous with assessed value. Sales prices of comparable land are used to estimate land values while building values are based on an amount representing the improvement's replacement cost less depreciation. 2. The allocation of the proportionate individual share of a common expense, as when the

owners of condominium or cooperative units are assessed for their proportionate share of unusual maintenance expenses for the building which benefit the project as a whole and are not funded through regular maintenance charges. 3. A specific levy for a definite purpose, such as adding curbs or sewers in a neighborhood. 4. An official determination of the just compensation to be paid a property owner for the taking of the property for a public purpose (condemnation). 5. An additional capital contribution of corporate shareholders or members of a partnership or association to cover a capital expenditure. (*See SPECIAL ASSESSMENT.*)

ASSESSMENT ROLLS   Public records of the assessed values of all lands and buildings within a specific area. Thus, an owner can compare his or her assessed valuation with that of similar properties and appeal if the owner feels the property was overassessed.

ASSESSOR   A public official who appraises property for tax purposes. He or she determines only the assessed value, not the tax rate.

ASSET   Something of value owned by a person; a useful item of property. Assets are either financial, as cash or bonds; tangible or intangible; or physical, as real or personal property. Accountants analyze financial balance sheets made up of assets and liabilities to determine net worth, which is the difference between the two.

ASSET DEPRECIATION RANGE SYSTEM (ADR)   The part of the Internal Revenue Service regulations covering guidelines and standards for determining the period over which to depreciate an asset. The ADR gives the taxpayer a choice of depreciating the property over a shorter or longer life than the guideline period. Effective for property placed in service after 1980, the ADR system no longer applies, and has been replaced by the Cost Recovery System created by the Economic Recovery Tax Act of 1981.

ASSIGNMENT   The transfer of the right, title, and interest in the property of one person (the assignor) to another (the assignee). There are assignments of, among other things, mortgages, sales contracts, contracts for deed, leases, and options.

Most contracts consist of rights and duties. Unless personal, duties can normally be delegated or assigned. For example, a listing contract is personal in nature and, therefore, the listing broker cannot assign the contract to another broker without the principal's consent. On the other hand, the duty to pay rent is not personal and normally can be assigned. Real estate contracts are usually assignable unless restricted in the contract itself.

In any assignment, the assignee becomes primarily liable and the assignor remains secondarily liable as surety, unless there is a novation agreement relieving the assignor from liability. The assignee acquires the same title, right, and interest in the particular contract that the assignor had. It is often said that an assignee stands in the shoes of the assignor, taking his or her rights and remedies subject to any defenses which another party has against the assignor.

An attempted assignment of a mortgage lien without the promissory note transfers nothing to the assignee; but the assignment of the note without the mortgage gives the assignee the right to the security. If an assignment of a mortgage or trust deed

(deed of trust) is recorded, constructive notice is given to all persons as to that assignment. The mortgagor must then pay the assignee, and is unprotected in the event payments are inadvertently made to the assignor (the original mortgagee).

Many contracts for deed provide that the buyer may not assign his or her interest in the contract without the prior written approval of the seller, although an assignment in violation of this provision is nevertheless valid between the assignor and assignee. When the seller wants an *anti-assignment clause,* the prudent buyer should require in the sales contract that the contract for deed contain language to the effect that the seller's consent to a proposed assignment shall not be unreasonably withheld. Mortgagees frequently use *nonassignment clauses* in mortgages to limit assignment of the obligation—this may be a factor in determining whether the seller should use a land contract or a purchase money mortgage. A prohibition against assignment of a contract does not prevent the assignment of a claim for damages caused by a breach of the contract, nor does it prevent assignment of the right to receive money payments due (or that will become due) under the contract. The prohibition is for the benefit of the vendor (seller, lender), who can waive it expressly or by conduct such as by accepting payments direct from the assignee.

When purchasing property subject to existing leases, the purchaser should obtain a written assignment of the seller's interest in those leases in recordable form.

With most leases, the tenant may sublet or assign the lease without the landlord's approval unless otherwise provided in the written rental agreement. The important distinction between an assignment and a sublease, from the landlord's viewpoint, is that the landlord cannot directly sue the sublessee whereas it is possible to sue the assignee. (See *ESTOPPEL, NOVATION, OPTION, SUBLEASE.*)

ASSIGNMENT OF LEASE The transfer of all title, right, and interest that a lessee possesses in certain real property. The document used to convey a leasehold is called an assignment of lease rather than a deed.

The assignee of a lease is liable on the basis of his or her holding the land, legally known as *privity of estate.* The assignor is liable on the basis of *privity of contract* with the landlord.

If a lease has an assignment clause requiring the consent of the landlord, the landlord may not unreasonably or arbitrarily withhold his or her consent. An assignment of a lease in violation of an anti-assignment restriction is not void, but is voidable at the lessor's discretion. Such an assignment is good between assignor and assignee. The issue that it is invalid on the basis of a lack of lessor's approval can be raised only by the lessor.

The tax effect of an assignment, as opposed to a sublease, depends on whether the basic rental is more or less than the value of the leasehold. If more, an assignment results in a capital loss, whereas subleasing results in an ordinary loss of income. If the basic rental is less than the value of the leasehold, an assignment results in a capital gain, whereas a sublease results in ordinary income. Costs of procuring a lease (commission, legal fees, concession, and so on) must be capitalized over the life of the lease.

ASSIGNMENT OF RENTS An agreement between a property owner and a mortgagee by which the mortgagee receives, as security, the right to collect rents from the mortgagor's tenants, although the mortgagor continues to have the sole obligation to the tenants under the lease.

ASSOCIATE BROKER　　A real estate license classification used in some states to describe a person who has qualified as a real estate broker, but still works for another broker; also called a broker-salesperson or broker-associate.

ASSOCIATION　　A group of people gathered together for a business purpose, sometimes treated as a corporation under tax law. The danger of a poorly drafted partnership or limited partnership agreement is that the Internal Revenue Service may attempt to treat the partnership as an association taxable as a corporation. The IRS uses the following test: If the organization has more corporate than noncorporate characteristics, it will be taxable as a corporation, with the resulting unfavorable tax features. The four major corporate characteristics generally are continuity of life, centralization of management, limited liability, and transferability of interest. (*See CONDOMINIUM OWNERS' ASSOCIATION, UNINCORPORATED ASSOCIATION.*)

ASSOCIATION OF UNIT OWNERS　　All of the unit owners of a condominium acting as a group for the administration of the project, in accordance with the declaration and bylaws. The association of unit owners may be either incorporated or unincorporated. (*See CONDOMINIUM OWNERS' ASSOCIATION.*)

ASSUMED BUSINESS NAME　　See *FICTITIOUS COMPANY NAME.*

ASSUMPTION OF MORTGAGE　　The act of acquiring title to property that has an existing mortgage, and agreeing to be personally liable for the terms and conditions of the mortgage, including payments. In effect, the buyer (grantee) becomes the principal guarantor on the mortgage note and is primarily liable for the amount of any deficiency judgment resulting from a default and foreclosure on the property. The original mortgagor (grantor) is still liable as surety on the note if the grantee defaults. The personal liability of the purchaser to pay the mortgage debt is usually created by an assumption clause placed in the deed (or assignment of lease if a leasehold mortgage is involved). Normally a deed need only be signed by the grantor, but where there is an assumption clause, both buyer and seller sign the deed so that the buyer becomes personally bound to the assumption. Because of the seller's continued liability, he or she usually asks a higher price for the property if the buyer is to assume a mortgage—the seller is in effect trading on the low interest rate of the existing mortgage. The lender is, in effect, a third-party beneficiary of the assumption agreement.

Since there is little reason for a lender to relieve the original seller from liability on the assumed note, most lenders prefer to have both the buyer and seller remain liable on the note. In certain cases, however, the lender will relieve the seller from continuing liability by way of a novation. Note that if the mortgagee changes any of the mortgage terms with the new owner, the original mortgagor may be released of all liability on the note. The lender normally charges an assumption fee, except that no such fee can be charged when either VA or FHA loans are assumed. Also, neither VA nor FHA assumptions require the prior approval of the lender or government. The current trend among lenders, especially in a climate of escalating interest rates, is to approve the assumption only after renegotiating the terms of the loan, raising the interest rate, and/or charging a fee. Some courts have sustained the right of the lender to require payment of an assumption fee and loan interest modification as consideration for its waiver of the acceleration clause in a mortgage. (See *ACCELERATION CLAUSE, DUE-ON-SALE CLAUSE, NOVATION, SUBROGATION.*)

AT-RISK RULES   Special rules set up by the Internal Revenue Service to restrict leverage opportunity by limiting the taxpayer's deductible losses to the amount he or she has "at risk." A taxpayer is generally considered "at risk" to the extent of cash contributed and amounts borrowed for which he or she is liable for payment from personal assets.

Under the federal tax law, limited partners in a partnership may deduct losses only to the extent of their investments. However, an important exemption exists for partnerships in which the principal activity is real estate (but not mineral property) investment.

The Economic Recovery Tax Act of 1981 also limits the availability of investment tax credit in certain situations where personal property is acquired with "no-risk" nonrecourse financing. (See *NONRECOURSE LOAN.*)

ATRIUM   Usually the main area of a structure with a ceiling of a translucent material that allows sunlight into the interior quarters.

ATTACHMENT   The legal process of seizing the real or personal property of a defendant in a lawsuit by levy or judicial order, and holding it in the custody of the court as security for satisfaction of a judgment. The lien is thus created by operation of law, not by private agreement. The plaintiff may recover such property in any action upon a contract, express or implied. Real property is attached by recording a copy of the *writ of attachment* in the public record. The attachment thus creates a lien against the property before entry of a judgment so that the plaintiff is assured there will be property left to satisfy the judgment. The lien can be enforced by issuance of an execution after a judgment for the plaintiff. An attachment may arise from an action for payment of money upon an unsecured contract. The property may not be sold or encumbered free of the attachment without satisfaction or release of the attachment, or the posting of a cash bond equal to plaintiff's claim plus costs. An attachment is not available when a party brings an action to collect payment of a secured obligation (mortgage). (See *LIS PENDENS.*)

ATTESTATION   The act of witnessing a person's signing of an instrument by a subscribing witness.

ATTIC   Accessible space located between the top of a ceiling and the underside of a roof. Inaccessible spaces are considered structural cavities.

ATTORNEY-IN-FACT   A competent and disinterested person who is authorized by another person to act in his or her place. In real estate conveyance transactions, an attorney-in-fact should be so authorized by way of a written, notarized, and recordable instrument called a power of attorney. An attorney-in-fact has a fiduciary relationship with his or her principal. The attorney-in-fact need not be an attorney at law, although people often give a power of attorney to their lawyers.

An attorney-in-fact may have a general or specific power; however, even one with general powers may not act in any way contrary to the principal's interests (for instance, selling the principal's property for inadequate consideration) or act in his or her own interests (for example, conveying the principal's land to himself). The listing broker should think carefully about the possible conflict of interest problems before accepting a power of attorney from the client and should also consider having separate written instructions detailing exactly what actions, and/or on what terms, the broker is authorized to act.

An attorney-in-fact appointed by a minor is not competent to convey title to real property owned by the minor.

A husband cannot be his wife's attorney-in-fact for purposes of releasing her dower rights. (See AGENT, POWER OF ATTORNEY.)

ATTORNEY'S FEES   Monies an attorney charges for his or her legal services. Unless provided for by statute or in a contract, attorney's fees usually cannot be recovered by an aggrieved party. It is therefore important to insert a clause in all contracts (especially promissory notes) to the effect that, in the event of litigation arising from the contract, the prevailing party shall be entitled to reimbursement of all attorney's fees and costs.

ATTORNMENT   The act of a tenant formally agreeing to become the tenant of a successor landlord; as in attorning to a mortgagee who has foreclosed upon the leased premises. Attornment establishes a new tenancy, with the mortgagee being the landlord, and acts as a defense against the defaulting mortgagor's claim for rent.

In a long-term lease situation, an attornment agreement is typically entered into by a sublessee with a fee owner of the land and a mortgagee holding a mortgage on the fee or on the master leasehold estate. The sublessee seeks to protect his or her estate from destruction by reason of the premature termination of the master leasehold or from loss by reason of the foreclosure of the mortgage when the sublessor defaults. The attornment agreement provides that, in the event of termination or foreclosure, the sublease shall continue, just as if the owner or the mortgagee were the lessor in a lease with the sublessee for a term equal to the unexpired term of the sublease, and upon the same terms and provisions. (See NONDISTURB-ANCE.)

ATTRACTION PRINCIPLE   The pulling force of a commercial business center due to one or more of the various existing merchandising factors. A shopping center, made up of many diverse businesses, holds cumulative attraction for consumers.

ATTRACTIVE NUISANCE   A doctrine of tort law stating that a person who maintains on his or her property a condition that is both dangerous and conceivably inviting to children owes a duty to exercise reasonable care to protect children from the danger. Thus, an owner who maintains a swimming pool, discarded refrigerator, or unmarked open pit may be liable for injuries to trespassing children. Construction sites should be adequately secured to prevent inquisitive children from being injured.

AUCTION   A form of selling land or personal property whereby verbal offers are taken and the property is sold to the highest bidder. Some states require auctioneers selling real estate to carry a special license. Real estate auctions are generally used in mortgage foreclosure sales, tax sales, and with hard-to-sell properties. If the auction is "without reserve", the auctioneer cannot withdraw goods or bid on them personally or through an agent.

In the secondary mortgage market, the Federal National Mortgage Association uses a unique auction-type purchasing procedure termed a Free Market System Auction.

AUTHORIZATION TO SELL   A listing contract whereby an agent is employed by a seller to procure a buyer for the property; it usually does not give the agent the authority to enter into a binding contract of sale. Such unusual authority typically requires a special authorization as in a limited power of attorney. (See *LISTING*.)

AUTRE VIE   French for "another life" and used to describe a life estate measured by the life of someone other than the life tenant, as in a life estate to Charlie during the life of Harry.

AVENUE   A fully improved through-roadway, serving local or minor collector traffic, which is landscaped and planted with trees.

AVULSION   The loss of land when a sudden or violent action of nature results in its washing away. A riparian owner generally does not lose title to land lost by avulsion—the boundary lines stay the same no matter how much soil is lost and the former owner can reclaim the lost land. In contrast, the riparian owner loses title to land washed away by erosion, the gradual and imperceptible washing away of soil. (See *ACCRETION, RIPARIAN*.)

AXIAL GROWTH   City growth that occurs outward along main transportation routes. This pattern is usually star shaped.

AZIMUTH   An azimuth of a boundary line is the direction of the line in relation to a north-south line or meridian, or the angle between a north-south line and the boundary line measured from the north point in the northern hemisphere and the south point in the southern hemisphere. Every line has two azimuths, depending on the direction one looks down the line. Thus, the azimuth of line A→B is 240°, but the azimuth of line B→A is 60°.

BACKFILL   The earth, or selected material such as aggregate, used to fill in around foundation walls after they are completed, or to fill other excavated voids, or to compact soil.

BACK-TO-BACK ESCROW   An escrow set up to handle the concurrent sale of one property and the purchase of another property by the same party. For example, in order for John Lark to obtain the $20,000 cash down payment to purchase a new three-bedroom home, he must close the sale of his present two-bedroom home. John may set up a back-to-back escrow with an escrow company, which will close the sale of his old home and then apply the necessary proceeds to close the purchase of his new home. (See DOUBLE ESCROW.)

BACK-TO-BACK LEASE   An agreement made by a landlord as a concession to a prospective tenant, in which the landlord agrees to take over the tenant's existing lease in return for the tenant's agreement to lease space in the landlord's commercial building (office building, industrial park). (See CONCESSIONS.)

BACKUP OFFER   An offer to buy submitted to a seller with the understanding that the seller has already accepted a prior offer; a secondary offer. Sometimes the seller accepts the backup offer contingent on the failure of the sales transaction on the part of the first purchaser within a specified period of time. The seller must be careful how to proceed, however, when the time for buyer's performance under the first contract has expired. Rather than just immediately treat the contract as terminated and arrange to convey the property to the backup buyer, the seller should make sure that the seller has fully performed, or made a full and adequate tender of such performance, to the first purchaser. Otherwise, the seller may be contractually bound to convey the same property to two different buyers. The best practice is to obtain a release from the first purchaser. (See TENDER.)

The real estate agent should be cautious about encouraging the seller-client to breach any existing contract in order to accept a better second offer. The agent might be sued by the first buyer for the tort of intentional interference with contract.

BAILMENT   The delivery of personal property from the bailor to the bailee with the agreement, express or implied, that the property shall be returned or properly accounted for when the special purpose is accomplished, such as parking a car at a parking lot. Property stored in a mini-warehouse may be subject to the special rules of bailment law.

BALANCE SHEET An itemized financial statement setting forth personal or corporate assets, liabilities, and net worth (the difference between assets and liabilities) as of a specified date. It is a cross-section analysis of the business. Most lending institutions require an applicant for real estate financing to submit a balance sheet, usually on a form attached to the loan application. Some lenders also require a profit and loss statement showing income and expenses. Some states have enacted False Statement Acts to penalize the falsification of statements used in the loan process. (See *PROFIT AND LOSS STATEMENT.*)

BALCONY An unroofed platform enclosed by a railing or parapet, which projects from the wall of a building for the private use of tenants, or for exterior access to the upper floors. When a balcony is roofed and enclosed and has operating windows, it is considered part of the room it serves. (See *LANAI.*)

BALLOON PAYMENT The final payment under an installment obligation that is substantially larger than the previous installment payments and repays the debt in full; the remaining balance that is due at the maturity of a note or obligation. Balloon payments are frequently used in second mortgages (to keep installments low when paying first and second mortgages concurrently) and in similar situations where the monthly payment does not fully amortize the principal balance over the life of the obligation. A note or obligation that provides for a lump-sum payment at the end of the term is sometimes called a *partially amortized loan.*

For example, Mr. Clay sells his condominium studio apartment for $50,000, with a down payment of $10,000 and a balance of $40,000 by way of a contract for deed at 10 percent interest, payable at $353.60 per month (amortized on a 30-year schedule), with the balance due in full at the end of five years. If the buyer makes the full five years of payments, at the end of that time, the buyer will have paid off only $1,764 of principal, leaving a balance of $38,236 to be paid in the final balloon payment. If the buyer elects to pay off the contract in a shorter period of time, the balloon payment will be correspondingly higher. The amount of the balloon payment can be easily determined by use of a loan progress chart. This chart can also be used to determine what portion of a fully amortized loan remains to be paid at any given moment in time.

When the federal truth-in-lending provisions apply, the amount of a balloon payment must be clearly stated in the contract.

The Federal Home Loan Bank Board now permits savings and loan associations to offer prospective homebuyers balloon mortgages in amounts up to 95 percent of the value of the home and for terms up to 40 years. In the past, mortgages were limited to 5 years and to 60 percent of the value of the home with the borrower having to make a down payment of at least 40 percent. Lenders can also adjust the interest rates of partially amortized balloon loans consistent with board rules covering adjustable mortgage loans.

BALTIMORE METHOD An appraisal method whereby a corner lot is calculated to be worth the total of the lots on each side of it. (See *CORNER-LOT APPRAISAL METHODS.*)

BALUSTER   One of a string of small poles used to support the handrail of a stairway.

BAND OF INVESTMENT   An appraisal technique used in evaluating income property to build the interest rate portion of the appropriate capitalization rate to apply to the subject property; the sum of the mortgage and equity positions of the buyer. This technique is popularly used to estimate an appropriate discount (risk) rate. Equity investors seek to obtain the best financing deal in order to maximize the advantage of leverage.

The band of investment for a particular property is derived from a synthesis of mortgage and equity rates that market data reveal to be applicable to comparable properties. The appropriate "cap rate" is the sum of the mortgage requirement rate (a constant representing the interest on and recapture of the mortgage component of the total value of the property) and the equity rate (the anticipated cash flow to the equity investment, as indicated by comparable sales). Thus, each portion of a property's interest or ownership is multiplied by the rate of return required to attract money into that type of ownership position.

For example, assume that an investor wishes to purchase a hotel. As her broker, you have investigated similar recent sales and have found that mortgage money is available for two-thirds of the property value at 9¼ percent interest for a term of 25 years. The mortgage requirement rate (constant) is 10.28 percent. The remaining one-third of the value of the property must be paid by your investor in cash, and she can expect an equity rate of 11 percent. The overall cap rate, then, is derived as follows:

	Percent of Value	Rate	Product
Mortgage	66.67	.1028	6.85
Equity	33.33	.11	3.67
Cap Rate (weighted average)			10.52

(See CAPITALIZATION RATE, CONSTANT, INTERNAL RATE OF RETURN.)

BAND or BOX SILL   In pier and beam foundations, the two horizontal members that connect the pier to the floor joist. The boards are joined to create a right angle and the joist is placed perpendicular to the upright angle. This perpendicular placement provides the foundation with the necessary rigidity.

BANK PARTITIONS   Floor-fastened partitions of approximately five feet in height.

BANKRUPTCY   A condition of financial insolvency in which a person's liabilities exceed assets and the person is unable to pay current debts. Bankruptcy may be voluntary, as when the debtor petitions the court of his or her own accord; or it may be involuntary, as when a creditor forces payment of a debt of $1,000 or more, which the debtor cannot pay.

When a person enters into federal bankruptcy proceedings, all assets become vested in a court-appointed trustee or receiver who liquidates these assets to pay claims held against the debtor by his general creditors. Bankruptcy discharges the debtor from further liability on all debts then owed, except for such exempted debts as tax claims, alimony and support payments, liability for malicious injury and fraud, and debts not scheduled.

Once declaring bankruptcy, a person cannot do so again for another seven years. Generally, a bankrupt person must wait at least two years before becoming eligible for a new loan. The fact that a person went bankrupt will usually be reported by most credit agencies for a period of eight years.

A creditor of the bankrupt, whose claim is secured by a mortgage on real property, is normally entitled to the proceeds of the mortgaged property prior to any distribution of the bankrupt's assets to general creditors. As a general rule, the discharge in bankruptcy affects a debtor's personal obligations but it does not destroy liens against the debtor's property. Fraudulent conveyances, however, are void, and transfer of the insolvent debtor's property to a creditor within prescribed periods (such as 90 days) of filing the bankruptcy petition may be voided by the trustee in bankruptcy, since it enables a preferred creditor to get a greater percentage of the debt over other creditors. One of the fundamental policies of bankruptcy is to insure equality of distribution among creditors.

The bankruptcy of either party to a real estate agency agreement (listing) terminates the agency because title to the property passes to the trustee in bankruptcy. A discharge in bankruptcy does not generally relieve a real estate licensee from the penalties resulting from payment out of the state licensing agency's real estate recovery fund to defrauded consumers.

Bankruptcy of a lessee or vendee is usually a stated ground for default under a lease or contract for deed. Many leases and contracts for deed contain bankruptcy default clauses that provide the owner/landlord with the right of termination if the buyer/tenant goes bankrupt. Under the Federal Bankruptcy Act, however, forfeiture and termination clauses conditioned on insolvency or bankruptcy are now unenforceable. The purpose of the law is to curtail the effectiveness of restrictions on the transfer of property and forfeiture clauses insofar as they concern the property's becoming part of the bankruptcy estate.

The bankruptcy of a mortgagor or a trustor to a trust deed note will affect foreclosure proceedings if the bankruptcy is initiated before the foreclosure proceedings have begun. In such cases, the title to the property passes to the trustee in bankruptcy, and the referee (usually the judge) of the bankruptcy court must authorize the foreclosure proceedings. The filing of the petition in bankruptcy acts as an automatic stay of the foreclosure. The stay restrains the enforcement of all judgments and all judicial and voluntary liens, as well as all acts to create liens, to collect or enforce claims, or to recover property until the case is discharged or the stay is vacated. Note that the trustee can seek to avoid the mortgage on any proper ground such as a lack of consideration.

There are several other types of bankruptcy actions designed to reorganize and save a debtor's business operation. These actions have the debtor's "rehabilitation" as their prime goal. Under the former federal Chapter X proceedings, available to corporations only, the reorganization may be either voluntary or involuntary. It does not affect secured debts, that is, those that are secured by liens (mortgage loans, real estate taxes), although it does suspend any pending foreclosure proceedings. A court-appointed referee is responsible for setting up the reorganization of the operation. The debtor is allowed to retain possession of the property while arranging a plan for payment. Although such proceedings deal only with unsecured property, the court can order a suspension of all actions by a mortgagee and thus prevent foreclosure. There is no trustee, but a receiver will be appointed by the court if the debtor is not permitted to remain in possession.

Chapter XII proceedings are available only to noncorporation debtors owning real property. All enforcement proceedings are suspended, including foreclosure. The trustor or debtor in possession has the right to immediate possession of any of the debtor's real property that a mortgagee may be holding under the mortgage. Note that the Bankruptcy Reform Act of 1978 substantially modified long-standing federal bankruptcy law and consolidated into a single chapter the earlier separate Chapters X, XI, and XII.

BARGAIN AND SALE DEED   A deed, formerly in the form of a contract between buyer and seller, that recites a consideration and conveys all of the grantor's interest in the property to the grantee. A bargain and sale deed usually does not include warranties as to the title of the property conveyed; however, the grantor asserts by implication that he or she has possession of, a claim to, or interest in the property conveyed. The courts usually hold that the grantor promises only that the grantor has done nothing to cause a defect in title and is thus not liable for unknown defects. Trustees, fiduciaries, executors, and officers of the court often convey the real property under their control by way of a bargain and sale deed, sometimes with a covenant against the grantor's acts. (*See COVENANT, QUITCLAIM DEED, WARRANTY DEED.*)

BARGAIN SALE   A sale of property for less than its fair market value. The Internal Revenue Service may treat such a sale as a part-gift and part-sale transaction. (*See GIFT TAX.*)

BASEBOARD   A board running around the bottom of the wall perpendicular to the floor. The baseboard is sometimes called wains. A baseboard covers the gap coating between the floor and the wall, protects the wall from scuffs, and provides a decorative accent.

BASE LINE   1. One of a set of imaginary lines running east and west used by surveyors for reference in locating and describing land under the government survey method of property description. 2. A topographic centerline of a survey, as for the route of a freeway. (*See GOVERNMENT SURVEY METHOD.*)

BASEMENT   A space of full story height below the first floor wholly or partly below the exterior grade, which is not used primarily for living accommodations. Space, partly below grade, which is used primarily for living accommodations or commercial use, is not defined by FHA as basement space.

BASE PERIOD   A time interval or starting point used for calculating certain business and economic data, frequently found in escalation clauses. The determination of the base year has great significance in commercial leases where it is used to establish the cut-off year preceding rent escalations. The parties usually arrive at a complex formula for determining the base index, which is adopted as 100, from which stem future rent increases to match increases in operating expenses, utilities, services, and property taxes.

For example, if 1981 were used in a lease as the base year, it would be given an index of 100; if costs increased 8 percent in 1982 in relation to 1981 costs, then the 1982 index would be 108 and lease rents would be raised if so specified in the lease document.

BASE RENT The minimum rental stipulated under a percentage lease. The first year is called the base year. The second and each succeeding year is called a comparison year. (*See PERCENTAGE LEASE.*)

BASE SHOE Molding used at the junction of the baseboard and the floor; also called a carpet strip.

BASE TOP MOLDING A thin strip placed on top of the baseboard and perpendicular to the wall to cover gaps between the wall and the baseboard and give the molding a finished appearance.

BASIS The dollar amount that the Internal Revenue Service attributes to an asset for purposes of determining annual depreciation or cost recovery, and gain or loss on the sale of the asset. The determination of basis is of fundamental importance in tax aspects of real estate investment. All property has a basis. If property was acquired by purchase, the owner's basis is the cost of the property plus the value of any capital expenditures for improvements to the property, reduced by any cost recovery depreciation actually taken or allowable. The basis is also reduced by any untaxed gain "carried over" to the new property in cases where the new property is a replacement of a former residence, or is acquired through a like-kind tax exchange or an involuntary conversion. This new basis is called the property's adjusted basis.

If property was acquired by a lifetime gift, the basis is the donor's basis at the time of the gift plus the value of any capital expenditures for improvements made to the property by the donee, reduced by any depreciation allowable or actually taken by the donee. In certain cases in which the transaction is part gift and part sale, the maximum basis is the fair market value of the property on the date of the transfer plus any capital expenditures by the new owner for improvements to the property, minus any depreciation allowable or actually taken by the new owner.

If the property was acquired by inheritance, the heir (or heirs) will assume, as the basis for determining gain, the stepped-up basis of the property, that is, the fair market value of the property as of the date of death (the federal estate tax value of the asset in the decedent's estate).

If the property was acquired in a totally or partially tax-deferred exchange, the basis of the new property received in the exchange is determined by reference to the basis of the old property exchanged. Frequently, however, tax-deferred exchanges become partially taxable because of the receipt of cash or other unlike property in addition to the property of a like kind. If cash or other property is received, the gain on the exchange is taxable to the extent of such cash or other property. Thus, when a gain is partly recognized, the basis of the property received will be the basis of the property exchanged, reduced by other property or cash received and increased by the amount of taxable gain.

A personal residence is not depreciable for tax purposes because it is neither "property used in a trade or business" nor "property held for the production of income" as required under the Internal Revenue Code. However, the original basis of residential property may be adjusted upward in the amount of any capital expenditures made for improvements to the residence; thus, the taxpayer should maintain accurate records and receipts of substantial household improvements. When a property is sold, the amount of gain or loss is determined by comparing the adjusted basis on the date of sale with the net proceeds of the sale.

If property, such as a rental unit, has been held for longer than one year for income purposes and the taxpayer has not declared any depreciation over the period it was held as a rental, the IRS will automatically apply straight-line depreciation to the property and reduce the basis accordingly. If an accelerated method of depreciation has been taken on residential property, the IRS will require the taxpayer to "recapture" as ordinary income (pay income taxes on) the excess depreciation taken during the year of sale and adjust the basis accordingly; if the property is nonresidential, then *all* depreciation taken is recaptured as ordinary income and the basis is adjusted. Another important aspect is the allocation of basis. If the taxpayer purchases depreciable real estate, he or she must allocate the basis between the land, which is not depreciable, and the improvements, which are depreciable. A taxpayer often uses the same allocation as that determined by the state tax assessor. The taxpayer must also allocate his or her basis between the building and the fixtures and furniture in the building for separate calculation of depreciation, gain, or loss.

In the development of a large tract of land, the developer should consider allocating the purchase price among different portions of the tract according to their relative values for the purpose of determining the tax basis in each portion. The determination of the cost of portions of land on the basis of the fair market value of each portion has been approved by the Tax Court, as has been the allocation of cost according to front footage, release prices, tentative sales prices, and assessed valuation.

Due to the importance of basis, the various adjustments to it, and the tax consequences arising from the various adjustments, real estate investors should seek competent advice on a real estate investment from a tax accountant, a tax attorney, or an experienced commercial-investment broker. (*See ACCELERATED DEPRECIATION, CAPITAL GAIN, DEPRECIABLE REAL PROPERTY, EASEMENT, RECAPTURE OF DEPRECIATION, RESIDENCE, STEPPED-UP BASIS.*)

BASIS POINT   One one-hundredth of one percent. Used to describe the amount of change in the market price of bonds and many debt instruments, including mortgages. For example, 50 basis points is the difference between a 13 percent and a 13½ percent loan. On a $40,000 loan to be paid over a 30-year period, this would be an increase of $5,000 in the total loan payments.

BASKET PROVISION   A provision contained in the regulatory acts governing the investments of insurance companies, savings and loan associations, and mutual savings banks that allows for a certain small percentage of total assets to be placed in investments not otherwise permitted by the regulatory acts. A loan made under this provision, such as a high-yield second mortgage, or wraparound mortgage, would be called a basket money loan. These acceptable miscellaneous types of transactions are collected into a separate basket, so to speak.

BATTEN — Narrow strips of wood or metal used to cover joints either on the interior or the exterior; used for decorative effect.

BAY — An unfinished area or space between a row of columns and the bearing wall typically found in industrial and warehouse facilities. Usually, the smallest area into which a building floor can be partitioned.

BAY WINDOW — A window that forms a bay in a room, projects outward from the wall, and is supported by its own foundation.

BEACH — Land on the margin of a sea, lake, or river. If the tide ebbs and flows over the land, it is called *tideland*; if the land is not subject to tidal action, it is called *shoreland*.

BEAM — A structural member that transversally supports a load.

BEARING — In survey terminology, a bearing is a horizontal angle measured from 0° to 90°, fixing the direction of a course or distance in relation to true north or south.

BEARING WALL — A main or supporting wall referred to as a load-bearing wall, usually supporting a roof above. In a condominium, all bearing walls are common elements and nonbearing walls, such as certain partitions, are owned by the apartment owners.

BEDROCK — The solid rock underlying soils and other surficial formations.

BEDROOM COMMUNITY — A section of the community that serves as a residential area for an adjoining or nearby metropolitan area. Also known as a *dormitory town*.

BEFORE-AND-AFTER METHOD — An appraisal method employed in determining just compensation of land which has been partially taken by condemnation. The value of the remaining property is the difference between its value before the partial taking and its value after. For example, assume a 100-acre parcel is worth $2.00 per square foot before the state condemns the front 50 acres. After the condemnation, the rear 50 acres is valued at $0.50 per square foot. Under the before-and-after method, the amount of compensation in the condemnation award due for the remaining property is the difference between the value of the whole property before the taking and the value of the remainder after the taking—or $1.50 per square foot. Thus, the condemnee is entitled to $2.00 per square foot for the 50 acres taken and $1.50 per square foot on the 50 acres remaining.

The before-and-after method is also used in modernization cases; that is, an appraiser may take the value of property before and after remodeling to determine if the value increased more than modernization costs. (*See CONDEMNATION, JUST COMPENSATION, SEVERANCE DAMAGES.*)

BENCH MARK   A permanent reference mark (PRM) affixed to a durable object, such as an iron post or brass marker embedded in a sidewalk, used to establish elevations and altitudes above sea level over a surveyed area; also used in tidal observation.

The elevations are based on the official datum and each bench mark has its own recognized official elevation. Thus, a surveyor can start at any bench mark to set the elevation measurements. Where there is no datum for an area, surveyors use the base elevations set by the U.S. Geological Survey. (*See DATUM, GEODETIC SURVEY SYSTEM, MONUMENT.*)

BENCHMARK   The standard or base from which specific estimates are made; or, a major court decision that serves as the precedent or guideline for future decisions.

BENEFICIARY   A person who receives the benefits from the gifts or acts of another, such as one who is designated to receive the proceeds from a will, insurance policy, or trust; the real owner, as opposed to the trustee who holds only legal title. (*See DEED IN TRUST.*)

BENEFICIARY STATEMENT   A statement of the unpaid balance of a loan and the condition of the indebtedness, as it relates to a deed of trust transaction.

BENEFIT-OF-BARGAIN RULE   A rule of damages in which a buyer who has been defrauded can recover the difference between the actual value of the property and the value of the property as represented to him or her, as opposed to merely recovering the out-of-pocket loss. (*See DAMAGES.*)

BEQUEATH   To leave personal property to another by will, as a bequest. To leave real property by will is to devise. In modern terminology it is frequently used to convey a gift by will, whether it be real or personal property. (*See LEGACY.*)

BETTERMENT   An improvement to real property, such as a sidewalk or road, that substantially increases the property's value. The measure of value is not in the improvement's actual cost, but rather in the enhanced value added to the property. It does not result from an acquisition of new property, nor is it a mere restoration of the property; it is a capital expenditure as compared to repairs or replacements. (*See SPECIAL BENEFIT.*)

BIANNUAL   Occurring twice a year; semi-annual. For example, real property tax payments may be due biannually, in November and May of each year.

BID   1. An offer to purchase property for a specified amount, such as at an auction or a foreclosure sale. Often the owner of property put up for auction will put in a *protective bid* to prevent the property from being sold at a sacrifice price. A mortgagee may bid in at a foreclosure auction up to the amount of the outstanding loan. (*See AUCTION.*)

2. Formal procedure of submission, by a list of contract bidders, of sealed proposals to perform certain work at a cost specified in the proposal, usually within a set period of time. Intended to ensure the client and contractors with an objective and competitive method of fulfilling job requirements at lowest cost.

BIENNIAL   Occurring every two years. Some states require biennial renewal of real estate licenses.

BILATERAL CONTRACT   A contract in which each party promises to perform an act in exchange for the other party's promise to perform.

The usual real estate sales contract is an example of a bilateral contract in which the buyer and seller exchange reciprocal promises respectively to buy and sell the property. If one party refuses to honor his or her promise and the other party is ready to perform, the nonperforming party is said to be in default. Neither party is liable to the other until there is first a performance, or tender of performance, by the nondefaulting party. Thus, when the buyer refuses to pay the purchase price, the seller usually must tender the deed into escrow to show that he or she is ready to perform. In some cases, however, tender is not necessary.

Depending on its wording, a listing form may be considered to be a bilateral contract, with the broker agreeing to use his or her best efforts to locate a ready, willing, and able purchaser for the property, and the seller promising to pay the broker a commission if the broker produces such a buyer or if the property is sold. Once signed by the broker and seller, such a listing contract becomes binding on both.

In a *unilateral contract*, one party must actually perform (and not just promise to perform) for the contract to be binding. For example, in an option, the optionor (seller) promises to keep a specific offer to sell open for a specific time in exchange for the performance of an act by the optionee (buyer); that is, the actual payment (not just the promise to pay) of the option money. When the option is exercised, a bilateral contract to buy and sell is created according to the terms set forth in the option. (*See OPTION, TENDER, UNILATERAL CONTRACT.*)

BILL OF SALE   A written agreement by which one person sells, assigns, or transfers to another his or her right to, or interest in, personal property. A bill of sale is sometimes used by the seller of real estate to evidence the transfer of personal property, such as when the owner of a store sells the building and includes the store equipment and trade fixtures. The transfer of the personal property can be effected by mention in the deed or, as is more common, by a separate bill-of-sale document. A bill of sale may be with or without warranties covering defects or unpaid liens of the property.

A bill of sale is normally used when the purchaser is an investor and, for tax reasons (faster depreciation write-off), he or she wants a separate accounting for the personal property involved, especially if the property is valued at an amount greater than the standard price for similar property. The broker in a transaction involving personal property should see that there is an accurate inventory taken of the items included in the bill of sale.

BINDER   1. An agreement formed by the receipt of an earnest money deposit for the purchase of real property as evidence of the purchaser's good faith and intention to complete the transaction. Used to bind the parties until a more formal contract can be prepared and executed. Receipt of the binder money, or deposit, is usually evidenced in the sales contract. (*See EARNEST MONEY.*)

2. A written instrument giving immediate fire and extended insurance coverage until a regular insurance policy can be issued, sometimes obtained pending the closing of a real estate transaction.

3. A temporary contract of title insurance in which the insurer agrees to issue a specified policy within a certain period of time. Excluded from coverage are any defects, liens, or encumbrances affecting the title that intervene between the date of the binder and the date of the conveyance to the proposed insured.

Since a preliminary report does not constitute a commitment to insure the title, it may sometimes be advisable to obtain a binder or commitment from the title insurer stating its willingness to insure the title, particularly in complex transactions with multiple simultaneous closings.

BIRD DOG   A saleperson whose sole job is to "flush out" new listings. Upon obtaining a lead, the bird dog salesperson turns everything over to his or her broker or to another salesperson better experienced to handle the transaction. Any person capable of furnishing leads, such as postal carrier, mover, or barber.

BLACKTOP   Asphalt paving used in streets and driveways.

BLANKET MORTGAGE   A mortgage that is secured by several properties or a number of lots.

A blanket mortgage is often used to secure construction financing for proposed subdivisions or condominium development projects. The developer normally seeks to have a "partial release" clause inserted in the mortgage so that he or she can obtain a release from the blanket mortgage for each lot as it is sold, according to a specified release schedule. For example, assume a developer obtains a $500,000 mortgage to cover the development of 50 lots. He might be required to pay off $12,500 of principal in order to get each lot released from under the blanket mortgage. Sometimes, land developers will have a "special recognition" clause put in the blanket mortgage whereby the lender agrees to recognize the rights of each individual parcel owner, even if the developer defaults and there is a foreclosure. Occasionally, the federal government will secure a blanket lien against all properties owned by a person who has defaulted on his or her income taxes.

A blanket mortgage may also be used when one desires to buy a house plus an adjacent vacant lot and finances the purchase with a single mortgage that covers both properties, or it may be used where the equity in one property is insufficient to meet the lender's requirements. (See PARTIAL RELEASE CLAUSE.)

BLIGHTED AREA   A declining area, usually in the inner city, in which real property values are seriously affected by detrimental influences, such as encroaching inharmonious property use mixture or rapidly depreciating buildings, with no immediate prospect of improvement. (See URBAN RENEWAL.)

BLIND AD   An advertisement that does not include the name and address of the person placing the ad; an ad that lists only a phone number or post office box address. Licensed brokers are generally prohibited by state license laws from using blind ads.

BLIND POOL   A securities offering of interests in unspecified and yet-to-be-determined properties; a nonspecified property offering. In a blind pool, an investor usually relies on the general partner's ability to locate and put together suitable investments. Some states, such as New York, prohibit blind pool offerings; that is, they only permit the offering of securities in existing, selected properties or specific properties proposed for development. Other states permit blind pool offerings that meet prescribed requirements. (See REAL PROPERTY SECURITIES REGISTRATION.)

BLOCK   See LOT, BLOCK, AND SUBDIVISION.

BLOCKBUSTING   An illegal and discriminatory practice whereby one person induces another to enter into a real estate transaction from which the first person may benefit financially, by representing that a change in the neighborhood with respect to race, sex, religion, color, or ancestry of the occupants may occur, which may result in the lowering of the property values, a decline in the quality of schools, or an increase in the crime rate. Such a practice generally violates both state and federal antidiscrimination laws. It may result from even giving the impression that panic selling exists.

The term blockbusting includes subtle as well as obvious forms of racial inducements, so that a representation may be unlawful even if race is not explicitly mentioned. For example, the uninvited solicitations of real estate listings in a racially transitional neighborhood are prohibited representations if it can be shown that the solicitations are made for profit, are intended to induce the sale of a dwelling, and that the solicitations would convey to a reasonable person, under the circumstances, the idea that members of a particular race are or may be entering the neighborhood. Also called panic peddling. (*See DISCRIMINATION, FEDERAL FAIR HOUSING LAW, PANIC PEDDLING.*)

BLOCK INTEREST   Interest computed on the original face amount of the loan which remains the same even as the principal declines. Thus, a $10,000 loan with block interest at 12 percent payable over three years would require equal annual interest payments of $1,200 until completely paid, regardless of the unpaid principal amount. As a general rule, to determine the effective rate of interest (true annual interest), double the stated block interest rate. Thus, in the example, the true annual interest on the $10,000 loan would be almost 24 percent. Also called ADD-ON INTEREST.

BLUE BOOK   One of any number of real estate or other reference books, such as *Amortization and Balloon Payment Tables,* published by Professional Publishing Corporation of San Rafael, California, and *Olcott's Land Values,* published by George C. Olcott & Company of Chicago.

BLUE LAWS   Religious laws handed down from colonial days restricting the transaction of business on Sundays and certain religious holidays; derived from the original practice of printing these laws on blue paper.

BLUEPRINT   A working plan used on a construction job by tradespeople; an architectural drafting or drawing that is transferred to chemically treated paper by exposure to strong light causing the paper to turn blue thus reproducing the drawing in white.

BLUE-SKY LAWS   State securities laws designed to protect the public from fraudulent practices in the promotion and sale of securities (such as promising the sky); for example, through limited partnerships, syndications, and bonds. Blue-sky laws normally require that securities be registered with the securities commissioner in the state where the offers are being made and that the issuer disclose (usually in a prospectus) all pertinent facts about the investment to prospective purchasers.

Unlike federal securities laws, some state laws also impose qualitative standards upon issuers of securities, and require that each offering be "fair, just and equitable." This term may be applied to limit the amount of commissions or other compensation paid, the nature of the investment, or other related matters.

BOARD   1. The local organization of the State Association of Realtors®, which belongs to the National Association of Realtors®. (*See NATIONAL ASSOCIATION OF REALTORS®.*) 2. Sometimes refers to the state real estate commission.

BOARD FOOT   A measure of lumber one foot square by one inch thick; 144 cubic inches = $1' \times 1' \times 1''$.

BOARD OF DIRECTORS The governing body of a corporation authorized to carry on and control the business affairs of the company, the members of which are elected periodically by shareholders. Unless required in the bylaws, the directors usually need not be shareholders of the corporation. State law establishes the minimum number allowed, as well as how many must be residents of the state.

A director who acts as a broker in negotiating the sale or purchase of corporate property cannot accept a commission for his or her services without express authorization from the board of directors to act as a broker and receive a commission.

A condominium owners' association is generally administered by a board of directors. Among other duties, the board is charged by law with the duty to see that adequate insurance is obtained if so required by the bylaws. Failure to do so would subject individual directors to personal liability. (*See ARTICLES OF INCORPORATION, CONDOMINIUM OWNERS' ASSOCIATION, CORPORATE RESOLUTION, CORPORATION.*)

BOARD OF EQUALIZATION *See EQUALIZATION BOARD.*

BOILER PLATE The standard, fixed language in a contract, such as is found in most mortgages, contracts of sale, contracts for deed, leases, and CC&Rs (covenants, conditions, and restrictions). Where such language is too one sided, the contract might be challenged as an adhesion contract. When a form contract or lease is used, any uncertain or ambiguous terms will be construed against the party who furnished the form. (*See ADHESION CONTRACT.*)

BOILER ROOM A questionable promotional technique whereby multiple "cold pitch" phone calls are made by land sales companies to the public to create leads for the sale of real estate, usually vacant land or property located in another area or state. These telephone solicitors are usually required to have real estate licenses.

BONA FIDE Real; actual; in good faith. A bona fide purchaser is one who acquires property in good faith and for a valuable consideration without knowledge, actual or constructive, of the prior rights or equities of third persons. Bona fide purchasers are usually protected under the state recording acts against the rights of third parties with a prior unrecorded interest in the same property. (*See CONSTRUCTIVE NOTICE, GOOD FAITH, POSSESSION, RECORDING.*)

BOND A promissory note that generally accompanies a mortgage and is the primary evidence of the debt obligation secured by the mortgage; may also refer to a completion bond or a performance bond. Also an interest-bearing certificate issued by a government as a means of financing real estate projects and community improvements such as schools and parks. General obligation bonds are designated to be repaid out of property taxes. (*See DEBENTURE, PERFORMANCE BOND, PROMISSORY NOTE.*)

BONUS CLAUSE   A prepayment clause in an installment contract, deed of trust, mortgage, or note providing for a special payment to be made to the lender in the event of full or partial payment before the scheduled due date. (*See PREPAYMENT.*)

BOOK VALUE   The amount at which an asset is carried on the financial books of a person, partnership, association or corporation.

Book value is the capitalized cost of an asset less depreciation taken for accounting purposes, based on the method used for the computation of depreciation over the useful life of the asset. It is the adjusted basis of an asset, and usually differs from appraised or market value. Book value serves as the basis of computing profits or losses derived from a sale. The book value of a property can be readily determined by adding the depreciated value of the improvement to the allocated value of the land. (*See BASIS.*)

BOOT   Money or other property that is not like-kind, which is given to make up any difference in value or equity between exchanged properties. Boot may be in the form of cash, notes, gems, the fair market value of an asset such as a mortgage, land contract, personal property, good will, a service, or a patent offered in an exchange. The taxable gain in an exchange is recognized immediately to the extent of boot, while other gain from the exchange may be deferred until subsequent transfer.

Where liabilities (mortgages, deeds of trust) are assumed by both parties to an exchange of property, the amount of the liabilities are netted to determine a net boot. An excess amount of liability assumed by one party to the exchange is boot to the other party. This is true whether the party to whom the property is transferred assumes the liability or merely takes the property subject to the liability. (*See BASIS, EXCHANGE.*)

BOTTOMLAND   Lowlands located in a valley, dale, or near a river or creek. Also, land that is often underwater, such as tideland or a flood plain.

BOULEVARD   A major collector with or without a median strip, generally shorter than a highway, usually serving through traffic on a continuous route.

BOUNDARIES   The perimeters or limits of a parcel of land as fixed by legal description.

Boundary disputes are controversies between adjoining owners as to the proper location of the dividing line between the properties. Some abutting owners enter into a boundary agreement in which they stipulate that a certain dividing line, such as a fence, serves as the true boundary of the properties.

A frequent dispute arises where the branches of a tree located on one owner's property extend over the boundary line onto a neighbor's property, thereby invading the neighbor's air rights. The neighbor can cut the branches up to the boundary line, or he or she can seek court action for money damages and an abatement of the nuisance. To lessen the risks of boundary disputes, prudent buyers require the seller to stake or survey the property. (*See AGREED BOUNDARIES.*)

BOUNDS A reference to direction, based on terminal points and angles. (*See* METES *AND BOUNDS*.)

BRACING Framing lumber nailed at an angle in order to provide rigidity.

BRANCH OFFICE Any secondary place of business apart from the principal or main office from which real estate business is conducted.

Each branch office usually must have a broker-in-charge, or branch manager, who is responsible for the operations of the branch. In some states, this manager need only be a salesperson. Most states require each branch office to be registered and a special license for it issued.

BREACH OF CONTRACT Violation of any of the terms or conditions of a contract without legal excuse; default; nonperformance. The nonbreaching party to the contract can usually seek one of three possible alternative remedies upon a material breach of the contract: rescission of the contract, action for money damages, or an action for specific performance. (*See ANTICIPATORY BREACH, DAMAGES, ELECTION OF REMEDIES, RESCISSION, SPECIFIC PERFORMANCE*.)

BREAK-EVEN POINT In residential or commercial property, the figure at which rental income is equal to all required expenses and debt service. It is the point at which gross income is equal to fixed costs plus all variable costs incurred in developing that income. Use of the break-even analysis is important to calculation of the profitability of a building. In large commercial projects, the standby financing commitments usually require that the project be leased up to its break-even point before a permanent lender will fund a take-out mortgage.

BRIDGE LOAN 1. Short-term loan to cover the period between the termination of one loan, such as the interim construction loan, and the beginning of another loan, such as a permanent take-out loan; or the loan between the acquisition of a property and its improvement or development to make it qualify for a permanent loan. It is sometimes used to provide the funds for the costs incurred in the conversion of an apartment house into a condominium. (*See GAP FINANCING, SWING LOAN*.)

2. A residential financing arrangement in which the buyer of a new home borrows money and gives a second mortgage on the buyer's unsold home to fund the acquisition of a new home. This loan is useful where the seller of the new home will not accept an offer "subject to the sale of the buyer's home" or where the buyer needs to raise the down payment by a certain date or else lose the new home.

BRIDGING Small wood or metal pieces placed diagonally between the floor joists. Bridgings disburse weight on the floor over adjacent joists thus increasing the floor's load capacity.

BRING-DOWN SEARCH   A continuation of a title search to verify that no liens have been filed against the property between the time of the original search and the recording of the deed or mortgage; also called a take-down search or a continuation. In many states, the buyer customarily pays the fee for this continuation. (*See CONTINUATION.*)

BRITISH THERMAL UNIT (BTU)   A unit of measure of heat, used in rating the capacity of air conditioning and heating equipment (radiators, boilers). A BTU represents the amount of heat required to raise the temperature of one pound of water one degree Fahrenheit at approximately 39.2°F.

BROKER   One who acts as an intermediary between parties to a transaction. A real estate broker is a properly licensed party (individual, corporation or partnership) who, for a valuable consideration or promise of consideration, serves as a special agent to others to facilitate the sale or lease of real property.

A real estate broker is an independent businessperson who sets the office policies. A broker hires employees and salespeople, determines their compensation, and supervises their activities. The broker is free to accept or reject agency relationships with principals.

Brokers represent their principals and accept the responsibility of exercising care, skill, and integrity in carrying out their instructions. Generally, a broker's duties are confined to advertising property and to finding a person ready, willing, and able to deal on the terms stipulated by and acceptable to the principal. However, legal restrictions are now imposed on brokers by legislative action, and in recent years, federal, state, and local fair housing laws have been passed which place new social obligations on them. Brokers cannot legally refuse, due to race, religion, sex, or national origin, to show, sell, rent, or otherwise negotiate regarding property listed with them. All offers must be submitted by the broker to the principal.

To qualify as a real estate broker, one must meet the requirements set forth in the real estate license law of the state in which the broker intends to practice. This generally involves passing a written examination, meeting educational requirements, evidencing good character, and paying the required fees.

A broker is permitted by law to hire others to assist the brokerage in representing its clients. While the broker can be a corporation or a partnership, its salespeople must be individuals. Some brokers continue as selling brokers, some are sales managers, and others are primarily administrative brokers doing little or no listing and selling.

In many states, a licensed broker cannot recover a commission from his or her principal unless the employment agreement (listing contract) is in writing. (*See AGENCY, EXAMINATION, FIDUCIARY, LICENSING, INDEPENDENT CONTRACTOR, LICENSE LAWS, LISTING, SALESPERSON.*)

BROKERAGE   The aspect of the real estate business that is concerned with bringing together the parties and completing a real estate transaction. Brokerage involves exchanges, rentals, and trade-ins of property, as well as sales.

In most cases, a real estate broker or salesperson will find a ready, willing, and able buyer to purchase a property, either on the terms specified by the seller in his or her listing contract or on new terms acceptable to the seller. For this service, the seller normally pays a commission based on a percentage of the gross sales price. This commission is paid directly to the broker (or brokerage company) who then may compensate the selling salesperson according to a prearranged schedule. (*See COMMISSION.*)

BROKERAGE COMMISSION

The rate of compensation a broker receives for performing his or her employment agreement (listing), or the compensation received by a cooperating broker who procures a ready, willing, and able buyer for another broker's listing, as through the multiple listing service.

There are no longer any established commission schedules; in fact, any attempt by a group of brokers to fix brokerage rates would be a violation of antitrust laws. Local custom and usage may prescribe the acceptable range of commission rates for various transactions. In larger transactions, commission rates are determined by negotiation between principal and broker, often on a graduated basis, such as 6 percent of the first $400,000 and 3 percent of the balance. Some state laws provide that in order for the broker to recover a commission, there must be a written employment agreement (listing). Some state laws require a disclosure in the listing agreement to the effect that commissions are negotiable. (*See COMMISSION, COOPERATING BROKER.*)

BROKER-IN-CHARGE

In many states, the broker-in-charge of a branch office is designated by the principal broker of a real estate brokerage company and registered with the state real estate license law officials as the person directly in charge of and responsible to said principal broker for the real estate operations conducted at a branch office. (*See BRANCH OFFICE.*)

BROWNSTONE

A row house constructed with reddish-brown sandstone; usually refers to a structure constructed during the nineteenth century and found in large cities such as New York. A dark-colored red sandstone, often used as facing for row houses.

BUDGET

A balance sheet or statement of estimated receipts and expenditures. Property managers must be well skilled in the preparation of an accurate budget for operating office buildings or condominium buildings.

Budgets take many different forms. The cash operating budget details the positive and negative cash flows of a property from month to month. It usually does not contain depreciation, bad debt losses, and other noncash items. The capital improvements budget outlines a fiscal program for making capital repairs, replacements, or additions to a property over a stated period of time. A budget is no more reliable than the person who prepares it.

BUDGET MORTGAGE

A mortgage with payments set up to cover more than interest and principal reductions. In addition to monthly amortized principal and interest payments, the monthly payments may include an amount equal to one-twelfth of the year's property taxes, a pro rata share of the fire insurance premium, and any other similar charges which, if not paid, could result in a foreclosure of the property. Such a mortgage with all-inclusive payments facilitates the payment by the purchaser of such expenses and protects the mortgagee in case the purchaser cannot make these payments when they become due as one large, lump-sum payment. The use of the budget mortgage is especially common in residential mortgage loans, especially VA and FHA loans.

BUFFER ZONE A zoning term meaning a strip of land separating one land use from another. Sometimes a developer of a large residential subdivision will leave certain land undeveloped as a buffer against adjoining land which might be incompatibly zoned, such as an industrial park.

BUILDER'S RISK INSURANCE Fire, liability, and extended-coverage insurance written to cover the special risks of a building under construction. Coverage increases automatically as the building progresses and terminates upon its completion. Such a policy should be replaced by permanent insurance when the building is ready for occupancy. Premiums may be based on the estimated "completed value" or based on a "full reporting clause" in which the builder periodically reports the increases in value as construction progresses.

BUILDING AND LOAN ASSOCIATION An incorporated mutual organization that invests its members' funds in residential mortgages and repays the interest earned to its member depositors in periodic dividends. (*See SAVINGS & LOAN ASSOCIATIONS.*)

BUILDING CODES Rules set up by local, state, or municipal governments to regulate building and construction standards. In many areas these codes are based on national standards. Building codes are designed to provide minimum standards to safeguard the health, safety, and welfare of the public by regulating and controlling the design, construction, quality, use and occupancy, location, and maintenance of all buildings and structures. The establishment of building codes is a valid exercise of the state's police power and thus they are valid restrictions on an owner's use of his or her property. Some codes are divided into specialized areas, such as plumbing codes, electrical codes, and fire codes. These codes are enforced by the issuing of building permits and certificates of occupancy and by inspections, and fines are imposed on violators. (*See BUILDING PERMIT, UNIFORM BUILDING CODE, ZONING.*)

BUILDING LEASE A long-term lease of raw land under which the tenant agrees to pay a set ground rent and further agrees to construct and maintain specified improvement of the premises. (*See GROUND LEASE.*)

BUILDING LINE A setback line; a line beyond which one may not build any improvement. Building line restrictions may be created by designating them on a recorded subdivision plat or by inserting a restriction in the subdivider's deed. Establishing building lines ensures a degree of uniformity in the appearance of buildings and creates a right to unobstructed light, air, and view.

BUILDING OWNERS AND MANAGERS ASSOCIATION (BOMA) A national organization of over 4,000 professionals in the highrise/office building industry, with over 80 local BOMA associations.

The Building Owners and Managers Institute (BOMI) is the related educational institute that provides professional training in all aspects of building management and operations via individual-study courses leading to professional certification as a Real Property Administrator (RPA). The seven required courses are Engineering and Building Structures, Real Property Maintenance, Risk Management and Insurance, Accounting and Financial Concepts, Law, Finance, and Management Concepts.

BUILDING PAPER Fiber-reinforced, waterproof paper treated with bitumen, a natural asphalt from coal, petroleum, or with some other water-resistant compound. Building paper is placed between siding and wall sheathing, around door and window frames, and in other areas to insulate the house and keep out moisture.

BUILDING PERMIT A written governmental permission for the construction of a new building or other improvement, the demolition or substantial repair of an existing structure, or the installation of factory-built housing. The proposed construction must conform to local zoning and building codes and must generally be inspected and approved upon completion. A building permit usually must be obtained before the start of a project and is therefore a convenient way for local authorities to check on actual compliance with the zoning code.

A prudent developer should include in the purchase agreement for a proposed development site a condition that the developer obtain a building permit. The seller should be sure that a deadline date is required for this condition, otherwise the developer could unreasonably delay in seeking the permit while keeping the seller's property off the market.

Any owner contemplating an addition and/or change to his or her property should first check with the appropriate county or municipal building department to avoid any violations. The existence of building code violations will generally render a seller's title unmarketable. Failure to disclose such violations would appear to constitute a material misrepresentation, entitling the buyer to rescind the transaction and obtain the return of his or her money. (See CERTIFICATE OF OCCUPANCY, ZONING.)

BUILDING RESIDUAL TECHNIQUE An appraisal term for a method of determining the contribution of an improvement to the present value of the entire property, normally used in appraising income property.

When the value of land is known, the appraiser deducts from the net income produced by the property the amount of net income which must be attributed to the land to justify its value. For example, if the land value is $10,000 and the going rate of interest is 12 percent, then the land itself must return 12 percent of its value, or $1200 per year, if it is to justify its purchase price. The balance or residue of the net income represents that income attributable to or earned by the building, which is then capitalized in order to arrive at the indicated value of the building. Land value is added to arrive at the value of the property as a whole. (See INCOME APPROACH.)

BUILDING RESTRICTIONS Limitations on the size or types of improvements established by zoning acts or by private restrictions inserted in a deed or ground lease. Violations of building restrictions render the title unmarketable. (*See MARKETABLE TITLE, RESTRICTION.*)

BUILDING STANDARDS The specific elements of construction the owner/developer chooses to use throughout a building. The building standard offered an office tenant, for example, would relate to the type of partitions, doors, ceiling tile, light fixtures, carpet, draperies, and like things.

BUILD-TO-SUIT An understanding or contract in which a lessor agrees to develop a property or finish certain space to the specifications of a lessee in return for a lease commitment on the part of the prospective tenant. The cost of work done, or a portion thereof, is usually amortized in the form of additional rental payments. Possession is given upon completion. (*See TURN-KEY PROJECT.*)

BUILT-INS Certain stationary equipment—such as some kitchen appliances, bookcases, desks, shelving, cabinets, and furniture—permanently affixed to real property and understood to be included when the property is sold. A built-in may also refer to a garage that is under the same roof as the main building it serves. (*See FIXTURE.*)

BUILT-UP METHOD An appraisal term meaning a method of determining the discount rate used in selection of the appropriate capitalization rate. The four basic components of the discount rate are the riskless rate, management, nonliquidity, and risk. Sometimes referred to as the summation method of rate selection.

BULK TRANSFER Any transfer in bulk (and not a transfer in the ordinary course of the seller's business) of a major part of the materials, inventory, or supplies of an enterprise. The Uniform Commercial Code (UCC) regulates bulk transfers to deal with such commercial frauds as a merchant selling out his stock, pocketing the proceeds, and leaving his creditors unpaid. The UCC requires the buyer of the goods to demand that the seller provide a schedule of all the property and a list of all creditors and that the buyer give notice to creditors of the pending sale. Failure to comply with the UCC means that the transfer or sale is ineffective in respect to the claims of any creditor of the seller. Bulk transfers usually become relevant upon the liquidation or sale of a business.

Under state law, a bulk sale must often be reported by the seller to the state tax authorities and the purchaser must withhold payment until the seller's tax clearance is received. The purchaser may become liable for any unpaid taxes that are a lien against the items sold if the tax clearance is not made.

BUMPER A device of wood, rubber, or other material used around a loading dock to cushion the impact of parking trucks.

BUNDLE OF RIGHTS   An ownership concept describing all those legal rights that attach to the ownership of real property, including the right to sell, lease, encumber, use, enjoy, exclude, and will. These rights also include the rights of use, occupancy, cultivation, exploration, the right to license, devise, dedicate, give away, share, mortgage, and trade or exchange. When purchasing real estate, one actually buys the rights previously held by the seller, except those that are reserved or limited in the sale. These rights are called beneficial interests associated with real property interests.

BUNGALOW   A small, one- or one-and-one-half-story house.

BUREAU RATE   A standard rate for hazard insurance, and for title insurance in some states, established by a rating bureau for all companies writing policies in a specific area.

BUS DUCT   Electrical conductors that group together multiple circuits used to provide service along a given line in an industrial plant.

BUSINESS DAY   A day of the week, except Saturdays, Sundays, and holidays; a normal working day. Because of accepted custom and practice, business day is preferable to the use of banking day or working day.

Some laws require notice within five business days such as notice to quit for tenant's failure to pay rent; other laws refer to calendar days. A possible dispute can arise if a contract fails to state whether the notice be business days or calendar days, although the usual interpretation is that it is calendar days unless specified otherwise. (*See DATE, HOLIDAYS.*)

BUSINESS ENERGY PROPERTY TAX CREDIT   Business taxpayers can qualify for a new 10 to 15 percent credit for investing in any of three categories of energy property: alternate energy property, solar or wind energy property, and specially defined energy property. The credit became effective on November 1, 1978. If energy property is also tangible personal property that qualifies for the regular investment tax credit, then both credits can be utilized.

To qualify, the equipment must be new and must be placed in service after September 30, 1978, and before January 1, 1983, or, if acquired by the taxpayer, the original use must begin during this period. Unlike most other investment credit property, energy property can qualify for the investment credit even if it is considered a structural component or is used in connection with lodging facilities.

The credit is available only to people engaged in a trade or business. If the property is disposed of before the end of the useful life claimed for the purposes of the credit, the credit will be recaptured according to the rules for the regular investment credit. The property must have a useful life of at least three years. Alternate energy property, solar or wind energy property and specially defined energy property are extensively defined in the Energy Tax Act of 1978.

BUSINESS LIFE INSURANCE   Life insurance purchased by a business enterprise on the life of a member of the firm. It is often bought by partnerships to protect the surviving partners against loss caused by the death of a partner, or by a corporation to reimburse it for loss caused by the death of a key employee. Also referred to as key man insurance.

BUSINESS OPPORTUNITY   Any type of business that is for sale; also called *business chance brokerage*, or simply *business brokerage*. The sale or lease of the business and goodwill of an existing business, enterprise, or opportunity. It includes a sale of all or substantially all of the assets or stock of a corporation, or assets of a partnership or sole proprietorship.

Generally, if real property is an asset of the business, a real estate broker's license is required to sell the business. Because a broker may not be aware of many of the special problems involved in selling a business, however, the advice of an experienced business counselor or attorney may be appropriate. Both seller and buyer should be aware of the application of the bulk transfer laws on the sale of the business. They should also be aware that, under the Uniform Commercial Code, any contract involving the sale of goods of $500 or more must be in writing in order to be enforceable. (*See BULK TRANSFER, GOOD WILL.*)

BUY-BACK AGREEMENT   A provision in a sales contract that provides that the seller (and in some cases, the broker) will buy back the property within a specified period, usually for the original selling price, upon the happening of a certain event, such as the purchaser being transferred from the area.

BUYDOWN   A financing technique used to reduce the monthly payment for the homebuying borrower during the initial years. Under some buydown plans, a residential developer, builder, or the seller will make subsidy payments (in the form of points) to the lender that "buy down," or lower, the effective interest rate paid by the homebuyer, thus reducing monthly payments for a set period of time.

The amount of the interest supplement may remain fixed for the entire buydown period, or it may be graduated, with the amount of the subsidy declining each year.

Buydowns are costly: A three-year buydown carries 2.7 points for each one percentage point drop of interest.

As interest rates on real estate loans climbed in the late '70s and early '80s many families could not qualify for loans of the size they needed to purchase a home. For example, to qualify for a $60,000 30-year loan (mortgage or deed of trust) at 15 percent interest requires an annual income of approximately $46,700 (under early '80s guidelines). While the same size loan at 10 percent requires an annual income of $35,600. To sell houses and have buyers qualify, many builders have turned to the buydown technique. Assume the builder of a house was to offer a 12 percent rate for the first three years of the above-mentioned loan, it would reduce the monthly payment from $758.67 to $617.17, a savings of $5,094 over the three years. The builder could do this by reducing the profit on the sale or by adding part of this cost of doing business to the price of the house.

At the end of the three-year period, the interest rate would go to the original rate of 15 percent. At that time, the owner could be making more income so the additional $141.50 a month could be paid, or if interest rates had dropped, the house could be refinanced at a lower rate of interest.

The Federal National Mortgage Association (Fannie Mae) has developed a unique buydown program, which it hopes will grow in popularity in the '80s.

BUYER'S MARKET An economic situation in which the supply of properties available for sale exceeds the demand. As a result, sellers are often forced to lower their prices and sometimes assist in the financing (with purchase-money mortgages) in order to attract buyers. A decline in prices resulting from an oversupply.

BUY-SELL AGREEMENT 1. An agreement among partners or shareholders to the effect that one party will sell and another party will buy a business interest at a stated price upon the occurrence of a stated event. This form of buy-sell agreement is popularly used in closely held corporations and partnerships to cover the possibility of death or disability of a key participant. Life insurance is commonly used to assure that funds will be available to effect the buy-out.

2. An agreement entered into by an interim and a permanent lender for the sale and assignment of a mortgage to the permanent lender when a building has been completed. Often the mortgagor is a party to this agreement on the theory that the mortgagor would have a contractual right to insist that the permanent lender buy the mortgage.

BYLAWS As it relates to condominiums, the regulations, rules, or laws adopted by a condominium owners' association or corporation for the condominium's management and operation. Bylaws cover such matters as the manner and selection of the board of directors and the duties and obligations of the corporation members. These self-imposed rules are a form of private law. While a corporate resolution applies to a single act of the corporation, a bylaw is a continuing rule to be applied on all future occasions. Condominium bylaws are initially established by the developer and then are subject to change when the owner's association takes over. The bylaws may be amended, usually by a vote of at least 75 percent of the owners. (*See CORPORATE RESOLUTION.*)

BY OPERATION OF LAW Refers to the effect and power of the law acting upon property; property rights determined by some positive legal rule or amendment, by which someone may acquire or lose rights without any act on his or her part. For example, a wife may acquire a one-third life estate in her husband's real property through the operation of the law of dower.

CADASTRAL MAP A map, used in connection with title recording, that indicates legal boundaries and ownership of real property. A cadastral program refers to a complete inventory of land in an area by ownership, description, and values as used in the tax assessment process.

CALL A reference, made in the surveying or platting of a parcel of land, to a course, distance, or monument when a boundary is being described or "run."

CALL PROVISION A provision in a mortgage or trust deed that gives the mortgagee or beneficiary the right to accelerate payment of the mortgage debt in full on a certain date or upon the happening of specified conditions; an acceleration clause. Also, refers to the borrower's ability to redeem, or call in, a bond.

CALL REPORT A report on mortgage delinquencies.

CANCELLATION CLAUSE A clause that may be included in a commercial or industrial lease granting the lessor or the lessee the right to terminate the lease term upon the happening of certain stated events or occurrences by the payment from one party to the other of definite amounts of money as consideration. Such consideration usually tends to cover expenses or damages of the party whose rights are being cancelled, such as unamortized costs of special improvements, brokerage fees, and possible loss of rental before the property is rerented.

If the tenant cancels, the consideration fee paid to the landlord, plus any unamortized cost of improvements, is a deductible income tax expense in the year of cancellation.

If the landlord cancels, the cancellation fee paid to the tenant is a capital expenditure of the landlord, and it is amortized over the remaining term of the cancelled lease. The cancellation payment to the tenant is akin to a sale and, if the lease is of land that is nondepreciable property, it is a capital asset and the tenant is entitled to report the cancellation fee as a capital gain in the year of receipt.

Also, a provision in a residential lease whereby the landlord can cancel the lease upon the sale of the fee simple property; otherwise, the new owner would have to take title subject to the lease.

Prior to accepting a "backup offer," the seller should insert a clause to the effect that acceptance is subject to the written cancellation of the prior accepted contract. (*See BACKUP OFFER.*)

CANTILEVER A projecting beam or overhanging portion of a structure supported at one end only, such as a bay window or balcony.

CAPACITY OF PARTIES The legal ability of people or organizations to enter into a valid contract. A person entering into a contract will fall into one of the following categories.

Full Capacity to Contract: The unlimited ability of a person to enter into a contract which is legally binding. Most adults, including those who are illiterate, have full capacity to contract and are said to be *competent* parties. (*See CONTRACT.*)

Limited Capacity to Contract: The ability of a person to enter into a contract which is legally binding upon him- or herself *only* under certain circumstances. For example, minors have limited ability to contract, which means that the contract of a minor is valid only if the minor does not disaffirm a contract entered into during his minority or shortly after reaching majority. Contracts made by minors to obtain such necessities as food, clothing, and shelter, however, are not voidable by the minor and will be enforced against him or her. (*See MINOR.*)

No Capacity to Contract: The inability of a person, under any circumstances, to enter into a valid contract, such as people who have been adjudicated insane or officers of a corporation who are not authorized to execute a contract in behalf of the corporation. It would also cover acts of a corporation beyond the powers as defined in the articles of incorporation (referred to as *ultra vires*). (*See CORPORATE RESOLUTION.*)

CAPITAL The money and/or property comprising the wealth owned or used by a person or business enterprise; the accumulated wealth of a person or business.

CAPITAL ASSETS All property *except* that which is held by a taxpayer primarily for sale to customers in the ordinary course of one's trade or business. Capital assets include such property as the taxpayer's personal residence, land held for investment, stocks, securities, and machinery and equipment used in business. If owned for more than twelve months, a capital asset is given favorable capital gains tax treatment when sold or exchanged. (*See CAPITAL GAIN.*)

CAPITAL EXPENDITURE The cost of a capital improvement, which is an improvement that has been made to extend the useful life of a property or to add to the value of the property, such as a new roof, boiler replacement, or extensive remodeling. In depreciable property, a capital expenditure usually must be amortized over the remaining useful life of the property or that portion of the property to which the improvement belongs. The expense is not currently tax deductible as are repairs, which are *recurring* expenditures. Under the accelerated cost recovery system, a "substantial improvement" (about 25 percent value increase) is given a depreciation schedule separate from the building itself. (*See BASIS, CAPITAL GAIN, REPAIRS.*)

CAPITAL GAIN   The taxable profit derived from the sale of a capital asset. The capital gain is the difference between the sales price and the basis of the property, after making appropriate adjustments for closing costs, capital improvements, and allowable depreciation.

A capital gain is considered a long-term gain if the asset was owned for more than twelve months, and a short-term gain if the asset was owned for exactly twelve months or less. Short-term gains are treated as ordinary income for tax purposes. Both long-term and short-term capital gains may now be included in income for purposes of income averaging.

Long-term capital gains receive preferential tax treatment, calculated accordingly: 60 percent of the gain on the sale of the asset may be excluded from the taxpayer's income, and the other 40 percent is taxed as ordinary income at the taxpayer's ordinary tax rate. Thus, the maximum long-term capital gains rate (for an individual in the maximum 50 percent bracket) is 20 percent of the total gain (i.e., 50 percent of 40 percent equals 20 percent). The portion of long-term capital gain excluded from ordinary income is a tax preference item, except on the sale of a principal residence. There is a special one-time exclusion of capital gain up to $125,000 in the sale of a principal residence by a taxpayer aged 55 years or older.

Corporations do not get a 60 percent deduction. A corporation can add its entire gain into regular income and pay regular corporate income tax or, under an alternate tax, the corporation would not be required to pay more than a specified amount of tax on the excess of net long-term capital gains over net short-term capital losses. (*See BASIS, FIXING-UP EXPENSES, GAIN, HOLDING PERIOD, RESIDENCE, TAX PREFERENCE.*)

CAPITAL IMPROVEMENT   Any structure erected as a permanent improvement to real property; any improvement made to extend the useful life of a property or to add to the value of the property. For example, the replacement of a roof is considered a capital improvement whereas the repair of screen doors is not. (*See CAPITAL EXPENDITURE.*)

CAPITALIZATION   1. A mathematical process for converting net income into an indication of value, commonly used in the income approach to appraisal; it involves discounting future incomes into present value. (*See APPRAISAL, CAPITALIZATION RATE.*)

2. Also refers to the par value of the stock of a corporation plus the face amount of outstanding bonds and loans. (*See THIN CAPITALIZATION.*)

CAPITALIZATION RATE (CAP RATE)   The percentage selected for use in the income approach to valuation of improved property. The cap rate is designed to reflect the recapture of the original investment over the economic life of the improvement to give the investor an acceptable rate of return (yield) on his or her original investment and to provide for the return of the invested equity. In other words, if the property includes a depreciating building, the cap rate provides for the return of invested capital in the building by the end of the economic life (the recapture rate which allows for the building's future depreciation) and the return on the investment in the land and the building (similar to yield).

For example, if a building has a 50-year economic life, then the recapture rate is set at 2 percent per year. If the rate of return on the investment is 8 percent and the recapture rate is 2 percent, then the overall capitalization rate applicable to the building is 10 percent.

The selection of an appropriate cap rate is influenced by the conditions under which the particular investment is being operated, as well as the availability of funds, prevailing interest rates, risk, and so on. If the property earns $100,000 per year and the cap rate is 9 percent, then, in determining what the property is worth to the investor, the investor would compute it as follows: $100,000 × 1/.09 = $1,111,111. Only an experienced appraiser can select the appropriate cap rate—a mere 1 percent difference in the suggested cap rate could make a 12½ percent difference in the value estimate.

The cap rate measures the risk involved in an investment. Thus, the higher the risk (a restaurant) the higher the cap rate; the lower the risk (a post office) the lower the cap rate. (See BAND OF INVESTMENT, INCOME APPROACH, INTERNAL RATE OF RETURN.)

CAPITALIZE 1. To provide cash; to fund. 2. An accounting procedure whereby a company records an expenditure as a capital asset on its books instead of charging it to expenses for the year. This is normally done with capital expenditures, such as the cost of a new roof. (See CAPITAL EXPENDITURE, CAPITAL IMPROVEMENT.)

CAPITALIZED-INCOME APPROACH See INCOME APPROACH.

CAPITAL LOSS A loss derived from the sale of a capital asset. Up to $3,000 of the net capital loss (reduced by capital gains during the year, if any) is deductible annually against taxable ordinary income, with the excess carrying forward to future years at a rate of $3,000 per year until the loss has been fully deducted. Whereas *long-term* gains receive special treatment, *short-term* capital losses receive preferential treatment. Losses on properties that have been held for less than 12 months are deductible in full (up to $3,000 per year) to offset ordinary income dollar for dollar. Long-term losses require $2 of loss for each $1 of offset; that is, they are halved before deduction. Capital losses are not recognized on the sale of taxpayer's personal residence. (See BASIS.)

CAP RATE See CAPITALIZATION RATE.

CARAVAN A group inspection tour of listed properties by a broker's sales staff.

CARPORT A roofed space having at least one side open to the weather. A carport is often made by extending the house roof to one side, and is primarily designed or used for motor vehicles. This term is usually related to small one- and two- family dwellings. In multifamily properties, a garage may have one or more sides open to the weather.

CARRYBACK FINANCING Refers to the seller taking back a note for part of the purchase price secured by a junior mortgage (a second or third mortgage), wraparound mortgage, or contract for deed.

CARRYING CHARGES
1. Costs incurred in owning property up to the time the development of the property is completed. Normal carrying charges include a developer's costs for payments of property taxes and interest on the land acquisition and construction loans during the time the property is under development. Also called *front money*.

Investors and developers are usually concerned with whether they can capitalize certain carrying charges. For instance, if a developer has a proposed development pending and has little or no income to absorb tax deductions, the developer will want to capitalize the carrying charges. The rule is that the developer can capitalize annual taxes, mortgage interest, and other true carrying charges over a ten-year period if the property is unimproved or unproductive. The election to capitalize is made annually when preparing a tax return. After the project is completed, the developer *must* deduct the expenses.

2. The regular costs of maintaining a property, such as taxes, insurance, utilities, and accrued interest. These costs are often apportioned between buyer and seller at the closing of a real estate transaction. (*See CLOSING.*)

CARRY-OVER CLAUSE
See EXTENDER CLAUSE.

CASH FLOW
The spendable income from an investment after deducting from gross income all operating and fixed expenses, including principal and interest. The amount of cash derived over a certain measured period of time from operation of income-producing property after debt services and operating expenses, but before depreciation and income taxes. "Net after tax" cash flow, or cash available for distribution, includes an allowance for income tax attributable to the income.

Two benefits of investing in improved, income-producing real property are the tax shelter provided during ownership and the anticipated appreciation in the property value which may be realized upon its sale. Thus, an investment can turn out to be profitable even if there is monthly negative cash flow. (*See INTERNAL RATE OF RETURN, NEGATIVE CASH FLOW.*)

The property manager is often responsible for preparing a cash-flow analysis so that the property owner can evaluate the return on the property investment.

CASHIER'S CHECK
A bill of exchange (check) drawn by a bank (usually signed by its cashier) upon itself as drawer and payable upon demand, like a promissory note executed by the bank. A cashier's check is preferred over an ordinary personal check, and it (or a certified check) is usually required of the purchaser of property by the contract terms to close a transaction.

A cashier's check is, however, still subject to a stop payment order of the maker. The certified check is only subject to a stop payment order if the maker obtains the bank certification, not in the case where the payee has the maker's check certified in the maker's bank. (*See CERTIFIED CHECK.*)

CASH METHOD
An accounting method of reporting income in the taxable year in which the income is actually or constructively received and reporting expenses when actually paid out. Income is constructively received when it is credited, set apart, or otherwise made available

to the taxpayer without substantial limitations or restrictions so that he or she could have received it on request. The cash method is sometimes called the *cash receipts and disbursements method*. It contrasts with the accrual method of accounting. The cash method is the usual method for real estate brokerage firms and other service businesses. (*See ACCRUAL METHOD.*)

CASH-OUT In a listing, cash-out refers to the fact that the seller desires to receive the complete sales price in cash, rather than accept less by taking back a purchase money mortgage or selling under a contract for deed; in other words, no carryback financing is acceptable. It could mean "cash to mortgage" where the buyer pays the seller's equity in cash and assumes or takes subject to the existing mortgage.

CASING A frame, as of a window or door.

CATWALK A narrow footing on a bridge or along a girder of a large building. A catwalk may also be a walkway strung from one girder to another or placed over uncovered attic joists.

CAULKING A flexible putty substance used to fill gaps at fixed joints on a building in order to reduce the passage of air and moisture; as in making watertight building windows.

CAVEAT EMPTOR Latin for "let the buyer beware." A buyer should inspect the goods or realty prior to purchase, because the buyer buys "as is" and at his or her own risk.

The modern judicial trend is to soften the effect of this ancient doctrine. Today, the seller has more of an affirmative duty to disclose any and all factors that might influence the buyer's decision to purchase. In fact, in some cases the trend is toward *caveat venditor*, "let the seller beware," and most recently, "let the broker beware." The exposure to liability of builders and contractors, for instance, who previously had hidden behind the caveat emptor doctrine, has been greatly expanded, especially in the sale of new homes and condominiums. However, the doctrine still applies to judicial sales.

Many state license laws require licensees to disclose to purchasers, sellers, or prospects any and all material knowledge they may have about the properties they handle. Generally, the courts assert that a prospective purchaser, as a member of the public, can rely on the statements made by a licensed salesperson or broker.

With respect to residential leases, the doctrine of caveat emptor has been substantially altered in recent years. In the past, a landlord would lease the premises "as is" with no obligation to make the premises habitable or to make repairs. In several states, this doctrine has been replaced in residential leases by an implied warranty of habitability, whereby the landlord has an obligation to make the premises fit before the tenant moves in and to continue to keep them fit during the lease. (*See "AS IS", IMPLIED WARRANTY OF HABITABILITY.*)

CC&Rs Covenants, conditions, and restrictions, which are private restrictions on the use of real property; in some states, simply called restrictions. (*See DECLARATION OF RESTRICTIONS.*)

CEASE AND DESIST ORDER An order from a government authority directing a person violating the law to refrain from continuing to do so. For example, many state agencies are authorized to issue cease and desist orders against a respondent found to have committed a discriminatory act; or against a seller of condominiums or subdivisions in violation of applicable regulations.

CEMETERY LOTS A special land-use designation created when the landowner or cemetery authority dedicates property exclusively to cemetery use. Cemetery owners are exempt from paying real property taxes in many states.

The subdivision laws usually are not applicable to the sale of cemetery lots. Cemetery lot salespeople do not generally need a real estate license, but often they are required to have a special cemetery salesperson's license. The purchaser of a cemetery lot often acquires only an easement or license right of burial—not a fee simple title to the lot. Joint tenant owners each have a vested right of interment.

With the current scarcity of developable land, some developers look to the development of the air space above cemeteries. The modern trend of cemeteries is toward the lawn cemetery with no upright tombstones and a open park appearance.

CENTRAL BUSINESS DISTRICT (CBD) A city's downtown area in which is concentrated the main business, governmental, recreational, professional, and service activities of the community.

CERTIFICATE OF CLAIM A contingent promise to reimburse an FHA-insured mortgagee for certain costs incurred during foreclosure of an insured mortgage, provided that the proceeds from the sale of the property are enough to cover the costs.

CERTIFICATE OF ELIGIBILITY A certificate issued by a Veterans Administration regional office to veterans who qualify for a VA loan.

The Veteran Housing Act permits regional administrators to restore a veteran's entitlement to loan-guarantee benefits after his or her property purchased with an existing VA-guaranteed loan has been disposed of and: 1. this loan has been paid in full; 2. the administrator is released from liability under the guarantee; 3. or any loss the administrator has suffered has been repaid in full. It is no longer required that property ownership was transferred for a compelling reason.

The act also authorizes regional administrators to restore a veteran/seller's entitlement to loan-guarantee benefits and release the veteran from liability to the VA when another veteran has agreed to assume the outstanding balance on the veteran/seller's existing VA-guaranteed loan and consented to the use of his or her entitlement to the same extent that the veteran/transferor had used the original entitlement. The veteran/transferee and the property must otherwise meet the requirements of the law. Reinstatement of eligibility is never automatic, but must always be applied for, preferably at the time of the sale of property purchased with an existing VA-guaranteed loan.

Many veteran-sellers presume that they are eligible for a new VA loan after selling their property by way of a loan assumption. In a loan assumption, the broker should point out that for the seller to have complete VA entitlement restored, the buyer must be a veteran and must agree in the sales contract to substitute his or her entitlement for the seller's. (*See VA MORTGAGE.*)

CERTIFICATE OF INSURANCE   A certificate in which an insurance company verifies that a particular policy insuring certain parties is in effect for given amounts and coverage. This certificate is often issued when a commercial lease requires the lessee to maintain certain specified insurance coverage. (*See PRIVATE MORTGAGE INSURANCE.*)

CERTIFICATE OF NO DEFENSE   A legal instrument executed by a mortgagor setting forth the exact unpaid balance of a mortgage, the current rate of interest, and the date to which interest has been paid. It further states that the mortgagor has no defenses or offsets against the mortgagee at the time of the execution of the certificate. Once the mortgagor has executed a certificate of no defense, the mortgagor cannot thereafter claim that he or she did not owe the amount indicated in the certificate.

Also called an *estoppel certificate,* a certificate of no defense is most frequently used when the mortgagee is selling the mortgage to a third party, and the purchaser wants to be assured of the amount and terms of the mortgage and that the mortgagor acknowledges the full amount of the debt. Most mortgage documents contain a clause obligating the mortgagor to execute a certificate of no defense upon written notice from the mortgagee.

In a landlord-tenant situation, a certificate of no defense is a statement by the tenant setting forth the amount of rent payable and the term of the lease and acknowledging that the tenant claims no defenses or offsets against the landlord. A certificate of no defense is sometimes required when the landlord is selling the property or is assigning the lease. This is also called an *offset statement.* (*See REDUCTION CERTIFICATE.*)

CERTIFICATE OF OCCUPANCY   A certificate issued by a governmental authority indicating that a building is ready and fit for occupancy and that there are no building code violations. Some condominium developers insert language into the sales contract to the effect that upon notification that the units are ready for occupancy the buyer must accept the unit despite any construction defects which may exist, although acceptance will not bar the buyer from obtaining redress for such defects. Once the building has been certified for occupancy, the developer can then close the individual sales, transfer title to the buyers, and, most important, begin to pay off the construction loan and eliminate the interest payments.

CERTIFICATE OF REASONABLE VALUE (CRV)   A certificate issued by the Veterans Administration setting forth a property's current market value estimate, based on a VA-approved appraisal. The CRV places a ceiling on the amount of a VA-guaranteed loan allowed for a particular property. If the purchase price exceeds the CRV, then the veteran usually pays for this excess in cash, since secondary financing is somewhat restricted under VA regulations. In practice, the CRV never exceeds the sales price. (*See VA MORTGAGE.*)

CERTIFICATE OF TITLE   A statement of opinion prepared by a title company, licensed abstractor, or an attorney on the status of a title to a parcel of real property, based on an examination of specified public records. This certificate of title should not be confused with the certificate of title that is issued to a titleholder of land registered under the Torrens system, or with a title insurance policy.

A certificate of title does not guarantee title, but does certify the condition of the title as of the date the certificate is issued, on the basis of an examination of the public records maintained by the recorder of deeds, the county clerk, the county treasurer, the city clerk and collector, and clerks of various courts of record. The certificate also may include records involving taxes, special assessments, ordinances, zoning, and building codes.

Note that a certificate of title does not offer protection against "off-the record" matters such as undisclosed liens, rights of parties in possession, and matters of survey and location. Nor does it protect against "hidden defects" in the records themselves, such as fraud, forgery, lack of competency, or lack of delivery. A title insurance policy, not a certificate of title, protects against certain off-the-record and hidden defects risks.

An owner's certificate of title normally will not be issued for less than the sales price of the property. A mortgagee's certificate will not be issued for less than the amount of the loan being certified. No certificate, either owner's or mortgagee's, will be continued when a change of ownership is involved, so when this occurs, a new certificate must be issued. Liability is usually limited to the party requesting the title evidence, such as a mortgagee, owner, or vendee.

The person who prepares the certificate of title is liable only for negligence in preparing the report, and this liability is usually limited to the extent of his or her personal assets or the assets of the local abstracting company by whom he or she is employed.

In many states, the seller provides a certificate of title at his or her own expense, certifying the condition of the title as of the closing date. If the buyer desires title insurance, the buyer must pay the difference between the cost of the certificate of title and the cost of the title insurance policy. (See *ABSTRACT OF TITLE, HIDDEN RISK, TITLE INSURANCE, TORRENS SYSTEM, TRANSFER CERTIFICATE OF TITLE*.)

CERTIFIED CHECK   A check that the issuer (usually a bank) guarantees to be good, and against which a stop payment is ineffective if the payee obtains the certification.

Payment by certified check immediately discharges the buyer's duty of performance under a contract. Payment by personal check, however, constitutes conditional performance and does not discharge the buyer's obligation until the check clears (that is, is paid by the depositor's bank).

Certified checks are normally required by escrow companies from purchasers who use out-of-state banks—a reason many brokers have their clients set up a local checking account and transfer funds for the closing of a purchase. Many escrow companies now require all parties to make their closing payment by way of a certified check, before escrow will record the conveyance documents. Some brokers require prospective buyers to use a certified check for an earnest money deposit. (See *CASHIER'S CHECK*.)

CERTIFIED COPY   A copy of a document (such as a deed, marriage or birth certificate) signed by the person having possession of the original and declaring it to be a true copy.

CERTIFIED PROPERTY MANAGER (C.P.M.)   A professional real property manager who has qualified, by the successful completion of the specified educational courses and written demonstration reports, for the CPM designation granted by the Institute of Real Estate Management of the National Association of Realtors®. It is the highest designation a real property manager can earn.

CERTIFY   To testify in writing; to confirm; to guarantee in writing, as in a certified check; to endorse, as with a proper seal.

CERTIORARI   A review by a higher court of a case or proceeding conducted by an inferior court, officer, board, or tribunal to certify the record of such proceeding. a means of obtaining a judicial review.

CESSION DEED   A form of deed used to transfer the street rights of an abutting owner to a government agency. A subdivider who dedicates his or her streets to the municipality would use a cession deed. (See DEDICATION.)

CESSPOOL   An underground porous pit used to catch and temporarily contain sewage and other liquid refuse, where it decomposes and is absorbed into the soil. (See EFFLUENCE.)

CHAIN   1. An engineer's chain is a series of 100 wire links each of which is one foot in length. 2. A surveyor's chain is a series of wire links each of which is 7.92 inches long. The total length of the chain is four rods, or 66 feet. Ten square chains of land are equal to one acre. It is a method of measurement used in the United States Public Land Surveys.

CHAIN OF TITLE   The recorded history of matters that affect the title to a specific parcel of real property, such as ownership, encumbrances, and liens, usually beginning with the original recorded source of the title. It shows the successive changes of ownership, each one linked to the next so that a "chain" is formed.

Ownership of a particular property frequently passes through many hands after the original grant. If there is any broken link in a property's chain of title, then the current "owner" does not have valid title to the property. For example, if there were a forged deed somewhere in the chain, then no subsequent grantee would have acquired legal title to the property.

An abstractor searches and notes the chain of title (also called *running the chain of title*) in an examination of the title at the office of the county recorder or clerk, tracing the title from the original grant up to the present ownership. In the United States, chains of title in colonial states frequently date back to a grant from the

King of England. In those states admitted to the Union after the formation of the United States, the deeds of conveyance in chains of title generally stem from the patent issued by the United States Government. In a few states, such as Louisiana and Texas, chains of title generally date back to a point prior to the acquisition of the land by the federal government.

To be within the unbroken chain of title, the instrument must be capable of being discovered or traced through linking conveyances from the present owner through successive owners to a common grantor. If this cannot be done, it is said that there is a "gap" in the chain. In such cases, there is a cloud on the title and it is usually necessary to establish ownership by a court action called a *suit to quiet title*.

All documents recorded in the chain of title give constructive notice to everyone of the document and its contents. However, if a document is not recorded in the chain of title, so that even a diligent search using the grantor-grantee index will not reveal its presence, then there is no constructive notice given of the existence of the unrecorded document. A deed not properly recorded is said to be a *wild deed*, and is not valid against a subsequent recorded deed to a good faith purchaser.

In practice, the abstractors rarely search back more than 60 years. Some states have adopted a Marketable Title Act that extinguishes certain interests and cures certain title defects that arose before the "root of title" was recorded. The root of title is the most recent conveyance (deed, court decree) which furnishes a basis for title marketability and has been of record for 40 years or more.

Other chain of title problems arise when a person acquires title using one name and then conveys the property under another name. In such cases, the grantor should indicate the name by which he or she acquired title; for example, "Sally Hines, who acquired title as Sally Fromm." Because of the importance of the chain of title, it is necessary that the parties' names be consistent and be spelled out properly in all documents. (*See GRANTOR-GRANTEE INDEX, RECORDING, TITLE SEARCH, WILD DEED.*)

CHAIN STORE   Any one of a number of retail stores under common ownership, under a central management, selling standard merchandise, and operating under a uniform policy. A major chain store is often an anchor tenant in a shopping center. (*See ANCHOR TENANT.*)

CHALET   A housing construction style originating in the Swiss Alps, found mainly in mountainous regions, especially ski resort areas. Its design features large, overhanging eaves that offer protection from heavy winter snowfall. An A-frame.

CHANGE OF NAME   Any person can change his or her name simply by using another name, so long as the name change is not made to defraud. Because of the difficulties of identification, most people changing their names prefer to go through a legal process to effect the change officially. This process is a relatively minor one, merely requiring a petition to be filed with the proper governmental office and notice of the changed name to be published in a newspaper. A corporation can change its name by an amendment to its articles of incorporation, which must be filed in the state of incorporation.

Whenever any person or corporation undergoes a change of name, care should be taken to reflect such change on any documents that were recorded under the previous name. For example, a recorded document should be amended to read, "Cathy Jones, being the same person who acquired title as Cathleen J. Arbuckle." (See *CHAIN OF TITLE; LEGAL NAME; NAME, CHANGE OF.*)

CHANGE ORDER An order to a contractor from the owner, architect, or engineer on a construction project authorizing changes or modifications to the original work as shown in the contract drawings, plans, or specifications. A standard AIA form is normally used. A change order usually changes the original contract price.

Condominium developers generally require purchasers of apartment units under construction to submit change orders and pay for special changes to the original apartment package, such as custom carpeting or appliances.

CHATTEL An item of tangible personal property. The word "chattel" evolved from the word "cattle," one of man's early important possessions. *Chattels real* are annexed to real estate, whereas *chattels personal* are movable. A lease is an example of a chattel real. Chattels are transferred by means of a bill of sale. The Uniform Commercial Code regulates the transfer of chattels and the use of chattels as security for debts. (See *FINANCING STATEMENT.*)

CHATTEL MORTGAGE A mortgage secured by personal property. Under the Uniform Commercial Code, chattel mortgages have been replaced by security agreements. (See *SECURITY AGREEMENT.*)

CHECK 1. A negotiable instrument authorizing a bank to pay money to the payee or bearer. 2. A government survey designation for a twenty-four square mile unit bounded by two guide meridians and two correction lines. Each check is divided into sixteen townships, each six miles square.

CHIMNEY A stack of brick or other masonry extending above the surface of the roof that carries the smoke to the outside. The smoke is carried inside the chimney through the flue.

CHIMNEY CAP Ornamental stone or concrete edging around the top of the chimney stack which helps protect the masonry from the elements and improves the draught in the chimney.

CHIMNEY FLASHING A strip of material, usually metal, placed over the junction of the chimney and the roof to make the joint watertight. Flashings are used wherever the slope of the roof is broken up by a vertical structure.

CHIMNEY POT A fire clay or terra cotta pipe projecting from the top of the chimney stack. The chimney pot is decorative and also increases the draft of the chimney.

CHURNING   The practice of transferring property to gain some advantage. The Internal Revenue Code contains various "antichurning" provisions to discourage certain tax avoidance transfers. For example, accelerated cost recovery is not allowed when one of the principal purposes of a transfer of property is to gain accelerated deductions on property placed in service before 1981. These antichurning restrictions affect property transferred to or from a related party and transfers of certain leased property.

CINDER FILL   A layer of cinders placed between the ground and the basement floor or between the ground and the foundation walls to aid in water drainage.

CIRCLE   A roadway having a circular form with only one access point to the adjoining street.

CISTERN   An artificial reservoir or tank, often underground, for the storing of rain water collected from a roof.

CLAIM OF RIGHT   Refers to the occupancy of property by one having no legal right to title but, nevertheless, claiming such a right. It is an adverse possessor's claim to a fee simple title, either under some apparent color of title or by mere naked claim. For example, assume a father gives his daughter the family farm and she works the farm for 25 years until the father dies. No deed was ever prepared as is required under the Statute of Frauds. Most courts would hold that while an oral grant itself is invalid, when accompanied by an actual entry and possession for the statutory period of time, it will ripen into title by adverse possession because of her claim of right.

There is a definite split of court decisions where the occupant places a fence two feet onto a neighbor's property thinking it is really the occupant's property. Some courts hold that there can be no adverse possession if the occupant believes he or she already owns the property, thus not asserting any *hostile* claim of right. (*See ADVERSE POSSESSION.*)

CLAPBOARD   Siding of narrow boards thicker at one edge, used as exterior finish for frame houses.

CLEANOUT DOOR   An exterior door located at the base of the chimney for convenient removal of the ashes that were put through the ash dump.

CLEARANCE LETTER   A letter from a licensed termite inspection company disclosing the results of a property inspection. FHA, VA, and some conventional lenders require a clearance letter prior to approving a loan. (*See TERMITE INSPECTION.*)

CLEARANCE POINT   As it relates to industrial properties, in the case of one rail track separating and diverging from another, that point at which a 13-foot spread is reached between the centers of the two tracks.

CLEARING TITLE   The process of examining all recorded and unrecorded instruments affecting a particular prop-
erty, and taking any necessary action to remove or otherwise cure the title of any
defects or clouds in order that the title may become a good, marketable title. (*See
MARKETABLE TITLE.*)

CLEAR SPAN   The condition within a building wherein a given
floor area is free of posts, support columns, or
shear walls.

CLEAR TITLE   Title to property that is free from liens, defects, or
other encumbrances, except those which the
buyer has agreed to accept, such as a mortgage to be assumed or a restriction of
record; established title; title without clouds. (*See CLOUD ON TITLE, MARKETA-
BLE TITLE.*)

CLIENT   The person who employs an agent to perform a
service for a fee. In real estate brokerage, typically
the client is the seller and the buyer usually is the prospect or customer. (*See
AGENT.*)

CLIENT TRUST   An account set up by a broker to keep a client's
ACCOUNT   monies segregated from the broker's general
funds; also called an *earnest money account.*
Each broker is generally required by state law to deposit funds, which are not to be
immediately released to escrow, into a trust fund account with a bank or recognized depository within one business day after receipt. The broker is to be the
trustee of the client trust account, and all funds deposited in the account must be
available for withdrawal upon demand. A single client trust account can usually
serve all of the broker's clients, provided that detailed records are maintained and
made subject to inspection by the proper state licensing agency. The principal
broker in an agency is responsible for all trust fund monies and, although the
broker will usually authorize a salesperson in writing to deposit client monies, the
broker may not authorize anyone to make withdrawals.

Article 8 of the National Association of Realtors® Code of Ethics provides that:
"The REALTOR® should keep in a special bank account, separated from his own
funds, monies coming into his possession in trust for other persons, such as
escrows, trust funds, client's monies, and other like items."

If substantial sums of money are involved, the broker should suggest the use of an
interest-bearing account—there should be a clear understanding of who will benefit from the interest (usually the buyer, not the seller).

One of the main reasons for requiring a broker to maintain a client trust account
separate from his general account is to protect these monies from possibly being
"frozen" during legal actions against the broker, such as creditor attachments or
probate of a deceased broker's estate. Also, since the account is custodial in nature, the Federal Deposit Insurance Corporation will personally insure each client's funds up to $100,000 if each account is specifically designated as custodial
and the name and interest of each owner in the deposit is disclosed on the depositor's records. This insurance will not apply if the broker allows any personal or
business funds to commingle with clients' funds.

In addition to a client trust account for use with earnest money deposits, it is good practice for a broker to set up a management trust account when acting as property manager for several income rental properties. It is not necessary to open a separate trust account for each transaction; rather, a simple ledger system is sufficient. (*See COMMINGLING, CUSTOMER TRUST FUND.*)

CLOSE CORPORATION   See *CORPORATION.*

CLOSING   The consummation of a real estate transaction, when the seller delivers title to the buyer in exchange for payment by the buyer of the purchase price. Closing in some areas may not occur until the documents are recorded; however, under general rules of real estate law, transfer of title takes place upon delivery of the deed to the grantee. In many states, there is not a joint meeting of buyer and seller; each performs separately.

In real estate practice, there are several informal meanings given to the word *closing*. For example, the phrase *closing a sale* is often used to describe the process of getting the buyer and seller to agree to and sign the purchase agreement; the term *legal closing* refers to the moment that title and money are exchanged; and *financial closing* refers to the actual disbursements of monies, as directed in the closing or settlement statements. When a person says, "I'm going to the closing this afternoon," that normally refers to the act of going to the broker's office, mortgagee's office, or escrow company to finalize the transaction (sign the final documents, such as a mortgage, deed, or assignment of lease).

The broker usually estimates the date of closing when the purchase agreement is drawn up. Forty-five days is a normal period, giving the buyer enough time to inspect the property, examine the title, and arrange financing, and permitting the seller to prepare the conveyance documents and clear any problems with the title. If the purchase agreement calls for a contract for deed, the processing time is usually shorter.

The details of closing are typically carried out according to local trade and custom. The procedures usually are not controlled by statute, although certain aspects of the closing may be regulated by laws such as the federal Real Estate Settlement Procedures Act (RESPA). Closing may be handled through licensed escrow companies, lenders, banks, attorneys, brokers, or the parties themselves.

In addition to the buyer and seller, the closing process could involve a third-party lender plus many other related parties such as appraiser, pest controller, surveyor, and attorney. In cases of loan refinancing, the closing process involves only the lender and the borrower.

Prorations of expenses, which are to be shared between the buyer and seller (usually for such operating items as real property taxes, and ground lease rent), are normally computed as of the closing date unless a different date (such as the date of occupancy) is specifically stated in the purchase agreement. The term *closing date* in this instance refers to the legal closing date—the date on which documents transferring title from the seller to the buyer are delivered and recorded. (*See ESCROW.*)

CLOSING COSTS   Expenses of the sale (or loan refinancing) that must be paid in addition to the purchase price (in the case of the buyer's expenses), or which must be deducted from the proceeds of the sale (in the case of the seller's expenses). Some closing costs result from legal requirements, others are a matter of local custom and practice. Typical expenses that might be incurred by the seller and buyer in an ordinary transaction are listed below.

Seller's Expenses	**Buyer's Expenses**
Cost of clearing title	New loan or assumption fees
Certificate of title	Deed and mortgage recording fees
Abstract, continuation, title insurance (when required by the sales contract)	Escrow fee (share with seller)
	Title insurance, if desired
Attorney's fees for drafting deed or assignment of lease, bill of sale	Appraisal and inspection fees
	Attorney's fees for drafting contract for deed
Conveyance tax	Condominium transfer fee
Broker's commission	
Escrow fee (share with buyer)	
Lessor's consent to assignment	
Prepayment penalty	
Survey and staking (if required)	
Termite inspection	

In addition to these closing costs, which are fixed at a specified amount regardless of the closing date, there are other variable expenses—items such as real property taxes, prepaid insurance premiums, interest on assumed obligations, rents, and so on—which must be prorated between the seller and the buyer. Because these expenses are directly related to property ownership, they are normally prorated as of the date that title to the property passes, thus making the seller responsible for expenses for the period that he or she owned the property, and the buyer responsible for expenses accruing from the date he or she takes title. In some areas, the buyer assumes the expenses as of the day of closing.

On VA and FHA loans, some typical buyer's costs are: a one-percent loan fee, an appraisal fee (VA: $350, FHA: $400), a termite inspection report (FHA only), tax prorations, recording deed and mortgage, a credit report, a hazard insurance premium, insurance and tax impounds, a title insurance policy, and interest on new-loan funding. Typical seller's costs on FHA and VA loans are: points, commissions, conveyance tax, attorney's fees to draft the deed, notary fees, termite work and a VA inspection fee, and a disclosure statement fee on new loans.

A purchaser under new VA financing is not allowed to pay any escrow fees, so all escrow fees will be the sole responsibility of the seller. The FHA limits the amount that a buyer under new FHA financing may pay for escrow fees; therefore, under FHA financing, a seller may have to pay more than one-half of escrow fees.

Under the provisions of the federal RESPA law, the lender is required to give the borrower a copy of a government booklet on closing costs entitled "Settlement Costs and You." The lender must also provide a good-faith estimate of closing costs likely to be incurred in financing the property. If both the booklet and estimate are not provided at the time of loan application, they must be mailed within three business days.

CLOSING PROTECTION LETTER   A form of additional title insurance coverage not arising out of the basic policy, given by the title insurance company to insured lenders and, in some unusual cases, to insured owners. It protects against loss resulting from errors or infidelity of the title company's agent or approved attorney in the handling of the transaction or closing ("quasi fidelity coverage").

CLOSING STATEMENT   A detailed cash accounting of a real estate transaction prepared by a broker, escrow officer, attorney, or other person designated to process the mechanics of the sale, showing all cash received, all charges and credits made, and all cash paid out in the transaction. A closing statement may also be called a *settlement statement* or adjustment sheet. The statement shows how all closing and adjustment costs plus prepaid and unpaid expenses are allocated between the buyer and the seller. In many areas, separate closing statements are prepared for the buyer, showing credits, charges, and the balance due from him or her at closing; for the seller, showing credits, charges, and the proceeds he or she will receive at closing; and for the broker, showing a detailed accounting of all monies received and disbursed in the transaction. For a sample, see the Appendix.

CLOSURE   Refers to the process in a metes and bounds description of returning to the point of beginning. Unless the described parcel is thus "closed," there is no legal description.

CLOUD ON TITLE   Any document, claim, unreleased lien, or encumbrance that may superficially impair or injure the title to a property or make the title doubtful because of its apparent or possible validity. Clouds on title are usually revealed by a title search, and may be removed from the record by a quitclaim deed or a quiet title proceeding initiated by the property owner. While the "cloud" remains, the owner is usually prevented from conveying a marketable title except when it is only a minor nuisance item. Typical clouds on title are: (1) a recorded contract for deed that has not been removed from the record, but under which the buyer has defaulted; (2) a recorded option that was not exercised, but which still appears on the record; (3) a recorded mortgage paid in full, but with no satisfaction of mortgage recorded; (4) property sold without the wife's release of her dower interest; (5) an heir of a prior owner with a questionable claim to the property; (6) the situation in which one of many heirs has not signed a deed; (7) a *lis pendens* (pending litigation) having been dropped but not removed from the record; or (8) a lessee in default having an option to purchase, which probably will not be enforceable if he or she breaches the lease; or (9) a prior conveyance with an incomplete legal description. (*See QUIET TITLE ACTION.*)

CLUSTER DEVELOPMENT The grouping of housing units on less-than-normal-size homesites, with remaining land used as common areas. For example, rather than build ten units per acre on a ten-acre site, a developer might cluster twenty units per acre and prepare five acres as a common area with facilities for recreation. (*See PLANNED UNIT DEVELOPMENT.*)

CLUSTER ZONING A zoning provision whereby a specific residential or unit density is prescribed for an entire area. The developer is free to concentrate or disperse the density within the area in accordance with flexible site-planning criteria. This differs from traditional zoning ordinances that allocate zoning on a lot-by-lot basis, prescribing the same maximum density for all single-structure lots within the zoning district. (*See PLANNED UNIT DEVELOPMENT, ZERO LOT LINE.*)

COASTAL ZONE MANAGEMENT ACT A federal law passed in 1972 recognizing the national interest in the effective planning, management, beneficial use, protection, and development of the salt water and Great Lakes coastal zones. The act calls for states to plan and develop management programs for the land and water resources of their coastal zones.

CODE OF ETHICS A written system of standards of ethical conduct. Because of the nature of the relationship between a broker and a client or other persons in a real estate transaction, a high standard of ethics is needed to ensure that the broker acts in the best interests of both his or her principal and any third parties.

Members of the National Association of Realtors® subscribe to a very strict code of ethics. In fact, many state real estate commissions have incorporated key sections of the code into their rules and regulations governing the conduct of licensees. The National Association of Realtors® has published a booklet called *Interpretation of the Code of Ethics,* applying the code to practical situations. There are also approved "Standards of Practice" which interpret some of the Articles of the Code of Ethics. These Standards of Practice may be cited as additional support for alleged violations of the code. The NAR Code of Ethics is reprinted in the Appendix.

CODICIL A supplement or addition to a will which normally does not revoke the entire will. A codicil must be executed with the same formalities as a will and be witnessed by the required number of people. (*See WILL.*)

COGNOVIT NOTE See *CONFESSION OF JUDGMENT.*

COINSURANCE A common provision in building insurance policies under which the insured agrees to maintain insurance on his or her property in an amount equal to at least 80 percent of the replacement cost. If the property is not insured to that amount and there is a loss, the insurance company will make the insured share in the loss on a pro rata basis. For example, if the building is insured for only 60 percent of its value and there is a \$10,000 loss, the insurance company will pay only \$7,500 (60%/80% [or $\frac{6}{8}$] ×

$10,000). Because property values are steadily increasing, it is important for the property owner to review his or her insurance policy from time to time to keep within the 80 percent minimum. In addition, the insured can pay for inflation guard coverage. In any event, liability under any insurance policy is limited to the face amount of the policy. One reason for the 80 percent rule is that generally no more than 80 percent of a building's value is destroyed by fire; a certain part of the structure will usually be available for salvage. Coinsurance requirements generally are included in commercial and industrial hazard policies, and a similar type of coinsurance coverage is found in homeowners' policies.

Also refers to insurance coverage that is underwritten by several different insurers. (*See INSURANCE.*)

COLD CANVASS Obtaining listings by door-to-door solicitation of homeowners; a cold call. Real estate salespeople usually employ this method when seeking listings in a specific area or when looking for homes of a certain type or with certain features.

COLLAPSIBLE CORPORATION The prearranged use of a corporation to convert ordinary income into capital gain—a situation prevented by a set of Internal Revenue Service rules. This concept is most easily understood by looking at a hypothetical situation: Two real estate dealers organize a corporation to develop a condominium. The corporation constructs the building, which substantially increases the value of the land. Before the units are sold, the dealers sell their stock in the corporation to a third party and claim capital gain treatment on the sale of their stock. If an IRS agent were to examine this transaction, the agent probably would apply the collapsible corporation rules if the property had been held for less than three years. The IRS then would claim that the sale of the stock was equivalent to the sale of the development, and taxable similarly, that is, taxable at ordinary income rates. The collapsible corporation rules penalize these stockholders by treating the sale of their stock as ordinary income, which it would have been considered if the corporation itself had sold the development.

COLLAR BEAM A horizontal beam connecting the rafter at the lower end. The collar beam adds rigidity and helps to divert the weight of snow on the roof from the exterior walls.

COLLATERAL Something of value given or pledged as security for a debt or obligation. The collateral for a real estate mortgage loan is the hypothecated mortgaged property itself.

COLLATERAL HEIRS Heirs descending from the same common ancestor but not from one another. Collateral heirs are not in a direct line of descent—they may be siblings, aunts, uncles, or cousins, but not a son or daughter, who are lineal descendants.

COLLATERALIZED MORTGAGE A collateralized mortgage loan is a loan secured by collateral in addition to real estate, as with a pledged savings account. Collateralization is taking an existing mortgage and using it as security or collateral for a loan (without having to discount it).

COLLECTION ACCOUNT An account established by someone to receive periodic payments on a debt or obligation, to make disbursements as requested by the payee, and to make an accounting to both parties. For example, many contracts for deed require the buyer to put his or her payments into a collection account at a bank or escrow company which, in turn, pays the real property taxes, lease rent, maintenance fees, mortgage payments (if any), and insurance payments. Typically, the collection fees charged for this service are split equally between the buyer and seller, though the seller may try to persuade the buyer to pay the entire fee since the collection account is generally considered to be for the buyer's protection (to insure that the seller makes timely payments of taxes, and so on). Collection fees are relatively slight, usually ranging from $10 to $15 per month, in addition to an initial setup fee. Also used in wraparound mortgage situations.

COLLECTION REPORT The form used by a loan correspondent (servicer) in reporting collections from mortgagors, including payments in full, repayment of advances, tax and insurance funds for foreclosed mortgages, and any other items remitted as regular installment payments.

COLOR OF TITLE A condition in which a title appears to be good, but because of a certain defect, it is in fact not valid (paper title).

For example, Penelope Smith conveys a ten-acre farm to Randall Brown by deed. Mr. Brown enters into possession unaware that Ms. Smith held title under a forged deed. Thus, Brown does not have valid title to the property. By occupying the premises for a prescribed period of time, Brown can acquire legal title to the entire ten-acre parcel by means of adverse possession under color of title, even though he physically occupied only part of the ten acres, because the adverse claimant under color of title need only possess a portion of the premises described in the ineffective conveyance to acquire title to the whole parcel. If there were no deed involved, and Brown adversely occupied just part of the ten acres, after the prescribed period he would acquire title only to the acreage he actually occupied (or fenced or cultivated). In addition, a claimant not under color of title has a stronger burden of proof on each of the required elements for adverse possession.

In some states, a possessor of property under color of title must be in good faith in order to acquire title by adverse possession. That is, the possessor must believe the deed is really valid even though it is actually defective (i.e., the possessor can't be a squatter). Thus, the defect in the deed must not be so obvious that a reasonable person would know the deed was not valid. (*See ADVERSE POSSESSION.*)

COMBED (STRIATED) PLYWOOD Common building material in modern homes, particularly for interior finish. The exposed surface is combed in parallel grooves.

COMMENCEMENT OF WORK The noticeable beginning of an improvement on real estate as determined under local law. This exact time has significance relative to the effective date of a mechanic's lien (and thus the priority against other liens such as mortgages), as well as protecting a builder against changes in the zoning rules. (*See MECHANIC'S LIEN, ZONING ESTOPPEL.*)

COMMERCIAL ACRE A term referring to that portion of an acre of newly subdivided land remaining after dedication for streets, sidewalks, parks, and so on; that portion on which the developer is free to build.

COMMERCIAL BANK A financial institution designed to act as a safe depository and lender for many commercial activities (usually short-term loans). Commercial banks rely heavily on demand deposits—checking accounts—for their basic supply of loanable funds, although they also receive capital from savings accounts, loans from other banks, short-term loan interest, and the equity invested by their owners.

COMMERCIAL LEASEHOLD INSURANCE Insurance to cover the payment of rent in the event the insured (tenant) cannot pay it. Sometimes required by a commercial lender in a shopping center development as a prerequisite to issuing a leasehold mortgage.

COMMERCIAL PROPERTY A classification of real estate that includes income-producing property such as office buildings, gasoline stations, restaurants, shopping centers, hotels and motels, parking lots, and stores. Commercial property usually must be zoned for business purposes.

COMMINGLING To mingle or mix; for example, to deposit client funds in the broker's personal or general account. A licensee found guilty of commingling funds may generally have his or her license suspended or revoked by the state licensing agency. Some commingling situations are rather obvious, others are more involved, such as a broker acting as property manager who takes a fee out of the tenant's security deposit. Commingling is covered under Article 18 of the Realtors® Code of Ethics.

It is often an act of commingling for a broker to fail to deposit trust funds into escrow, a client trust, or earnest money account at a bank or recognized depository by the next business day following receipt of the funds. It does not constitute commingling for the broker to keep a minimum amount of his own money in the client trust account (say $50) in order to keep the account open, nor is it commingling to hold an uncashed check until acceptance of an offer when directed to do so by the buyer (offeror); however, before the seller accepts the offer, the broker must specifically disclose the fact that the check is being held in an uncashed form. Similarly, it is not commingling to hold an uncashed check after acceptance of an offer when directed to do so by the seller (offeree).

As a matter of policy, not cashing checks until an offer is accepted may prevent problems for the broker. Often a buyer submits an offer with a personal check as an earnest money deposit. If the broker deposits the check in his or her client's trust account and the offer is rejected, then the broker is in a position of having to refund the earnest money deposit before the broker knows whether the buyer's check has cleared. If the broker delays in returning the earnest money deposit, the buyer will be irritated and their business relationship ruined. Yet, if the broker returns the deposit and the check bounces, the broker is out the money.

A more serious offense than commingling is *conversion*, which is the actual misappropriation of the client's monies. (*See CONVERSION*.)

COMMISSION   The compensation paid to a real estate broker (usually by the seller) for services rendered in connection with the sale or exchange of real property. In order to collect a commission, the broker must be licensed in the state, have a written employment agreement (listing) with the seller, and sell the property and/or execute a valid contract of sale for the property.

The commission is normally stated as a percentage of the gross sales price, and the exact rate is subject to negotiation (because fixed rates would be in restraint of trade and in violation of anti-trust laws). Leasing commissions are usually based on graduated percentages over the entire lease term. In most areas, commission rates are established by custom. Rates cannot be fixed by law or by agreement among brokers. Many listing contracts now provide a statement to the effect that "commission rates are negotiable and are not fixed by law." The broker usually receives no monetary compensation for time and expenses involved with showings that do not lead to sales.

Often a broker will share the commission with another broker who has cooperated in the transaction. In order to share a commission with a salesperson associated with another broker, a broker must process the money through the salesperson's employing broker, except in the case of deferred commissions earned under a prior broker.

Once the seller accepts the offer from a ready, willing, and able buyer, the seller is technically liable to the broker for the full commission, regardless of whether or not the buyer completes the purchase. However, in a case where the broker knew or should have known that the buyer was not financially able to complete the purchase, the courts tend to prevent a broker from seeking a full commission from the seller. Of course, if the offer is made subject to a condition, the broker cannot collect a commission until the condition is satisfied. Also, if a property is listed and is later taken under condemnation or sold at a foreclosure sale, the broker usually receives no commission, since the broker did not negotiate the sale.

A broker who has produced a ready, willing, and able buyer on the listing terms is generally still entitled to his or her commission if the transaction is not consummated for any of the following reasons:

1. The owner (seller) changes his or her mind and refuses to sell.

2. The buyer defaults and refuses to buy. Some state courts now refuse to enforce the commission agreement where the buyer defaults, through no fault of the seller.

3. The owner's spouse refuses to sign the contract or deed.

4. There are defects in the owner's title which have not been corrected.

5. The owner commits fraud with respect to the transaction.

6. The owner is unable to deliver possession within a reasonable time.

7. The owner insists on terms not in the listing, such as the right to restrict the use of the property.

8. The owner and buyer agree to cancel the signed contract to purchase.

Note that most license laws make it illegal for a broker to share a commission with someone who is not licensed as a salesperson or broker. Commission here has been construed to include such things as certain items of personal property (a broker giving a new TV to "a friend" for providing a valuable lead) and other premiums (vacations and so on), as well as finder's fees and actual percentages of the commission.

The courts have held that a real estate broker or salesperson buying property through his or her own brokerage firm for personal use must still be taxed on the commission he or she would have received for the sale, even though it is reflected as a discount (or a "contra") against the purchase price. Commission income, whether it is received by an employee or independent contractor, is considered "personal service" or "earned" income.

Once the commission has been received by the broker, it is then divided according to a prearranged formula between the brokerage agency ("the house") and the salespeople involved in the transaction. Virtually all brokerages retain a portion of the commission—often as much as 40 to 50 percent—to pay overhead costs, salaries, and profits. Since commission splits vary considerably from company to company, it is necessary that the salesperson have a clear understanding (preferably in writing) with the employing broker as to how he or she is to be paid, when, and at what percentage of the gross commission earned. Note that a salesperson is acting as a subagent through his or her broker and, as such, cannot negotiate as an independent agent for the client.

An innovation in commission arrangements is the 100-percent plan, whereby certain salespeople who achieve a minimum sales level pay monthly service charges to their brokers (to cover the costs of office space, telephones, and supervision) and receive 100 percent of the commissions they generate. (See DEFERRED COMMISSION, DRAW, FINDER'S FEE, LISTING, ONE HUNDRED PERCENT COMMISSION, PROCURING CAUSE.)

COMMISSIONER   1. A member of a state real estate commission. 2. A person appointed by a court of equity in a partition proceeding to advise the court as to the best method of partitioning a property among co-tenants. 3. A person appointed by a court to supervise a mortgage foreclosure sale. (See PARTITION, REAL ESTATE COMMISSION.)

COMMITMENT   A pledge or promise to do a certain act, such as the promise of a lending institution to loan a certain amount of money at a specified rate of interest to a qualified buyer provided that the loan is made by a certain date. Unlike a contract for sale, a party, such as a lender bound by a commitment, cannot be forced judicially to specifically perform; however, an aggrieved party may seek money damages upon refusal to loan on the commitment.

A conventional loan commitment may be either firm or conditional. The borrower applies directly to the lender, usually on a standard form application. The lender then analyzes the applicant's purpose and financial ability to repay the loan and, if they are acceptable, writes the borrower a commitment letter. This commitment letter is, in effect, a detailed offer to loan money according to specific terms. If the borrower accepts the commitment and satisfies any conditions the lender may have made, such as providing satisfactory appraisal and credit reports, the lending institution prepares the proper mortgage documentation. When the mortgage papers have been executed and the title approved, the lending institution will release the mortgage proceeds to be applied for the purposes for which the loan was made, such as refinancing.

Under FHA loans, a conditional commitment is an agreement to loan a definite amount of money on a particular property subject to FHA's approval of a presently unknown borrower whose credit and eligibility will have to be checked. A firm FHA commitment is an agreement to insure a loan in a certain amount on a specific property to a designated borrower. A conditional loan commitment fee is usually refunded from the closing costs when the loan is actually made. FHA conditional commitments are good for six months and may be renewed for another six months upon payment of an additional fee.

In large developments, developers often pay for or "purchase" a commitment for permanent takeout financing. (See BUYDOWN, STANDBY FEE.)

Commitment also refers to an agreement by a title insurance company to issue a policy in favor of a proposed insured upon acquisition of a specific property. Unlike a binder, however, it is not a contract for temporary insurance. The commitment is for a short period of time and identifies the type of policy to be issued, the estate or interest of the insured, vesting of title, legal description of the property being covered, and any exceptions to coverage.

COMMON AREAS   Land or improvements in a condominium development designated for the use and benefit of all residents, property owners and tenants. Common areas frequently include such amenities as corridor or hall areas and elevators, and parks, playgrounds, and barbecue areas, which are sometimes called green belts. In shopping centers, the common areas are parking lots, malls, and traffic lanes.

COMMON ELEMENTS   Parts of a property that are necessary or convenient to the existence, maintenance, and safety of a condominium, or are normally in common use by all of the condominium residents. All condominium owners have an undivided ownership interest in the common elements. Maintenance of the common elements is paid for by the condominium owners' association, and each owner must pay a monthly maintenance assessment prorated according to his or her individual common interest. Typical common elements are elevators, load-bearing walls, floors, roofs, hallways, swimming pools, and so on. (See COMMON AREAS, COMMON EXPENSES, COMMON INTEREST, LIMITED COMMON ELEMENTS.)

COMMON EXPENSES   The operating expenses of condominium common elements, together with all other sums designated as common expenses by or pursuant to the condominium declaration or bylaws.

COMMON INTEREST   The percentage of undivided ownership in the common elements belonging to each condominium apartment, as established in the condominium declaration. The applicable percentage is usually computed as the ratio of the square footage of a particular apartment to the total square footage of all the apartment units, or as the ratio of the apartment's purchase price to the total sales price of all the apartment units. The ratio is expressed as a percentage, such as 1.47 percent or .0147. The percentage of common interest determines an owner's interest in the common elements, the amount an owner will be assessed for maintenance and operation of the common properties, the real estate tax levied against an individual unit, and the number of votes an owner has in the condominium owners' association.

COMMON LAW   That body of law which is based on usage, general acceptance, and custom, as manifested in decrees and judgments of the courts; judge-made law ("case law") as opposed to codified or statutory law (or civil law as found in a few states like Louisiana). This manner of jurisprudence originated in England and was later incorporated into this country's legal system, either by statute or custom.

COMMON PROFITS   1. In a condominium, the balance of all income, rents, profits, and revenues from the common elements remaining after the deduction of the common expenses. 2. The profits derived from the operations of a partnership or corporation.

COMMON WALL   A wall separating two living units in a condominium project. Most developers declare the common walls between two apartments to be common elements and thus traditional party-wall rules would not apply. (See PARTY WALL.)

COMMUNITY ASSOCIATIONS INSTITUTE (CAI)   The CAI is an independent, not-for-profit research and educational organization formed in 1973 to develop and distribute the most advanced and effective guidance for the creation, financing, operation, and maintenance of the common facilities and services in condominiums, townhouse projects, planned unit developments, and open-space communities.

COMMUNITY PROPERTY   A system of property ownership based on the theory that each spouse has an equal interest in the property acquired by the efforts of either spouse during marriage. This system stemmed from Germanic tribes and, through Spain, came to the Spanish colonies of North and South America. The system was unknown under English common law.

In those states which maintain a community property system, such as California and other states with laws of Spanish origin (see list below), there are two classifications of property—separate property and community property. Separate property is property that either the husband or wife owned at the time of marriage, or that which was acquired by one spouse during marriage by inheritance, will, or gift. Separate property is entirely free from all interest or claim on the part of the other spouse. All other property is community property and is automatically owned equally by each spouse regardless of whose name record title is held under.

The signature of both husband and wife are required to appear on a listing contract or any instruments of conveyance if community property is involved. In determining the proper tenancy for a buyer to take title, expert tax advice should be obtained.

Either husband or wife may transfer his or her separate property and the other spouse need not sign the deed. However, as a matter of practice, title insurance companies and others prefer the signature of both spouses to eliminate any question as to whether the property is actually separate property or community property. In keeping with this practice, a licensee who wishes to prevent unnecessary disappointment later will recognize the need for obtaining, among other things, the signature of both parties on an instrument of conveyance, or on any other instrument that might affect the title to real property. In the event that a grantor is a bachelor, spinster, widow, or widower, it is wise to include, after the party's name, the above appropriate description in order to communicate immediately to anyone seeing the instrument that there was no community property interest in the grantor.

Neither dower, curtesy, nor survivorship rights exist in community property states. Upon the death of one spouse, half of the property passes to the decedent's heirs and the surviving spouse retains his or her half-share in the community property. The community property states are Arizona, California, Idaho, Louisiana, Nevada, New Mexico, Texas, and Washington. (*See DOWER.*)

COMMUNITY SHOPPING CENTER   A shopping center of approximately 150,000 square feet, classified between the smaller neighborhood center and the larger regional center. (*See SHOPPING CENTER.*)

COMPACTION   Matted down or compressed extra soil which may be added to a lot to fill in the low areas or raise the level of the parcel.

COMPARABLES   Recently sold or leased properties that are similar to a particular property being evaluated and are used to indicate a reasonable fair market value for the subject property. A comparable property need not be identical with the subject property. To qualify as a comparable property, the property used for comparison must have the same highest and best use and should be reasonably similar to the subject with respect to size, design, type of construction, physical condition, and location. Adjustments of value must be made to compensate for differences in these respects. The multiple-listing service records are an excellent place to start looking for comparables, especially with condominium apartments and subdivisions. However, in an active residential real estate market, most comparable references over three months old are outdated. Also called "comps." (*See MARKET-DATA APPROACH.*)

COMPARATIVE UNIT METHOD   A method used to determine the reproduction cost in which all components of the building are added together on a unit basis, such as cost per square foot. Some components would be framing, exterior finish, and floor and roof construction. (*See REPRODUCTION COST.*)

COMPARISON METHOD   See MARKET-DATA APPROACH.

COMPASS POINTS   The 32 positions marked on a compass to indicate directions, usually used when recording a metes and bounds or other legal description.

COMPENSATING BALANCE   Funds deposited by a borrower with a lending institution as a means of inducing the lender to make a loan or extend a line of credit to the borrower. Usually applies to commercial loans but not to mortgage loans.

COMPLAINANT   A person who makes a complaint or instigates legal action against another (the respondent).

COMPLETION BOND   A surety bond posted by a landowner or developer to guarantee that a proposed development will be completed according to specifications, free and clear of all mechanics' liens. A completion bond is distinct and separate from a *performance bond*, which is given to an owner by a party to a contract (normally the contractor or subcontractor) to assure that party's performance of the contract provided he or she is paid. With a completion bond, the landowner or developer may have no underlying contract to perform. Most county subdivision ordinances require the subdivider to post a cash completion bond as a condition to the county's granting approval of a proposed subdivision. Some lenders require an owner to provide a completion bond in addition to a performance bond from the contractor, thus assuring the lender that the development (which is the security for the loan) will be completed whether or not the owner pays the contractor. The bond is drawn in the amount of the total construction cost and is exercisable only if the developer can't complete the project. If this happens, the lender can use the bond proceeds to complete and then sell the building to recover the interim loan funds. (*See PAYMENT BOND, PERFORMANCE BOND, SURETY.*)

COMPLIANCE INSPECTION   1. Inspection by a public official of a structure to ensure that all building codes and specifications have been complied with. 2. Inspection of a construction site or structure by either a lending institution (for conventional mortgage loan) or a government representative (for an FHA or VA loan) to ensure that it complies with all relevant requirements before a mortgage is made or before advances are made under a construction loan. (*See INSPECTION.*)

COMPONENT BUILDING   A prefabricated structure. Completed sections of walls, floors, beams, trusses, roofs, and other housing parts are delivered to a construction site where they are assembled into one housing unit.

COMPONENT DEPRECIATION   A tax-saving method of depreciating the components of a building separately (in contrast to *composite* or *unitary depreciation*, where the entire asset is depreciated at the same rate). Component depreciation is advantageous in that it provides considerably faster depreciation deduction on those structural elements which have a much shorter life than the building as a whole. The shorter-lived the component and the higher its cost in relation to the building as a whole, the greater the potential tax savings will be. For example, the useful life of a building may be 40 years, but certain of its component parts will have shorter lives, such as air conditioning—10 years; elevator—15 years; wiring—15 years; plumbing—15 years; roof—15 years.

The principal advantage of component depreciation over accelerated depreciation is the larger depreciation write-offs are not subject to the recapture-of-depreciation rule. The useful lives and cost basis assigned to the various components must be supportable. With new buildings, a relative cost breakdown should be obtained from the general contractor.

As a result of the Economic Recovery Tax Act of 1981, component depreciation is not permissible for any property placed in service after 1980. However, where component depreciation was begun by the taxpayer for property placed in service in or before 1980, that method may be continued for the useful life of the property, or until its prior sale by the taxpayer. (*See ACCELERATED COST RECOVERY SYSTEM, USEFUL LIFE.*)

COMPOUND INTEREST Interest computed on the principal sum *plus* accrued interest. At the beginning of the new interest period, all interest is added to the principal, forming a new principal figure on which interest is then calculated. This process repeats itself each interest period—interest may be compounded daily, monthly, semiannually, or annually. Thus, on a $1,000 savings account at 5 percent interest compounded annually, for the first year the amount of interest is $50. In the second year, the new principal balance is $1,050, thus making the second year interest $52.50.

Some states specifically prohibit (as usurious) actions to recover compound interest on loans, so that contracts charging interest on interest cannot have the extra interest enforced. However, after simple interest has become due, interest upon it may be contracted for and collected under a new special agreement. (*See INTEREST.*)

CONCENTRIC CIRCLE THEORY An economic theory of city growth which states that, if there are no barriers, cities tend to expand in concentric circles from their point of origin. The model city consists of five zones: the central business district, a zone of transition, a zone of independent workingpeople's homes, a region of better residences, and a group of commuter zones.

CONCESSIONS 1. Discounts given to prospective tenants by landlords to induce them to sign a lease. Concessions are frequently encountered in commercial leases, where landlords may give the first two months' rent free or provide an allowance to the tenant for renovating or customizing the demised space. A purchaser of a commercial or income-producing property should check all existing leases to see if there are any lease concessions that would reduce the amount of rent receivable in the future (such as free cable TV or one month's free rent per year for the term of the lease). If so, the value of these concessions should be computed to reduce the amount of contract rent specified. An estoppel certificate should also be obtained from the tenant. Some state laws require concessions to be noted on a lease by special wording. Concessions are negotiable points in a lease that are resolved in favor of the prospective tenant. Another example in leasing a new office building would be the owner's assumption of the lessee's remaining obligation under the lessee's existing lease in another building.

2. A lease of a portion of a premises for a particular purpose, such as a refreshment stand at a recreational center.

3. A franchise right granted by a governmental agency to conduct a business.

CONCILIATION AGREEMENT A settlement or compromise agreement. Under the Federal Fair Housing Act, the Department of Housing and Urban Development (HUD) shall endeavor to obtain a conciliation agreement with the respondent charged with a discriminatory practice. The agreement may require the respondent to do affirmative acts such as selling or renting to the complainant, or to refrain in the future from committing discriminatory acts.

CONCRETE BASEMENT FLOOR   Generally constructed of concrete reinforced with steel bars within the concrete. The basement floor, along with the foundation walls and the piers provide the support for the structure. Concrete is used because it is moistureproof and inexpensive.

CONCURRENT LEASE   A lease that overlaps the term of an existing shorter-term lease in which the new lessee takes subject to the rights of the first lessee. In effect, the new lessee takes control of the property in the place of the lessor and is entitled to the rents until the first lease expires, at which time the new lessee will be entitled to exclusive possession. The concurrent lease may cover all or part of the same premises as the earlier lease.

CONDEMNATION   A judicial or administrative proceeding to exercise the power of eminent domain; that is, the power of the government (federal, state, local, improvement district) to take private property for public use. The agency taking the property is the condemnor and the person whose property is being taken is the condemnee. In the taking of private property for public use, a fee simple estate or any lesser right, such as an easement, may be acquired. A common example of condemnation is the taking of an owner's access to a street entrance when the county builds a highway or dedicates the area for county use.

The right of eminent domain is limited by the Fifth Amendment to the U.S. Constitution, which states: "No person shall be deprived of life, liberty, or property without due process of law; nor shall private property be taken for public use without just compensation." Private property may be taken without the consent of the owner, whose defenses may be that the land was not taken for a sufficient public use or, as is more frequently the case, that just compensation was not paid. The modern trend of the courts is to define the term "public use" broadly to include not only public facilities such as streets, railroads, schools, and parks, but also property which would provide intangible public benefits, such as scenic easements.

The actual appraised value of the property at the date of the summons is generally the measure of valuation used to determine the amount of "just compensation." However, there is usually disagreement as to the appropriate appraised value, and this becomes the basis for most condemnation lawsuits.

Certain items *are not considered* in determining the fair market value of condemned property, such as loss of goodwill, relocation expenses, inconvenience, and the value of improvements added to the property after the date of the summons. This exclusion is especially harmful to operating businesses whose real estate value is much lower than the value of the business as an ongoing concern. After a property has been condemned, all preexisting liens and encumbrances are extinguished and their claims must be asserted against the condemnation award. Typically, the condemnee will be paid the condemnation award within two years after final judgment is rendered. If listed property is condemned, the listing broker typically is not entitled to a commission since the broker did not negotiate the sale.

Under a lease, tenants are entitled to their share of the condemnation award to compensate them for the loss of their leasehold estates. To avoid this, many lessors insert a *condemnation clause* into the lease, which provides that the lease will be cancelled upon condemnation, with all proceeds going to the lessor.

Condemnation also refers to the decision by the appropriate public agency that a property is no longer fit and must therefore be closed or destroyed.

When property is condemned, or sold under a threat of condemnation, the owner may defer any profit realized by treating the disposition as an involuntary conversion. The owner must replace the converted property with property similar in use within three taxable years following the end of the tax year in which the conversion occurs. Any excess of the condemnation proceeds over the cost of the new property is then taxable. (*See ACQUISITION APPRAISAL, BEFORE-AND-AFTER METHOD, EMINENT DOMAIN, INVOLUNTARY CONVERSION, JUST COMPENSATION, POLICE POWER, SEVERANCE DAMAGES, SPECIAL BENEFIT.*)

CONDITIONAL SALE CONTRACT   A contract in which the seller retains title to the item sold, but the item is given to the purchaser so long as he or she is not in default on any of the conditions of the contract; sometimes called an *executory contract*. Under this kind of contract, the seller has a *security interest* in the property and the buyer has an *equitable interest*. Usually, personal property (such as an air conditioner or an appliance) is the subject of a conditional sale contract. When real property is the subject of the contract, the contract is called a *contract for deed*. Upon the buyer's full performance of the conditions of the conditional sale contract, the seller must transfer legal title to the buyer. The conditional sale contract creating a security interest in a fixture or in an article that will become a fixture has been replaced under the Uniform Commercial Code by an instrument known as a *security agreement*. (*See CONTRACT FOR DEED, SECURITY AGREEMENT.*)

CONDITIONS   See *COVENANTS AND CONDITIONS*.

CONDITIONAL USE ZONING   A special land use tentatively approved by a zoning ordinance, which ordinarily requires compliance with stated standards. Such zoning might permit the use of a hospital in a residential zone, but limit the types of functions the hospital can perform. Also called *special use* zoning.

CONDO   A common reference to a condominium unit or development; refers to either a particular unit or the entire building. (*See CONDOMINIUM OWNERSHIP.*)

CONDOMINIUM   See *CONDOMINIUM OWNERSHIP*.

CONDOMINIUM MAP   The detailed site plan of a condo project containing the layout, location, unit numbers, and dimensions of the condominium units, which is filed for record at the same time as the condominium declaration. The condominium map is generally certified by an architect, land surveyor, or engineer. Also called *condominium plan*.

CONDOMINIUM OWNERS' ASSOCIATION   An association of the owners of condominium units. It is often in an unincorporated association form, and its main purpose is to control, regulate, and maintain the common elements in the condominium. The voting power of each owner in an association is usually measured by his or her percentage of undivided interest in the condominium. Through the bylaws, the board of directors of a condominium owners' association is authorized to regulate and administer the affairs of the condominium, especially in regard to the maintenance and repair of the common elements. The association has the authority to assess and collect sufficient money to maintain the common areas and to assure the financial stability of the condominium. When a unit owner is in default of the monthly charges or special assessments, the association may place a lien against the individual apartment, which can be foreclosed to satisfy the debt.

Under the 1976 Tax Reform Act, the condominium owners' association can elect to be treated as a tax-exempt organization. If such an election is made, the association will not be taxed on membership dues, fees, and assessments received from members of the association who own residential units, but the association must meet certain income and expenditure tests referred to below.

Membership dues and assessments will not be treated as taxable income, provided that at least 60 percent of the association's gross income comes from membership dues, fees, or assessments; that at least 90 percent of its expenditures are used to acquire, manage, maintain, or improve association properties; and that substantially all of the units or lots owned by members are used as residences (although they need not be owner-occupied).

The association is still taxed as a corporation on investment income and income from trade or business (for example, rental income or fees from third parties for use of the association's facilities).

CONDOMINIUM OWNERSHIP

An estate in real property consisting of an individual interest in an apartment or commercial unit and an undivided common interest in the common areas in the condo project such as the land, parking areas, elevators, stairways, exterior structure and so on. Each condominium unit is a statutory entity that may be mortgaged, taxed, sold, or otherwise transferred in ownership, separately and independently of all other units in the condo project. Units are separately assessed and taxed based on the combined value of the individual living unit and the proportionate ownership of the common areas. The unit also can be separately foreclosed upon in case of default on the mortgage note or other lienable payments. In effect, the condominium permits ownership of a specific horizontal layer of airspace as opposed to the traditional view of vertical property ownership from the center of the earth to the sky. Typically, the unit, the percentage of common interest, and the limited common elements are appurtenant to each other and cannot be sold or transferred separately.

Condominium ownership is popular in many urban and resort areas due to the general scarcity of desirable and usable land and the tax and other advantages of fee ownership and apartment living. In addition to residential condominiums, many office and professional buildings, industrial plants, medical clinics, warehouses, recreational developments, and combined apartment and office buildings are using the condominium form of ownership. Each condominium owner has exclusive ownership of his or her individual unit but must, nevertheless, comply with the requirements of the declaration, bylaws, and house rules set up for the protection and comfort of all the condominium owners.

Under individual state laws, the developer/owner of a condominium must usually execute and record a master deed together with a condominium declaration. The declaration, when recorded, must generally be accompanied by a true copy of the bylaws, a condominium map, floor plans, and elevations. Note that the establishment of a condominium is not an irrevocable step—state statutes generally permit the removal of a building from condominium ownership with the consent of all or most owners and lienholders. The unit owner's voting power is typically based on a percentage of common interest (note that in a cooperative, each owner has one equal vote regardless of the unit size).

In 1976, the U.S. Department of Housing and Urban Development (HUD) released data from the first national study of condominiums. Over 3 million people in the United States were living in approximately 1.25 million condominium units. The number of condominium units had increased 15-fold since 1970, with nearly 50 percent of all units located in Florida, California, or New York. The National Association of Home Builders estimates there will be nearly 200,000 condominium units constructed annually in the 1980s.

By the year 2000, it is estimated that more than 50 percent of all new housing starts will be condominiums. Even mortgage financing tends to favor condominium ownership. For example, construction mortgages for rental properties often carry interest rates 1.5 percent higher than those for condominiums.

Resales of a condominium may be subject to the right of first refusal of other owners. Generally speaking, however, resales are not as restricted as in the cooperative form of common ownership.

Condominium units tend to sell at prices below those of single-family homes. However, the life-cycle costs of a condominium (mortgage, utilities, maintenance, and condominium fees) may be equal to or, in some cases, greater than those of other forms of housing.

Although all types of consumers own condominiums, couples of 45 to 64 years of age who previously owned single-family residences and whose children have left home ("empty-nesters") or the elderly are dominant buyers.

The HUD study reported that the greatest problem consumers have with condominiums is their inability, as an association of property owners, to operate and maintain their common elements. The failure of these associations to properly maintain the common properties, the study concluded, directly affects the value of each owner's unit.

The study also looked into consumer problems and abuses: complexity of documents, association operating problems, imperfect disclosure of terms and conditions of the condominium project, and underestimated operating expenses. (*See COMMON INTEREST, CONVERSION, COOPERATIVE OWNERSHIP, DECLARATION, HORIZONTAL PROPERTY ACTS, INSURANCE, INTERSTATE LAND SALES, PROPERTY TAX.*)

CONDUIT A metal pipe in which electrical wiring is installed.

CONFESSION OF JUDGMENT The act of a debtor in permitting judgment to be entered against him or her by a written statement to that effect without the necessity for the creditor to institute any legal proceedings. Leases and judgment notes generally include a judgment clause (also called a *cognovit*) by which a tenant or debtor authorizes an attorney to make a confession of judgment against him or her in case of default. This allows the creditor to get a speedy judgment by simply having an attorney file an affidavit to the effect that a default has taken place. A confession of judgment may also generally give a lender a judgment lien against all real and personal property (usually within a certain jurisdiction) owned by the debtor. Some state laws prohibit lessees and others from executing confession of judgment clauses before they are in default in payment of rent or other debts.

CONFIRMATION OF SALE   A court approval of the sale of property by an executor, administrator, guardian, conservator or commissioner in a foreclosure sale. In most cases, the amount of the broker's commission must also be approved by the court. (*See PROBATE.*)

CONNECTION LINE   A line used in surveying land that connects a surveyor's monument with a permanent reference mark. (*See SURVEY.*)

CONSEQUENTIAL DAMAGES   1. A money award made by a court to compensate an injured party for all losses resulting from a breach of contract, which losses a reasonable person could have foreseen at the time the contract was made.

2. That damage arising from the acts of public bodies or adjacent owners to a given parcel of land that impairs the value of that parcel without actually condemning its use in whole or in part. For example, in an inverse condemnation proceeding, consequential damages might be awarded when land is used for a public sewage treatment plant and private land located downwind of the plant suffers a loss in value due to noxious odors.

CONSERVATION   A practice by federal, state, and local governments and private landowners of protecting and preserving the natural and scenic resources in order to ensure the highest long-term benefits for all residents. Also, a specific land use designation in land use and zoning laws restricting the property to noncommercial uses. (*See ENVIRONMENTAL PROTECTION AGENCY.*)

CONSERVATOR   A guardian, protector, preserver, or receiver appointed by a court to administer the person and property of another (usually an incapable adult) and to ensure that the property will be properly managed. A conservator may not need a real estate license to sell the protected real estate, although the sale does require court approval.

CONSIDERATION   An act or the promise thereof, which is offered by one party to induce another to enter into a contract; that which is given in exchange for something from another. It could also include the promise to refrain from doing a certain thing, like filing a justifiable lawsuit (the forbearance of a right). Consideration distinguishes a contract from a gift. Consideration is usually something of value, such as the purchase price in money, though it may be personal services or exchanged property. It is the price bargained for and paid for a promise, and it may be a return promise. Thus, the mere promise to pay money is sufficient consideration, and an earnest money deposit is not necessary for purposes of creating a binding contract.

Even though the sales price is stated in the contract to purchase real property and earnest money is actually received, the actual consideration that supports the contract is the mutual exchange of promises by buyer and seller to legally obligate themselves to do something they were not legally required to do before; that is, the seller agrees to sell a property for a certain price and the buyer agrees to pay that price to buy the described property.

As a general rule:

- There should be a recital of consideration in a deed as presumptive evidence that something of value was given for the transfer of the realty. While most contracts must be supported by a valuable consideration, a good consideration (love and affection) is sufficient to support a gift deed. Except when a fiduciary executes a deed, the actual consideration need not be stated but may be proved by any other legal evidence. A recital of some consideration in a deed is prima facie evidence that no trust resulted to benefit the grantor and that any executory and contractual provisions in the deed are enforceable.

- In practice, the price paid for property can be calculated by checking the deed to find the transfer tax paid (if applicable) and computing the taxable consideration.

- A broker's license may be suspended for being a party to naming a false consideration, but not if it is obviously a *nominal consideration.* (*See DUAL CONTRACT, NOMINAL CONSIDERATION.*)

- An option must be supported by actual consideration.

- In a lease, the periodic payment of rent over the rental term is the consideration for the use and occupancy of the premises. However, suppose there is a lease for one year at a rent of $400 per month and, after four months, the landlord decides to raise the rent to $500 per month. The tenant promises to pay the increase, but fails to do so, so the landlord brings an action to evict. The tenant will probably win the case, unless the landlord gave additional consideration to support the tenant's promise to pay the increased rent.

- There must be present consideration to support a contract. Assume Betty rescues wealthy Charley from a burning house. Charley then promises in writing to convey his farm to Betty in gratitude for her rescue efforts. Charley's promise is not supported by *present* consideration and, if Charley should change his mind, Betty could not have the promise specifically enforced. Likewise, a mortgage is not valid when given to secure a preexisting debt without any new consideration, such as an extension of time, as an inducement for the execution of the mortgage.

- Courts will not usually inquire into the adequacy of consideration to support a contract. A court will, however, deny an action for specific performance if the parties were not in an equal bargaining position and if the party bringing the action had not paid a fair and sufficient consideration. For example, if the fair market value of the property in question is $20,000 (at the time the contract is made), and a buyer (who did not disclose that he was a licensed broker) seeks specific performance of a purchase contract in which the purchase price agreed upon is $2,000, a court would probably deny the action.

The question of adequacy of consideration also arises in cases involving an alleged fraudulent conveyance under the Uniform Fraudulent Conveyance Act. That is, when a conveyance is made by the seller who is or who will thereby be rendered insolvent, and who is bankrupt within four months of the conveyance, the trustee in bankruptcy will be able to set aside the conveyance as fraudulent if the price was inadequate. In certain cases, inadequacy of consideration is asserted as evidence of undue influence and as evidence that the buyer was not a "bona fide purchaser" for value under the recording laws. (*See DEPOSIT, NOMINAL CONSIDERATION, VALUABLE CONSIDERATION.*)

CONSOLIDATE　　To unite, combine, or incorporate by reference; such as to combine two mortgages on one property into a single loan; to combine two or more parcels of land (the reverse of the subdivision process); or to join a land sales registration with an earlier registration, especially when the property is developed and sold in succeeding phases or increments. For example, a developer owning a 100-acre parcel may subdivide 50 acres into 100 half-acre lots, and register that as a subdivision with the appropriate state and federal agencies. Later, when the owner develops the remaining 50 acres, he or she can consolidate this new registration with the 50-acre subdivision registered earlier, and sell both increments under the same registration. Consolidated registration of subdivided land is permitted under both state and federal (HUD) regulations.

CONSTANT　　1. A percentage that is applied directly to the face value of a debt. It develops into the annual amount of money necessary to pay a specified net rate of interest on the reducing balance and to liquidate the principal debt in a specified time period; a method for determining rate and term *on an annual basis.*

2. The annual payment required per dollar of mortgage money, including both interest and amortized principal. The mortgage constant varies with each change in interest rate and each change in the amortization term, as illustrated in the table below.

ANNUAL CONSTANT TABLE

Interest Rate	20 Years	25 Years	30 Years
9.50	11.19	10.49	10.10
10.00	11.59	10.91	10.54
10.50	11.99	11.34	10.98
11.00	12.39	11.77	11.43
11.50	12.80	12.20	11.89
12.00	13.22	12.64	12.35

CONSTRUCTION ALLOWANCE　　Money or other financial inducement to a lessee that is provided by the lessor to cover the cost, in whole or in part, of preparing a structure for the lessee's occupancy. This could cover costs for partitions, wiring, lighting, and standard carpeting. Also called *tenant improvements.*

CONSTRUCTION LOAN　　A short-term or interim loan to cover the construction costs of a building or development project, with loan proceeds advanced periodically in the form of installment payments as the work progresses. In this manner, the outstanding loan balance is matched to the value of the collateral as it grows. Interest on the borrowed money is not normally charged until the incremental construction draws are advanced. When interest is charged on the entire amount even before it is advanced, it is called *Dutch interest.* Upon completion of the project, one or more long-term permanent loans, such as those end loans taken out by the buyers of individual condominium units, will *take out* (pay off) the construction loan. The loan-to-value ratio for these loans is usually 75 percent of the appraised value. Primary sources of construction loans are commercial banks and savings and loan associations. (*See INTERIM FINANCING, SUBORDINATION AGREEMENT, TAKEOUT FINANCING.*)

CONSTRUCTIVE   An inference created by the law, as in constructive eviction or constructive notice.

CONSTRUCTIVE   Acts done or not done by the landlord which so
EVICTION   materially disturb or impair the tenant's enjoyment of the leased premises that a tenant is effectively forced to move out and terminate the lease without liability for any further rent. This concept is a product of modern property law, which now tends to place more emphasis on the quality of possession or habitability under a lease. Constructive eviction might occur when a landlord cuts off the electricity or fails to provide heating, makes extensive alterations to the premises, or attempts to lease the property to others. Another example would be if the landlord of a high-rise apartment building failed to provide elevator service. There can be no constructive eviction without the tenant's vacating of the premises within a reasonable time of the landlord's act. It is a wrongful eviction. The tenant's duty to pay rent is not terminated if the tenant remains in possession. The tenant can sue to recover possession or bring an action for damages based on breach of the covenant for quiet enjoyment. (*See EVICTION.*)

CONSTRUCTIVE   Notice of certain facts that may be discovered by
NOTICE   diligence or inquiry into a public record; a legal presumption that a person is responsible for knowing these facts. The proper recording of a document gives constructive notice to the world of the document's existence and contents. Possession of property also imparts constructive notice of the rights of the party in possession. Examples of rights of parties in possession would be rights under an unrecorded deed, contract for deed, lease-option, and rights of adverse possession. Constructive notice is also referred to as *legal notice,* in contrast to *actual notice,* which is express or direct knowledge acquired in the course of a transaction. (*See ACTUAL NOTICE, CHAIN OF TITLE, INQUIRY NOTICE, RECORDING.*)

CONSTRUCTIVE   A theory of tax law to the effect that the unre-
RECEIPT   stricted right to receive money is the same as the actual receipt of that money. For example, receipt of a demand promissory note would be the same for tax purposes as money received. Thus, if a person has the right and ability to receive payment, which includes profit or income, that profit will be taxed when the right to receive it arises, regardless of when the payment is actually accepted.

CONSUMER PRICE   As prepared by the Bureau of Labor Statistics of
INDEX (CPI)   the Federal Department of Labor, the index is a statistical measure of changes in the prices of

goods and services. The CPI measures the purchasing power of consumer dollars by comparing today's costs of a sample of goods and services with the costs of the same sample at an earlier date.

The CPI is often used as a standard in making rent adjustments in commercial leases. The Bureau intends to review the CPI in 1983 to treat housing costs as if the owner were renting the building, with the expectation that this change will result in the calculation of a lower inflation rate. (*See BASE YEAR, COST OF LIVING INDEX.*)

CONSUMMATE   To bring to completion. A sale of real property is generally consummated upon the closing of the transaction, usually evidenced by the delivery of the deed and funds and the recording of the conveyance documents. (*See CLOSING.*)

CONTIGUOUS   In close proximity; adjoining or abutting; near, coterminous (having the same boundaries). Many state subdivision laws define a subdivision to include any land consisting of two or more lots, contiguous or not, offered as part of a common promotional plan of advertising and sale. Condominium property does not have to be contiguous either (a parking lot located across the street), but it must be in the same vicinity.

Contiguous owners must yield to a reasonable degree their desired privacy to the general welfare of the community. For example, reasonable inconvenience may be suffered by owners contiguous to commercial enterprises and railroads.

Often, a partial release clause in a mortgage may require that a partial release will be given only on a parcel which is contiguous to a parcel previously released. The term "contiguous" should be precisely defined so the release clause will not be challenged on grounds of uncertainty and vagueness.

CONTINGENCY   A provision placed in a contract that requires the completion of a certain act or the happening of a particular event before that contract is binding. Often a buyer will submit an offer to purchase contingent upon obtaining financing or rezoning. In such a case, the seller should be sure the contingency is specifically detailed and unambiguous and that there is a definite cut-off date; otherwise the buyer could tie up the seller's property indefinitely as the buyer attempts to get financing or rezoning. A party may waive any contingency clause which was inserted for his or her benefit. For example, the buyer could force the seller to sell the property even though the buyer was not able to obtain the zoning—the original contingency in the contract for sale. Contingency implies a promise to use one's best efforts to bring it about.

Contingency clauses must be drafted precisely because they frequently become the focal point of a dispute. Consider the following questions when drafting a contingency: what is the condition; for whose benefit is it; can it be waived and by whom; when must it be met; is there a right to extend; and what are the rights and obligations of buyer and seller if the condition is not met despite good faith efforts.

If a contingency is worded too loosely, such as contingent on "my deciding whether it is a good deal or not," then the entire contract is considered "illusory" and unenforceable by either party due to lack of "mutuality of obligation." If the sale is contingent on a "satisfactory" inspection or attorney's review of lease, the courts will try to impose standards of good faith and reasonability so a party cannot back out just because of a change in that party's plans.

A contingent sale must be distinguished from an option. In an option, the optionee has absolute discretion whether or not to exercise the option. In a contingency, the buyer must buy upon the occurrence or nonoccurrence of a specified event, such as loan qualification.

If the buyer inserts a contingency in the offer, the seller may want to counteroffer. For example, if the offer is contingent upon the closing of the sale of buyer's home, the seller might add a clause to the effect that "if seller receives another offer (or decides to withdraw the property from sale), buyer will have 72 hours to remove or waive the contingency, otherwise the contract is cancelled."

The financing contingency is not only the most frequently used contingency; it is also the most controversial. Even a well-written contingency statement can cause problems. For instance, assume that a financing contingency stated that the offer was contingent upon buyer obtaining a first mortgage loan commitment for $67,500 with interest not to exceed 12 percent per annum and for a term of not less than 30 years, and monthly payments for principal and interest not to exceed $680 plus 1/12 the estimated annual real property taxes and 1/12 the annual insurance premium. Buyers agreed to use good faith and due diligence in obtaining such loan. Buyers qualified for the loan but refused to take the loan because the lender added an interest rate escalation clause. While a court might allow some deviation in the financing commitment, the inclusion of an escalation clause is a material deviation of the terms of the offer to purchase and thus the buyer would not be in breach of the contract for refusing to complete the purchase; the buyer is entitled to a return of the deposit money. However, a buyer who did qualify for financing on the terms stated in an offer but who later gets divorced or otherwise changes circumstances so as to not be qualified at the time of closing may have difficulty defending a lawsuit for enforcement of the purchase contract. Sometimes a cautious seller might add a clause to the effect that "the execution of any loan documents by the buyer shall be deemed to be an acceptance of such loan and a waiver of this contingency." (*See SPECIAL CONDITIONS.*)

CONTINGENCY LISTING A type of listing used in a multiple-listing service which has unusual or special conditions; sometimes designated by the letter "C" placed in front of the MLS number. Contingencies may include shorter-than-normal listing duration, an unusual structure, or an *office exclusive*. (*See OFFICE EXCLUSIVE.*)

CONTINUATION An update of a title search. The search of title is "run to date." In a typical transaction, the title company will issue a preliminary title report soon after a sales contract or an offer to purchase is signed or escrow is opened. At the closing date, the title company usually will be asked to continue the search down to the time of recording the final documents by checking the public record to be sure no intervening rights in the property have arisen. The final title report will then show title in the grantee. The buyer usually pays for the continuation. (*See TITLE SEARCH.*)

CONTOUR MAP A topographic map showing the lay of the land of an area by means of a series of lines that connect points of equal elevation at set intervals depending on the scale used.

CONTRACT A legally enforceable agreement between competent parties who agree to perform or refrain from performing certain acts for a consideration. In essence, a contract is an enforceable promise.

In real estate, there are many different types of contracts, including listings, contracts for sale, options, mortgages, assignments, leases, deeds, contracts for deed, escrow agreements, and loan commitments. Each of these contracts must meet the minimum requirements as described in the following paragraphs.

Competent Parties: There must be at least two bona fide parties to any contract. (Thus, John Sharp cannot agree to deed property to himself. He could, however, convey property to himself and Bob Smith as tenants in common.) Both parties must possess at least limited capacity to contract. Thus, minors cannot deed property they own since they lack the capacity to convey property. Such a deed would be voidable by the minor. (In some states, it is automatically void.) A minor does possess, however, the limited capacity to enter into a valid contract to purchase property from an adult; such a contract would be enforceable by the minor against the adult, but would be voidable by the minor if the minor chose not to complete the purchase during his or her minority. A fiduciary and a corporation must have the proper authority to enter into a contract. Depending on the terms of the contract, when a party to a contract dies, his or her heirs and assigns may be bound to the contract. (*See CAPACITY OF PARTIES, DEED, MINOR.*)

Writing: Unless otherwise required by law, oral contracts can be just as valid as written contracts. Generally, however, real estate contracts, except those for leases of one year or less, must be in writing to be enforceable. All essential terms of the contract must be complete and certain so that the entire agreement is set forth in writing and nothing material is left to be agreed upon in the future. Until the contract is signed, everything is negotiable. Once the contract is signed, nothing is negotiable and new consideration is needed to modify the terms of the contract. (*See STATUTE OF FRAUDS.*)

Description: If the contract involves real property, then the property must be accurately described so that the parties can identify the subject matter of the contract. A deed, mortgage, or assignment of lease should contain a complete legal description. Most contracts for sale contain a good description of the property (address, size, and tax map number), but usually not a full legal description. (*See LEGAL DESCRIPTION.*)

Meeting of the Minds: There must be a valid offer and an unqualified acceptance of that offer, so that the seller understands the terms of the buyer's offer and the buyer understands the method of purchase of the identified property. (*See OFFER AND ACCEPTANCE.*)

Consideration: The contract must be supported by consideration; that is, both parties must be required to do something they were not previously obligated to do. Most contracts require a *valuable consideration,* such as a promise to pay money. A *gift deed,* however, is valid if it recites a good, rather than valuable, consideration, such as "for love and affection." (*See CONSIDERATION, OPTION.*)

Legal Purpose: To be enforceable, a contract must contemplate a legitimate purpose. Thus, a contract to lease a building for an illegal gambling casino would not be enforceable, nor would a listing contract to pay a commission to an unlicensed person. A usurious contract is not fully enforceable.

Signature: To be bound by a contract, a party must have signed it. In the usual real estate transaction, both buyer and seller sign the contract for sale.

If there is any ambiguity in a contract, the courts will construe the contract most strictly against the party who prepared it. For example, since the broker prepares the listing contract, it is construed very strictly against the broker. Thus, if there were any doubt whether the listing was an exclusive agency or an exclusive right to sell, the courts would construe it to be an exclusive agency.

It is not necessary that there be one formal document representing the contract of the contracting parties, though it is often preferable in order to eliminate any disputes as to whether a contract was formed. Sometimes the essentials of a contract (the offer and acceptance) arise from separate correspondence between the parties, so one formal contract is never actually signed. All parties must agree, however, on all essential terms in the contract, and should not leave anything to subsequent agreement. If this happens, the "contract" may be construed as preliminary negotiations rather than as a true contract.

Some contracts may be discharged due to impossibility of performance. For example, if the promisor of a personal-service contract dies, the contract is ordinarily discharged. Thus, a contract with a renowned architect to design a special building would probably be discharged by his or her death. However, if the work and/or services are of such a character that they may be performed by others, such as with a plumbing contract, the obligation will survive the death and bind the promisor's estate. Contracts pertaining to real estate are normally binding on the heirs and assigns of the deceased. The courts will sometimes discharge a contract when it feels the terms would be impossible for a reasonable person or organization to perform.

The essential element in every contract is that both parties clearly understand what is their agreement. Poorly drafted documents, especially those containing extensive legal language, are subject to various interpretations and often lead to litigation. In most instances, the parties involved in a real estate transaction would be best advised to engage the services of an experienced real estate attorney to draft a contract that accurately reflects the true intentions of the parties. Note that a broker who drafts legal contracts may be guilty of the unauthorized practice of law. (*See CONTRACT FOR SALE, DEED, LEASE, PRACTICE OF LAW, STATUTE OF FRAUDS.*)

CONTRACT DOCUMENTS In terms of real estate development, the agreement between two parties together with all supporting elements which assist in defining, amending, or modifying the agreement and its attendant conditions (drawings, specifications, change orders, addenda). The term is used in standard form documents used by the American Institute of Architects (AIA), such as those between the owner, architect, and general contractor.

CONTRACT FOR DEED An agreement between the seller (vendor) and buyer (vendee) for the purchase of real property in which the payment of all or a portion of the selling price is deferred. The purchase price may be paid in installments (of either principal and interest or interest only) over the period of the contract, with the balance due at maturity. When the buyer completes the required payments, the seller must deliver good legal title to the buyer by way of a deed or assignment of lease (if the property is leasehold property). Under the terms of the contract for deed, the buyer is given possession of the property and equitable title to the property while the seller holds legal title and continues to be primarily liable for payment of any underlying mortgage. The features of the buyer's equitable title and obligation to purchase are what distinguishes a contract for deed from a lease-option.

The contract for deed document usually contains the names of the buyer and seller, the sales price, the terms of payment, a full legal description, and a lengthy statement of the rights and obligations of the parties, similar to those under a mortgage, including use of premises, risk of loss, maintenance of premises, payment of taxes and insurance, and remedies in case of default. Specific rights, such as acceleration or the right to prepay without penalty, must be expressly written into the agreement. The contract is usually signed by both parties, acknowledged, and recorded.

The contract for deed is used quite extensively in many areas where it may be called a land contract, agreement of sale, installment contract, conditional sales contract, bond for deed, or real estate contract. In a dynamic and rapidly appreciating real estate market, the contract for deed enables buyers to purchase property on reasonable financial terms and thereby benefit from the appreciation of the property values. Many buyers then sell the property at a profit before their final payment becomes due. In a tight money market where it is difficult to qualify prospective buyers for conventional financing, the contract for deed is frequently the best method to sell or purchase a property. Especially benefited by the contract for deed are young couples, who would have difficulty qualifying for a bank loan at the time of entering into the contract for deed, but whose incomes will increase before maturity of the agreement, enabling them to refinance and pay off the contract for deed.

Some sellers prefer to sell on a contract for deed because it can create an installment sale, which will enable them to defer payment of a large capital gains tax. In addition, if the buyer defaults, the seller can sue for strict foreclosure, something he or she cannot do if a mortgage is used. However, a seller who chooses this remedy is rescinding the contract, and cannot seek a deficiency judgment for the unpaid balance. (See CONTRACT PRICE, FORFEITURE, INSTALLMENT SALE.)

Some contracts for deed provide that seller and/or buyer can convert the contract into a conventional security transaction. For example, upon payment of 40 percent of the purchase price the seller may be required to deliver a deed and take back a purchase money mortgage from the buyer for the balance of the purchase price.

It should be pointed out that use of a contract for deed is not without some disadvantages. From the buyer's viewpoint:

First: Since the seller need not deliver good marketable title until the final payment, the buyer must, at the risk of default, continue to make payments even when there may be a doubt whether the seller will be able to perform when all payments are made. This can be especially serious when the seller is a corporation, since its directors and shareholders have only limited liability. Some attorneys try to minimize this problem by inserting a clause to the effect that "the property is to be conveyed free and clear of all encumbrances except [those specified herein] and to remain free and clear except for the above stated encumbrances." The seller is then discouraged from placing further mortgages and encumbrances on the property during the period of the contract for deed.

Second: The buyer may have difficulty getting the seller to deed the property upon satisfaction. By withholding a large enough final payment, the buyer often can persuade a seller to pay the costs of drafting the deed. In addition, at the time of final payment, the seller might be suffering a legal disability, or be missing, bankrupt, or dead, and the property might be tied up in probate.

Third: The buyer might be restricted from assigning his or her interest in the contract for deed by covenants against assignment.

Fourth: Liens that arise against the seller could cloud the title.

Fifth: Unless a collection account is used, problems could arise if the seller does not apply the buyer's payments to pay the underlying mortgage.

From the seller's viewpoint:

First: In the event the buyer defaults, the process of clearing record title may be time consuming and costly, especially if the buyer is under a legal disability or is bankrupt, is a nonresident, or has created encumbrances in favor of persons who might have to be joined in any quiet title action.

Second: The seller's interest in the contract for deed is less salable than a mortgagee's interest would have been had the seller sold under a purchase-money mortgage.

Third: By its very nature the contract for deed is a contract, and all contracts are subject to differing interpretations with the possibility of disputes and litigation. (*See COLLECTION ACCOUNT, HOLDING ESCROW.*)

CONTRACT OF SALE   Also called a *sales contract;* a contract for the purchase and sale of real property in which the buyer agrees to purchase for a certain price and the seller agrees to convey title by way of a deed or an assignment of lease (for leasehold property). In addition to binding the parties to the purchase and sale of the property during the period of time required to close the transaction, the contract frequently serves as the initial directions to the closing agent or escrow company to process the mechanics of the transaction. Thus, it is most important that the parties agree in the contract on all of the pertinent closing details, such as who pays the various expenses of the sale, who bears the risk of loss, the date of occupancy, and the proration date. In essence, the contract of sale is an executory contract to convey property, serving as the vehicle to get to the deed, which finally conveys title. It is the blueprint for the entire transaction. Once the contract is signed, the remainder of the transaction is primarily mechanical.

To be enforceable, the contract of sale must be in writing, be signed by both parties, contain the buyer's and seller's names, contain an adequate description of the property (a full legal description is advisable, however, in the sale of unimproved land), state the sales price, and have a legitimate purpose. If the seller is married, the spouse should sign the contract so that he or she will be bound to release all marital rights (if applicable) when the deed is delivered. For example, if a wife fails to sign, the contract is nonetheless valid; however, she must be willing to join in the deed to release her dower and/or homestead.

Most contracts of sale are not recorded unless the parties anticipate a particularly long period of time to close the transaction. Normal residential closings take approximately 45 days from the date the contract is signed. However, a contract for deed should be recorded to protect the buyer, because it is often a period of years before the buyer pays off the contract and obtains legal title to the property.

If the buyer defaults and does not purchase the property, the seller can elect one of the following remedies: keep the deposit as liquidated damages; sue the buyer for money damages; or sue the buyer to complete the purchase under the terms of the agreement. This last remedy of specific performance is possible only if money damages cannot adequately compensate the seller for his or her loss. If the seller defaults, the buyer can rescind the agreement and obtain the return of his or her deposit money, or sue the seller for specific performance to have the court compel the seller to sell the property on the agreed terms.

A broker typically uses a standard contract of sale form. If a broker does not charge a separate fee for completing this form, it is not the unauthorized practice of law to assist one's client in filling it out and advising on the insertion of appropriate special conditions. As long as this service is rendered incidental to representing the client in the purchase or sale of the property, it is permissible. (*See CONTRACT, CONTRACT FOR DEED, EQUITABLE CONVERSION, SPECIFIC PERFORMANCE.*)

CONTRACTOR   One who contracts or covenants, either with a public body or private parties, to construct works or erect buildings at a certain price. A contractor is ordinarily understood to be the person who undertakes to supply labor and materials for specific improvements under a contract with an owner or principal. A *general contractor* is a contractor whose business operations require the use of more than two unrelated building trades or crafts whose work the contractor superintends or does in whole or in part; the term "general contractor" does not include an individual who does all work personally without employees or other "specialty contractors." A contractor may contract a complete job as the prime contractor or may contract with a general contractor to do part of a job as subcontractor.

CONTRACT PRICE   A tax term used in computation of gain realized from an installment sale. The contract price represents a property's selling price, minus any mortgages assumed or taken subject to by the buyer, plus the excess (if any) of any such liens collected in addition to the seller's adjusted basis at the time of sale. In essence the contract price is the seller's equity in the property.

One of the advantages of the contract for deed for the seller is that it permits the "contract price" to be the same as the selling price and thus defer taxes much better than if the buyer assumed or took subject to the mortgage. As an example, taxpayer sells property for $100,000, basis of $70,000 and the gain is $30,000; the down payment is $20,000 with an assumption of an existing $60,000 first mortgage and a purchase money second mortgage of $20,000. Although the selling price is $100,000, the contract price is only $40,000. Thus, of the total amount the seller is to receive ($40,000), the gain ($30,000) represents 75 percent. Therefore, 75 percent of the down payment and of each principal payment on the purchase money mortgage is gain, and only the remaining 25 percent is considered return of basis.

Alternatively, if the property is sold on a contract for deed, the entire $100,000 selling price would also be the contract price. Therefore, only 30 percent of the down payment would be gain. The remaining gain consists of 30 percent of principal payments received under the contract for deed, which would be taxable only as those principal payments are received. (*See INSTALLMENT SALE.*)

CONTRACT RENT   The rental income as stipulated by the parties in a lease. Appraisers often contrast this with economic rent, which is the amount of rent that could be obtained if the property were vacant and available on the open market. Where the contract rent exceeds the economic rent, it is often called a *negative leasehold*.

CONTRIBUTION   An appraisal principle in which the worth of an improvement is what it adds to the entire property's market value, regardless of the actual cost of the improvement. A remodeled basement may not contribute its entire cost to the value of the property, whereas a new bedroom usually will increase a house's value by more than its installation cost.

CONTRIBUTION, RIGHT OF   Cotenants who pay more than their pro rata share of necessary expenses to preserve the property may require a contribution from all other cotenants. These expenses include real property taxes, special assessments, and necessary repairs (but not unique improvements). (*See RIGHT OF CONTRIBUTION.*)

CONVENTIONAL ESTATE   An estate that is purposely created by the parties to a transaction, as opposed to an estate created by operation of law, such as a life estate created under dower laws.

CONVENTIONAL LOAN   A loan made with real estate as security and not involving government participation in the form of insuring (FHA) or guaranteeing (VA) the loan. The mortgagee can be an institutional lender or a private party. The loan is conventional in the sense that it conforms to accepted standards and the lender looks solely to the credit of the borrower and the security of the property to assure payment of the debt. Conventional loans include those loans insured by private mortgage insurance companies. Since the lender is not subject to the more stringent government regulations of the FHA and VA, conventional loans are frequently more flexible with respect to terms and interest rates, although they do reflect a higher interest rate and larger down payment requirements due to the higher risk involved. Nonconventional loan interest rates (FHA, VA, FmHA) are fixed by federal regulation. Conventional loans are subject to institutional regulation, which may be statutory (federal, state) or self-created.

CONVERSION   1. The process of transforming an income-producing property, such as a rental apartment building or hotel, into condominium apartments for sale to separate owners. The building is often renovated, the existing leases are allowed to lapse or are terminated, and the project is registered with the proper state agency and the title brought under the condominium act. The process requires considerable expertise in each of the following stages: cost and market analysis, purchase, initial remodeling, appraisal, interim and long-term financing, tenant relocation, and sales. State law often requires the developer to give existing tenants a long period in which to relocate if they elect not to purchase their unit. Due to increased construction costs, many developers are exploring condominium conversion as the answer to housing shortages. Yet, because of tenant displacement problems, many communities have placed restrictions (and even moratoriums) on condominium conversions.

2. The appropriation of property belonging to another. The conversion may be illegal (as when a broker misappropriates the funds of his or her client) or it may be legal (as when the government condemns property under the right of eminent domain). (*See COMMINGLING, INVOLUNTARY CONVERSION.*)

CONVEYANCE   The transfer of title or an interest in real property by means of a written instrument such as a deed or an assignment of lease. Note that a decree of divorce or a property settlement agreement involving real property does not in itself act as an effective conveyance. The Uniform Land Transactions Act proposes a simplified method of transferring title to real property.

CONVEYANCE TAX   Also called a *transfer tax*; a state tax imposed on the transfer or conveyance of realty or any realty interest by means of deed, lease, sublease, assignment, contract for deed, or similar instrument. One purpose of the tax is to acquire reliable data on the fair market value of the property to help establish more accurate real property tax assessments. The seller, grantor, or lessor is liable for the tax. Generally exempt from the tax are mortgages, correction deeds, transfers of realty if the tax was paid when the underlying contract for deed was recorded, transfers between husband and wife or parent and child, and transfers in which the actual consideration is $100 or less. When the transaction is exempt, the document normally must be accompanied by a form certificate setting forth the grounds for the exemption. Some transfers, such as a deed of easement, are totally exempt and the grantor is not required to file even an exemption certificate. (*See RECORDING, TRANSFER TAX.*)

COOLING-OFF PERIOD   A kind of grace period provided by law or by contract in which a party to a contract can legally back out of a contract; a right of rescission. Under the federal Truth-in-Lending law there is a specified cooling-off period in security transactions involving a borrower's personal residence. The federal Interstate Land Sales Act has a cooling-off period of seven calendar days. Many states have their own statutory cooling-off periods for condominium, timesharing, and subdivision sales. Contrary to some popular belief, however, there is no automatic right to rescind a real estate purchase contact unless so specified by statute or by contract. (*See RESCISSION.*)

COOPERATING BROKER   A broker who assists another broker (usually the "listor") in the sale of real property. Usually, the cooperating broker is the (selling) broker who found the buyer who offers to buy a piece of property, which is listed with another (listing) broker. The cooperating broker has no contractual relationship with the seller and therefore must look solely to the listing broker for a commission, often split on a 50/50 basis.

The Realtor® Code of Ethics provides that a Realtor® cooperating with a listing broker should not invite the cooperation of a third broker without the consent of the listing broker. Also, the Realtor® should cooperate with other brokers on property listed by him or her exclusively whenever it is in the interest of the client, sharing commissions on a previously agreed basis. Negotiations concerning property listed exclusively with one broker should be carried on with the listing broker, not with the owner (except with the consent of the listing broker).

Under some multiple-listing rules, the cooperating broker is deemed to act as the subagent for the listor on behalf of the seller in trying to find a ready, willing, and able buyer. If the cooperating broker decides to represent the buyer, then this fact must be made very clear in writing to all parties, especially as regards the right to a commission. (*See SUBAGENT.*)

COOPERATIVE OWNERSHIP   Cooperative ownership of an apartment unit means that the apartment owner has purchased shares in the corporation (or partnership or trust) which holds title to the entire apartment building. The cooperative owner is, in essence, a shareholder in a corporation whose principal asset is a building. In return for stock in the corporation, the owner recieves a proprietary lease granting occupancy of a specific unit in the building. The owner thus occupies under lease but does not own the unit, and his or her interest is treated as personal property. Each unit owner must pay his or her pro rata share of the corporation's expenses, which includes any mortgage charges, real estate taxes, maintenance, payroll, and so on. The owner can deduct for tax purposes his or her share of the taxes and interest charges (provided 80 percent of a cooperative's income is derived from tenant/owner rentals). Note that the stock certificate usually is freely assignable; however, the proprietary lease typically has severe restrictions on its assignability.

There are basic differences between a "co-op" and a condominium. In a co-op, the corporation owns the building and the dweller owns a proprietary lease and a corresponding number of shares in the corporation. In a condominium, each unit is individually owned. Voting power in a co-op is usually one vote per unit whereas, in a condo, an owner's voting power is relative to the size or value of the owner's unit (the percentage of common interest).

In a co-op, the corporation may take out or assume a single mortgage on the entire building. In a condominium, there is no mortgage on the building but there may be individual mortgages on units whose owners have not paid all cash. Thus, financing is often easier for a condominium unit purchaser than for a co-op, although some states now permit banks to lend on individual co-op units.

Since condominium owners actually own their own units, they are less restricted in the use of their apartments than are co-op tenants under proprietary lease. Upon resale, the co-op tenant normally must obtain the co-op's board of directors' approval of the proposed purchaser or lessee. Some boards may not want rock musicians, movie stars, or even ex-Presidents.

Only individuals (not corporate owners) may deduct real estate taxes and mortgage interest attributable to ownership of a co-op, and, of course, the owner of a co-op is a corporation. Corporations, however, can deduct taxes and interest on condominium units they own. Because of this tax situation, the promoter of a condominium is in a much better position to sell units to national corporations and other business enterprises for housing their executives or use by customers.

Since condominium owners obtain their own financing and are responsible for their individual property tax assessments, they are not responsible for any default on another owner's mortgage or property taxes. In a co-op, when an owner (tenant/shareholder) defaults on his or her mortgage or tax payments, the other shareholders must cure the default or risk having the entire project sold for taxes or foreclosed under the blanket mortgage. This contingent liability is one of the major drawbacks of co-op ownership. To protect against this risk, many co-ops assess a monthly charge to set up a prepayment reserve fund to cover real property taxes.

Developers of cooperatives sometimes help in finding ways to finance the purchaser's often substantial down payment requirement. One method is for the developer to take back a second mortgage on the buyer's leased premises, while the buyer in turn uses the proceeds of the second mortgage in order to buy the stock from the cooperative corporation. The buyer then deposits the cooperative stock with the developer as collateral until the debt is paid off.

When preparing a sales contract involving a co-op, the following language may be used to describe the property: "Ten shares of stock in Paige Apartments, Inc., entitling owner to proprietary use of Apartment 67 and parking stall #3, and co-use of common elements."

CO-OWNERSHIP   *See COTENANCY.*

CORE SPACE   *See RENTABLE AREA, USABLE AREA.*

CORNER-LOT   Methods of appraising business property that as-
APPRAISAL   sume that a corner lot is worth more than inside
METHODS   lots through corner influence or value.

CORNER STAKES   Used by a surveyor in running a survey by metes
                       and bounds. Such stakes are needed to fix the sur-
vey on the ground and are set at every change of direction.

CORNICE   A horizontal projection or molding at the top of
                       the exterior walls under the eaves. The cornice is
decorative and aids water drainage. Any molded projection at the top of an interior or exterior wall, in the enclosure at the roof eaves, or at the rake of the roof.

CORPORATE   A summary of a specific action taken by the board
RESOLUTION   of directors of a corporation. The corporate secre-
                       tary normally records the resolution in the min-
                       ute book of the corporation.

Lenders often request a certificate of resolution to verify that the corporate board
has authorized the borrowing of money or the opening of an account. This is
called a borrowing resolution, and usually uses language similar to the following:
"Upon motion duly made, seconded and unanimously passed, the following resolution was adopted on the 5th day of October, 1982. RESOLVED that the Corporation hereby authorizes the borrowing of $25,000 from the Bank of Paradise to
purchase a grocery store."

When a corporation is the seller of real property, the purchaser should request a
resolution from the seller's board of directors authorizing the sale and designating
an authorized officer to sign the conveyance instruments. If the corporation is
selling most of its assets, a resolution of the shareholders to authorize the sale is
also usually required. (*See CORPORATION.*)

CORPORATION   A legal entity created under state law, consisting
                       of an association of one or more individuals but
regarded under the law as having an existence and personality separate from such
individuals. The main characteristics of a corporation are its perpetual existence
(that is, the corporation exists indefinitely and only ceases to exist when and if it
is properly dissolved through legal proceedings); centralized management in the
board of directors; liability of a shareholder limited to the amount of one's investment; and free transferability of corporate shares.

A corporation has independent capacity to contract and to hold title to real property consistent with the powers given it in its articles of incorporation. Contracts
which the corporation has not been empowered to enter into (*ultra vires*, or beyond its powers) may not be valid. It is therefore important to ascertain whether
the corporation is empowered to enter into the contract, and whether the person
signing on behalf of the corporation is authorized to sign. This information is

verified by requesting a copy of the certificate of resolution of the board of directors authorizing the contract and the person signing it on behalf of the corporation. Normally, board approval is sufficient to authorize a sale of corporate property, but when the sale constitutes most of the corporate assets, shareholder approval (often three-fourths of the shares under state law) may be required.

When a new corporation is buying real property, it is important to verify that the articles have been filed and the corporation has in fact been legally formed; otherwise the deed is invalid for lack of grantee.

A corporation (except a Subchapter S corporation) is taxed at special corporate income tax rates, and the stockholders must pay an added tax on dividends or other profits received from the corporation.

A closely held corporation is one owned by a relatively few people, all or most of whom are directly involved in the conduct of the business, with very little stock held by outside investors.

Corporations are subject to regulation in the state where they were incorporated and in the states where they do business. (See ASSOCIATION, CORPORATE RESOLUTION, DOUBLE TAXATION, FOREIGN CORPORATION, SUBCHAPTER S CORPORATION, TAX BRACKET, ULTRA VIRES.)

CORPOREAL PROPERTY Tangible real or personal property, such as buildings, fixtures, and fences. Incorporeal property includes intangibles, such as rents, easements, and good will.

CORRECTION DEED A deed used to correct a prior erroneous deed, as when the grantor's name has been misspelled or when some minor mistake of fact has been made. A correction deed is also used to correct or change an inaccurate description of a parcel, often when a property is resurveyed. Also called a *deed of confirmation, reformation deed,* or a "confirmatory deed." Though exempt from the conveyance tax, the correction deed is subject to the appropriate recording fee. A grantor can be forced to execute a correction deed if he or she gave a covenant of further assurance in the original deed.

CORRECTION LINES Provisions in the government survey method made to compensate for the curvature of the earth's surface. Every fourth township line (at 24-mile intervals) is used as a correction line on which the intervals between the north and south range lines are measured and corrected to a full six miles. (See GOVERNMENT SURVEY METHOD.)

CORRELATIVE WATER RIGHT A modern law in some states holds that a riparian owner who has rights in a common water source is entitled to take only a reasonable amount of the total water supply for the beneficial use of the land (such as irrigation). Under the *appropriative water right* favored in some states, the owner has the exclusive right to take all the water for specific beneficial uses.

CORRELATION See RECONCILIATION.

CORRIDOR   A passageway or hallway which provides a common way of travel to an exit. A deadend corridor is one which provides only one direction of travel to an exit.

COST APPROACH   An approach to the evaluation of property based on the property's reproduction cost. Because most people will not pay more for a property than it would cost to acquire a similar site and erect a similar structure on it, the current reproduction cost of the building plus the value of the land tends to set the upper limit of a property's value. The cost approach is also called the *summation approach* since it involves adding together the building and land values, each computed separately. The primary steps are to: (1) estimate the land value; (2) estimate the reproduction cost of the building new; (3) deduct all accrued depreciation from the reproduction cost; and (4) add the estimated land value to the depreciated reproduction cost.

To estimate land value, the land is presumed to be vacant and the appraiser looks at sales of comparable land. While land does not depreciate, it is affected by the current use to which it is being put.

To determine reproduction cost, the comparative cost method is used based on current market costs to construct buildings that are similar in design, type, size, and quality of construction. From this reproduction cost is deducted accrued depreciation due to physical deterioration, functional obsolescence, and economic obsolescence. Finally, the estimated land value is added to the depreciated reproduction cost of the building. Note that if accrued depreciation exceeds 25 percent, the effectiveness of this approach is severely diminished and an alternative method (the market-data approach or income approach) should be employed, if possible.

The cost approach is most helpful in the appraisal of special-purpose buildings such as schools, churches, and post offices. Such properties are difficult to appraise using other methods because there are not many comparable sales and there usually is no income produced by the properties. This method is only appropriate if the property is being used for its highest and best use. (*See APPRAISAL, COMPARABLES, REPRODUCTION COST.*)

COST-OF-LIVING INDEX   An index number indicating the relative change in the cost of living between a selected period of time (using a factor of 100) and another period of time. Escalator clauses in commercial leases often refer to an increase in maintenance expenses to match the increase in the cost of living or an increase in the U.S. Department of Labor's Consumer Price Index (which uses a 1967 reference base of 100). (*See BASE PERIOD.*)

COST-PLUS CONTRACT   A construction agreement in which the owner will pay the cost of all labor and materials plus a certain additional amount based on a set percentage of the cost, representing profit and contractor's overhead. This type of contract contrasts with a fixed-price contract.

COST RECOVERY   A form of deduction applicable to real and personal property used in a trade or business, or held for the production of income. This method was adopted by the Economic Recovery Tax Act of 1981 in place of depreciation and applies to new and used real or personal property "placed in service" by the taxpayer after 1980. "Placed in service" means the day the property is available for its business use. It is the day on which income property is available for rent, not necessarily the day the property is acquired. Unlike depreciation, cost recovery does not depend upon the "useful life" or the "salvage value" of property. Rather, the entire cost (of the depreciable portion) of property may be deducted over an arbitrary period of time.

The Internal Revenue Service has published cost recovery tables to help the taxpayer compute the deduction. These tables are a helpful tool in analyzing a potential investment and preparing income and expense projections for income property.

To use Table A, simply compute the unadjusted basis of the property as of the time the property is placed in service. Cost recovery starts the month the property is first placed in service. Simply locate that month on the table and use that same column for each year the property is held. For example, the taxpayer buys an apartment building for $350,000 with $100,000 allocated to the land. The property is placed in service on June 18, 1982. The taxpayer is a calendar-year taxpayer (fiscal year taxpayers use a different column). Under the June column the cost recovery deduction for the first recovery year is 7 percent of the adjusted basis of $250,000 or $17,500; for the third recovery year it is 10 percent or $25,000. (*See ACCELERATED COST RECOVERY SYSTEM.*)

ACCELERATED COST RECOVERY TABLE A

15-YEAR REAL ESTATE (EXCEPT LOW-INCOME HOUSING)

RECOVERY YEAR	USE COLUMN FOR MONTH IN FIRST YEAR PROPERTY PLACED IN SERVICE											
	JAN	FEB	MAR	APR	MAY	JUN	JUL	AUG	SEP	OCT	NOV	DEC
1	12	11	10	9	8	7	6	5	4	3	2	1
2	10	10	11	11	11	11	11	11	11	11	11	12
3	9	9	9	9	10	10	10	10	10	10	10	10
4	8	8	8	8	8	9	9	9	9	9	9	9
5	7	7	7	7	7	8	8	8	8	8	8	8
6	6	6	6	6	7	7	7	7	7	7	7	7
7	6	6	6	6	6	6	6	6	6	6	6	6
8	6	6	6	6	6	5	5	6	6	6	6	6
9	6	6	6	6	5	5	5	5	5	6	6	6
10	5	6	5	6	5	5	5	5	5	5	6	5
11	5	5	5	5	5	5	5	5	5	5	5	5
12	5	5	5	5	5	5	5	5	5	5	5	5
13	5	5	5	5	5	5	5	5	5	5	5	5
14	5	5	5	5	5	5	5	5	5	5	5	5
15	5	5	5	5	5	5	5	5	5	5	5	5
16	-	-	1	1	2	2	3	3	4	4	4	5

COTENANCY A form of concurrent property ownership in which two or more persons own an undivided interest in the same property. When title to one parcel of real estate is vested in (or owned by) two or more persons or other entities, such persons or entities are said to be co-owners of the property. There are several forms of co-ownership, each one having unique legal characteristics. The forms of co-ownership most commonly recognized by the various states are tenancy in common, joint tenancy, tenancy by the entirety, community property, condominium and cooperative, and partnership property. Each of these forms of co-ownership is discussed separately. (*See COMMUNITY PROPERTY, GRANTEE, JOINT TENANCY, PARTNERSHIP, RIGHT OF CONTRIBUTION, TENANCY BY THE ENTIRETY, TENANCY IN COMMON, UNDIVIDED INTEREST.*)

COUNSELING   A relatively recent specialty within the real estate industry that involves providing skilled, independent advice and professional guidance on a variety of real estate problems. A counselor attempts to provide the client with direction in choosing from among alternative courses of action. By meeting certain rigid standards, an individual can qualify for the professional designation, C.R.E. (Counselor, Real Estate) conferred by the American Society of Real Estate Counselors.

COUNTEROFFER   A new offer made in response to an offer received from an offeror. This has the effect of rejecting the original offer, which cannot thereafter be accepted unless revived by the offeror's repeating it.

Usually, the buyer submits his or her offer to buy for the seller's acceptance. If the seller makes any change to the offer, no matter how slight, it constitutes a counteroffer, terminates the original offer, and bars its subsequent acceptance. Thus, if the seller changes the suggested closing date from 10:00 a.m. November 10, 1982 to 11:00 a.m. November 10, 1982, initials the change, and signs the sales contract, he or she has made a counteroffer. The roles of the parties are thus reversed and the counteroffer itself can be accepted or rejected as an original offer would be. To create a valid contract, the buyer must accept the terms of the counteroffer within a certain period of time. Note that a simple inquiry as to whether the offeror would be willing to change the terms of an offer is not sufficient to constitute a rejection of the offer or a counteroffer.

A common practice has been for the seller to make a change to the buyer's sales contract, initial and date the change, and transmit it to the buyer for acceptance. If the buyer then wanted to make a change to the altered contract, he or she would, in effect, be making a counter-counteroffer.

It is poor practice to rely on a contract that has many initialed changes, since it is difficult to determine at what point in time there actually exists a valid contract. It is a good idea to have the parties execute a written counteroffer. There are counteroffer forms specially designed by local boards of Realtors®. If a buyer wishes to make a counteroffer in response to the seller's counteroffer form, the buyer should probably begin the process anew, by completing a new sales contract offer.

Because it is important to be able to determine the chronology of events, each change should be time dated. Also, the broker must give a copy of the changes to the signing party at the time such changes are made, not afterward.

COUNTERPART   A duplicate or copy of a document. Sometimes used in preparing conveyance documents when there are multiple parties and inadequate time to send a single document to parties located throughout the country for signatures. In such a case, a copy of the document can be sent to each signing party and then all the executed copies can be recorded as one document. Normally counterparts will be treated as a single document although not created simultaneously.

COUNTY   A governmental division of a state. It is usually the largest administrative division within a state.

COURT   1. A short roadway partially or wholly enclosed by buildings giving the impression of a small open square. 2. An open area enclosed on two or more sides by walls or buildings. 3. An official session for the administration of justice—a court of law.

The federal court system consists of the United States Supreme Court, which is the highest court in the land; courts of appeals and circuit courts—the intermediate courts; and district courts—the lower courts. The United States also has specialized courts, such as the United States Tax Court, Patents Court, Court of Claims, and Customs Court.

State court systems vary, but their fundamental concepts are basically the same as the federal system. Generally, there is a high court, usually called the supreme court; intermediate courts, often labeled appellate courts; and lower courts, usually called district courts, county courts, lower claims courts, or small-claims courts. There are also special courts to handle traffic violations, probate, and land matters (such as the Torrens system).

COURTESY TO BROKERS   The practice of sharing commissions between listing and cooperating brokers. For example, in the sale of a large condominium project, the listing real estate broker may work for the developer. If a prospective buyer is a client of another broker, the listing broker may extend "courtesy" to the buyer's broker (called the selling broker), and share part of the commission with him or her. It is not uncommon for a developer who controls his or her own brokerage company to decide not to extend courtesy to "outside" brokers unless there are marketing difficulties in selling the project.

In a "For Sale by Owner" situation, it is common to have the owner agree to a buyer's broker courtesy fee.

COVENANT   An agreement or promise between two or more parties in which a party or parties pledge to perform or not to perform specified acts on a property; or a written agreement that specifies certain uses or nonuses of the property. Covenants are found in such real estate documents as leases, mortgages, contracts for deed, and deeds. Damages may be claimed for breach of a covenant.

Covenants found in warranty deeds (general and special) are promises made by the grantor, binding both the grantor and the grantor's heirs and assigns, warranting that the title is of a certain character and that if the title should be found to be not of that character, the grantor or his or her heirs will compensate the grantee for any loss suffered. In many areas, covenants are implied by use of certain language in a deed, such as "convey and warrant," "warrant generally," or "warrant specially." Some typical covenants found in warranty deeds follow:

Covenant against grantor's acts: This covenant is used in special warranty deeds in which the grantor is a fiduciary, such as an executor, trustee, or guardian. In effect, the covenant states that the grantor has not done or suffered anything to encumber the property, but that he or she makes no warranties concerning the title prior to taking title. This covenant does not "run with the land" (it does not benefit future grantees).

Covenant of seisin: The grantor guarantees that at the time of the conveyance he or she owns and is in possession of the property and has the good right to sell it. This covenant relates to the time of transfer and is broken, if at all, at the time of delivery of the deed. The covenant is not broken if there is a lien on the land, but it is broken if the title is held by a third person or if the grantor has not the extent of the estate he or she purports to convey. For instance, the covenant of seisin is breached where the grantor warrants that he or she is seized of a fee simple estate, yet only possesses a life estate.

Covenant against encumbrances: This covenant warrants that the property is clear of any and all encumbrances not specifically excepted in the deed. Therefore, it is important to state all encumbrances as exceptions in the deed. Otherwise, if any encumbrance exists against the property and is not excepted in the deed, the grantee can recover his or her expense in paying off the encumbrance, such as unpaid taxes. Like the covenant of seisin, this covenant limits any recovery to the price paid, and is broken, if at all, at the time of delivery of the deed. It covers all encumbrances, including those that are known and those that are unknown to both grantor and grantee. A covenant against encumbrances is not breached, however, when there are open and visible physical encumbrances, such as an easement for power lines or an irrigation ditch.

Covenant of quiet enjoyment: The grantor warrants that the grantee and his or her heirs and assigns will have the right to a property free of interference from the acts or claims of third parties. The innocent grantees are thus protected from title disputes arising between the grantor and a former claimant. The covenant of quiet enjoyment is breached only by an eviction, actual or constructive, by reason of a title superior to that of the grantor.

Covenant of warranty of title: This covenant assures the grantee that the grantor will bear the expense of defending the grantee's title to the property if any person asserts a rightful claim to the property. If the covenant is broken due to some third person having a better title, then the grantee may sue for damages up to the value of the property at the time of sale. It usually reads, "That the grantor will forever warrant the title to said premises."

Covenant of further assurance: This covenant obligates the grantor to perform any acts necessary to perfect the title in the grantee. It is also used to force a grantor to execute a correction deed when there has been some error in the original deed. The covenant is breached when the grantor refuses to pay the proper expenses and charges for obtaining the necessary documents, such as failure to record a satisfaction of mortgage where required or failure to obtain a quitclaim deed releasing an unrecorded interest in property or a dower interest. This covenant is usually enforced in an action for specific performance rather than in a suit for damages. Also called the *covenant of further assistance.* (See *DEED, SPECIAL WARRANTY DEED, WARRANTY DEED.*)

COVENANT NOT TO COMPETE Agreement given by a seller of a business not to compete against the purchaser in an agreed area for a specified time. This protects the purchaser of the business against the seller opening a competing business and regaining all of the old customers. It also allows the purchaser to amortize and write off the payment for the covenant over the life of the covenant. Also, a similar agreement may be made by employees in an employment contract.

Such covenants are not favored by the courts and are closely scrutinized for possible violation of antitrust laws and as unreasonable restraints on doing business or employment.

COVENANTS AND CONDITIONS   Covenants are unconditional promises contained in contracts, the breach of which would entitle a person to damages. Conditions, on the other hand, are contingencies, qualifications, or occurrences upon which an estate or property right (like a fee simple) would be gained or lost. Covenants are indicated by words such as promise, undertake, agree; conditions are indicated by words such as if, when, unless, and provided. Because they are limitations only and do not create obligations, failure of the condition to occur will not entitle either party to damages against the other party. Conditions may be either precedent or subsequent. A *condition precedent* is one that must happen or be performed before a right or estate is gained; a *condition subsequent* is one that will cause a right to be lost or an estate to be terminated, upon its occurrence.

For example, a lease may contain covenants to repair, pay taxes and assessments, or pay rent. If the tenant breaches a covenant, the landlord may sue the tenant for damages. If the lease contains a certain condition and the tenant breaches the condition, then his or her leasehold interest will be terminated. Thus, a commercial lease often contains a condition in a defeasance clause that the tenant will forfeit his or her lease upon the tenant's being declared bankrupt or upon illegal use of the premises.

Promises may be both conditions and covenants. For example, the concurrent conditions found in contracts for sale are also covenants. The delivery of the deed by the seller and the payment of the purchase price by the buyer are concurrent conditions. Also, they are covenants. Thus, the buyer could sue the defaulting seller for damages only after the buyer met the condition of tendering performance (by placing the purchase money into escrow). (*See* CONTINGENCIES, COVENANT.)

COVENANTS, CONDITIONS AND RESTRICTIONS (CC&Rs)   *See* RESTRICTIONS.

COVENANTS RUNNING WITH THE LAND   Covenants that become part of the property rights and benefit or bind successive owners of the property. In order for the burden of a covenant to run with the land, the covenant must have been created in writing by a promise between a grantor and grantee of the property, it must "touch and concern" the land, it must have been the intention of the original parties that the covenant would run with the land, and subsequent grantees must have notice of the existence of the covenant. An example of a restrictive covenant may be a prohibition contained in a deed against erecting a pigpen on the property. (*See* RESTRICTIVE COVENANT.)

CRAM DOWN   A provision in the federal Bankruptcy Act that permits a settlement of a bankruptcy in certain situations even without the consent of all classes of creditors.

CREATIVE FINANCING   A generic term used to describe a wide variety of new and innovative financing techniques used to market a property. (*See* ALTERNATIVE MORTGAGE INSTRUMENTS.)

CREDIT   1. Obligations that are due or are to become due.
2. In closing statements, that which is due and payable to either the buyer or seller—the opposite of a charge or debit. The credit appears in the right-hand column of the accounting statement.

CREDITOR   The person to whom a debtor owes a debt or obligation; a lender.

CREDIT RATING   A rating given a person or company to establish credit worthiness based upon present financial condition, experience, and past credit history.

CREDIT REPORT   A report detailing the credit history of a person or business, used to determine credit worthiness. The financial status of commercial or industrial tenants can be checked by consulting a Dun and Bradstreet reference book, a credit reporting agency, or a local Chamber of Commerce or Better Business Bureau.

CREDIT UNION   A cooperative nonprofit organization in which members (labor unions, clubs, churches, Realtors®) place money in savings accounts, usually at higher interest rates than at other savings institutions. Credit unions usually make only short-term installment loans, buy may occasionally make loans secured by a lien on real property—typically second mortgages. Credit unions are a good source for home improvement loans.

Under the Federal Credit Union Act, credit unions do have authority to make 30-year real estate loans to members to finance their principal residence. Credit unions can also make loans for FHA/VA loans at interest rates comparable to the market value (above 12 percent). Deposits in federally chartered credit unions and state-chartered ones that apply and qualify are insured by the National Credit Union Share Insurance Fund. The fund is administered by the National Credit Union Administration (NCUA), an independent agency of the federal government, which regulates and supervises the activities of the federal credit unions.

CROSS-DEFAULTING CLAUSE   A provision in many junior mortgages stipulating that a default in one mortgage also triggers a default in the mortgage in which the clause appears.

CUL DE SAC   A street that is open at one end only and usually has a circular turnaround at the other end; a blind alley. The use of cul de sacs is becoming more popular in residential subdivisions in place of the traditional grid pattern with numerous intersections. (See *PLANNED UNIT DEVELOPMENT*.)

CURTAIL SCHEDULE   A listing of the amounts by which the principal sum of an obligation is to be reduced by partial payments and of the dates when each payment will become due. Also called a *mortgage amortization schedule*.

CURTESY   The interest recognized in some states of a husband in property owned by his wife at the time of her death. During her life, the husband has no curtesy interest whatsoever in his wife's property and thus does not need to sign off his curtesy rights (as a wife would her dower rights) on any conveyance document executed by the wife. Upon her death, the husband may have a vested life interest in one-third of the wife's real estate, depending on the state's law. The husband is usually not entitled to curtesy if he is guilty of desertion or neglect. (*See DOWER.*)

CURTILAGE   The enclosed ground space surrounding a dwelling, such as the lawn or patio.

CURVILINEAR   Having boundaries of curved lines. Usually refers to the use by subdivision developers of curves in street and lot layouts, as opposed to the older grid patterns. This type of design pattern is more aesthetically pleasing and results in fewer traffic accidents.

CUSHION   An amount of money computed into a contractor's bid for a project to protect the contractor against possible unforeseen occurrences such as delays in governmental approvals, poor weather, and bidding mistakes.

CUSTODY   1. The care and keeping of something. 2. Responsibility for a property, as when a mortgagee turns foreclosed property over to the VA (if it was a VA loan). This specialized VA term may or may not include the right of possession of the property.

CUSTOMER   A prospective buyer of real estate. Not to be confused with a property seller, who is the listing broker's client.

CUSTOMER TRUST FUND   An impound account maintained for the purpose of setting up a reserve to pay certain periodic obligations such as real property taxes, insurance premiums, lease rent, and maintenance fees. Many lenders require the borrower/owner of a condominium apartment or other residence to maintain such funds to assure that the carrying charges will be paid on time. (*See IMPOUND ACCOUNT.*)

CYCLICAL MOVEMENT   An economics term used to describe shifts in the business cycle of the national economy from prosperity through recession, depression, recovery, and back again to prosperity.

DAMAGES The compensation recoverable by a person who has sustained an injury, either to his or her person or property, through the act or default of another. There is a complex area of law directly concerned with determining the appropriate measure (amount) of damages for specific types of injuries. In cases of fraud, courts often use the benefit-of-bargain rule, awarding as damages the cash difference between the actual value of the property and the value of the property as fraudulently represented to the buyer. In some cases, the courts apply the "out of pocket" rule, awarding as damages the difference, if any, between the actual value of that which the plaintiff (the person seeking damages) paid (i.e., the consideration) and the actual value of that which was received, and any amounts expended in reliance upon the fraudulent party.

Often the seller in a real estate contract retains the buyer's deposit money as damages when the buyer decides not to perform the contract to purchase the property. Sometimes the parties agree at the time of signing their contract that a defaulting party will pay a certain amount to liquidate or settle any damages. Damages recoverable by an owner for a lessee's breach of contract to lease would be the excess (if any) of the agreed or contract rent, over and above the rental price the owner would be forced to accept in reletting the premises in a pressure situation. The burden of proving damages is always on the plaintiff. (*See BENEFIT-OF-BARGAIN RULE, CONSEQUENTIAL DAMAGES, LIQUIDATED DAMAGES.*)

DAMPER An adjustable valve at the top of a fireplace that regulates the flow of heated gases into the chimney.

DAMPPROOFING A horizontal layer of plastic, lead, asphalt, or other water resistant materials placed between the interior and exterior walls to exclude moisture.

DATE Usually the exact day a legal document is signed. Certain documents, such as deeds or long-term leases, often contain several dates evidencing different events, such as the day the parties signed the document, the day the document was acknowledged, and/or the day it was recorded.

Though a date is not essential for the validity of most real estate contracts, it has considerable evidentiary value for proving a deed was delivered on the date specified, determining priority between unrecorded deeds, establishing time limits for performance (such as "seller has 48 hours to accept from the date of this offer"), and proving whether or not the statute of limitations has run.

When the parties to a purchase agreement intend the closing to take place on a certain date (with no extensions of time), they should specify the date and expressly declare that "time is of the essence."

In a contract for deed, the date may be important in determining which party is liable for a casualty loss, personal injuries to a guest, or liability for a special assessment.

To avoid confusion, it is best to be quite specific about terms stating, for instance, that "the seller pays up to and including March 28." A period running "to" a certain date does not include that date unless the words "to and including" are used. Rather than say "to 12:00 a.m." and have doubt whether it is midnight or noon, use 11:30 a.m. or 11:30 p.m. Rather than say a 90-day period, put a specific termination date so you avoid arguments whether it is calendar days or 30-day months and whether first and last days are counted.

DATUM   A level surface to which heights and depths are referred; the datum plane. The datum may be an assumed point, such as a monument, or it may be tidal in nature (that is, mean sea level). (*See BENCH MARK.*)

DBA   An abbreviation for the phrase, "doing business as"; used to identify a trade name or a fictitious business name.

DEALER   An Internal Revenue Service designation for a person who regularly buys and sells real property. A person is classified as a dealer if, at the time of a property's sale, he or she held the property "primarily" for sale to customers in the ordinary course of business. Courts have interpreted "primarily" to mean principally or of first importance. A dealer must pay tax at ordinary income rates on any gains from the sale of property but may also take ordinary deductions for losses. The dealer thus loses the benefit of capital gains treatment. In addition, dealer property does not qualify for tax-deferred treatment in an IRC 1031 exchange.

The determination of dealer status is made on a case-by-case basis. One may be a dealer with respect to some properties and an investor with respect to others, depending on the facts of each case. Since it is difficult for anyone who deals with many properties to prove he or she is only an investor and not a dealer, detailed records of each transaction should be kept. Some of the factors that the IRS considers in determining if one is a dealer are the purpose for purchasing the property, the length of time the property was held, the number of sales activities of the owner, the existence of other income and other businesses, and the extent of improvements made on the property by the taxpayer. If the owner subdivides and develops the property, it is likely the owner is a dealer; there are exceptions, however, especially with one-time subdividers.

To avoid being classified as a dealer, a person should seek advice from a qualified tax accountant, attorney, or investment counselor. Depending on an owner's individual financial situation, it may be to the owner's advantage to purchase fewer, though more expensive, properties, hold on to the properties for a longer period of time, and spread the gains from transactions over several tax years. (*See CAPITAL GAIN.*)

DEBENTURE   A type of long-term note or bond given as evidence of debt. Unlike a mortgage note, a debenture is not secured by a specific property. Usually, the issuer executes an indenture or agreement with a trustee such as a bank. The indenture states the amount, interest rate, maturity, and special features of the bond issue, such as its ability to be accelerated or converted. To avoid restriction of future borrowing power, many issuers use *subordinated debentures;* that is, loans that may be subordinated to other company loans in the terms provided for in the debenture. *Sinking fund debentures* require a certain amount to be escrowed annually so there will be funds available for redemption.

The Federal National Mortgage Association issues debentures to finance the acquisition of mortgages in the secondary mortgage market. If there is a default on an FHA loan, the government will give interest-bearing debentures to the mortgagee after title is transferred to the FHA. (*See FEDERAL HOUSING ADMINISTRATION.*)

DEBIT   A charge on an accounting statement or balance sheet (appearing in the left-hand column); the opposite of a credit. Used in bookkeeping and in preparing the closing statement in a real estate transaction.

DEBT COVERAGE RATIO   The ratio of annual net income to annual debt service. For example a lender may require that a qualified corporate borrower have net income of 3.5 times the debt service of the loan being approved.

DEBT FINANCING   The payment, in whole or in part, for a capital investment with borrowed monies, as opposed to investing one's own funds. Usually, in real estate, the property itself serves as the security for the debt.

DEBTOR   One who owes money; a borrower, a maker of a note; or a mortgagor.

DEBT SERVICE   The amount of money needed to meet the periodic payments of principal and interest on a loan or debt that is being amortized. If the periodic payments are constant, in equal amounts, then a portion will pay off accrued interest with the remainder reducing principal. (*See AMORTIZATION.*)

DECK   A partition or dividing wall found in a building that houses two or more tenants, separating the area leased by one party from that leased by others.

DECLARATION   The legal document that the developer of a condominium must generally file and record in order to create a condominium under state law. The declaration usually contains a precise description of the land on which the project is located; whether it is fee or leased; a description of the apartments, common elements, and limited common elements; a statement indicating the use of the building or buildings and apartments, including restrictive uses; and a statement of other detailed legal requirements, such as service of process and provision for amendment of the declaration. The declaration must generally be recorded, for amendment of the declaration. The declaration must generally be recorded, together with a true copy of the by-laws governing the operation of the project and a condominium map showing the floor plan, elevations, and so forth. The developer usually must also record a master deed or lease. (*See CONDOMINIUM.*)

DECLARATION OF HOMESTEAD See *HOMESTEAD.*

DECLARATION OF RESTRICTIONS A statement of all the covenants, conditions, and restrictions (CC&Rs) that affect a parcel of land. A subdivider may note the restrictions on the map or plan when recording the subdivision plat. If the restrictions are numerous, the subdivider may also prepare a separate document called a Declaration, listing all the restrictions, and then record this Declaration. The restrictions usually aim at a general plan of development and require all lot owners to comply with certain building standards and conform to certain restrictions. For example, the CC&Rs may require lot owners to construct homes valued at more than $60,000 or to obtain prior design approval from a designated architectural control committee. Once recorded, these restrictions in the declaration run with the land and bind all future lot owners. Any owner can enforce the restrictions against any other owner who violates any of the restrictions. A Declaration of Restrictions can be terminated by lapse of a specified time or by agreement of all benefited parties. (*See RESTRICTION.*)

The following are typical provisions of a Declaration of Restrictions:

"Each building or other structure shall be constructed, erected, and maintained in strict accordance with the approved plans and specifications."

"No building shall be located on any lot nearer than 35 feet to the street lot line, nearer than 30 feet to the rear lot line, or nearer than 10 feet to the side lot lines."

"No building or structure shall be more than 25 feet in height as measured from the highest natural grade at any point on the perimeter of the foundation of the structure to the highest point of the roof."

"No animals, livestock, or poultry of any kind shall be raised, bred or kept on any land in the subdivision except by special permit issued by the board of directors. However, a reasonable number of dogs, cats, or other common household pets may be kept without the necessity of obtaining such permit."

Lawsuits frequently arise over interpretation of questionable language in a Declaration of Restriction; for example, if trailers are prohibited, does that also exclude mobile homes? Or does the word "structure" include a swimming pool or fence? Restrictions should be carefully drafted to avoid ambiguity.

DECLINING-BALANCE METHOD An accounting method of depreciation for income-tax purposes designed to provide larger-than-straight-line deductions in the early years of a property's life, and applicable to property placed in service prior to 1981. Tax laws provide for the use of accelerated depreciation in certain instances. Using an accelerated rate of 175 percent of the straight-line rate, the investor can realize an even greater amount of depreciation in the early years of the property's 15-year useful life.

To compute declining-balance depreciation: find the rate used under the straight-line method; multiply that by the percentage of the declining-balance method rate; and then apply the resulting rate against the remaining basis each year. For example, in 1980 investor John Brillo purchased a new apartment building with a useful life of ten years and a depreciable basis of $250,000. Using the 200 percent, or "double-declining," method, the following rate of depreciation occurs:

Year	Remaining Basis	Rate of Decline	Depreciation	Accumulated Depreciation
1	$250,000	20%	$50,000	$ 50,000
2	200,000	20	40,000	90,000
3	160,000	20	32,000	122,000
4	128,000	20	25,000	147,000
5	102,000	20	20,480	167,000
6	81,920	20	16,384	183,864
7	65,536	20	13,107	196,971
8	52,429	20	10,485	207,456
9	41,944	20	8,388	215,844
10	33,556	20	6,711	222,555

As you can see, this method would permit investor Brillo to write off better than half of his investment's value—$147,600—in only four years.

The Economic Recovery Tax Act of 1981 replaces depreciation with cost recovery, and declining balance methods with the accelerated cost recovery system (ACRS), which is based in part upon the former declining balance methods.

For property placed in service between July 24, 1969, and December 31, 1980, the Internal Revenue Code allowed the use of accelerated depreciation when applied to the following types of structures:

New residential buildings	up to 200%
Used residential buildings with a remaining life of 20 years or more	125%
New nonresidential buildings	up to 150%
Used nonresidential buildings	straight-line only

For pre-1981 property, gain realized from the sale of property depreciated by a declining-balance method in excess of that which would have been realized using the straight-line method will be "recaptured" as ordinary income; that is, not taxed at the favorable capital gains rate. For property placed in service after 1980, and for which accelerated cost recovery was taken, recapture of depreciation remains the same for residential property. For nonresidential property, however, *all* depreciation taken is recaptured as ordinary income. (*See ACCELERATED DEPRECIATION, FIRST USER, RECAPTURE OF DEPRECIATION, STRAIGHT-LINE METHOD, SUM-OF-THE-YEARS'-DIGITS METHOD.*)

DEDICATION   The transfer of privately owned land to the public without consideration, with the intent that the land will be accepted and used for public purposes. A landowner may dedicate the entire fee simple interest or an easement such as a public right-of-way across the landowner's property.

There are two types of dedication: statutory and common law. A statutory dedication is accomplished by recording a subdivision map approved by local officials and expressly indicating on the map those areas dedicated to the public, such as parks and streets.

A common law dedication is a matter of contract and thus requires an offer, evidenced by an intention and an unequivocal act of dedication on the part of the owner and acceptance on the part of the public. The dedication may be either express—as when a developer or subdivider deeds roads to the county, or inplied—as when the owner has acquiesced to the public use of the owner's property, usually for the prescriptive period. (See CESSION DEED.)

For example, in order to prevent the public from claiming a dedication, the Rockefeller Center closes off its streets and sidewalks for one day out of the year. This is done to evidence that the public's right to use the property is a mere license and that Rockefeller Center has a definite intention not to dedicate its property to the public. Some owners also imbed into their sidewalk a metal plaque stating "Private Property, Permission to Use Revocable." "No Trepassing" signs may not be sufficient for purposes of preventing the public from claiming a dedication.

The fee interest acquired by dedication is similar to a qualified fee; for example, upon an abandonment of the dedicated public use, the fee goes to the owner under a possibility of reverter, while the government is usually prevented from diverting the property to a new use.

Dedication of property such as streets and open spaces is sometimes made a prerequisite to governmental approval of a proposed development. In some cases, the developer can pay a fee rather than dedicate land. (See TRANSFER DEVELOPMENT RIGHTS.)

DEED   A written instrument by which a property owner as "grantor" conveys and transfers to a "grantee" an ownership interest in real property. There are many types of deeds, including warranty deeds, grant deeds, bargain and sale deeds, quitclaim deeds, gift deeds, guardian's deeds, executor's deeds, sheriff's deeds, and deeds of trust. The major difference in each case is the type of covenant made by the grantor. Perhaps the most commonly used deed is the general warranty deed. Title to leasehold property is transferred by way of an "assignment of lease" document rather than a deed. (See FREEHOLD, LEASEHOLD.)

The deed is unique in that it signals the end of one ownership and the beginning of another. In order to be valid as between grantor and grantee a deed must contain the following elements:

Grantor: There must be a grantor named in the deed who is of age and of sound mind. A mistake in the spelling of the grantor's name or signature will not invalidate the deed if the grantor's identity is otherwise clear. If there are multiple grantors, each must be named as a grantor in the deed to convey his or her interest, or each may convey separately in separate deeds. (See GRANTOR.)

Grantee: There must be an actual grantee. Thus, a deed delivered to a corporation prior to its coming into legal existence (by filing its articles of incorporation) is void for lack of a grantee. A deed delivered to the estate of a dead grantee is void although a deed delivered to a minor or incompetent is valid. While a deed to a fictitious person is void, a deed to a person using a fictitious name is valid. It is good practice to include the status of the parties, such as married, minor, trustee or personal representative. While a grantor cannot be the sole grantee, the grantor could convey the deed jointly to the grantor and another person or the grantor's corporation.

A deed is not operative as a valid conveyance until the grantee's name is inserted in it by the grantor personally, by someone at the grantor's request and in his or her presence, or by the grantor's agent duly authorized in writing.

Consideration: A deed should recite some consideration, although in most instances it need not be the actual consideration. Most deeds recite a nominal consideration, such as "for $10 and other good and valuable consideration." Deeds granted by fiduciaries, however, must state the actual consideration, and in all cases the contract of sale states the actual consideration. (*See CONSIDERATION.*)

Words of conveyance: There must be words of conveyance, such as, "I hereby grant and convey." The deed can thus be distinguished from a mortgage instrument. (*See MORTGAGE.*)

Legal description: There must be a legal description of the land conveyed, either by metes and bounds, by lot, block, and subdivision, or by a government survey description. In a condominium deed, however, the apartment designation and post office address is generally sufficient because the full legal description is already recited in the recorded declaration. Note that if the deed attempts to convey more property that the seller actually owns (through an incorrect legal description), the deed is not void but is usually valid for that portion of the description actually owned by the grantor.

Signature: The grantor must sign the deed. If the grantee is assuming an existing mortgage or is agreeing to abide by a restrictive provision in the deed, then the grantee also must be required to sign. In some states, the signature must be witnessed and/or notarized. A date of execution is not essential but is customary and tends to establish the date of delivery.

Delivery: A deed must be delivered to be valid. Delivery is the final act of the grantor, signifying an intention that the deed shall currently take effect. However, when transferring Torrens registered property, it is the registration of the deed and not the act of delivery which conveys title.

Upon valid delivery of the deed by the grantor and acceptance by the grantee, title passes and the deed ceases to be an operative instrument. Thereafter, in law, it is merely evidence of a conveyance of title and thus, its loss or destruction does not adversely affect the grantee's title.

Delivery must be made during the lifetime of the grantor and grantee. Assume, for example, that a grantor entered the hospital and delivered a deed to his brother saying, "The property is yours in case I die" (as opposed to "when I die"). In this case, there is no delivery since the grantor's intent is to keep the title to the property should he live.

The delivered deed must be accepted by the grantee. This requirement is often presumed by the courts where beneficial to the grantee (called "constructive acceptance"); as in cases of a beneficial conveyance to a person incapable of consenting, such as a deed to a minor or an incompetent person. The acceptance can be presumed by the grantee retaining the deed, recording the deed, encumbering the title, or any other act of ownership.

The destruction of a deed normally has no effect on the deed since the deed is simply evidence of the title, it is not the title itself. Therefore, title cannot be re-invested in the grantor by the grantee destroying the deed even with the intent to restore the grantor's original title. (*See DELIVERY.*)

Though not essential for validity, a deed is normally recorded to protect the grantee against claims of any third party. To be validly recorded, a deed must be properly recorded in the chain of title. (*See ACCEPTANCE, CHAIN OF TITLE, CORRECTION DEED, COVENANT, GIFT DEED, INDENTURE DEED, MERGER, QUITCLAIM DEED, RECORDING, WARRANTY DEED.*)

DEED IN LIEU OF FORECLOSURE A deed to a lender given by an owner conveying mortgaged property in which the mortgage is in default. It is an alternative to a foreclosure action. Its main disadvantage to a lender is that the deed does not wipe out junior liens, as a foreclosure action would. (*See FORECLOSURE.*)

DEED IN TRUST A form of deed by which real estate is conveyed to a trustee, usually to establish a land trust. Under the terms of such an instrument, full powers to sell, contract to sell, mortgage, and subdivide are granted to the trustee. The trustee's use of these powers, however, is controlled by the beneficiary under the provisions of the trust agreement. Deeds in trust are used in those states that recognize land trusts. (*See LAND TRUST.*)

DEED OF RECONVEYANCE A document used to transfer legal title from the trustee back to the borrower (trustor) after a debt secured by a deed of trust has been paid. (*See DEED OF TRUST.*)

DEED OF TRUST A legal document in which title to property is transferred to a third-party trustee as security for an obligation owed by the trustor (borrower) to the beneficiary (lender). A deed of trust is similar to a mortgage—the main difference is that it involves three parties. In some states such as California, a judicial foreclosure proceeding is avoided when the trustee can sell the property under a power of sale after allowing the trustor a legally prescribed period of time to reinstate the delinquent loan. In some states, the borrower-trustor is given a short period of time, such as three months, in which he or she can pay back the amount due plus a reinstatement fee (one-half of one percent of the unpaid balance) and reinstate the loan. Thus, the trustee can't accelerate the entire note immediately upon the trustor's default, but must wait the statutory period.

When a borrower repays the note secured by a deed of trust, the trustee must reconvey title back to the borrower by way of a deed of reconveyance, also called a *release deed*. A deed of trust is also called a *trust deed*. (*See MORTGAGE.*)

Lenders in many states prefer to make residential property loans under a trust deed because: (1) in states that permit it, a trustee may be given the power to sell property after default without going through the time-consuming judicial foreclosure process; (2) the statute of limitations may bar an action on the note in a mortgage transaction; however, this is not so with a deed of trust containing a power of sale, since the trustee has legal title and thus can sell the property at any time to pay off the debt; (3) deeds of trust can be used to secure more than one note; (4) the lender need not be named in the deed of trust in the event he or she wishes to remain anonymous; and (5) there is usually no statutory right of redemption after the sale under the power of sale.

One disadvantage to naming a noninstitutional trustee under a deed of trust is that problems sometimes arise in locating such trustee to obtain a reconveyance after the debt has been paid. The preferred practice is to name a corporate trustee in the document.

The deed of trust is not really another method of financing; rather, it is an alternative to the mortgage document as a security device. In some states, a deed of trust may still be legally enforceable even though there is no promissory note; this is not true of a mortgage.

DEED POLL

A deed signed by only the grantor. In ancient practice, such a deed had a clean-shaven edge, whereas an indenture deed, signed by both grantor and grantee, had a wavy or indented edge and could be proven by matching up the edges of both copies. The deed poll (like a lease) binds the grantee upon acceptance to any covenants of the grantee contained in such deed, even though the deed is not signed by the grantee. In this sense, it is an exception to the Statute of Frauds. (*See INDENTURE DEED.*)

DEFAULT

The nonperformance of a duty or obligation that is part of a contract. The common occurrence of default on the part of a buyer or lessee is nonpayment of money when due. A default is normally a breach of contract and the nondefaulting party can seek legal remedies to recover his or her loss. Defaults in long-term leases or contracts for deed other than nonpayment might be failure to renew insurance policies, failure to pay real estate taxes, damaging the property, and so forth.

Note that a buyer's good faith inability to obtain financing under a contingency provision of a purchase agreement is not considered a default (the performance of the contract depends on the buyer getting the property financed), and in this case the seller must return the buyer's deposit.

Junior mortgages usually contain a clause authorizing the holder of the junior mortgage to advance money to cure any default of the mortgagor under a prior mortgage. Were the first mortgage to remain in default and the lender to foreclose, it would have the effect of wiping out the junior mortgage. (*See JUNIOR MORT-GAGE, NOTICE OF DEFAULT.*)

DEFAULT JUDGMENT

A court order in favor of the plaintiff resulting from the defendant's failure to answer a complaint or appear in court to defend the action.

DEFEASANCE CLAUSE

A clause used in leases and mortgages to defeat or cancel a certain right upon the happening of a specified condition. A defeasance clause typically found in mortgages provides that if the borrower repays the debt when due (by the "law day"), then the words of grant are void and the mortgage is thereby cancelled, divesting the mortgagee of title and reinvesting title in the mortgagor. Automatic defeasance was important under the common law and in title theory states where title is transferred under a mortgage. Note that a satisfaction, reconveyance, or release deed must generally be obtained and recorded to clear the lien of a paid mortgage or trust deed debt from the record title.

A document that the parties call a deed or sale-leaseback might be treated by the courts as actually being a mortgage if it contains a defeasance clause permitting reconveyance back to the grantor upon full satisfaction of a debt.

DEFEASIBLE FEE SIMPLE See *FEE SIMPLE DEFEASIBLE.*

DEFECT OF RECORD Any encumbrance on a title that is made a part of the public record. Recorded defects include judgments, deeds of trust, mortgages, other liens, and easements. (*See CLEAR TITLE.*)

DEFENDANT The person being sued by the plaintiff in a lawsuit; the person charged with the wrong and from whom recovery is sought. (*See RESPONDENT.*)

DEFERRED COMMISSION A commission that has been earned but not yet fully paid; also called residuals.

A salesperson may not ordinarily receive compensation from anyone other than his or her present employer. In the case of deferred commissions from a previous employer, however, the salesperson may usually receive such commissions direct from his or her former employing broker. A cash-basis taxpayer/salesperson would not have to pay income tax on the amount earned until he or she actually receives it.

Often commissions are deferred in situations in which not enough cash has been received by the seller in an installment sale. For example, in the sale of a condominium to be constructed, the broker may receive part of the commission from the down payment and the remainder when the project is completed and the buyer pays in full and receives title.

DEFERRED MAINTENANCE Physical depreciation or loss in value of a building resulting from postponed maintenance to the building. This type of depreciation is normally curable by making the necessary repairs and improvements. It is sometimes called curable physical depreciation.

A prospective purchaser of a building in which there is a significant amount of deferred maintenance should be especially careful to compute the estimated repair and replacement costs into an investment analysis of the property.

DEFERRED-PAYMENT METHOD An accounting method of reporting taxable income on a deferred basis, also called the cost-recovery method or the return-of-capital method. Under the deferred payment method, no gain is taxed to the seller until payments received from the buyer exceed the basis of the property and the cost of sale. This method can be used only in those cases in which the seller receives part of the sales price in the year of the sale, but the balance of the payment is not evidenced by any promissory note having a fair market value. While use of this method can defer part of the gain, one disadvantage of the method is that the taxpayer will not be able to have capital gain tax treatment on the deferred portion. The benefits of this method were lessened when the IRS eliminated the 30 percent ceiling on installment sale reporting. (*See INSTALLMENT SALE.*)

DEFICIENCY   A judgment against a borrower, endorser, or guar-
JUDGMENT   antor for the balance of a debt owed when the se-
                    curity for a loan is insufficient to satisfy the debt.
A deficiency occurs when the foreclosure sale of a property produces less than the
amount needed to pay the costs and expenses of the action and to satisfy the
obligation secured by the foreclosed mortgage. For such deficiency, a personal
judgment is entered against the original mortgagor. This judgment operates as a
lien on the judgment debtor's assets and is enforceable and collectible in the same
manner as any judgment at law. If this judgment proves to be uncollectible, the
lender is probably entitled to claim a bad debt deduction on the lender's income
taxes. In the case of a corporate mortgage, this would be a bad business debt and
may fully offset against ordinary income.

In those states where mortgages generally carry a power of sale, creditors must
bring a separate action to obtain a deficiency judgment because the jurisdiction of
a court is not invoked. The parties can agree that the lender can look only to the
collateral (the mortgaged property) in the event of a default. To accomplish this,
the parties place in the note language to the effect that "this note is without recourse," which has the effect of preventing a deficiency judgment. In California
and a few other states, the mortgagee cannot recover a deficiency judgment on a
purchase money mortgage; these states have enacted so-called antideficiency legislation.

Note that deficiency judgments are not allowed in connection with foreclosed
FHA mortgages and are frowned upon by the VA.

If a purchaser assumes the seller's existing mortgage, the purchaser thereby becomes personally liable (along with the seller) for any deficiency. However, when
the purchaser buys the property "subject to" the existing mortgage, he or she
cannot be held personally liable for any deficiency; thus, upon default, the purchaser's liability would extend only to the loss of the property. (*See DRY MORT-
GAGE, FORECLOSURE, JUDGMENT LIEN, POWER OF SALE.*)

DEFLATED   A mortgage in which the parties agree to reduce
MORTGAGE   the amount of the principal debt and increase the
                    interest rate. In this way, the seller receives the
same amount of dollars but the buyer obtains a greater interest deduction.

DEGREE   A surveying term meaning 1/360th part of a full
                    rotation about a point in a plane. (*See ANGLE.*)

DELAYED   Refers to an attempt to qualify a real estate trans-
EXCHANGE   action as an IRC Section 1031 exchange where the
                    "exchange" of the properties is not simultaneous.
As a result of a limited number of federal court rulings, (the "Starker" cases), some
tax practitioners set up elaborate procedures to put the sales proceeds in a trust to
be used to purchase properties in the future. Subsequent cases and tax rulings
have severely restricted the effective use of the delayed exchange and have reas-
serted the requirement of simultaneous transactions. (*See EXCHANGE.*)

DELIVERY   The legal act of transferring ownership. Docu-
                    ments such as deeds and mortgages must be de-
livered and accepted before becoming valid. Legal delivery does not refer to the
act of manually transferring the document; rather, it refers to the *intention* of the

grantor. The grantor must intend that the deed be currently operative and effective to transfer title to the grantee, and intend that the grantee become the legal owner. For example, a grantor may voluntarily hand over a deed to a grantee only for review by the grantee's attorney. This would not be a valid delivery since the grantor did not have the intention to relinquish all control over the deed. To be a legal delivery, the grantor must have been competent, not only at the time of signing and acknowledging the deed, but also at the time of its delivery.

If this requisite intention is present, there is a valid delivery of the deed even though the grantee's right to possession and enjoyment of the property may be deferred to a future date—delivery need not be physical or direct. Thus, when the deed is given to a third person by the grantor with instructions to give it to the grantee upon satisfaction of a condition which is certain to occur, there is an effective delivery and the third person holds the deed as agent for the grantee. For instance, when Sam Dunphy gives a deed to an escrow agent with instructions to deliver it to Elmer Key "when I die," with no other conditions being imposed on the delivery, then it is a valid delivery and effectively transfers title to Elmer Key with possession and enjoyment delayed until Sam Dunphy's death. But if Sam had instructed the agent to give the deed to Elmer "in case I die," then there would be no valid delivery since Sam did not intend a present transfer of title. When the grantor makes a constructive delivery to a third person, the grantor must relinquish all control over the deed—otherwise there is no effective delivery. There is no valid delivery upon an unauthorized delivery by an escrow agent prior to full performance of the stated escrow conditions.

Once there is a valid delivery and acceptance, the act of the grantee in surrendering the property or the deed will not put title back in the original grantor. To accomplish this, the grantee must execute a new deed back to the original grantor.

While a deed does not generally have to be recorded to be valid, some states provide that the settlement agent shall not close a transaction and disburse the proceeds of sale until the deed (or assignment of lease or contract for deed, if applicable) is recorded. Thus, the transaction is finally closed *after* the time title technically has passed to the buyer. Title to Torrens registered property, however, is not transferred upon delivery of the deed. It is transferred only upon registration of the deed on the certificate of title with the registrar of titles and the issuance of a transfer certificate of title to the new owner.

A deed is presumed to have been delivered if the deed is found in the possession of the grantee or if the deed is recorded. Conversely, a deed still in the possession of the grantor is presumed not to have been delivered, although these presumptions may be rebutted. This issue sometimes arises when the grantor intends immediate transfer of title yet does not want the transfer made public at the time of transfer. The grantor thus will request that the grantee delay recordation until after the grantor's death.

Historically, title to real property was transferred by *livery of seisin*, the act of giving possession of the property to the grantee. This act was sometimes symbolized by the grantor's standing on the property and handing the grantee a twig or a handful of earth. Sometimes a witness recorded the act on a document. Today, the transferring of possession is represented by delivery of the document reflecting the grantor's intent to transfer title to the property. (*See ACCEPTANCE, DEED, ESCROW.*)

DEMAND   1. A letter from a creditor requesting payment of the amount due, as in a loan or lease. 2. The quantity of economic goods that can be bought at a certain price, in a given market, at a particular time; what the marketplace will demand. Effective demand is the desire to buy coupled with the ability to pay. Demand is an essential element of value.

DEMISE   A conveyance of an estate or interest in real property to someone for a certain number of years, for life, or at will—most commonly for years, as in a lease. A lease often refers to the "demised premises." The use of the word demise often implies a covenant of quiet enjoyment by which the lessor undertakes to guarantee that the lessee will not be disturbed in the lessee's use of the premises by superior claims of others. A synonym for the term "let" in a lease.

DEMISING WALL   A partition or dividing wall found in a building housing two or more tenants, separating the area leased by one party from that leased by others.

DEMOGRAPHY   The statistical study of human populations, especially in reference to size, density, and distribution. Demographic information is useful in evaluating commercial locations, or shopping center sites.

DEMOLITION LOSS   1. A loss in value due to physical destruction of the premises. Generally, a loss due to the voluntary demolition of a building is deductible as an ordinary loss. However, if an owner purchases the property with the intent of demolishing the existing building, the demolition loss is not an ordinary loss but a cost that must be allocated to the basis of the land. In addition, the cost of demolishing a certified historic structure cannot be deducted—such costs must be treated as additional land cost.

2. Some leases contain a clause that gives the lessor the right to cancel the lease upon proper notice in the event that the lessor chooses to demolish the building. The clause is usually required only by owners of older buildings who want to leave their option open for new construction at some indefinite future date.

DENSITY   When used in connection with zoning requirements, a term meaning the number of building units per acre or the number of occupants or families per unit of land area (acre, square mile); usually the ratio of land area to improvement area. For example, if a parcel of real property were zoned R-10, the maximum density per net usable acre would be 10 units. (See *FLOOR AREA RATIO, LAND-USE INTENSITY.*)

DENSITY ZONING   A type of zoning ordinance, generallly associated with subdivisions, that restricts the average maximum number of houses per acre that may be built within a particular subdivision. For example, if a subdivision were zoned at a 15,000 square-foot-lot-minimum, the developer could build only 2.5 houses per acre. On the other hand, if the area is density zoned at an *average maximum* 2.5 houses per acre, the developer is free to achieve an open, clustered effect by slightly reducing the individual lot sizes. Regardless of lot size or the number of units clustered, the subdivider will be in compliance with the ordinance as long as the average number of units in the development remains at or below the maximum density. This average is called *gross density.*

Developers often try to work closely with zoning officials to develop ordinances and standards most beneficial to living comfort and aesthetic values.

DEPARTMENT OF HOUSING AND URBAN DEVELOPMENT (HUD)   *See HUD.*

DEPLETION   Reduction in size or quantity. The exhaustion of an asset, such as gas, oil, mineral oil, or timber-producing real estate. Depletion may be deducted in certain mineral programs, and thereby provides attractive tax-shelter benefits.

DEPOSIT   Money offered by a prospective buyer as an indication of good faith in entering into a contract to purchase; earnest money; security for the buyer's performance of a contract. An earnest money deposit is not necessary to create a valid purchase contract because the mutual promises of the parties to buy and to sell are sufficient consideration to enforce the contract. If the buyer completes the purchase, the deposit money is applied toward the purchase price. If the buyer defaults, the contract may provide that the seller can retain the deposit money as liquidated damages. Contracts also often require the seller to split the deposit money with the broker, up to an amount not exceeding the broker's commission (per the terms of the listing or the contract of sale). If the seller defaults, the deposit should be returned in full to the buyer.

For protection, the seller should require a deposit large enough to cover the broker's commission, the cost of the title search, and the loss of time and opportunity to sell elsewhere. A deposit of 10 percent of the purchase price should be adequate. If the seller requires too substantial a deposit, however, a defaulting buyer might seek a return of part of it, claiming that the deposit did not accurately serve as liquidated damages, but rather as a forfeiture or penalty. Some states set a standard such as three percent; if the deposit exceeds that amount, the seller has the burden of proving that the deposit was, in fact, reasonable and not a penalty.

If the deposit involves a large amount of money, it is good practice to provide that the deposit be placed in an interest-bearing account for the buyer's benefit.

The buyer should be careful to make sure there are sufficient funds to cover the deposit check. If the deposit check bounces, the seller could try to terminate the contract by arguing that no valid contract exists, since the seller's acceptance is conditional on receiving a proper deposit.

The question, "who owns the deposit," sometimes arises. If the seller authorizes the broker to accept deposit money on his or her behalf, the deposit money belongs to the seller when the broker accepts it. In some states, the deposit money must be placed in a neutral escrow and cannot be withdrawn until the transaction is consummated. It never belongs to the broker, although the broker may share in the deposit money if the buyer defaults and the seller retains the deposit as liquidated damages. Consider the situation where the broker absconds with the deposit money. If the seller has not authorized the broker to accept the deposit money, the broker is acting as the buyer's agent in handling the money until such time as the seller accepts the buyer's offer to purchase. Thus the buyer would suffer the loss if the broker were to steal the money. On the other hand, if the seller had authorized the broker to accept the deposit, the seller would suffer the loss. Such authoriza-

tion is specifically contained in many exclusive-right-to-sell listing contracts. (*See
ADDITIONAL DEPOSIT, EARNEST MONEY, ELECTION OF REMEDIES, LIQUI-
DATED DAMAGES, SECURITY DEPOSIT.*)

DEPOSITION   The formal testimony made by a witness or a
party to a lawsuit (the deponent) prior to the trial.
Any party may take the testimony of any other person in a deposition by using an
oral examination or written questions (called "interrogatories") for the purpose of
discovery (ascertaining evidence) or use as evidence, for preserving testimony in
the legal action, or both.

DEPRECIABLE LIFE   The time period over which cost recovery of an
asset is to be allocated. For tax returns, deprecia-
ble life may be shorter than estimated service life. (*See DEPRECIATION [TAX]*).

DEPRECIABLE REAL   Depreciable property must be of a type that is sub-
PROPERTY   ject to wear and tear, and must be property used
in a trade or business, or held for the production
of income. Consequently, land and the taxpayer's personal residence are not depreciable. If the taxpayer uses part of his or her residence for business purposes, a
pro rata depreciation deduction can be taken for that allocated use. (However, the
latest tax act has imposed stringent requirements on the business purpose deduction.)

It is not essential that the property actually produce income; it is usually sufficient
that the property is held with the expectation of producing income or making a
profit. However, if a property is determined to be a "hobby," the depreciation of it
will be limited. Only improvements to real property can be depreciated, such as
buildings, sidewalks, and fences. Although depreciation deductions have now
been replaced with "cost recovery," this latter deduction is still limited to depreciable property, and the depreciable portion thereof. (*See COST RECOVERY, DE-
PRECIATION [TAX], VACATION HOME.*)

DEPRECIATION   The accounting charge made to allow for the fact
ALLOWANCE   that the asset may become economically obsolete
before its physical deterioration. The purpose is
to write off the original cost by distributing it over the estimated useful life of the
asset. It appears in both the profit and loss statement and the balance sheet. [*See
COST RECOVERY, DEPRECIATION (TAX).*]

DEPRECIATION   A loss in value due to any cause; any condition
(APPRAISAL)   that adversely affects the value of an improvement. For appraisal purposes, depreciation is di-
vided into three classes according to its cause: physical deterioration, functional
obsolescence, and economic obsolescence. The most common method of measuring depreciation was once the straight-line method, but today most appraisers use
the *breakdown method* in which depreciation is broken down into all three
classes with each class measured separately, whether such depreciation is curable
or incurable.

Physical deterioration of an improvement is indicated by decay or disintegration,
cracks, wear and tear, settling of foundations, structural defects, actions of the
elements, any loss of physical soundness, and termite damage.

Functional obsolescence (inside property lines) is indicated by obsolete boilers, ancient plumbing, unnecessarily high ceilings, out-of-date lighting fixtures, and out-moded architecture.

Economic obsolescence (outside property lines) is indicated by population decreases, incongruous uses of property, legislative action (city, state, and national), changes in a neighborhood, and invasion of other conditions that lower values.

Accrued depreciation, also called *past depreciation*, is depreciation existing as of the date of appraisal. In contrast, *future depreciation* is an estimation of the loss in value that is likely to occur in the future.

Because of depreciation factors, it isn't likely that any two properties will be valued exactly alike. Assume, for example, that two buildings were constructed at the same time, using similar materials. After two years, the properties would have different values due to the independent effect of depreciation forces on the separate buildings; for example, one of the buildings may now have termites. (*See APPRAISAL, COST APPROACH.*)

DEPRECIATION (TAX)

For income tax purposes, depreciation is an expense deduction taken for an investment in depreciable property to allow for the recovery of the cost of the investment. It can occur even when the market value of a property increases. (Non-income-producing property, such as a personal residence, cannot be depreciated.)

The annual amount of the depreciation deduction results from an arbitrary apportionment of the investment in the building systematically spread over its useful life. Thus, tax depreciation is a statutory concept that occurs even though the property itself may have actually appreciated in value. Land is not depreciable (although the cost of landscaping may be depreciated in certain cases). Therefore, there must be an allocation of basis between the land and the building. Most taxpayers use the allocation as set by the state tax assessor.

Prior to the Economic Recovery Act of 1981 the three main methods of computing depreciation were the straight-line method (equal annual installments); the declining-balance method (up to double straight-line); and the sum-of-the-years'-digits method (rate is a fraction in which the numerator is the property's remaining useful life at the start of the tax year, and the denominator being the sum of all the years' digits corresponding to the estimated useful life at acquisition). (*See DECLINING-BALANCE METHOD, STRAIGHT-LINE METHOD, SUM-OF-THE-YEARS'-DIGITS METHOD.*)

The 1981 Tax Act established one uniform method of depreciation for an asset acquired after 1980. (*See ACCELERATED COST RECOVERY SYSTEM.*)

Pre-1981 personal property, such as the furniture in a furnished rental apartment, can receive special first-year depreciation treatment if the taxpayer so elects, and if the property has a useful life of six years or more. This additional depreciation deduction is 20 percent of the original cost of the property, up to a total investment of $10,000 for an individual return, or a total investment of $20,000 for a joint return. The maximum deduction is thus $2,000 for an individual and $4,000 for a joint return, and this amount may be taken **in addition** to normal depreciation allowable for the property.

If the taxpayer does not take depreciation, the Internal Revenue Service will compute the allowable straight-line depreciation for the taxpayer and apply it to reduce the basis upon the sale of the property. The taxpayer who is entitled to take the depreciation deduction is the one who suffers the economic loss due to the decrease in value. Usually this is the owner, though bare legal title alone is not sufficient. For example, a life tenant is entitled to the deduction as if he or she were the absolute owner of the property. When the life tenant dies, the depreciation deduction, if any, passes to the remainderman. (*See ACCELERATED DEPRECIATION, BASIS, COMPONENT DEPRECIATION, COST RECOVERY, DEPRECIABLE REAL PROPERTY, RECAPTURE OF DEPRECIATION, USEFUL LIFE.*)

DEPTH TABLES   Tables of percentage used by appraisers and assessors to provide a uniform system of measuring the additional value to lots, which value accrues because of added depth, with the extra depth valued according to the added utility that it creates (called "depth influence."). Depth tables are used by tax assessors seeking to achieve uniformity in assessment practices. One of the earliest depth tables established was the "4-3-2-1 rule," which provided that the front quarter of the lot holds 40 percent of the value; the second, 30 percent; the third, 20 percent; and the fourth, 10 percent. This rule has been recently expanded to provide percentages for each few feet of the lot.

DERAIGN   To prove ownership of land; to trace title.

DESCENT   The acquisition of an estate by inheritance when an heir succeeds to the property by operation of law. Descent literally means the hereditary succession of an heir to the property of an ancestor who dies intestate.

Rights under laws of descent vary from state to state. The law of the state in which the property is located will not only prescribe the persons to inherit the property, but will also provide the respective shares each is to receive. When a person dies leaving a spouse and one child, the spouse and child usually take the entire estate between them—some states dividing it equally and some allowing only one-third to the surviving spouse. If, however, a spouse and two or more children survive, it is customary for the spouse to take one-third and the children to divide the remaining two-thirds equally among them. If a spouse but no children or descendants of the children exist, some state laws give the spouse one-half of the estate and the other half is divided equally among collateral heirs, such as parents, brothers, and sisters of the decedent; in some states, however, the surviving spouse would take all.

All states make provisions for adopted children. When they have been legally adopted, they are usually considered heirs of the adopting parents, but will not be considered heirs of ancestors of the adopting parents.

In most states, illegitimate children inherit from the mother, but not from the father unless he has admitted parentage in writing, or parentage has been established legally. Of course, if he legally adopts such a child, that child will inherit as an adopted child. State law should be consulted. (*See CURTESY, DOWER, ELECTIVE SHARE, INTESTATE, PROBATE.*)

DESCRIPTION   The portion of a conveyance document that defines the property being transferred. In order to be valid, documents such as deeds, assignments of leases, certain leases, and mortgages must contain a full legal description of the property to be conveyed. Usually a contract for the sale of real property need only contain a description sufficient to identify the property, such as street address and/or tax map key number.

In a deed, the description is normally divided into two parts: the general and the specific descriptions. The general description usually identifies the parcel in question by location, name, or reference to previous known owners. It leads into the specific description with the phrase "more particularly described as follows," or by reference to public maps, plats, or other recorded information.

The specific description exactly defines the limits of the property involved. These limits may be defined by one (or any combination) of three basic methods of real estate description: metes and bounds, government (rectangular) survey, and subdivision plat.

Great care must be exercised to avoid ambiguities. For example, the "next contiguous 40 acres" is ambiguous because an acre can have any shape; the "south one-half of the farm" is adequate if the lot is rectangular but not if it is irregular.

Some contracts for large, bulk real estate sales include what are known as *Mother Hubbard clauses*. These clauses state that the description includes all property owned by the seller at the location or, if appropriate, all real estate owned by the seller in that particular area. (*See GOVERNMENT SURVEY METHOD, LEGAL DESCRIPTION, METES AND BOUNDS, PLAT.*)

DETERMINABLE FEE   *See FEE SIMPLE DETERMINABLE.*

DEVELOPER   One who attempts to put land to its most profitable use through the construction of improvements, such as commercial condominiums or subdivision projects. The developer organizes and supervises the entire project, usually from the acquisition of land all the way through construction and final sales, and sometimes continuing with the maintenance of the project. While the developer's financial rewards are sometimes substantial, the risks are also high. All aspects of development are becoming so specialized and highly technical that developers frequently retain consultants, such as construction and finance experts, to assist them throughout the various stages of development. (*See ENTREPRENEUR.*)

DEVELOPMENT IMPACT FEE   An amount of money charged a developer by a local governmental body to cover the costs of providing essential services to the proposed project, such as fire and police protection, and road maintenance.

DEVELOPMENT LOAN   A loan to cover the costs of improving property; an interim loan. In a typical case, a subdivider acquiring land seeks financing to cover the costs of both on-site and off-site improvements (site preparation, roads, sewer, water, drainage) to bring the individual lots up to a standard so they can be profitably marketed. Often the development loan will specify a schedule of partial releases to permit individual lots to be sold free and clear from the lien of the loan. Development loans on large subdivisions are often structured in phases to match the incremental development of the project.

DEVELOPMENT RIGHTS   The rights a landowner sells to another to develop and improve the property. In some areas, where residential units are to be built on land to be leased at economic or market levels, development rights are the premium paid by the developer for the privilege of improving the property and bringing the future seller and the landowner together to create the leasehold estate. Sometimes only the development rights themselves are sold, and, after the improvements are built and sold, the purchasers lease the land directly from the landowner. Often the developer purchases a master lease in conjunction with the development rights and then subleases the improved lots to the ultimate purchasers. Development rights may be sold by the developer to a subdeveloper, provided the landowner consents to such assignment. (See *TRANSFER OF DEVELOPMENT RIGHTS*.)

DEVISE   A transfer of real property under a will. The donor is the *devisor* and the recipient is the *devisee*. When there is no will, the real property *descends* to the heirs. In some states, a deed is not required to transfer property by devise because the will acts as the instrument of conveyance upon the donor's death. (See *BEQUEATH, DESCENT*.)

DIFFUSED SURFACE WATERS   Those waters that come from rain, snow, or underground springs and are diffused over the surface of the ground.

DILUVION   The gradual and imperceptible washing away and resultant loss of soil along a watercourse; opposite of alluvion.

DIRECTIONAL GROWTH   The direction or location toward which a community appears destined to grow. This directional growth is considered in mortgage underwriting and appraisal because it plays a role in determining the present and future value of real estate.

DIRECT PARTICIPATION PROGRAM LICENSES   National Association of Securities Dealers (NASD) licenses issued on a national basis for securities salespeople selling real estate securities (such as resort condominiums with rental pools) and tax shelters in programs providing a direct "pass-through" of tax benefits (limited partnerships, REITs, but not stock in ordinary corporations). The two types of licenses are the Limited Representative License and the Limited Principal's License. Developed through the cooperation of the National Association of Securities Dealers (NASD) and Real Estate Securities and Syndication Institute (RESSI).

DIRECT REDUCTION MORTGAGE   A mortgage that requires payment of a fixed amount of principal each period (loan recapture). The total payment will vary, as the interest portion will reduce with each payment. Most likely found in financing between private parties.

Under the direct reduction payment plan, the mortgagor is able to easily calculate how much has been paid on the principal since this amount remains the same each month. What varies is the amount applying to interest. Thus, in the early years of the loan, the combined monthly principal and interest payments are larger than in a constant or level mortgage payment plan.

DISBURSEMENT   Money paid out, or expended, in an accounting process such as an escrow closing. Disbursements may be entered as a credit on the closing statement such as when the net proceeds of sale are disbursed to the seller, or as a debit, as when attorney's fees or title search are paid. Other examples of disbursements are construction loan draws and advances.

DISCHARGE OF CONTRACT   Cancellation or termination of a contract. Some of the common grounds in which the obligations of a contract may be discharged are: mutual cancellation; rescission; performance or nonperformance; accord and satisfaction; illegality; and, in certain circumstances, to the extent a court will not enforce the contract, by the Statute of Limitations, the Statute of Frauds, and the Bankruptcy Act. There is no discharge in the event of a breach of contract, but there are remedies to the nonbreaching party.

DISCLAIMER   A statement denying legal responsibility, frequently found in the form of the statement, "There are no promises, representations, oral understandings, or agreements except as contained herein." Such a statement, however, would not relieve the maker of any liabilities for fraudulent acts or misrepresentations. Also called an *exoneration clause* or *exculpatory clause*. A common disclaimer found in brokers' information fact sheets is this: "The information contained on this fact sheet is taken from sources deemed reliable. However, we cannot guaranty the accuracy of such information." Note that this type of disclaimer may be effective to protect one against an innocent misstatement of fact but will not protect one from making an intentionally false statement. (*See EXCULPATORY CLAUSE.*)

DISCLOSURE STATEMENT   An information report required under the Federal Truth-in-Lending law to be given consumer borrowers by creditors. State statutes often require disclosure reports in condominium, time sharing, and subdivision sales. (*See TRUTH-IN-LENDING.*)

DISCOUNT   To sell at a reduced value; the difference between face value and cash value. There are companies that specialize in buying mortgages and real estate contracts (often referred to as *paper*) at a discount. Often the original lender will want to cash out on the loan and will thus sell the mortgage at the current published mortgage discount rate. If the discount rate were 12 percent, for example, the lender could sell a $100,000 mortgage at 88 percent of its worth ($88,000 or 12 percent below par). Discounting any type of loan usually increases its effective yield to the lender and/or interest cost to the buyer.

In tight money situations, a developer seeking permanent takeout financing for a condominium project might have to "buy down" permanent mortgages at a set interest rate for purchasers of the units by paying a discount charge to the lender. For example, to get a lender to agree to provide the financing for individual purchasers at 14 percent interest, the developer may have to buy down the commitment by paying the lender a discount of five percent of the loan amount. There are conventional buydown and FNMA buydown programs. (*See BUYDOWN, END LOAN, ORIGINATION FEE, POINTS, TAKE-OUT FINANCING, USURY.*)

DISCOUNTED CASH FLOW   Used in measuring return from a real estate investment; it is the present value of a future income stream as determined by a given discount rate (using present value tables). This measure weighs dollars received early in the life of an investment more heavily than those received later. Two common methods are the internal rate of return method and the net present value method. Also known as present value analysis. (*See INTERNAL RATE OF RETURN, PRESENT VALUE.*)

DISCOUNT POINTS   An added loan fee charged by a lender to make the yield on a lower-than-market-interest VA or FHA loan competitive with higher interest conventional loans. One discount point is equal to one percent of the loan amount. By law, the buyer may not pay any discount points on an FHA or VA loan, although the buyer does usually pay a one percent origination fee. The amount of discount points is set by each individual lender and usually reflects the spread between the conventional rates and FHA/VA rates at the time the loan is made. Each point represents an approximate equivalent increase in the FHA/VA interest rate of 1/8 percent. For example, if a lender charges a discount of eight points on a $100,000 loan at 14 percent interest, this increases the lender's effective yield from 14 percent to 15 percent (1/8 × 8 = 1%). The entire discount fee is collected from the seller at the start of the loan. When interest rates go up, the number of discount points goes down. (*See POINTS.*)

DISCOUNTING   The appraisal process of mathematically computing the present worth estimate of a property based on an anticipated future income stream. (*See PRESENT VALUE OF ONE DOLLAR.*)

DISCRETIONARY FUNDS   Money available for investment; money in excess of that needed for basic needs.

DISCRIMINATION   The act of making a distinction against or in favor of a person on the basis of the group or class to which the person belongs; the failure to treat people equally. The Civil Rights Act of 1866 prohibits any discrimination based on race. In 1968, this act was upheld by the United States Supreme Court in the case of *Jones v. Alfred H. Mayer Company*, when the court ruled that the 1866 federal law "prohibits all racial discrimination, private and public, in the sale and rental of property."

The Federal Fair Housing Act, contained in Title VIII of the Civil Rights Act of 1968, took the 1866 law one step further, making it unlawful to discriminate on the basis of race, color, religion, sex, or national origin when selling or leasing residential property or vacant land for the construction of residential buildings.

The law lists various types of prohibited discriminatory practices but generally covers all prejudice in real estate transactions, including related financial practices.

Discrimination in financing transactions is further regulated under the Federal Equal Credit Opportunity Act.

However, it is not a violation of the law to discriminate in the following situations:

1. The sale or rental of single-family homes is exempted when the homes are owned by an individual who does not own more than three such homes at one time, even though he or she is not living in the dwelling at the time of the transaction or was not the most recent occupant (*only one such sale by an individual is exempt within any 24-month period*). Furthermore, the transaction must not involve a broker, salesperson, or agent, and discriminatory advertising cannot be used.

2. The rental of rooms or units in an owner-occupied building designed for four or fewer families.

3. Dwelling units owned by religious organizations and not operated commercially may be restricted to persons of the same religion if membership in the organization is not restricted on the basis of race, color, sex, or national origin.

4. A private club that is not in fact open to the public may restrict the rental or occupancy of lodgings that it owns to its members as long as the lodgings are not operated commercially.

The Federal Fair Housing Act of 1968 also prohibits "blockbusting" and "steering." Refer to each of these topics for more information.

The Act is administered by the Secretary of the Department of Housing and Urban Development. Any aggrieved person may file a complaint with the secretary or a delegate of the secretary within 180 days after a discriminatory act occurs. The secretary's efforts to resolve the dispute are limited to conference, conciliation, and persuasion. Several state and municipal fair housing laws have been ruled as "substantially equivalent" to the federal law. All complaints in that state or locality, including those filed with HUD, are referred to and handled by the state agencies.

An aggrieved party may also take the alleged violator to court, either U.S. District Court or a state court if the state's fair housing laws are substantially equivalent. Court actions may also be brought by the U.S. Attorney General in cases where accused violators of the federal law are engaged in a pattern of discrimination or practices that raise an issue of general public importance. Complaints brought under the Civil Rights Act of 1866 must be taken directly to a federal court.

Brokers as well as property owners are charged with upholding the discrimination law. A broker should inform his or her principal of the provisions of the discrimination law, and if the principal still insists on discrimination, the broker should terminate the agency.

Both FHA and VA regulations prohibit the use of discriminatory restrictive covenants by those participating in their respective loan programs. In addition, discriminatory restrictive provisions in deeds are not enforceable under the U.S. Supreme Court's decision in *Shelley v. Kraemer*.

The National Association of Realtors® and HUD and the Justice Department have created *affirmative marketing agreements* to assure minorities free and open access to housing via comprehensive, voluntary programs. NAR has adopted a Code for Equal Opportunity. The code includes suggested conduct for Realtors® belonging to member boards who have adopted it and who wish to comply with both the letter and the spirit of the fair housing laws. (*See BLOCKBUSTING, FEDERAL FAIR HOUSING LAW, STEERING.*)

DISINTERMEDIATION   The process of individuals investing their funds directly instead of placing their savings with banks, savings and loan associations, and similar institutions for investment by such institutions. This bypassing of financial institutions occurs when proportionately higher yields are available on secure investments (such as high-grade corporate bonds, money market funds, and government securities) than can be obtained on savings deposits. Disintermediation has a direct influence on the scarcity of mortgage money since diverted savings rarely find their way into mortgages.

DISPOSAL FIELD   A drainage area, not close to the water supply, where waste from a septic tank is dispersed. The waste is drained into the ground through tile and gravel.

DISPOSSESS PROCEEDINGS   Legal action to evict someone not legally in possession. (*See EVICTION, SUMMARY POSSESSION.*)

DISSEISIN   The ouster or wrongful dispossession of someone lawfully possessed of real property (one seized of a freehold).

DISTRAINT   The right of a landlord, pursuant to court order, to seize a tenant's belongings for rents in arrears. Also called *distress for rent due* or *landlord's warrant.* (*See ABANDONMENT.*)

DISTRESSED PROPERTY   Property that brings an insufficient return to the owner or is in difficulty for other reasons. Sometimes it is property that must be sold due to pending foreclosure or probate of an insolvent estate.

DIVIDED INTEREST   An interest in various parts of a whole property, such as the interest of the fee owner, lessee, or mortgagee.

DOCK-HIGH BUILDING   An industrial building in which the floor level of the main floor is constructed at a height sufficient to permit direct loading onto the beds of trucks parked at ground level outside.

DOCUMENTARY TAX STAMPS   A transfer tax in the form of stamps affixed to legal documents. Prior to 1968, the federal government imposed a documentary tax on real estate conveyance instruments such as deeds and mortgages. When the federal government repealed its tax, the states imposed their own conveyance or transfer tax. Most states now mark the amount of tax on the first page of the document rather than actually affix any stamps. (*See CONVEYANCE TAX.*)

DOCUMENTS   Legal instruments such as conveyancing documents (deeds, leases, and mortgages), contracts (options, exchange, and purchase agreements), and other legal forms (wills and bills of sale).

DOMICILE   The state where an individual has his or her true, fixed, permanent home and principal business establishment and where that person has the intention of returning whenever he or she is absent from it. Once established, a domicile is never lost until there is a concurrence of specific intent to abandon the old domicile, intent to acquire a specific new domicile, and actual physical presence in the new domicile. Though a person may have residences in different states and reside there at different times of the year, it is only possible to have one domicile. Since domicile consists of physical presence plus an intention to make the state one's permanent abode, such factors as local registration of autos, driver's license, voting, paying taxes, membership in local organizations, local bank accounts and local business interest are all important in establishing the requisite intent. *Domus* is the Latin word for house. (*See RESIDENCE.*)

DOMINANT ESTATE (TENEMENT)   The estate that is said to attach to and derive benefit from the servient estate in reference to an easement appurtenant; as where an easement road passes over an owner's land (the servient estate) to give access to an adjacent parcel (the dominant estate). The dominant estate usually adjoins the servient estate. (*See EASEMENT, EASEMENT IN GROSS.*)

DONOR   One who gives or makes a gift. The recipient of the gift is called the donee. (*See GIFT TAX.*)

DOORSTOP   A device attached to the wall or floor to prevent a door from opening too far and damaging the wall.

DORMER   A projection built out from the slope of a roof, used to house windows on the upper floor and to provide additional headroom. Common types of dormers are the gable dormer and the shed dormer.

DOUBLE CORNER STUD   Two vertical studs joined at right angles to form the corner of the frame. The double studs are heavier than regular studs and give greater support.

DOUBLE-DECLINING BALANCE   See *DECLINING-BALANCE METHOD.*

DOUBLE ENTRY   In reference to a settlement or closing statement, it is the practice of entering a dollar amount as both a debit entry and a credit entry. For example, taxes paid in arrears would be prorated and appear as a credit to the buyer and a debit to the seller.

DOUBLE ESCROW   A situation in which the seller attempts to use the buyer's money to acquire title to property "X" from the owner in one escrow in order to be able to convey title to property "X" to the buyer in the second escrow. A real estate licensee is under a duty to fully disclose to his or her principal that the buyer's funds in the second escrow are being used to complete the seller's purchase in the first escrow, usually at a profit.

For example, assume a seller had a contract in escrow to purchase certain property for $40,000. The seller then contracted to sell the same property for $50,000, the buyer put down $5,000 as a deposit, and a second escrow was set up. The seller expected to use the buyer's money to acquire title in the first escrow and simultaneously transfer title to the buyer in the second escrow. When the buyer failed to put the balance of the purchase price in escrow, the seller was forced to default on the original $40,000 contract. The buyer asked for return of the $5,000 deposit and a court held that since the seller was unable to place the deed in escrow, the seller was also in default and could not hold the buyer's deposit because, "in a contract for the sale of real estate, the delivery of the deed and the payment of the purchase price are dependent and concurrent conditions. Neither party could place the other in default unless he was able to perform or tender performance." (See BACK-TO-BACK ESCROW, ESCROW.)

DOUBLE-LOAD CORRIDOR   A building term used to describe a design in which apartment units are located on both sides of a corridor, as in many hotels. As one walks down the corridor, there are units on both sides, as opposed to a single-load corridor, which has units on only one side.

DOUBLE PLATE   Two horizontal boards on top of and connecting the studs. The plate serves as a foundation for the rafters.

DOUBLE TAXATION   Paying income tax at the corporate level and then paying another tax on the same income at the personal level. This term is often used in connection with the tax aspects of an ordinary corporation. Under the corporate form of ownership, income is subject to a double tax; i.e., the corporation must pay a corporate income tax on its earnings and a shareholder must pay a second tax when he or she draws earnings out of the corporation in the form of dividends. One method of avoiding this double taxation is by passing on earnings to key employees in the form of large (but reasonable) salaries. However, a corporation must be careful not to pay excessive compensation to employees because if the IRS determines that the compensation to stockholder-employee is excessive, it will treat such excess as a dividend and thus not deductible to the corporation and thus taxable to both the corporation and the stockholder-employee.

Subchapter S corporations, Real Estate Investment Trusts (REITs), mutual funds, and partnerships avoid double taxation by allowing profits and losses to pass through to the individual with no tax paid by the corporate entity.

Double taxation also refers to the situation of paying two separate taxes on the same property, such as the payment of state and federal taxes in more than one state. May also refer to the situation when federal estate taxes are paid once upon the death of one joint tenant and again upon the death of the surviving joint tenant. (See CORPORATION, LIMITED PARTNERSHIP, SUBCHAPTER S CORPORATION, TAX BRACKET.)

DOUBLE WINDOW HEADER Two boards laid on edge that form the upper portion of a door or window.

DOWER The legal right or interest recognized in some states that a wife acquires in the property her husband held or acquired anytime during their marriage. During the husband's life, the dower is an expectant, or inchoate, interest which does not actually become a legal estate (called *consummate dower*) until the husband's death. The parties must be validly married (note that some states recognize common-law marriages). In those states still recognizing dower, in order for the husband to convey clear title to his own property, it is necessary for the wife to sign a release of her dower.

Dower rights have been eliminated in many states, and in states that have adopted the Uniform Probate Code, dower has been replaced by the surviving spouse's right to an elective share upon the death of one spouse. (*See ADMEASUREMENT OF DOWER, CURTESY, ELECTIVE SHARE, JOINTURE.*)

DOWN PAYMENT The amount of cash a purchaser will pay at the time of purchase. While it usually includes the earnest money deposit, the terms are not synonymous. The earnest money is applied toward the total amount of cash down payment due at the closing. (*See EARNEST MONEY.*)

DOWNSIDE RISK The risk that an investor will lose his or her money in a particular venture.

DOWNSPOUT A vertical pipe made of cement, metal, clay, or plastic which carries rainwater from the eaves through to the ground.

DOWNSTROKE Slang term meaning the amount of money needed to enter into an investment. In the purchase of real property, it would include the total down payment plus closing costs.

DOWNZONING A change in zoning from a higher to a lower or from a more active to less active classification, such as from residential to conservation, or multi family to single-family use. In these cases, there is no taking under eminent domain and thus no compensation paid to the affected landowner who helplessly sees the property reduce in value. (*See ZONING.*)

DRAGNET CLAUSE A clause in a mortgage which extends the lien of the mortgage to secure repayment of other debts of the mortgagor, past, present, or future. Dragnet clauses are strictly construed by the courts who may require a direct relationship between the original debt and the other debts. Problems for a buyer could arise where a buyer purchases property subject to a mortgage containing a dragnet clause. (*See ANACONDA MORTGAGE.*)

DRAINAGE A system of gradually drawing off water and moisture from land, naturally or artificially, by means of pipes and conduits.

DRAW   An advancement of money. A real estate broker-age company will sometimes advance money to its more experienced sales associates to be applied against either commissions earned but not paid or future commissions. Court cases have held that a broker cannot recover the difference between the amount advanced and the commission actually earned when the commission is less than the advance. Also refers to the periodic advancing of funds under a construction loan agreement.

DRILL TRACK   A segment of rail track that is intermediary be-tween a main line and the individual industry tracks (spurs) that serve private industrial property.

DRIVE   A long winding collector roadway; usually through a valley, mountainous area, or plateau, having scenic qualities.

DRY MORTGAGE   A mortgage or deed of trust in which the lender looks solely to the real property for recovery of the debt in case of default; i.e., there is no personal liability for any deficiency upon foreclosure; a nonrecourse mortgage. (See *DEFICIENCY JUDGMENT*.)

DRY ROT   Fungus-caused decay in timber, which reduces the wood to a fine powder.

DRYWALL CONSTRUCTION   Any type of interior wall construction not using plaster as finish material. Wood paneling, ply-wood, plasterboard, gypsum board, or other types of wallboard are usually used for drywall.

DUAL AGENCY   Representing both principals to a transaction. In many states, it is unethical and illegal for a broker to represent both buyer and seller in a real estate transaction. Most license laws provide that a real estate license will be revoked or suspended if a licensee repre-sents both parties without obtaining their written consent. Although state laws seem to imply that it would be permissible to represent both parties as long as each consents in writing, such laws merely state that the real estate authorities will not take disciplinary measures against the licensee in such a case. It is thus still necessary to examine the common-law principles.

Common-law agency principles stress the fiduciary duties of loyalty an agent owes to his or her principal. Thus, there is a conflict of interest if a broker repre-sents both the seller, who wants the highest price, and the buyer, who wants the lowest price. This is common where the buyer and seller are working with differ-ent salespeople from the same brokerage company. The most practical solution, in addition to obtaining written consent, is for the selling broker to state clearly to the buyer that he is the seller's agent and owes his first loyalty to the seller, but that he will also assist the buyer according to the highest ethical standards of the real estate profession. Dual agency rules apply similarly when a real estate broker-age company has a listing on a property and one of its salespeople wants to repre-sent the buyer. In such a case, the brokerage company should specifically disclose to the buyer that the company's first loyalty is to the seller. Sample language inserted in the sales contract could be, "Buyer understands that Sellwell Realtors, Inc., is representing the seller in the transaction."

Article 13 of the Realtors® Code of Ethics goes further, stating, "The Realtor® shall not accept compensation from more than one party even if permitted by law, without the full knowledge of all parties to the transaction." In interpreting this article, the professional standards committee noted that, "it is more professional for a broker to represent one of the parties; that representing both, even with consent, is poor policy."

The fact that a broker is getting paid by one party does not necessarily make the broker the exclusive agent of that party, although it is evidence of that fact.

A cooperating broker who acts as a subagent of the listing broker would have the same conflict of interest/ dual agency problem in trying to also act as the buyer's agent. (See AGENCY, SUBAGENT.)

DUAL CONTRACT An improper or fraudulent contract to buy property which contains terms and financial conditions different from the original or true agreement and falsely represents the parties' true intentions. The fraudulent dual contract may then be submitted to a lending institution in hopes of obtaining a larger loan. This fraudulent practice is sometimes known as "kiting." An example of such a contract might be one in which the parties show a lower purchase price than was actually agreed on so that the buyer will be eligible for a maximum FHA loan or the broker may accept a large earnest money deposit in the form of a check, which he or she agrees never to deposit, in an attempt to impress the mortgage company with the buyer's financial resources. In addition to notifying the seller about the agreement not to deposit, the broker must take steps to ensure that the mortgagee is not defrauded.

A broker who participates in any way in the preparation of a dual contract may be subject to license suspension or revocation, a fine for misconduct, or civil damages. Also, the broker cannot be a party to the naming of a false consideration.

Some brokers have been accused of using an addendum which commits the seller to provide a sum of money to the buyer at closing for replacing carpeting or repairing fences when, in fact, there is no intention to use this money for the stated purpose. What happens instead is that the buyer assigns the funds to the closing agent as all or part of the equity investment in the property being purchased. Such addendum is not shown with the FHA application since such a kickback effectively lowers the purchase price to the buyer and the buyer is not providing an equity investment out of his own funds. When a federally chartered lender is involved, this type of dual contract practice would be a federal criminal offense.

DUCT A tube, pipe, or channel for conveying or carrying fluids, cables, wires, or tempered air. Under-floor duct systems are commonly used to provide for telephone and electrical lines.

DUE DILIGENCE 1. A fair, proper, and due degree of care and activity. An expressed or implied requirement in certain real estate contracts stating that a person use good faith efforts to perform that person's obligations under a contract. A buyer who makes an offer contingent on obtaining financing must use due diligence in seeking such financing.

2. Also, a term used in securities law to refer to the duty of the issuer or broker to insure that the offering prospectus is accurate and does not misstate or omit material information.

DUE-ON-SALE   A form of acceleration clause found in some mort-
CLAUSE   gages, especially savings and loan mortgages, requiring the mortgagor to pay off the mortgage debt
when the property is sold, thus resulting in automatic maturity of the note at the
lender's *option*; also referred to as a *nonassumption clause*. This clause effectively
eliminates the possibility of the new buyer's assuming the mortgage unless the
mortgagee permits the assumption, in which case the mortgagee might increase
the interest rate or charge an assumption fee. Also called an *alienation clause, call
clause*, or a *right-to-sell clause*, it can be found in contracts for deed and deeds of
trust.

While such clauses are upheld in a majority of the states, some state courts and
legislatures have invalidated such clauses on the grounds of unreasonable restraint against alienation, at least without a showing that the transfer will impair
the lender's security in the property (the "bankrupt-arsonist buyer").

The Federal Home Loan Bank Board (FHLBB) issued regulations in 1976 that
specifically authorize the insertion of a due-on-sale clause in a residential mortgage given by a federal savings and loan association. In several cases, the courts
have held that these federal rules "preempt" the state rules. For example, a state
law banning due-on-sale clauses would be effective against state-chartered savings
and loans but not federally chartered associations. However, in *Nalore v. San
Diego S & L*, 9th Circuit, September, 1981, a federal appellate court held that state
law controls enforcement of the due-on-sale clause. The U.S. Supreme Court later
decided this issue in favor of the federal lenders.

The FHLBB regulations do list certain situations where the due-on-sale clause will
not be enforced, such as a transfer after the death of a joint tenant, a leasehold
interest of three years or less provided there is no option to purchase, and upon
transfer to immediate family as in a divorce case.

Related to the due-on-sale clause is a "due-on-encumbrance" clause, found in a
mortgage or a deed of trust, which would allow the holder of a mortgage to accelerate the mortgage note if the mortgagor places junior financing on the property. The
justification for the clause is that the mortgagee feels that any additional financing
reduces the mortgagor's equity in the property and increases the likelihood of
default. Some courts have also invalidated such clauses on grounds they constitute unreasonable restraints on the free marketability of property.

VA and FHA mortgages do not contain due-on-sale clauses. (*See ACCELERATION
CLAUSE, PARAGRAPH 17.*)

DUMMY   A person who buys property for another to conceal the identity of the true purchaser; also called
a straw man or nominee. If a broker or a salesperson attempts to use a dummy
buyer to purchase property for which he or she has a listing, the real estate person
must specifically disclose in writing to the seller this relationship to the buyer.
Failure to do so may result in license suspension or revocation. (*See NOMINEE,
STRAW MAN.*)

DUPLEX   A structure that provides housing accommodations for two families and supplies each with sep-
arate entrances, kitchens, bedrooms, living rooms, and bathrooms. A two-family
dwelling with the units either side by side (in some areas called a "twin") or one
above the other.

In subdivisions that are restricted to single-family dwellings, some duplex owners argue that a duplex is merely the combining of two separate single-family dwellings with a party wall. To prevent arguments of this type, many subdividers restrict use to "*detached* single-family dwellings." A duplex apartment is one in which there are rooms on two floors.

DURESS   Unlawful force or action by one person against another into performing some act against his or her will. The threat of force is called *menace*. Duress is a defense against enforcing a contract because there is no genuine meeting of the minds. A contract entered into under duress is not enforceable against the forced party. (*See UNDUE INFLUENCE*.)

DWELLING   Any building, structure, or part thereof, used and occupied for human habitation or intended to be so used, including any appurtenances. Many municipalities have adopted ordinances relating to the repair, closing, and demolition of dwellings unfit for humans to live in.

DWELLING UNIT   As defined in many zoning codes, a room or rooms connected together, constituting an independent housekeeping unit for a family and containing a single kitchen, unlike a hotel room.

Under the Federal Fair Housing Act, the term "dwelling" includes residences and land intended for a residence, but excludes hotel and motel accomodations.

EARLY OCCUPANCY   Refers to the practice of allowing the buyer to take possession of the real property prior to closing. Such a practice should be carefully evaluated because of the risks of mechanics' liens, inadequate insurance coverage, and "buyer's remorse" with possible lawsuit.

EARNEST MONEY   The cash deposit (including initial and additional deposits) paid by the prospective buyer of real property as evidence of good-faith intention to complete the transaction; called *bargain money, caution money, hand money,* or a *binder* in some states. The amount of earnest money deposited usually does not exceed 10 percent of the purchase price and its primary purpose is to serve as a source of payment of damages should the buyer default. Earnest money is *not* essential to make a purchase agreement binding if the buyer's and seller's exchange of mutual promises of performance (that is, the buyer's promise to purchase and the seller's promise to sell at a specified price and terms) constitute the consideration for the contract. Thought should be given to placing the money in an interest-bearing account for the buyer's benefit.

The deposit, or earnest money, is usually given to the broker at the time the sales contract is signed. The broker's authority to hold this money on behalf of the seller should be specifically set forth in the listing, since such authority is not implied in law. The broker has the responsibility under the license laws to deposit this money into a client trust account or neutral escrow, or with the knowledge and consent of both parties, the broker may hold the earnest money until the offer has been accepted. The broker may not, however, commingle this money with his or her own general funds. When the transaction is consummated, the earnest money is credited toward the down payment. In the event that the *seller* defaults, the broker should check with the buyer before returning the earnest money. The buyer may not want the earnest money returned directly if he or she wishes to sue the seller for specific performance.

There is some uncertainty as to exactly who owns the earnest money once it is put on deposit. Until the offer is accepted, the money is, in a sense, the buyer's. Once the seller accepts the offer, however, the buyer may not get the money back, even though the seller will not be entitled to it until the transaction is completed. At this point, the money does not belong to the broker either, for it must be deposited in a special trust account maintained especially for such purposes. This uncertain nature of earnest money deposits makes it absolutely necessary that such funds be properly protected pending a final decision on how it is to be disbursed. (*See BINDER, COMMINGLING, DEPOSIT, DOWN PAYMENT.*)

EARNEST MONEY   *See CLIENT TRUST ACCOUNT.*
ACCOUNT

EASEMENT   A nonpossessory (incorporeal) property interest
(short of an estate) which one person (the bene-
fited party) has in land owned by another (the burdened party), entitling the
holder of the interest to limited use or enjoyment of the other's land. Because an
easement is an actual interest in land, the Statute of Frauds applies and an express
grant of easement must be in writing, usually in the form of a separate deed or a
reservation in a deed. Thus, an easement is an interest in land rather than a mere
contractual agreement. Easements are also created by necessity (as in landlocked
situations), by implication, or by prescription.

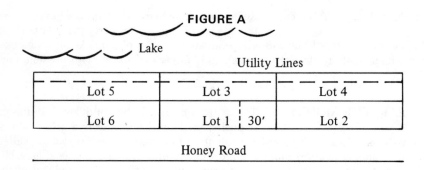

FIGURE A

Lake

Utility Lines

| Lot 5 | Lot 3 | Lot 4 |
| Lot 6 | Lot 1 | 30' | Lot 2 |

Honey Road

Easements are classified as either appurtenant or in gross. An *easement appurtenant* is a right in another's land (servient estate) which benefits and attaches to the
owner's land (dominant estate). In Figure A, Lot 3 has a 30-foot roadway easement
across Lot 1. This easement is appurtenant to and passes with Lot 3 regardless of
whether the owner of Lot 3 expressly transfers the easement when Lot 3, the
dominant estate, is sold. It also binds the succeeding owner of Lot 1 whether or
not the deed to Lot 1 refers to the easement. Common examples of easements
appurtenant are the right to travel over another's property, party walls, and shared
driveways. In a condominium, the right to walk over the parking area, to have
utility lines running through the walls, or a sewer pipe running beneath the land
surface are also examples of easements appurtenant.

An *easement in gross* is personal in nature and does not pass with the land because it does not benefit or attach to any dominant estate. Common examples of
this type of situation are utility easements, power line easements, billboard-site
easements, and the like.

In Figure A, the owners of Lots 5 and 6 may agree that the owner of Lot 5 will not
build a building so high that it cuts off the view of the lake which the owner of Lot
6 enjoys. This is called a *negative easement*. The right of aircraft to fly below
certain altitudes over or near property bordering an airport is called an *avigation
easement* (aerial navigation).

When an easement or right-of-way is located by a grant that does not define its
specific width, such width is assumed to be one that is suitable and convenient for
ordinary, free passage. Some of the major sources of litigation involving easements
are the initial easement grant's failure to adequately define the easement area (the
floating easement problem), the uses to which it may be put, or which party has
responsibility for repair and upkeep.

Since the easement is both a benefit to the holder and a burden to the servient property owner, it significantly affects the value of the respective properties and the extent of the easement should be clearly understood. Since most easements originate by express grant, the drafter should clearly express the rights and duties associated with the easement. An easement can be an affirmative easement, such as a right of way to cross the property, or a negative easement, such as a restriction on height of a fence. It can also be created for different periods of time—for a term of months, years, or for life.

Easements should not be confused with profits or licenses. A *profit* is the right to take the soil, mineral, or products of the land. A *license* is not an interest in land; it is merely permission to use the land of another for some limited purpose, and it can be revoked at any time.

Easements may be terminated:

1. when the owner of the dominant estate becomes the owner of the servient estate. The easement is thus terminated by merger.

2. when the owner of the dominant estate abandons the easement. Mere nonuse is insufficient cause, as there must be clear acts showing an intent to abandon, such as the owner of the dominant estate erecting a fence across his or her easement right-of-way.

3. when the owner of the easement releases his or her interest, usually by means of a quitclaim deed.

4. when an easement has been created for a particular purpose and that purpose ceases.

5. when the easement is taken by eminent domain or lost by adverse possession.

6. when the grantee makes use of the easement for an improper purpose (called *overburdening*).

Note that an easement cannot be terminated due to any inconvenience or hardship experienced because the owner of the servient tenement cannot develop the property without added expense. The owner of the servient tenement cannot relocate the easement simply to suit personal needs—to do so would be, in essence, a private right of eminent domain. (See *EASEMENT BY NECESSITY, EASEMENT BY PRESCRIPTION, EASEMENT IN GROSS, IMPLIED EASEMENT, LICENSE, SCENIC EASEMENT, SERVIENT ESTATE.*)

EASEMENT BY NECESSITY   An easement created by a court of law in cases where justice and necessity dictate it, especially in a classic landlocked situation (see Lot 3, Figure A). Two essential elements of this type of easement are that there must have been a common grantor of the dominant and servient estates and that there must be a reasonable necessity for the easement, not just mere convenience. For example, if George Brown had owned Lots 1-6 (see previous Figure A) and then conveyed Lot 3 to Jane Lee without mention of any easement of passage across Lot 1, most courts would imply an easement by necessity. This easement is based on the presumed intention of the parties. Since it is created by operation of law, the Statute of Frauds is not applicable and no written agreement is required. Also called an *easement by implied grant.*

EASEMENT BY PRESCRIPTION A right acquired by an adverse user to use the land of another. As with acquiring title through adverse possession, the use that results in an easement by prescription must be adverse, hostile, open, notorious, and continuous for the statutory period. An easement by prescription cannot usually be acquired on public land or on Torrens registered property. Unlike easements by express or implied grant, an easement by prescription may be extinguished by nonuse for the prescriptive period without evidence of actual abandonment. (See *ADVERSE POSSESSION, ADVERSE USER, LOST-GRANT DOCTRINE*.)

EASEMENT IN GROSS The limited right of one person to use another's land (servient estate) when such right is not created for the benefit of any land owned by the owner of the easement. In such a case, there is no dominant estate because the easement attaches personally to the owner, not to the land. The easement in gross is an encumbrance on the servient estate. If there is uncertainty as to whether an easement is appurtenant or in gross, most courts favor the interpretation that it is an easement appurtenant.

An easement in gross is similar to a license, except that it is irrevocable for the period of the owner's life. For example, the owner of Lot 3 in Figure A may give his friend Mary White a nonrevocable right to cross over Lot 3 and fish in the lake. This right, or easement in gross, will terminate upon the death of Ms. White or upon the conveyance of Lot 3 to a new owner, whichever occurs first. Ms. White may not assign her right to anyone else. A personal easement in gross may not be assigned by the owner to a third party. Commercial easements in gross, however, such as rights given utility companies to install pipe lines and power lines, are a more substantial property interest and are assignable.

EAVE The overhang of a sloping roof that extends beyond the walls of the house. Also called roof projection.

EAVE DRIP The drainage of water from the eaves of a structure onto the land of another which, if continued for the statutory time, could develop into a prescriptive easement right.

EAVE TROUGH A channel, usually metal pipe, placed at the edge of the eaves to carry rain water to the downspout.

ECONOMIC-BASE ANALYSIS An appraisal term to describe a means of measuring the economic activity of a community that enables it to attract income from outside its borders; the study of the relationship between basic and nonbasic employment patterns as a means of predicting population, income, and other variables having an effect on real estate and land utilization. This term refers to the ways in which people in a community make their livings.

ECONOMIC LIFE The estimated period over which an improved property may be profitably utilized so that it will yield a return over and above the economic rent attributable to the land itself; the period during which an improvement has value in excess of its salvage value. In the case of an older structure or improvement, economic life refers to the period during which the *remaining* improvements to the real property (not land) are depreciated for tax purposes. The economic lives of such improvements are normally shorter than their actual physical lives. Also called service life. (*See USEFUL LIFE.*)

ECONOMIC OBSOLESCENCE   A loss of value (typically incurable) resulting from extraneous factors that exist outside of the property itself; a type of depreciation caused by environmental, social, or economic forces over which an owner has little or no control. If there is a change in zoning, economic obsolescence is likely to occur, as in the following examples: to a residence if an industrial plant is built next to it; to a well-maintained house in a deteriorating neighborhood; and to a motel if a new highway is built that results in difficult access to the motel. Other causes might be proximity to nuisances and changes in land use or population. Also called locational or environmental obsolescence. (*See COST APPROACH, OBSOLESCENCE.*)

ECONOMIC RENT   The rental income which real estate can command in an open, competitive market at any given time, as contrasted with contract rent, or the income actually received under a lease agreement. For example, if there is a new plant being built, yet there is no new housing being built, the appraiser should consider this fact since rents will increase under normal supply and demand principles. (*See CONTRACT RENT.*)

EFFECTIVE AGE   The age of the improvements to real property at the time of inspection, which differs from actual age by such variable factors as depreciation, quality of maintenance, and the like. Thus, remodeling can extend the economic life of a structure by reducing or mitigating the impact of actual age.

EFFECTIVE GROSS INCOME   The estimated potential gross income from a rental property less an allowance for vacancy and bad debts.

EFFECTIVE INTEREST RATE   The actual rate or yield of a loan, regardless of the amount stated on the debt instrument. (*See ANNUAL PERCENTAGE RATE.*)

EFFECTIVE RATE   The average lease rate of a property per square foot after deducting negotiated concessions such as free rent, construction allowances over and above the cost of building standard items, or the costs of the landlord's assumption of a tenant's existing lease.

EFFICIENCY UNIT OR APARTMENT   A small, compact apartment unit, sometimes called a studio apartment. It consists of a combination living room, bedroom, kitchenette, and bathroom areas.

EFFLUENCE   A flowing out; excrement deposited by a soil-absorption waste system that may seep or flow out onto the ground or into a creek, stream, river, or lake, particularly in times of flooding or high ground-water levels.

EGRESS   A way to exit from a property; the opposite of ingress.

EJECTMENT   A legal action by an owner to regain possession of real property when there is no landlord-tenant relationship between the owner and the occupant; an action to oust someone who is not legally in possession of real property, such as a trespasser (potential adverse possessor) or a tenant at sufferance whose lease has expired, or in an action by a mortgagee to get possession from a defaulting mortgagor. (*See EVICTION.*)

ELECTION OF REMEDIES   Selection from several alternative courses of action to remedy a breach of contract. For example, if the buyer defaults on an agreement to purchase, the seller elects whether to retain the deposit as liquidated damages, tender the deed and sue for specific performance, or sue for damages. The seller, however, cannot elect to pursue all possible remedies.

Where the buyer defaults and the seller elects to retain the deposit as liquidated damages, the seller normally splits the deposit with the broker (up to the amount of the previously agreed-upon commission). (*See CONTRACT FOR SALE, DAMAGES, LIQUIDATED DAMAGES, SPECIFIC PERFORMANCE.*)

ELECTIVE SHARE   In some states, usually those that have abolished dower and curtesy, a minimum share of a deceased spouse's probate estate (one-third for example) which a surviving spouse may claim in lieu of any amount specified in the deceased spouse's will, or which the surviving spouse may claim if the other spouse died intestate. (*See DESCENT.*)

ELEEMOSYNARY CORPORATION   A corporation formed for charitable and benevolent purposes and subject to special statutory controls. (*See NONPROFIT CORPORATION.*)

ELEVATION SHEET   Drawings that provide views of the front and sides of a building as it will appear when completed.

EMBLEMENT   A growing crop (called *fructus industriales*), such as grapes or corn, which is produced annually through labor and industry, also called a "way-growing crop." Emblements are regarded as personal property even prior to harvest; thus, a tenant has the right to take the annual crop resulting from his or her labor, even if the harvest does not occur until after tenancy has ended. A landlord cannot lease land to a tenant farmer and then terminate the lease without giving the tenant the right to reenter the land to harvest any crops grown by the tenant.

EMINENT DOMAIN   The right of government (both state and federal), public corporations (school districts, sanitation districts), public utilities, and public service corporations (railroads, power companies) to take private property for a necessary public use, with just compensation paid to the owner. Generally, however, the law will not allow compensation for loss of profits, inconvenience, loss of goodwill, and the like, although severance damages may be awarded for a loss in value to adjacent property which is not actually condemned. Through eminent domain, the state may acquire land (either fee, leasehold, or easement) for streets, parks, public buildings, public rights-of-way, and similar uses. No private property is exempt from this exercise of government power.

If the owner and the government cannot negotiate a satisfactory voluntary acquisition of the property, the government can initiate a condemnation action to take the property. In such a case, an owner's main grounds for complaint would usually be that the intended use is not a sufficient public use or that the valuation given the property in the condemnation proceeding is not a just valuation. Generally speaking, the courts will not permit a taking in fee if an easement will do; an entire piece can't be taken if only a part is needed.

Whether a taking is for a public purpose is broadly construed. For example, a public purpose exists in condemnation for urban renewal purposes. The government can, for instance, condemn a blighted area and then sell it to a private developer for private purposes.

Eminent domain differs from the taking of land through police power in that eminent domain is an outright acquisition of property with payment of compensation. It is not an uncompensated regulation of the use of property as in the case of restrictive zoning.

Upon the vesting of title in the government, all preexisting liens and encumbrances are extinguished; anyone affected by this change, such as mortgagees, must look to the award of condemnation money for satisfaction of their claims.

Generally, when an owner's property is taken by eminent domain, recognition of gain realized from the condemnation money can be deferred if qualified replacement property is purchased within three years from the end of the year in which the taxable gain is realized. In most cases, in order for the replacement property to qualify, it must be similar or related in use ("like kind" property).

A lessee is usually given the right to cancel his or her lease when a large portion of the leased premises is taken. Long-term leases usually provide for a condemnation award to be apportioned between lessor and lessee, according to the value of the parties' respective estates. (See CONDEMNATION, POLICE POWER, SEVERANCE DAMAGES.)

EMPTY NESTER   An older family whose children have grown and left home. Statistics show that such families are major condominium buyers.

ENABLING LEGISLATION   A statute creating the power or authority to carry out an activity, as under the provisions of a federal housing program, or to do something not previously authorized, such as a condominium law creating the unique condominium form of ownership.

ENCROACHMENT   An unauthorized invasion or intrusion of a fixture or other real property or another's property, thus reducing the size and value of the invaded property. Common examples of encroachments are the roof of a building which extends over the property line or the front of a building that extends over the building setback line or extends onto a neighbor's property. Most encroachments are the result of carelessness or poor planning rather than bad intent, as in the case of a driveway or fence built without a survey to find the lot line.

Since an undisclosed encroachment could render a title unmarketable, its existence should be noted on its listing, and the contract of sale should be made subject to the existence of the particular encroachment.

An encroachment is a *trespass* if it encroaches on the land and a *nuisance* if it violates the neighbor's airspace, as in the case of overhanging tree branches. The injured party can seek a judicial remedy in ejectment, quiet title, or injunction and damages. A court is empowered to order the removal of the encroachment. However, if the encroachment is slight, the cost of its removal is great, and its creation was unintentional, a court may decide to award money damages in lieu of ordering removal.

An accurate land survey will disclose most encroachments and is usually required by lenders and buyers of any substantial parcel of real property. Most purchasers will obtain their own surveys when purchasing property if there is any doubt as to possible encroachments. If such a survey reveals any encroachments not previously disclosed by the seller, the buyer may compel the seller to remove the encroachment (or reduce the purchase price accordingly) and also to pay for the survey.

Encroachments are not normally revealed in the chain of title and thus are not warranted against in a title insurance policy. Also, most standard title insurance policies do not insure against matters which an accurate survey would reveal. An extended coverage title policy will usually insure against encroachments. (*See EXTENDED COVERAGE, SURVEY, TRESPASS.*)

ENCUMBRANCE   Any claim, lien, charge, or liability attached to and binding on real property which may lessen its value, or burden, obstruct, or impair the use of a property but not necessarily prevent transfer of title; a right or interest in a property held by one who is not the legal owner of the property. Also spelled incumbrance. There are two general classifications of encumbrances: those that affect the title, such as judgments, mortgages, mechanics' liens, and other liens which are charges on property used to secure a debt or obligation; and those that affect the physical condition of the property such as restrictions, encroachments, and easements.

A covenant against encumbrances guarantees that there are no encumbrances against the property except those specifically disclosed. If no encumbrances are disclosed as exceptions in the contract of sale, the buyer may proceed with the purchase on the assumption that there are no encumbrances against the property.

Encumbrances should be noted on the deed following the property description. (*See DEED, EASEMENT, LIEN.*)

END LOAN   A permanent mortgage which a consumer uses to finance the purchase of a new condominium unit or a lot within a developed subdivision; often called *take-out financing*. The lender who makes the development or interim loan for a construction project might also provide the permanent financing to individual unit buyers to "take out" the developer after the project is completed and sold; hence the terms *take-out financing* and *end loan* (See PERMANENT FINANCING.)

ENDORSEMENT   1. A method of transferring title to a negotiable instrument, such as a check or promissory note, by signing the owner's name on the reverse side of such instrument. A blank endorsement guarantees payment to subsequent holders. An endorsement which states that it is without recourse does not guarantee payment to subsequent holders. A special endorsement specifies the person to whom or to whose order the instrument is payable. 2. A notation added to an instrument after its execution that is made to change or clarify the document's contents. In insurance policies, coverage may be restricted or enlarged by endorsing the policy. For example, there are over 100 special endorsements that may be added to the standard title insurance policy. In FHA loans, an endorsement is placed on the note by the FHA to indicate that the loan is insured under the National Housing Act.

ENGINEERING   An appraisal method of estimating accrued depre-
BREAKDOWN   ciation, which considers separate estimates of
METHOD   each major building component, such as roof, elevators, and air conditioning.

ENJOIN   To forbid performance or, in some cases, to command performance of an act. The courts can issue injunctions against a pattern of discrimination in real estate transactions. Both federal and state agencies generally have injunctive powers against subdividers who sell land in violation of land sales laws. (See INJUNCTION.)

ENTITY, LEGAL   A person, actual or artificial, that is recognized by law. Usually refers to an artificial being such as a corporation or partnership. There are many tax considerations for a buyer in choosing the appropriate entity to hold title to a real estate investment. (See OWNERSHIP.)

ENTREPRENEUR   One who takes the initiative to organize and manage an enterprise or business, usually assuming a substantial portion of risks, losses, and profits; a promoter; a developer. Entrepreneurs solve real estate problems themselves, whereas real estate counselors are hired to solve them for others.

ENVIRONMENTAL   A report that includes a detailed description of a
IMPACT STATEMENT   proposed development project with emphasis on the existing environmental setting, viewed from both local and regional perspectives, and a discussion of the probable impact of the project on the environment during all phases. The National Environmental Policy Act (NEPA), enacted in 1969, requires federal agencies to file environmental impact statements with the Federal Council on Environmental Quality and obtain the council's approval for all proposed government actions. Government actions have been interpreted as including anything from approval of a federal

license or permit to policy determinants, provisos, and proposed legislation. Such impact statements must include the following information:

1. a detailed description of the proposed action

2. a discussion of the direct and indirect impact on the environment that might result from the action

3. identification of unavoidable adverse environmental effects

4. an assessment of any feasible alternatives to the proposd action

5. a description of the action's cumulative and long-term effects on the earth's surface

6. identification of any irreversible commitment of resources that might result from the action.

Under the National Environmental Policy Act (NEPA), to ensure that environmental amenities and values are given systematic consideration equal to economic and technical considerations in the federal decision-making process, each federal agency must prepare a statement of environmental impact in advance of each major action, recommendation or report on legislation that may significantly affect the quality of the human environment. Such actions may include new highway construction, harbor dredging or filling, nuclear power plant construction, large-scale aerial pesticide spraying, river channeling, new jet runways, munitions disposal, bridge construction, and more.

ENVIRONMENTAL PROTECTION AGENCY (EPA) A federal agency created in 1970 by bringing together various federal pollution-control activities that had been scattered among a number of federal departments and agencies. The EPA is involved with environmental problems of air and water pollution, solid waste management, pesticides, radiation, and noise. In these areas, the EPA sets standards, determines how much pollution is tolerable, establishes timetables to bring polluters into line with its standards, and enforces environmental laws. The EPA conducts an extensive environmental research program, provides technical, financial, and managerial help to state, regional, and municipal pollution control agencies, and allocates funds for sewage-treatment facilities. The original authority of the EPA has subsequently been increased by the passage of the Clean Air Amendments and the Resource Recovery Act in 1970; the Federal Water Pollution Control Act Amendments, the Federal Environmental Pesticide Control Act, the Noise Control Act and the Marine Protection Research and Sanctuaries Act in 1972; and the Safe Drinking Water Act in 1974. (See ENVIRONMENTAL IMPACT STATEMENT.)

EOLIAN SOIL See AEOLIAN SOIL.

EQUAL CREDIT OPPORTUNITY ACT In 1974, federal legislation was passed to ensure that the various financial institutions and other firms engaged in the extension of credit exercise their responsibility to make credit available with fairness and impartiality and without discrimination on the basis of race, color, religion, national origin, sex or marital status, age, receipt of income from public assistance programs (food stamps, social security); and good faith exercises of any right under the Consumer Credit Protection Act (creditor must state reasons for denial of credit). The act applies to all who regularly extend or arrange for the extension of credit. A real estate licensee would be considered a "creditor" if the licensee routinely assists sellers in determining if a proposed buyer in a land contract or purchase money mortgage is creditworthy. Regulation B, implementing the act, contains partial exemptions from procedural provisions for business, securities, and public utilities credit.

Principal provisions of Regulation B are that:

1. Creditors may not make statements discouraging applicants on any discriminatory basis.

2. Creditors may not refuse to grant, on any discriminatory basis, a separate account to a creditworthy applicant.

3. Creditors may not ask the marital status of an applicant applying for an unsecured separate account, except in a community property state or as required to comply with state law governing permissible finance charges or loan ceilings.

4. Neither sex nor marital status may be used in credit-scoring systems.

5. Creditors may not inquire into child-bearing intentions or capability, or birth control practices, or assume from an applicant's age that an applicant or an applicant's spouse may drop out of the labor force due to childbearing and thus have an interruption of income.

6. With certain exceptions, creditors may not require or use unfavorable information about a spouse or former spouse when an applicant applies for credit independently of that spouse and can demonstrate that the unfavorable history should not be applied.

7. A creditor may not discount part-time income, but may examine probable continuity of an applicant's job.

8. A creditor may inquire about and consider whether obligations to make alimony, child support, or maintenance payments affect an applicant's income.

9. A creditor may ask to what extent an applicant is relying on alimony, child support, or maintenance payments to repay the debt. The applicant must first be informed that such disclosure is unnecessary if the applicant does not rely on such income to obtain the credit.

10. Creditors must provide the reasons for terminating or denying credit to applicants who so request.

11. Creditors must have informed holders of existing accounts of their rights to have credit history reported in both spouses' names.

12. Creditors must, with certain exceptions, give applicants the following written notice: "The Federal Equal Credit Opportunity Act prohibits creditors from discriminating against credit applicants. The federal agency that administers compliance with this law concerning this (insert appropriate description— bank, store, etc.) is (name and address of the appropriate agency)."

13. With certain exceptions, creditors may not terminate credit on an existing account because of a change in an applicant's marital status without evidence that the applicant is unwilling or unable to pay.

The legislation provides for civil liability for violations of this act. Types of liabilities are:

1. Any creditor who fails to comply with any requirement imposed under this title shall be liable to the aggrieved applicant in an amount equal to the sum of any actual damages sustained by such applicant acting either in an individual capacity or as a representative of a class.

2. Any creditor who fails to comply with a requirement imposed under this title shall be liable to the aggrieved applicant for punitive damages in an amount not greater than $10,000, as determined by the court, in addition to any actual damages provided in section 706(a). However, that in pursuing the recovery allowed under this subsection, the applicant may proceed only in an individual capacity and not as a representative of a class.

3. Section 706(b) notwithstanding, any creditor who fails to comply with any requirement imposed under this title may be liable for punitive damages in the case of a class action in such amount as the court may allow, except that as to each member of the class, no minimum recovery shall be applicable, and the total recovery in such action shall not exceed the lesser of $500,000 or one percent of the net worth of the creditor.

EQUAL DIGNITIES RULE A rule of agency law which stipulates that when a contract is required by law to be in writing, the authority of an agent to enter into such a contract on behalf of his or her principal must also be in writing. For example, a power of attorney for real estate contracts must be in writing because state statutes of fraud generally require that all real estate contracts be in writing and that the agent's authority likewise be in writing. Usually the power of attorney must also be recorded if the real estate contract (such as a land contract for deed) is expected to be recorded. (See POWER OF ATTORNEY.)

EQUALIZATION BOARD A state or county reviewing agency with the power to adjust certain inequities in tax assessments. Equalization is the adjustment of the assessed valuation of real property in a particular taxing district to achieve a parity with the level of assessment in other districts. Such reviewing agencies establish equalization factors to assure that all property owners in the state pay an equitable and uniform share of the state tax. Inequities could arise when the state bases its taxes upon the assessments made by local assessors under local rules. For example, if one county appears to have assessments that are 15 percent lower than the state average assessment, this underassessment may be corrected by applying a 115 percent factor to each assessment in that county. (See PROPERTY TAX.)

EQUITABLE CONVERSION A rule of law created to give the buyer under an executory contract of sale title to the property for certain purposes prior to the date set for closing. Because a court of equity "regards as done that which ought to be done," the doctrine of equitable conversion holds that immediately upon the making of the contract, the seller holds the legal title for the buyer, who has the beneficial, equitable title. Thereafter, the seller holds legal title only as security for the purchase price. In essence, the seller's interest (legal title of the real estate) is converted into an interest in personal property (the money to be paid to purchase the property). Conversely, the buyer's interest (purchase money) becomes an interest in real estate. Thus, if, at the time of the sales contract's execution, the seller is still in possession of the property (as is the usual case), he or she holds the property subject to a legal obligation to take care of it for the buyer and must be sure it does not suffer damage. The doctrine applies in cases involving the valuation of the seller's interest at his or her death, and also in cases involving risk of loss or destruction of the premises. For example, a seller had agreed to sell her farm for $100,000, but died before closing. She had willed her personal property to Mike Waters and her real property to Pat Parker. Through the doctrine of equitable conversion, the seller's interest in the farm is treated as personal property and thus the proceeds from the sale would pass to Mr. Waters. (*See EQUITABLE TITLE, RISK OF LOSS.*)

EQUITABLE LIEN   A lien arising out of a written contract which shows an intention of the parties to charge some particular property as security for a debt or obligation. A court may decide that an equitable lien exists based on principles of fairness and justice, such as when the parties intended to create a lien but there was a defective execution of a mortgage instrument. Examples of equitable liens include a vendee's lien, which a buyer holds against a property in the amount of the deposit when a seller defaults in the performance of a sales contract, and a vendor's lien, which is the security lien behind a purchase-money loan that is not secured by a mortgage. Occasionally, a lender will make an unsecured loan but have the borrower agree not to convey or encumber the real property owned by the borrower.

EQUITABLE SERVITUDE   An easement of use enforced in equity which permits restrictive covenants not running with the land to be enforced as though they do run with the land. To enforce such equitable servitudes, it must appear that the restrictive covenants are designed for the benefit of the lot owners in a particular subdivision or tract, that there is a dominant or benefited land, that there is a general scheme or plan of improvement or development for the entire tract, and that the covenants are intended as restrictions on the land conveyed and incident to its ownership, the purchaser accepting the lot subject to that burden. The doctrine of equitable servitudes might be asserted by a homeowner against a person attempting to build an apartment building in a tract designed for single-family homes. (*See SERVITUDE.*)

EQUITABLE TITLE   The interest held by a vendee under a purchase contract, contract for deed, or an installment purchase agreement; the equitable right to obtain absolute ownership to property when legal title is held in another's name. This interest is transferable by deed, assignment, subcontract, or mortgage and passes to the vendee's heirs and devisees upon death. The concept stems from the fact that the buyer can sue in equity to get specific performance if the seller refuses to sell once a contract of sale is signed and the buyer tenders performance. In such cases, the courts say that the buyer becomes "the owner of the land in equity." Though the vendor retains the bare legal title, the vendee has the right to demand that legal title be transferred upon payment of the full purchase price. Thus, the vendee will benefit from any

increase in value between the date of the purchase agreement and delivery of the
.deed. The vendee will, however, also take the risk of any adverse circumstances,
such as a change in zoning.

Under a trust deed in some states, the trustee holds the bare legal title and the
trustor has the equitable title. (*See CONTRACT FOR DEED.*)

EQUITY 1. That interest or value remaining in property
after payment of all liens or other charges on the
property. An owner's equity in property is normally the monetary interest the
owner retains over and above the mortgage indebtedness. If the property is encumbered with a long-term mortgage, the mortgagor's equity in the property increases
with each monthly principal mortgage payment (not to mention increased value
through appreciation).

In the early years of the mortgage, the equity build-up is gradual, as most of the
monthly payment is applied to the interest on the loan rather than to the principal.
The greater an owner's equity, the less risk for a mortgagee who lends money based
on the security of the property.

2. A *court of equity* is a type of court originally set up under the early English legal
system to handle complaints for which there was no adequate remedy in the regular law courts, particularly cases in which money damages would not adequately
compensate the aggrieved party. For example, if a seller refused to perform his
contract to sell his farm to a buyer, the buyer's only remedy at law would be to sue
for money damages. A court of equity, however, could force specific performance
of the contract. Most states no longer have separate courts of equity and law, but
the distinction between legal and equitable remedies in regard to specific performance and proceedings that do not involve injury is still of importance. (*See AP-
PRECIATION, SPECIFIC PERFORMANCE.*)

EQUITY BUILD-UP The gradual reduction of outstanding principal
due on the mortgage, usually through periodic
amortized payments. Such payments build up the difference (equity) between the
property value and the amount of the mortgage.

**EQUITY OF
REDEMPTION** The right of a mortgagor, *before* a foreclosure sale,
to reclaim property which had been forfeited due
to mortgage default. The mortgagor can redeem
the property by paying the full debt plus interest and costs. Any attempt to have
the mortgagor waive his or her equity of redemption is unenforceable and void as
being contrary to public policy. This equity of redemption has been held to be an
interest in real estate and is thus affected by the ordinary laws and rules concerning conveyances, including the Statute of Frauds. Any right to redeem *after* a
foreclosure sale must be created by state statute. In those states which permit a
power of sale to be inserted in the mortgage document, most foreclosures of property are conducted pursuant to the nonjudicial foreclosure statute. Upon a foreclosure sale, the equity of redemption is terminated. (*See FORECLOSURE, POWER
OF SALE, REDEMPTION PERIOD, TAX DEED.*)

**EQUITY
PARTICIPATION** Refers to the arrangement between a potential
buyer and an investor in which the investor
shares an equity interest in a real property pur-
chase in exchange for assisting with the financing of the acquisition. The investor

may provide all or part of the down payment, closing costs, or monthly payment. Investors may be private parties, corporations, mortgage lenders, or even the seller. It is most important to obtain competent tax advice on the proper allocation of tax deductions such as mortgage interest, depreciation, and property tax.

EQUITY SHARING LOAN A loan where a resident-owner splits his or her equity or the increase in the value of the home with an investor-owner, who contributes toward the down payment and also to monthly payments and benefits in deducting a share of the tax write-offs. (*See SHARED APPRECIATION LOAN.*)

EROSION The gradual loss of soil due to the operation of currents, tides, or winds; the opposite of accretion. (*See ACCRETION, AVULSION.*)

ERRORS AND OMISSIONS INSURANCE A form of insurance which covers liabilities for errors, mistakes, and negligence in the usual listing and selling activities of a real estate office or Bscrow company. It does not, however, cover fraudulent behavior. Considering the enormous exposure to liability a broker or salesperson has under the broad liability provisions of the law, the importance of having errors and omissions insurance is obvious. Called "E&O" insurance.

ESCALATOR CLAUSE 1. A clause in a contract permitting an adjustment of certain payments either up or down in order to cover certain contingencies. Many fixed-rental net leases, particularly long-term commercial leases, contain a clause in which the parties agree to an adjustment of rent based on set increases in such things as taxes, insurance, maintenance, and other operating costs. Similarly, the rent may be tied into the cost-of-living index to cover increases in the maintenance expenses and raised at stated intervals (every two years). An escalator clause protects the lessor's investment position against a reduction in the rate of return over the term of the lease by increasing the yield during periods of inflation. (*See CONSUMER PRICE INDEX.*)

2. A clause contained in some mortgages, allowed in some states, permitting the lender to increase or decrease the agreed-upon interest rate based on fluctuations in prevailing interest rates or the prime rate or based on changes in some economic index such as Treasury bill rates. Some lenders reserve the right to increase the monthly payments and/or interest rates upon the occurrence of a certain event— for example, if it is later discovered that the mortgagor-purchaser is an investor rather than an owner-occupant. This type of agreement is also sometimes called a *price adjustment clause.* In addition, some mortgage escalator clauses provide for the interest on the mortgage note to escalate up to the maximum legal rate in the event of the borrower's default.

Sample language for an escalator clause might read: "At any time from date hereof, and from time to time thereafter, the legal holder of this note may, upon three month's prior written notice, decrease or increase the interest rate of this note then in effect, provided, however, that after receipt of any notice to increase the interest rate, the undersigned may within such three months' period prepay the balance remaining unpaid hereunder without payment of any prepayment charges as are provided in this note." (*See VARIABLE INTEREST RATE.*)

ESCAPE CLAUSE   A clause in a contract relieving a party of liability for failure to perform, as where a stated contingency does not occur. If such a clause allows the party to cancel the contract for no reason whatsoever, there really is no enforceable contract since mutuality of obligation is lacking. (*See CONTINGENCY*.)

Also refers to a clause in a proprietary lease of a tenant-stockholder which permits the tenant to surrender the stock and lease back to the cooperative association and thereby terminate continuing liability for payments due under the lease.

ESCARPMENT   A long, steep face of a rock or land.

ESCHEAT   The reversion of property to the state or county, as provided by state law, in cases where a decedent dies intestate and there are no heirs capable of inheriting or when the property is abandoned. In some states, bank accounts that are unused for more than seven years will escheat to the government.

ESCROW   The process by which money and/or documents are held by a disinterested third person (a stakeholder) until the satisfaction of the terms and conditions of the escrow instructions (as prepared by the parties to the escrow). When these terms have been satisfied, there is delivery and transfer of the escrowed funds and documents. Although in some states a real estate broker is authorized to handle an escrow, the common practice is often to employ the services of a licensed escrow company, title company, or lending institution to carry out the escrow functions.

Escrow can generally be used to close the following types of real estate transactions: sales, mortgages, and exchanges; sales by means of a contract for deed; and leases of real estate. In all cases, the escrow holder acts as a fiduciary and retains documents and entrusted assets until specified conditions are fulfilled. The holder is the special and impartial agent for *both* parties and acts in accordance with the escrow instructions given by both. The sales contract usually serves as the basis for escrow instructions for both seller and buyer because it contains (or should contain) the agreement of the parties concerning who must pay the various expenses, proration date, and the like. This underscores the critical role of the real estate salesperson or broker whose responsibility it is to advise the parties and properly prepare the sales contract. If the contract has been unprofessionally prepared, the escrow company may be delayed or even prevented from closing the transaction. It is important to remember that an escrow agent does not prepare or review the legal documents—escrow merely takes directions from the parties to the contract and acts on them in a confidential manner. The parties should not rely on the escrow agent to discover defects in the transaction. If an established escrow company is not involved in the transaction, an attorney should be consulted about the preparation of proper escrow instructions.

Because of the escrow's limited duties of disclosure and the confidentially of the escrow in general, facts known to the escrow holder are normally not imputed or implied to the other party. Escrow is a limited agent for both parties, but once the conditions to the escrow transaction have been performed, the nature of the dual agency changes—escrow then becomes the agent for the seller for the money and the buyer for the deed. Escrow acts as the "clearing house" for the details of the transaction. Escrow cannot be unilaterally revoked and in the event of disagreement the escrow can only be amended, changed, or revoked by mutual agreement.

In closing a real estate transaction, the escrow company may perform such duties as paying liens, computing prorations, ordering title evidence, having new documents prepared, drawing up closing statements, obtaining necessary signatures, recording documents, and receiving and disbursing funds. After payment of their respective closing costs, the buyer is thus assured of receiving a clear title and the seller is assured of receiving the appropriate funds. Escrow fees are typically split equally between buyer and seller.

Some special situations to which an escrow arrangement is most appropriate are: closing of sale and immediate resale or purchase; closing when several lenders are involved either in new mortgages or releases of prior encumbrances; closing an entire condomininum project when purchasers' funds must be escrowed under state law; closing a VA or FHA loan (this is an FHA/VA requirement).

When a valid escrow has been set up and a binding and enforceable contract of sale has been deposited with the escrow holder along with a fully executed deed, the death or incapacity of one of the parties to the escrow will not terminate the escrow. Upon performance of the decedent's part of the contract, the other party is entitled to have escrow concluded according to the terms of the contract.

An escrow is usually not opened until major contingencies in the contract of sale have been met. Such major contingencies might be the arrangement of new financing or the approval of a loan assumption, building permit, zoning change, or the like. Among the contingencies which can be taken care of *after* the start of escrow are appliance check, termite inspection, and signing of bylaws or house rules. (*See BACK-TO-BACK ESCROW, CLOSING COSTS, DELIVERY, DOUBLE ESCROW, HOLDING ESCROW, INTEREST, INTERPLEADER, RELATION-BACK DOCTRINE.*)

ESCROW INSTRUCTIONS In a sales transaction, a writing signed by buyer and seller that details the procedures necessary to close a transaction and directs the escrow agent how to proceed. Sometimes the buyer and seller execute separate instructions and sometimes the contract of sale itself serves as the escrow instructions. A broker who does not join in the escrow agreement could find the seller successfully ordering the escrow company not to pay the broker the listing commission.

ESTATE 1. The degree, quantity, nature, and extent of ownership interest that a person has in real property. It refers to one's legal interest or rights, not to the physical quantity of land. To be an estate, an interest must be one that is (or may become) possessory and whose ownership is measured in terms of duration. A *freehold estate* (a fee simple or a life estate) is an interest in land for an uncertain duration. All other interests are less than freehold, and include leasehold interests, such as an estate for years or an estate at will. Not all interests in land are estates. For example, a mortgage is a lien or charge on land, but it is not a part of ownership and thus is not an estate. Also, an easement is an interest in land but not an estate because it cannot vest in possession. Estates that are created by operation of law (such as dower) are known as *legal estates,* as distinguished from *conventional estates,* or those created by the parties. The word "estate" has its origin in the historic feudal system in which a person's "status" was determined primarily by the extent of that person's land ownership. (*See TENANCIES.*) 2. The property owned by a decedent and which may be subject to probate administration, federal and state tax, and claims by creditors.

ESTATE AT WILL   Leasehold estate that can be terminated at any time by either landlord or tenant. (*See TENANCY AT WILL.*)

ESTATE OF INHERITANCE   A freehold estate that can be passed by descent or by will after the owner's death, such as a fee simple absolute. A life estate is not an estate of inheritance.

ESTATE TAX, FEDERAL   An excise tax imposed under the Internal Revenue Code by the federal government upon the transfer of property from the estate of a deceased to a beneficiary upon, or by reason of, the decedent's death. All property in which the deceased had an interest, *including* jointly held property, life insurance proceeds, and property in which the decedent had retained a life estate may be subject to federal estate tax. The Tax Reform Act of 1976 reflected substantial change in the area of federal estate taxation. Three of the major changes include: (1) No longer would lifetime transfers (gifts) receive preferential treatment over transfers effective at death; in addition, gift taxes and estate taxes were set up under a common rate schedule. Gift tax rates had previously been three-fourths of estate tax rates. (2) Lifetime transfers (gifts) and transfers effective at death would be cumulated for determining estate tax; however, any gift tax paid would be subtracted from any estate tax due. (3) Under certain conditions, real property used for farming or trade or business may be valued on the basis of its use instead of on the basis of "highest and best" use.

The Economic Recovery Act of 1981 adopted the following changes in the area of federal estate taxation: (1) The amount exempt from taxation would be increased over a six-year phase-in period from $175,000 in 1981 to $600,000 in 1987; (2) after 1981 unlimited amounts of property may be transferred to a spouse tax free; (3) generally, the value of gifts (other than gifts of life insurance) made by a decedent within three years of death is not includable in the gross estate. In addition, post-gift appreciation will not be included in the gross estate. However, transfers made within three years of death (other than gifts qualifying for the annual gift tax exclusion) are includable in the gross estate for purposes of determining the estate's qualification for special use valuation, deferral of estate taxes and stock redemptions, and for purposes of determining property that is subject to estate tax liens.

The basis of inherited property is the value at the time of the death of the decedent or six months later.

The federal estate tax is due and payable within 9 months after the decedent's death. Extension on payment of the tax may be granted upon petition showing that the estate would have to sell an asset at a "sacrifice" price. Beneficiaries inheriting a family farm or business may be granted an extension to pay the estate tax. Where this extension is granted, the U.S. Treasury has a lien on the property. Lenders are reluctant to lend money to owners of such real estate. Now, the Treasury may subordinate its lien to that of a bank. In the sale of real property, the preliminary title report will raise the exception of unpaid estate taxes.

Competent legal advice, careful estate planning, the proper choice of form of ownership, and the use of *inter vivos* trusts can serve to eliminate much of the estate tax burden and the cost of probate administration. (*See CONSIDERATION, GIFT TAX, INHERITANCE TAX, PROBATE, STEPPED-UP BASIS.*)

ESTOPPEL   A legal doctrine by which a person is prevented from asserting rights or facts which are inconsistent with a previous position or representation made by act, conduct, or silence. For example, a mortgagor who certifies that he or she has no defense against the mortgagee would be estopped to later assert any defenses against a person who purchased the mortgage in reliance on the mortgagor's certificate of no defense. An estoppel differs from a waiver in that a waiver generally refers to a voluntary surrender or relinquishment of some known right, whereas estoppel creates an inability to assert a defense or right.

If the conduct of one party to an agreement is such that it misleads another, and the first party relies on that conduct, an estoppel will be created to prevent the first party from denying the effect of his or her conduct (called estoppel in pais). When a grantor conveys more interest in land than he or she in fact has, and later acquires the full title, such grantor can be barred by estoppel from denying the grantee's full interest in the land. When a real estate owner allows another person to act as if he or she is the true owner, and an innocent purchaser buys the land from that other person, the true owner is estopped from asserting ownership.

In boundary cases, a landowner is sometimes estopped to assert that the true boundary line is different from the line previously agreed upon by the owner and his or her neighbor. This is especially true if the neighbor has acted in reliance on the landowner's representations of the location of the line and built a fence or driveway, planted crops, made improvements, or the like.

Sometimes a seller under an *oral* contract of sale is estopped to assert the Statute of Frauds as a defense to the buyer's suit for specific performance when the buyer has entered into possession, paid money, or made improvements, *and* the buyer can show that he or she would suffer irreparable injury and hardship if the contract were not enforced.

Equitable estoppel may be asserted by a developer who obtained a building permit but then finds the government has downzoned the parcel or changed the land use. (*See NONCONFORMING USE.*)

A purchaser of rental property might have the existing tenants execute estoppel statements acknowledging their obligation to pay the proper amount of rent according to the specified terms of their leases. (*See CERTIFICATE OF NO DEFENSE, LACHES, REDUCTION CERTIFICATE.*)

ESTOPPEL BY DEED   A legal doctrine that applies to a person who, without having legal title to a property, deeds the property to another and then *subsequently* obtains good title to the property. The grantor is then estopped from denying his or her lack of title at the time of the original conveyance, thus automatically vesting complete legal title in the grantee. Also called title by estoppel. (*See AFTER-ACQUIRED.*)

ESTOPPEL CERTIFICATE   See CERTIFICATE OF NO DEFENSE.

ESTOVERS   Necessities allowed by law, such as the right of a tenant to use whatever timber there may be on leased premises in order to support his or her minimum needs for fuel, repairs, and tools.

ET AL.   Latin abbreviation for *et alii*, meaning "and others."

ETHICS   A system of moral principles, rules, and standards of conduct. High ethical standards are more important in real estate than in other transactions where the clients may be more familiar with the services performed. Good ethics is concerned with fidelity, integrity, and competency. (*See CODE OF ETHICS.*)

ETHNIC GROUP   People belonging to the same race having a common heritage of language, culture, and customs. (*See DISCRIMINATION.*)

ET UX.   Latin abbreviation for *et uxor*, meaning "and wife."

ET VIR.   Latin for "and husband."

EVICTION   The disturbance of a tenant's enjoyment of all or any material part of the leased premises by act of the landlord or by claim of a superior title by a third party. The legal process of removing a tenant from the premises for some breach of the lease. In the case of a *partial eviction*, the tenant is deprived of the use of part of the premises. Upon eviction, the tenant is no longer responsible for paying rent, unless the lease contains a survival clause stating that the tenant's liability for rent survives eviction.

Typical grounds for the eviction of a tenant include nonpayment of rent, unlawful use of the premises violating the use provisions of the lease (such as conducting a business in a rental unit leased strictly for residential purposes), and noncompliance with health and safety codes. (*See CONSTRUCTIVE EVICTION, EJECTMENT, SUMMARY POSSESSION.*)

EVIDENCE OF TITLE   Proof of ownership of property. Common examples of such evidence are a certificate of title, title insurance policy, or, with Torrens registered property, a Torrens certificate of title.

A person who contracts to sell property must furnish the buyer with a marketable title to the property. Unless the contract provides otherwise, however, the seller is not obliged to furnish the buyer with any evidence that the title is good and marketable. Generally, either party (or in some states, both parties) may pay for a lawyer's abstract of title or title insurance policy. This usually depends on local practice and custom as reflected in the contract terms. (*See CERTIFICATE OF TITLE, TAX AND LIEN SEARCH, TITLE INSURANCE.*)

EXAMINATION, LICENSING   In *all states*, anyone seeking a real estate license must take a written examination and demonstrate a reasonable knowledge of general real property laws and principles, documents, and state licensing laws. Separate examinations are generally given to salespeople and brokers. Requirements vary from state to state, and details and qualifications for each state's exam can be obtained from the appropriate state licensing officials.

EXCEPTION   1. As used in a conveyance of real property, an exception is the exclusion from the conveyance of some part of the property granted. The title to that withdrawn part remains in the grantor by virtue of the original title rights. A conveyance by Grant Park to Bob Lee of a ten-acre parcel "excepting therefrom a strip of land ten feet wide running along the northerly boundary" constitutes a legal exception. An exception is to be distinguished from a *reservation,* which is the creation on behalf of the grantor of a new right issuing out of the thing granted, such as the reservation of an easement by the grantor to cross the property or the reservation of a life estate in the conveyed property. 2. Liens and encumbrances specifically excluded from coverage under a title insurance policy. 3. Those matters noted in the "subject to" clause of the contract of sale, in which the seller agrees to convey clear and marketable title "subject to the following exceptions." (*See RESERVATION.*)

EXCESS CONDEMNATION   The taking of more land than is actually used to meet the public purpose of the condemnation. The excess is sometimes sold at public auction after the project is completed.

EXCHANGE   A transaction in which all or part of the consideration for the purchase of real property is the transfer of property of "like kind" (i.e., real estate for real estate). The original attraction of an exchange was in those cases where it was difficult to produce a cash buyer. Under present income tax laws, however, the exchange (Internal Revenue Code Section 1031) has become a popular device for deferring capital gains taxes. The *tax-free exchange,* as it is sometimes called (erroneously, since it only defers the tax), involves the exchange of property held for investment or the production of income for property of a like kind (which includes improved and unimproved property). In such an exchange, payment of any capital gains tax is not avoided but, rather, is deferred until the property is later disposed of in a taxable transaction. The underlying philosophy behind an exchange is that income tax should not apply as long as an investment remains intact in the form of real estate. The exchange of a personal residence does not qualify for this tax-deferred treatment but does qualify for deferral of tax treatment under IRC § 1034 when "replaced" within 24 months. A leasehold with 30 or more years remaining under the lease is considered "like" a fee title to improved or unimproved property. One disadvantage to an investor in a tax-free exchange is that the basis in the new property is lower than it would have been had the new property been purchased and the old property been sold in separate transactions. Such a reduced basis thus results in smaller depreciation deductions. It is important that the contract indicate the taxpayer's intention to *exchange* rather than to *sell* the property.

The most frequent types of exchanges are the "three-cornered" exchanges. In one type, the exchanging party (A) conveys his property (1) to the purchaser (B) in exchange for new property (2) which the purchaser obtains pursuant to the exchanging party's directions.

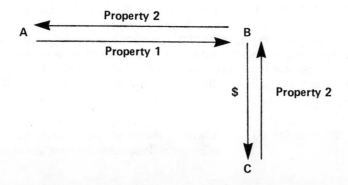

In another type, the exchanging party (A) conveys his property (1) to the purchaser (B) in exchange for new property (2) received directly from a third-party seller (C).

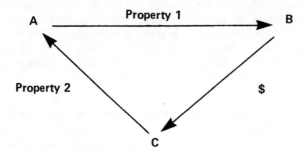

It is rare to find two properties of equal value; therefore, to balance the equities, one party usually also pays some money or assumes a larger amount of underlying debt. If received by the party seeking the tax-free exchange, this money or additional debt from which a person is relieved would be treated as *boot* and gain will be taxable to the extent of that boot. For example, Angelo Domni wants to exchange his $500,000 apartment building subject to a $400,000 mortgage lien for Howard Long's apartment building, valued at $450,000 with a $400,000 mortgage. Domni's equity is $100,000 and Long's equity is $50,000. Therefore, Long would have to pay $50,000 in boot to equalize the equities. Or, if the equities were the same, but Howard's property had only a $350,000 mortgage (so that Angelo was relieved of $400,000 but assumed only $350,000) then Angelo would again be considered to have received $50,000 of boot. If any of the *exchangors* are married, the involved spouse should release any marital rights in the exchange deed. (*See BOOT, DELAYED EXCHANGE, DOWER, LIKE KIND, MULTIPLE ASSET EXCHANGE.*)

EXCISE TAX A tax not imposed on property. It is a direct tax, imposed without assessment, and is measured according to the amount of services performed, income received, or similar criteria. Examples are license fees, sales tax, and federal estate tax.

EXCLUSIONARY ZONING The zoning of an area in such a way as to exclude minorities and low-income people. For example, the requirement of minimum lot or house size might have a discriminatory effect, whether intentional or not, unless justified on grounds of protecting the general health, safety, and welfare of the community.

EXCLUSIVE AGENCY A written listing agreement giving a sole agent the right to sell a property for a specified time, but reserving to the owner the right to sell the property himself without owing a commission. The exclusive agent is entitled to a commission if he or she personally sells the property or if it is sold by anyone other than the seller. It is exclusive in the sense the property is listed with only one broker. (*See EXCLUSIVE RIGHT TO SELL.*)

EXCLUSIVE LISTING A written listing of real property in which the seller agrees to appoint only one broker to sell the property for a specified period of time. The two types of exclusive listings are the exclusive agency and the exclusive right to sell. All exclusive listings must stipulate a definite termination date. A listing for an indefinite period is frowned on by the courts, is illegal in many states, and is generally poor practice. This is to protect sellers who, unaware that the listing is still in effect after the end of the initial listing period since they failed to give a cancellation notice, may list the property with another broker and thus find themselves liable for the payment of two full commissions.

Article 6 of the Realtors® Code of Ethics provides that "To prevent dissension and misunderstanding, and to assure better service to the owner, the Realtor® should urge the exclusive listing of property unless contrary to the best interest of the owner." This Article 6 has come under recent attack on antitrust grounds. (*See EXTENDER CLAUSE.*)

EXCLUSIVE RIGHT TO SELL   A written listing agreement appointing a broker the exclusive agent for the sale of property for a specified period of time. The listing broker is entitled to a commission if the property is sold by the owner, by the broker, or by anyone else. The phrase "right to sell" really means the right to find a buyer; it does not mean that the agent has a power of attorney from the owner to sell the property. Unless the contract clearly states it is an exclusive right or authorization to sell, most courts will treat it as being a mere exclusive agency listing. (*See EXCLUSIVE AGENCY, LISTING, TERMINATION OF LISTING.*)

EXCULPATORY CLAUSE   1. A clause sometimes inserted in a mortgage note in which the lender waives the right to a deficiency judgment. 2. As used in a lease, a clause that intends to clear or relieve the landlord from liability for tenants' personal injury in common areas and property damage. It may not, however, protect the landlord from injuries to third parties. Some states have passed legislation banning the use of exculpatory clauses in multifamily residential leases. The issue in these cases is freedom to contract versus the social policy of the state. (*See DISCLAIMER.*)

EXECUTE   The act of making a document legally valid, such as formalizing a contract by signing, or acknowledging and delivering a deed. In some cases, execution of a document may refer solely to the act of signing; in other cases it may refer to complete performance of the document's terms.

EXECUTION   A judicial process whereby the court directs an officer to levy upon (seize) the property of a judgment debtor in satisfaction of a judgment lien. State laws usually protect certain properties from execution. (*See HOMESTEAD, WRIT OF EXECUTION.*)

EXECUTOR   A person appointed by a testator to carry out the directions and requests in his or her last will and testament, and to dispose of his or her property according to the provisions of the will. State probate laws generally refer to this person as a "personal representative of the decedent."

The executor is entitled to possession and control of the testator's real estate pending determination of heirs, payment of claims, and distribution of the property.

Unless the power to sell the decedent's real property is given to the executor in the will, he or she must request court approval prior to selling the property. The executor does not generally need a real estate license in order to sell the property, but must be authorized to do so by the probate court. When the will authorizes the executor to sell real property, the property may be sold either at public auction or private sale, without prior notice to the court (however, title does not pass until the sale is confirmed by the court). Usually, the executor must make a final accounting within one year of having been appointed. (*See ADMINISTRATOR, PROBATE.*)

EXECUTORY CONTRACT
A contract in which one or both of the parties has not yet performed, such as a contract for sale. An *executed contract,* on the other hand, is one in which there is nothing left to be done by either party; it has been completely performed by both parties. The instrument is no longer a contract but rather is evidence of an executed agreement. The distinction is important. For example, the Statute of Frauds does not generally apply to an executed *oral* agreement; thus, one who conveys property by deed in accordance with an oral contract of sale cannot later assert the Statute of Frauds to try to rescind the contract and regain the property. If executory, however, the seller could not be forced to convey the deed under oral contract.

EXECUTORY INTEREST
An interest in real property which shifts title from one transferee to another (i.e., "to Harry Green and his heirs, but if Alice Gorski marries Mike Cwik, then to Alice Gorski and her heirs") or "springs out" of the grantor in the future (i.e., "to Harry Green and his heirs when and if Harry Green marries Carol Kaiser"). A fee simple subject to an executory interest is an estate where, upon the happening of an event designated in the grant, the fee simple is automatically transferred to a third person and not to the original grantor or his or her heirs. For example, Jim Winn grants his farm "to George Zito so long as it is used during the next 20 years to grow wheat, and if not so used, then to Ed Schultz and his heirs."

The distinction between an executory interest and a *possibility of reverter* (when the property reverts to the grantor) is important because the executory interest must generally become possessory within the period allowed under state law. (*See FUTURE INTEREST, POSSIBILITY OF REVERTER, RULE AGAINST PERPETUITIES.*)

EXHIBIT
A document or section of a document presented as part of the supporting data for the principal document. For example, a contract of sale may have a legal description attached as an exhibit; an inventory of furniture may also be attached as an exhibit. (*See ADDENDUM.*)

EXPANSION OPTION
A provision in a lease granting a tenant the option to lease additional adjacent space after a specified period of time.

EXPOSURE
1. Where and/or how a property is situated in terms of compass direction or its accessibility to air, light, or facilities. For example, many properties are offered as having a southern exposure or a high degree of exposure to sunlight.

Many commercial tenants prefer the south and west sides of business streets because the pedestrian traffic seeks the shady side of the street in warm weather. In addition, merchandise displayed in store windows on this side of the street is less prone to damage by the sun.

2. In marketing terms, a property must be exposed for sale in the open market. A property's exposure to the market includes how it is displayed, exhibited, and/or allowed to be seen by qualified buyers.

EXTENDED COVERAGE 1. A term used extensively in fire insurance policies to denote that the policies cover damage by wind, hail, explosion, riots, smoke, and other perils. 2. A title insurance policy which covers risks normally excluded by most standard coverage policies. The standard policy normally insures the title only as shown by the public records. It does not cover unrecorded matters that might be discovered by an inspection of the premises. Most lenders require extended-coverage mortgage title insurance policies. Extended coverage indemnifies the insured against such things as mechanics' liens, tax liens, miscellaneous liens, encumbrances, easements, rights of parties in possession, and encroachments, which may not be disclosed by the public records. (See AMERICAN LAND TITLE ASSOCIATION, TITLE INSURANCE.)

EXTENDER CLAUSE 1. A clause, once found in most listing forms, which provided that the listing would continue for a set period of time, such as 90 days, and then would be automatically renewable until the parties agreed to terminate it. Use of such clauses in listing contracts is frowned on by the courts and is a violation of many state license laws. The use of such a clause by an organization may be a violation of the antitrust laws. Such clauses, however, do not violate antitrust laws if inserted by individual brokers in their own exclusive listing forms, though the clause must state a final termination date.

2. A "carry-over" clause (often referred to as a *safety clause*) may be contained in a listing. It provides that a broker is still entitled to a commission for a set period of time after the listing has expired if the property is sold to a prospect of the broker introduced to the property during the period of the listing. A clause stating such conditions for payment might read: "If within 90 days after expiration of the listing agreement, the property is sold to or exchanged with any person who physically inspected the property with the broker or any cooperating broker during the listing period if the broker gave the seller the name of such a person in writing within five days after the stated expiration date of the listing agreement." The owner should disclose to any broker seeking a listing whether there are any expired listings. Unless careful disclosure is made of any extender clauses in such expired listings, the owner could be faced with a claim for commissions from both the former broker who had shown the buyer the property and the new broker. (See NEGOTIATION, OVERRIDE.)

EXTENSION An agreement to continue the period of performance beyond a specified period. For example, under the terms of a sales contract, the seller's broker may have the right to extend the time for closing an additional 30 days.

In periods of tight money, when buyers with maturing contracts for deed find it difficult to sell or refinance their property prior to the maturity date of their contract for deed, many buyers are willing to pay a premium in order to extend the agreement and thus avoid a default. However, care should be taken by a mortgagee in extending a debt since, in the case of deed assumptions, an extension may have the effect of changing the original contract so that guarantors and prior grantees are released from liability.

A lease extension is an agreement by which the lease is made effective for an additional period of time beyond its effective date; it is often referred to as a lease renewal.

FACADE　　　The exposed or front face of a building; often used to describe an exterior that features a unique architectural design or concept.

FACE VALUE　　　The amount due at the maturity of an instrument; the par value as shown on its face, not the real value or the market value. Mortgage notes are often sold at a discount below their face value.

FAIR CREDIT REPORTING ACT　　　A federal law designed to protect the public from the reporting of inaccurate information by credit agencies. Under the Fair Credit Reporting Act, an individual has the right to inspect information in his or her file at the credit bureau, correct any errors, and make explanatory statements as a supplement to the file. The act also requires that if a seller of real estate refuses to sell to a particular prospective buyer or to extend the buyer credit under a contract for deed because of the buyer's credit report, the seller must disclose to the prospective buyer the identity of the credit agency making the report. Most adverse information about a debtor is dropped after 7 years (except bankruptcy information, which is held 14 years).

A related law is the federal Fair Debt Collection Practices Act, concerned with regulating the activities of collection agencies in the collection of consumer debts, that is, debts incurred by a natural person to obtain money, property, insurance, or services primarily for personal, family, or household use. Also related is the Freedom of Information Act.

FAIR HOUSING ACT　　　See *FEDERAL FAIR HOUSING LAW.*

FAIR MARKET VALUE　　　An appraisal term for the highest price which a property, if offered for sale for a reasonable period of time in a competitive market, would bring to a seller who is willing, but not compelled to sell, from a buyer who is willing, but not compelled to buy, both parties being fully informed of all the purposes to which the property is best adapted and ways it is capable of being used. Fair market value is used as a basis for determining property taxes in some states. It is not to be confused with purchase price since factors such as negotiating ability and timing may make the fair market value more of a theoretical value. (*See ASSESSED VALUATION.*)

FALSE ADVERTISING   Advertising that contains blatantly false or misleading information. False advertising by a seller constitutes misrepresentation and thus gives the buyer relying on it grounds for cancelling his or her contract to purchase. In certain cases, false advertising may constitute fraud and would be grounds for a court to award a money judgment for any damages suffered. Generally, a real estate licensee responsible for false advertising is subject to suspension or revocation of his or her real estate license. A nonlicensee who makes false representations (for instance, in respect to a subdivision) may be subject to criminal prosecution. (See *ADVERTISING, BLIND AD.*)

FAMILY   In the traditional sense, family refers to persons related to each other by blood or marriage. In the more modern sense, the term family is being given a broader interpretation, to include certain nontraditional living arrangements. It is important to check definitions under local zoning ordinances to see whether "single-family dwellings" permit unmarried, unrelated groups such as the elderly or disabled to live together. (See *RELATED PARTIES.*)

FANNIE MAE   Nickname of the Federal National Mortgage Association (FNMA). Other agencies active in the secondary mortgage market are Ginnie Mae and Freddie Mac. (See *FEDERAL NATIONAL MORTGAGE ASSOCIATION.*)

FARM AND LAND INSTITUTE   A national organization which is a section of the National Association of Realtors ®. It is concerned with all aspects of the sale of land. The professional designation conferred to qualified members is AFLM, Accredited Farm and Land Member.

FARM AREA   A selected geographical area or one specific building to which a real estate salesperson devotes special attention and study. A good salesperson learns everything there is to know about a particular farm area, including all recent comparable sales, and tries to solicit listings from this community. The salesperson is thus an expert on his or her farm area.

FARM ASSETS   The true concept of a ranch or farm, offered for sale or exchange, separated into its component assets (particularly for income tax purposes) consists, among other things, of: farmland; personal residence; other residences and structures used in the business of farming or ranching; vines, trees, pipelines, fences, irrigation systems, livestock; and unharvested crops sold to the purchaser.

These assets are subject to special treatment for income tax purposes, as provided for in the Internal Revenue Code and the Regulations of the Internal Revenue Service. Therefore, price allocation upon sale, exchange, or lease of the whole ranch or farm property, or some part thereof, is important.

FARM CREDIT SYSTEM   A federal program inaugurated under the Federal Farm Loan Act of 1916, designed to serve the unique financial requirements of farmers, ranchers, producers and harvesters of agricultural products, rural homeowners, and owners of selected farm-related businesses. The 50 states are divided into 12 Farm Credit Districts, operating independently under the supervision of the Federal Farm Credit Administration.

FARMER'S HOME ADMINISTRATION (FmHA)

A federal agency under the U.S. Department of Agriculture, originally designed to handle emergency farm financing, that channels credit to farmers and rural residents and communities. Loans can be made for housing located in open country and in all rural communities with populations under 10,000, and in most towns with populations between 10,000 and 20,000 that are outside of Standard Metropolitan Statistical Areas (SMSAs) and have a serious lack of mortgage credit.

There are a variety of credit programs to be used to help purchase or operate farms, provide new employment and business opportunities, enhance environment, and acquire homes. Most of the loan programs fall into two categories; guaranteed loans, in which the loan is made and serviced by a private lender and guaranteed for a specified percentage by the FmHA, and insured loans that are originated, made, and serviced by the agency. Discounts, or points, are not allowed with such loans and preference is given to eligible veterans.

FARMLAND

Land used specifically for agricultural purposes, in the raising of either crops or livestock. Also land so designated in zoning laws for agricultural purposes.

FEASIBILITY STUDY

An analysis of a proposed subject or property with emphasis on the attainable income, probable expenses, and most advantageous use and design. A feasibility study is often used by a developer to entice investors to put up the front money for a proposed development. Such a study is required by some mortgage investors and lending institutions prior to granting a loan commitment. In addition to being a decision-making tool for the developer and lender, it is also a valuable sales tool. However, it is different from a marketability study which is more concerned with demand for the contemplated use. (See ABSORPTION RATE, FRONT MONEY.)

The purpose of a feasibility study is to estimate the rate of return obtainable for a specific project and to determine whether the proposed project is economically feasible.

Also, a survey of an urban area using federal funds to determine if it is practicable to undertake an urban renewal project within that area.

FEDERAL FAIR HOUSING LAW

In 1968, Congress enacted Title VIII of the Civil Rights Act, called the Federal Fair Housing Act, which declared a national policy of providing fair housing throughout the United States (Reference Sections 3601-3631 of Title 42, United States Code). This law makes discrimination based on race, color, sex, religion, or national origin illegal in connection with the sale or rental of most dwellings and any vacant land offered for residential construction or use. The federal law does not prohibit discrimination in other types of real estate transactions, such as those involving commercial or industrial properties. The law is administered by the Office of Equal Opportunity (OEO) under the direction of the Secretary of the Department of Housing and Urban Development (HUD).

As amended in 1972, the law instituted the use of equal opportunity posters (11″ × 14″) for display at brokerage houses, model home sites, mortgage lenders' offices, and other related locations. Failure to display the poster constitutes prima facie evidence of discrimination if a broker who does not display the sign is investigated by HUD on charges of discrimination. The poster must have the equal housing opportunity slogan: Equal Housing Opportunity. It must also carry the equal housing opportunity statement: "We are pledged to the letter and spirit of U.S. policy for the achievement of equal housing opportunity throughout the Nation. We encourage and support an affirmative advertising and marketing program in which there are no barriers to obtaining housing because of race, color, religion, sex, or national origin." There also must be the following equal housing opportunity logo on the poster:

The fair housing law provides protecton against the following acts of discrimination, if they are based on race, color, sex, religion, or national origin:

- Refusing to sell or rent to, deal, or negotiate with any person.

- Discriminating in terms or conditions for buying or renting housing.

- Discrimination by advertising that housing is available only to persons of a certain race, color, sex, religion, or national origin; such as placing sold signs when the property is not, in fact, sold.

- Denying that housing is available for inspection, sale, or rent when it really is available. (This includes a practice called *steering*, whereby certain brokers may steer members of minority groups away from some of their listings in racially unmixed areas.)

- Blockbusting, a practice whereby a broker hopes to make a profit through persuading owners to sell or rent housing by telling them that minority groups are moving into the neighborhood, also called "panic-peddling."

- Denying or requiring different terms or conditions for home loans made by commercial lenders, such as banks, savings and loan associations, and insurance companies.

- Denying to anyone the use of or participation in any real estate service, such as broker's organizations, multiple-listing services, or other facilities related to the selling or renting of housing.

The Fair Housing Act applies to the following:

- Single-family housing owned by private individuals when a broker or other person in the business of selling or renting dwellings is *employed* (includes use of MLS) *and/or* discriminatory advertising is used.

- Single-family housing not owned by private individuals, such as those owned by development corporations.

- Single-family housing owned by a private individual who owns more than three such dwellings or who, in any two-year period, sells more than one dwelling in which he or she was not the most recent resident.

- Multifamily dwellings of five or more units.

- Multifamily dwellings containing four or fewer units, if the owner does not reside in one of the units.

Exceptions: The following situations are exempt from the Fair Housing Act (but covered by the post-Civil War 1866 antidiscrimination civil rights law, if based on race):

- The sale or rental of single-family housing if neither a broker nor discriminatory advertising is used, and no more than one dwelling in which the owner was not the most recent resident is sold during any two-year period.

- The rental of rooms or units in owner-occupied multiple dwellings for two to four families, if discriminatory advertising is not used (the "Mrs. Murphy exemption"—Mrs. Murphy represents the small investor struggling to earn a living by taking in roomers in a small rooming house).

- The sale, rental, or occupancy of dwellings owned and operated by a religious organization for other than commercial purposes to persons of the same religion, if membership in that religion is not restricted on account of race, color, sex, or national origin; the religious organization can give preference to its members (e.g., it could assess a surcharge to nonmembers).

- The restriction of lodgings owned or operated by a private club for other than a commercial purpose to rental or occupancy by its own members.

There are two separate remedial avenues, one administrative and one judicial. An aggrieved person may take his or her complaint directly to a U.S. District Court within 180 days of the alleged discriminatory practice, whether or not a verified complaint has been filed with the Secretary of the Department of Housing and Urban Development. However, in states with equivalent antidiscrimination judicial rights and remedies, such a suit would have to be brought in the state court. The burden of proof is on the complainant. The court can grant permanent or temporary injunctions, temporary restraining orders, or other appropriate relief, and may award actual damages and not more than $1,000 in punitive damages. Criminal penalties are provided for those who coerce, intimidate, threaten, or interfere with a person's buying, renting, or selling housing, making a complaint of discrimination, or exercising any rights in connection with this law. Licensees should keep detailed records of all transactions and rentals in order to defend themselves against possible discrimination complaints. Violations are frequently proven through the use of "testers" and the courts have ruled that there is no requirement that the testers actually be bona fide purchasers or renters. (See *BLOCKBUSTING, DISCRIMINATION, STEERING.*)

Under 1980 regulations, HUD has identified certain words which should be avoided because they may tend to convey discriminatory intent, for example: White, Black, Colored, Catholic, Jew, Protestant, Chinese, Chicano, Irish, restricted, ghetto, disadvantaged, private, membership approval.

Advertising should never state or imply that the rental of separate units in a dwelling is restricted to persons of only one sex unless the sharing of living areas is involved. Even directions to the real estate for sale may be discriminatory, such as references to synagogues or "near Martin Luther King memorial," or close to a specific country club or private school that caters to particular racial, religious, or ethnic groups.

The selective use of advertising media or content based on ethnic considerations could be considered as violating the intent of the law. For example, the sole use of an English language newspaper in an area like Miami, Florida, where there are many Hispanic publications. While you cannot be forced to advertise in a minority media, such failure will be a factor to consider in a discrimination hearing, as would be a policy of using as human models members of only one sex, race, or other group (it is not necessary, however, to have an exact percentage of the various groups in the local population).

Discrimination in federally subsidized housing projects is prohibited under Title VI, Civil Rights Act of 1964, which states that: "No person in the United States shall, on the ground of race, color, or national origin, be excluded from participation in, be denied the benefits of, or be subject to discrimination under any program or activity receiving federal financial assistance."

FEDERAL DEPOSIT INSURANCE CORPORATION (FDIC) An independent executive agency designed to insure the deposits of all banks entitled to federal deposit insurance. Individual accounts are insured up to $100,000. The FDIC is currently a self-supporting agency, of which the premiums are well in excess of the claims and expenses.

FEDERAL HOME LOAN BANK SYSTEM (FHLB) Established by Congress in 1932 to provide reserve funds for member institutions, it serves much the same purpose with respect to savings and loan associations as the Federal Reserve System performs for commercial banks (except, of course, it does not print money).

The twelve regional FHL banks constitute a permanent pool of reserve credit to maintain liquidity of members and to provide a means for mortgage lending when local funds are insufficient. For example, in one particular month, the Federal Home Loan Board reduced the liquidity requirement from 5½ percent to 5 percent for federally insured savings and loan associations, making more than $1 billion available for mortgage-lending purposes. The FHLB enforces the federal truth-in-lending provisions concerning savings and loan associations. All federally chartered savings and loan associations are required to become members of their regional home loan banks.

To illustrate the impact the board can have on the mortgage market, here is a list of major policy revisions made in 1981:

• Savings and loan associations may offer 40-year mortgages with 10 percent down payments instead of the current 30-year mortgages and 20 percent down payments. The 40-year mortgages do not apply to condo or cooperative conversions unless the buyer is the principal occupant.

• Dollar limits on home loans are removed, a plus for buyers in high-cost areas who wish to buy multifamily units.

- The first lien restriction on home loans is canceled, permitting buyers to borrow additional mortgage money for other purposes.

- Restrictions on the geographical locations of loan security properties have been removed, which should provide an inflow of mortgage money to areas with fund shortages from areas with surplus funds.

- The current $15,000 limit on home improvement loans is lifted.

FEDERAL HOME LOAN MORTGAGE CORPORATION (FHLMC)

A federal agency established in 1970 to buy mortgages in the secondary mortgage market from commercial banks having insured deposits or from federally insured savings and loan associations belonging to the Federal Home Loan Bank System. Although its main purpose is to provide an outlet for conventional mortgage loans originated by savings and loan associations, it does include FHA and VA loans as well. FHLMC does a high volume of trading in conventional mortgage-backed securities, conventional mortgages, FHA and VA loans, and GNMA loans.

Commonly called "Freddie Mac" or The Mortgage Corp, it has become an important auxiliary source of mortgage funds for condominium mortgages since entering the field. Many condominium lenders use the standardized forms and follow the guidelines issued by Freddie Mac, as use of these forms is mandatory for lenders desiring to make use of the Freddie Mac secondary market. The standardized documentation includes not only legal documents, such as mortgage and note, but preliminary documentation as well, such as loan application, credit reports, and appraisal forms.

Lenders must not only use the standard forms but must also comply with Freddie Mac regulations. As a result, this agency plays an important role in shaping the financial practices in the real estate industry. As an example, Freddie Mac has issued regulations detailing the situations in which a "due-on-sale" clause can be exercised by the lender.

A local lender might offer to sell a participation loan package to FHLMC. For example, the lender might package up 10 of its mortgages and sell a 90 percent interest and retain 10 percent plus continue to service the loan.

FHLMC has created and marketed a new type of security called a guaranteed mortgage certificate. The certificates are backed by residential mortgages purchased by FHLMC and held in trust on behalf of the certificate holders. An investor in such certificates is investing in an undivided pool of home mortgage loans rather than individual loans. Timely payment of principal and interest on the certificates is unconditionally guaranteed by the government. (See PARTICIPATION SALE CERTIFICATE, SECONDARY MORTGAGE MARKET.)

FEDERAL HOUSING ADMINISTRATION (FHA)

History and Achievements:

FHA was established in 1934 under the National Housing Act to encourage improvement in housing standards and conditions, to provide an adequate home financing system through the insurance of housing mortgages and credit, and to exert a stabilizing influence on the mortgage market. FHA was the government's response to a lack of quality housing, excessive foreclosures, and a building industry which had collapsed during the depression.

Important achievements of the FHA program have been the general acceptance of the fully amortized loan, standardization of appraisal processes, and better planning and land utilization by developers. Additionally the introduction of high loan-to-value ratios combined with a small down payment requirement expanded significantly the number of potential homebuyers. FHA loans have traditionally played an important part in home financing even though such loans have never exceeded 30 percent of the total loans made. In recent years FHA loans have received heavy competition from conventional mortgages, which also offer high loan-to-value ratios backed by private mortgage insurance (such as MGIC).

Mutual Mortgage Insurance:

FHA, which is part of the Department of Housing and Urban Development, neither builds homes nor lends money directly. Rather it insures loans on real property, including condominiums, made by approved lending institutions. Should the homeowner default on his mortgage, the lending institution will not incur any significant losses since FHA has insured the lender against that risk. This is accomplished under a mutual mortgage insurance plan. All FHA loans regardless of type or amount require the borrower to pay an insurance premium of one-half of one percent per year on the average scheduled mortgage balance outstanding during the year. The insurance premiums decline each year as the outstanding balance declines (except in the early years of the FHA-245 Graduated Payment Mortgage). Mortgage insurance premiums are paid as part of the mortgagor's regular monthly obligation along with the principal and interest on the loan and the impounds for real property tax and hazard insurance. The homeowner who keeps his FHA mortgage loan on the books for ten years can request a refund of his share of mortgage insurance premiums collected in excess of the program's actual operating expenses.

In the event of default, the mortgagee can elect to keep the property after foreclosure and thus, in effect, disregard the insurance. It is more probable that the mortgagee will notify the FHA of default, foreclose on the property, and then convey title to the FHA. In return, the mortgagee receives interest-bearing government bonds (debentures), cash, or a combination of both. Although the debentures are guaranteed by the United States government, and are thus readily marketable, the lender may still have to take a discount. Since the debentures mature after 20 years and bear low interest rates, the mortgagee in a debenture-backed situation may have to bear some financial loss (although with most single-family homes, the FHA will usually pay cash). The foreclosed property will generally be sold at a foreclosure sale, and the lender will file a claim with the FHA for the deficiency plus foreclosure expenses (which are fixed by statute). FHA-acquired properties are often fixed up and sold on the open market through local real estate brokers.

Interest Rate and Loan Limits:

The maximum interest rate on FHA loans is set by the Secretary of Housing and Urban Development, who is responsible for adjusting the interest rate as necessary to reflect increases and decreases in the cost of mortgage money in the open marketplace. The usual term of an FHA loan is 30 years for residential loans and 40 years for multifamily-dwelling loans. Loans are made in five-year increments. Two factors limiting the length of the mortgage are: 1. the term of the loan cannot exceed three-fourths of the dwelling's remaining useful economic life as determined by the FHA appraisal; and 2. the term of the loan can be rounded only to the next higher five-year increment beyond the fixed rental period on a ground lease property. FHA makes only 20-, 25-, and 30-year loans.

Maximum loan amount limits are established by Congress although higher limits may be authorized by FHA itself in high cost-of-living areas. Loans are made in increments of $50. The maximum loan amount available on a specific property is based on the purchase price or the FHA-appraised value, whichever is less. (It should be noted that FHA recognizes VA appraisals, but not conventional appraisals.) FHA requires that the real estate sales contract on a property include a contingency provision (usually in the form of an addendum) that should the property appraise for less than the sales price, the seller agrees to refund the buyer's good faith deposit and cancel the contract if the buyer wishes not to complete the transaction.

No secondary financing is permitted at the time an FHA-insured loan is made. Thus the borrower must be prepared to pay cash for all closing costs (it is permissible for the seller to pay closing costs) and for the difference between the sales price and the maximum loan amount, which the seller cannot pay or otherwise credit to the borrower. In fact the borrower must provide evidence of the needed funds before FHA will make its commitment to insure the loan. There is no prohibition against placing secondary financing on the property after the FHA mortgage is closed and FHA has issued FHA mortgage insurance to the lender.

Loan Fees and Discount Points:

An FHA loan applicant is allowed to pay a loan origination fee of not more than one percent of the amount borrowed (or 2½ percent for construction loans when the lender makes inspection and partial disbursements during building construction). The buyer is *not* permitted to pay any loan discount points except in the case of refinancing and builder-mortgagors. The lender normally finds it necessary to charge loan discount points to increase the yield on the loan from the set FHA interest rate to a level reflective of the cost of funds in the financial market place. One point equals one percent of the total mortgage loan amount. During periods when credit is difficult to obtain, FHA discount points have run as high as 10 or 12 points. While this is not the usual situation, the discount paid by a seller on a $50,000 loan could amount to as much as $5,000 or $6,000. A more normal range for discount points would be from two to five points.

Programs:

Title I FHA loans are granted for home improvements, alterations, and repairs. These loans are for relatively low amounts with a repayment term of no longer than 7 years and 32 days.

Title II FHA loans are granted for construction or purchase of a home. They may also be obtained to refinance existing mortgage debt. While there are a number of Title II programs, the most popular are:

> Section 203(b): The most widely used program, this mortgage is available for both owner-occupants and nonowner occupants purchasing or refinancing one- to four-family homes. The maximum loan-to-value ratio is 97 percent.

> Section 203(b) - Veteran: Qualified veterans may purchase one- to four-family homes as owner-occupants with a loan-to-value ratio which may exceed 97 percent due to a slightly lesser down payment than the standard 203(b) loan requires.

> Section 234: Condominiums are covered under this program, which in most respects is similar to the basic 203(b) program. To obtain an FHA loan in a condominium, it is necessary that the condominium itself be FHA approved.

> Section 245: The Graduated Payment Mortgage was introduced by FHA in 1978 to permit lower monthly payments in the early years of

the mortgage through negative amortization. Payments increase approximately 7½ percent the first five years to reach a level high enough to retire the increased principal balance during the last 25 years of the loan. Because of the negative amortization the loan-to-value ratio is lower than on the 203(b) and 234 programs. Depending on interest rates, the loan-to-value ratio might range from 87 to 93 percent. Because buyer qualification is based on first-year payment amount, a greater number of potential home owners can qualify for the mortgage. The primary purpose of this program is to make it possible for young homebuyers starting out with a good potential for future income growth ahead of them to qualify to buy a home sooner.

Assumptions:

At this writing FHA loans remain fully assumable with no escalation of interest rates or other modifications or changes to the underlying loan. They may be assumed either with or without a release of liability granted to the seller. If the seller seeks such a release of liability, then the new buyer must qualify with FHA and meet FHA underwriting income and credit standards.

Commitments:

A developer or builder sometimes seeks an FHA commitment to insure the mortgages on a project to be constructed. In such cases, the FHA may give a conditional commitment to ensure that is dependent upon the structures or houses being satisfactorily completed according to FHA standards as verified by FHA inspection. Some commitments are dependent upon the sale of the building to a purchaser satisfactory to the FHA. (See CLOSING COSTS, COMMITMENT, CONVENTIONAL LOAN, DEBENTURE, GRADUATED PAYMENT MORTGAGE, IN-SERVICE LOAN, INSPECTION, MINIMUM PROPERTY REQUIREMENT, MUTUAL MORTGAGE INSURANCE FUND, PRIVATE MORTGAGE INSURANCE, VA MORTGAGE.)

FEDERAL LAND BANK A privately owned cooperative organization administered by the Farm Credit Administration to provide low-cost, long-term loans to farmers and livestock corporations who belong to the Federal Land Bank Association. There are 12 federal land banks, one in each farm credit district.

FEDERAL NATIONAL MORTGAGE ASSOCIATION (FNMA) "Fannie Mae" is the popular name for the Federal National Mortgage Association, originally a federal agency created to provide a degree of liquidity in the mortgage market by establishing a secondary market for existing mortgages. The agency does not loan money directly, but rather buys mortgages with bond-generated funds, which are originated by other lending institutions. It is the nation's largest purchaser of home mortgages, about $50 billion worth. Thus, in periods of tight money, the purchase of these original loans releases more money to the lending institutions to make additional mortgages. This gives loan originators a chance to roll their funds over continuously, thus earning immediate profits and at the same time stimulating the construction activities in the economy. Fannie Mae raises cash for its purchase of mortgages by selling its own government-guaranteed debentures at market interest rates. Sometimes Fannie Mae agrees to purchase a certain number of mortgages even before the mortgages are originated; these commitments to purchase mortgages, however, usually last for only a short period of time.

FNMA originally purchased only VA and FHA loans at a discount, but now it purchases and sells conventional loans as well. These loans are assumable and contain no prepayment clause or escalator clause. Under the Housing Act of 1968, FNMA was divided into two separate and distinct corporations. One, still called Fannie Mae, is now a private corporation owned by stockholders who pay full federal corporate income taxes, and whose operations are regulated by the federal government. The other is a government agency called the Government National Mortgage Association (GNMA, popularly known as "Ginnie Mae"), which also operates in the secondary market, especially with federally subsidized projects.

Mortgage banking firms are generally quite active with the FNMA. These firms often originate mortgage loans and sell them to the FNMA, but retain the under-writing and servicing functions. The FNMA currently reimburses such lenders three-eighths of one percent of the mortgage loan balances as a fee for these serv-ices. Many lending institutions sell their mortgages to the FNMA at a discount during periods of rising interest rates and financial disintermediation. When in-terest rates fall and savings are redeposited, these institutions will generally pay a premium price to reacquire these mortgages. In order to raise funds to purchase such mortgages in the secondary market, the FNMA issues bonds collateralized by pools of mortgages acquired through the FNMA's commitment program. Lending institutions selling FHA and VA mortgage loans to the FNMA must buy capital stock in the amount of 2 percent of all mortgages sold. This stock is listed in the name of the FNMA on the New York Stock Exchange. The FNMA purchases mort-gages at market prices and may, in turn, sell them at weekly auctions in large blocks to big institutional investors such as insurance companies. (See DEBEN-TURE, GOVERNMENT NATIONAL MORTGAGE ASSOCIATION, SECONDARY MORTGAGE MARKET, TANDEM PLAN.)

FEDERAL RESERVE SYSTEM   A central banking system designed to manage the nation's economy. Each of the 12 districts is served by a federal reserve bank. The "Fed" has a great impact on real estate investment activity through its regulation of member banks' reserves, i.e., money unavailable for loans or any other use; determination of discount rates, i.e., the rate that the district banks charge member banks for the use of the Fed's money (thus impacting interest rates); decisions to buy or sell government securities; and the supervision of truth-in-lending and equal credit opportunity laws. To illustrate how the Fed can regulate lending practices, the Fed has the power to place a 2 percent surcharge on loans to member banks that bor-row quite frequently from the Fed.

FEDERAL REVENUE STAMP   A documentary transfer tax which, up until 1968, was levied by the federal government upon the transfer of title to real property. The rate was $.55 per $500 of consideration and payment was evidenced by red stamps placed on the document. After repeal of this federal tax, many states instituted their own conveyance or transfer taxes. (See CONVEYANCE TAX, TRANSFER TAX.)

FEDERAL SAVINGS AND LOAN ASSOCIATION   A savings and loan institution that is federally chartered and privately owned by shareholders (stock savings and loan) or depositors (mutual savings and loan). Such institutions are required to be members of their regional Federal Home Loan Bank and the Federal Savings and Loan Insurance Corporation (FSLIC), which performs a function similar to that of the Federal Deposit Insurance Corporation (FDIC) by insuring deposits up to $100,000 in federal savings and loan associations. State-chartered savings and loan associations who wish to be insured by FSLIC must belong to the Federal Home Loan Bank System. Savings deposit insurance, together with uniform lending policies and accounting supervision, has greatly increased public confidence in savings and loan institutions and has resulted in a considerable increase in the total assets and outstanding mortgage loans of such organizations. Federal savings and loan associations are now the leading source of residential real estate loans. (See *SAVINGS AND LOAN ASSOCIATIONS.*)

FEDERAL TAX LIEN   A federal lien which attaches to real property if either the federal estate tax is not paid or the taxpayer has violated the federal income tax or payroll tax laws.

Under the Federal Tax Lien Act of 1966, a junior federal tax lien will not be divested by a nonjudicial foreclosure proceeding (under a power of sale) taken under state law unless the federal government consents in writing to the sale or written notice of the proposed sale is given, thus providing the federal government an opportunity to collect its lien from the proceeds of the sale. Accordingly, most attorneys obtain a current title report prior to commencing a nonjudicial foreclosure in order to ascertain that there are no outstanding federal tax liens on the subject property.

A federal tax lien is generally subject to the interest of purchasers and creditors who record their interest prior to the time that notice of the federal tax lien is recorded. As with other liens, a federal tax lien is subject to liens of real property taxes and special assessments owed to the state or county, regardless of whether they are recorded before or after notice of the federal tax lien is recorded.

The above rules do not apply, however, if the taxpayer becomes insolvent. In such cases, the federal government follows different and more complex rules, claiming the priority of its lien over previously recorded liens.

The Tax Reform Act of 1976, providing for the priority of federal tax liens, is contingent on public indexing of the liens at Internal Revenue Service offices. An index of liens affecting real property is maintained in the district office for the area in which the property is located. An index of liens affecting personal property is maintained in the district office for the area in which the taxpayer resides at the time of the filing of the notice of a lien.

A tenant in common could be surprised to find the real property sold or partitioned to satisfy a federal tax lien against a cotenant in common. This potential threat of partition is also a concern to a purchaser in a timesharing project.

Under the Tax Reform Act of 1976, where the estate elects special (lower) valuation for estate taxes with respect to a "family farm" or certain real property used in a family business, a special tax lien attaches to that property for 10 years or more so that, if the property is sold during that period, the taxes "saved" as a result of that special valuation will be "recaptured."

FEDERAL TRADE   A federal agency created to investigate and elimi-
COMMISSION (FTC)   nate unfair and deceptive trade practices or unfair
                          methods of competition in interstate commerce.
Deceptive practices generally include such actions as an affirmative misstatement of fact—an express statement that is false, as well as any false implication that may reasonably be implied from such a statement. This could encompass a developer's misleading representations of his or her intent to resell property for pur-

chasers. Unfair practices would generally include any practice in which the following three elements are present: the practice offends public policy; it is immoral, unethical, oppressive, or unscrupulous; it causes injury to consumers. This would include such actions as inducing purchasers to buy through scare tactics or high-pressure gimmicks. The FTC also enforces the federal Truth-in-Lending laws as they relate to brokers.

FEE APPRAISER   A professional who, for a charge or a fee, renders an appraisal of a parcel of real property and typically submits an appraisal report.

FEE SIMPLE   The maximum possible estate one can possess in real property. A fee simple estate is the least limited interest and the most complete and absolute ownership in land; it is of indefinite duration, freely transferable, and inheritable. Fee simple title is sometimes referred to as "the fee." All other estates may be created from it, which means that all other estates must be something less than fee simple (such as life estates, leaseholds, etc.). Any limitations that exist on the control and use of the land held in fee do not result from the nature of the estate itself, but are founded on public or private controls governing the use of the land (zoning ordinances and building codes or restrictions and conditions). The fee may also be encumbered, either by voluntary (mortgage) or involuntary (tax lien) encumbrances. Such encumbrances tend to reduce the value of the fee interest. (*See FREEHOLD, RESTRICTIONS.*)

FEE SIMPLE DEFEASIBLE   An estate in land in which the holder has a fee simple title subject to being divested upon the happening of a specified condition; also called a *qualified fee* or a *defeasible fee*. There are two categories of fee defeasible estates—fee simple determinable and fee simple subject to a condition subsequent.

The term *fee simple determinable* implies that the duration of the estate can be determined from the deed itself. This is not true of a *fee simple subject to a condition subsequent*, in which case the estate's duration depends on the grantor's independent choice of whether or not to terminate the estate.

A fee simple determinable is an estate in real property that exists "so long as," "while," or "during the period" that a certain prescribed use continues. Such use is described in the grant of conveyance. For example, a conveyance to the University of Knowitall "so long as" the real estate is used for educational purposes would give the university title provided the granted land is used as prescribed. If, at some future time, the university were to stop using the property for educational purposes, title would revert to the original grantor, if living, or to his or her heirs, if the grantor is deceased. A fee simple determinable *automatically* ends when the purpose for which it has been prescribed terminates. Upon the grant of a fee simple determinable, there remains in the grantor a possibility of reverter.

A fee simple subject to a condition subsequent, on the other hand, is an estate conveyed "provided that," "on the condition that," or "if" it is used for a specific purpose. If it is no longer used for that purpose, it reverts to the original grantor or his heirs. This type of estate is much the same as a fee determinable, except that in a fee determinable conveyance, the words are of duration while a fee condition subsequent refers strictly to a specific *condition*. In addition, unlike a fee determinable, when fee condition subsequent property is no longer used for its prescribed purpose, the original grantor (or heirs) must physically retake possession of the property within a reasonable period of time after the breach (i.e., the grantor must exercise his or her right of reentry). Any transaction involving a fee simple defeasible estate should be referred to an attorney for a professional opinion. (*See POSSIBILITY OF REVERTER, RIGHT OF REENTRY.*)

FEE TAIL   A freehold estate which has the potential of continuing forever, but will necessarily cease if and when the first fee tail tenant's lineal descendants die out. It is an estate in which the right of inheritance is limited to a fixed line of succession, consisting of the direct "issue of the body," or blood relatives. Under common law, words of inheritance and procreation were needed to create a fee tail estate, that is, "Harry Hopes and the heirs of his body." The property is said to be "in entail." This type of estate is opposed to a fee simple estate, which can pass to *both* collateral and lineal heirs.

FELONY   A serious crime punishable by imprisonment in a state or federal prison. Violation of certain real estate laws are felonies. (*See MISDEMEANOR.*)

FELT JOINT COVER   A covering of tightly woven wool treated with a bitumen tar derivative that prevents seepage at the joints of plumbing pipes.

FHA   A popular reference to the Federal Housing Administration. (*See FEDERAL HOUSING ADMINISTRATION.*)

FIABCI   The acronym for the "Federation Internationale de Biens Consuls Immobliers," the former name for IREF, the International Real Estate Federation.

FICTITIOUS COMPANY NAME   A business name other than that of the person under whom the business is registered. An example would be "XYZ Real Estate," or "Greenfields Realty." Most state license laws require such brokerage offices to be jointly registered under the supervising broker's name and the business's fictitious name, such as "Elmo Schwartz, broker, also known as Bonanza Real Estate Brokers." Most states require the filing of a fictitious name certificate or a trade name registration.

FIDELITY BOND   Also known as a *surety bond*, a fidelity bond is purchased by an employer to cover his or her employees who are entrusted with sums of money or are responsible for valuable assets. Such bonded persons are required by the bonding or insurance company to carry out their duties and responsibilities effectively and honestly. Property managers and escrow companies often are required to post a fidelity bond.

FIDUCIARY   A relationship which implies a position of trust or confidence wherein one person is usually entrusted to hold or manage property or money for another. The term fiduciary describes the faithful relationship owed by an attorney to a client or by a broker (and salesperson) to a principal. Among the obligations that a fiduciary owes to his or her principal are the duties of loyalty, obedience, and full disclosure; the duty to use skill, care, and diligence; and the duty to account for all monies. When an agent breaches any of these fiduciary duties, the principal can usually bring civil action for money damages, sue to impress a constructive trust upon any secret profit, or compel the agent to forfeit any compensation.

Because of the close personal relationship between broker (agent) and seller (principal), the broker often learns certain confidential information about the seller's property and financial situation of the principal. This information cannot be used by a broker even after the transaction is completed and the fiduciary relationship terminated. One of the reasons it is so difficult to adequately represent both parties in a real estate transaction is that the broker has a duty to keep confidential that information learned from the principal and also a duty to disclose all pertinent information to the principal. (See AGENCY, DUAL AGENCY, SUBAGENT.)

FILE   To place an *original* document on public record. Most legal documents are *recorded*, i.e., kept in the form of a literal copy produced by electrostatic process and microfilm. After a document has been recorded, the original is returned to the person noted on the top left portion of the document. Documents relating to registered property (Torrens system) are filed with the registrar of titles, who retains the document. (See RECORDING, REGISTRAR, TORRENS SYSTEM.)

FILLED LAND   An area where the grade has been raised by depositing or dumping dirt, gravel, or rock. The seller, and thus the broker, of such land would, under most circumstances, have a duty to disclose to the buyer the fact that the property is on filled land. Failure to disclose such information would make the seller and broker liable if an unaware buyer subsequently were to suffer damages (for example, if the land were to slip or subside during construction) and seek to rescind the transaction upon discovery that the property is on filled land. Naturally, this disclosure rule does not apply if it is obvious that the entire community is on filled land which has been utilized for a relatively long period of time without any adverse effects. (See CAVEAT EMPTOR.)

FILTERING DOWN PROCESS   The process by which housing units originally or once occupied by middle- and upper-income families decline in relative quality and become available to occupants of lesser income.

FINANCE CHARGE   The total of all costs imposed directly or indirectly by the creditor and payable either directly or indirectly by the customer, as defined by the federal Truth-in-Lending laws. (See ANNUAL PERCENTAGE RATE, TRUTH-IN-LENDING LAWS.)

FINANCE FEE   A mortgage brokerage fee to cover the expenses incurred in placing a mortgage with a lending institution; a mortgage service charge or origination fee. With VA and FHA loans, this placement fee is limited to one percent of the loan amount, except in special cases. The usual conventional loan finance fee is approximately 1½ percent of the loan amount for an existing building and 2 percent for new construction. The finance fee is sometimes stated in points, with each point being equal to one percent of the loan amount (for example, two percent would become two points). (*See ORIGINATION FEE, POINTS.*)

FINANCIAL INSTITUTION An intermediary organization that obtains funds through deposits and then lends those funds to earn a return. Some of the prime types of financial institutions are savings and loan associations, commercial banks, credit unions, and mutual savings banks. Also known as thrift institutions.

FINANCIAL STATEMENT A formal statement of the financial status and net worth of a person or company, setting forth and classifying assets and liabilities as of a specified date. Sometimes the requester of the financial statement may require that it be certified by a recognized certified public accounting firm. The recent trend among mortgage bankers is to require certified financial statements from all loan applicants.

Under some state subdivision laws, the subdivider must present a current financial statement when registering a proposed subdivision. Financial statements are required by HUD in interstate land sales in accordance with the Interstate Land Sales Practices Act. Such statements must be certified if the subdivision is over a certain value and number of lots.

FINANCING That part of the purchase price for a property, exclusive of the down payment. Examples of instruments securing financing are mortgages, deeds of trust, contracts for deed, and the like. Typical sources of financing are banks, savings and loan associations, insurance companies, credit unions, mortgage bankers, and private parties. According to the Federal Reserve Board, residential mortgage credit represents the largest single category of credit outstanding in the United States.

Normally there are several instruments used in financing real estate. There is a note, evidencing the obligation of the borrower to repay, and the security instrument, which may be a mortgage or deed of trust. In the case of a purchase under a contract for deed, there is no note. The cost of financing real estate may include some or all of the following: appraisal fee, credit report fee, title insurance fee, correspondents' fee, attorney's fee, survey charge, closing fee, recording fee, and broker's fee. The cost to a borrower in obtaining financing varies directly with the availability of lenders seeking investments in real estate. (*See CONTRACT FOR DEED, DEED OF TRUST, MORTGAGE.*)

The 1980s will see the use of novel types of financing devices such as mortgages involving a renegotiable rate, graduated payment, wraparound, flexible loan insurance plan, shared appreciation, buydown, and a greater use of syndication in lieu of traditional debt financing. Some sellers have even used the lottery system to help finance the buyer's purchase of their property.

FINANCING STATEMENT A brief document (required under the Uniform Commercial Code) filed to perfect or establish a creditor's security interest in a chattel or other personal property. This is important in real estate in order to protect the creditor's interest in personal property which is used as security for a debt, but which becomes a fixture when it is attached to realty. For example, if Sue Brown buys a sink from the D.S. Count Department Store on a conditional sales contract and then installs the sink in her home, the sink becomes a fixture subject to all existing recorded liens. The store, however, may protect its security interest by immediately recording a copy of the financing statement (Form UCC-1), which would give it a prior secured right to the sink that would be superior to the rights of the home mortgagee. Thus, the store has a prior right to the sink in the event that Brown defaults on her home mortgage and the bank forecloses on the realty.

It is the security agreement between debtor and creditor, not the financing statement, that creates the lien. However, it is the filing of the financing statement that "perfects" the lien, i.e., makes the lien effective against later creditors. While the use of a financing statement is not applicable to real property mortgages, many mortgagees still file a financing statement in those borderline cases where there is uncertainty whether the security is to be treated as personal or real property.

When filed, a financing statement is effective for five years from the date of filing and lapses upon expiration of that period unless it is extended by a continuation statement filed any time within the six-month period preceding the expiration of the five-year period. (See FIXTURE, SECURITY AGREEMENT, UNIFORM COMMERCIAL CODE.)

FINDER'S FEE   A fee paid to someone for producing either a buyer to purchase or a seller to list property; also called a referral fee. A finder is a person who finds, interests, introduces, or brings together parties in a deal, even though the finder has no part in negotiating the terms of the transaction.

In many states, a broker can split a commission only with another real estate licensee or with a real estate broker from another state (not another country) who does not participate in any of the negotiations within the state. The question sometimes arises as to whether an owner can pay a finder's fee to an unlicensed person such as a tenant in a building. In accepting such a fee, the finder runs the serious risk of being classified as a real estate salesperson and found in violation of state license laws for accepting compensation without being licensed.

Under the federal Real Estate Settlement Procedures Act, no person can pay a fee or other thing of value in exchange for having a referral where the transaction itself involves an original federally related mortgage loan. This provision prohibits kickbacks for referrals; it does not cover payments made for services actually rendered or performed by a finder.

FINISH FLOORING   The visible interior floor surface that is usually made of a decorative hardwood such as oak. The finish flooring may be laid in strips or in a block design such as parquet.

FIRE INSURANCE   A form of property insurance covering losses due to fire, often including additional coverage against other hazards, such as smoke or windstorm. (See INSURANCE.)

FIRE SPRINKLER SYSTEM   A fire protection system activated by heat within a given building area, which automatically provides a flow of pressurized water from overhead nozzles when the temperature exceeds a certain predetermined level. To prevent the water-supply pipes from freezing, they are often filled with compressed air to hold the water behind the dry valve; the system is called a dry system.

FIRE STOP Short boards placed horizontally between the studs or joists that decrease drafts and thus help retard fires.

FIRE WALL A wall constructed of fire-retardant materials, the purpose of which is to prevent the spread of fire within a building. The fire wall carries a standard rating that designates its ability to constrain fire in terms of hours.

FIRE YARD An area, the length of one or more sides of a building, which must be kept clear in order to facilitate the passage of fire vehicles, according to certain building codes.

FIRM COMMITMENT A definite undertaking by a lender to loan a set amount of money to a specified interest rate for a certain term; also, a commitment by the FHA to insure a mortgage on certain property to a specified mortgagor (as opposed to a commitment conditioned on approval of a yet-to-be-determined mortgagor).

A real estate broker has a duty to see that financial obligations and commitments regarding real estate transactions are in writing and express the exact agreements of the parties and that copies of such agreements are placed in the hands of all parties involved at the time that the agreements are executed. (See CONDITIONAL COMMITMENT.)

FIRST MORTGAGE A mortgage on property that is superior in right to any other mortgage. It is not enough that a mortgage is the first to be executed or that the parties call it a first mortgage; absent subordination, it must be recorded first. (See SECOND MORTGAGE, SUBORDINATION AGREEMENT.)

FIRST REFUSAL, RIGHT OF A right, usually given by an owner to a lessee, which gives the lessee the first chance to buy the property if the owner decides to sell. The owner must have a legitimate offer which the lessee can then match or refuse. In a condominium conversion, the tenant is often given by state law the first right to purchase the tenant's apartment. (See RIGHT OF FIRST REFUSAL.)

FIRST USER As it relates to depreciable property acquired prior to 1981, any owner who develops or acquires new property and who first puts the property to the use for which it was intended. Since there has been no prior owner benefiting from the improvements thereon, the first user is entitled to certain tax benefits not permitted to subsequent owners, such as certain accelerated rates of depreciation and special first-year depreciation. This concept was abolished by the Economic Recovery Tax Act of 1981. (See ACCELERATED DEPRECIATION, DEPRECIATION, FIRST-YEAR DEPRECIATION.)

FIRST-YEAR DEPRECIATION A special, increased amount of depreciation which could be taken in the first year of ownership of tangible, depreciable personal property with a remaining useful life of six years or more; also called *bonus depreciation*. This concept was abolished by the Economic Recovery Tax Act of 1981.

FISCAL YEAR   A business year used for tax, corporate, or accounting purposes, as opposed to a calendar year. For example, a commonly used fiscal year is the 12-month period from July 1 through June 30 of the following year. It may not coincide with a calendar year. Individuals and partnerships ordinarily use a calendar year.

FIXED EXPENSES   Those recurring expenses which have to be paid regardless of whether or not the property is occupied, such as real property taxes, hazard insurance, and debt service. As opposed to operating expenses necessary to maintain the production of income from the operation of a property. (*See OPERATING EXPENSES.*)

FIXED RATE LOAN   A loan with the same rate of interest for the life of the loan. Until the late 70s and early 80s the fixed rate loan was the usual type of real estate loan. With the arrival of highly volatile interest rates, lenders attempted to adjust interest rates with a variety of new different type loans. As the quasi-governmental agencies changed their guidelines, establishing a marketplace for these new adjustable interest loans, it became evident that the fixed rate loan would be seen less and less in the real estate market.

FIXING-UP EXPENSES   Expenses (such as painting and carpet cleaning) incurred in repairing and refurbishing a primary residence in order to facilitate its sale. If such expenses are for work performed during the 90-day period before a contract of sale is signed and are paid for within 30 days after the sale, they may be deducted from the contract sale price of the house in order to determine the adjusted sale price, provided the expenses are not deducted elsewhere on the return and are not accounted for as improvements. (*See RESIDENCE, SALE OF.*)

FIXTURE   1. An article that was once personal property but has been so affixed to real estate that it has become real property (such as stoves, bookcases, plumbing, track lighting, and tile). Whether an article is a fixture depends on the intention of the parties and may be determined by the manner in which the item is attached, its type and adaptability to the real property, the purpose it serves, and the relationship of the parties. Generally, the test of whether or not an item is a fixture as a result of its method of attachment depends more on the firmness of its installation rather than on the size of the hole that might be caused by its removal. The fact that removal leaves a dirty or unpainted spot is irrelevant. If an article is determined to be a fixture, it passes with the property even though it is not mentioned in the deed. Some articles are so closely associated with a structure that they are deemed to be fixtures under the constructive annexation theory (as in the case of house keys, which pass to the buyer upon sale of the property). When a fixture is wrongfully removed from property, damages are generally measured in terms of the value of the fixtures as part of the realty, not the price it would command on the open market after removal.

An exception to the fixture rule is made for *trade* or *tenant fixtures.* A tenant can normally remove trade fixtures at the termination of the lease because the courts reason that the parties did not intend that the tenant's fixtures would become a permanent part of the building. The trade fixture rule applies only to articles installed by the tenant and not those installed by the landlord. If the tenant fails to remove his or her fixtures, the landlord takes title to the abandoned property.

The question of whether or not an item is a fixture, and thus part of the real estate, arises in several cases: in determining real estate value for tax purposes; in determining whether or not a real estate sale included the item or items in question; in determining whether or not the item in question is part of the security given by a mortgagor to a mortgagee; in determining the ownership of the item in question when the lease is terminated; and in determining coverage under a hazard insurance policy which excludes personal property items.

The question of whether or not an item is a fixture has become especially important in modern transactions because of the different rules of lien priority for fixtures and nonfixtures set forth by the Uniform Commercial Code.

Even though an item of personal property is not a fixture, it can still cause disputes. For example, a prudent broker who spots a junk pile of old cars or an old dissheveled portable tool shed on the land might want to provide in the sales contract for its removal at seller's expense.

A seller must deliver all fixtures unless noted as exceptions in the contract of sale. This applies to unowned fixtures as well. A broker taking a listing should inspect the premises carefully and determine whether any of the apparent fixtures, such as air conditioners or carpeting, are rented or being purchased under a UCC financing statement. The contract of sale should specify who is to own certain doubtful items, such as television antennas and mirrors. (*See EMBLEMENT, FINANCING STATEMENT, PERSONAL PROPERTY, TRADE FIXTURE.*)

2. Also refers to the permanent parts of a plumbing system such as toilets and bathtubs.

FIXTURING PERIOD   In a commercial lease situation, the period during which the lessee enters the premises to install its improvements in preparation for opening its business.

FLAG LOT   A land parcel having the configuration of an extended flag and pole. The pole represents access to the site, which is usually located to the rear of another lot fronting a main street. A parcel may be subdivided into one or two flag lots as shown below:

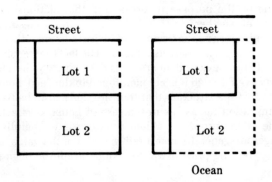

FLASHING   Sheet metal or other impervious material used in roof and wall construction to protect a building from seepage of water.

FLAT An apartment unit or an entire floor of a building used for residential purposes.

FLAT LEASE A lease that requires periodic, equal rental payments to be made throughout the term of the lease. Whether payments are to be made monthly, annually, or otherwise is stipulated in the contract.

FLEXIBLE-PAYMENT MORTGAGE A loan in which the payment schedule is based on the borrower's particular financial condition. Often, interest rates are initially lower than ordinary mortgages and the initial payments are below those of an amortized mortgage. This mortgage repayment plan enables younger buyers to purchase homes by allowing them to make smaller payments in the early years and larger payments later, when their incomes have increased. For example, under a regular payment plan, a $60,000 mortgage for 30 years at 15 percent interest would be repaid with monthly installments of $758.67. Under the flexible-payment plan, the payments might be as small as $710.00 during the first five years and rise to $775 during the remaining 25 years in order to pay off the entire balance.

The Federal Home Loan Bank has authorized federally chartered savings and loan associations to make flexible-payment mortgages provided that each monthly payment at least covers interest costs and the loan payments become fully amortized by the end of the fifth year. (*See VARIABLE PAYMENT PLAN.*)

Under the Flexible Loan Insurance Payment, or FLIP, potential buyers could reduce their monthly payments by as much as 20 percent during the initial year of the mortgage and then graduate upward over the next five years. The buyer places the down payment in an interest-bearing savings account as pledged cash collateral. Only the lender can draw on the pledged account and the monies can be used to supplement the buyer's monthly payment or to apply against principal if the borrower defaults or the property is sold. Private mortgage insurance covers the top 20 percent of the loan, thus reducing the lender's risk.

FLIP® 1. A FLIP mortgage is a flexible loan insurance program mortgage. (*See FLEXIBLE-PAYMENT MORTGAGE.*)

2. A FLIP transaction is one in which one party contracts to buy a property with the intention to quickly transfer (flip) the property over to the ultimate buyer. (*See BACK-TO-BACK ESCROW.*)

FLOAT 1. A mortgage banking term that refers to the spread of the variable interest rate on a loan; the "pegged rate"—for example, the interest on a development loan might be set at 3 percent above the local prime rate. A float can have a floor or a ceiling, such as, "in no event below 9 percent or above 15 percent"; or it can have no limitation, as in a *full float.* A typical float clause is: "Three and three-fourths percent (3¾%) over and floating with Bank of Equity prime, but not less than three and three-fourths percent (3¾%) over Bank of Equity prime at the time of loan closing."

2. A banking term that refers to a check that has not yet been cleared for collection. Local checks may float for two or three days before clearing. This term may also refer to the bank's use of the money prior to the check's clearing. (*See PRIME RATE, VARIABLE RATE.*)

FLOATING LIEN A lien, such as a mortgage, which will attach to property that is later acquired. To be a floating lien, the mortgage must contain a special clause, otherwise the security is limited to the property existing at the time of the mortgage. (*See ANACONDA MORTGAGE.*)

FLOATING ZONE A land area described in the text of zoning regulations but not placed on the zoning map until a developer applies for rezoning.

FLOOD INSURANCE Insurance offered by private companies and subsidized by the federal government, designed to provide coverage for damage from floods or tidal waves. Lending institutions subject to Federal Deposit Insurance Corporation regulations require flood insurance in order to complete a mortgage loan transaction involving any building, or its condominium apartments, located in a designated flood or tidal wave zone. The premium is in a fixed amount nationwide. Because the law places the sole responsibility on the lending institutions to initiate, maintain, and renew the flood insurance, lenders are very conservative in interpreting whether or not a property is in such a zone. Even the owner of a condominium apartment on the thirty-sixth floor of a building near a beachline may have to obtain flood insurance.

The Federal Insurance Administration of HUD expects about 20,000 communities nationwide to fall within a flood hazard area, as identified in a flood hazard boundary map or a flood insurance rate map. These communities must adopt land use controls requiring new structures built in the flood plain to either be elevated above the 100-year flood level or take other preventive measures. (*See FLOOD-PRONE AREA.*)

FLOOD PLAIN The flat portions of land located along watercourses and streams, which are subject to overflow and flooding; building in these areas is usually restricted by governmental controls.

FLOOD-PRONE AREA A flood-prone area is one having a 1 percent annual chance of flooding, or a likelihood that a flood may occur once every 100 years.

FLOOR AREA RATIO The ratio of floor area to land area, often land on which the building sits. It may be expressed as a percent or decimal, and is determined by dividing the total floor area of the building by the lot area; used in zoning ordinances as a formula to regulate building volume; a restriction on the amount of building per lot area; a density restriction.

FLOOR DUTY The frequent practice in real estate brokerage offices of assigning one sales agent the responsibility for handling all telephone calls and office visitors for a specified period of time. The person "on floor" often has the opportunity to meet new clients if the caller does not ask to speak to a particular salesperson. This person must be a licensed real estate agent, not a secretary. Independent contractor licensees cannot be required to sit floor duty.

FLOOR JOIST Horizontal boards laid on edge resting on the beams that provide the main support for the floor. The subflooring is nailed directly to the joists. Joists are also found in ceilings.

FLOOR LOAN A loan amount that is below the maximum loan approved. That part of the loan that will be disbursed when the physical improvements are complete. For example, a lender may agree to make a $2,000,000 permanent loan as follows: $1,200,000 upon closing and the balance of $800,000 provided the premises are 75 percent leased by a certain date. The $800,000 *gap* will be funded only if the occupancy level specified is attained within the specified period after the funding of the floor loan. If this occupancy is not obtained, the developer must seek *gap financing*, which is very expensive because of the high risks involved. (*See GAP FINANCING.*)

FLOOR PLAN The architectural drawings showing the floor layout of a building, including the exact room sizes and their interrelationships. Under many state condominium laws, a developer must file a set of floor plans and elevations of a building together with a verified statement of the architect or engineer showing the layout when the developer records the declaration.

An examination of the floor plan is an important consideration in the appraisal valuation process. A poor floor plan or room layout could result in devaluation because of incurable functional obsolescence.

FLUE An enclosed passage in a chimney or any duct or pipe through which smoke, hot air, and gases pass upward. Flues are usually made of fire clay or terra cotta pipe.

FOOTCANDLE A determination of light intensity. One footcandle is the illumination measured on a surface one foot distant from the source of one candle. Therefore, the light level in an office space may be described as, say, 85 footcandles.

FOOTING A concrete support under a foundation, chimney, or column that usually rests on solid ground and is wider than the structure being supported. Footings are designed to distribute the weight of the structure over the ground.

FORBEARANCE The act of refraining from taking legal action despite the fact that payment of a promissory note in a mortgage or deed of trust is in arrears. It is usually granted only when a borrower makes a satisfactory arrangement by which the arrears will be paid at a future date. (*See CONSIDERATION, WORKOUT.*)

FORCE MAJEURE A term, originally used in insurance law, meaning a superior or irresistible force, one that cannot be foreseen or controlled (a "vis major"). It refers to a clause found in many construction contracts that is designed to protect the parties when part of the contract cannot be performed or the time of performance must be delayed due to causes which are beyond the control of the parties and cannot be prevented by the exercise of due care and prudence. For example, a subcontractor might agree to pay $500 per day in damages for each day past December 31 that his installation of the plumbing is not complete, except if the delay is caused by acts of God, labor disputes, inability to obtain materials, fire, and the like. Thus, if a shipping strike were to cause a 30-day delay in the arrival of the plumbing lines, the subcontractor would not have to pay the $500 per day, at least through January 31.

Sometimes a force majeure clause is inserted in a ground lease to protect a tenant who is obligated to complete an improvement by a certain date from a default caused by unavoidable delays in completing the project. (*See ACT OF GOD.*)

FORECAST   Estimate of the outcome of future occurrences; particularly, financial statements of future periods based on such estimates.

FORECLOSURE   A legal procedure whereby property used as security for a debt is sold to satisfy the debt in the event of default in payment of the mortgage note or default of other terms in the mortgage document. The foreclosure procedure brings the rights of all parties to a conclusion and passes the title in the mortgaged property to either the holder of the mortgage or a third party who may purchase the realty at the foreclosure sale, free of all encumbrances affecting the property subsequent to the mortgage.

There are three general types of foreclosure proceedings—judicial foreclosure, nonjudicial foreclosure, and strict foreclosure.

Judicial foreclosure, normally used in those states in which there is no power of sale included in the mortgage document, provides that the property may be sold by court order upon sufficient public notice. If a mortgagor defaults in making payments or in fulfilling any of the requirements of the mortgage, such as paying taxes, the mortgagee can enforce his or her rights. The mortgagee's first action may be to accelerate the due date of all remaining monthly payments. The attorney for the mortgagee can then file a suit to foreclose the lien of the mortgage. Upon presentation of the facts in court, the property will be ordered sold by court order. A public sale will be advertised and held, and the real estate be sold to the highest bidder.

Some states allow *nonjudicial foreclosure* procedures to be used when a power of sale is contained in a mortgage or trust deed. Under this form, a lender, or the lender's trustee (if a deed of trust is used), has the right to sell the mortgaged property upon default without being required to spend the time and money involved in a court foreclosure suit. In fact, under this form of lender control, a borrower's redemption time is shortened considerably by the elimination of the statutory redemption period sometimes granted in the judicial process. Notice of default is recorded by the trustee at the county recorder's office within the jurisdiction's designated time period to give notice to the public of the intended auction. This official notice is accompanied by advertisements in public newspapers that state the total amount due and the date of the public sale. The purpose of the notice is to give publicity to the sale, not to give notice to the defaulting mortgagor. After selling the property, the mortgagee or trustee may be required to file a copy of a notice of sale of affidavit of foreclosure.

Although the judicial and nonjudicial foreclosure procedures are the prevalent practices today, it is still possible in some states for a lender to acquire the mortgaged property by a *strict foreclosure* process. After appropriate notice has been given to the delinquent borrower and the proper papers have been prepared and filed, the court will establish a specific time period during which the balance of the defaulted debt must be paid in full. If full payment is not made, the borrower's equitable and statutory redemption rights are waived, depending on the special circumstances involved in the case, and the court awards full legal title to the lender. There can be no deficiency judgment in strict foreclosure cases.

A few states permit foreclosure by entry and possession. By the mortgagee holding possession for the redemption period, the mortgage debt is deemed paid to the extent of the value of the real property.

In preparing a foreclosure proceeding, a current title report should be obtained because all prior and subsequent mortgage creditors must be joined as parties to the judicial action, and junior federal tax liens are not divested by nonjudicial foreclosure proceedings unless the federal government consents or is given notice of the sale. If the state statute of limitations pertaining to real estate actions has run, the mortgagee is barred from exercising its power of sale.

Most states allow a defaulted mortgagor a period of time during which the property may be redeemed after the foreclosure sale. During this statutory redemption period (which may be as long as one year), the court may appoint a receiver to take charge of the property, collect rents, or pay operating expenses. If the mortgagor can raise the necessary funds to redeem the property within the statutory period, the redemption money is paid to the court. Since the mortgage debt was paid from the proceeds of the sale, the mortgagor can take possession free and clear of the former defaulted mortgage. Historically, the right of redemption is inherited from the old chancery proceedings in which the court sale ended the "equitable right of redemption." In many states, a statutory redemption period is provided by state law to begin after the sale to give the mortgagor an opportunity to regain title to the land. (Note, however, that if the mortgagee accepts any payment on the mortgage debt after default and before the right of redemption expires, most courts hold that the mortgagee has waived the right to complete the foreclosure.)

If redemption is not made, or if no redemption period is allowed by state law, then the successful bidder at the sale receives a deed to the real estate; sometimes called a commissioners deed. This is a statutory form of deed that may be executed by a sheriff or master-in-chancery to convey such title as the mortgagor had to the purchaser at the sale. There are no warranties with such a deed; the title passes "as is," but free of the former defaulted mortgage. The purchaser obtains no better title than the mortgagor held.

If there are any excess proceeds of the foreclosure sale after deducting expenses, they are paid to the mortgagor. If, on the other hand, the proceeds from the sale are not sufficient to repay the foreclosed debt, further action may usually be taken against the debtor in order to recover the deficiency. If such a deficiency occurs in a judicial foreclosure, the court can enter a deficiency judgment, which operates as a general lien on the debtor's assets. If a deficiency results from a sale under nonjudicial foreclosure, however, the mortgagee must institute new proceedings to obtain a deficiency judgment.

There are several tax consequences a defaulted mortgagor must consider upon foreclosure. Primary of these concerns is that in terms of tax laws, the defaulting owner is considered to have sold his or her property for a price equal to the unpaid debt at the time of disposition. Assuming that the mortgage balance is in excess of its adjusted basis (reduced by depreciation), the defaulting owner may realize a taxable gain as a result of the foreclosure sale even though (no money is received) from the sale. This could be a particular problem for investors in a failing syndication who not only lose their investment but are saddled with a tax bill from the government. The courts have held this rule to apply to defaults of contracts for deed as well as terminations of mortgages and trust deeds. There is also a recapture of any accelerated depreciation.

The FHA rules require that a homeowner be at least three months behind in mortgage payments, that his or her delinquency span a six-month period, and that he or she be in breach of the mortgage before a lender can foreclose an FHA loan.

A borrower who files bankruptcy can effectively interfere with the foreclosure proceedings. Once bankruptcy is filed, no creditor can take any action against the debtor outside of bankruptcy court. Therefore, any foreclosure action is automatically stayed (or delayed) while the bankruptcy is pending. Also, if the foreclosure sale takes place within one year before the filing of the bankruptcy, the sale can be voided if the foreclosure sale price is substantially less than the actual fair market value of the secured property.

An alternative to foreclosure would be for the mortgagee to accept a *deed in lieu of foreclosure* from the mortgagor. This is sometimes known as a *friendly foreclosure*, since it is settled by agreement rather than civil action. The major disadvantage to this type of default settlement is that the mortgagee takes the real estate subject to all junior liens, whereas foreclosure eliminates all such liens. (*See DEED OF TRUST, DEFICIENCY JUDGMENT, EQUITY OF REDEMPTION, FEDERAL TAX LIEN, MORTGAGE, POWER OF SALE, UPSET PRICE.*)

FOREIGN CORPORATION Any corporation not organized under a given state's laws but which conducts a portion of its business in that state. All foreign corporations which undertake to do business in a state or attempt to take, hold, demise, sell or convey real estate there must generally qualify to do business and obtain an annual license to do business in the state. (*See CORPORATION.*)

FOREIGN INVESTMENT IN REAL PROPERTY TAX ACT OF 1980 The purpose of the law is to subject nonresident aliens and foreign corporations to U.S. income tax upon their gain from the disposition of a United States real property interest in: 1. an interest in real property located in the U.S., and 2. an interest in any domestic corporation that was a "United States real property holding corporation" at any time during the five-year period prior to the disposition of the interest, or during the period the taxpayer held the interest after June 18, 1980, if shorter.

A United States real property corporation is a domestic or foreign corporation, whose interest in U.S. real property is 50 percent or more of its total assets. The test can apparently be made on any day of the calendar year.

For purposes of computing the tax, a nonresident alien or foreign corporation is treated as being "engaged in a trade or business within the United States," and the gain is treated as "effectively connected" with the U.S. trade or business. Thus, a foreign investor is subject to tax at regular rates. Expenses attributable to the gain may be deducted, and nonresident aliens are allowed the capital gains deduction.

The gain resulting from most dispositions will qualify for long-term capital gain treatment. For foreign corporations, there is no minimum tax on the gain; however, the legislation requires nonresident alien individuals to compute the alternative minimum tax.

FORESHORE LAND   Land that is above sea level only at low tide. Because of the action of the tide, this land alternates between wet and dry. (*See SHORELINE.*)

FORFEITURE   The loss of the right to something as a result of nonperformance of an obligation or condition. A forfeiture loss usually bears no true relationship to the amount of damages allowed by law, and thus there is strong public policy against enforcing forfeitures. Courts frequently refuse to enforce provisions in contracts which require the defaulting party to forfeit all amounts paid under an installment purchase contract (that is, a contract for deed). Even where forfeitures are recognized by some courts, the right to forfeiture must be specifically provided for in the contract or else the sole remedy is rescission.

Real property may be acquired by forfeiture, such as when a grantor has conveyed real estate subject to a condition subsequent. Should the condition be breached, the grantor can reacquire the property by forfeiture by exercising the right of reentry.

When a buyer defaults on a mortgage or trust deed in which he or she holds substantial equity, forfeiture may be inequitable. In such cases, upon proper application, the court may prohibit the forfeiture and order the property sold, with the proceeds necessary to pay off the note distributed to the mortgagee and the balance paid to the mortgagor. (*See FORECLOSURE, RESCISSION.*)

A real estate license may be lost through forfeiture when the licensee fails to pay the appropriate renewal fees or to fulfill any continuing education requirements.

FORGERY   The illegal act of counterfeiting documents or making a false signature, alteration, or falsification. A forged deed is void and ineffective to transfer any title to the grantee, and recording will not make it valid. Even if a later purchaser for value acquires the property with no notice of the prior forged deed, he or she does not obtain valid title; i.e., the forged owner (or heirs) would still have legal title. A title insurance policy will compensate such a purchaser for a loss from forgery in the chain of title.

FORMICA   A trade name for a plastic material used primarily for the top of counter areas, but which is also used for wall covering, as a veneer for plywood panels, or as a wallboard where a fire-resistive material is desirable. Similar and competitive materials are produced under other trade names.

FOR SALE BY OWNER (FSBO)   A situation in which the owner attempts to sell his or her property without listing with a real estate broker. Many owners will cooperate with and compensate a broker representing a buyer. Experienced brokers actively solicit listings from FSBOs (pronounced "fizz-bows"). The FSBO often gets discouraged in a short time, especially after having to deal with unqualified buyers and mere lookers. (*See COURTESY TO BROKERS.*)

FORUM SHOPPING CLAUSE   The clause in an agreement specifying the state in which the parties agree lawsuits may be brought and designating which state laws will apply. Typical language is: "This contract shall be interpreted and construed under and governed by the laws of the state of Homestate, and any lawsuit arising out of or because of this contract shall be brought in the state courts. The judgment of the State Supreme Court shall be final and binding on all parties hereto."

Such a clause will generally be upheld if the state designated as the one whose laws govern the transaction and the state in which the lawsuit is filed bear some relationship to the place of making or place of performance of the original contract.

FOUNDATION DRAIN LINE   A pipe, usually clay, placed next to the foundation footing to aid in water run-off.

FOUNDATION WALL   The masonry or concrete walls below ground level that serve as the main support for the frame structure. Foundation walls form the side walls of the basement.

FOUR-THREE-TWO-ONE RULE (4-3-2-1)   See DEPTH TABLE.

FRANCHISE   1. A right or privilege conferred by law, such as a state charter authorizing the formation and existence of corporations. The privilege granted to conduct certain service businesses, such as the operation of a taxicab company, is a franchise. 2. The private contractual right to operate a business using a designated trade name and the operating procedures of a parent company, (the franchisor) such as McDonald's restaurant. In the financing of income property, a franchise may have value as additional security to a loan. It may also be assigned to the lender.

A recent development in real estate operations is the advent and growing popularity of the franchised brokerage. Such firms as Century 21, ERA, and Realty World operate franchised brokerages on a national level. These organizations do not own and operate the individual offices outright; rather, they license their standardized trade names, reputations, operating procedures, and referral services to independently owned and operated brokerages. These referral services take the multiple-listing-service idea one step further, having the capability to refer prospects across town or across the country. State laws, however, are moving toward stricter legislation of these firms, particularly in the areas of advertising, antitrust, fee splitting, and out-of-state licensing.

A general summary of the major advantages and disadvantages usually cited for real estate franchises is shown below:

ADVANTAGES: 1. Market identification is available through the use of a trademark and trade name; 2. A good market image is provided through mass advertising techniques; 3. Association with a successful operation can be beneficial in several ways; 4. A referral system by which franchise members trade leads and listings has certain advantages; 5. Brokers can receive volume discounts not otherwise available (e.g. advertising); 6. Recruitment of sales personnel is easier; 7. Management help and services are provided; 8. Franchises obtain good sales training programs not otherwise available.

DISADVANTAGES: 1. Fees, whether initial or a royalty override, may be higher than necessary in terms of the benefits derived; 2. There is an original identity loss that cannot be recaptured; 3. There are certain bookkeeping requirements that many brokers feel are unnecessary; 4. Because of the necessity of group approval for certain activities, specifically those related to marketing, there are difficulties in agreeing on concerted unified actions; 5. Referrals can sometimes lead to tensions between individual franchisees in large market areas; 6. Reduced ability to choose business associates, particularly where franchisors are more interested in quantity than quality; 7. In some instances, a franchisor may not live up to initial promises; 8. A trade name and trademark may turn out to be a poor substitute for a long established local name.

In 1979, the Federal Trade Commission adopted a business and franchise rule designed to alleviate "widespread evidence of unfair practices in connection with the sale of franchises" where the franchisee operates under the trade name of a franchisor or where the franchisor has significant control or gives significant assistance to the franchisee. The FTC rules go far beyond many state laws governing franchises and creates a whole new set of protection for franchisees. The FTC rule was designed to curb abuses by franchisors, while allowing continued development of the franchise system that is growing into a dynamic and mature business activity.

FRAUD   Any form of deceit, trickery, breach of confidence, or misrepresentation by which one party attempts to gain some unfair or dishonest advantage over another. Unlike negligence, fraud is a deceitful practice or material misstatement of a material fact, known to be false, and done with intent to deceive, or with reckless indifference as to its truth, and relied upon by the injured party to his or her damage. For example, in response to a buyer's question regarding termites, the seller produces a falsified termite report. Not disclosing known defects or remaining "silent" can be considered fraud.

It is important to distinguish between fraud in the inducement and fraud in the execution of a contract. If the party knows what he or she is signing, but the consent to sign is induced by fraud, the contract is voidable. If the party does not actually know what he or she is signing because of deception as to the nature of such an act, and if the deceived party doesn't intend to enter into a contract at all, then the contract is void. The voidable contract is binding until rescinded, whereas the void contract has no force or effect whatsoever.

The state statute of limitations for a court action based on fraud is generally computed from the date of the fraud or from the time at which the defrauded person could discover or should have discovered the fraud.

In accordance with the Realtors® Code of Ethics, it is the duty of a Realtor® to protect the public against fraud, misrepresentation, or unethical practices in the real estate field. All state licensing laws provide that a broker's license can be suspended or revoked for fraudulent acts. (See MISREPRESENTATION, NEGLIGENCE.)

FREDDIE MAC   Popular name for Federal Home Loan Mortgage Corporation. (See FEDERAL HOME LOAN MORTGAGE CORPORATION.)

FREE AND CLEAR TITLE   Title to real property which is absolute and unencumbered by any liens, mortgages, clouds, or other encumbrances. (See MARKETABLE TITLE.)

FREEHOLD An estate in real property, the exact termination date of which is unknown (for a described, yet indefinite period of time); those estates that have a potentially indefinite duration (*fee simple*) or a period of years incapable of exact determination (*life estate*). Freehold estates may be categorized as *estates of inheritance*, such as fee simple, and lesser *estates for life*, which extend only for the life of an individual (includes dower and curtesy). Nonfreehold (leasehold) estates can be measured in calendar time. In the Old English court system, only an owner of freehold property could bring a real action (as opposed to a personal action for money damages). Thus, only freehold estates were regarded as real property. The two principal elements of a freehold estate are actual ownership of real property and unpredictable duration.

FREEHOLDER One who owns land that he or she can transfer without anyone's permission. Some state license laws require a license applicant to furnish character references from at least two "freeholders" of the county where he or she resides.

FREE-STANDING BUILDING A building containing one business rather than a row of stores or businesses with a common roof and side walls.

FREEWAY A divided arterial roadway for through traffic with full control of access with grade separations at intersections.

FRIEZE BOARD A horizontal exterior band or molding, often decorated with sculpture, resting directly below the cornice.

FRONTAGE The length of a property abutting a street or body of water, that is, the number of feet that front the street or water. Frontage differs from width, which sometimes decreases or increases as the lot extends back from the street.

FRONTAGE STREET A street that is parallel and adjacent to a major steet providing access to abutting properties, but protected from heavy through traffic.

FRONT-ENDING Recognition of profit from a transaction prior to periods during which it is earned or despite significant risks that could result in subsequent losses; also called front-loading.

FRONT FOOT A measurement of property frontage abutting the street line or waterfront line, with each front foot presumed to extend the depth of the lot. Lots of varying depth but with the same front foot may compared for valuation purposes by using a depth table. When a lot measurement is given, such as 75' × 150', the first figure (75') refers to the front feet. If such a lot were valued at $22,500, it would be worth $300 per front foot. (*See DEPTH TABLES, SPECIAL ASSESSMENT.*)

FRONT MONEY   A popular expression in the real estate development business that refers to the amount of hard money (cash as opposed to borrowed monies) the developer must have ready in order to purchase the land, and to pay attorney's fees, loan charges, and other initial expenses prior to actually developing the project. Front money is sometimes called *start-up costs* or *seed money. End money* represents the amount of money held in reserve in case project costs exceed estimates. Called "over and above" money in FHA rental housing projects.

FROST LINE   The depth of frost penetration in the soil. The frost line varies throughout the U.S. and footings should be placed below this depth to prevent movement of the structure.

FRUCTUS NATURALES   Uncultivated crops and perennial plantings, such as trees and bushes, which are generally classified as real property. *Fructus industriales*, on the other hand, are annual plantings that require cultivation and are generally classified as personal property. (*See EMBLEMENT.*)

FULL DISCLOSURE   A requirement to reveal fully and accurately all material facts. This requirement is based on the theory that no fraud is committed if the purchaser has accurate and full information regarding the property to be purchased. A broker is under a fiduciary obligation to disclose in full to a client all known, relevant facts affecting a proposed transaction. Many state subdivision and condominium laws as well as the Federal Interstate Land Full Disclosure Act (concerning subdivisions) require a developer to disclose fully all material facts of a project to each prospective purchaser or lessee through required distribution of a public report.

FULL RECONVEYANCE   Upon payment in full of the debt secured by a deed of trust, the trustee reconveys the property to the person or persons entitled thereto on written request of the grantor and the beneficiary, or upon satisfaction of the obligation secured and written request for reconveyance made by the beneficiary or his assignee. It is acknowledged by the trustee and should be recorded immediately. (*See DEED OF TRUST.*)

FUNCTIONAL OBSOLESCENCE   A loss in value of an improvement due to functional inadequacies, often caused by age or poor design. For example, functional obsolescence may be attributable to such things as outmoded plumbing or fixtures, inadequate closet space, poor floor plan, excessively high or low ceilings, or antiquated architecture. Thus, a warehouse with nine-foot ceilings would probably suffer a loss in value because a modern forklift could not operate in such a small space. Functional obsolescence may be incurable, as in the case of wide columns, or curable, as in the case of an inadequate electrical system that can be replaced with new wiring. Functional obsolescence is dependent on the changing requirements of the buying public and thus involves features that are unfashionable or unnecessary, such as a kitchen without modern built-in cabinets and sinks.

GABLE   The triangular portion of an end wall rising from the level top wall under the inverted "v" of a sloping roof. The gable can be made of weatherboard, tile, or masonry and can extend above the rafters. The gable aids in water drainage.

GAIN   The profit received upon the sale of an asset. If it is a depreciable capital asset, then the gain technically consists of two elements: recaptured depreciation, if any, which would be taxed at ordinary income rates, and capital gain (the balance of the gain after deducting excess depreciation), which is taxed at favorable capital gain rates if the asset was held for more than twelve months. (*See CAPITAL GAIN, RECAPTURE OF DEPRECIATION.*)

GAMBREL ROOF   A curb roof, having a steep lower slope and a flatter one above, as seen in Dutch colonial architecture.

GAP GROUP   Homebuyers in the moderate-income bracket who need some type of assistance or subsidy to qualify for financing.

GAP FINANCING   The financing used to make up the difference between the underlying loan (*floor loan*) and the total amount required. Gap financing usually fills a temporary need until permanent financing is obtained, and thus is sometimes called a *bridge mortgage* or *swing loan.*

Gap financing may also be used when permanent takeout financing is difficult to obtain or is too expensive. By obtaining gap financing and waiting, it is possible that more favorable terms may be reached. (*See RENT-UP.*)

GAP IN TITLE   A break in the chain of title, such as when the records do not reflect any transfer to a particular grantor. This could happen if that grantor had failed to record his or her deed. (*See CHAIN OF TITLE.*)

GARDEN APARTMENT   A type of multiple-unit dwelling providing for a lawn and/or garden area, typically found in a low-rise condominium project.

GARNISHMENT A legal process designed to provide a means for creditors to safeguard for themselves a debtor's personal property which is in the hands of a third party (*garnishee*). The types of properties that may be garnished include goods or effects of the debtor concealed in the hands of third parties, debts owed to the debtor by the garnishee, wages payable by the garnishee as allowed by law, and security interests of the debtor in the hands of the garnishee. The procedures usually require the service of a *writ of garnishment* upon the garnishee, who must secure in his hands all property of the creditor in order to pay the creditor-plaintiff the amount of judgment the plaintiff has recovered (post-judgment) or may recover (prejudgment). The debtor may obtain release of the garnished property by filing a bond with the court in the amount sufficient to pay the claim of the creditor, together with costs and interest, and conditioned upon judgment in favor of the creditor.

If garnishment takes place *after* judgment, then the property is paid over to the creditor. If the debt is disputed, then the garnishee should deposit the property with the court. Generally, the complaint and writ of garnishment are issued pursuant to the creditor's petition for process or by subsequent motion of the creditor requesting the court to insert in the process a direction to the officer serving the garnishment papers to leave a copy with the garnishee and to summon the garnishee to answer certain questions. Because of recent U.S. Supreme Court decisions requiring notice and a hearing prior to a garnishment of wages or property, the entire garnishment process *prior* to a judgment and without a hearing may be subject to challenge on constitutional grounds.

GAZEBO An ornamental garden structure from which a view may be enjoyed, often constructed of light metal or wood.

GENERAL AGENT One who is authorized by a principal to perform any and all acts associated with the continued operation of a particular job or a certain business of the principal. The essential feature of a general agency is the continuity of service, such as that provided by a property manager of a large condominium project. Most real estate brokers are treated as special agents. (*See AGENCY, SPECIAL AGENT.*)

GENERAL CONTRACTOR A construction specialist who enters into a formal construction contract with a developer to construct a real estate building or project. Also called the *prime contractor*, this person often negotiates individual contracts with various subcontractors who specialize in particular aspects of the building process, such as plumbing, electricity, air conditioning, drywall, and the like. If the general contractor fails to pay them, the subcontractors can assert mechanics' liens against the entire project. To become a general contractor, one must usually pass a qualifying examination and obtain a license from the appropriate state regulatory agency. (*See CONTRACTOR, MECHANIC'S LIEN, PERFORMANCE BOND.*)

GENERAL IMPROVEMENT DISTRICT A local public entity created to perform a specific governmental function, such as a water district. It issues bonds and levies general taxes to carry out its functions. (*See SPECIAL ASSESSMENT.*)

GENERAL LIEN   The right of a creditor to have all the debtor's property sold to satisfy a debt. Unlike a specific lien against certain property, a general lien is directed against the individual debtor and attaches to all of his or her property. Common examples of general liens are judgment liens and government tax liens arising from unpaid taxes, such as income, gift, estate, inheritance, and franchise taxes. (*See LIEN.*)

GENERAL PARTNER   A co-owner of a partnership who is empowered to enter into contracts on behalf of the partnership and who is fully liable for all partnership debts. The general partner may be a corporation or an individual. In a limited partnership, the general partner is in charge of managing the partnership, has authority to act unilaterally on behalf of the partnership, is accountable to the limited partners as a fiduciary, and has full liability for the debts and obligations of the partnership. (*See PARTNERSHIP.*)

GENERAL PARTNERSHIP   A form of business organization in which two or more co-owners carry on a business for profit. All the owners are general partners and share a full liability for the debts and obligations of the partnership. Although advisable, a written agreement is not required. A general partnership is subject to dissolution by reason of the death, withdrawal, bankruptcy, or legal disability of any general partner. (*See PARTNERSHIP.*)

GENERAL PLAN   A long-range governmental program to regulate the use and development of property in an orderly fashion; a plan aimed at a well-balanced community growth.

In planning a subdivision, a developer might establish a general building scheme, or general plan, in order to achieve a degree of uniformity in the subdivided community. When a general plan exists, the subdivider will make each conveyance subject to recorded restrictions in order to keep the general plan in operation. Then, any lot owner can enjoin any other lot owner from violating the general plan. For example, in a subdivision generally planned for residential use only, one lot owner could prevent another lot owner from constructing a restaurant. (*See EQUITABLE SERVITUDE, RESTRICTION.*)

GEODETIC SURVEY SYSTEM   The United States Coast and Geodetic Survey System. The skeleton of the system consists of a network of bench marks covering the entire country. Each bench mark is located by its latitude and longitude. The system was initiated to identify tracts of land owned by the federal government, but has gradually been extended throughout the nation.

GHETTO   A term which originated in Eastern Europe, used to describe a particular section of a city in which people of a certain race, religion, or nationality reside in heavy concentrations; sometimes used to refer to a densely populated area in which low-income families live in generally run-down housing. Lenders must be careful not to violate federal and state redlining discrimination laws in refusing to make loans in these areas. (*See REDLINING.*)

GIFT CAUSA MORTIS   A gift made in view of death; a gift that is made in contemplation of death, or intended to take effect only in the event of, or upon, death of the donor. For federal estate tax purposes for decedents dying prior to 1982, a gift made within three years of death was considered as a gift made in contemplation of death and, except to the extent of the annual exclusion, was automatically included in the estate of the decedent. For persons dying after 1981, this provision will no longer apply, except in the case of a gift of a life insurance policy. (*See GIFT TAX.*)

GIFT DEED   A deed in which the consideration is "love and affection." Because the deed is not supported by valuable consideration, the donee (recipient of the gift) may not be able to enforce against the donor certain promises or agreements contained in the deed. A gift deed is valid unless made to defraud creditors. Usually, an attorney in fact is not authorized to execute a gift deed.

When a gift deed has been used to transfer real estate, a title report will usually show the possibility of an unpaid gift tax, a cloud that must then be eliminated by a clearance from tax officials. (*See DEED, GIFT TAX.*)

GIFT TAX   A graduated federal tax paid by a donor upon making a gift. For the purposes of the gift tax, a gift is defined as the transfer by an individual of any type of property for less than adequate consideration in money or money's worth ("detached and disinterested generosity"). There is a $10,000 ($3,000 prior to 1982) per donor, per donee (recipient of the gift), per year exclusion, which can be deducted by the donor from the taxable value of gifts to each donee. Also, to the extent that his or her gifts exceed this exclusion, each donor has a set lifetime credit that can be applied to gifts, regardless of the donee. This credit is set at $47,000 in 1981 and thereafter increases in stages. The credit and the equivalent exemption amount is stated below.

For example, assume that Marilyn Poorman gave each of her five children a gift of $10,000 in 1982. There would be no gift tax because of the $10,000 per donee exemption. Now assume that in 1983 Marilyn Poorman gave $25,000 to each of her five children ($125,000 total). There would be no gift tax on the first $50,000 ($10,000 × 5), and no gift tax on the remaining $75,000 (because of the credit). She would have to file a *gift tax return*. Regardless of value, a gift tax return must be filed if the gift is of a future interest, such as a remainder fee. A gift tax return must also be filed annually if individual gifts exceed $10,000.

On January 1, 1977, the provisions of the Tax Reform Act of 1976 came into effect. The Tax Reform Act was a major overhaul of our federal gift tax law. Some of the major changes included:

1. No longer would lifetime transfers (gifts) receive preferential treatment over transfers effective at death; in addition, gift taxes and estate taxes were set up under a common rate schedule. Gift tax rates had previously been approximately three-fourths of estate tax rates.

2. Lifetime transfers (gifts) and transfers effective at death would be cumulative for determining estate tax; however, any gift tax paid would be subtracted from any estate tax due.

3. A unified credit replaces the gift tax exemption. Any part of the credit used to offset gift tax is not available to offset federal estate tax. The unified credit was

introduced in stages, with the $47,000 figure being reached in 1981. The Economic Recovery Tax Act of 1981 adds six more steps.

Year	Credit	Exemption Equivalent
1982	$ 62,800	$225,000
1983	79,300	275,000
1984	96,300	325,000
1985	121,800	400,000
1986	155,800	500,000
1987	192,800	600,000

Thus, in 1987, there will be no estate or gift tax on taxable transfers aggregating $600,000 or less.

4. The marital deduction is liberalized by providing an unlimited deduction for the lifetime gifts between spouses.

The donee tax basis in property acquired by gift is the same as the donor's basis. Both the basis and the holding period follows the property. If, however, the transfer of property results in a loss, then the basis is the lower of either the donor's basis or the fair market value as of the date of the gift. Though the donor is obligated to pay the tax, the donee may pay it, in which case that amount is added to his or her basis. (See BASIS.)

If the donor is unable to pay the gift tax due, the donee may be held responsible for the tax under the theory of "transferee liability."

One of the primary purposes of the $10,000 annual exclusion is to avoid the necessity of determining the motivation involved in relatively small transfers between persons, regardless of relationship.

The Economic Recovery Tax Act of 1981 also created an annual exclusion for gifts made for the purpose of paying medical expenses or educational expenses (specifically, tuition); note that payments for room and board do not qualify.

GI LOAN Government-guaranteed loan. (See VA MORTGAGE.)

GIRDER A heavy wooden or steel beam supporting the floor joists. The girder provides the main horizontal support for the floor.

GOING CONCERN VALUE The value existing in an established business property as compared to the value of selling the real estate and other assets of a concern whose business is not yet established. The term takes into account the good will and earning capacity of a business. Sometimes used in the test of determining solvency or insolvency or in computing value for purposes of corporate merger or issuance of stock.

GOOD CONSIDERATION A consideration founded on love and affection for kindred by blood or marriage, which may be found in a gift deed. However, a good consideration is not sufficient to support a contract. For example, if a father promises in writing to give his farm to his daughter on her 21st birthday, and he later changes his mind, the daughter would have no legal basis to sue for breach of contract since she had not given any valuable consideration to support his promise. (*See GIFT DEED.*)

GOOD FAITH   Bona fide. An act is done in good faith if it is in fact done honestly, whether negligently or not. The recording laws are designed to protect a "good faith" purchaser. Most discrimination laws require a broker to transmit all good faith offers to lease or buy. Many states add a requirement of good faith for a person to acquire title to someone else's real property by adverse possession.

Sometimes an act done in "bad faith" is punishable as a crime. For instance, if an investor-borrower applies for an owner-occupant loan and lies about his intent to occupy, this type of falsehood is punishable as a misdemeanor under the National Banking Act. (*See BONA FIDE, RECORDING.*)

GOOD WILL   An intangible, salable asset arising from the reputation of a business; the expectation of continued public patronage; including other intangible assets like trade name and going concern value. When a business is sold, the sales price often reflects its good will value. Good will is not a depreciable asset, although it is a capital asset. Thus a seller prefers to place a high value on the good will (and obtain a capital gain) while a buyer prefers a lower value (since good will can't be depreciated). (*See BUSINESS OPPORTUNITY, CONDEMNATION.*)

GOVERNMENT LOT   See QUARTER SECTION.

GOVERNMENT NATIONAL MORTGAGE ASSOCIATION (GNMA)   A federal agency created in 1968 when the Federal National Mortgage Association (FNMA) was partitioned into two separate corporations. "Ginnie Mae," as it is popularly called, is a corporation without capital stock and is a division of the United States Department of Housing and Urban Development (HUD). The GNMA operates the special assistance aspects of federally aided housing programs and has the management and liquidating functions of the old FNMA. The FNMA is authorized to issue and sell securities backed by a portion of its mortgage portfolio, with the GNMA guaranteeing payment on such securities. The GNMA also guarantees similar securities issued by other private offerors (banks, mortgage companies, savings and loan associations) if they are backed by accumulated pools of VA, FHA, or FmHA mortgages. For an initial fee of $500 plus an annual fee paid to the GNMA, the private issuer can obtain the guaranty of the GNMA, backed by the full faith and credit of the United States government.

Under the so-called *tandem plan*, the GNMA generally acquires from lenders the kinds of mortgage loans that would not otherwise be made because either their high-risk factors or low interest rates (such as those offered under government-subsidized housing programs) make them uneconomical for the private lending community. If the GNMA did not commit itself to purchasing such loans at prevailing market yields, lenders would not make them, particularly in low- and moderate-income areas. For example, a lender may agree to issue a mortgage at an interest rate of 9¼ percent—well below the current market. The GNMA buys the mortgage, then resells it at a discounted price, which will yield the buyer 10¾ percent. The 1½ point spread represents a federal government subsidy that enables a home purchaser to finance a home at a more affordable rate.

Now gaining popularity among investors is the "Ginnie Mae pass-through." This is a security interest in a pool of mortgages that provides for a monthly pass-through of principal and interest payments directly to the certificate holder. Such certificates are guaranteed by Ginnie Mae. These securities have provided funds used for financing more than half of all FHA and VA mortgage originations. (See *GUARANTEED MORTGAGE CERTIFICATE, MORTGAGE-BACKED SECURITY, TANDEM PLAN.*)

GOVERNMENT PATENT	The original United States land grant which conveyed government-owned land to the people.

GOVERNMENT SURVEY METHOD A system of land description that applies to much of the land in the United States, particularly in the Western States; also called the *geodetic* or *rectangular survey system*. It is based on pairs of principal meridians and base lines, with each pair governing the surveys in a designated area. Principal meridians are north and south lines, and base lines extend east and west. The government survey method was designed to create a checkerboard of identical squares covering a given area. The largest squares measure 24 miles on each side and are called *quadrangles*. Each quadrangle is further divided into 16 squares called *townships*, whose four boundaries each measure 6 miles. A column of townships extending north-south is called a *range* and is numbered numerically east and west according to its distance from the principal meridian. There are now 36 principal meridians located in different parts of the United States.

Because of the curvature of the earth, the north-south lines, or range lines, converge as they extend northward. In order to keep them as close to 6 miles apart as possible and thus preserve the square shape of the township, the lines are laid out for approximately 24 miles and then adjusted so that they are again 6 miles apart.

A township is 6 miles square and contains 36 square miles. Townships are numbered north and south from the base line. Each square mile, which is equivalent to 640 acres, is designated as a section. Sections within a township are numbered from the northeast corner, following a back and forth course, until the last section (36) is reached in the southeast corner. This method of numbering ensures that any two sections with contiguous numbers also have contiguous boundaries. For purposes of land description, sections are commonly divided into half-sections containing 320 acres, quarter sections containing 160 acres, and so forth. Land acreage descriptions are then generally made by referring to a particular quarter of a particular township, or tier, either north or south of a particular base line, and either east or west of a particular meridian.

A section is the smallest subdivision usually surveyed by government surveyors, and at each section corner, there is a marker known as a *survey monument*. A sample government survey description would be:

> The E ½ of the NW ¼ of the SE ¼ of Section 17, and the N ½ of the NE ¼ of the SE ¼ of Section 17, Township 14 North, Range 4 West of the 6th Principal Meridian.

Note that generally, the longer the description, the smaller the parcel of land. This method is good for identifying large parcels, but not for pinpointing small lots.

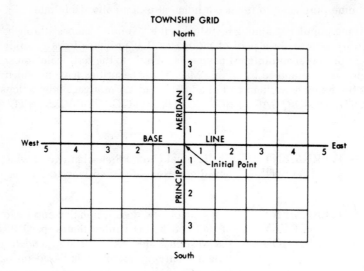

TOWNSHIP GRID

**NUMBERING
OF SECTIONS IN TOWNSHIP**

Adjoining Sections

SECTION 20

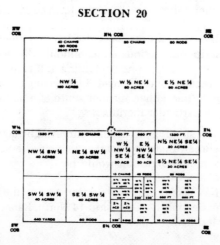

GRACE PERIOD   An agreed-upon time after an obligation is past due during which a party can perform without being considered in default. For example, a mortgage payment is due March 1, but the mortgage contains a ten-day grace period, so the mortgagor is not in default as long as payment is made by March 10. Also known as days of grace.

With monetary defaults, there is usually no requirement of prior written notice to the debtor. But with nonmonetary defaults such as waste or failure to keep a property insured, the grace period usually begins to run only after written notice is given.

GRADE   The elevation of a hill, road, sidewalk, or slope to the degree that it is inclined from level ground. The slope of an inclined surface of a road or lot is generally expressed as a percentage of the level or horizontal distance; a 5 percent grade rises 5 feet in each 100 feet of level distance. The *grade level* of a lot refers to the general elevation of the land. *Rough grade* is a surface on which topsoil will be spread to bring the lot up to a finished grade.

GRADIENT   The slope, or rate of increase or decrease in elevation, of a surface, road, or pipe. Gradient is expressed in inches of rise or fall per horizontal linear foot of ascent or descent.

GRADUATED PAYMENT MORTGAGE   A mortgage in which the monthly payment for principal and interest graduates by a certain percentage each year for a specific number of years and then levels off for the remaining term of the mortgage. There are five different versions of the plan available in the FHA-245 program. The most popular is Plan III in which payments increase at the rate of 7½ percent per year for five years (see chart).

The FHA-245 program is especially attractive to persons just starting their careers and anticipating increases in their incomes to obtain a home with initially a lower monthly installment obligation than would be available under a level payment plan. Since FHA underwriting guidelines are based on the first year's monthly requirement for principal and interest amortization, persons using FHA-245 can qualify for larger loan amounts than would ordinarily be available under other forms of financing.

Comparison of Payment Schedules of Level Payment Mortgage and FHA Graduated Payment Mortgage (Plan III)

$100,000 loan, 11½% interest, 30-year term
(rounded to nearest dollar)

Year	Level Payment	Graduated Payment	Difference
1	$991	$ 760	− 231
2	991	817	− 174
3	991	878	− 113
4	991	944	− 47
5	991	1014	+ 23
6-30	991	1091	+100

GRADUATED RENTAL LEASE A lease in which the rent payments commence at a fixed, often low, rate, but increase at set intervals as the lease term matures. Such increases might be based on a percentage of the increased value of the land based on a periodic appraisal. This gives long-term commercial tenants an opportunity to get started in business without a heavy financial burden during the early years. It may also be preferred by the lessor for tax purposes in order to reduce cash flow in a certain high-tax period. A graduated rental lease is often an excellent device for attracting tenants in a tough market or difficult to lease facility. Also called a graded lease. (See CASH FLOW, ESCALATOR CLAUSE, STEP-UP LEASE.)

GRANDFATHER CLAUSE A common expression used to convey the idea that something which was once permissible continues to be permissible despite changes in the controlling law. For instance, a developer with prior county planning approval to build 10,000 square foot minimum-sized lots can build such lots even if the current zoning regulations are amended to require 12,000 square foot minimum-sized lots. The developer is "grandfathered" under the originally approved subdivision plan. This situation is similar to nonconforming use.

In terms of recent state legislation regarding real estate prelicensing educational requirements, current licensees may be "grandfathered," or exempted, from such new requirements. (See NONCONFORMING USE.)

GRANNY FLATS A slang term to describe accessory apartments in single-family zoned areas. These separate rental units, such as above the garage, are illegal under most zoning laws.

GRANT The act of conveying or transferring title to real property. Historically, the operative words in a conveyance of real estate are grant, bargain, sell, warrant, convey. The grantor delivers the grant, in the form of a deed to the grantee. If a leasehold is involved, an assignment of lease is used to transfer the leasehold title. (See DEED.)

GRANT DEED A type of deed in which the grantor warrants that he has not previously conveyed the estate being granted to another, that he has not encumbered the property except as noted in the deed, and that he will convey to the grantee any title to the property he may later acquire. Grant deeds are very common in California, especially where the buyer also receives a title insurance policy.

GRANTEE The person who receives from the grantor a conveyance of real property. The grantee must be a person, either natural or otherwise, who exists at the time of the conveyance and is capable of taking title. As a general rule, a grantor cannot convey title to himself alone. He may, however, convey title to himself and others; for example, John Park conveys title to John Park and George Ant as joint tenants.

Some general applications of the above principles are:

1. If the grantee is dead at the time of delivery of the deed, the deed is void. (Delivery is deemed to have taken place when the executed deed is placed in escrow, not necessarily when it is actually delivered to the grantee.)

2. If the grantee is a corporation, or an informal club or society, which had not filed its incorporation papers before delivery of the deed, the deed is void for lack of a competent grantee.

3. A deed conveying an estate to the heirs of a living person is void since no person can be an heir during the lifetime of his or her ancestor. (The correct wording would be "to Joe Young and his heirs and assigns. . . .")

4. When the grantee's name has been omitted, the deed generally is ineffective to convey full title until the name is filled in with the grantor's permission.

When title is transferred to multiple grantees, there are many possible variations of title ownership. For example, if a mother and father decide to buy a home with their daughter and son-in-law, title may be held as follows: "To James Lynch and Carolee Lynch, husband and wife, as joint tenants, an undivided one-third interest and Paul Jones and Mary Jones, husband and wife, as tenants by the entirety, an undivided two-thirds interest of Lot 123. . . ." Thus upon the death of James Lynch, Carolee will own a one-third undivided interest as tenant in common with Paul and Mary Jones, who continue to own their two-thirds undivided interest as tenants by the entirety. (*See DEED; OWNERSHIP, FORM OF.*)

GRANTOR   The person transferring title to, or an interest in, real property. A grantor must be competent to convey; thus, an insane person cannot convey title to real property. A deed from a minor usually is voidable (not void) and may be disaffirmed before or within a reasonable time after the grantor reaches majority. A corporate grantor must have legal existence, be authorized to hold and convey title to real property, and be represented by a duly authorized officer of the corporation.

The grantor must be clearly identified in the deed. Misspellings do not render the deed inoperative unless the discrepancy is so extensive that the grantor cannot reasonably be identified. The grantor should convey title under the same name in which he or she acquired title. If the grantor has changed names, the conveyance should reflect such change; for example, "Joan Henry, who acquired title under the name Joan H. Adams. . . ."

Both grantor and grantee must be living and cannot be the same person. For example, a husband cannot convey his interest in a joint tenancy to himself as a tenant in common. A conveyance to "Joe Gomez and Fred Jackson, their heirs and assigns" would be valid, however, even if Gomez and Jackson were dead at the time of the conveyance.

When title is vested in two or more persons, each must convey his or her separate interest. Usually all co-owners will join in one deed, although separate deeds are perfectly valid to transfer the complete title to the grantee.

Even though one spouse may not be a co-owner of the property, he or she should join in the deed conveying the other spouse's property in order to release dower, curtesy, and/or homestead rights (if applicable). The marital status of the grantor should, therefore, be inserted in the deed. In fact, the recorder may not accept a deed for recordation unless it contains the marital status and address of the grantor. (*See DEED.*)

GRANTOR-GRANTEE   Public record books which are maintained in the
INDEX   official recorder's office, listing all recorded instruments and the liber (book) and page numbers where the complete and exact document can be found in the record books. Sepa-

rate index books are maintained for grantors and grantees so that a document can be located by searching under either name. These books are indexed by year and are in alphabetical order by grantor in the grantor index and by grantee in the grantee index. They contain the following information: kind of instrument; name of grantor; name of grantee; date of instrument; book, page, and date of recording; and description. Also called "name-indices."

Here is an example of one method for searching a title using the grantor-grantee indexes. In this case, Abe Adams owned a farm in 1890. In 1925, Adams conveyed the farm to Bill Benny by deed. In 1950, Benny conveyed the farm to Clarice Carver by deed. In 1960, Carver borrowed $50,000 from the Commercial Bank and gave a mortgage on the property. In 1974, Carver conveyed the farm to Diane Dealer by deed and now Dealer enters into a contract to sell the property to Elbert Edwidge.

The basic title search procedure is that each owner, beginning with the most recent, is traced back through the grantee index to the source of his or her ownership. Thus, the title searcher would start by looking in the grantee index under Dealer's name from the present back to 1974, where he finds the deed to Dealer from Carver. He would then look under Carver's name from 1974 back to 1950, where he finds the deed from Benny to Carver; then under Benny's name back to 1925, where he finds the deed from Adams to Benny; then under Adam's name from 1925 back to 1890. The searcher will then look in the grantor index under Adams's name from 1890 and "search up" to 1925, then under Benny's name from 1925 to 1950, then under Carver's name from 1950 to 1974, then under Dealer's name from 1974 to the present. In this way, the searcher will find the mortgage to the Commercial Bank, which is recorded in 1960 in the grantor's index under Carver's name. (*See RECORDING, TITLE SEARCH.*)

GRI (GRADUATE, REALTORS INSTITUTE) A professional designation, which may be earned by any member of a state-affiliated Board of Realtors® who successfully completes prescribed courses approved by the State Board of Realtors®. State associations generally sponsor the GRI courses covering law, finance, investment, appraisal, office management, and salesmanship.

GRIDIRON A term used to describe the rectangular street pattern of cities or subdivision developments.

GRIEVANCE PERIOD A specified day or group of days during which the public may register complaints about tax assessments or other problems on the local level.

GROSS AREA The total floor area of a building, measured from the exterior of its walls (excluding uncovered areas such as courtyards or patios). In *commercial* leasing, the gross floor area is the entire square footage within the floor's perimeter, measured to the *inside* finish of the permanent outer building walls or to the glass line in newer buildings.

GROSS INCOME The total income derived from a business, wages, or from income-producing property, before adjustments or deductions for expenses, depreciation, taxes, and similar allowances; that is, all income, "the top line."

GROSS INCOME
MULTIPLIER
A rule of thumb for estimating the market value of industrial and commercial properties. The ratio to convert annual income into market value. (*See GROSS RENT MULTIPLIER.*)

GROSS LEASE
A lease of property under which the lessee pays a fixed rent and the lessor pays the taxes, insurance, and other charges regularly incurred through ownership; also called a *fixed* or *flat lease*. In a *net lease*, the lessee pays all these charges. Most residential and commercial office leases are gross leases. Most residential ground leases and commercial and industrial building leases are net leases.

GROSS RENT
MULTIPLIER
A useful rule of thumb for estimating the market value of income-producing residential property. The multiplier is derived by using comparable sales divided by the actual or estimated monthly rentals in order to arrive at an acceptable average. By multiplying the estimated rent of the property under consideration by the multiplier, one can compute a rough estimate of the property's market value. Only a rough estimate of value is thus produced because the gross rent does not allow for variations in vacancies, uncollectable rents, property taxes, management, and similar unpredictable circumstances. To be most accurate, the estimate should generally be based on unfurnished rentals.

The use of the gross income multiplier, sometimes called the *gross rent multiplier*, has slowly been going out of use during the last ten years in recognition of the fact that it is a very crude guideline that does not take into consideration the tax ramifications of different possible investors and does not recognize alternate methods of financing.

GROUND LEASE
A lease of land alone, sometimes secured by improvements placed on the land. The ground lease is a means used to separate the ownership of the land from the ownership of the buildings and improvements constructed on the land. In most areas, it is a net lease that creates a tenancy for years, typically for a term of 55, 75, or 99 years. Ground leases do not generally run for longer than 99 years due to some early state laws that held leases of 100 years or longer to be transfers of fee simple title rather than leases. The lease rent (called *ground rent*) normally is fixed for an initial period of 30 years (calculated as a percentage of the assessed valuation of the land on the date of lease execution), with the balance of the rent to be renegotiated on or before the expiration date of the fixed term. The new rent is usually based on a set percentage of the then appraised value of the property minus the cost of on-site and off-site improvements. Sometimes the rent increase is determined at the time of execution of the lease, and a graduated lease, with fixed increases at stated intervals, is agreed upon.

In some states a ground lease is used in both residential and condominium developments; however, it is also popular in commercial property development. Since land ownership is separated from improvement ownership, capital gains taxes on land sale may be avoided and financing requirements may be decreased. (*See NET LEASE, PERCENTAGE LEASE, RENEGOTIATION OF LEASE.*)

GROUNDWATER
Water under the surface of the earth, regardless of the geological structure in which it is standing or moving. Groundwater does not include water flowing in underground streams with identifiable beds and banks.

GUARANTEED MORTGAGE CERTIFICATE (GMC) A debt instrument issued by Freddie Mac to raise money for its activities in the secondary mortgage market. These certificates are backed by a pool of mortgages previously purchased by Freddie Mac and further backed by the U.S. government itself.

GUARANTEED SALE PROGRAM A service offered by some brokers in which they agree to pay the owner of a listed property a predetermined price if the property is not sold within a specified period of time. This enables the owner to purchase a replacement property regardless of how long it takes to sell the listed property.

The broker generally charges a fee in addition to the sales commission—usually one or two percent of the sales price. Brokers should be aware that the Internal Revenue Service will consider that the property acquired through a guaranteed sales program is treated as dealer property by the IRC. (*See DEALER.*)

The guaranteed sale agreement must be well drafted to cover all rights and obligations. State licensing officials take a close look at these programs since owners have complained that some brokers refuse to perform their promises.

GUARANTY A pledge or security made by one person (the guarantor) to assure that another person (the obligor) will perform his or her contract or fulfill his or her obligations to a third person (the obligee). There is a growing tendency among lenders to require a mortgagor to obtain someone who will collaterally guarantee the repayment of a secured loan, especially when the borrower is either a new or financially weak corporation. (*See PERSONAL JUDGMENT.*)

GUARDIAN A person, appointed by court or by will, who is given the lawful custody and care of the person or property of another (called a *ward*). The ward might be a minor, an insane person, or a spendthrift. The guardian may, upon court approval and without necessity of obtaining a real estate license, sell the ward's property, if it is in the best interest of the ward. The grantee would receive valid title under a guardian's deed. A *guardian ad litem* is a person appointed by a court to bring or defend a legal action on behalf of his or her ward.

GUEST-CAR RATIO For purposes of site planning, the number of parking spaces for each living unit for use of guests.

GUIDE MERIDIANS As used in the government (rectangular) survey method, the survey lines running due north and south, 24 miles apart. Guide meridians correct for the convergence of principal meridians due to the earth's curvature. (*See GOVERNMENT SURVEY METHOD.*)

HABENDUM CLAUSE   That part of a deed beginning with the words "to have and to hold," following the granting clause and reaffirming the extent of ownership that the grantor is transferring. The habendum clause defines or limits the extent of ownership in the estate granted as, for instance, a fee simple, life estate, or easement: "To have and to hold unto said Jane Henley, grantee, a life estate in . . . ." If there is a discrepancy between the extent of ownership as specified in the granting clause and that specified in the habendum clause, the granting clause prevails. Consequently, a habendum clause is *not* an essential part of the deed. (*See QUANTUM.*)

HABITABLE   Being in a condition that is fit to live in. A residential landlord has an obligation to keep the leased premises in a habitable condition. If any condition within the premises renders the dwelling unit uninhabitable or poses imminent threat to the health or safety of any occupant, a tenant may terminate the rental agreement by following certain procedures prescribed in the state landlord and tenant code.

Courts are now enforcing implied warranties of habitability against builders of new residences when the defects render the building uninhabitable. (*See IMPLIED WARRANTY OF HABITABILITY.*)

HABITABLE ROOM   A room used for living purposes, such as a den, bedroom, or kitchen, as opposed to a bathroom or hallway. Usually, habitable rooms are the only ones counted in the number of rooms in a house.

HANGOUT   A balloon loan that occurs when a long-term loan exceeds the term of a lease for the same property. If a lender makes a commitment to a 24-year loan on a property with a 20-year lease, the four-year difference is called a hangout. When the terms call for the balance of the loan to be paid at the expiration of the lease, the loan is called a *balloon loan.*

HARD MONEY MORTGAGE   Any mortgage loan given to a borrower in exchange for cash, as opposed to a mortgage given to finance a specific real estate purchase. Often, a hard money mortgage will take the form of a second mortgage given to a private mortgage company in exchange for the cash needed to purchase an item of personal property or solve some personal financial crisis. The borrower in this case would pledge the equity in his or her property as collateral for the hard money mortgage. (*See SOFT MONEY.*)

HAZARD INSURANCE   A property insurance policy which indemnifies against loss resulting from physical damage to property due to hazards such as fire, flood, and windstorm. (*See INSURANCE.*)

HEAD CASING   The strip of molding placed above a door or window frame.

HEARING   An administrative legal proceeding with definite issues of fact to be determined and with the parties having the right to be heard and have counsel present much the same as at a trial. The rules of evidence are usually less strict than in a trial.

A real estate licensee is generally assured the right to a hearing under the state license laws when his or her license is in danger of being suspended, revoked, or not renewed.

HEARTH   The floor of the fireplace. The front hearth, which extends out into the room, may be made of brick or decorative stone. The back hearth inside the fireplace is usually made of fire brick.

HEAVY INDUSTRY   Businesses that require ample property to accommodate their nature and function, such as factories, packing plants, or mills. The term connotes noise, pollution, heavy truck traffic, vibration, and fumes.

HECTARE   A metric unit of land measurement equal to 2.471 acres, or 100 ares. An are is 100 square meters. The prefix *hect-* means "100 times"; thus, a hectare is 100 ares.

HEIGHT, BUILDING   Vertical distance measured from curb or grade level, whichever is the higher, to the highest level of a flat roof or to the average height of a pitched roof, excluding penthouse or other roof appendages occupying less than 30 percent of the roof area.

HEIR   A person who inherits under a will or a person who succeeds to property by the state laws of descent if the decedent dies without a will (intestate). State probate codes (laws of descent and distribution) set up the method of determining heirs for distributing an intestate decedent's real property. When real and personal property descend to more than one heir, the heirs take title as tenants in common. The words "heirs and assigns" are no longer necessary to convey or devise title in fee simple. In modern usage, the word heir is used to indicate those persons who acquire in any manner (by descent, devise, or bequest) the ownership of any property by reason of the death of the owner. (*See DESCENT, LEGACY.*)

HEIRS AND ASSIGNS   Heirs are recipients of an inheritance from a deceased owner, whereas assigns are successors in interest to a property. The words "heirs and assigns" are customarily inserted in deeds and wills and are considered to be words of limitation, not words of purchase. Words of limitation in a conveyance indicate what type of estate is created. Words of purchase indicate who takes the estate. For example, in a conveyance "to Harry Howe and his heirs," the words "to Harry Howe" are words of purchase. The words "and his heirs" are words of limitation indicating a fee simple estate; they would not be present in the transfer of a life estate. Heirs and assigns are also generally responsible for the contracts of their predecessors, such as leases, options, mortgages, and contracts for deed.

HEREDITAMENT   Every kind of inheritable property, including real, personal, corporeal, and incorporeal; those things appurtenant to the land. An incorporeal hereditament would be the right to receive future rents or insurance proceeds.

HIATUS   1. A gap in the chain of title. 2. A space existing between adjoining parcels due to a faulty legal description.

HIDDEN RISK   A title risk which cannot be ascertained from an examination of the public records. The most common hidden risks include forgery or lack of delivery in the chain of title; corporate forgery (the execution of an instrument not authorized by the appropriate officers); minority of a party to an instrument; death of a principal prior to execution of an instrument by his or her attorney-in-fact; conveyance in fraud of creditors; elective share rights of the spouse of a first party who falsely represented him- or herself to be single; and potential vulnerability of the subject property to mechanics' liens. All such hidden risks are covered under standard policies of title insurance, but not under a standard certificate of title or an attorney's opinion which certifies record title. (See CERTIFICATE OF TITLE, TITLE INSURANCE, TORRENS SYSTEM.)

HIGHEST AND BEST USE   An appraisal term meaning that reasonable use which, at the time of the property appraisal, is most likely to produce the greatest net return to the land and/or the building over a given period of time. The use must be legal and in compliance with regulations and ordinances within the police power of the county and state, including health regulations, zoning ordinances, building code requirements, and other regulations. The highest and best use is determined by evaluating the quantity and quality of income from various alternative land uses. Net return normally is interpreted in terms of money, although consideration may be given to such things as amenities.

For example, vacant land in a central business district currently used as a parking lot may or may not be employed at its highest and best use, depending upon whether the surrounding market is ready for further commercial development. A gas station site may be more effective as a fast-food facility or a dry cleaners.

For appraisal purposes, land is always valued as if vacant and available for development to its highest and best use. The estate taxes and the real property tax paid by an owner of unimproved real estate is usually based upon the highest and best use of the land rather than the use to which it is actually devoted. (See APPRAISAL, DEDICATION, INCOME APPROACH.)

HIGH RISE   A popular expression for a condominium or apartment building generally higher than six stories. However, there is no national height standard.

HIGH-WATER MARK   That line on the shore reached by the shoreward limit of the rise of medium tides "between the spring and the neap." In most states, this mark, also called *mean high water*, is the seaward boundary of privately owned lands and is the dividing line between public and private property. The shoreline, however, may be determined in a few areas by the high wash of the waves, as usually evidenced by the vegetation line, not the high water mark. (*See SHORELINE.*)

HIGHWAY   A roadway generally serving through traffic on continuous route providing the primary access between communities.

HIP ROOF   Pitched roof with sloping sides and ends.

HISTORIC STRUCTURE   The Tax Reform Act of 1976 adopted certain tax incentives and deterrents to encourage the preservation of historic buildings and structures. To qualify as a historic structure, the property must be listed in the National Register of Historic Places, located in a registered historic district, and certified by the Secretary of the Interior as being of historic significance to the district, or located in a historic district designated under an appropriate state or local government statute that has been certified by the Department of the Interior. There is a 25 percent investment tax credit for certified historic structures.

An individual will be permitted to elect a five-year write-off of rehabilitation expenditures for property which is used in trade or business or held for the production of income. The 1981 Economic Recovery Tax Act increased the expenditure deduction to $40,000 per unit effective for expenditures made after 1980, but the increased limit only applies to programs that permit responsible tenants to purchase their units at prices that limit the seller's profit. An alternative tax break is the right given the owner to treat the historic structure as new property so that accelerated depreciation could be used for the total investment in the improvement. The taxpayer cannot choose both of these tax breaks.

The 1976 Act penalizes an individual who demolishes or substantially alters a historic structure. Demolition costs will not be permitted as a deduction and substantial alterations or completely new improvements will not be eligible for any form of accelerated depreciation. (*See SCENIC EASEMENT.*)

HOLDBACK   1. That portion of a loan commitment which will not be funded until some additional requirement has been attained, such as pre-sale or rental of 70 percent of the units or completion of all building work. 2. In construction or interim financing, a percentage of the contractor's draw held back until satisfactory completion of the contractor's work and assurance of no mechanic's or materialman's liens. The holdback is designed to provide additional protection for the interim lender and the developer, and is often 10 percent of the contract price or an amount equal to the contractor's projected profits from the project. (*See FLOOR LOAN.*)

HOLDER IN DUE COURSE   A person who has obtained a negotiable instrument (promissory note, check) in the ordinary course of business before it is due, in good faith and for value, without knowledge that it has been previously dishonored and without notice of any defect or setoff at the time it was negotiated.

A holder in due course enjoys a favored position with respect to the instrument because the maker cannot raise certain "personal defenses" in refusing payment. Personal defenses include lack of consideration, setoff, and fraud.

This facilitates trade and commerce because people are more willing to accept such instruments without careful investigation of the maker's credit or the circumstances surrounding the creation of the instrument.

A holder in due course is insulated against a claim by the maker that the promissory note has been paid in part or in full or has been forged. Thus, the maker of the note should have the note marked "paid" and returned to him in order to avoid the risk of the holder's negotiating it to another holder in due course who could force the maker to pay it again. (See NEGOTIABLE INSTRUMENT.)

HOLD HARMLESS CLAUSE   A clause inserted in a contract whereby one party agrees to indemnify and protect the other party from any injuries or lawsuits arising out of the particular transaction. Such clauses are usually found in leases in which the lessee agrees to "indemnify, defend, and hold harmless" the lessor from claims and suits of third persons for damage resulting from the lessee's negligence on the leased premises. Hold harmless clauses are also found in property management contracts when the owner holds the agent harmless for all damages except those caused by the agent's own negligence or fraud.

HOLDING COMPANY   A company that owns, directs, or controls the operations of one or more other corporations, usually directly owned subsidiaries; a corporation organized to hold the stock of other corporations, such as a bank holding company.

HOLDING ESCROW   An arrangement whereby an escrow agent holds the final title documents to a contract for deed. Holding escrows are often suggested as the solution for the problems that arise under a contract for deed when the buyer is ready to pay off the balance owing on the contract but the seller either cannot be found or is not cooperative about executing the deed. Under a holding escrow, the seller, at the time that the contract for deed is signed, deposits with the escrow agent an executed deed or assignment of lease and instructs the escrow agent to deliver the conveyance to the buyer when full payment is made under the contract. Many escrow companies are reluctant to handle holding escrows, even when they are indemnified against loss, because of the following possible complications:

1. It may be difficult for the holding escrow to ascertain whether there has been a full payoff, whether the amount deposited in escrow is the correct amount, and whether the buyer is in default under any other terms of the contract for deed.

2. Difficulties may arise if the seller dies, particularly in terms of determining the rights of his or her heirs. Other problems may arise if the seller remarries, and new dower, curtesy, or marital rights must be considered. (See RELATION-BACK DOCTRINE.)

3. If the buyer has resold the property still under contract, and used a different escrow agent, the seller will be requested to draft new documents conveying title directly to the new buyer. Thus, there sometimes are added costs.

While the holding escrow practice is good in theory, these practical problems may prevent its effective use. A good alternative is to establish a collection account with the lending institution where the seller has his existing mortgage. The collecting agent will know how to contact the seller if the buyer wants to quickly pay off the outstanding balance and receive a deed to the property. Also, the buyer can thus be assured that the seller's mortgage payments are being made as long as he makes his contract for deed payments—and, vice versa—the seller can be notified if the buyer is in default in making his payments. This situation is sometimes called a *true escrow*. (See *COLLECTION ACCOUNT, CONTRACT FOR DEED.*)

HOLDING PERIOD   The period during which a person retains ownership of a capital asset. The Tax Reform Act provides that if property is held for a specific holding period and then disposed of, the gain will be treated as long-term gain and may be taxed at favorable capital gains rates. If the property is not held for the specified holding period, any gain on disposition will be a short-term gain and taxed at ordinary income rates. The holding period required to qualify for capital gains is twelve months plus one day.

The holding period commences on the date that ownership is established, whether that is by way of deed or possession under contract for deed. It is technically measured from the day after the date of purchase to the date of closing the sale. With an option, it is measured from the day the option is exercised. It is computed in terms of months, not days. (See *CAPITAL GAIN.*)

As regards a personal residence, the taxpayer can add ("tack on") the replacement residence to the present residence for purposes of meeting the 12-month requirement.

Where the property is acquired by purchase, the holding period generally commences with the closing or settlement date. Where the basis to the purchaser is determined by reference to its basis in the hands of the prior owner, such as in the contribution of property by a partner to a partnership, or donor of a gift, the period the asset was held by the prior owner (the partner or donor) will be included in the holding period for the acquirer (partnership).

The holding period of property acquired in a tax-deferred exchange includes the period the exchanged property was held.

The holding period of improvements made after the acquisition of real estate is computed separately from the holding period of the real estate itself. Therefore, a building subsequently constructed on raw land will have a shorter holding period than the land itself. (See *TACKING.*)

HOLDOVER TENANT   A person who stays on the leased premises after his or her lease has expired. The landlord normally has the choice of evicting the holdover tenant or permitting him or her to remain and continue to pay rent. The landlord may also elect to treat the holdover tenant as a tenant whose lease would continue from period to period, with the period to be that of the original lease, and for the same rent. The lease, however, would generally not exceed one year, since most state statutes of frauds require that leases for one year or longer be in writing. A holdover tenant usually has no rights whatsoever to the leased property—he or she is little better than a trespasser. (See *TENANCY AT SUFFERANCE.*)

HOLIDAYS

The following is a list of significant holidays recognized by most banks and many businesses, as well as state and federal offices.

New Year's Day	January 1
Lincoln's Birthday	February 12
Washington's Birthday (observed)	Third Monday in February
Washington's Birthday (traditional)	February 22
Memorial Day (observed)	Last Monday in May
Memorial Day (traditional)	May 30
Independence Day	July 4
Labor Day	First Monday in September
Columbus Day (observed)	Second Monday in October
Columbus Day (traditional)	October 12
Election Day	First Tuesday in November
Veteran's Day	November 11
Thanksgiving Day	Fourth Thursday in November
Christmas Day	December 25

Legal public holidays recognized by the federal government are specified in Section 6103(a) of Title 5 of the United States Code.

Usually, whenever an act is to be performed upon a particular day which happens to fall upon a holiday, the act may be performed upon the next business day with the same effect as if performed upon the day appointed. This rule is generally not true where the parties have clearly indicated that "time is of the essence." In any event, a prudent contract drafter should foresee possible problems and make the appropriate adjustments.

HOLOGRAPHIC WILL

A will that is written, dated, and signed in the testator's handwriting, but not witnessed. Some states permit a holographic will to be valid even though it was not witnessed, presumably on the theory that the handwriting can be analyzed to verify authenticity and demonstrate competency.

HOME LOAN

A loan secured by a residence for one, two, three, or four families under either a mortgage or a deed of trust.

HOMEOWNERS' ASSOCIATION

A nonprofit association of homeowners organized pursuant to a declaration of restrictions or protective covenants for a subdivision, PUD, or condominium. Like other nonprofit associations, a homeowners' association does not have shareholders—it has members.

In a typical subdivision development, a developer will record a declaration of restrictions, covenants, and easements to ensure the orderly and harmonious development of the subdivision and to protect against future depreciation of values resulting from deterioration of the neighborhood. After sale of the lots has commenced, the developer will normally transfer his or her right to enforce the restrictions, liens, and covenants to the homeowners' association. In connection with condominiums, the homeowners' association is also responsible for maintaining the common elements, such as the swimming pool and elevators, and for hiring a managing agent to implement its policies.

The Tax Reform Act of 1976 allows two types of housing associations—condominium management associations and residential real estate management associations—to elect to be treated as tax-exempt organizations for taxable years beginning after 1973. But this tax-exempt status will protect the association from tax only on its exempt function income, such as membership dues, fees, and assessments received from member-owners of residential units in the particular condominium or subdivision involved. On any net income that is not exempt function income, the association is taxed at corporate rates but is not permitted the corporate surtax exemption granted to regular domestic corporations, although it may use the alternative tax on its net long-term capital gain.

Some homeowners' associations today are incorporated, nonprofit associations, since an unincorporated association could expose its members to the risk of unlimited liabilities, such as damages for personal injuries to others. Another added benefit of a nonprofit corporation is the established body of law that exists, which can be used to guide the corporation's operations.

HOME OWNERSHIP The status of owning the residence in which one lives. There are certain income tax advantages derived from owning a home, such as deduction of real estate taxes and mortgage interest payments, deferment of capital gain tax on the sale of the residence, and certain casualty losses. (*See RESIDENCE, SALE OF.*)

HOMEOWNERS' WARRANTY PROGRAM (HOW) An insurance program offered by a subsidiary of the National Association of Home Builders that offers a buyer of a new home a ten-year warranty against certain physical defects, such as faulty roofing, heating, electrical services, and plumbing. The one-time insurance premium averages about $2 per thousand of the home's selling price. The cost may be paid by ". . . broker, seller, or buyer, or it may be shared."

The major provisions of the program are that a new home is protected for ten years against major structural defects. (This is the builder's obligation for the first two years. The next eight years are covered by a national insurance plan.) During the first year the builder provides a warranty that materials and workmanship in the new home meet HOW's Approved Standards. During the second year the HOW builder continues to be responsible for the wiring, piping, and duct work on the systems in the home. During these first two years, the national insurance coverage provided through HOW assumes the builder's responsibilities to the homeowner if, for any reason, he cannot or will not meet the warranty's obligations.

HOMESTEAD A tract of land that is owned and occupied as the family home. In many states, a portion of the area or value of this land is protected or exempt from judgments for debts. The purpose of the state homestead laws is to protect the family against eviction by general creditors and to protect each spouse individually by requiring that both husband and wife join in executing any deed conveying the homestead property. The homestead value that is exempt from creditor's claims is specifically defined by state law. In some states a single person may claim a homestead exemption in the same manner as a married couple. Also in some states, the homestead interest attaches by operation of the law, but in others the homestead interest must be protected by filing a notice as required by local statute. Usually state laws do not exempt homesteads from annual real estate taxes levied against the property or to a mortgage for purchase money or for the cost of improvements. The rights to occupy the homestead and to enjoy the exemption benefits generally continue for the life of the husband and wife and the survivor of them and also for minor children. Homestead rights may be released by both husband and wife joining in a deed. Homestead rights in property may be lost by abandonment, as when the home is sold and the householder plans to move to a new home. Intention of the householder is a key factor in the legal establishment of a homestead.

Some states authorize a probate homestead to provide a home for the surviving children and minor children out of the decedent's lands.

HOMOGENEOUS   An appraisal term meaning of the same or similar kind. As used in appraisal, this term describes an area or neighborhood in which the property types or uses are similar and harmonious and the inhabitants have similar cultural, social, and economic backgrounds. A homogeneous neighborhood tends to stabilize property values in the area.

HORIZONTAL   The name generally given to the laws pertaining
PROPERTY ACTS   to condominiums that permit ownership of a specified horizontal layer of airspace, as opposed to the traditional method of vertical ownership of property from the earth below to the sky above. In a condominium, the horizontal planes appear as the floor and ceiling, and the vertical planes appear as the walls.

In order to ensure that each apartment will be eligible for the individual rights of private property in terms of taxation and conveyance, a developer generally has to disclose (by way of a declaration) all plans to a state Real Estate Commission or other legal governing body for approval. If approval is given, the governing body usually issues a public report of its findings, which each buyer of an individual unit must read and sign a receipt for. Once the condominium building has been completed, it is turned over to the owners (by way of the owners' association) to operate and manage according to the bylaws which have been established pursuant to general guidelines imposed by the law. (See *CONDOMINIUM OWNERS' ASSOCIATION, CONDOMINIUM OWNERSHIP.*)

HOSTILE   Possession of real property by one person which
POSSESSION   is in contradiction, or adverse to, the possession of the title owner. The word "hostile" does not mean there is any real hatred. It means that the possessor's claim neither recognizes the title of the true owner nor is subordinate to that title. Hostile possession is one of the essential elements to establish a claim to title under adverse possession. (See *ADVERSE POSSESSION.*)

HOTEL   As defined in many zoning codes, a building or group of attached or detached buildings containing lodging units in which 50 percent or more of the units are lodging units. A hotel includes a lobby, clerk's desk, or counter with 24-hour clerk service and facilities for registration and keeping of records relating to hotel guests.

While the reserving of hotel spaces does not require a real estate license, the rental of real property does. The distinction is sometimes rather narrow, especially for resort properties.

HOUSE RULES   Rules of conduct adopted by the board of directors of a condominium homeowner's association and designed to promote harmonious living among the owners and occupants.

Such rules are usually enforced by the resident manager with the support of the board. Since it is generally easier to change the house rules than to amend the condominium bylaws, condominium associations often use the house rules to regulate the condominium use, as in the case of rules governing the use of certain common areas such as the picnic grounds, pool, or guest parking, or rules prohibiting pets or loud noises.

Landlords of apartment buildings usually require their tenants to abide by the published house rules. The house rules must be fair and apply equally to all tenants. (*See LANDLORD-TENANT CODE.*)

HOUSING FOR THE ELDERLY   A project specifically designed for elderly persons (62 years of age or older) which provides living unit accommodations and common use space for social and recreational activities and, when needed, incidental facilities and space for health and nursing services for the project residents.

HOUSING STARTS   Housing units actually under construction, as distinguished from building permits issued. The use of national and regional statistics in housing starts is helpful in analyzing real estate and mortgage trends; it is a key economic indicator. (*See STARTS.*)

HUD   A federal cabinet department officially known as the Department of Housing and Urban Development, HUD is active in national housing programs. Among its many programs are urban renewal, public housing, model cities, rehabilitation loans, new FHA-subsidy programs, and water and sewer grants. The Office of Interstate Land Sales Registration is under HUD's jurisdiction, as are the Federal Housing Administration (FHA) and the Government National Mortgage Association (GNMA.)

HUD PROGRAMS GENERALLY IDENTIFIED BY NUMBER

Title

I   Home Improvement Loans
Mobile Home Loans

1   Community Development Block Grants
(Housing and Community Development Act of 1974)

VI   Equal Opportunity in HUD-Assisted Programs
(Civil Rights Act of 1964)

VIII   Fair Housing
(Civil Rights Act of 1968)

Section

8   Lower-Income Rental Assistance
(U.S. Housing Act of 1937)

23   Low-Rent Leased Public Housing
(U.S. Housing Act of 1937)

202   Direct Loans for Housing for the Elderly or Handicapped
(Housing Act of 1959)

203(b) and(i)	One-to-Four Family Home Mortgage Insurance (National Housing Act of 1934)
207	Multifamily Rental Housing (National Housing Act (1934))
213	Cooperative Housing (National Housing Act (1934))
221(d)(2)	Homeownership for Low- & Moderate-Income Families (National Housing Act (1934))
221(d)(3) and(4)	Multifamily Rental Housing for Low- & Moderate-Income Families (National Housing Act (1934))
223(f)	Existing Multifamily Rental Housing (National Housing Act (1934))
231	Mortgage Insurance for Housing for the Elderly (National Housing Act (1934))
232	Nursing Homes and Intermediate Care Facilities (National Housing Act (1934))
234	Condominium Housing (National Housing Act (1934))
235	Homeownership Assistance for Low- & Moderate-Income Families (National Housing Act (1934))
244	Single-Family Home Mortgage Coinsurance (National Housing Act (1934))
244	Multifamily Housing Coinsurance (National Housing Act (1934))
245	Graduated Payment Mortgage (National Housing Act (1934))
312	Rehabilitation Loans (Housing Act of 1964)
701	Comprehensive Planning Assistance (Housing Act of 1954)

Executive Order

11246	Equal Employment Opportunity (September 24, 1965)
11063	Fair Housing (Title VIII) (Civil Rights Act of 1968)

HUNDRED-PERCENT Generally refers to the location in the downtown
LOCATION business district which commands the highest
land value. This type of location usually reflects
the highest rental prices and the highest traffic and pedestrian count. This term
sometimes refers to the site which is ideal for the requirements of a specific user.

HYPOTHECATE To pledge specific real or personal property as
security for an obligation without surrendering
possession of it. For example, a long-term tenant could hypothecate the tenant's
leasehold rights as security for a loan. The lender could even use its rights in a
receivable mortgage as collateral for some loan to the lender.

In a typical purchase of a house, the buyer pays a portion of the purchase price
with his or her own cash and borrows the balance from a lending institution. The
lender requires the buyer to hypothecate the property, or pledge it as security for
repayment of the loan, which is accomplished by use of a mortgage or trust deed.
The borrower retains the rights of possession and control, while the lender secures
an underlying equitable right in the pledged property. (See PLEDGE.)

IDEM SONANS   Sounding the same. Legally, names improperly spelled need not void an instrument, provided the written name sounds the same as the correctly spelled name, and there is no evidence of any intent to deceive by incorrect spelling. An important rule in title insurance practice.

IMPACT FEES   A municipal assessment against new residential, industrial, or commercial development projects to compensate for the added costs of public services generated by the new construction. Such indirect service requirements would be to cover hook-up costs for water and sewer lines.

IMPLIED AGENCY   An actual agency which arises by deduction or inferences from other facts and circumstances, including the words and conduct of the parties (i.e. implied in fact). (*See AGENCY.*)

IMPLIED CONTRACT   An unwritten contract inferred from the actions of the parties. Such an agreement is created by neither words nor writing; it is inferred from the conduct of the parties. Also, a contract in which the terms are understood and agreed to, but not fully stated in the document. Note that, for obvious reasons, this is not a very businesslike or effective way of transacting real estate business.

A contract implied in law is one which is not considered to have been actually intended by the parties but which the law creates in the interest of fairness and equity (also called a quasi-contract).

IMPLIED EASEMENT   An easement arising by implication from the acts or conduct of the parties. For example, a person acquiring mineral rights on a property also acquires an implied easement to enter the property for the purposes of removing the minerals. (*See EASEMENT.*)

IMPLIED LISTING   A listing which arises by operation of law as implied from the acts of the parties; in some states, a listing which arises by implication from the conduct of the broker and seller and may be enforceable even though not in writing. In many other states, however, all listing contracts must be in writing, and all parties signing it must receive a copy; and no listing agreement will be implied. (*See CONTRACT, EXCLUSIVE LISTING, LISTING, STATUTE OF FRAUDS.*)

IMPLIED WARRANTY OF HABITABILITY   A legal doctrine that imposes a duty on the landlord to make the leased premises habitable and ready for occupancy and to continue to maintain them in a state of repair throughout the entire term of the lease. This is a reversal of the common law *caveat emptor* doctrine, under which the landlord was released of responsibility and the tenant took the premises "as is," regardless of habitability.

Many state landlord and tenant codes specifically provide that the landlord shall make all repairs and arrangements necessary to put and keep the premises in a habitable condition. The landlord must protect the tenant from all latent defects— that is, hidden conditions which the tenant is not aware of and could not be expected to know.

The implied warranty of habitability has recently been held to apply to the seller or builder of a new home, who can be held liable for defects that make the dwelling unfit. For example, courts have ruled that the implied warranty of habitability protects the purchasers of new condominium units with defective air-conditioning systems. (*See* HABITABLE.)

IMPLY   To indicate, suggest, or communicate something, not by express statement but by conduct or actions that lead to a logical inference. Most real estate transactions must be *express*, as opposed to *implied*, and must be in writing.

IMPOUND ACCOUNT   A trust account established to set aside funds for future needs relating to a parcel of real property. Many mortgage lenders require an impound account to cover future payments for taxes, assessments, private mortgage insurance, and insurance in order to protect their security from defaults and tax liens. In the case of FHA loans, many lenders require a tax reserve of six months and an insurance reserve of one year. Also, the FHA mutual mortgage insurance premium ($\frac{1}{2}$ of 1 percent) is usually collected at least one month in advance. When the property is sold and the buyer assumes the seller's mortgage, the lender does not usually return the escrow account balance to the owner. The sum remains with the lender, and it is the responsibility of the buyer and seller to prorate the balance between them. Impound accounts are required for FHA loans, and although VA regulations do not require an impound account for taxes and insurance premiums on GI loans, many lenders customarily require that such accounts be established and maintained. Under RESPA, the amount of reserves in the impound account is limited to one-sixth of the estimated amount of taxes and insurance that will become due in the twelve-month period beginning at settlement.

Sometimes, part of the purchase price due the seller may be impounded or put aside by escrow to meet the post-closing expense of clearing title or repairing the structure. (*See* CUSTOMER TRUST FUND.)

IMPROVED LAND   Real property whose value has been enhanced by the addition of such on- and off-site improvements as roads, sewers, utilities, and buildings, as distinguished from raw land.

IMPROVEMENTS   Valuable additions made to property which amount to more than repairs, costing labor and capital, and are intended to enhance the value of the property. Improvements *of* land would include grading, sidewalks, sewers, streets, utilities, and the like. Improvements *to* land would include buildings, fences, room additions, new roof, and similar constructions. It could also be an alteration of the land's surface, such as an irrigation channel.

Based on modern appraisal methods, the value of an improvement is generally determined by what it adds to the land in terms of production of income or amenities. A reasonable relationship should exist between a site and the character of the improvement placed on it. An overimprovement, underimprovement, or misplaced improvement detracts from the combined value of a lot and the building on it.

For income tax purposes, improvements must generally be capitalized, with deductions taken over a period of years, whereas maintenance and repairs which do not add to the value of the property can be deducted on income property as business expenses in the year incurred. (*See BASIS, REPAIRS.*)

IMPUTED INTEREST Interest implied by law. When an installment contract, such as a land contract or a mortgage note, fails to state an interest rate or sets a rate under 9 percent simple annual interest, the IRS will impute, or assign, interest at 10 percent per year (computed semiannually). This rule does not apply to installment sales under $3,000.

Section 483 of the Internal Revenue Code, "Interest on Certain Deferred Payments," was enacted in 1964 to prevent the seller from treating as capital gain that part of the selling price which really represented interest on deferred payments. In effect, it prevents deferred payments from being treated wholly as principal. Prior to the enactment of this Section, parties to a real estate installment sale frequently would omit interest from the contract and raise the purchase price to reflect this omission. The seller would thus try to generate favorably taxed capital gains rather than interest that would be fully taxed as ordinary income.

If a contract between family members does not specify at least 6 percent, the IRS will assign a rate of 7 percent for the transaction. For sales in excess of $500,000, the imputed rate will be 10 percent, unless the contract specifies at least 9 percent. Also, once a taxpayer reaches the $500,000 limit, one year must elapse before a sale may again qualify for the 6 percent rate.

Buyers may deduct for tax purposes, even though no interest is paid, 10 percent per annum on the unpaid balances. The face amount of the note is the total amount of principal and interest over the term of the note at 10 percent per annum compounded semiannually. By reallocating the face amount of the note to part interest and part principal, the buyer may not only carve out an interest deduction, but also reduce the basis of the property acquired.

Prior to the elimination of the 30 percent rule on installment sales, the imputed interest rules often were used by the IRS to render certain transactions ineligible for the installment sale provisions. (*See INSTALLMENT SALE.*)

IMPUTED NOTICE An agent's knowledge that is binding upon the principal because of the agency relationship between them. If, for example, the buyer's agent is notified of the seller's acceptance of the buyer's offer, the buyer could not thereafter withdraw the offer even though the buyer had no actual notice yet of the accepted contract.

INACTIVE LICENSE In many states, a real estate licensee can place the license in an inactive status. During this time, the licensee cannot transact any real estate business, including splitting fees with active licensees for referrals. The licensee usually must continue to pay license fees, although many states charge a lesser fee than for an active license.

INCHOATE   Incomplete, imperfect, begun but not completed. In most states where dower is recognized, a wife's interest in the lands of her husband during his life is an inchoate dower interest. A husband's curtesy right, however, is typically *not* an inchoate right; it only takes effect upon the wife's death. Also describes a mechanic's lien that has not yet been filed but will take effect when filed and relate back to the visible commencement of work. (See *DOWER, MECHANIC'S LIEN.*)

INCLUSIONARY ZONING   A land-use concept in which local zoning ordinances require residential developers to include a certain percentage of dwelling units for low- and moderate-income households as a condition to governmental approval of development of the project. In some areas, developers can pay a fee in lieu of allocating space for low- or moderate-income units. Certain communities have even tried to impose resale price controls on developers as a condition to approval.

INCOME APPROACH   An approach to the valuation or appraisal of real property as determined by the amount of net income the property will produce over its remaining economic life. With this method, the market value is equal to the present worth of future income. The four main steps in calculating valuation using the income approach are:

1. Estimate the annual gross income, that is, the income that would accrue if all units were rented at their fair market value.

2. Determine the effective gross income by deducting an allowance for vacancy and collection loss.

3. Determine the annual net income by then deducting the annual expense of operation.

4. Apply the appropriate capitalization rate to the annual net income.

The most difficult step in this process is the determination of the appropriate capitalization rate. This rate must be selected to reflect accurately the recapture of the original investment over the economic life of the improvement, give the investor an acceptable rate of return on his or her original investment, and provide for the return of borrowed capital. Note that an income property that carries with it a great deal of risk will generally require a higher rate of return than a safe investment. The appraiser must use residual techniques to provide for the recapture of the investment in the improvement but not the land because the land is not a wasting asset. The main advantage of using this approach is that it best approximates the expectations of the typical investor of commercial property who is looking for a money return on the investment. It is rarely used on single-family residential properties. (See *APPRAISAL, BUILDING RESIDUAL TECHNIQUE, CAPITALIZATION RATE, ECONOMIC RENT, LAND RESIDUAL TECHNIQUE, PROPERTY RESIDUAL TECHNIQUE.*)

INCOME AVERAGING   A method of reducing income taxes especially for an individual taxpayer who earns a disproportionately high amount of money in comparison to the preceding four tax years. Of special importance to real estate investors is the fact that income averaging can be applied to long-term capital gains whether the taxpayer elects to itemize deductions or not.

INCOME PROPERTY   Property purchased primarily for the income to be derived plus certain tax benefits, such as accelerated depreciation. Income property can be commercial, industrial, or residential.

INCOMPETENT   A person who is not legally qualified to perform a valid act; one who lacks the power to act with legal effectiveness; any person who is impaired by reason of mental illness, physical disability, drugs, age, or other cause to the extent that he or she lacks sufficient understanding or capacity to make or communicate responsible decisions concerning his or her person. Thus, insane and, in certain cases, intoxicated people are incapable of entering into valid contracts. A corporation not authorized by its articles of incorporation to purchase real property is incompetent to contract for the purchase of real estate. Similarly, an officer not so authorized by the board of directors is incompetent to sell corporate real estate. An illiterate person, however, is not incompetent to contract as long as he or she understands the nature of his or her acts. If a person is adjudged incompetent, the court will generally appoint a guardian to contract with all persons doing business with the incompetent. (*See CAPACITY OF PARTIES, CONSERVATOR, GUARDIAN.*)

INCORPORATE   The act of forming a corporation by preparing the necessary articles of incorporation and filing them with the appropriate state governmental business-registration division. (*See ARTICLES OF INCORPORATION, CORPORATION.*)

INCORPORATION BY REFERENCE   A method of including all the terms of one document into another document merely by reference. For example, a sales contract may refer to an addendum or an Exhibit A and incorporate the terms of such addendum to the same extent as if it were fully set forth. A short-form mortgage or lease may refer to a previously recorded lengthy document containing the many "boilerplate" provisions of the mortgage or lease transaction.

INCORPOREAL RIGHTS   Intangible or nonpossessory rights in real property, such as easements, licenses, profits, mining claims, insurance claims, and future rents; possessing no physical body.

INCREMENT   An increase in quantity or size, commonly used to refer to the development of large subdivisions in phases, or in increments. (*See UNEARNED INCREMENT.*)

INCUMBRANCE   *See ENCUMBRANCE.*

INCURABLE DEPRECIATION   An appraisal term meaning the deterioration of an item that would make it impossible or too expensive to restore or replace. All items physically deteriorated are treated in an appraisal of real property as incurable if it appears to be not economically feasible or profitable to cure the deterioration on the date of the appraisal. If the depreciation is due to functional obsolescence, it is treated as incurable if it is not profitable to cure it. Economic obsolescence is generally incurable. (*See APPRAISAL.*)

INDENTURE DEED A deed in which both grantor and grantee bind themselves to reciprocal obligations. Normally, a deed need only be signed by the grantor (called a *deed poll*) but an indenture deed is signed by the grantee as well, who might thereby agree to assume the mortgage or agree to special covenants. The word *indenture* stems from an ancient custom whereby deeds were made for each of the parties on the same sheepskin and then torn apart on an uneven line. They could later prove genuineness by matching up their indentures. Many leases to be signed by both lessor and lessee also begin with the words "This Indenture. . . ." (*See DEED POLL.*)

INDEPENDENT CONTRACTOR One who is retained to perform a certain act, but who is subject to the control and direction of another only as to the end result and not as to how he or she performs the act. The critical feature, and what distinguishes an independent contractor from an employee or agent, is the degree of control the employer has over such a person's activities.

An employer, as defined or interpreted by the FICA and income tax laws, must withhold income tax from and pay social security taxes on commissions paid to an employee but does not need to do so in the case of an independent contractor, who must personally pay FICA and taxes.

Many brokers treat their salespeople as independent contractors and therefore do not withhold federal taxes on money paid to them. Brokers should be aware, however, that it is not sufficient merely to label a salesperson as an independent contractor in a written agreement, nor can such an agreement be called an *employment agreement*. There are other important factors often necessary in order to maintain the independent-contractor status of sales personnel. Some of these factors are:

1. The salespeople must pay for their own license fees and board membership fees.

2. The broker may not reimburse the salespeople for business-related auto, transportation, and entertainment expenses.

3. The broker may not require an independent contractor's attendance during any set hours or at any sales meetings, nor may he or she require such salespeople to meet any quotas.

4. The salesperson must pay his or her own income and FICA taxes and may receive no minimum salary.

A broker who wants to maintain the independent-contractor status of his or her salespeople must be careful not to exercise a high degree of control over their activities; as control increases, so does the likelihood that the broker will be considered an employer. For instance, requiring attendance at weekly sales meetings might be just enough control for the IRS to challenge successfully the broker's treatment of his or her salespeople as independent contractors. If this status is overturned, the broker then would be required to pay federal withholding and

FICA for the "former" independent contractors and may also be required to pay back taxes not withheld.

The amendments to the tax law in 1978 provided there would be a forgiveness of any pre-1979 taxes the Internal Revenue Service may have assessed against brokers who had a "reasonable basis" for treating sales associates as independent contractors. Further congressional action can be expected.

A person who hires an independent contractor is not usually liable for injuries caused by the negligence of the independent contractor. An employer, on the other hand, is liable for employees' acts within the scope of their employment. Thus, an employer would be liable for the automobile accident of an employee who was driving in the course of conducting company business. In view of the complex issues involved in determining whether real estate salespeople are employees or independent contractors, most brokers carry public liability insurance that covers all their salespeople and office personnel. In addition, many brokers request their salespeople to name the broker as "additional insured" in their personal automobile policies.

Because many licensing laws make brokers responsible for the activities of their salespeople, even if they are independent contractors, many brokers want to exercise a high degree of control over such activities. However, the state licensing laws do not preclude the establishment of independent-contractor status for tax purposes, provided the relationship is carefully structured to avoid possible classification of such a person as an employee. A broker should always consult a tax attorney concerning such matters. (See PRINCIPAL BROKER, SALESPERSON.)

INDEX LEASE   A lease that provides for adjustments of rent according to changes in a price index such as the consumer price index. The index used in establishing the escalation must be reliable and bear a close relationship to the nature of the tenant's business. The most frequently used indices are the consumer price index, also called the cost-of-living index, and the wholesale price index.

INDIRECT COSTS   Development costs not related to the land or structure, such as legal and architectural fees, financing, and insurance costs during construction.

INDIRECT LIGHTING   The light which is reflected from the ceiling or other object external to the fixture.

INDIVIDUAL RETIREMENT ACCOUNT (IRA)   A retirement savings program which an individual may institute if he or she is not covered under a qualified retirement plan or is self-employed (such as an independent contractor). For tax purposes, persons establishing and maintaining such accounts are allowed to deduct IRA contributions from their gross income up to a certain amount in each year they qualify. A person maintaining an IRA is, in effect, creating a tax-sheltered retirement fund, the contributions to and earnings of which are not taxable until retirement.

Under the Economic Recovery Tax Act of 1981 for tax years beginning after 1981, an individual, whether or not an active participant in a qualified employer plan or in a government plan, may take an income tax deduction for his or her cash contributions to an IRA each year to the extent of the lesser of the following amounts: (1) $2,000 or (2) 100 percent of the individual's annual compensation (earned income) that is includable in his or her gross income. Where a working spouse shares an IRA with a nonworking spouse, the limit is 100 percent or $2,250. (*See KEOGH PLAN.*)

INDORSEMENT   An additional provision attached to a title or other insurance policy. Standard title coverage may be altered, enlarged, or reduced by an appropriate indorsement. Among the more common indorsements are protection against loss or damage incurred from CC&R's (the "100 series"); mechanic's liens; easements and encroachments; and loss due to noncompliance with applicable zoning ordinances. An inflation protection indorsement, typically limited to owners of residential homes or condominiums, provides for increases in the face amount of insurance by application of a formula, which is typically tied to the U.S. Department of Commerce composite construction cost index.

INDUSTRIAL PARK   An area zoned for industrial use that contains sites for many separate industries and is developed and managed as a unit, usually with provisions for common services to its users; a relatively modern real estate concept which has proven very successful.

Typically, an industrial developer will acquire a large parcel of land (usually 400 to 500 acres), obtain industrial zoning, and add streets, water and sewer systems, and utilities. Then the developer records a declaration of restrictions that sets up a property owners' association and regulates setback lines, landscaping, architecture styles, and so forth. The developer might sell a site to a particular industry which will build its own plant, or the developer might build the plant and lease it to the industry. The advantage of acquiring a site in an industrial park is that it avoids the problems and costs involved in acquiring prepared industrial property and saves money through the sharing of common expenses for items such as sewers, security, utilities, and the like.

INFILTRATION   The gradual alteration of a neighborhood due to displacement of residents or change in the existing uses of the property caused by shifts in the economic, social, and physical forces creating the environment.

INHERITANCE TAX   A state "estate" tax imposed on heirs for their right to inherit property. The tax is not levied on the property itself, but rather on the heirs for their right to acquire the property by succession or devise. Therefore, the rates or the deductions may vary depending upon the degree of the relationship. (*See ESTATE TAX, FEDERAL; GIFT TAX.*)

At the time of a person's death, a statutory lien usually attaches to all real property interests owned by the decedent, which lien remains in effect until the inheritance taxes have been paid and a "tax clearance" issued. This applies even if property was held in joint tenancy with right of survivorship.

INITIALS   Abbreviation of a name. Initials are effective as a person's signature as long as the signer intends them to be equivalent to his or her legal signature.

Any changes to a contract should be initialed by all parties and dated. A notary must usually initial all erasures on a document; otherwise, the document may not be accepted for recordation. A conservative approach to signing a lengthy document is to have all parties initial each page. This is sometimes done with a will.

In the more formal Torrens system of title registration, the recorder will not generally accept for recordation any document on which the parties have not signed their full names; no initials are accepted. If an initial is only part of a given name or a party has no middle name, the document should state the fact. Similarly, a power of attorney used to execute documents must usually be signed with the full name of the principal. (See *LEGAL NAME, SIGNATURE.*)

INJUNCTION A legal action whereby a court issues a writ which forbids a party defendant from doing some act. An injunction requires the person to whom it is directed to refrain from doing a particular thing, such as violating deed restrictions or house rules prohibiting pets.

INNER CITY An urban area which is generally recognized as a central residential or commercial part of a city despite the fact that it does not necessarily have political, geographic, racial, or economic boundaries.

INNOCENT PURCHASER FOR VALUE One who purchases real property without notice, actual or constructive, of any superior rights or interests in the property. The state recording statutes are designed to protect an innocent purchaser for value from the secret claims of a prior purchaser. Also called a *bona fide purchaser for value.* (See *POSSESSION, RECORDING.*)

INQUIRY NOTICE Legal notice which is presumed by law when factors exist which would make a reasonable person inquire further. For example, if someone is in possession of the property offered for sale, the purchaser is charged with knowing whatever facts an inspection of the property would have disclosed; purchasers therefore take title subject to the rights of the occupant. (See *ACTUAL NOTICE, CONSTRUCTIVE NOTICE, POSSESSION.*)

IN-SERVICE LOAN Refers to the National Housing Act's Section 222 mortgage insurance for housing for military personnel. Under this program, HUD allows the Departments of Defense, Transportation, and Commerce to pay the HUD mortgage insurance premium on behalf of the personnel on active duty under their jurisdiction. The mortgages may finance single-family dwellings and condominiums insured under standard HUD home mortgage insurance programs.

INSIDE LOT Any lot located between the corner lots on a given block; interior lot.

INSPECTION   A visit to and review of the premises. A purchaser
of property should always inspect the premises
before closing. Since possession of property gives constructive notice of any
claims of ownership, an inspection is an important step in discovering any possible claims of others. An inspection might also reveal any encroachments or unrecorded easements.

It is good practice for a broker to inspect the listed premises in order to ascertain
that his or her representations to prospective buyers will be accurate. The broker
should also search the public records for unrecorded leases, particularly those
relating to billboard signs and farming/grazing rights, and especially those which
might contain options to purchase the real estate.

Many brokers insert a clause in the sales contract to the effect that all appliances
and electrical and plumbing fixtures will be in normal working order and shall be
inspected by the buyer prior to closing. The buyer must make such an inspection a
few days before the closing. If such a clause is inserted in the contract when the
transaction is to be closed in escrow, the escrow company will not close until it
has received an inspection approval letter from the buyer. The FHA and VA require that inspections be made prior to their approval of residential loans in order
to ensure that the buyer will not have to make major repairs (wiring, roof, and the
like) during the first year of ownership. The VA prohibits the buyer from being
charged inspection fees, and the seller should be aware that he or she may have to
make repairs prior to VA approval of the loan application.

A title insurance company issuing an owner's policy may have one of its inspectors search for easements not shown in the public records, building restrictions,
and improvements not within the stated lot lines.

A residential landlord generally reserves the right to inspect leased premises after
having given appropriate notice. (*See ACCESS.*)

INSTALLMENT   *See CONTRACT FOR DEED.*
CONTRACT

INSTALLMENT NOTE   A promissory note providing for payment of the
principal in two or more definite stated amounts
at different times. (*See INSTALLMENT SALE.*)

INSTALLMENT SALE   An income tax method of reporting gain received
from the sale of real estate when the sales price is
paid in installments, i.e. where at least one payment is to be received after the
close of the taxable year in which the sale occurs. No down payment is required.
Section 453 of the Internal Revenue Code no longer requires there be two installments of principal; i.e. the buyer could make a down payment of prepaid interest
only, and a balloon payment of principal in a later year. If the seller provides any
financing, it is an installment sale. Some or all of the purchase price must be paid
in a year(s) subsequent to the tax year of the sale.

If certain conditions are met, the taxpayer can save on taxes by postponing the
receipt of an installment and reporting of such income to future years when his or
her other income may be lower. Thus, a taxpayer can avoid paying the entire tax
on the gain in the year of sale. A gain from the installment sale is recognized for
any tax year with respect to principal payments received in that tax year in the
same ratio as the gross profit from the sale bears to the total "contract price."

In addition to cash received, the sales price includes the fair market value of any property or notes received from the buyer and any existing mortgage on the property, whether assumed by the buyer or not. The year of sale is the tax-reporting year of the seller, and the date of the sale is the date of transfer of title to the property or, under a contract for deed, the date of possession. Note that the installment method of reporting is automatic with respect to qualifying sales of real estate, although the taxpayer can elect not to use the installment method. This can be accomplished by reporting the entire gain on the taxpayer's tax return for the tax year.

Money received in the year of sale includes option money (even if paid in a prior year), down payment, payment of seller's indebtedness, excess of mortgage over basis, and subsequent principal payments. Mortgages assumed by the buyer are not normally included in computing payments in the year of sale. However, if the amount of the mortgage exceeds the seller's basis in the property, the excess is treated as payment in the year of sale. Note that the rule only includes money paid on the purchase price of the property. Payment of interest is not considered to be a payment made on the purchase price but rather a payment made in consideration of the right to defer all or part of such payment.

Because the seller can defer all or a substantial part of his or her gain until receipt of the unpaid balance of the purchase price, the seller can accept a small cash down payment and thus expand the market of potential buyers. This may also put the seller in a position to negotiate for a higher sales price. In addition, the seller pays income tax only on the profit portion of each installment payment. Only that portion of the principal that represents gain is taxable, and the portion that represents the return of capital investment (basis) is not taxable. The seller thus retains a larger amount of each payment, which can be used for further investments. Interest, of course, is fully taxable as ordinary income.

The three steps in determining tax liability under an installment sale are:

1. Determine the total taxable gain on the transaction.

2. Determine the seller's total proceeds from the sale (i.e. that money to be paid directly to seller) but don't include proceeds to others, such as a loan assumption (often called the *contract price*).

3. Determine the amount of gain to be realized each year (the ratio of the total taxable gain to the total "contract price," multiplied by the amount of cash received in that year).

For example, an investor sells a property for $135,000, accepts a down payment of $40,500, and takes back a purchase-money mortgage from the buyer in the amount of $94,500, to be paid over 20 years beginning in the following year. The total gain that the investor realizes from the sale is $30,375. Thus, the investor must claim 23 percent of the down payment as a capital gain—23 percent being the ratio between the $30,375 gain and the $135,000 contract price, or:

$$\text{contract price } \$135,000 \overline{)30,375} \text{ total gain} = .225, \text{ or } \textbf{23\% ratio}$$

The investor, therefore, reports an initial capital gain of $9,315—23 percent of the original down payment:

$40,500 down payment
×   .23 ratio
———————
$ 9,315 initial capital gain

The investor's capital gains for the next 20 years (the mortgage loan period) would be as follows:

$$\text{number of years } 20\overline{)\underset{\text{\$94,500 owed to seller after down payment}}{4,725 \text{ paid to seller each year}}}$$

$$\begin{array}{r} \$4,725 \\ \times \quad .23 \text{ ratio} \\ \hline \end{array}$$

$1,086.75 capital gain each year

The Installment Sale Revision Act of 1980 made the following significant changes in the installment sale reporting rules:

1. The 30 percent limitation on principal received in the year of sale was eliminated.

2. The two-payment rule was eliminated.

3. An election to report on the installment basis is no longer required; it is now automatic.

4. The rule now applies to contingent sale price contracts. For example, buyer agrees to pay $60,000 down and 10 percent of gross revenues up to a maximum of $60,000 per year for 3 years.

5. The same transaction can be both an installment sale and a like-kind exchange. Receipt of like-kind property is not treated as a payment for installment sale purposes.

6. A third-party guarantee does not convert a purchaser obligation into a payment.

7. The new law requires payment of tax despite installment payment of the purchase price if the purchaser is related to the seller and if that purchaser resells the property within two years. "Related parties" include spouse, parents, children, grandchildren, and various controlled corporations, partnerships, and trusts.

8. If an installment payment is forgiven or waived by the seller, it is still deemed to be received.

A taxpayer cannot report a loss when selling by installment method. (*See CONTRACT PRICE, IMPUTED INTEREST.*)

INSTITUTIONAL LENDER Financial institutions such as banks, insurance companies, savings and loans, or any lending institution whose loans are regulated by law. Such institutions invest depositors' and customers' money in mortgages, as opposed to private lenders, such as pension and trust funds or credit unions, which invest their own funds. Institutional lenders are frequently represented by mortgage brokers who act as loan correspondents for out-of-state institutional lenders. Because they are actually lending other people's money, institutional lenders are carefully regulated by government rules.

For many years, life insurance companies ranked first among institutional lenders for total mortgage investments. Recently, however, savings banks and savings and loan associations have closed the gap. Savings and loan associations usually lend on one- to-four family dwellings, life insurance companies frequently deal with multifamily building mortgages, and both commercial banks and life insurance companies lend large amounts on commercial properties.

INSTRUMENT   A formal legal document such as a contract, deed, or will. The term *document* is a more comprehensive term referring to any paper relied upon as the basis, proof, or support of anything else.

INSULATION   Pieces of plasterboard, asbestos sheeting, compressed wood-wool, fiberboard, or other material placed between inner and outer surfaces, such as walls and ceilings, to protect the interior from heat loss. Insulation works by breaking up and dissipating air currents.

INSULATION DISCLOSURE   The Federal Trade Commission requires that real estate brokers, builders, and sellers of new houses must disclose in their sales contracts the type, thickness, and R-value of the insulation installed in the house. In addition, brokers are required to show the required facts in all listing and earnest money agreements. (*See* R-VALUE.)

INSURABLE INTEREST   A right or interest in property that would cause the person who has that right or interest to suffer a monetary loss if the property were destroyed or damaged. Thus an insurable interest would exist not only for a property owner or lessee, but for any involved mortgagee or other lien creditors as well. To collect damages from an insurance policy, one must be able to prove an insurable interest at the time of loss. (*See* INSURANCE.)

INSURABLE TITLE   A title on which a title insuring company is willing to issue its policy of insurance. (*See* TITLE INSURANCE.)

INSURANCE   Indemnification against loss from a specific hazard or peril. There are many kinds of insurance available to cover property or liability against various risks. Fundamentally, insurance may be written on objects such as buildings, contents of buildings, and equipment. Or it may be written to cover activities such as loss of income resulting from damage or some other unforeseen happening. Insurance can also be obtained to cover the insured's legal liability to other people. Note that when a building is insured under an insurance policy, it is insured against specific risks, such as fire, windstorm, and explosion. All-risk coverage is available under some circumstances so that one policy provides complete coverage for the owner in the event that the insured object is damaged. Property and liability insurance policies are personal contracts made by an insurer with a particular insured person. Such policies, therefore, do not run with the land and cannot be assigned without the consent of the insurer. If a loss occurs, however, the right to the insurance proceeds may be assigned. When a loss of property does occur, the policy may be reduced by the amount of the loss. An additional premium is then required to reinstate the policy back to the full amount of insurance.

Most insurance policies contain a pro rata liability clause which usually provides that "the insurer is not liable for a greater portion of any loss than the amount insured against bears to the total insurance carried on the property against the peril involved, whether collectible or not." This prevents the owner from collecting a greater amount than the actual loss by carrying policies with several insurance carriers.

Public liability insurance covers the risk which an owner assumes when the public may enter the owner's building. A situation that might be covered by such a liability policy would be a claim made for hospital expenses and doctors' bills submitted by a person who was injured in a building and claimed that the injury was due to the landlord's negligence in not properly maintaining the stairs. These policies are usually referred to as *owners', landlords', and tenants' liability insurance*.

When a claim is made under a policy that insures a building or other physical object, there may be two possible methods of determining the amount of the claim. One is based on the depreciated value, or actual cash value, of the damaged property, and the other is based on the replacement cost. If a part of a 30-year-old building is damaged, the timbers and the materials are 30 years old and therefore do not have the same value as new material. In determining the amount of the loss according to actual cash value, the cost of new material would be obtained, and this would be reduced by the estimated depreciation which the item had suffered during the time it had been in the building. The alternate method is to cover replacement cost. This would represent the actual amount a builder would charge to replace the damaged property at the time of the loss.

Insurance rates are set by rating bureaus which are supervised by state authorities. Under this system, the cost of the risk of possible damage is spread over all properties in the state by the establishment of a premium rate based upon the losses experienced during the past year or several years for the risk involved. Rates are revised by underwriting bureaus and are kept current in accordance with the loss ratio and cost of repairing the damage.

If a person owned a $1 million building and thought the building was in such fine condition and so well protected and cared for that it would be impossible to suffer a loss for more than $100,000, he or she might then buy a policy for $100,000. This policy on a commercial building will include what is called a *coinsurance clause*. This clause requires that in the event of loss, the total insurance carried on the building must equal the stated percentage of the value of the insured building. The penalty for not carrying the proper amount of insurance is a reduction in the amount of the claim which the insurance company is required to pay. For instance, most commercial properties include an 80 percent coinsurance clause. If the building owner carries the proper amount of insurance at the time of loss, his or her claim will be paid in full to the limit of the amount of the policy. The purpose of a coinsurance clause is to require the insured to carry the proper amount of insurance so that he or she will pay an adequate premium for this coverage.

Residential insurance policies also contain a coinsurance clause. For example, assume a house costing $100,000 to rebuild today would be insured for $80,000 to meet the 80 percent requirement (note that some policies are increasing this percentage). All losses, total or partial, would be fully paid up to the $80,000 face value. But if the house is only covered for $40,000, then it is insured for only one-half of the minimum. Therefore, if the property loss is total, the homeowner would be reimbursed up to the full face value; but if the loss is partial, the homeowner would be reimbursed either for the actual cash value (i.e. current replacement cost less depreciation) or for one-half of the loss, whichever is greater.

The three most popular types of homeowner policies are the Basic (HO-1), Board (HO-2), and the Comprehensive (HO-5). The Comprehensive covers all perils except flood, earthquake, and war.

In order to obtain hazard insurance, one must have an insurable interest in the property. Both vendor and vendee have an insurable interest in property sold under a contract for deed. Most contracts for deed require that the buyer maintain insurance to a stated amount and make the loss payable to the seller. If the sales contract provides for the assignment and proration of the seller's insurance policy, the transfer should be made at the closing. The seller then signs a form called an *assignment of policy*. This form is not effective until it has been accepted by the insurance company or by its authorized agent. (*See COINSURANCE.*)

Real estate brokerage firms should consider carrying errors and omissions insurance. This is professional liability insurance much like a doctor's malpractice coverage. It provides protection if the broker is sued for misrepresentation or concealment of a material fact, whether intentional or not.

A property manager is often responsible for securing adequate insurance protection for properties under its management. Some of the most common categories of insurance coverage are: standard fire; extended coverage and collateral fire; machinery and equipment; consequential loss, use, and occupancy coverage such as for business interruption and rental income; general liability, and worker's compensation insurance.

Many times property owners decide to pay small casualty losses and deduct it on their tax returns instead of filing a claim against the insurance company, so as to avoid rate increases or cancellation. But the IRS will not allow such deductions because the taxpayer made a voluntary election not to claim reimbursement. Since the IRS will allow all losses suffered up to the deductible portion of the insurance policy, some owners might consider increasing the deductible portion of the insurance coverage, which should also result in a reduction of the insurance premium.

INTEREST   The sum paid or accrued in return for the use of money. Interest is usually stated in terms of an annual rate, although the parties may not always call this payment interest, since it may be disguised in the form of points or mortgage prepayment penalties. Interest on a promissory note is usually charged and due in arrears at the end of each payment period (monthly, semiannually, or as required by the lender).

The maximum rate of interest that may be charged on mortgage loans is usually set by state law. Charging interest in excess of this rate for a loan is called usury, and nonexempt lenders are penalized for making usurious loans. In some states, a lender who make a usurious loan will be permitted to collect the borrowed money, but only at the legal rate of interest. In other states a usurious lender may lose the right to collect any interest or may lose the entire amount loaned in addition to the interest. Loans made to corporations and FHA and VA loans are generally exempt from state usury laws.

Unlike amortization payments, interest payments are deductible for income tax purposes. Note that interest (and real property taxes) related to the construction period of buildings must be amortized over a ten-year period (previous to the 1976 Tax Reform Law, they were deductible in full when paid or incurred). Low-income housing was scheduled to remain exempt from this capitalization requirement until 1982, but the Economic Recovery Act of 1981 permanently exempts low-income housing from the requirement.

Interest rates for FHA, VA, and FmHA loans are periodically fixed by statute. The rate, as set by the FHA, is the same among all three of these types of loans.

Interest rates are quoted for a one-year period. This annual interest amount is divided by 12 to find the interest due for one month. A shortcut to finding a month's interest charge is to multiply the principal balance of the loan by the interest factor shown in the following table:

INTEREST FACTOR TABLE

ANNUAL RATE (%)	FACTOR
8%	.66667
8¼	.68750
8½	.70833
8¾	.72917
9	.75000
9¼	.77083
9½	.79167
9¾	.81251
10	.83333
10¼	.85417

Note that there is a difference between *nominal interest*, the amount (percentage) of annual interest stated in the loan document, and *effective interest*, the amount of interest the borrower actually pays. The difference usually results from the manner in which the debt is collected, such as the use of discount points to increase the gross rate or principal plus interest (add-on) methods. In addition, see the explanation under *TRUTH-IN-LENDING LAWS* for the difference between interest and the annual percentage rate. (*See BLOCK INTEREST, COMPOUND INTEREST, IMPUTED INTEREST, POINTS, PREPAID INTEREST, TRUTH-IN-LENDING LAWS, USURY, VARIABLE INTEREST RATE.*)

INTEREST IN PROPERTY A legal share of ownership in property, whether the entire ownership, as in a fee simple interest, or partial ownership, as in a leasehold estate.

INTERIM FINANCING A short-term loan usually made during the construction phase of a building project; often referred to as a *construction loan*. The proceeds from the interim loan are disbursed in increments as the construction progresses. Long-term or permanent financing is usually arranged to "take out" the interim loan. (*See CONSTRUCTION LOAN, TAKEOUT FINANCING.*)

INTERLOCUTORY DECREE A judicial order that does not take final effect until a specified time or the occurrence of a certain event. Besides divorce decrees, which often have a bearing on the division of real property, condemnation actions also frequently involve interlocutory decrees.

INTERNAL RATE OF RETURN (IRR) A rate of discount at which the present worth of future cash flows is exactly equal to the initial capital investment. An investor in real estate or any other investment is interested in two factors when analyzing a potential investment: the return *of* the original invested capital and a return *on* the original investment. Usually this return on investments is expressed as an annual return, or yield. The internal rate of return is a sophisticated mathematical measurement which, in the last few years since its inclusion in the Realtors® National Marketing Institute commercial investment courses, has seen a growing popularity. The advantages of using the internal rate of return as a measurement of an investment's worth is that all types of investments—stocks, bonds, real estate, and business ventures—can be analyzed so they can be compared in an objective manner. Internal rate of return is calculated on the basis of the projected cash flows from the initial investment.

Although the internal rate of return is becoming more and more widely used, it does present some problems. The primary one does not directly relate to the validity of the IRR but probably presents the greatest difficulty—it is that most real estate sales personnel and investors do not understand what it entails. The particular problem with the use of the IRR mathematical formula is that it requires the assumption that the investments being analyzed have similar risk factors, and the projected cash flows used as measurements are only as good as the person preparing the projections. Also called *discounted cash flow*. (*See* INWOOD TABLE, PRESENT VALUE OF ONE DOLLAR.)

INTERNAL REVENUE CODE (IRC)   The body of statutes codifying the federal tax laws and administered by the Internal Revenue Service (IRS), an agency which issues its own regulations interpreting those laws.

INTERPLEADER   A legal proceeding whereby an innocent third party (stakeholder), such as an escrow agent or broker, can deposit with the court property or money which he or she holds and which is subject to adverse claims so that the court can distribute it to the rightful claimant.

The distribution of deposit or earnest money held in escrow is often a problem when the buyer and seller are in dispute over the purchase contract. Generally, the escrow agent will not release the funds until all of the parties, including the broker, sign a cancellation of escrow form. When one of the parties refuses to cancel the escrow, then no one can recover the deposit money. If the escrow agent cannot get the parties to agree on the disposition of the deposit money, the recourse is to file an interpleader action asking the court to accept the money and distribute it to the rightful claimant. Under such circumstances, escrow agents strongly urge the parties to compromise because the total costs of the interpleader action incurred by both parties often exceeds the amount of the deposit; thus nobody but the attorneys gets any money. When the broker is holding the earnest money, the broker may originate the interpleader. (*See* ESCROW.)

INTERSTATE LAND SALES   The Interstate Land Sales Full Disclosure Act is a federal law, enacted in 1968, which regulates interstate land sales by requiring registration of real property with the Office of Interstate Land Sales Registration (OILSR) of the United States Department of Housing and Urban Development (HUD). The main purpose of the act is to require disclosure of full and accurate information regarding the property to prospective buyers *before* they decide to buy. To comply with the act, the developer must prepare a *statement of record* and register the subdivision with HUD. After the registration is effective, the developer must deliver to the purchaser (and obtain a receipt for) the *property report* prior to execution of the purchase agreement. The developer must give prospective buyers a cooling-off period of 7 calendar days to consider the material contained in the property report. Many large subdivisions are registered with HUD because HUD regulations apply if the developer uses the mails or any other means of interstate commerce in the sale of lots.

There is an intrastate exemption to the regulations of the Act that is limited in scope and very narrowly construed. If the subdivision contains fewer than 300 lots which are sold or leased to residents of the same Standard Metropolitan Statistical Area (SMSA) in which the subdivision is located (leeway is given so that 5 percent or less of sales in any one year may be made to residents of another state), the subdivider may apply for the exemption.

Some of the more common exemptions from HUD filing requirements are:

1. subdivisions in which there are fewer than 100 lots. If fewer than 25 lots, there is a total exemption from the act, not just the registration and disclosure requirements.

2. subdivisions in which *all* the lots are 20 acres or more in size (inclusive of easements)

3. subdivisions in which the land is improved by a building or in which there is a contract obligating the seller to erect such a building within a period of two years

4. bulk sales of lots to another developer

5. sale to a contiguous owner

6. fewer than 12 sales per year

7. sales to a governmental agency

8. sales of a single-family residential subdivision when the subdivision meets local code standards, title passes within 180 days after the contract, and the seller refrains from promotional techniques such as gifts and dinner programs

It should be noted that condominum units are considered by HUD to be lots "in the sky," and thus the developer may have to register a condominium with HUD as well as the local regulatory agency. The risk of noncompliance is greatest in those larger projects in which the developer is building in separate increments but promotes the use of common facilities which may not be completed for more than two years (such as a golf course).

A developer need not register with HUD a condominium in which each unit has been completed prior to sale. In this regard, *completed* means habitable and ready for occupancy. The developer can also avoid registration (and thus not be required to furnish buyers with a property report) if the unit is sold under a contract that obligates the seller to complete construction of the development within two years following the sale, as long as construction is not delayed by conditions beyond the developer's control. Also, the developer does not have to give a prospective buyer a HUD property report before the buyer signs a reservation but only before he or she signs a contract to buy.

A registered subdivider who sells on an installment contract must refund any payments over 15 percent of the purchase price (excluding interest owed) if the purchaser defaults on the contract. This requirement can be avoided if the contract requires the subdivider to deliver legal title within 180 days after the execution of the contract.

The three-year statute of limitations for fraud does not begin to run until the discovery of the fraud is made or should have been made.

Note that even though a particular subdivider or subdivision may be exempt from registration under the law (e.g. a 60-lot subdivision), it is still *unlawful to make false statements regarding such sales* by means of interstate commerce. However, if there are less than 25 lots, then the subdivider is not subject to any provision of the act. (*See PROPERTY REPORT, STATEMENT OF RECORD.*)

INTER VIVOS TRUST   A "living" trust which takes effect during the life of the creator, as opposed to a testamentary trust, which is created within a person's will and does not take effect until the death of the creator. Inter vivos transfers are those made between living persons (for example, deeds, leases).

The inter vivos trust is frequently utilized to allow the trustee to provide investment services when the trustor is either unwilling or too unsophisticated to administer his or her assets or as a vehicle for a trustor to dispose of insurance proceeds, pension benefits, and his or her estate (pour-over trust). The use of an inter vivos trust owning property will be a way to avoid probate proceedings on the death of the trustor. (*See LAND TRUST.*)

INTESTATE   To die without a will or having left a will which is defective in form. The decedent's property passes to his or her heirs according to the laws of descent in the state where such real property is located. These laws of descent vary from state to state and determine who is entitled to the decedent's property which then must pass through probate in the state. Descent laws do not affect the distribution of jointly held property or life insurance proceeds.

State laws of descent vary greatly; in some states, an unmarried person's estate passes to his or her parents; in other states, the decedent's parents may have to share the estate with the intestate person's lineal brothers and sisters. A married person's property may pass to the spouse and children or descendants of children in varying shares; if the deceased left no children or descendants of same, the surviving spouse may be the sole heir in some states or may have to share with the decedent's parents in other. Many states allow a surviving spouse to take a special marital share of the estate, such as dower, curtesy, or an elective share. In states that recognize community property, a surviving spouse legally owns one-half of all community property, so it is only the half-interest owned by the decedent that passes to his or her heirs according to the state laws of descent. (*See DESCENT, ESCHEAT, WILL.*)

INTRASTATE   An exemption from federal securities registration
EXEMPTION   requirements afforded to securities which are offered and sold only to residents of one particular state, where the issuer of the security is a resident of and doing business within that state. The exemption will apply to a corporation if it is incorporated by and doing business within that state and the assets and activity of the partnership are also located within that state. Though exempt from the burdensome registration requirements of the Securities and Exchange Commission, the intrastate offering is

still subject to the full-disclosure and antifraud provisions of the Securities Act of 1933 and the Securities Exchange Act of 1934. The intrastate exemption is strictly construed and enforced. If one sale or resale or even an offer is made to a nonresident, the exemption will be lost; the issuer will then have to register the entire issue and offer rescission rights to prior purchasers.

The SEC has adopted Rule 147 to clarify the rules regarding the intrastate exemption. Under Rule 147, if at least 80 percent of the corporate assets are located within the state and it uses 80 percent of its proceeds from sales of the securities within the state, the corporation is deemed to be doing business in the state. A developer will therefore have difficulty using an intrastate offering to raise money for projects outside the state. A developer may even have difficulty if he or she has other projects or assets located outside the state. (*See PRIVATE OFFERING, REAL PROPERTY SECURITIES REGISTRATION, RULE 147.*)

INTRINSIC VALUE   An appraisal term meaning the result of a person's individual choices and preferences for a given geographical area based on the features and amenities the area has to offer. For example, to most people, property located in a well-kept suburb near a shopping center would have a greater intrinsic value than similar property located near a sewage treatment plant. As a rule, the greater the intrinsic value, the more money a property can command upon its sale. Most land speculation is based on this principle of present versus future intrinsic value. What was farmland a few years ago could very well be a booming communty today, and it is the wise investor who knows how to spot, buy, and sell such speculative properties at the most advantageous times.

INVENTORY   1. An itemized list of property. Many brokers recommend that their clients attach to the sales contract an inventory of property to be included in the sale of a residential property, including a condominium dwelling. Such a procedure lessens misunderstandings concerning which items in the seller's home will pass to the buyer with the sale. Of course, an inventory should definitely be included in the sale of income-producing property, such as a furnished apartment building, and the agent should verify the inventory.

2. A list of goods on hand held for sale in the ordinary course of business. Profits from the sale of inventory goods is taxed as ordinary income and does not qualify for capital gains treatment. (*See DEALER.*)

INVERSE CONDEMNATION   An action for just compensation brought by a person whose property has been effectively taken, substantially interfered with, or taken without just compensation. For example, when a governmental authority announces it will condemn an owner's property and then unduly delays in taking the property, the owner can bring legal action to force a condemnation and payment for the taking. Of, if the noise of low-flying aircraft damages the owner in the use of the land, there may be inverse condemnation, or a taking of property for which compensation must be paid. Another example is where some public works are undertaken with resultant damage to a private owner, but no condemnation action is taken by a public body. It is referred to as inverse condemnation because it is started by an owner who seeks compensation from the condemning agency and is payment for land not directly condemned. (*See CONDEMNATION.*)

Courts have held that a zoning action which merely decreases the market value of property does not constitute a compensable taking actionable under a theory of inverse condemnation as long as a reasonably viable economic use exists. An inverse condemnation suit is not available before there has been an actual taking or physical interference with the subject property.

INVESTMENT CONTRACT A contract, transaction, or scheme whereby a person invests money in a common enterprise and is led to expect profits solely from the efforts of the promoter or a third party. The sale of real property using "investment contracts" is deemed to be the sale of a security thus requiring compliance with federal and state securities laws. (See REAL PROPERTY SECURITIES REGISTRATION.)

INVESTMENT CREDIT (FEDERAL TAX) Federal tax law has provided for an investment credit to encourage the growth of small businesses including real estate investments and farming activities. A tax credit is a special credit against taxes restricted to certain tangible personal property. In a real estate investment, personal property which would be included would be elevators, escalators, and coin-operated vending washers and dryers, but not furniture (except when used in a hotel operation).

The Tax Reform Act of 1976 provides an investment credit up to 10 percent of the cost of the eligible property as a reduction in taxes to be paid in the year of purchase. The exact amount depends on the life of the asset. The asset must have a cost recovery period of at least three years to be eligible for the credit. As the useful life of the asset increases, so does the taxpayer's right to take advantage of it. The full credit is available only if the asset has a cost recovery period of seven years or more.

Asset Life	Amount of Investment Credit Available
3 to 4 years	1/3 of the 10% (3-1/3%)
5 to 6 years	2/3 of the 10% (6-2/3%)
7 years or more	the entire 10% credit

Assets placed in service in 1981 or later: Under the Economic Recovery Act of 1981 the class Life ADR System of depreciation is generally replaced by the accelerated cost recovery system (ACRS) for property placed in service after 1980 in tax years ending after 1980. (See ACCELERATED COST RECOVERY SYSTEM) The investment credit rate is applied to qualified investment in property placed in service after 1980 determined on the basis of the ACRS recovery period rather than by the useful life of an asset. For eligible 10-year, or 5-year property, 100 percent of the investment qualifies for the investment credit. For 3-year recovery property, only 60 percent of the investment qualifies for the credit.

Qualified investment for investment credit purposes is subject to an at-risk limitation.

The 1981 tax act also established a new recapture system of investment credit allowed and taken if during any tax year prior to the close of the recapture period (ACRS life) the property is disposed of. The amount of the increase in tax is determined by applying the recapture percentage to the decrease in investment credit that would have resulted from reducing to zero the qualified investment utilized in computing the credit for such property in previous years.

The following table is used in determining the recapture percentage.

If the recovery property is disposed of within	The recapture percentage is: 10-year and 5-year property	For 3-year property
(1) One full year after placed in service	100	100
(2) One full year after the close of the period described in clause (1)	80	66
(3) One full year after the close of the period described in clause (2)	60	33
(4) One full year after the close of the period described in clause (3)	40	0
(5) One full year after the close of the period described in clause (4)	20	0

The increase in tax due to recapture is limited to investment credits that were used to reduce tax liability. For investment credits not used to reduce tax liability, investment credit carrybacks and carryovers are to be adjusted.

"Recapture period" is the period consisting of the first full year after the property is placed in service and the four succeeding full years (or the two succeeding full years in the case of 3-year property).

New property has an unlimited eligibility, while used property is limited to $100,000 per year. The limitation on cost of used property qualifying for the investment tax credit is increased from $100,000 to $125,000 for tax years beginning in 1981 through 1984, and to $150,000 thereafter. The increases are effective for property placed in service after 1980. There is a maximum to which the regular tax of an individual may be offset in any year by the investment credit. A single taxpayer or a married couple filing a joint return may offset regular tax by $25,000 plus 80 percent of any tax liability exceeding $25,000 in 1981 and 90 percent for a tax year ending in 1982 or thereafter. Any unused investment credit may be carried forward for up to seven years.

The act provides for recapture of investment credit if the asset is sold prior to the expiration of the asset's life as set up at the time of acquisition. The recapture is on a pro rata basis of the unused portion of the asset's life. The excess investment credit previously taken would be added to the tax liability in the year of sale.

The investment credit is a tax provision not utilized by all investors and business people. It is an actual credit against taxes and is not a reduction in basis. It is an important tax-planning item to be discussed with a CPA or attorney.

In addition to this regular investment credit, business taxpayers may qualify for a credit for investing in qualified energy property. (See BUSINESS ENERGY PROPERTY TAX CREDIT.)

The 1981 tax act provides a new investment tax credit for rehabilitating qualified buildings and for rehabilitating qualified certified historic structures. The credits amount to 15 percent of expenditures for qualified buildings 30 to 39 years old, 20 percent of expenditures for buildings at least 40 years old, and 25 percent of expenditures for certified historic structures. The regular investment credit and the energy investment credit do not apply to any portion of the basis that qualifies for this rehabilitation credit.

The 15 and 20 percent credits are limited to nonresidential buildings. However, the 25 percent credit for certified historic structure rehabilitation is available for both nonresidential and residential buildings. These credits are available only if the taxpayer elects to use the ACRS straight-line method of cost recovery for property with a 15-year recovery period for the rehabilitation expenditures. In addition, there must be a substantial rehabilitation of the building to qualify for the credit. This means that the qualifying expenditures over the tax year and the preceding tax year must exceed the greater of the adjusted basis of the property or $5,000.

INVESTMENT INTEREST The amount of interest incurred to purchase or carry investment property. This does not include personal interest, such as that incurred in the financing of a residence or business interest. The 1976 Tax Reform Act limited the interest-payment deduction that an investor can claim to $10,000 plus net investment income. Any interest exceeding this limitation can be carried forward to succeeding years, subject to further limitation in those years.

INVOLUNTARY CONVERSION A tax term referring to a loss of property through destruction or condemnation. Such a "conversion" is considered a "sale" and is subject to income tax unless the proceeds of the condemnation award or insurance proceeds are reinvested in similar property. In the event that property has been condemned and the owner replaces the property, the basis in the replacement property is deemed to be the same as that which is replaced, except that it is increased by any debt assumed above the amount of the condemnation award, and gain is recognized to the extent that the award exceeds the price paid for the replacement property. Under Section 1033 of the Internal Revenue Code, the replacement property must be purchased within three years of the end of the tax year in which there was a threat of condemnation. (See CONDEMNATION.)

INWOOD TABLE A set of interest tables widely used by appraisers in computing the present value of an annuity for a number of years at various interest rates. Among its many uses, it enables an appraiser to estimate the value of a leasehold interest when the income stream (cash flow) is constant. Also referred to as the *Inwood coefficient*.

The principle underlying the system is that a series of equal annual payments to be made in the future is not an annuity's present worth. The annuity is worth only the amount which, if deposited today at a fixed rate of interest compounded annually, would provide for the withdrawal at the end of the year of an amount equal to one annual payment. (See INTERNAL RATE OF RETURN, PRESENT VALUE OF ONE DOLLAR.)

IRONCLAD AGREEMENT An agreement that cannot be broken by the parties to it.

IRRIGATION DISTRICTS Quasi-political districts created under special state laws to provide water services to property owners in the district and given the power to levy assessments to finance the districts' operations.

j

JALOUSIE Adjustable glass louvers in doors or windows used to regulate light and air or exclude rain.

JAMB A vertical surface lining the opening in the wall left for a door or window.

JOINT AND SEVERAL LIABILITY A situation in which more than one party is liable for repayment of a debt or obligation and a creditor can obtain compensation from one or more parties, either individually or jointly. General partners are jointly and severally liable for partnership debts and obligations, as are the grantee and grantor for any unpaid common expenses in the sale of a condominium unit. Employees, affiliates, and agents of a subdivider who violates the Uniform Sales Practices Act may be liable jointly and severally and to the same extent as the subdivider. There is usually a right of contribution among persons who are jointly and severally liable so that the person who is actually forced to repay the debt can try to collect equal amounts from the others who also are liable. (*See RIGHT OF CONTRIBUTION.*)

JOINT TENANCY An estate or unit of interest in real estate that is owned by two or more natural persons with rights of survivorship. Only one title exists, and it is vested in a unit made up of two or more persons, all owning equal shares. The basic idea of a joint tenancy is that of unity of ownership; title is held as though all the owners collectively constituted one person, a fictitious entity. The death of one of the joint tenants does not destroy the owning unit—it only reduces by one the number of persons who jointly own the unit. The remaining joint tenants receive the deceased tenant's interest by the right of survivorship. Thus, the decedent's interest cannot be transferred by will or descent. As each successive joint tenant dies, the remaining tenants acquire the interest of the deceased. The last survivor takes title in severalty, fully inheritable at his or her death by his or her heirs and devisees. Some form of joint tenancy is recognized in most states, although several states have opted to eliminate the right of survivorship as a distinguishing characteristic. The fact that one holds title to property as a joint tenant is no reason for a person not to make a will. Joint tenancy does avoid a formal probate proceeding, however.

Traditionally, four unities are required to create a joint tenancy: unity of title, unity of time, unity of interest, and unity of possession. Unless all four of the unities are present, a joint tenancy is not created. Such unities are present when title is acquired by one deed, executed and delivered at one time, and conveying equal interests to all the grantees who hold undivided possession of the property as joint tenants. A joint tenancy can be created *only* by grant or purchase (by a deed of conveyance), or by devise (will)—it cannot be created by operation of law. The grantees or devisees must be specifically named as joint tenants. In most states, a deed or will that is unspecific about the grantees' or devisees' tenancy will pass title to the parties as tenants in common. Typical wording used to create a joint tenancy may be as follows: "To Morton Charles and Seymour Berkowitz, and to the survivor of them, and his or her heirs and assigns as joint tenants, with rights of survivorship, and not as tenants in common."

Note that a combination of interests can exist in one parcel of real estate. For example, if Jack and Betty Redundo hold title to an undivided one-half as joint tenants, and Irving and Bernice Proszek hold title to the other undivided half as tenants by the entirety, the relation between the two sets of joint tenants is that of a tenancy in common.

A joint tenancy can be terminated when any of the essential unities referred to above have been terminated. This can occur either by mutual agreement of the parties or by one of the parties selling his or her interest in the joint tenancy. For example, if Bob Burns, Bob Smith, and Bob Roberts hold title to certain farm land as joint tenants, and Roberts conveys his interest to Rebecca Sunnybrook, then Sunnybrook will own an undivided one-third interest and Smith and Burns will continue to own an undivided two-thirds interest as joint tenants. Rebecca Sunnybrook will own the farm as a tenant in common with the joint tenants Smith and Roberts. The same destruction occurs if one or more of the joint tenants' interests are defeated by an action of law, such as the appointment of a receiver in bankruptcy, or the sale of property to satisfy a judgment. In title-theory states, a mortgage is a conveyance of land to the lender. The land is then subject to being reconveyed upon payment of the debt, and a joint tenant in such states who mortgages his or her interest without the other joint tenants joining the mortgage will, therefore, destroy the existing joint tenancy by removing his or her interest from the joint tenancy.

Many state laws hold that there is no dower in joint tenancy. Thus, business associates can hold title to a parcel of real estate as joint tenants and their spouses, if any, are not required to join in a conveyance in order to waive dower and/or homestead rights. A corporation cannot be a joint tenant because a corporation has perpetual existence and, at least in legal theory, never dies.

A common misconception is that a debtor can protect him- or herself from creditors' claims by taking title to property in joint tenancy. The creditor has every right to attach the debtor's interest in jointly held property and force a partition. However, if the joint tenant dies before the creditor seizes that tenant's interest, the creditor loses his or her interest because the surviving tenant takes the property free from the claims of the decedent's creditors. On the other hand, a creditor of the surviving joint tenant has substantially increased his or her security.

One of the principal advantages of joint tenancy is the avoidance of the delay and expense of probate proceedings since the surviving joint tenant immediately becomes the sole owner of the property. Thus, the current value of the property is not included in the total value of the estate on which probate fees are assessed. In addition, the survivor holds the property free from the debts of the deceased joint tenant and from heirs against his or her interest. However, the savings in probate fees are partly offset by the legal costs of terminating the joint tenancy of record and may be totally offset by the added taxes. Typically, the probate delay is not unreasonably long. However, probate proceedings may sometimes be necessary in order to cover the furnishings and personal property of the deceased because such property is not usually held in joint tenancy. In addition, each joint tenant gives up his or her right to dispose of his or her interest by will and, as a result, precludes the use by an estate planner of various tax-saving devices to minimize the estate taxes. These estate taxes can be substantial since the value of the jointly held property is included in the decedent's estate for estate-tax purposes even though it does not pass through probate proceedings. In fact, the federal estate tax may be applied to the entire value of all jointly held property—not just the original cost per owner—except to the extent that the surviving joint tenant can provide detailed records clearly proving the extent of his or her contribution. That contribution must be demonstrated in money, earnings, or inheritance, but not in time spent working on the property. There are exclusions, however, such as the rule that each spouse is considered to own one-half of jointly owned property, regardless of which spouse furnished the original consideration or whether the creation of the joint interest constituted a gift.

Joint tenancies are subject to gift taxes, income taxes, and inheritance taxes in addition to federal estate taxes. A purchaser should discuss these tax consequences with experienced tax counsel before deciding whether to hold title to the property in joint tenancy. In addition, joint tenancy or tenancy by the entirety may not be appropriate for people in second marriages with prior children.

In many states, a property owner can create a joint tenancy (also a tenancy by the entirety with a spouse) by conveying to him- or herself and another as joint tenants without the necessity of conveying through a third person (called a *straw man*). This is a statutory exception to the common-law "four unities" rule that requires the creation of a joint tenancy by one and the same instrument at the time that title to the property is acquired. Another approach would be for Able, Baker, and Charley to convey to Baker, Charley, and Daniel as joint tenants.

In the event all joint tenants die in an common disaster, the Uniform Simultaneous Death Act will, in effect, treat them as equal tenants in common. Rather than avoid probate, however, the unfortunate effect would be to multiply the number of probate proceedings.

Upon the death of a joint tenant, the survivor(s) should, as a matter of good title practice, record an affidavit of death and a death certificate with the county recorder. This is often required under state inheritance tax laws to obtain a tax clearance. If the property is registered in Torrens, the certificate of title must be amended to reflect such death. (*See* COTENANCY, DOWER, GIFT TAX, INHERITANCE TAX, PROBATE, PROPERTY TAX, SEVERANCE, STRAW MAN, SURVIVORSHIP, TENANCY (*all forms*), TITLE-THEORY STATES, UNDIVIDED INTEREST, UNITY.)

JOINTURE   A freehold estate in land for the life of the wife to take effect upon the death of the husband; a life estate in lieu of dower. A jointure or any pecuniary provision that is made for the benefit of an intended wife, and in lieu of her dower, shall bar her right to dower provided she assents to the jointure. (*See* DOWER.)

JOINT VENTURE   The joining of two or more people in a specific business enterprise, such as the development of a condominium project or a shopping center. They may pool their respective resources such as money, expertise, property, or equipment. It is necessary that there be an agreement, express or implied, to share in the losses or profits of the venture. Joint ventures are a business form of partnership and are treated as partnerships for tax purposes. The main difference between the two is that a joint venture is a special joining of the parties for a specific project with no intention on the part of the parties to enter into any continuing partnership relationship (a "one-shot partnership"). If the joint parties combine their efforts on several different projects, the relationship becomes more like a general partnership than a joint venture. Also, while a partner can bind the partnership to a contract, one party to a joint-venture agreement cannot bind the other joint venturers to a contract. (*See LIMITED PARTNERSHIP, PARTNERSHIP.*)

JOIST A heavy piece of horizontal timber, to which the boards of a floor, or the lath of a ceiling, are nailed. Joists are laid edgewise to form the floor support.

JUDGMENT The formal decision of a court upon the respective rights and claims of the parties to an action or suit. After a judgment has been entered and recorded with the county recorder, it usually becomes a general lien on the property of the defendant. (*See EXECUTION.*)

JUDGMENT LIEN A purely statutory general lien on real and personal property belonging to a debtor. Usually the lien covers only property located within the county where the judgment is rendered; notices of the lien must be filed in other counties when the creditor wishes to extend the lien coverage. To collect the amount of the judgment, the court will be asked to issue a legal document called a *writ of execution* directing the sheriff to seize and sell as much of the debtor's property as is necessary to pay the debt and the expenses of the sale. A judgment lien differs from a mortgage in that a judgment lien does not have a specific parcel of real estate given as security at the time that the debtor-creditor relationship is created.

As provided or required by the law of the state in which the real estate is located, a judgment will take its priority as a lien on the debtor's property on one or a combination of the following dates: (1) the date the judgment was entered by the court, (2) the date the judgment was filed for record in the recorder's office, or (3) the date an execution was issued. Judgments are enforced through the issuance of an execution and the ultimate sale of the debtor's real or personal property by a sheriff. When the property is sold to satisfy the debt, the debtor should demand a legal document known as a *satisfaction judgment,* which should be filed with either the clerk of the court, or, in some states, with the recorder of deeds, so that the record will be cleared of the judgment. (*See ATTACHMENT, EXECUTION, LIS PENDENS.*)

JUDGMENT-PROOF A term used to describe a person who has no assets to satisfy a judgment for money. Under many states' real estate recovery fund procedures, a person who has been defrauded by a real estate licensee can collect damages from the fund only if he or she can show that the licensee is judgment-proof. (*See RECOVERY FUND.*)

JUDICIAL FORECLOSURE A method of foreclosing on real property by means of a court-supervised sale. In a judicial foreclosure, there is an appraisal, after which the court determines an upset price below which no bids to purchase will be accepted. (*See FORECLOSURE, POWER OF SALE, UPSET PRICE.*)

JUNIOR MORTGAGE   A mortgage, such as a second mortgage, which is subordinate in right or lien priority to an existing mortgage on the same realty. Since this mortgage contains more risk than a first mortgage, it usually carries a higher interest rate. When there is a substantial modification of the prior, or senior, encumbrance which materially affects the obligation or the security of the junior lien, the modification is probably not effective unless the junior lienor consents and subordinates his or her interest to it. Thus, if the senior lienor extends the term of the underlying obligation, it is not enforceable against an existing junior lien. Also, if the senior obligation is increased by additional obligation advances by the mortgagee, the advances are subject to the junior lien. As a general rule, the foreclosure of a senior lien extinguishes all junior liens, whereas the foreclosure of a junior lien has no effect on a senior lien—that is, the purchaser at the junior foreclosure sale buys the property subject to the senior lien. There is no legal limit on the number of junior mortgages that can be placed on a property, but there is a practical limit. A lender would never want the loan amount to exceed the borrower's equity in the secured property. (See *SECONDARY FINANCING, SECOND MORTGAGE, SUBORDINATION CLAUSE, WRAPAROUND MORTGAGE.*)

JURAT   The clause written at the bottom of an affidavit by a notary public stating when, where, and before whom the affidavit was sworn.

JURISDICTION   The authority or power to act, such as the authority of a court to hear and render a decision that binds both parties. Real estate matters are usually within the jurisdiction of the court of the county in which the property is located. A state real estate commission or department generally has jurisdiction over the licensing and conduct of real estate salespeople and brokers in the state.

JUST COMPENSATION   An amount of compensation to be received by a party for the taking of his or her property under the power of eminent domain. Under both federal and state constitutions, private property may not be taken for public use without just compensation having first been determined by the court. This determination of just compensation is probably the most difficult problem in condemnation proceedings. A condemnee can generally accept the offered compensation or can request and receive a court hearing for determining the appropriate amount of compensation. (See *BEFORE-AND-AFTER METHOD, CONDEMNATION, EMINENT DOMAIN, SPECIAL BENEFIT.*)

KEOGH PLAN   A federal tax law designed to encourage business-people to set money aside for retirement years by giving them a substantial tax advantage. The plan (also known as an *HR-10 plan*) permits a self-employed individual to set aside a certain percentage of his or her compensation in a trust each year and to deduct this amount on his or her tax return as an ordinary business expense. This money can be invested by the trust on behalf of the individual, and all earnings and gains on these investments are compounded tax free. When the individual retires, he or she can take a lump-sum distribution of the whole fund. A tax is due when the fund is distributed upon retirement, but then the taxpayer is probably in a lower tax bracket, and if the money is distributed over a ten-year period, a special ten-year averaging formula will reduce the tax even further.

Under the Pension Reform Act, a self-employed individual can make a deductible contribution into a trust of 15 percent of his or her annual compensation up to a maximum amount of $15,000. An individual in a 50-percent tax bracket could thus achieve a yearly tax break of $7,500 via this business deduction. There is a $200,000 limit of self-employment income to be taken into account in computing a Keogh contribution. A self-employed person with a Keogh plan can also put $2,000 into an Individual Retirement Account per year in addition to the $15,000 and thus deduct all $17,000 from taxable income. (*See INDIVIDUAL RETIREMENT ACCOUNT.*)

KEY LOT   A lot that has added value because of its strategic location, especially when it is needed for the highest and best use of contiguous property; a lot which adjoins the rear property line of a corner lot and fronts on a secondary street.

KEYMAN INSURANCE   A life insurance policy paid for by a company to cover the estimated cost of replacing a key person in the company; it may be either a life or disability policy, or a combination of both. Some lenders require keyman insurance when the borrower is a small corporation that relies primarily on the talents of one executive.

KICKERS   Different types of equity participations a lender may seek as a condition for lending money, such as participation in rentals, profits, or extra interest. Serious legal questions are often raised concerning whether such equity participations constitute additional interest in terms of the usury laws.

KILN   A large oven-like chamber used for baking, drying, and hardening various materials such as lumber, brick, and lime.

KIOSK   A small structure, usually constructed of wood, with one or more sides open and typically used as a newsstand, photo film center, or ice cream stand. Such an enterprise usually pays rent on a fairly high-percentage lease basis.

KITCHENETTE   Space, less than 60 sq. ft. in area, used for cooking and preparation of food.

KNOCKDOWN   Prepared construction materials which are delivered to the building site unassembled but complete and ready to be assembled and installed.

L

LACHES   An equitable doctrine used by courts to bar or prevent the assertion of a right or claim because of undue delay or failure to assert the claim or right. For example, a neighbor who watches the construction of an adjacent thirty-story building and, after the building reaches the twenty-ninth floor, asserts a claim that the building encroaches five feet onto his or her property and demands that it be torn down. Laches is similar to the Statute of Limitations, which is a legal (as opposed to an equitable) doctrine used to bar a claim asserted after the passing of a statutory period of time. (*See STATUTE OF LIMITATIONS.*)

LANAI   Popular term in the western or southern states for a balcony, veranda, porch, or covered patio.

LAND   The surface of the earth extending down to the center and upward to the sky, including all natural things thereon, such as trees, crops, or water, plus the minerals below the surface and the air rights above. The term *real property* includes the land and all artificial things attached to the land, such as houses, fences, fixtures, and the like, together with all rights appurtenant to the property, such as easements, rents, and profits. In customary usage, the term land has become synonymous with *real property* and *real estate*.

LAND BANK   Land purchased and held for future development. In some communities, the government will condemn and preserve certain scenic property in an effort to prevent adverse development and to control urban or suburban development or sprawl. (*See SCENIC EASEMENT.*)

LAND BANKER   A developer who improves raw land for construction purposes and maintains an inventory of these types of lots as a function of this ongoing business.

LAND CONTRACT   An installment contract for sale with the buyer receiving equitable title (right to possession) and the seller retaining legal title (record title). (*See CONTRACT FOR DEED.*)

LAND DESCRIPTION   A description of a particular piece of real property. In the case of a deed, assignment of lease, or mortgage, the description of the property should be a complete legal description.

In the case of a sales contract, however, the description need only be sufficient to identify the property; often a street address would suffice for this purpose.

In writing a sales contract, it is best to also describe the type of property, such as "that certain fee simple property containing *approximately* 12,000 square feet together with a three-bedroom house with detached garage." It is important to insert the word *approximately* to avoid any claim that might later be made by one of the parties in an effort to rescind the contract on the grounds, for example, that the lot was only 11,999 square feet. If only raw land is involved, the better practice is to use a complete legal description. If the property is leasehold, most brokers also insert the current lease rent plus the lease renegotiation and expiration dates. (*See LEASEHOLD, LEGAL DESCRIPTION.*)

LAND ECONOMICS The scientific study of land and the methods of determining and implementing land's highest and best use.

LAND GRANT A grant of public lands by the government usually for roads, railroads, or agricultural colleges (thus the term "land grant college").

LAND LEASEBACK A creative financing device (often used with raw land which a developer wants to improve) by which a developer sells the land to an investor, who leases the land back to the developer under a long-term net lease and subordinates the fee ownership to the lender, who provides development financing. The net effect of the land leaseback transaction is to obtain maximum leverage, including 100 percent land financing, and, since the land is subordinated to development financing, probably 100 percent development financing as well. (*See SALE-LEASEBACK, SUBORDINATION AGREEMENT.*)

LANDLOCKED Real property that has no access to a public road or way, such as parcel C in the drawing below.

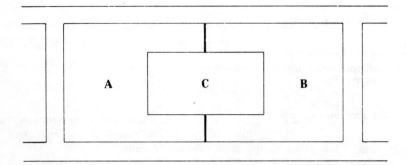

If parcel C had ever been a part of parcel A or B, a court would grant the owner of parcel C an easement of necessity over the parcel with which it had once been joined. This easement of necessity continues only during the period of necessity. Landlocked parcels are sometimes created as a result of condemnation for a limited access highway. (*See EASEMENT BY NECESSITY.*)

LANDLORD The lessor or the owner of leased premises. The landlord retains a reversionary interest in the property so that when the lease ends, the property will revert to the landlord.

LANDLORD-TENANT CODE See *UNIFORM RESIDENTIAL LANDLORD AND TENANT ACT.*

LANDMARK A stake, stream, cliff, monument, or other object or feature which is used to fix or define land boundaries; also a prominent feature of a landscape or property that is the symbol for the place. (*See MONUMENT.*)

LAND POOR The state of being short of money because of owning an excess of real property which does not produce income.

LAND RESIDUAL TECHNIQUE A method of real property appraisal similar to the *building residual technique* of capitalization, except that the amount of income earned by the improvements (the return *on* and recapture *of* the capital investment) is deducted from the annual net income, and the resulting figure (the land residual) is capitalized and is then added to the improvement cost to arrive at the appraised value of the real property. (*See INCOME APPROACH, RESIDUAL PROCESS.*)

LANDSCAPING Shrubs, bushes, trees, and the like, on the grounds surrounding a structure. Under certain circumstances landscaping costs can be depreciated. According to a recent IRS ruling, apartment-building developers can take depreciation for landscaping over the life of the building. The general rule, however, is that land itself is not depreciable for tax purposes (pasture land, however, is depreciable).

LAND, TENEMENTS, AND HEREDITAMENTS A feudal phrase used to describe all types of immovable realty, including the land, buildings, and all appurtenant rights thereto; the complete ownership of all the bundle of rights in a freehold estate.

LAND TRUST A trust originated by the owner of real property, in which real estate is the only asset. As in all trusts, the legal and equitable title to the property is in the trustee's name under a deed into trust. The beneficial interest in the trust property is in the beneficiary, who is usually the trustor (that is, the person who created or established the trust). Generally, only living persons may create a land trust, but corporations as well as living persons can be the beneficiaries. The beneficial interest in real estate held in a land trust is considered to be *personal property*. The beneficiary has the rights to the possession, income, and proceeds of sale of such property. Under a land trust agreement, the trustee deals with the property only upon the written direction of the beneficiary. The land trust agreement is executed by the trustor and the trustee. A beneficial interest under a land trust can be transferred merely by assignment, without the necessity of a deed and all its formal requirements. It can be pledged as collateral for a loan without a mortgage being placed on record (through a collateral assignment). Courts have held that real estate held in a land trust cannot be partitioned by the beneficiaries because their interest is not one in real estate, but one in personal property.

A land trust generally continues for a definite term, such as 20 years. At the expiration of the term, if the beneficiary does not extend the trust term, the trustee is usually obligated to sell the real estate and to return the net proceeds to the beneficiary.

Land trusts are popular where there are multiple owners who seek protection against the effects of divorce, judgments, or bankruptcies of the other owners. Because ownership is kept private, a land trust is sometimes used for secrecy when assembling separate parcels. Land trusts can also avoid title liens and partition suits, reduce probate expenses, and help nonresidents to avoid ancillary probate costs and inheritance taxes in the state where the land is located. In the event the real property is to be sold, the trustee should execute the contract of sale and the deed.

LAND-USE INTENSITY A system of land use under local zoning codes designed to relate land, building coverage of the land, and open space to one another. The land-use intensity (LUI) scale provides a series of density ratings (percentages) which include floor area, open space, living space, and recreation space. In applying land-use intensity, the floor area ratio creates a maximum amount of floor area in a building in relation to the land area of the lot upon which the building is to be constructed. Open space requirements are minimum requirements based upon and computed from a percentage of the actual floor area to be developed in a particularly zoned lot. The LUI has become an important tool in the development of Planned Unit Developments (PUD). (*See PLANNED UNIT DEVELOPMENT.*)

LANE A narrow roadway without curbs or sidewalks; generally applies to old developments.

LARGER PARCEL A term used in condemnation cases when the court considers the extent of severance damages in cases where a partial taking has occured. There is usually a requirement of unity of ownership, use, and contiguity. However, it has been held that integrated use, not physical contiguity, is the test of whether condemned land is part of a single tract that would warrant an award of severance damages. (*See SEVERANCE DAMAGES.*)

LATE CHARGE An added charge a borrower is required to pay for failure to pay a regular loan installment when due. It is generally not treated as interest, but as a service charge for the extra work and inconvenience suffered by the creditor. The courts, however, will not enforce excessive late charges (such as 10 percent or more of the unpaid principal), which would be deemed to be a penalty.

LATE DATE ORDER The commitment to a buyer for an owner's title insurance policy issued by a title insurance company, which covers the seller's title as of the date of the contract. At the closing, the buyer orders the title company to record the deed and extend its examination to show the buyer as the present owner of the real property. (*See CONTINUA-TION.*)

LATENT DEFECTS   Hidden structural defects presumably resulting from faulty construction, known to the seller but not to the purchaser, and not readily discoverable by inspection. If the seller *or the broker* is aware of such defects, such as a defective water heater or a dangerous stairway behind a basement door, he or she must disclose them to the prospective purchaser. Failure to disclose such information is a tacit misrepresentation and grounds for the buyer to rescind the contract. (*See "AS IS," MISREPRESENTA-TION.*)

LATERAL AND SUBJACENT SUPPORT   The support a parcel of real property receives from the land adjoining it is called *lateral support*. It is not a right in the land of an adjoining owner—rather, it is a right incident to ownership of the property entitled to the support. *Subjacent support* is that support which the surface of the earth receives from its underlying strata. The basic rules of support are the same for both. In essence, an adjoining landowner (or holder of mineral or other rights beneath the land of another) has a duty to support a neighbor's land in its natural state. This duty of support does not run specifically to any of the improvements on the land, but does impose liability for damage to improvements on the neighbor's land if the land would have subsided as a result of a landowner's excavation, even without the weight of the improvements. In general, an owner of property can lessen any exposure to liability by giving his or her neighbors adequate notice of any intent to perform excavation work on the property so neighbors can take the necessary precautions.

LATH   Thin strips of wood or metal nailed to rafters, ceiling joists, or wall studs to form a groundwork for slates, tiles, shingles, or plaster.

LAW   That body of rules by which society governs itself. Real estate law derives from state and federal constitutions, state and federal legislation, regulations of federal and state boards and commissions, county and municipal ordinances, and last and most important, court decisions. In addition there is *private law*, which refers to the law that the parties create for themselves in their legal documents. For example, the bylaws and house rules of a condominium set forth detailed private rules of conduct for the owners, and violation of these rules gives the owners legal recourse against the violator. (*See COMMON LAW.*)

LAW DAY   The date an obligation becomes due; sometimes refers to the closing date. Under common law, the mortgagor had to pay off the mortgage debt by the law day. Failure to pay on time would result in the mortgagor's automatically losing the mortgaged property to the mortgagee. If payment was made by the law day, the mortgage became void, and the mortgagee would be divested of any title to the property pursuant to the defeasance clause. (*See DEFEASANCE CLAUSE.*)

LAWFUL INTEREST   The maximum interest rate permitted by law, with any amount above the rate being usurious. (*See INTEREST, USURY.*)

LEACHING CESSPOOL In plumbing, any cesspool which is not watertight and permits waste liquids to pass into the surrounding soil by percolation.

LEAD LENDER Typically, a local lender who funds the initial portion of a large loan and arranges for one or more institutional lenders to fund the balance of the financing. The lead lender handles the servicing of the loan. (*See PARTICIPATION MORTGAGE.*)

LEASE An agreement, written or unwritten, transferring the right to exclusive possession and use of real estate for a definite period of time. To create a valid lease, the lessor must retain a reversionary right; that is, the lessor (landlord) grants the right of possession to the lessee (tenant), but retains the right to retake possession after the lease's term has expired. The lease is, in effect, a combination of both a conveyance (to transfer the right of occupancy) and a contract (to pay rent and assume other obligations). It is an exchange of the possession and profits of the land in return for rent. The lessor's interest is called the *leased fee estate* and consists of the right to recover the contract rent plus the reversion. The lessee's interest is called the *leasehold estate* and consists of the right to the exclusive use and occupancy of the leased estate. An "agreement for a lease" contemplates the execution of a lease at a later time.

The law controlling landlord-tenant relations originally developed from early agricultural leases. With such leases, the landlord's obligation was limited to providing the tenant with peaceful possession; in return the tenant agreed to pay rent. Under this agreement the landlord was not expected to assist in the operation of the land. Rather, leased lands were under the exclusive control of the tenant without interference from the landlord. In the simplest terms, the tenant-landlord relationship was a strict possession-rent relationship. If a tenant defaulted in his or her rent payment, eviction would be forthcoming. In a rural setting, this was a workable arrangement.

In modern times, however, the courts apply the rules governing contracts in determining the validity of a lease. Usually, no special wording is necessary to create the relationship of landlord and tenant. A lease should be in writing; however, if it is not written, the law will write it for the parties involved, just as the law writes a will for someone who dies intestate. Although, depending on the circumstances, the lease may be written, oral, or implied, the provision of the statutes of the state in which the real estate is located must be followed. The lessor, being the owner of the real estate, is usually bound by an implied covenant of *quiet enjoyment* for the benefit of the lessee. By this covenant, the lessor asserts that the lessee will not be evicted by a person who successfully claims to be the real owner of the premises with a title which is paramount to the lessor's. The requirements for a valid lease are similar to those of a contract and are generally as follows:

Capacity to Contract: The parties must be legally capable of entering into a contract. (Note, however, that a minor can generally enter into binding contracts for necessities, of which essential housing may be considered one of the most basic needs.)

Mutual Agreement: The parties must reach a mutual agreement and support it by valid consideration.

Legal Objectives: The lease's objectives must be legal; that is, it would generally be illegal to lease a building as a house of prostitution, so a lease for such a purpose would be invalid.

Statute of Frauds: State statutes of frauds generally apply to leases. They usually provide that leases for more than one year (one year plus one day) or leases which will not be fully performed within one year from the date of making must be in writing. Note that a lease for exactly one year could fall short of the requirements of the Statute of Frauds if the lease period commences subsequent to the date of entering into the agreement. Similarly, a lease for less than one year may fall under the Statute of Frauds if more than one year elapses between the signing of the lease and its termination date. Even though a lease might be for a term of less than one year, as a matter of good business practice, it should be put into writing to lessen the chances of dispute and misunderstanding between the parties. A lease not in conformance with the Statute of Frauds is generally considered unenforceable. Even a short-term lease should be put in writing because it will be good proof in case of trial, usually falls under a longer statute of limitations, provides for attorney's fees, and acts as a preliminary screening device for spotting potentially troublesome tenants.

Signatures: The lease must be signed by the landlord because the courts consider the lease as a conveyance of real estate. When the lessor holds his or her interest in severalty, most states require the spouse to join in signing the lease. A lease need not be signed by the lessee (although it is good practice for the lessee to do so), since his or her taking possession and paying rent with knowledge of the lease constitutes an acceptance of the lease terms. When a lease is signed by two or more tenants, they become jointly and severally liable and can only avoid this by signing separate leases specifying their separate obligations.

Description of the Premises: A description of the leased premises should be clearly stated. Usually, this involves only a street address and/or apartment number for residential, apartment, and small commercial properties. Large commercial site leases, on the other hand, must be more detailed, including such things as a floor plan, total square footage, storage areas, parking, and the like. If the lease affects land, as with a ground lease, a legal description should be used.

Use of the Premises: The lessor may restrict the use of the leased property through provisions included in the lease. This is particularly important with leases for stores or commercial space. For example, a lease may contain a provision that the property is "to be used for the purpose of a Big Beltbuster Burger Bonanza Bazaar drive-in restaurant, and no other." If the lease does not state a specified purpose, the tenant may use the premises for any lawful purpose.

Term of the Lease: The term of the lease is the period for which the lease will run, and it should be stated precisely. Good practice requires that the beginning and ending of the term dates be stated, together with a statement of the total period of the lease—for example, "for a term of thirty years beginning June 1, 1968 and ending May 31, 1998." Courts do not favor leases with an indefinite term and will hold that such perpetual leases are not valid unless the language of the lease and the surrounding circumstances clearly indicate that such is the intention of the parties. Leases are controlled by the statutes of the various states and must be in accordance with those provisions. In some states, terms of agricultural leases are limited by statute. Also, some states by statute prohibit leases for 100 years or more. The maximum long-term lease is traditionally 99 years, since there were some early state court decisions holding that a lease of 100 years or more actually passed fee simple title to the lessee. The term of the lease is generally unaffected by the death of either landlord or tenant.

Possession of the Leased Premises: In most states, the landlord must give the tenant actual occupancy or possession of the leased premises. Thus, if the premises are occupied by a holdover tenant, or adverse claimant, at the date of a new lease, the landlord owes a duty to the new tenant to bring whatever action is necessary to recover possession and to bear the expense of this action. However, in a few states, the landlord is bound to give the tenant only the right of possession, and then it is the tenant's obligation to bring any necessary court action to secure actual possession. It is this right to exclusive possession that distinguishes a lease from a mere license to use property.

Consideration: Rent is the usual consideration granted for the right to occupy the leased premises. However, the payment of rent is not essential as long as consideration was granted in the creation of the lease itself. Some courts have construed rent as being any consideration which supports the lease, thus not limiting its definition to the monthly payment of a specified amount. After a lease has been executed and is in force, most courts will not enforce an agreement to reduce or increase the rent during the term for which the lease was originally drawn. These courts consider the lease to be a contract and therefore not subject to change unless the changes are in writing and tantamount to cancellation of the original lease. Under common law principles, the rent was payable at the end of the lease term unless the parties agreed otherwise. This was based on the concept that rent is a return for the lessee's enjoyment of the use of the land and thus not payable until after the enjoyment had occurred. Most modern leases, however, provide for rent to be paid in advance. Most land leases and long-term leases provide, in addition to the payment of rent, that the tenant will be required to pay all property charges, such as real estate taxes, special assessments, water and sewer taxes, and all necessary insurance premiums to protect the property. Most leases provide for some form of security. This security for payment of rent may be established: (a) by contracting for a lien on the tenant's property, (b) by requiring the tenant to pay a portion of the rent in advance, (c) by requiring the tenant to post security, and/or (d) by requiring the tenant to have a third person guarantee the payment of the rent.

There are three main classifications of leases:

1. Leases based on the type of realty involved, such as *office leases, ground leases, proprietary leases, residential leases.*

2. Leases classed according to the term of the lease, such as short-term and long-term leases. Most short-term leases are *gross leases* requiring the landlord to pay all taxes, assessments, and operating costs (such as most apartment leases). Long-term leases (generally 10 years and longer) are often *net leases* that give the tenant greater rights and responsibilities. Particularly in long-term leases, attention should be given to the rights of both parties in the event of condemnation of the leased premises.

3. Leases classed according to the method of rent payment, such as *fixed-rental, graduated, percentage, gross, and net leases.*

Most states provide that leases can be filed for record in the county in which the leased property is located. However, unless the lease is for a relatively long term (three years or more) or is security for a mortgage, it usually is not recorded.

A lessee may assign his or her lease or sublet the premises if the terms of the lease do not prohibit it. A tenant who transfers the entire remaining lease term assigns the lease. A tenant who transfers most of the term, but retains a small part of it, sublets. Most leases prohibit a lessee from assigning or subletting without the landlord's permission. When a lease is assigned, the assignee becomes the principal obligor and the lessee assumes the position of a surety.

If the landlord sells the property, the grantee takes title subject to the lease and becomes liable for all covenants in the lease. Tenants who make improvements to a landlord's property usually do so for the benefit of the landlord. Such improvements, if classified as fixtures, become part of the real estate. However, a tenant may be given the right to install trade fixtures or chattel fixtures by the terms of the lease. It is customary to provide that such trade fixtures may be removed by the tenant before the expiration of the lease provided the tenant puts the building back into the condition it was at the time of possession.

In land leases involving agricultural land, the courts have held that damage or destruction of the improvements does not relieve the tenant from the obligation to pay rent to the end of the term. This ruling has been extended in most states to include leases of land on which the tenant has constructed a building. It also has been extended in many instances to include leases which give possession of an entire building to the tenant. Since the tenant is leasing an entire building, the courts have held that he or she is also leasing the land on which that building is located. In those cases where the leased premises are only a part of the building (such as office or commercial space or an apartment in an apartment building), upon destruction of the leased premises, the tenant is not required to continue to pay rent. Furthermore, in some states, if the property was destroyed as a result of negligence on the part of the landlord, the tenant is able to recover damages from the landlord. Under most commercial and industrial leases, the tenant must maintain and repair the interior and often the exterior of the premises as well.

A lease may be terminated by:

1. expiration of the term

2. merger of the leasehold and fee estates

3. destruction or condemnation of the premises

4. abandonment

5. agreement of the parties (surrender)

6. forfeiture due to default or breach of the leasing terms and conditions. (Note that under the Federal Bankruptcy Act tenant bankruptcy is no longer a permitted ground for default.)

7. commercial frustration of purpose, such as if the proposed use is made illegal (but not if the tenant can't obtain a needed business license)

(See *ABANDONMENT, EVICTION, FIXTURE, FLAT LEASE, GRADUATED RENTAL LEASE, GROSS LEASE, GROUND LEASE, LANDLORD, LEASEHOLD, LEASE OPTION, MONTH-TO-MONTH TENANCY, NET LEASE, PERCENTAGE LEASE, SECURITY DEPOSIT, SURRENDER, TRADE FIXTURE, UNIFORM RESIDENTIAL LANDLORD AND TENANT ACT, WASTE.*)

LEASED FEE   The interest and rights of the lessor in real estate that the lessor has leased is called a leased fee. The lessor has a right to receive rental income and a right to possess the property at the end of the lease. The value of the rental payments plus the remaining property value at the end of the lease period (the reversionary interest) is the leased fee interest, which may be sold or mortgaged subject to the rights of the tenant. In valuing the leased fee, the appraiser usually will capitalize the present value of the income received by the lessor and adding the reversionary value of the land, or land and building, at the expiration of the lease term (the annuity method of capitalization). The reversionary value of the land is difficult to predict so it is usually calculated to be the same as its present value, discounted to its present value by multiplying the value times the appropriate Inwood factor. (See *INWOOD TABLE.*)

LEASEHOLD   A less-than-freehold estate which a tenant possesses in real property. In a lease situation, the tenant possesses a leasehold and the landlord possesses the reversion estate (that is, when the lease terminates, the property will revert to the landlord). Leasehold estates are generally classified as estates in personal property. Some states, however, provide for certain leasehold estates to be considered as real property while also retaining their characteristics as personal property. Under common law, an estate for years was termed a "chattel real" and classified as personal property. The four principal types of leasehold estates are the estate for years, the periodic tenancy (estate from year to year), the tenancy at will, and the tenancy at sufferance. The estate for years runs for a specific period of time; the periodic tenancy runs for an indefinite number of time periods; the estate at will runs for an indefinite time; an estate at sufferance runs until the landlord takes some action.

Unlike other uses of land, the leasehold is a transfer of the exclusive right to possession, as opposed to the mere privilege to use the land. Thus, a hotel guest is different from a tenant. The significance between various types of authorized usages of property (licenses, easements, profits, and leases) becomes important in terms of the remedies available upon breach of contract. The tenant in a leasehold can be removed from the property only by strict statutory eviction procedures, whereas a license can usually be revoked at any time.

The term or duration of the leasehold estate varies, depending on the purposes of utilization of the land. Many residential apartment leases are short term, that is, for one year or month to month. Most ground leases usually run for 55 years, while some run for 75 years or longer. For FHA leasehold-mortgage purposes, it is required that leases have a minimum term that exceeds the fixed rental term of the loan. These long-term leases are transferred by *assignment of lease* rather than by deed. Both the assignor and assignee of a leasehold estate must sign the assignment of lease, since the assignee assumes the obligations of the assignor under the lease.

Under common law, improvements constructed by the lessee on the leased premises would revert to the landlord at the termination of the leasehold estate. Many ground leases, however, specifically provide in the reversion clause for the right of the lessee to remove all improvements at the end of the lease term. This provision simplifies the arrangement of financing and negotiation for an extension or renewal of the lease.

The valuation of a lessor's interest is a complex procedure that involves the use of capitalization rates and present value tables to ascertain the present value of the landlord's reversion interest and the present value of the rental income. As a general rule of thumb, most landlords seek a 6 percent return, though certain large landholding companies will take a 4 percent return during the initial rental period. In comparing properties for valuation purposes, leaseholds should be compared only with other leaseholds and not with fee simple properties.

In areas where leaseholds are popularly used, such as Hawaii and Maryland, it is common practice to make leasehold estates subject to a recorded declaration of restrictions, usually by reference in the lease to the book and page number of the declaration. A purchaser should examine the lease and all referenced documents well in advance of closing in order to ascertain exactly what he or she is buying. (*See ASSIGNMENT OF LEASE, GROUND LEASE, LEASEHOLD MORTGAGE, LESS-THAN-FREEHOLD ESTATE, PERIODIC TENANCY, TENANCY AT SUF-FERANCE, TENANCY AT WILL.*)

LEASEHOLD IMPROVEMENTS   The improvements to leased property made by the lessee. Improvements by the lessee are generally tax depreciable by the lessee. If the improvement's useful life or cost recovery period is less than the term of the lease, the improvement is depreciable over its useful life or cost recovery period. If the useful life of the improvement is longer than the lease, the lessee may be able to amortize the improvement's cost over the remaining life of the lease.

LEASEHOLD MORTGAGE   A mortgage placed upon the lessee's interest in the leased premises. Leasehold mortgage financing is a specialized form of secondary financing because the mortgage is subordinate to the position of the fee owner. The prime lenders in leasehold financing are life insurance companies, major mutual savings banks, and major commercial banks.

In the development of a large project, the fee owner will sometimes lease the land to a developer and subordinate his or her fee to the leasehold mortgage. The subordination may be limited to loans of a certain type or term (such as a construction loan but not any refinancing), or the subordination might take place only upon full completion of construction of the proposed improvement. Often, the lender will attempt to persuade the fee owner to mortgage the fee along with the leasehold mortgage. (*See SUBORDINATION CLAUSE.*)

LEASE OPTION   A lease containing a clause that gives the tenant the right to purchase the property under specified conditions. Some important features of a lease option are:

1. It usually runs with the land, so that if the lease is assigned, the option to purchase is likewise assigned.

2. It does not usually extend beyond the term of the lease.

3. The supporting consideration can be the rent being paid. A default in rent may result in termination of the option.

4. It can be assigned separately from other provisions in the lease.

A recent purchaser of real property considering a quick resale might use a lease option instead of a sale in order to extend the holding period to one year to achieve the capital gains tax benefit. The lessor/optionor must be careful to structure the transaction so that the economic reality of the transaction will make it a lease rather than an outright sale. For example, if the total payments under the lease are substantially equal to the purchase price payment under the option, and the payments are applicable to the purchase price, the IRS may characterize the deal as a sale (rather than as lease) because the lessee has no other economic choice but to exercise the option.

An option in a lease is inseparable from the integrated lease contract and therefore an extension of the lease usually prolongs the life of the option, unless the lease states otherwise.

In addition to an option to purchase, other lease options include options to renew and options to extend. Under the latter, the original lease is continued on the same terms, including the extension provision. With an option to renew, the lessee is entitled to a new lease on set terms, not including the original renewal provision. (*See OPTION.*)

LEGACY   A disposition of money or personal property by will, as in a bequest. The recipient is called the legatee.

LEGAL AGE   The statutory age at which a person attains majority and is no longer a minor. (*See MINOR.*)

LEGAL DESCRIPTION   A description of a piece of real property which is acceptable by the courts of the state where the property is located for use in real property conveyance documents by which land may be known with certainty. It is usually complete enough that an independent surveyor could locate and identify that specific parcel of land. Oral testimony is not admissible as a way of describing the property more fully, except in certain cases involving fraud or mistake. Such descriptions are usually based on the field notes of a surveyor or civil engineer. Methods of description include lot, block, and subdivision; government survey; and metes and bounds.

A legal description is required on all deeds, assignments of lease, and mortgages, and is used in most contracts for deed. Street addresses, tax-bill descriptions, and general descriptions (the Smith farm) are generally inadequate for use in recorded title documents since such identifying characteristics may not endure indefinitely. Use of such temporary descriptions could lead to obvious difficulties for someone searching the chain of title or trying to locate the property in the distant future. In general, a legal description should be used in any instrument which is to be recorded. If the description is not correct, then the document may be improperly indexed and thus may not be sufficient constructive notice to a third person under recording laws.

The general rules in case of conflicts in legal descriptions are:

1. Natural or artificial monuments prevail over courses and distances.

2. Natural monuments prevail over artificial monuments.

3. Courses govern over distances.

4. Stated acreage or area is the least reliable method of describing a parcel.

(*See LAND DESCRIPTION; LOT, BLOCK, AND SUBDIVISION; GOVERNMENT SURVEY METHOD; METES AND BOUNDS.*)

LEGAL NAME   The given, or Christian, name in combination with the surname, or family name. Under common law, an insertion, omission, or error in a middle name or initial is immaterial to the validity of a conveyance document.

An application for a real estate salesperson's or broker's state examination or license generally requires the applicant to supply his or her full legal name. The use of initials only is strongly discouraged, especially with common surnames, such as Smith, Lee, Brown, and the like. This policy is designed to eliminate confusion and misidentification of applicants with similar names.

LEGAL NOTICE   That notice which is either implied or required by law. Under the recording law, constructive notice is also referred to as legal notice.

LEGAL RATE OF INTEREST   The rate of interest prescribed by state law which will prevail in the absence of any agreement fixing the rate. For example, state law may provide for 6 percent interest on monies due after the maturity date of a promissory note. The usury limit is referred to as the lawful interest.

LEGEND STOCK   A security certificate which has a notation on its face indicating that its transferability is restricted. Such stock usually cannot be transferred for a certain period of time or until registered. Securities which claim exemption from SEC registration under the intrastate exemption (Rule 147) or the private offering exemption (Rule 146) must contain a restricted transfer legend. (*See RULE 146, RULE 147.*)

LESSEE   The person to whom property is rented or leased; called a *tenant* in most residential leases.

LESSOR   The person who rents or leases property to another. In residential leasing, he or she is often referred to as a *landlord*.

LESS-THAN-FREEHOLD ESTATE   The estate held by a person who rents or leases property. This classification includes an estate for years, periodic tenancy, estate at will, and estate at sufferance. (*See FREEHOLD, LEASEHOLD.*)

LETTER OF CREDIT   An agreement or commitment by a bank (issuer) made at the request of a customer (account party) that the bank will honor drafts or other demands of payment from third parties (beneficiaries) upon compliance with the conditions specified in the letter of credit. Through the issuance of its letter of credit, the bank agrees to pay the seller's draft, thereby substituting the bank's credit for that of the buyer. This often takes the form of a letter from a bank in one area of the country to a bank or merchant in another area introducing the person named, vouching for the customer and specifying a sum of money to be extended.

A letter of credit might also be used when a long-term tenant has to put up a substantial security deposit. Or a borrower seeking a large mortgage commitment might be required to put up a substantial deposit in the form of a letter of credit that is forfeitable if the commitment is not exercised. The account party prefers a letter of credit to placing cash in escrow on deposit because he or she can thus avoid borrowing costs or losing return on such funds. Sometimes it is necessary for a developer of a large hotel or other sizable development project to obtain a letter of credit at the start of the project in order to cover the costs of furniture that will not be needed until some future date. This gives assurance to the mortgagee and others that the developer will have adequate funds to complete the project when it comes time to fund the furniture purchase.

A bank charges a small annual fee for issuing a letter of credit, which, naturally, is issued only to customers with the highest credit ratings. Unlike direct loans, the bank need not report obligations under letters of credit as liabilities in its financial statements, nor is the bank required to maintain a certain amount of bank reserves to back up its letter of credit obligations.

Article 5 of the Uniform Commercial Code extensively covers the law concerning letters of credit. (See *LINE OF CREDIT*.)

LETTER OF INTENT An expression of intent to invest, develop, or purchase without creating any firm legal obligation to do so. It may refer to a specific project, or it may be a general letter of intent without regard to any specific project. The following is the kind of language used in a letter of intent to negate any legal duty to carry out the terms of the letter: "Since this instrument consists only of an expression of our mutual intent, it is expressly understood that no liability or obligation of any nature whatsoever is intended to be created as between any of the parties hereto. This letter is not intended to constitute a binding agreement to consummate the transaction outlined herein nor an agreement to enter into contract. The parties propose to proceed promptly and in good faith to conclude the arrangements with respect to proposed development, but any legal obligations between the parties shall be only those set forth in the executed contract and lease. In the event that a contract and lease are not executed, we shall not be obligated for any expenses of the developer or for any charges or claims whatsoever arising out of this letter of intent or the proposed financing or otherwise and, similarly, the developer shall not be in any way obligated to us."

LETTER OF PATENT A legal instrument transferring title to real property from either the United States or an individual state to the person named in the patent.

LETTER REPORT 1. A short appraisal report limited to the property characteristics, valuation, and recommendations. 2. A report by a title company as to the condition of title as of a specific date; it gives no insurance on that title, however.

LEVEL-PAYMENT MORTGAGE A mortgage which is scheduled to be repaid in equal periodic payments which include both principal and interest. Since payments are credited first against interest on the declining principal balance, the amount of money credited to principal gradually increases, while that credited to interest gradually decreases. Under VA and FHA loans, the mortgagee payments must include taxes and insurance in addition to principal and interest. (See *AMORTIZATION, BUDGET MORTGAGE, DIRECT REDUCTION MORTGAGE*.)

LEVERAGE The impact of borrowed funds on investment return. The use of borrowed funds to purchase property with the anticipation that the acquired property will increase in return so that the investor will realize a profit not only on his or her own investment, but also on the borrowed funds; the employment of a smaller investment to generate a larger rate of return through borrowing.

The term *high leverage* often is used when the investor has made a very low down payment. For example, Sam Lee purchases a $75,000 condominium unit for $4,000 down with a five-year, interest-only contract for deed for the balance. Lee hopes to sell the property for $85,000, thus making a profit from the use of other people's money. His expected profit on the purchase price of $75,000 is 13 percent, but the profit on his principal investment of $4,000 is 250 percent, which shows the advantage of leveraging. In addition, Sam can receive the tax benefits of depreciation on the entire improvement (including the leveraged portion). The term *reverse leverage* is used to describe a situation in which an investor pays a higher rate to borrow money than the rate of net income received from the property. Reverse leverage is also called *debt financing*.

LEVY   To assess; to seize or collect. To levy a tax is to assess a property and set the rate of taxation. To levy an execution is to officially seize the property of a person in order to satisfy an obligation. Usually the sheriff levies upon and brings within his or her control the personal property of a judgment debtor. Levying is not a judicial act, but rather a ministerial one. (*See ATTACHMENT, WRIT OF EXECUTION*.)

LIABILITY   1. In a double entry accounting system, all amounts appearing on the credit side, including all amounts owed. In a personal financial statement, assets minus liabilities equals net worth. (*See ASSET, NET WORTH*.)

2. Legal responsibility for an act. (*See DAMAGES*.)

LIBER   Latin term for "book." Usually refers to the record books at the county recorder's office which contain copies of all recorded documents relating to real estate in the county. When a document is recorded, it is given a liber volume and page (also called *folio*) number. Anyone wishing to examine this document can then locate an exact copy of the document by reference to the appropriate liber and page number. (*See RECORDING*.)

LICENSE   1. Permission or authority to do a particular act upon the land or property of another, usually on a nonexclusive basis. A license is a personal, revocable, and nonassignable right, but unlike an easement, it is not considered to be an interest in the land itself. If a right to use another person's land is given orally, it will generally be considered to be a license rather than an easement. The landowner may revoke such a right at any time, unless it has become irrevocable by estoppel. A license ceases upon the death of either party and is revoked by the sale of the land by the licensor. A landowner who grants a friend permission to enter his or her property for hunting purposes thus grants the friend a license to use the land. (*See EASEMENT, ESTOPPEL*.)

2. Formal permission from a constituted authority (such as a state real estate commission) to engage in a certain activity or business (such as real estate brokerage). (*See LICENSE LAWS*.)

LICENSEE   A person who has a valid license. A real estate licensee can generally be a salesperson or broker, active or inactive, or an individual, corporation, or partnership.

LICENSE LAWS   Laws enacted by all states, the District of Columbia, and certain Canadian provinces which provide the states with the authority to license and regulate the activities of real estate brokers and salespeople. Certain details of the laws vary from state to state, but the main provisions of each remain much the same. Many state license laws are based on the pattern law recommended by the National Association of Realtors®. The general purposes of license laws are to: (1) protect the public from dishonest or incompetent real estate practitioners; (2) prescribe certain standards and qualifications for licensing; (3) raise the standards of the real estate profession; and (4) protect licensed brokers and salespeople from unfair or improper competition.

All states require license applicants to pass an examination designed to test their real estate knowledge and competency. Sizable portions of such exams are based on the state license laws. Licenses or registration certificates are issued to qualified individuals and generally to partnerships and corporations. These licenses are legal permits to operate a real estate brokerage business as described and permitted by the state law. Each state law must be examined to determine whether a license is required for such activities as appraising, mortgaging, auctioning, or exchanging real estate. State licensing usually pre-empts attempts by municipal governments to assess local licensing fees.

Licenses are issued for definite terms and must be renewed within specified time limits. Each license is a personal right and terminates upon the death of the individual or the dissolution of the partnership or corporation. While a license or registration certificate is in effect, the activities or each licensed person or entity are subject to the control of the authorized state officials as prescribed by the state law. For this reason, every licensed person must be thoroughly familiar with the applicable state license laws. Violation of the license law provisions is usually cause for refusal, revocation, or suspension of a real estate license. A court conviction for acting as a real estate broker or salesperson without a license is generally considered a misdemeanor, punishable by a fine and/or imprisonment.

Each state law exempts certain persons from the license laws. Such exemptions usually include owners dealing with their own property; trustees, executors, receivers and others operating under court orders; public officials acting in the line of their duties; and, in some cases, attorneys at law.

LIEN   A charge or claim which one person (lienor) has upon the property of another (lienee) as security for a debt or obligation. A lien always arises from a debt and can be created by agreement of the parties (mortgage) or by operation of law (*tax lien*). A lien may be general (thus affecting only a particular property, as when a mortgage is given on one piece of property). Liens can also be statutory or equitable, voluntary or involuntary. For example, a *mechanic's lien* is an *involuntary, statutory, special lien*, whereas a mortgage is a *voluntary, equitable, special lien*. However, if the mortgage lien were foreclosed and the proceeds from the foreclosure sale did not cover the debt, the resulting deficiency judgment, when recorded, would be a general lien upon all of the debtor's property. Lien procedure, of course, is based on each state's statutes. Liens do not transfer title to the property—until foreclosure, the debtor retains title. Certain statutory liens (mechanics' liens and judgments) become unenforceable after a lapse of time from origination or recording unless a foreclosure suit is filed.

The priority of a lien is normally determined by the date of recordation. Thus, it is important to record the appropriate document as soon as the lien has been created. State property tax liens and assessments, however, take priority over all liens, even those previously recorded. Since the lien is an encumbrance on the title, the lienor should (at the lienee's expense) execute and record a satisfaction of the lien as soon as the lien has been paid in order to remove this cloud on the title. (*See* ENCUMBRANCE, JUDGMENT LIEN, MECHANIC'S LIEN, MORTGAGE, TAX LIEN.)

LIEN LETTER   *See* TAX AND LIEN SEARCH.

LIEN STATEMENT   A statement of the unpaid balance of a promissory note secured by a lien on property, plus the status of interest payments, maturity date, and any claims that may be asserted. Also called an offset statement. (*See* CERTIFICATE OF NO DEFENSE, REDUCTION CERTIFICATE.)

LIEN-THEORY STATES   Those states which treat a mortgage solely as a security interest in the secured real property with title retained by the mortgagor. The mortgagor has use of the property and is entitled to all rents and profits. The lien theory, or *equitable theory of mortgages*, regards the debt as the principal fact and the mortgage merely as collateral. It treats the mortgagor as the owner of the equitable title and the mortgagee merely as the holder of a lien for the security of his or her debt. This differs from a title-theory state, where legal title is actually transferred to the mortgagee and is only reconveyed back to the mortgagor when the mortgage debt is satisfied. (*See* DEED OF TRUST, DEFEASANCE CLAUSE, TITLE-THEORY STATES.)

LIFE ESTATE   Any estate in real or personal property that is limited in duration to the life of its owner or the life of some other designated person. If the estate is measured by the lifetime of a person other than its owner, it is called a *life estate pur autre vie*. Although classified as a freehold estate because it is a possessory estate of indefinite duration, a life estate is not an estate of inheritance. For example, Bob Smith conveys his home to his son John and reserves a life estate for himself. Bob (the life tenant) has a life estate, and John has a reversionary interest in the property. When Bob Smith dies, the fee simple property reverts to John.

A life estate may arise by agreement of the parties, in which case it is called a conventional life estate; or it may arise by operation of law (as with homestead, curtesy, or a wife's dower rights), in which case it is referred to as a *legal life estate*.

A life tenant:

1. is entitled to possession and ordinary uses and profits of the land, just as if he or she were the fee owner.

2. is obligated to keep the premises in a reasonable state of repair and free from waste so that the realty will later revert to the grantor or the remainderman in approximately unchanged condition in terms of its characteristics and value.

3. is obligated to pay the ordinary taxes, interest on encumbrances (not mortgage

principal amortization), and a prorata share of special assessments (along with the remainderman).

4. is barred from creating any interest in the property which extends beyond the measuring life.

5. is under no obligation to insure the premises for the benefit of the future interest holders, each of which has a separate, insurable interest and is responsible for obtaining his or her own insurance.

The life tenant may sell his or her interest or encumber it subject to any deed restrictions to the contrary, and the interest is subject to execution sale if there is a money judgment against him or her. The transferee receives no greater interest than the life tenant had—that is, an estate which ends at the expiration of the measuring life. Thus it is difficult to sell or mortgage a life estate. The mortgagee of a life tenant's interest would therefore probably require the life tenant to make the mortgagee the beneficiary of a term life insurance policy.

For tax depreciation purposes, a life tenant deducts depreciation over the useful life of the property and not on the tenant's life expectancy. After the death of the life tenant, the remainderman gets the deduction.

Where a taxpayer makes a gift of real property but retains a life estate, the entire value of the property is includable in the deceased taxpayer's estate for federal estate tax purposes.

A life estate is terminated by the death of the person whose existence is the measuring life. While no probate proceeding is necessary to establish title in the remainderman (the person now entitled to the property), it is good title practice to record a death certificate to show the fact of death. If the life tenant acquires the fee simple title to the property, the life estate is terminated by merger. (See FREEHOLD, PUR AUTRE VIE, REMAINDERMAN, WASTE.)

LIFTING CLAUSE

A clause included in a junior loan instrument that allows the underlying mortgage or deed of trust (senior loan) to be replaced or refinanced as long as the amount of the new senior loan does not exceed the amount of the first lien outstanding at the time the junior loan was made. (See SUBORDINATION AGREEMENT.)

LIGHT AND AIR

An owner has no natural right to light and air and cannot complain when a neighbor erects a structure which cuts off his or her light and air. To eliminate this possibility, some abutting owners attempt to purchase an easement for light and air over the neighbor's property. Such an easement should, of course, be granted in writing. For example, an owner with a beautiful view of the mountains might seek to obtain from a neighbor an easement of light and air over the neighbor's property. If the easement had been properly created and recorded, then neither the neighbor nor any successor could build a structure in this airspace. It is not possible to acquire a light and air easement by prescription—that is, a person cannot claim to have acquired a prescriptive right to airspace because he or she has used the view for the prescriptive statutory period of, for example, 20 years. (See AIR RIGHTS.)

LIGHT INDUSTRY

A zoning designation for industrial use encompassing mostly unobjectionable light manufacturing, as opposed to those industries which cause noise, air, or water disturbances and pollution. It includes such "clean" industries as bakeries, dry cleaning, and food processing.

LIKE-KIND PROPERTY A federal tax term relating to the nature of real estate rather than its quality or quantity. Only like-kind property will qualify for a real estate exchange and the resulting tax benefit.

Like-kind property is any real property, whether improved or unimproved, held or to be held by the taxpayer for investment or income purposes, thus excluding dealer property and residences. The property need only qualify as like property to the party seeking the tax-deferred benefit of the exchanges of like property.

One property may be improved and the other raw land, one can be domestic and the other foreign realty, or one a shopping center and the other an apartment building. Both properties must, however, be of the same ownership interest. Thus, a fee simple interest could not be exchanged for a leasehold. However, an IRS regulation does state that a leasehold interest of 30 years or more is to be deemed a fee simple. The Tax Court has upheld the exchange of general partnership interests in partnerships with substantially the same kind of underlying assets. (*See CONDEMNATION, EXCHANGE.*)

LIMITATIONS OF ACTIONS Time within which legal actions must be commenced or else action will be barred. (*See LACHES, STATUTE OF LIMITATIONS.*)

LIMITED ACCESS HIGHWAY A highway with access only at specific intervals, usually by way of ramps. Such a highway is designed to benefit through traffic and to avoid interference from neighboring traffic. Also called a controlled access highway.

LIMITED COMMON ELEMENTS That special class of common elements in a condominium project that is reserved for the use of one or more apartment(s) to the exclusion of other apartments. This would include assigned parking stalls, storage units, or any common areas and facilities available for use by one or more, but less than all, unit owners.

Any amendment of the condominium declaration that affects the limited common elements requires the unanimous consent of all those to whom the use is reserved. Any addition or alteration to a limited common element usually requires the prior approval of the board of directors, which acts on behalf of the apartment owners' association.

LIMITED PARTNERSHIP A partnership agreement in which one person (or group of persons) organizes, operates, and is responsible for the entire partnership venture. This person is called the *general partner*. The other members of the partnership are merely investors and have no say in the organization and direction of the operation. These passive investors are called limited partners. The limited partners share in the profits and compensate the general partner for his or her efforts out of such profits. Unlike a general partnership, in which each member is responsible for the total losses (if any) of the syndicate, the limited partners only stand to lose as much as they invest—usually nothing more. The general partner, then, is totally responsible for any large-scale losses incurred by the investment. Note, however, that when a limited partner receives cash distributions, either upon dissolution of the partnership or during the investment period, and the partnership's creditors' obligations remain unsatisfied, the limited partner may be required to return such distributions in order to satisfy the creditor's claims.

The form of limited partnership has been popularly used in the syndication of real estate ventures because it permits investors with only small amounts of capital to participate in real estate projects that require much capital and expertise in management, restricts their potential liability to their contribution, and also permits "pass-through" of tax benefits of real property ownership.

It is important for the organizer of a limited partnership to be careful that the IRS does not treat the partnership as an association taxable as a corporation (resulting in double taxation of income). Careful drafting of the limited partnership agreement by an experienced real estate tax attorney will usually assure the partnership of the appropriate tax status, in which all profits or losses pass through the partnership and are taxed only at the individual level. Partnership status thus combines the direct tax advantages of an immediate write-off of losses, if any, plus the elimination of a second tax at the corporate level.

The Tax Reform Act of 1976 provides that fees paid in connection with syndicating a partnership must be capitalized. Organizational expenditures, which are those expenditures incidental to the creation of the partnership, may be capitalized, or amortized, over a 60-month period commencing with the month that the partnership begins business. The Act also provides that it is no longer permissible to allocate a full share of a partnership loss for the entire year to any partner who did not hold his or her interest for the entire duration of that year. A partnership share of income or losses must correspond to the portion of the year that a partnership interest is held.

Many states have adopted the Uniform Limited Partnership Act to regulate the formation and operation of limited partnerships. Under this act, a certificate listing the names and investments of each participant in the partnership must be filed at the Business Registration Division or County Recorder's office. A limited partnership is not effective until a certificate is filed. Since a limited partner's interest is personal property, his or her death will not dissolve the partnership. Also, judgment and federal tax liens against a partner do not affect the partnership property, although they may affect the partner's right to receive profits.

Because the sale of a limited-partnership interest involves the sale of a security, it is subject to state and federal laws dealing with the sale of securities and, unless exempt, would have to be registered with the SEC and the appropriate state securities authorities. (*See AT-RISK RULES, DOUBLE TAXATION, FORECLOSURE, NET WORTH, REAL PROPERTY SECURITIES REGISTRATION, SAFE HARBOR RULE.*)

LIMITED POWER OF ATTORNEY

A power of attorney that is limited to a particular task, such as the transfer of a specific parcel of property. Most lenders and title insurance companies prefer the use of limited or special powers of attorney in real estate transactions as opposed to the use of general powers of attorney. (*See POWER OF ATTORNEY.*)

LIMITED SERVICE BROKER

A broker who offers the consumer less than the full line of services usually provided by a real estate broker. Such limited services might include writing offers, writing ads, assisting a buyer to obtain financing, and following up in escrow; but might not include advertising, showing, or holding open houses.

LINEAL 1. As it relates to family relationships, lineal is used to describe direct-line descendants, such as children or grandchildren, as opposed to *collaterals* (nephews, cousins, etc.); also applies to living descendants (blood or adopted), however remote from the deceased. 2. As it relates to measurements, lineal applies to a measurement made on a line. The lineal measure of a square that is four feet on each side is sixteen feet. Lineal measure is also called *linear measure.*

LINE OF CREDIT The maximum amount of money a bank will lend one of its more reliable and credit-worthy customers without the need for a formal loan submission. The borrower is thus assured of quick loan service without the delay of a credit review prior to disbursement of any funds. A customer's line of credit is subject to periodic reviews of the customer's credit standing and the overall banking relationship. (*See LETTER OF CREDIT.*)

LINE-OF-SIGHT EASEMENT A right that restricts the use of land within the easement area in any way that interferes with the view.

LINE STAKES Stakes set along the boundary lines of a parcel of land surveyed by metes and bounds.

LINTEL A horizontal board that supports the load over an opening such as a door or window.

LIQUIDATED DAMAGES An amount predetermined by the parties to an agreement as the total amount of compensation an injured party should receive in the event that the other party breaches a specified part of the contract. Often in building contracts the parties will anticipate the possibility of a breach (for example, a delay in completion by a set date) and will specify in the contract the amount of the damages to be paid in the event of the breach. To be enforceable, the liquidated damage clause must set forth an amount which bears a reasonable relationship to the actual damages as *estimated* by the parties; otherwise, the court will treat the amount as a penalty for failure to perform. If a defaulting buyer had deposited earnest money over 20 percent of the purchase price and the buyer failed to complete the contract, the courts would probably permit the buyer to recover some of the deposit money on the theory that the seller would be unjustly enriched by keeping it all. In addition, courts look with disfavor on penalty clauses and tend to declare them void and unenforceable. The clause should therefore specify for what damage the party is being compensated (loss of rent, attorney fees, and the like). As a general rule, a court will not enforce a liquidated damage clause in an installment contract or contract for deed when the clause tends to effect a forfeiture of all installment payments made.

If a seller elects to keep deposited earnest money as liquidated damages, it may prevent the seller from successfully pursuing other remedies, including additional money damages. For example, if a buyer deposits $1,000 earnest money on a $75,000 house and later defaults, the seller who keeps the $1,000 as liquidated damages and later sells the house for only $70,000 cannot later recover from the first buyer for the difference in the two purchase prices.

Some forms for contracts of sale have a special box for the parties to initial if they desire to treat the earnest money as liquidated damages. Some states have statutory guidelines as to what is a reasonable amount for liquidated damages; for example, in California if the amount is over 3 percent of the sales price, the seller has the burden of proving that such excess is reasonable, otherwise it would be treated as a penalty and returned to the buyer. (*See DAMAGES, ELECTION OF REMEDIES, UNJUST ENRICHMENT.*)

LIQUIDITY

The ability to sell an asset and convert it into cash at a price close to its true value. Stocks that are traded publicly (not stocks in small or closely held corporations) are a relatively liquid investment. Real estate is traditionally considered to be a longer-term investment, and is not highly liquid.

One test of the liquidity of a person or company is a ratio which measures the immediate debt-paying ability of the person. It considers cash in hand and anything that can be instantly turned into cash, called *quick assets*. A 1:1 quick ratio is generally acceptable for a business firm. The quick ratio is *Quick Assets: Current Liabilities.*

LIS PENDENS

A recorded legal document which gives constructive notice that an action affecting a particular piece of property has been filed in a state or federal court. Lis pendens is a Latin term which means "action pending" and is in the nature of a "quasi" lien. A person who subsequently acquires an interest in that property takes it subject to any judgment that may be entered; that is, a purchaser *pendente lite* (pending a lawsuit) is bound by the result of the lawsuit. The theory behind lis pendens is that a multiplicity of lawsuits can be avoided if all persons who might become involved with the property are first put on notice that the property is the subject of a lawsuit.

A notice of lis pendens is not the same as placing a lien on or attaching real property. It is only notice of a pending action involving title or possession of real property. The action must affect title, or right to possession, of real estate. Thus, it could not be used in a suit to recover attorney's fees or real estate commissions. A lien, however, is a charge or security interest against the property, and an attachment is a procedure to preserve the property for collection purposes. The end result of filing a lis pendens, however, is the same; that is, the property may not be freely sold or encumbered, and title is thereby effectively rendered unmarketable during the litigation.

The notice of pending action must generally contain the names of the parties, the object of the action, and a description of the affected property. Some states require a court hearing prior to rendering a lis pendens. From and after the time of recording the notice, the purchaser or encumbrancer of the affected property is considered to have constructive notice of the pendency against the designated parties. An attorney should be consulted prior to filing a lis pendens. An improperly filed lis pendens could lead to a lawsuit by the property owner for slander of title or malicious prosecution. Such a lis pendens could be removed from the record by filing a "motion to expunge." (*See ATTACHMENT, SLANDER OF TITLE.*)

LISTING

A written employment agreement between a property owner and a real estate broker authorizing the broker to find a buyer or a tenant for certain real property. Listings can take the form of *open listings, net listings, exclusive agency listings,* or *exclusive right-to-sell listings.* The most common form is the exclusive right-to-sell listing.

Note that *oral listings,* while not specifically illegal, are unenforceable under many state statutes of frauds and therefore are not generally recommended.

A broker should be careful to check the true ownership of the property at the time of listing in order to avoid taking listings signed by unauthorized parties. The broker also has the legal and ethical duty to inspect the listed property to ensure that all the information included in the listing agreement is accurate and complete. The owner should not be relied upon to confirm the accuracy of technical or detailed matters about which he or she couldn't really be knowledgeable, such as the legal effect of certain recorded restrictions on the property.

Listings are personal service contracts, and as such, they may not be assigned to another broker. This does not, however, prevent the broker from delegating to his or her sales office the task of procuring buyers for the property.

The time limit included in the listing agreement is extended by implication if negotiations to sell the property are in progress at the time the listing expires. (Note that the national average time required to sell the average listed house at its current market price is 97 days.)

The listing usually states the amount of commission the seller will pay the broker upon the happening of certain stated conditions. If a listed property is transferred by way of an involuntary sale, such as a foreclosure, condemnation, or tax sale, the broker is usually not entitled to a commission.

The broker must give a copy of the listing to all the parties signing it. The broker should not show the listing contract (including MLS listings) to the buyer, since the listing is an employment contract strictly between the seller and broker. A buyer who has read the listing might then be able to sue the seller if the buyer had relied on misstatements or omissions in the listing and thereby suffered damages. (*See EXCLUSIVE AGENCY, EXCLUSIVE RIGHT TO SELL, EXTENDER CLAUSE, NET LISTING, OFFER, OPEN LISTING, TERMINATION OF LISTING.*)

LISTOR A real estate salesperson who obtains the listing on a particular property. In most brokerage companies, the listor will receive a certain percentage (perhaps 25 percent) of the total commission if the property is sold. The listor will receive more if he or she also is responsible for making the sale (the "selling broker").

LITTORAL LAND Land bordering on the shore of a sea or ocean and thus affected by the tide currents. Littoral land is different from riparian land, which borders on the bank of a watercourse or stream. (*See RIPARIAN.*)

LIVABILITY SPACE RATIO For purposes of site planning, the minimum square feet of nonvehicular outdoor area in a development which is provided for each square foot of total floor area.

LIVE LOAD A moving or variable weight which may be safely added to the intrinsic weight of a structure. For example, a modern high-rise office building may have a live load capacity of 60 lbs. per square foot to accommodate office furniture and equipment.

LOAD   Weight supported by a structural part such as a load-bearing wall.

LOADING DOCK   The area, either within an industrial building and adjacent to its loading doors, or outside of the structure, which is used for the shipping or receiving of merchandise and the movement of merchandise between the warehouse area and trucks or rail cars.

LOAN COMMITMENT   A commitment by a lender to loan a certain amount of money to a qualified borrower on a particular piece of real estate for a specified amount of time under specific terms. It may be a conditional or qualified commitment or it may be a firm commitment. After reviewing the borrower's loan application, the lender usually decides whether to make a commitment to loan the requested funds. This application contains such information as the name and address of the borrower, his or her place of employment, salary, bank accounts, credit references, and the like. (See LOAN SUBMISSION.)

LOAN CONSTANT   See CONSTANT.

LOAN CORRESPONDENT   One who negotiates loans for conventional lending institutions or other lenders. The correspondent often continues to service the loan for the lender and acts as the collecting agent. (See MORTGAGE BANKER.)

LOAN SUBMISSION   A package of pertinent papers and documents regarding a specific property or properties which a lender receives for review and consideration for the purpose of making a mortgage loan. The following papers and documents are generally included: letter of transmittal; appraisal; financial statements; credit reports and/or Dun and Bradstreet reports; application; sales or purchase agreements on existing properties; leases, if applicable; photographs; plat plan and survey; cost breakdown, if applicable; set of plans and specifications on proposed construction; and other pertinent information which would help the lender in considering a particular submission, such as zoning ordinances, utilities map, strip maps, and aerial photographs.

LOAN-TO-VALUE RATIO   The ratio of a mortgage loan principal to the property's appraised value or its sales price, whichever is lower. Loan-to-value ratios depend on the individual lender's policy. Most lenders realize that the greater the equity a borrower has in a property, the less inclined he or she will be to default and lose the property through foreclosure. Savings and loan associations traditionally allow the highest loan-to-value ratio. When private mortgage insurance is used, the lender can sometimes offer 90 to 95 percent loan-to-value ratios (usually restricted to owner/occupants). Investors might qualify for 80 percent financing. FHA ratios are fixed by statute. There are no ratios for VA loans. A maximum loan-to-value ratio is set by law for institutional lenders, such as commercial banks and savings and loan associations.

LOBBY   1. A public waiting area or meeting place in hotels, motels, apartment buildings, office buildings, or other similar structures. 2. To work for or against passage of a bill or resolution pending before a legislative body.

**LOCAL
IMPROVEMENT
DISTRICT**
A separate legal entity, activated under state law by the inhabitants of a particular geographical area. The district is governed by a board of directors and possesses many of the characteristics of a city, particularly in terms of taxation. As a rule, the district issues its own bonds to finance particular improvements, such as water distribution systems, drainage structures, irrigation works, and a host of other types of developments. To repay the funds borrowed through the issuance of bonds, these districts have the power to assess all lands included in the district on an *ad valorem* basis.

LOCK BOX
A special lock placed on the door of a listed property designed to facilitate the showing by brokers of that property. A cooperating broker who wanted to inspect the property quickly need not go to the listing broker's office to get the house keys; the broker could merely call the listing office to obtain the combination to the lock box. Some lock boxes have locks that open with keys.

Lack of ordinary care in installing the lock box or providing the combination or special key could result in liability for property damage, theft, or personal injury. Some errors and omissions insurance policies now have a special lock box liability endorsement.

LOCK-IN CLAUSE
A clause in a promissory note that prohibits the prepayment of the note.

LOCUS SIGILLI
Latin for "place of seal," using the abbreviated form, *L.S.*, at the end of the signature line in some formal legal documents; used instead of the actual seal. (*See SEAL.*)

LOFT
Building area which is unfinished; also refers to open space, normally on the first or second floor and typically used for a low-cost manufacturing operation. The tenant pays a lower rent for loft space than for finished space, and amortizes the cost of finishing the area over the term of the lease. Banks, savings and loan associations, and retail stores usually rent on a loft-space rate basis.

LOOP
A looped roadway having two access points off the same roadway.

LOSS FACTOR
A commercial leasing term, also known as the *load factor* or *partial floor factor,* which is the square-footage difference between the rentable area and the usable area expressed as a percentage. For example, an office-building floor with a rentable area of 10,000 square feet and a usable area of 9,000 square feet has a load factor of 10 percent. The 1,000 square feet is used up by bathrooms, corridors, and elevator shafts.

The loss factor is a simple gauge for a tenant to use in evaluating separate rental sites which may have comparable rents but greatly different loss factors.

LOSS PAYEE
The person designated on an insurance policy as the one to be paid in case the insured property is damaged or destroyed. A secured lender often requires a borrower to carry adequate insurance on property used as security and to name the lender as the loss payee.

LOST-GRANT DOCTRINE   A rarely used rule of real property law relating to the claim of title to real property against the sovereign. Tracing its roots to the field of incorporeal hereditaments, its application to realty has been recognized in the United States largely in claims relating to lands allegedly held under now lost grants from the Spanish crown prior to the extension of American sovereignty over such territories. The lost-grant doctrine is similar to adverse possession in that the possession must be actual, open, and exclusive. For a claim against the sovereign, however, a higher degree of proof is required (for example, a chain of conveyance and payment of taxes). The claimant need only show the legal possibility of a lost grant, not its actual existence. (See ADVERSE POSSESSION.)

LOT, BLOCK, AND SUBDIVISION   A description of real property that identifies a parcel of land by reference to lot and block numbers appearing on maps and plats of recorded subdivided land. For example, the description might read: "Lot 6, Block 8, Breezy Hills Subdivision, Serene County, Anystate, according to the plat thereof on file and of record in the office of the Registrar of Deeds in and for the said county and state."

A lot is an individual parcel of land intended to be conveyed in its entirety to a prospective buyer. A block is typically a group of contiguous lots bounded by streets, as in a city block. Blocks are separated by roads.

LOT SPLIT   The division of land by separating its ownership or otherwise dividing it into several parcels. Lot splitting is typically regulated by local ordinances. Also called "land division."

LOTTERY   A chance for a prize in return for paying a price. In tight credit markets, sellers sometimes look to the lottery method to sell their real property. Many states have specific provisions in their real estate license act preventing real estate brokers from selling real estate by means of a lottery or offering prizes for the listing or selling of real estate.

The U.S. Code, Title 18, Section 1302 prohibits any reference, in any publication that uses the U.S. mail, to a lottery or a similar enterprise. The offering of real estate under a lottery cannot be transmitted by mail or published by mail. The violation of this act could bring a fine of not more than $1,000 or imprisonment of not more than two years or both. For a second offense imprisonment is not more than five years.

LOUVER   Slats or fins over an opening, pitched so as to keep out rain or snow yet permit ventilation. A finned sunshade on a building. The diffusion grill on fluorescent light fixtures. Also spelled louvre.

LOVE AND AFFECTION   A type of consideration. Love and affection is a good and sufficient consideration when a gift is intended. It is different from a *valuable consideration*. The difference between the two is important in those areas of the law requiring a valuable consideration, such as under the recording acts, which protect the rights of bona fide *purchasers for value*. A common example of a grant deed supported by love and affection is a gift transfer of the family home by a father to his son "for love and affection." (*See CONSIDERATION, GIFT DEED, VALUABLE CONSIDERATION.*)

LUMINOUS CEILING   A ceiling emitting light from its entire surface, through the use of fluorescent light above translucent glass or plastic.

LUMP SUM PAYMENT   Repayment of a debt by a single payment, including principal and accrued interest. A straight note may provide for periodic interest payments with one lump sum principal payment.

MAGGIE MAE   Nickname for the first nonfederal secondary market for conventional mortgages. It provides a market where a lender can sell Mortgage Guaranty Insurance Corporation (MGIC) insured mortgages to other investors.

MAGIC-WRAP   A mortgaging procedure in which MGIC insures a mortgage and sells it on the secondary market when the mortgage wraps around an existing VA or FHA mortgage.

MAI   "Member, Appraisal Institute"; the designation given by the American Institute of Real Estate Appraisers to a qualified appraiser. An MAI must be at least 28 years of age and have a minimum of five years of creditable appraisal experience. He or she must also submit two acceptable demonstration appraisal reports, and must pass certain required examinations. MAI appraisers subscribe to a high code of professional standards and ethics, and thus, most lenders requiring an appraisal will request a report done by an MAI or another professional such as a member of the Society of Real Estate Appraisers (SREA).

MAIL, USE OF   See *ACCEPTANCE.*

MAIN LINE   The principal or through track of a railroad line on which traffic moves through yards or between stations. The main line is operated by timetable or train order and governed by block signal indication.

MAINTENANCE   The care and work put into a building to keep it in operation and productive use; the general repair and upkeep of a building. If maintenance is deferred, the building will suffer a loss in value. (*See DEFERRED MAINTENANCE.*)

MAINTENANCE FEE   A charge levied against property owners to maintain their real estate in operation and productive use, especially in condominiums. In condominium living, the amount of the maintenance fee is usually determined by the board of directors upon review of the budgets. There are usually two budgets. The first is designed to anticipate the month-by-month needs with totals by category for the year. Financial statements are usually prepared each month. These statements compare the actual receipts and disbursements with the operating budget figures, giving a clear financial picture for basing management decisions.

A second budget, called a five-year capital budget, is prepared or updated yearly. This budget is designed to anticipate major expenditures such as painting the building, purchasing association insurance for the common areas, recarpeting corridors, and replacing any items of substantial cost. The income for these expenditures is obtained from monthly maintenance fee assessments, and is processed in the monthly financial statement through the condominium reserve fund. This reserve fund money is kept in regular savings accounts or higher yield time certificate deposits, and is withdrawn for disbursements when the need arises. (See OPERATING EXPENSES.)

MAJORITY The age at which a person is no longer a minor and is thus able to freely enter into contracts. The age of majority in most states for contract purposes is 18. (See MINOR.)

MAKER The person (borrower) who executes a promissory note and thus becomes primarily liable for payment to the payee (lender). The maker of a check is known as the drawer.

MALL A landscaped public area set aside for pedestrian traffic. Malls are popular features of large retail shopping centers. They are now also being created in established downtown retail areas to revitalize existing businesses and are being built in suburban areas to generate new business.

MANAGEMENT AGREEMENT A contract between the owner of income-producing property and the individual or firm who will manage that property. The management agreement establishes the scope of the agent's authority, as well as duties, compensation, termination procedures, and other matters such as payment of expenses. In addition to the essential elements of a valid contract, the written management agreement should contain, at a minimum, the legal description of the property to be managed, "hold harmless" clauses, scope of services, rate and schedule of compensation, accounting and report requirements, the starting date, the termination date, and any provisions for renewal options. (See PROPERTY MANAGEMENT.)

MANAGEMENT SURVEY A detailed analysis of the economic, physical, and operational aspects of a property, with recommendations as to changes and improvements that could enhance the property's profitability.

MANDAMUS A writ issued from a court ordering or prohibiting performance of a certain activity. A court might, for example, order a reluctant public official to issue a real estate license if the complainant is qualified; or, it might order a governmental agency to issue a building permit.

MANTEL   The decorative facing placed around a fireplace. Mantels are usually made of ornamental wood and topped by a shelf.

MAPS AND PLATS   Surveys of particular pieces of land showing monuments, boundaries, area, ownership, and the like, prepared by registered surveyors or civil engineers.

A subdivider must generally submit maps and plats of a proposed subdivision with his or her application for recordation and registration (if under the Torrens system) of the subdivision. Thereafter, when lots are sold in the subdivision, the legal description need only refer to the subdivision, lot, and block number which may be taken from the recorded map. (*See TAX MAP.*)

MARGINAL LAND   Land which is of little value because of some deficiency, such as poor access, lack of adequate rainfall, or steep terrain. Modern land reclamation and development techniques have successfully converted some marginal lands into attractive and functional developments. Former desert land, for instance, has been successfully developed into attractive subdivisions.

MARGINAL RELEASE   Notation of a satisfaction or release of mortgage by a county recorder, as evidenced by a note of its liber (book) and page number on the margin of the recorded mortgage.

MARINA   A docking and mooring facility for boats which is generally equipped with repair facilities, gas, supplies, and other conveniences; a boat basin.

MARITAL DEDUCTION   Prior to 1982, a deduction against federal estate tax equal to the value of certain property passing to the surviving spouse, up to the greater of $250,000 or one-half of the decedent spouse's estate. After 1981, the deduction is equal to 100 percent of the assets passing to the surviving spouse. (*See ESTATE TAX, FEDERAL.*)

MARK   A symbol used for a signature. (*See X.*)

MARKETABLE TITLE   Good or clear salable title reasonably free from risk of litigation over possible defects; also referred to as merchantable title. A marketable title is one which (1) is free from undisclosed encumbrances; (2) discloses no serious defects and is not dependent on doubtful questions of law or fact to prove its validity; (3) will not expose a purchaser to the hazard of litigation or embarrass him or her in the peaceful enjoyment of the property; and (4) would be accepted by a reasonably well-informed and prudent person, acting upon business principles and willful knowledge of the facts and their legal significance with the assurance that he or she could, in turn, sell or mortgage the property at fair market value.

Marketable title does not necessarily mean a perfect title, just one which is free from plausible or reasonable objections. The title must be such that a court would order the buyer to accept it if asked to decree specific performance of the sales contract.

A seller under a contract of sale is required to deliver marketable title at final closing; that is, a title which is so free from significant defects, other than those specified in the contract, that the purchaser can be assured against having to defend the title. This requirement of marketable title is implied in law and thus need not be stated in the contract. Title would not be marketable if there were a significant risk of litigation. The buyer cannot be forced to buy a lawsuit along with the property.

Sometimes a buyer will insert in the contract a provision that the seller shall deliver title "free from all defects or encumbrances." A seller should be aware that in these cases the buyer could probably reject title even if there were only a small or insignificant encroachment or defect. Unless the contract provides otherwise (in a "subject to" clause), any of the following could render title unmarketable: easements, restrictions, violations of restrictions, zoning ordinance violations, existing leases, encroachments (except those that are slight), and outstanding mineral and oil rights.

Although an unmarketable title does not mean that the property cannot be transferred, it does mean that there are certain defects in the title which may limit or restrict its ownership, and the purchaser cannot be forced to accept a conveyance which is materially different from the one bargained for or "marketed" in the contract of sale.

A zoning ordinance does not generally render title unmarketable. However, if a seller incorrectly represents that a zoning ordinance would not prohibit a purchaser's required use when, in fact, it would, a zoning ordinance may be equivalent to a lien or encumbrance. Furthermore, the seller's failure to inform the buyer of a zoning ordinance violation may constitute actionable fraud or entitle the purchaser to rescind.

Questions of marketable title must be raised by the purchaser prior to acceptance of the deed. Once the buyer accepts the deed, his or her only recourse is to sue on the covenants of warranty, if any, contained in the deed. (See MERGER, "SUBJECT TO" CLAUSE, UNMARKETABLE TITLE, WARRANTY DEED.)

MARKET-DATA APPROACH A method of appraising or evaluating real property based on the principle of comparison. Using this method the value of property is figured by comparing the prices paid for similar properties and establishing the value accordingly. The three main steps in the market-data approach are:

1. Locate comparable properties (properties with the same "highest and best use") which have sold recently, usually within the last three months, in "arm's-length transactions." This excludes certain sales, such as bankruptcy or foreclosure sales, sales by the government, sales between relatives, and so on.

2. Compare these properties with the subject property and make all necessary adjustments in the sales prices for any significant differences in the property, such as age, location, and physical characteristics. Adjustments are necessary even in comparing vacant land, such as hookups for utilities, soil composition, and location. There should be similarities in the number of rooms, bathrooms, bedrooms, size of lot, building age, style, and condition.

3. Reconcile all the comparable information and draw a conclusion of value.

The market-data approach is the most reliable gauge of the market and is most frequently used in appraising residential property, where the amenities are often so difficult to measure. This approach is also a component for use in the other two methods of determining value. In the cost approach market data is used to determine the depreciation figure, and in the income approach market data is used to determine the capitalization rate. The market-data approach requires an active real estate market for the type of property being appraised. (*See APPRAISAL, COMPARABLES.*)

MARKET VALUE   The highest price, estimated in terms of money, which a property will bring if exposed for sale in the open market, allowing a reasonable time to find a purchaser who buys with knowledge of all the uses to which the property is adapted and for which it is capable of being used. Market value is often referred to as the price at which a willing and informed seller would sell and a willing and informed buyer would buy, neither being under any pressure to act. However, market value is different from market price, which is the actual price the property sells for. (*See FAIR MARKET VALUE.*)

MASTER DEED   The principal conveyance document used by the owners of land on which condominiums are located. The master deed, together with a declaration, must generally be submitted when recording or registering the condominium pursuant to state laws. (*See DECLARATION.*)

MASTER FORM INSTRUMENT   An instrument containing various forms such as covenants and other clauses in a mortgage or deed of trust which may be recorded with the county registrar as a master form instrument. Such an instrument need not be acknowledged (notarized and witnessed). It is indexed under the name of the person recording it. Thereafter any of the provisions of a master form instrument may be incorporated by reference in any mortgage or deed of trust if the reference states that the master is recorded in the county and gives its recording date, file number, volume, and page. Such a reference should also state that a copy of the master was furnished to the person executing the mortgage or deed of trust.

MASTER LEASE   The dominant lease in a building or development. For example, a developer might lease land from a fee owner, construct a building or condominium, and then sublease space to others. The subleases will generally have provisions that conform to the terms of the master lease, since the sublease is subject to the terms of the master lease. (*See SUBLEASE.*)

MASTER PLAN   A comprehensive plan to guide the long-term physical development of a particular area. (*See GENERAL PLAN, ZONING.*)

MASTER SWITCH   An electrical wall switch that controls more than one fixture or outlet in a room.

MATERIALMAN   The supplier of materials used in the construction of an improvement. The materialman is entitled to a lien on the property for monies overdue, whether they be due from the owner or the prime contractor. The materialman must file a lien within the time specified by state law. This is usually measured from the completion date. (*See MECHANIC'S LIEN.*)

MATURITY   The time when an indebtedness, such as a mortgage note, becomes due and is extinguished if paid in accordance with the agreed upon schedule of payments. (*See CURTAIL SCHEDULE.*)

MEANDER LINE   An artificial line used by surveyors to measure the natural, uneven, winding property line formed by rivers, streams, and other watercourses bordering a property. The meander line is primarily a device to measure area, not to delimit title or determine a boundary line. Surveyors sometimes use straight lines on courses approximating the natural line. In a conveyance of land described as bounded by a meander line, the true boundary is the stream or waters themselves.

MEASURE OF DAMAGES   The rule of law set by statute or case law as to the amount of damages a plaintiff can recover against a defendant for a breach of contract or other civil wrong. (*See BENEFIT OF BARGAIN, DAMAGES.*)

MEASUREMENT TABLES   Here are some U.S. measurements and their metrical equivalents that might be useful to one in the real estate business. Under the Metric Conversion Act of 1975, the U.S. agreed to a conversion from its present system to the International Metric System.

UNIT	MEASUREMENT	METRIC EQUIVALENT
mile	5,280 feet; 320 rods; 1,760 yards	1.609 kilometers
rod	5.50 yards; 16.5 feet	5.029 meters
sq. mile	640 acres; 102,400 sq. rods	2.590 sq. kilometers
acre	4,840 sq. yards; 160 sq. rods; 43,560 sq. feet	4,047 sq. meters; 0.405 hectares
sq. yard	9 sq. feet	0.836 sq. meters
sq. foot	144 sq. inches	0.093 sq. meters
chain	66 feet or 100 links	20.117 meters
kilometer	0.62 mile (3,280 ft., 10 in.)	1,000 meters
hectare	2.47 acres	10,000 sq. meters

ACRE EQUIVALENT One Acre Equals a Rectangle of the Following Size:

LENGTH (Feet)*		WIDTH (Feet)*
16.5	by	2640
33	by	1320
50	by	871.2
66	by	660
75	by	580.8
100	by	435.6
132	by	330
150	by	290.4
208.7	by	208.7

*Note—multiply by 0.3048 to arrive at the equivalent measurement in *meters*.

CONVERSION FROM CUSTOMARY TO METRIC AND VICE VERSA

When you know:		You can find:	If you multiply by:
LENGTH	inches	millimeters	25
	feet	centimeters	30
	yards	meters	0.9
	miles	kilometers	1.6
	millimeters	inches	0.04
	centimeters	inches	0.4
	meters	yards	1.1
	kilometers	miles	0.6
AREA	square inches	square centimeters	6.5
	square feet	square meters	0.09
	square yards	square meters	0.8
	square miles	square kilometers	2.6
	acres	square hectometers (hectares)	0.4
	square centimeters	square inches	0.16
	square meters	square yards	1.2
	square kilometers	square yards	0.4
	square hectometers (hectares)	acres	2.5
MASS	ounces	grams	18
	pounds	kilograms	0.45
	short tons	megagrams (metric tons)	0.9
	grams	ounces	0.035
	kilograms	pounds	2.2
	megagrams (metric tons)	short tons	1.1
LIQUID VOLUME	ounces	milliliters	30
	pints	liters	0.47
	quarts	liters	0.95
	gallons	liters	3.8
	milliliters	ounces	0.034
	liters	pints	2.1
	liters	quarts	1.06
	liters	gallons	0.26

MECHANIC'S LIEN   A statutory lien created in favor of materialmen and mechanics (and architects and designers in some states) to secure payment for materials supplied and services rendered in the improvement, repair, or maintenance of real property. This right did not exist in common law. Note that materialmen are suppliers, while mechanics are laborers.

The purpose of this lien is to give security to those who perform labor or furnish materials in the improvement of the real property (usually not public property). In general, the mechanic's lien right is predicated upon the "enhancement of value" theory. By reason of the labor performed and the materials furnished, the real estate has been enhanced in value. Therefore, the parties performing the work or supplying materials should be given a right-of-lien on the real estate on which the work was done as security for the payment of the proper charges. The lien accrues in favor of subcontractors, materialmen, and laborers independently of the original contractor, and not by way of subrogation to the rights of the latter. Thus, any person furnishing labor or material for the improvement of real estate can assert a mechanic's lien provided there is a valid contract. The lien is for work and materials which become a permanent part of the building only, and thus does not cover certain costs for furnishing tools, or office overhead like telephone, stationery, and other similar expenses.

The mechanic's lien attaches to the improvement as well as to the interest of the owner of the real property who contracts for the improvement, including the equitable interest of a buyer under a contract for deed. The term "owner" also includes a lessor whose lease requires the erection of buildings, even though only the lessee contracted for the building.

To be entitled to a mechanic's lien, the work which was done must be by contract (express or implied) with the owner or owner's authorized representative. Usually such a lien is relied on to cover situations in which the owner has not paid for the work, or when the general contractor has been paid but he or she has not paid the subcontractors or suppliers.

In some states, mechanics' liens may be given priority over previously recorded liens such as mortgages. Inasmuch as the rights of the claimant are statutory, they are controlled by the requirements of the statute of the state where the real estate is located. It is usually provided that a claimant must take steps to enforce his or her lien within a certain time or the lien will expire. The time limit is usually one or two years after the filing of the lien claim. Enforcement usually requires a court action to foreclose the lien through the sale of the real estate to produce money to pay the lien.

The effective date of the lien is usually the time of visible commencement of operations; that is, when enough work is performed to give notice that the real property is being improved or is about to be improved. In the event that the property is transferred after the lien is effective, but before the filing of the notice of lien, the mechanic's lien has priority. Thus, a good faith purchaser for value who is without notice of the visible commencement of operation takes title subject to the possibility of a subsequent notice of lien. A prudent purchaser should obtain proper title insurance (an extended coverage policy) as protection against this type of risk.

In many states, mechanics' and materialmen's liens have priority over all other liens of any nature, except: (1) liens in favor of any branch of the government; (2) mortgages, liens, or judgments recorded or filed prior to the time of visible commencement of operations; and (3) mortgages recorded prior to the date of completion, under which all or a portion of the monies advanced and secured up to that time have been used to pay for the improvement. The mortgage must include such a statement.

Once a mechanic's lien has been paid off, a written notice (generally called a satisfaction of lien) should be filed in the proper court at the expense of the lienee (owner). If the liened property is Torrens registered property, the satisfaction of lien must be filed with the registrar of titles.

Usually, an owner of property can find protection against mechanic's liens for work authorized by his or her lessee or vendee (under contract for deed) by posting or recording a "notice of nonresponsibility." This notice would, in effect, inform the contractor that he would have to look solely to the person authorizing the work for his or her payment. (See NOTICE OF COMPLETION, NOTICE OF LIEN, NOTICE OF NONRESPONSIBILITY.)

MEETING OF THE MINDS   Mutual assent or agreement between the parties to a contract regarding the substance of the contract. If the parties by their words and acts manifest an intention to be bound to a contract, they can be held accountable. Thus, while parties may not *intend* to bind themselves to a contract, they may be deemed bound in law because of their outward indications of assent. There can be no contract unless there is a meeting of the minds; that is, there must be a valid offer which is properly accepted. (*See* ESTOPPEL, *OFFER AND ACCEPTANCE.*)

MEGALOPOLIS A large, densely populated metropolitan area, consisting of a number of major urban areas, such as the Eastern Seaboard area, which includes New York City, Washington, D.C., Philadelphia, Boston, and smaller surrounding cities. (*See* METROPOLITAN AREA.)

MERCHANTABLE *See* MARKETABLE TITLE.
TITLE

MERGER The uniting or combining of two or more interests or estates into one.

An easement may be extinguished upon the merger of a servient and a dominant estate. For example, Abner O'Brian, the owner of lot 1, the servient estate, gives Jayne Green, the owner of the adjacent lot 2, the dominant estate, an easement to cross over lot 1. Subsequently Ms. Green acquires title to lot 1. If Ms. Green later sells lot 2 to Bill Porter, the easement is not revived; it has been merged into lot 1 and would have to be created anew.

As a general rule, when a greater and lesser estate become vested in the same person, the lesser estate merges into the greater estate. For example, if a landlord sells property to a tenant, there is a merger of the leasehold estate with the original freehold estate. Obviously the lease is terminated, and the tenant is relieved of the duty to pay rent. This is also true when the tenant inherits the leased fee.

When a deed is delivered pursuant to a contract for deed, all the terms of the contract for deed are merged into and superceded by the deed, unless otherwise provided in the contract or the deed. Thus, if the vendor wants representations, warranties, or restrictions in the contract for deed to continue and *survive* the deed, he or she must insert them in the deed or specify which covenants and conditions in the contract are to survive delivery of the deed or assignment of the lease. In essence, the contract merges into the deed and ceases to exist. Also, when a sales contract calls for something to be done *after* closing and delivery of the deed, such as the installation of a sewer system, this requirement would usually survive the deed and be enforceable, that is, matters collateral to the conveyance are not merged.

A merger clause in a contract states that this writing constitutes the entire agreement between the parties and all other prior negotiations and representations are not a part of the contract. (*See* SURVIVAL CLAUSE.)

MERIDIAN One of a set of imaginary lines running north and south used by surveyors for reference in locating and describing land under the government survey method of property description. (*See* GOVERNMENT SURVEY METHOD.)

MESNE An intermediate or middle conveyance; any con-
CONVEYANCE veyance between the first conveyance and the most recent conveyance in the chain of title.

MESNE PROFITS   Profits derived from the wrongful possession of
land. Usually mesne profits are recoverable by the
lawful owner.

METES AND BOUNDS   A common method of land description that identifies a property by specifying the shape and
boundary dimensions of the parcel, using terminal points and angles. A metes and
bounds description starts at a well-marked point of beginning and follows the
boundaries of the land by courses and metes (measures, distances, and compass
direction) and bounds (landmarks, monuments) and returns to the true point of
beginning. Generally, however, in verifying such a description, monuments prevail over courses and distances. A description which fails to enclose an area by
returning to the point of beginning is defective. If there is any discrepancy in the
distance between monuments and linear measurements, the actual measured distance between the monuments prevails. An example of a metes and bounds description would be as follows:

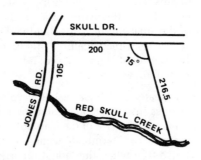

A tract of land located in Red Skull, Virginia, is described as follows:
beginning at the intersection of the east line of Jones Road and the
south line of Skull Drive; thence east along the south line of Skull
Drive 200 feet; thence south 15° east 216.5 feet, more or less, to the
center thread of Red Skull Creek; thence northwesterly along the center line of said Creek to its intersection with the east line of Jones Road;
thence north 105 feet, more or less, along the east line of Jones Road to
the place of beginning.

When used to describe property within a town or city, a metes and bounds description may begin as follows:

Beginning at a point on the southerly side of Kent Street, 100 feet
easterly from the corner formed by the intersection of the southerly
side of Kent Street and the easterly side of Broadway; thence . . .

When used to describe land in rectangular survey states, a metes and bounds
description may begin as follows:

That part of lots 7, 8, and 9 in Block R of Lightwater's Subdivision in
the NW ¼ of the SE ¼ of Section 16, Township 39 north, Range 12 east
of the 5th principal meridian bounded and described to wit as follows,
beginning . . .

(*See LEGAL DESCRIPTION, MONUMENT, POINT OF BEGINNING.*)

METROPOLITAN AREA   The area in and around a major city. For example, the Chicago metropolitan area is often construed to include certain areas in western Indiana as well as the surrounding suburbs in Illinois.

MEZZANINE   An intermediate floor between two main stories of a building or between the floor and ceiling of a one-story structure. A mezzanine usually covers a relatively small portion of the Botal floor space.

MGIC   *See MORTGAGE GUARANTY INSURANCE CORPORATION.*

MILE   A linear measurement of distance equal to 1,760 yards or 5,280 feet, or 1.609 kilometers. (*See MEASUREMENT TABLES.*)

MILITARY CLAUSE   A clause inserted in some residential leases to allow a military tenant to terminate the lease in case of transfer, discharge, or other circumstances making termination appropriate. Example:

> It is expressly agreed that if the lessee herein should receive official orders relieving him or her from duty at Fort Shafter or from active duty in the army or ordering him or her to live in service quarters, he or she may terminate this lease upon written notice of intention to do so. Such termination shall become effective 30 days after the date of the service of the notice upon the lessor. If the date of such termination falls between the days on which rent becomes due, there shall accrue on the first day of the rental period in which termination takes effect a proportionate part only of the rent which would be due but for such termination.

(*See SOLDIERS AND SAILORS CIVIL RELIEF ACT.*)

MILL   One-tenth of one cent. Some states use a mill rate to compute property taxes. For example, if the mill rate is 52 and the property is assessed at $40,000 the tax would be 0.052 × $40,000, or $2,080. This tax can also be quoted or computed as $52 per $1,000. (*See TAX RATE.*)

MINERAL RIGHTS   Rights to subsurface land and profits. Normally, when real property is conveyed, the grantee receives all right and title to the land including everything above and below the surface, unless excepted by the grantor. (*See OIL AND GAS LEASE.*)

MINIMUM LOT AREA   A zoning ordinance requirement establishing a minimum lot size upon which a building may be erected.

MINIMUM PROPERTY   Under FHA loan requirements, a property must
REQUIREMENTS   be livable, soundly built, and suitably located as
                         to site and neighborhood before the agency will
underwrite a residential mortgage loan. A broker, in estimating the seller's closing
costs, should consider repair expenses to comply with these requirements. The
parties in a FHA loan cannot avoid meeting the FHA standards by using an "as is"
clause.

MINOR   A person who is under the legal age of majority; a
              legal infant who is not a completely competent
legal party. The legal age of majority is set by state law and may vary depending on
the purpose of the law such as the legal age to drive, drink, or enter into contracts.
Most contracts, except those for necessities such as food and clothing, entered into
by a minor are generally voidable at his or her option. However, if the minor does
not disaffirm the contract within a reasonable time after attaining majority, then
the contract becomes fully enforceable against him or her. For example, if a minor
lists property with a broker, the broker would not be able to collect his or her
earned commission if, when the broker finds a ready, willing, and able buyer, the
minor decides to repudiate the listing contract. Note that, in any event, a minor
could not sell the property without court approval since a minor does not have the
legal capacity to transfer title to property nor does a minor have power to make a
valid will.

Even if the minor misrepresents his or her age, the minor can still disaffirm the
contract although he or she may be subject to an action in damages for fraud.

Since the grantor of a deed must be competent, a deed by a minor is voidable,
although a minor may be a grantee, and may receive realty by gift or inheritance. A
minor is generally deemed incapable of appointing an agent to sell his or her
property; thus any power of attorney executed is void.

If it is necessary for land owned by a minor to be sold for the minor's maintenance
or for investment, court proceedings to appoint a guardian must be instituted. The
minor is, then, the ward of the court. The court can grant the guardian a special
license to sell the property if the guardian posts a bond. The guardian does not
need a real estate license.

Title by adverse possession cannot generally be established against a minor unless
the adverse possession continues for the prescription period *after* the minor
reaches majority. (See *GUARDIAN, MAJORITY, VOIDABLE*.)

MINIWAREHOUSE   A structure containing self-storage units. A
                      miniwarehouse is typically found in an industrial
park and is designed to provide small, secure storage (10 to 200 sq. ft.) for individuals and small businesses (old records or files). A problem area for operators is the
legal disposition of goods which appear to have been abandoned by the renter.

MISDEMEANOR   A crime, less serious than a felony, usually pun-
                    ishable by imprisonment for one year or less. (See
                    FELONY.)

MISNOMER   A mistake in name. When a misnomer occurs in a
                 deed, the proper procedure is to prepare and re-
cord a correction of deed so as to avoid future title disputes. The misnomer of a

corporation in a deed is not material if the corporation can be reasonably identified, as when the deed states "Abby, Ltd.," when the real name is "Abby, Limited." A seller can be compelled to execute a correction of deed if his or her deed
to the grantee contains a covenant of further assurance. (*See* COVENANT.)

MISPLACED   A poorly located improvement; an improvement
IMPROVEMENT   that is poorly planned in that it either is too costly
or does not conform to the best utilization of the
site, such as a modern dwelling among a group of Victorian mansions.

MISREPRESENTATION   A false statement or concealment of a material
fact made with the intention of inducing some
action by another party. A court will grant relief in the form of damages or rescission if the misrepresented fact is material to the transaction. Misrepresentation
can be an affirmative statement, such as "this house does not have termites." It
can also be a concealment of a material fact known to one party which that party
knows is not reasonably ascertainable by the other party. An example of this
would be a case where a seller knows of a serious defect in the support beams, yet
does not disclose this fact to the buyer. This is sometimes called "negative fraud."
However, if the buyer clearly does not believe or rely on the misrepresentations, or
makes his or her own inspection and relies only on this investigation, the contract
cannot be rescinded due to misrepresentation.

Statements of opinion are not normally material facts, and thus are not actionable.
For example, "this house is a great buy at $50,000 since it is worth much more
than that," is a statement of opinion, often known as "puffing." Note the difference between the statement "the taxes are low" and "the taxes are $500" in a case
where the actual taxes are $1,000. It would be no defense to a broker that the seller
told the broker the taxes were $500—this type of information the broker should
verify. However, if the person making the representation possesses some superior
knowledge, then the representation, though opinion, is treated as one of fact. If a
builder, for instance, says, "the foundation appears to be properly laid," he or she
is liable if, in fact, it is not. Courts have held that when a broker represents that he
or she does not think the property is on filled land, he or she may be liable if it
turns out that the land is fill and the buyer thereby suffers damages. Although
misrepresentations usually take the form of verbal or written statements, they
could be such things as a nod of the head, pointing out false boundaries, or dis-
playing a forged map—in other words, any action that may tend to convey a false
message. Common subjects for misrepresentation lawsuits are statements regarding easements, sewer connections, high water, proposed special assessments,
number of legal units, and condition of roof.

It is not necessary that a person actually *intend* to misrepresent a fact. A broker or
salesperson is liable if he or she *knows* or *should have known* of the falsity of a
statement. Thus, if a broker makes a negligent misrepresentation of a material fact
to induce the buyer to buy, and the buyer relies on this fact to the buyer's detriment, then the broker is liable. The seller is also liable because the statement was
made by the seller's agent within the scope of authority of the agency. If the broker
fails to disclose a material fact, an aggrieved buyer usually has a successful case
against the broker when:

• the broker has knowledge of facts unknown to or beyond the reach of the buyer
  which materially affect the value or desirability of the property, and the broker
  fails to disclose these facts

- the broker intends to defraud the buyer by such nondisclosures

- the buyer suffers actual damages as a result of the misrepresentation

Some of the consequences of misrepresentation are:

- the broker or salesperson guilty of misrepresentation can have his or her license suspended or revoked

- the defrauded party can collect damages or have the contract rescinded

- the seller may not have to pay a commission to a misrepresenting broker

- under the federal Interstate Land Sales Act, a broker making a misrepresentation may be jointly and severally liable to the purchaser

- the buyer may be able to keep the property and sue the seller for the difference between the purchase price and the lesser actual value

- the buyer may be able to collect damages for expenditures made in reliance upon the misrepresentation

(See "AS IS," FRAUD, LATENT DEFECTS, PUFFING, SCOPE OF AUTHORITY.)

MISTAKE   An error or misunderstanding. A contract is voidable if there is a mistake that is mutual, material, unintentional, and free from negligence; such as both parties honestly contracting for a different lot in a subdivision (mistake of fact). Innocent mistakes seldom serve to void a contract. A party cannot claim mistake to get out of a contract on the basis that he or she did not read the contract he or she signed and was therefore mistaken as to its material terms; neither ignorance nor poor judgment is a mistake of fact. Nor can a party claim mistake in that they did not know the legal consequences upon signing the contract (mistake of law). (See ADHESION CONTRACT.)

When there is an ambiguity known by one party who fails to explain the mistake to the innocent party, the innocent party's interpretation generally will prevail.

MITER   In carpentry terminology, the ends of any two pieces of board of corresponding form cut off at an angle and fitted together in an angular shape.

MITIGATION OF DAMAGES   A principle of contract law that refers to the obligation of an injured party to take reasonable steps to reduce or eliminate the amount of damages that party may be entitled to. For example, a landlord may have a duty to try to locate a replacement tenant for space vacated or abandoned by a prior tenant in breach of the lease.

MIXED USE   The use of real property for more than one use, such as a condominium building that has residential and commercial units.

MOBILE HOME   Prefabricated trailer-type housing units that are semipermanently attached to land, either the owner's fee land or a leasehold, such as in a mobile home park. Mobile homes are usually affixed to a concrete foundation and connected to utilities. Although they may not be as mobile as the word implies, they may be removed from such attachments and hauled to a new location. In this respect mobile homes possess the features of both real and personal property. They are like real property when the units are attached to the earth's surface, and like personal property when they are detached and moved. The courts, however, generally consider a mobile home as a *fixture*, and thus treat it as real property. Some states require the mobile home salesperson to have a real estate license or a special mobile home license.

Many areas of the U.S. have initiated zoning legislation restricting mobile homes and mobile-home parks within the community. While some restrictions single out mobile homes by name, others may restrict them indirectly by prohibiting any housing unit containing less than a prescribed area of living space.

Currently, mobile homes represent 20 to 25 percent of all housing units built each year. Mobile-home financing is similar to automobile financing. However, loan terms are generally longer for mobile homes, running 10 to 12 years. Such loans are generally secured by a lien on the mobile home's title registered with the state licensing agency. Mobile-home loans may be underwritten by either the VA or FHA.

MOBILE-HOME PARK   An area zoned and set up to accommodate mobile homes and provide water hookups and sewage disposal for each home. Mobile-home parks are also called *trailer parks*.

MODEL HOME   A house built as part of a land-development program to demonstrate style, construction, and possible furnishings of similar houses to be erected and sold. A model home is also known as a *demonstration home* or a spec home. It is an excellent selling aid if properly handled, and is often sold with some of the furnishings after it has served its purpose. The first house completed in the development may be used as the model and is generally the last to be sold.

MODULAR HOUSING   A relatively recent concept in building homes which aims at producing housing at a cheaper and faster rate through prefabricating processes; also called prefabricated housing. Modular methods expedite construction because the house itself can be built in the factory while the building site is being prepared. This often eliminates costly delays.

Some courts have held that the sale of an unattached modular home is the sale of personal property and thus no written listing nor real estate license is required to earn a commission.

MODULE   A common dimensional element that influences the placement of window mullions, ceiling tiles, light fixtures, columns, electrical distribution systems, partitions, and like things. The module selected may greatly enhance the flexibility of office design.

MOLD   The cornice; wood molding applied to cover the junction of roof boards and outside wall. On the interior, the picture mold is placed where a wall joins a ceiling.

MONEY MARKET FUND   A form of mutual fund that trades primarily in short-term debt obligations, such as certificates of deposits (CD's), commercial paper, Treasury bills, and other U.S. government securities. (See *DISINTERMEDIATION.*)

MONTH-TO-MONTH TENANCY   A periodic tenancy where the tenant rents for one period at a time. In the absence of a rental agreement (oral or written), a tenancy is generally considered to be month-to-month or, in the case of boarders, week-to-week. Under such a tenancy, the estate continues for an indefinite period of time until either lessor or lessee gives the statutory notice of termination. This notice, as outlined by the various state statutes, must generally be given at least one rental period before termination. In other words, if the rent is due each month, one month's notice must be given; if the rent is due each week, one week's notice must be given, and so forth. In some states the required notice can be given at any time during the month.

A month-to-month tenancy may be created when a tenant holds over after his or her lease term expires. When no new lease agreement has been made, the landlord may either evict the tenant if he or she chooses, or acquiesce in the holdover tenancy. Acceptance of rent is usually considered conclusive proof of the landlord's acquiescence. The courts customarily rule that tenants holding over will do so for a term equal to the term of the original lease, providing the period is for one year or less. Some courts have ruled that a holdover tenancy will never exist for longer than one year. If the original lease, then, was for six months and the tenancy is held over, the courts usually consider that the holdover is for a like period, that is, six months. However, if the original lease was for five years, the holdover tenancy would not exceed one year (the Statute of Frauds period). Some written leases stipulate that in the absence of a renewal agreement a tenant who holds over does so as a month-to-month tenant. This is usually a valid agreement. (See *LEASE, PERIODIC TENANCY, RENT.*)

MONUMENT   A visible marker, either a natural or artificial object, set by the government or surveyors, which is used to establish the lines and boundaries of a survey. Monuments include artificial immovables like stakes, iron pins or posts, and metal or stone markers, as well as natural objects, like marked trees, streams, and rivers. A possible problem with natural monuments is the fact that they sometimes move from their original locations. An example of an intangible monument would be the corner of a section in a government survey system. While not visibly identifiable, it can still be accurately located by survey. The use of monuments is essential to the accuracy of a metes and bounds description. A metes and bounds description commences with a point of beginning at a monument such as an iron pin or the intersection of two streets.

In a contested issue as to who owns a particular property, monuments prevail in the event that courses or distances, as set forth in a metes and bounds description in deeds or other documents, show otherwise. (See *METES AND BOUNDS.*)

MORAL TURPITUDE   An act of baseness, vileness, or depravity in private social duties, that is, duties which one owes to a fellow person or to society generally; contrary to the accepted customary rule of right and duty between persons; conduct contrary to justice, honesty, modesty, or good morals. For example, embezzlement, perjury, robbery, and crimes of larceny are generally moral turpitude, whereas failure to pay income tax, speeding, or possession of small amounts of marijuana probably are not. Felonies are crimes of moral turpitude.

Note that the states' licensing authorities may not issue a license to any person who has been convicted of a crime involving moral turpitude unless the person has received a full and free pardon or presents satisfactory proof to the authorities that he or she has lived an upright and moral life for a certain period of time. (*See FELONY.*)

MORATORIUM   A temporary suspension of payments due under a financing agreement in order to help a distressed borrower recover and avoid a default and foreclosure. A moratorium also refers to a temporary suspension of issuing building permits pending governmental study of more restrictive zoning controls. This may happen especially with regard to shoreline development and no-growth policies and is sometimes called "zoning freeze."

MORE OR LESS   As used in the description of real property, this phrase indicates that the dimension or size is approximate. Any slight variation from the true size will have no effect on the enforceability of the contract. But a material or gross discrepancy could justify a rescission of the contract. Some courts have ruled that the "more or less" phrase indicates a sale in gross as opposed to a sale by acre. (*See SALE BY THE ACRE.*)

MORTGAGE   A legal document used to secure the performance of an obligation. The term mortgage is derived from the French words *mort* meaning "dead" and *gage* meaning "pledge." The word well expresses the meaning since the pledge is extinguished when payment of the debt is made. In the usual real estate transaction, the buyer of real estate needs or wants to borrow money to pay the seller the difference between the down payment and the purchase price. When the lender (mortgagee) loans the money, the buyer/borrower (mortgagor) is required to sign a promissory note for the amount borrowed and execute a mortgage to secure the debt. The purpose of the mortgage note is to create a personal liability for payment on the part of the mortgagor; the purpose of the mortgage is to create a lien on the mortgaged property as security for the debt. The note and the mortgage may appear in the same document, though it is customary to have separate instruments. For there to be a valid mortgage there must be both a debt and a pledge. The mortgage follows the debt and acts as security for the life of the debt. When the debt is satisfied or becomes unenforceable, for example when the statute of limitations expires, the mortgage is no longer effective security. The mortgage document is frequently lengthy and contains many clauses such as provisions for acceleration, subordination, release schedule, defeasance, and waivers. Also included are covenants to pay taxes, to keep the premises in repair, and to maintain adequate insurance.

Most mortgages contain an assignment-of-rents clause which allows the lender to collect rents in the event of default if the borrower continues to collect rental income from the property without paying on the note.

If the mortgagor fails to pay taxes, insurance premiums, and so on, the mortgagee can advance these costs and add the amount to the mortgage debt. Such advances usually bear the same interest rate as the original obligation. Note that some mortgages only refer to a "note of even date," that is, a mortgage in which the rate and terms are specified only in the mortgage note and not in the mortgage document. This is to prevent the practice of "raiding," in which mortgage brokers search the records to find clients for refinancing at currently more attractive interest rates.

In effect, the mortgage provides that the lender can depend on possessing the property in the event that the borrower defaults in payment of the note. Although not always the case, the mortgaged property is *usually* the property that the borrower purchases with the loan proceeds; called a purchase money mortgage. Therefore, the lender (mortgagee), upon default by the borrower (mortgagor), can bring foreclosure proceedings to sell the property and retain that part of the proceeds representing the monies still due on the note. If the proceeds of the sale are less than the amount owed, the mortgagee, in most states, would obtain a deficiency judgment against the mortgagor for the difference.

The rules of contract law apply to mortgages. The mortgage must be in writing, name the parties (who must be competent to contract), legally describe the mortgaged property, state a consideration, contain a mortgaging clause, state the debt, and be signed by the borrower (mortgagor). In addition, the mortgagor should state his or her marital status and, if a married man, his wife should also sign the mortgage because of her marital rights in the property. In addition, regardless of sex, a spouse should always sign because of his or her homestead rights in the property. The mortgage is usually acknowledged and then recorded, with the priority of the lien determined by the date of recordation. The rationale behind recording the mortgage is that the mortgage creates rights and interest in real property. The mortgage note, however, need not be recorded because it represents only a personal obligation. The number of signatures on the note does not have to conform to the number of persons signing the mortgage.

Sometimes a mortgage may appear to be a deed. One test of whether an instrument is a deed or a mortgage is whether the relation of the parties to each other as debtor and creditor continues.

Some states recognize the mortgagee as the owner of the mortgaged property, subject to defeat upon full payment of the debt or performance of the obligation. Such states recognize the mortgage document as a conveyance of property, and are called title-theory states. Those states that interpret the mortgage purely as a lien on real property are called lien-theory states.

Under the lien theory, the mortgagee is required to foreclose, offer the property for sale, and apply the funds received from the sale to reduce the debt. As protection to the mortgagor, some state laws give the mortgagor a statutory period within which to redeem after the foreclosure sale. Regardless of whether a state follows the title or lien theory of mortgages, the security interest of the mortgagee in the land is legally classified as personal property and can only be transferred with the transfer of the debt which the mortgage secures.

When property is sold, the existing mortgages may be assumed, made subject to (unless restricted by a due-on-sale clause), or paid off. When paid in full, the mortgagor should be sure to have the note returned "cancelled" and to record a *satisfaction of mortgage* or release of mortgage as notice that the mortgage is no longer a lien on the property.

The 1980s will use a variety of types of mortgages such as the adjustable mortgage loan, the graduated payment mortgage, the wraparound mortgage, the shared appreciation mortgage, the flexible loan insurance plan, and the buydown mortgage, among many others.

There are many types of mortgages which are discussed under their individual headings, such as blanket mortgages, budget mortgages, open-end mortgages, package mortgages, participation mortgages, and purchase-money mortgages. (*See ACCELERATION CLAUSE, CERTIFICATE OF NO DEFENSE, DEED OF TRUST, DEFEASANCE CLAUSE, DEFICIENCY JUDGMENT, FORECLOSURE, MARGINAL RELEASE, MORTGAGE LIEN, PROMISSORY NOTE, REDEMPTION PERIOD, SATISFACTION OF MORTGAGE, SUBORDINATION CLAUSE, WAIVER.*)

MORTGAGE-BACKED SECURITY   Securities that are secured by pools of mortgages and are used to channel funds from securities markets to housing markets. Ginnie Mae has a popular MBS program recognized for its low risk and high yield. The Ginnie Mae MBS security is a pool of VA and FHA mortgages put together as a bond. Freddie Mac and Fannie Mae also have MBS programs. (*See PARTICIPATION SALE CERTIFICATE.*)

MORTGAGE BANKER   A person, corporation, or firm not otherwise in banking and finance which normally provides its own funds for mortgage financing as opposed to savings and loan associations or commercial banks that use other people's money—namely that of their depositors—to originate mortgage loans. Although some mortgage bankers do supply permanent long-term financing, the majority of mortgage bankers specialize in supplying short-term and interim financing, either through their own resources or by borrowing from commercial sources. It is said that what a mortgage banker lends, it must sell.

The activities of mortgage bankers have been greatly expanded due to the development of the mortgage correspondent system. Under this system, a mortgage banker or mortgage banking company will seek to originate a great number of loan transactions and then sell these mortgages at a discount to large investors, such as insurance companies, commercial banks, and retirement and pension funds. Mortgage bankers are also a major source of construction loans and are very active in lending money on commercial real estate such as shopping centers and office buildings.

Most of the funding for mortgage banking is from the secondary mortgage market. A typical mortgage banking arrangement not involving the secondary market would be set up as follows:

1. A local mortgage banker negotiates a commitment with a savings and loan association in New York to sell $5 million of loans within a certain time.

2. Loans are made to individuals.

3. The local mortgage banker services the loans for the association.

4. The loans are sold to the New York investor under the terms of the previously arranged commitment.

In addition, these loan administrators are specialists in originating FHA and VA loans in areas where mortgage money is tight. They will generally sell such mortgages for an origination fee to financial institutions in other parts of the country where funds are not as tight. Typically, then, they are not the ultimate lenders in the mortgage transactions. The mortgage banker's objective is ultimately to sell the loan in the secondary mortgage market at a profit, while personally underwriting the risk. This is in contrast to the mortgage broker who will not act without the principal's consent. The mortgage banker normally remains in the picture and services the underlying mortgage for major investor clients. Such services include collecting monthly payments, disbursing the funds to pay taxes and property insurance, supervising the loan, preventing any delinquencies, and taking proper remedial action in the event of delinquency. (*See LOAN CORRESPONDENT, ORIGINATION FEE, SERVICING, WAREHOUSING.*)

MORTGAGE BROKER   A person or firm which acts as an intermediary between borrower and lender; one who, for compensation or gain, negotiates, sells, or arranges loans and sometimes continues to service the loans; also called a loan broker. Loans originated by the mortgage broker are closed in the lender's name, and are usually serviced by the lender. This is opposed to mortgage bankers, who not only close loans in their own names, but continue to service them as well. Many mortgage brokers are also licensed as real estate brokers and provide these financing services as supplements to their realty services.

MORTGAGE DISCOUNT   *See DISCOUNT POINTS, POINTS.*

MORTGAGEE   In a mortgage transaction, the one who receives and holds a mortgage as security for a debt; the lender; a lender or creditor who holds a mortgage as security for payment of an obligation.

MORTGAGE GUARANTY INSURANCE CORPORATION (MGIC)   An independent insurance corporation that will insure the top 5 to 20 percent of the principal of loans made by approved lenders to qualified borrowers. When regulations limit a lending institution's mortgage loans to definite percentage of appraised value (80 percent, for example), it is possible to obtain a larger loan with an MGIC (or, as it is sometimes called, MAGIC) guarantee without violating those regulations. There are several coverage plans available depending upon the ratio of the loan to the appraised value. For example, if a residence is appraised at $40,000, and a qualified purchaser wishes to make a cash payment of only $4,000, he or she will need 90 percent conventional mortgage loan of $36,000. Even though the lender's limit is 80 percent, this loan may be obtained with an MGIC guarantee under one of the following plans:

1. The borrower must pay a one-time insurance charge at the time of closing, with the exact percentage of the charge determined by the number of years it will take to reduce the loan balance to 80 percent of the appraised value.

2. The borrower must pay an initial charge of ½ of 1 percent of the loan, $180, at the time of closing, and ¼ of 1 percent of the remaining loan balance must be paid annually until the outstanding mortgage debt is reduced to 80 percent of property value.

In addition, the borrower is charged a $20 appraisal fee with either payment plan if the amount of the loan is 80 percent or more of the appraised value.

In consideration of either of these plans, MGIC guarantees, at its option, either to take possession of a foreclosed property and pay the insured lender the outstanding debt, including defaulted interest and foreclosure costs, or to pay the insured percentage of this amount without taking possession of the property. In many cases MGIC chooses the latter alternative, thus avoiding the problems associated with maintenance and resale of the property. (*See MAGGIE MAE, PRIVATE MORTGAGE INSURANCE.*)

MORTGAGE INSURANCE   A kind of insurance plan which will pay off the mortgage balance in the event of the death or, in some plans, disability of the insured mortgagor. In essence, mortgage insurance is decreasing-term life insurance. The premiums are paid with the regular monthly mortgage payment. Protection for a $40,000 policy over a 25-year loan period for a 35-year-old mortgagor would, for example, cost approximately $19.00 per month.

MORTGAGE LIEN   A lien or charge on the property of a mortgagor, which secures the underlying debt obligation. The mortgage lien is a voluntary lien created by the property owner, as opposed to the tax lien, which is an involuntary lien imposed by law. As with other liens affecting real property, the mortgage lien receives its priority through recording. Until recorded, the mortgage generally operates only as a contract between the parties and creates no lien affecting any recorded mortgage or lease. Regardless of whether a recorded mortgage is entitled "first mortgage," "second mortgage," or "third mortgage," it has priority over all subsequently recorded mortgages or other liens, unless it is subordinated to such subsequent liens. As with all liens, a mortgage lien becomes junior to any state real estate tax liens or liens for special assessments. The mortgage lien does not affect property which is registered in Torrens until such time as the mortgage itself is registered with the registrar of titles and noted on the certificate of title.

Sometimes a mortgage is intended to secure future advances which the mortgagee (the lender) may make to the mortgagor (the borrower), as in a construction loan, when obligatory progress payments are made as various stages in the construction are completed. Such future advances would be superior in priority to mortgages or other liens taking effect between the date of recording of the mortgage and the future advance, only where the future advance relates to the same transaction or series of transactions and the mortgage specifically refers to this particular advance as being secured by the previously recorded liens. (*See ANACONDA MORTGAGE, FUTURE ADVANCES, LIEN, RECORDING, SUBORDINATION AGREEMENT.*)

MORTGAGE SPREADING AGREEMENT   A contract that extends a prior mortgage lien to properties not previously covered. This gives added security to the lender and is often used when the mortgagor seeks additional financing.

MORTGAGE SUBSIDIES   A method of financing where a home builder permits a new home purchaser to occupy the new home for a period of time (e.g., six months) without monthly payments. The money saved goes towards a down payment, into a savings account to act as a reserve to help make the monthly payments after permanent financing is in place or to be a fund to buy down the interest rate of permanent financing. A builder may offer a lowered monthly payment, or subsidy, for a certain period of months. (*See BUYDOWN, CREATIVE FINANCING.*)

MORTGAGOR   The one who gives a mortgage as security for a debt; the borrower; usually the landowner, though it could be the owner of a leasehold estate; the borrower or debtor who hypothecates or puts up his or her property as security for an obligation. (*See HYPOTHECATE.*)

MOST FAVORED TENANT CLAUSE   A provision in a lease which assures a tenant that any negotiating concessions given to other tenants will also be given this tenant. Such a clause is especially helpful in the early stages of renting a building, since the tenant is assured that later tenants will not get better concessions.

MOTEL   A structure designed to provide convenient rental quarters for transients. Motels sometimes have common facilities for guests such as dining rooms, meeting rooms, pools, or lounges.

MUD ROOM   A vestibule or small room used as the entrance from a play yard or alley. The mud room frequently contains a washer and dryer.

MULLION   Thin vertical strips inside the window sash that divide the window glass into panes.

MULTIPLE ASSET EXCHANGE   An exchange of property for income tax purposes, usually involving two businesses, in which the values of many related assets—land, buildings, machinery, good will—are added together to reach a composite figure on which to compute the exchange.

Even if the individual component values differ in a multiple asset exchange, income tax on any gain realized from the transaction can be deferred if the composite values are the same. For example, Company A exchanges all of its operating assets for like-kind assets of Company B. The following breakdown of each company's assets occurs:

	Company A	Company B
Land	$150,000	$100,000
Buildings	175,000	200,000
Machinery	75,000	50,000
Goodwill	50,000	100,000

Traded on an asset-by-asset basis, Company A would be taxed on boot valued at $75,000—the $25,000 difference in the building values, plus the $50,000 difference in good will values. However, classified as a multiple asset exchange, both composite values are the same and no boot is involved. Note that multiple asset exchanges are generally complicated and are subject to many tax laws and rulings too detailed and specific for this discussion. (*See BOOT, EXCHANGE.*)

MULTIPLE DWELLING A tenement house. Any structure used for the accommodation of two or more families or households in separate living units. An apartment house.

MULTIPLE LISTING A listing agreement used by a broker who is a member of a multiple-listing organization. The multiple-listing agreement is, in effect, an exclusive right to sell with an additional authority and obligation on the part of the listing broker to distribute the listing to other brokers making up the multiple-listing organization. These listings are then distributed in an MLS periodic publication. The contractual obligations between the member brokers of a multiple-listing organization vary widely. Most provide that upon the sale of the property the commission is divided between the listing broker and the selling broker. The terms for division of the commission can vary from broker to broker. As a general rule, the participating brokers act as subagents on behalf of the seller.

In recent years, the multiple-listing service has come under close scrutiny by consumer groups and justice departments for alleged antitrust practices.

Under most multiple-listing contracts, the broker securing the listing is not only authorized, but is usually obligated to turn the listing over to a multiple-listing organization within a definite period of time so that it can be distributed to the other member brokers. The length of time the listing broker has to offer the property exclusively, without notifying the other member brokers, varies widely.

There is an advantage to both the broker and the seller in multiple listing. The broker develops a sizable inventory of properties to sell and to be sold and is assured of a portion of the commission if he or she lists the property or participates in the sale. The seller also gains under this form of listing agreement since all members of the multiple-listing organization are offering this property to prospective buyers. (*See CONTINGENCY LISTING, COOPERATING BROKER, LISTING, OFFICE EXCLUSIVE, POCKET LISTING, SUBAGENT.*)

MUNICIPAL ORDINANCE Enactments by the governing body of a municipality, such as building codes, traffic laws, and zoning regulations.

MUNIMENT OF TITLE A legal document evidencing title to real property, such as a deed or contract, which is proof of ownership and enables an owner to defend his or her title. An applicant, in order to register property in the Torrens system, must file with his or her application a file plan, an abstract of title, and all original muniments of title within his or her control mentioned in the schedule of documents.

MUNTIN The narrow vertical strip that separates two adjacent window sashes.

MUTUAL MORTGAGE INSURANCE FUND One of four FHA insurance funds into which all insurance premiums and other specified FHA revenues are paid, and from which any losses are met.

MUTUALITY OF CONSENT

A meeting of the minds; a mutual assent of the parties to the formation of the contract.

MUTUAL SAVINGS BANKS

Savings institutions which issue no stock and are mutually owned by their investors. These institutions operate similarly to savings and loan associations, and are located primarily in the northeastern section of the United States (now numbering about 500 institutions).

Although mutual savings banks do offer limited checking account privileges, they are primarily savings institutions and are highly active in the mortgage market. They invest in loans secured by income property, as well as residential real estate. In addition, since mutual savings banks usually seek low-risk loan investments, they prefer FHA-insured or VA-guaranteed mortgages.

MUTUAL WATER COMPANY

A water company organized by or for water users in a given district with the object of securing an ample water supply at a reasonable rate. Stock is purchased by and issued to users.

n

N² An abbreviation of "north one-half", often used in the government survey method of land description.

NAME, CHANGE OF Use of a new name. A person may change his or her name merely by using another name with the intention to make that his or her legal name, as long as the change is not done to defraud anyone. However, because of all the identification problems which may arise, most parties desiring to change their name go through a formal name change. This is a relatively simple procedure which usually involves filing a petition with the proper state authorities. People wishing to change their names may also be required to publish the change of name in the newspaper for a required period of time.

A name change can also be embodied in a divorce decree permitting the married woman to resume the use of her maiden name, or the name of a former husband. When people do change their names, they should be sure that their new name is properly noted at the registrar of titles if they own registered property, and at the recorder's office if they own any other recorded properties.

If a person uses one name as a grantee of property and then grants the same property under another name, there will be a potential defect in the recorded title. When the second deed is recorded, then, it will not be recorded in the proper chain of title and therefore will not give constructive notice to the world of its contents. For example, if Patty Lee, a single woman receiving title as such and later changing her name through marriage, should convey title as Patty Wilson, there would be a defect in the record title. Patty Lee should convey title as "Patty Wilson, formerly known as Patty Lee." An appropriate entry would therefore be made in the grantor-grantee index so a title company searching the title would be able to see that the new deed was derived from the chain of title in which Patty Lee was the grantee.

It is helpful to title searchers for a married woman to continue to use the name given her by her parents. For instance, Patty Ann Lee would become Mrs. Patty Ann Wilson or Mrs. Patty Lee Wilson and not Mrs. Robert Wilson. (*See LEGAL NAME.*)

NAME, FICTITIOUS *See FICTITIOUS COMPANY NAME.*

NAME, RESERVATION OF The exclusive right to the use of a trade name or a corporate name. This right may be reserved by any person intending to organize a corporation or change the name of an existing corporation. Reservation of a name is usually made by filing an application with the proper state authorities and paying the appropriate fee.

The National Association of Realtors® has zealously protected the exclusive use of its trade name, "REALTOR®."

NARRATIVE REPORT A complete appraisal report in which the appraiser presents all information pertinent to the property and the market for the property. The report is quite lengthy compared to the short form or check report and the letter report. (See LETTER REPORT.)

NATIONAL ASSOCIATION OF REAL ESTATE BROKERS See REALTIST.

NATIONAL ASSOCIATION OF REAL ESTATE LICENSING LAW OFFICIALS (NARELLO) NARELLO serves as a clearing house of real estate information and statistical data for its members. It consists of both real estate commissioners and real estate administrators. Members come from all 50 states, three Canadian provinces, Guam, Puerto Rico, and the Virgin Islands. A joint committee of NARELLO and the National Association of Realtors® has drafted several model license laws since the early 1960s. Many of the recommendations have since been adopted by the various states.

NATIONAL ASSOCIATION OF REALTORS® (NAR) Formerly known as the National Association of Real Estate Boards (NAREB), it is the largest and most prestigious real estate organization in the world. NAR has over 700,000 members, and includes Realtors® and Realtor-Associates® representing all branches of the real estate industry. The national organization functions through local boards and state associations. Active brokers who have been admitted to membership in state and local NAR boards are allowed to use the trademark REALTOR®. Salespeople are admitted on a Realtor-Associate® active status. Members of NAR subscribe to a strict code of ethics. (See CODE OF ETHICS, REALTOR®.)

The national professional organizations directly affiliated with the National Association of Realtors® are the Realtors National Marketing Institute (formerly known as the National Institute of Real Estate Brokers, NIREB), the Society of Industrial Realtors, the Institute of Real Estate Management, the Farm and Land Institute, the American Institute of Real Estate Appraisers, Real Estate Securities and Syndication Institute, the American Society of Real Estate Counselors, the Women's Council of Realtors, and the American Chapter of the International Real Estate Federation.

NATIONAL HOUSING PARTNERSHIP A private, profit-making company, in conjunction with its sole and general partner and administrative arm, the National Corporation for Housing Partnership, which specializes in housing for low- to moderate-income families, the handicapped, and the elderly. It has some 350 multifamily projects in the United States.

NATURAL   A phrase describing that feeling presumed to exist
AFFECTION   between close relatives such as father and son
                     and husband and wife. In contract law, such af-
fection is regarded as "good consideration" as opposed to "valuable consideration." To support a promise in a contract and make the contract enforceable, however, there must be a valuable consideration. (See CONSIDERATION, GIFT
DEED.)

NATURAL PERSON   An individual; a private person, as distinguished
                        from an artificial entity such as a corporation or
                        partnership.

NAVIGABLE WATERS   A body of water, either salt or fresh, capable of
                          carrying a commercial vessel, and large enough to
ebb and flow (a "highway for commerce"). The U.S. Army Corps of Engineers has
jurisdiction over navigable waters. With non-navigable waters, the bordering landowners have what are called riparian rights. (See RIPARIAN.)

NEGATIVE   A financing arrangement in which the monthly
AMORTIZATION   payments are less than the true amortized
                      amounts and the loan balance increases over the
term of the loan rather than decreases. In some cases, such difference is added
back to the loan and payable at maturity. For example, amortized payments for
the first six months of a 30-year adjustable mortgage loan would be based on a 13
percent rate, but interest would be charged against equity at 18 percent and such
interest rate charged would fluctuate every six-month period. In some loans, the
negative amounts may be made up by applying such deficits against the borrower's down payment equity.

NEGATIVE   A situation in which cash expenditures to main-
CASH FLOW   tain an investment (taxes, mortgage payments,
                      maintenance) exceed the cash income received
from the investment. For example, an investor in a $70,000 condominium apart-
ment pays $10,000 down and finances the balance through a contract for deed
which provides that he or she pay the $60,000 in $600 monthly payments (all
expenses included). The apartment rents for only $400 a month. In this case the
owner would have an out-of-pocket monthly loss of $200. Stated another way, this
owner has a $200 negative cash flow. The reason some investors will voluntarily
purchase a real estate investment that operates on a negative-cash-flow basis is
that they expect that the favorable yield on their investment will come in the form
of appreciated value upon the sale of the property. (See TAX SHELTER.)

NEGATIVE   An easement, such as a building restriction or a
EASEMENT   view easement, which has the effect of preventing
                      the servient landowner from doing an act other-
                      wise permitted.

NEGOTIABLE   Any *written* instrument which may be transferred
INSTRUMENT   by endorsement or delivery so as to vest legal title
                      in the transferee. Common examples of negotiable
instruments are checks, publicly traded stocks, and promissory notes. Negotiability, here, is the quality that allows negotiable instruments to circulate as money

does. To be negotiable, a promissory note, for example, must be an unconditional promise, made in writing by one person to another and signed by the maker engaging him or her to pay on demand, or at a fixed or determinable time, a certain sum of money *to order or to bearer*. It is essential to use words of negotiability such as "pay to Bob Reninski," or "order," or "bearer." Note that only the person (or persons) whose name appears on the instrument is liable for it. Thus, a principal is not liable unless his or her name appears on the instrument.

One who takes a negotiable instrument in good faith, for a valuable consideration and without notice of any defect, is a *holder in due course*, against whom the maker of the note cannot assert personal defenses (such as lack of consideration) in order to refuse payment.

Under the Uniform Commercial Code, a transferor implies certain warranties concerning the negotiable instrument, such as: that it is genuine and is what it purports to be; that the transferor has good title; that all involved parties have the capacity to contract; and that the transferor does not know of any fact that would impair the validity of the contract or make it valueless. (*See ENDORSEMENT, HOLDER IN DUE COURSE, UNIFORM COMMERCIAL CODE.*)

NEGOTIATION   The transaction of business aimed at reaching a meeting of the minds among the parties; bargaining. A real estate sale illustrates the negotiation process. Often the first offer received for property is considered to be merely an intention to deal. Thereafter a series of counteroffers follow, leading up to the consummation of the transaction. Usually, however, negotiation takes place only if the broker's efforts have proceeded to the point where the prospect would be considered a likely purchaser.

Most listing forms contain a safety clause, also called an *extendor* or *override clause*, allowing the broker to recover his or her commission for a specified period of time after the termination of the listing if the listed property is sold to anyone with whom the broker was negotiating prior to the time the listing ended. This applies provided that the broker has registered the names of such persons with the seller at the time the listing ended. In this regard, negotiation means more than putting the parties in touch; it means actually transacting business, bargaining, and arousing interest to effect a purchase and sale.

In commercial lease situations, concessions (such as temporary free rent) are negotiable points in the lease terms that are decided in the prospective tenant's favor.

Real estate commission rates are not fixed by law but are the subject of negotiation between the parties. (*See PROCURING CAUSE.*)

NEIGHBORHOOD   Contiguous areas showing common characteristics of population and homogeneity of land use.

NEIGHBORHOOD SHOPPING CENTER   A group of retail buildings, usually 10 to 30, providing a limited variety of convenience stores (barber shop, dry cleaning), and having common parking and management.

NET AFTER TAXES   The net operating income after all charges, including federal and state income taxes, have been deducted.

NET INCOME The sum arrived at after deducting from gross income the expenses of a business or investment, including taxes, insurance, and allowances for vacancy and bad debts. Net income is what the property will earn in a given year's operation. It is generally calculated before accounting for depreciation.

NET LEASE A lease, usually commercial, in which the lessee not only pays the rent for occupancy, but also pays maintenance and operating expenses such as taxes, insurance, utilities, and repairs. The rent paid is "net" to the lessor. This kind of lease is popular with investors who want to obtain a steady stream of income without having to handle the problems associated with management and maintenance. Commercial or industrial leases, ground leases, and long-term leases are typically net leases.)

Because the common interpretations given to the term "net lease" are so broad, it is essential to review the lease document to determine what expenses the tenant is to pay. In the true net lease the tenant is responsible for expenses relating to the premises exactly as if the tenant were the owner. Examples of such expenses are real estate taxes; special assessments; insurance premiums; all maintenance charges, including labor and materials; cost of compliance with governmental health and safety regulations; payment of claims for personal injury or property damage; and even costs of structural, interior, roof, and other repairs.

It is helpful to distinguish between the net rent, called "base rent," and the total of base rent and expenses, called "effective rent." (*See GROSS LEASE, PERCENTAGE LEASE, TRIPLE NET LEASE.*)

NET LISTING An employment contract in which the broker receives, as his or her commission, all excess monies over and above the minimum sales price agreed upon by broker and seller. Because of the danger of unethical practices in such a listing, its use is discouraged in most states. In some states, such as Massachusetts and New York, a net listing is illegal. (*See LISTING.*)

NET OPERATING INCOME (NOI) The balance remaining after deduction against the gross rental receipts for all fixed and operating expenses but before deducting any debt service.

NETTING OUT A slang expression that describes the amount of money the seller wants to receive on a sale of property; the amount that can be put in the seller's pocket after expenses and payment of liens. The broker's commission, however, is typically calculated on the gross sales price, not the seller's net price.

NET USABLE ACRE That portion of a property which is suitable for building. A 20-acre parcel may have 20 gross acres and only 15 net usable or buildable acres. Density requirements under local zoning regulations are often based on the net usable acreage of the property.

NET WORTH The value remaining after deducting liabilities from assets. Many private real estate syndicates establish their own suitability standards for prospective investors. They often require, for instance, that the investor be in the 50 percent federal income tax bracket and maintain a net worth of at least $75,000 or more.

The law sometimes requires a corporation to have a certain minimum net worth before it can manage the funds of others. For example, in real estate syndications, each corporate general partner must have and maintain a fair market value net worth (without considering its interest in the partnership) equal to the lesser of $250,000 or 15 percent of the amount invested by the limited partners if the amount invested is $2,500,000 or less. The "safe harbor" rule also provides that the corporate partner must maintain a fair market net worth equal to 10 percent of the amount invested if that amount exceeds $2,500,000. If a general partner of a partnership does not maintain this minimum net worth the Internal Revenue Service will not give a favorable written ruling that this partnership be treated as a partnership, rather than an association taxable as a corporation. When a limited partner joins a partnership and cannot ascertain if the partnership will be taxed as an association or as a partnership, he or she is taking a substantial risk. Most general partners, therefore, try to comply with the safe harbor rule. (*See LIMITED PARTNERSHIP, SAFE HARBOR RULE.*)

NET YIELD That portion of gross yield which remains after all costs, such as loan servicing and reserves, are deducted.

NEW TOWN A modern concept of urban planning characterized by a development which offers a complete range of services including housing, recreation, schools, and churches as well as a thoroughly planned and controlled balance of land uses. The New Town is usually a new municipality built in a previously undeveloped area close to an existing municipality, such as Foster City in California or Reston in Virginia. It is intended to be self-governing and relatively self-contained.

The "New Town in town" is a concept for a new town located within a city area, such as in an urban renewal clearance area. A prime example is Roosevelt Island, linked to New York City by a five-minute aerial tramway ride.

"NO ACTION" LETTER A written opinion from the staff of the Securities and Exchange Commission (SEC). "No action" letters cover many items including informing an applicant that the SEC will not require, based on the facts presented in the request for opinion, that a proposed project be registered as a security. If a project is classified as a security, it is subject to various complicated restrictions and regulations. It is advantageous, then, for project developers to avoid being considered a security in order to avoid these regulations. A developer of a proposed resort condominium may seek an interpretation from the SEC that its project does not involve the offering of a real estate security. The developer will do this in the form of a request for a "no action" letter in accordance with the procedure set forth in regulations under the Securities Act of 1933. A developer might also request a "no action" letter to certify that its project is exempt from registration under the federal interstate land sales subdivision regulations. (*See REAL PROPERTY SECURITIES REGISTRATION.*)

**"NO DEAL,
NO COMMISSION"
CLAUSE**   A clause inserted in a listing contract which stipulates that a commission is to be paid *only if and when title passes*. This nullifies the generally accepted principle that a broker earns a commission when the broker has brought an acceptable "ready, willing, and able" buyer to the seller for the price and under the terms specified in the listing agreement.

**NOMINAL
CONSIDERATION**   A consideration bearing no relation to the real value of a contract used so as not to reveal the true value of the property being conveyed. Consideration in name only, and not having any relation to actual market value. A deed often recites a nominal consideration, such as "ten dollars and other valuable consideration," rather than the full selling price. Such nominal consideration makes it clear that the grantee is a purchaser rather than a donee (receiver of a gift) and thus is protected under the state's recording act as a subsequent good faith purchaser.

A broker must not be a party to the naming of a false consideration in any document, unless it is the naming of an obviously nominal consideration. To do so would not only violate the Realtors® Code of Ethics but would generally be cause for suspension or revocation of the broker's license. (*See DUAL CONTRACT, RECORDING.*)

**NOMINAL INTEREST
RATE**   The stated interest rate in a note or contract, which may differ from the true or effective interest rate, especially if the lender discounts the loan and advances less than the full amount. (*See EFFECTIVE INTEREST RATE.*)

NOMINEE   One designated to act for another as a representative in a limited sense. A nominee corporation is sometimes used to purchase real property where the principals do not wish to be known. Care should be taken in structuring a purchase through the nominee corporation so that there are no adverse tax consequences, such as double taxation to the nominee corporation and then to the shareholders.

The term nominee is not a synonym for assignee. Especially if the purchase is based on seller carryback financing, the real buyer may not be able to get specific performance of the sales contract to the nominee on the grounds that there is no real mutuality of agreement and by reason of indefiniteness.

The nominee form is often used by a real estate syndicator who is the buyer but not the ultimate purchaser. It is also used in a Section 1031 tax-free exchange situation for acquiring the replacement property.

Nominee status is simply a name substitution—no legal rights are transferred. On the other hand, assignee status is a substitution of legal rights. Therefore, in most cases, the use of the word assignee rather than nominee will better achieve the parties' intended result of effectively transferring legal rights to the ultimate purchaser.

The offer should always identify the offeror; that is, neither the words "buyer or nominee" or "buyer or assignee" should be used in the deposit receipt portion of the offer. Otherwise, the named buyer could simply walk away from the deal and tell the seller to look to the nominee for recovery. Most courts would thus rule the contract illusory and unenforceable. (*See ASSIGNMENT.*)

NONCOMPETITION CLAUSE
A provision in a contract or lease prohibiting a person from operating or controlling a nearby business which would compete with one of the parties to the contract; also called a "no-compete" clause. The courts will enforce this kind of provision as long as it is reasonable as to time and location. In addition, if insertion of a noncompetition clause gives the contract added value, such value is generally considered as ordinary income to the benefited party. This value, then, is capitalized by the maker of the clause and amortized over the life of the covenant. Noncompetition clauses are frequently found in percentage leases for shopping centers where a shoe store tenant, for example, agrees not to establish a competing shoe store across the street. In recent years, such clauses have been given close scrutiny under federal and state antitrust laws.

NONCONFORMING USE
A permitted use of real property which was lawfully established and maintained at the time of its original contruction but which no longer conforms to the current zoning law. The nonconforming use might be the structure itself, the size of the lot, the use of the land, or the use of the structure. The use will eventually be eliminated, although the nonconforming use status does not necessarily have to be discontinued upon the sale or lease of the property. By allowing the use to continue for a reasonable time, the government can assure itself that the use will not continue indefinitely and, at the same time, avoid having to pay just compensation for taking the property through condemnation.

When purchasing a nonconforming structure, a buyer should be made aware that in case of substantial destruction by fire or otherwise, the zoning statutes may prohibit its reconstruction. In such a case, a buyer should discuss the possibilities of purchasing demolition insurance from an insurance agent. A nonconforming use can also terminate upon abandonment of the property. (*See VARIANCE.*)

NONDISCLOSURE
The failure to reveal a fact, with or without the intention to conceal it. (*See MISREPRESENTATION.*)

NONDISTURBANCE
1. A clause inserted in a mortgage which states that the mortgagee agrees not to terminate the tenancies of lessees who pay their rent in the event that the mortgagee forecloses on the mortgagor/lessor's building. Without such a clause, a lessee whose lease was signed subsequent to the mortgage could have his or her lease terminated by a foreclosure action. (*See ATTORNMENT.*) 2. When a seller chooses to keep mineral rights to conveyed property, a nondisturbance agreement is made between seller and buyer to the effect that the seller will not interfere with any building or development on the surface of the land itself.

NONJUDICIAL FORECLOSURE
The process of selling real property under a power of sale in a mortgage or deed of trust which is in default. (*See FORECLOSURE, POWER OF SALE.*)

NONPROFIT CORPORATIONS Corporations formed for a nonprofit purpose, such as a charity, or a political, fraternal, educational, or trade organization. These organizations are sometimes referred to as eleemosynary corporations. Such corporations do not have any shareholders as do profit-making corporations. They only have members who are not personally liable for debts of the corporation but who also have no right to dividends or to the assets of the corporation. These corporations' properties are controlled and their affairs are conducted by a board of directors. They may make contracts, and acquire and dispose of real or personal property in their own names. The special tax rules covering nonprofit corporations are found in IRC §501. (See *ELEEMOSYNARY CORPORATION.*)

NONRECOURSE LOAN A loan in which the borrower is not held personally liable on the note. The lender of a nonrecourse loan generally feels confident that the property used as collateral will be adequate security for the loan. Also called a dry mortgage. (See *DEFICIENCY JUDGMENT.*)

Nonrecourse financing is used in real estate syndications in order to enable the limited partners to add their proportionate share of the mortgage in their tax basis for the purpose of computing depreciation deductions or taking other losses in a real estate syndication.

NORMAL WEAR AND TEAR That physical deterioration which occurs with the normal use of a property, without negligence, carelessness, accident, or abuse of the premises, equipment, or chattels by the occupant, members of the occupant's household, or their guests. The tenant of residential property is not responsible for loss in value due to normal wear and tear. The landlord, then, cannot hold back the security deposit for such damage. As defined in the Uniform Residential Landlord and Tenant Act, normal wear and tear is deterioration or depreciation in value by ordinary and reasonable use. This specifically excludes, however, items which are missing from the dwelling unit. Normal wear and tear is a major cause of property depreciation, along with functional and economic obsolescence.

An important element in determining the reasonableness of a unit's wear and tear is the length of the tenant's residency. For instance, if an apartment has been inhabited by the same renter for three years, it may be reasonable to expect that the walls need to be painted and that the carpeting needs to be cleaned.

NOSING The rounded outer face of a stair tread.

NOTARY PUBLIC A public officer whose functions are to administer oaths; to attest and certify documents by his or her signature and official seal, giving them credit and authenticity; to take acknowledgments of deeds and other conveyances; and to perform certain official acts, such as protesting rates and bills; an official witness. In the absence of a seal, the notarization is void. One who has a beneficial interest in a document cannot act as a notary public to the same document. In some states the notary must post a fidelity bond. (See *ACKNOWLEDGMENT.*)

NOTE A document signed by the borrower of a loan, stating the loan amount, the interest rate, the time and method of repayment, and the obligation to repay. The note is the evidence of the debt. When secured by a mortgage, it is called a mortgage note and the mortgagee is named as the payee. In a trust deed, the note is usually made payable to the bearer or holder. The note may also contain some of the provisions as in the mortgage or trust deed document, such as prepayment or acceleration. (*See PROMISSORY NOTE.*)

NOTICE 1. Legal notice is notice which is required by law, or notice which is imparted by operation of law as a result of the possession of property or the recording of documents. When deeds are recorded, subsequent purchasers are thereby put on notice as to the contents of such documents. This is called *legal* or *constructive notice.* 2. Information which may be required by the terms of a contract. When two parties agree to terminate a lease, for example, written notice must be given by either party 30 days prior to its termination. Though notice can be oral, it is always advisable to give notice in writing, so that it is easy to prove that necessary notice was given. Such written notice should be personally served by the sheriff. Contracts frequently contain a standard paragraph covering the details of proper notice. For instance, "Notices, requests, or demand by either party shall be in writing and shall be given personally or by Registered or Certified Mail, postage prepaid, addressed to seller and buyer at the addresses set forth herein. Notice shall be deemed given, when mailed." (*See ACTUAL NOTICE, CONSTRUCTIVE NOTICE, INQUIRY NOTICE, NOTICE OF DEFAULT.*)

NOTICE OF ASSESSMENT A notice issued by the state or local taxing agency to the owner of real property specifying the assessed valuation of the property. For example, assume that the market value of a home is $70,000, of which $40,000 is allocated to the fee simple land and $30,000 to the improvements. The assessed value will be 70 percent of the fair market value. Thus, the assessed valuation for the improvement would be $21,000, and the assessed valuation of the land would be $28,000. (*See ASSESSED VALUATION, CONVEYANCE TAX, PROPERTY TAX.*)

NOTICE OF COMPLETION A document filed in some states to give public notice that a construction job has been completed and that mechanics' liens must be filed within a specified time to be valid. The owner or the general contractor may publish the notice of completion, though the notice generally may not be published by the contractor until after he or she has made a written demand upon the owner to publish and the owner has failed to publish.

If a mechanic does not file a notice of lien in writing in the office of the clerk of the appropriate court where the property is situated within the specified period, then lien rights will be waived. Note that recording or filing the notice of lien is generally not enough to create a lien. The lien must be recorded with the clerk of the appropriate circuit court and a hearing must be held to establish if there exists probable cause to enforce the lien. (*See MECHANIC'S LIEN, NOTICE OF LIEN.*)

NOTICE OF DEFAULT A notice to a defaulting party that there has been a default. The defaulting party is usually provided a grace period in which to cure the default. Notices of default are frequently provided for in contracts for deed and mortgages and are sometimes required by operation of law. Care should be taken to make the grace period at least 5 *business* days, otherwise a defaulting party receiving a notice of default sent on Thursday before a long holiday weekend might not have sufficient time in which to cure.

Under a contract for deed, in order to avoid a forfeiture of the property through an inadvertent default, the prudent purchaser will insert a clause requiring that notice of default be given along with a grace period to correct the default. Such notice should be in writing and should be sent to the defaulting party by registered or certified mail, return receipt requested, at an address specified in the contract. (*See GRACE PERIOD.*)

NOTICE OF DISHONOR   A document issued by a notary public at the request of a note holder who has been refused payment of a note by its maker. This is legal evidence that the note has been unpaid.

In a law action between the holder against the endorser or drawer, the notice of dishonor is an essential element, unless waived (as it usually is in most mortgage notes). Related rights of the holder are "presentment" (to demand payment of amounts due) and "notice of protest" (to obtain an official certification of nonpayment).

NOTICE OF LIEN   A specific written notice required in some states in an application for a mechanic's lien. Notice of lien must be made to the appropriate court where the property is located. A copy of the notice must be served on the owner and on any other interested persons in the same manner as provided by law for the service of a summons. The notice is usually posted on the improvement, and must set forth the amount of the claim, the labor or material furnished, a sufficient description of the property, the names of the parties who contracted for the improvement, the names of the general contractor, the names of the owners of the property, and any other person or persons with an interest in the property. Service upon any one of several joint owners of a proper notice of lien is generally deemed to be service upon all of the owners. The notice of lien must be filed within a certain time period after the date of completion of the improvement against which it is filed.

The lien attaches only after the court has determined that there is probable cause to believe there is a basis for the mechanic's claim. The requirement of a "probable cause" hearing has been added in many states in response to recent U.S. Supreme Court decisions supporting an individual's constitutional right to notice and a hearing prior to the deprivation of any property rights. (*See MECHANIC'S LIEN, NOTICE OF COMPLETION.*)

NOTICE OF NONRESPONSIBILITY   A legal notice designed to relieve a property owner of responsibility for the cost of improvements ordered by another person, such as a tenant. The owner usually gives notice that he or she will not be responsible for the work done by posting notice in some conspicuous place on the property, and by recording a verified copy in the public records. (*See MECHANIC'S LIEN.*)

NOTICE OF PENDENCY   See LIS PENDENS.

NOTICE TO QUIT   A written notice given by a landlord to the tenant stating that the landlord intends to regain possession of the leased premises and that the tenant is required to leave and yield up the property. The notice to quit can stipulate that the tenant must quit either at the end of the lease term or immediately if there is a breach of lease or if the tenancy is at will or by sufferance. Usually a notice to quit based on nonpayment of rent gives less time to correct the default than a notice to quit based on damage to the premises or some other grounds. This term sometimes refers to the notice given by a tenant to the landlord that he or she intends to give up possession on a stated day.

NOVATION   The substitution of a new obligation for an old one; substitution of new parties to an existing obligation, as where the parties to an agreement accept a new debtor in place of an old one. For example, in the assumption of a loan, the lender may release the seller and substitute the buyer as the party primarily liable for the mortgage debt. A novation requires an intent to discharge the original contract, and, being a new contract, it requires its own consideration and other essentials of a valid contract. Note, however, that unless there is a novation, a tenant assigning his or her lease to another will still remain liable for the original lease. (See ASSIGNMENT.)

NUISANCE   Conduct or activity which results in an actual physical interference with another person's reasonable use or enjoyment of his or her property for any lawful purpose. A private nuisance is one affecting only a limited number of people, whereas a public nuisance is one affecting the community at large, such as excessive noise from jet airliners. If a use is considered to be a nuisance, the injured party can seek an abatement of the nuisance either by way of damages or by injunction, such as restraining a neighbor from operating an open garbage dump. Common examples of nuisances are activities resulting in unreasonable noise, odors, and fire hazards. (See ATTRACTIVE NUISANCE, TRESPASS.)

NULL AND VOID   Having no legal force or effect; of no worth; unenforceable; not binding. Discriminatory restrictive covenants contained in a deed or other instrument are null and void. (See VOID.)

NUNCUPATIVE WILL   An oral will declared by the testator in his or her final sickness, made before witnesses and shortly afterwards reduced to writing. Such a will is not valid in most states and is usually limited to military personnel or to disposition of personal effects. (See HOLOGRAPHIC WILL.)

NUT   A slang term referring to the carrying charge on a property, such as the monthly nut for an investment piece of real estate. (See DEBT SERVICE.)

OATH   A solemn pledge made before a notary public or other officer. A person taking an oath is often referred to as "affiant." An oath often takes the form of an appeal to a Supreme Being to attest to the truth of a person's statement. An example of an oath would be: "You do solemnly swear that the contents of this affidavit, which you subscribe to, are true as therein stated." In all cases, the notary must require the affiant either to raise his or her hand or to place it on a Bible before administering the oath. If the affiant cannot or will not use the term "swear," an affirmation is permissible. (*See AFFIRMATION.*)

OBLIGATION BOND   A bond signed by a mortgagor in excess of the loan amount, executed to serve as a safeguard to the lender against nonpayment of taxes, insurance premiums, or any overdue interest that may accrue over the life of the loan.

OBLIGOR   A promisor; one who incurs a lawful obligation to another (the *obligee*). The maker of a promissory note is an obligor. In a performance bond, the contractor is the obligor. One who guarantees the performance of the obligation is a surety; also called a guarantor. (*See SURETY.*)

OBSERVED CONDITION   An appraisal method used to compute depreciation. The appraiser arrives at a total depreciation figure for physical deterioration, functional obsolescence, and economic obsolescence (both curable and incurable), and then subtracts each of those figures in turn from the building reproduction or replacement cost.

OBSOLESCENCE   A type of depreciation of property. Functional obsolescence is a loss of value due to some defect in a structure, such as outmoded plumbing, or inadequately designed fixtures. An example of functional obsolescence would be one bathroom in a 12-bedroom house. Economic obsolescence is a loss in value from causes in the neighborhood, but outside the property itself, such as a change in zoning.

OCCUPANCY AGREEMENT   An agreement to permit the buyer to occupy the property prior to the close of escrow in consideration of paying the seller a specified rent, usually on a daily prorated basis. An occupancy agreement should be in writing to avoid the possible friction which could arise between buyer, seller, and broker over the right to early occupancy and the amount of rent to be paid. It is not prudent for the buyer to be allowed to occupy the premises prior to the close of escrow without having a written occupancy agreement; in most cases, it would also be prudent to first have the buyer waive any contingencies to the purchase. The buyer in this situation should take out a homeowner's insurance policy, or at least receive an endorsement on the seller's policy in order to be properly covered. Disputes between sellers and buyers who occupy early have been a fertile area for litigation, especially as to the habitable condition of the premises. (See EARLY OCCUPANCY.)

OCCUPANCY PERMIT   A permit issued by the appropriate governing unit to establish that a property is habitable and meets necessary health and safety standards.

OFFER   A promise by one party to act or perform in a specified manner provided the other party acts or performs in the manner requested. An offer demonstrates an intention to enter into a contract as opposed to merely inviting offers from others, as with a listing contract. An offer creates the power of acceptance in the other party.

The sales contract transmits to the seller a prospective buyer's offer to purchase the seller's property (also called a "proposition"). All offers should be dated. This is especially important if an offer does not contain a specific expiration date. The courts usually declare that an offer should remain open, unless withdrawn, for a reasonable time. This requires evidence of the time and date at which an offer was made.

OFFER AND ACCEPTANCE   The two components of a valid contract; a meeting of the minds. An offer is a manifestation of an intention to enter into an agreement. When dealing with a real estate contract, the offer must be communicated to the offeree and must be definite and certain, with all terms reduced to writing. The offer creates the power of acceptance in the person to whom it is communicated. Upon acceptance by the offeree of all the terms of the offer, a valid contract is created. Unless the offer is in the form of an option, the offeror can revoke the offer at any time before the offeree has communicated acceptance to the offeror, but the revocation usually is not effective until received by the offeree. Immediately upon an effective revocation, the offeree no longer has the power to accept the contract. An offer may be terminated by lapse of time, communication or notice of revocation, qualified acceptance as in a counteroffer, rejection, death, or insanity of either the offeror or offeree.

The acceptance of an offer must be definite, unambiguous, and unqualified. If the acceptance is qualified in any way or changes the terms of the offer in any way, then it constitutes a counteroffer and a contract can only be created when this counteroffer is accepted by the original offeror. In real estate transactions, the acceptance should be in writing and signed by the party to be bound. It is also advisable that the time of the acceptance be indicated. There is a presumption in commercial transactions that an offer made in writing normally must be accepted in writing.

Most offers to purchase real property are made in the sales contract. There is no legal requirement the offer be accompanied by an earnest money deposit, though this is the usual case. It is common for the offeror, normally the prospective buyer, to give the offeree a limited time, such as 48 hours, in which to accept the offer. The purpose, here, is to limit the time in which the seller has the power to accept. The offeror could, nevertheless, withdraw the offer at any time during this 48-hour period, since an offer can be revoked at any time prior to notification of acceptance. An exception would be a case where the offeror's agreement to hold the offer open is supported by independent consideration, such as in an option. If accepted *after* the 48-hour deadline, the acceptance would constitute a counteroffer.

A written offer mailed to the offeree is accepted and a contract is created when the offeree places the acceptance in the mail. If the offeror attempts to revoke the offer after the offeree has mailed the acceptance but before the acceptance is received by the offeror, the revocation is ineffective. The rationale is that the offeror has chosen the mail as the agent and when the offeree delivers to the agent, that is, puts the acceptance in the mail, it is deemed to be effectively communicated to the offeror, even if the acceptance is lost in the mails. (*See ACCEPTANCE, COUNTEROFFER, MEETING OF THE MINDS, OPTION.*)

OFFERING SHEET   A one-page loan summary that describes the loan's important features. This summary assists the investor in evaluating the purpose of the mortgage loan being submitted by the loan correspondent.

OFFER TO SELL   Broadly defined in most statutes to include any inducement, solicitation, or attempt to encourage a person to buy property or acquire an interest in property.

Under the various licensing laws, one who offers to sell, buy, or rent real estate or any options on real estate, for others, for a consideration, is required to have a real estate license.

Under state and federal securities law, an "offer to sell" is any specific discussion of an investment that is available for purchase. The law may limit the number or manner of such offers in nonregistered securities transactions.

OFFICE BUILDING   A building usually divided into individual offices, used primarily by companies to conduct business.

In general, an office building is appraised like any other income property. Appraisal is, however, a complex process, involving special problems. In evaluating an office building, an appraiser must particularly consider the economic background of the area in which the building is located. Such factors usually include population growth, monthly industrial payrolls, total bank clearances, building permits over a period of years, school enrollment, public utilities, transportation facilities, rentals of comparable properties, percentage of vacancies, and the nature of tenancies. (*See APPRAISAL.*)

OFFICE EXCLUSIVE   A listing in which the seller refuses to submit the listing to a multiple-listing service. Many MLS rules require that the seller be subsequently informed of the advantages of MLS, and sign a certification to that effect. The seller, in essence, wants only the listing broker to show the property. It is a listing which is retained by one real estate office to the exclusion of other brokers.

In certain cases the MLS may write to the seller enumerating the advantages of MLS, and request that the seller reconsider listing with the MLS. A copy of any such letter must be sent to the listing broker. An office-exclusive listing does not relieve the listing broker from the obligation to cooperate fully with other members in selling the property. This is in accordance with the bylaws of the board and the Code of Ethics of the National Association of Realtors®. (*See MULTIPLE LISTING, See also the REALTOR® CODE OF ETHICS—APPENDIX B.*)

OFFICE OF EQUAL OPPORTUNITY (OEO)
The federal agency under the direction of the Secretary of the Department of Housing and Urban Development, which is in charge of administering the Fair Housing Act. (*See FEDERAL FAIR HOUSING LAW.*)

OFFICE OF INTERSTATE LAND SALES REGISTRATION (OILSR)
The federal agency which regulates interstate land sales. The agency was established as part of HUD in 1969 to prevent abuse, such as fraud and misrepresentation, perpetrated on the public in the promotion and sale of recreational property across state lines. (*See INTERSTATE LAND SALES.*)

OFFICE OF THE COMPTROLLER OF THE CURRENCY (OCC)
A federal agency that regulates nationally chartered banks, akin to the Federal Home Loan Bank System's function to federal savings and loan associations.

OFF-RECORD TITLE DEFECT
A defect in title to real property which is not apparent from an examination of public records. A recorded document may not effectively transfer title to property if it was forged, was never delivered to the grantee, or was signed by an incompetent party. A party whose signature has been forged on a deed still retains legal title to the property and can enforce the title even against a good faith purchaser for value who records the forged deed. A certificate of title does not reveal or insure against such off-record risks. To protect against losses incurred as a result of off-record risks, a buyer should obtain title insurance. (*See CERTIFICATE OF TITLE, HIDDEN RISK, TITLE INSURANCE.*)

OFFSET STATEMENT
1. A statement by an owner or lienholder to the buyer as to the balance due on existing liens against property being purchased. 2. A statement by a tenant of a rental property to a buyer, setting forth the terms of the rental agreement, including the rent and amount of security deposit.

OFFSITE COSTS
Developer's costs for sewers, streets, and utilities which are incurred in the development of raw land, but are not connected with the actual construction, or onsite costs, of the building.

OFF-STREET PARKING
Parking spaces located on private property, usually on an area provided especially for such use; provides vehicular parking spaces with adequate aisles for maneuvering to provide access for entrance and exit.

OIL AND GAS LEASE A grant of the sole and exclusive right to extract oil and/or gas from beneath the surface of the land. Such a lease is generally for a designated term of years, and is subject to a payment of royalties in the event of production, the commencement of drilling operations on or before a specified date, and the performance within a specified time of a certain amount of development work. Typically, there is an express or implied easement to enter the property in order to drill. (*See IMPLIED EASEMENT, PROFIT A PRENDRE, ROYALTY.*)

ON OR BEFORE A phrase in a contract referring to the time for performance of a specified act, such as the payment of money or the closing of a transaction. Such a provision in a promissory note may be so written to permit prepayment without penalty. If a seller wanted a transaction to close in tax year 1983, the seller should not permit the contract to have the closing set for "on or before January 1, 1983."

ONCE IN A LIFETIME EXCLUSION Refers to the provision in the Internal Revenue Code that permits a homeowner 55 years of age or older to exclude up to $125,000 of gain from the sale of a principal residence occupied any three of the prior five years. This is a once-in-a-lifetime exclusion. For example, if a homeowner excludes the $75,000 profit on one home, the homeowner cannot later exclude a $50,000 profit on a subsequent home. (*See RESIDENCE, SALE OF.*)

ONE HUNDRED PERCENT COMMISSION A commission arrangement between a real estate broker and a salesperson, usually an independent contractor, in which the salesperson receives the full net commission on certain real estate sales provided the salesperson meets specified sales quotas and/or pays the broker for specified administrative overhead costs. The State Real Estate Commission closely scrutinizes such arrangements to be certain that there is continued compliance with the licensing law requirement of adequate supervision by the managing broker of all salespeople.

OPEN AND NOTORIOUS POSSESSION Possession which is sufficiently clear that a reasonable person viewing the property would know that the occupant claimed some title or interest in it. An owner does not lose property to adverse possession unless he or she has notice, actual or constructive, of the occupant's claim to the property. The construction of buildings or the fencing and cultivating of land would certainly be sufficiently open and notorious possession. The mere posting of a "no trespassing" sign probably would not be sufficient. (*See ADVERSE POSSESSION.*)

OPEN-END MORTGAGE An expandable loan in which the borrower is given a limit up to which may be borrowed, with each incremental advance to be secured by the same mortgage. The advances may be in amounts up to but not exceeding the original borrowing limit. This practice reduces closing costs on future loans under the same mortgage and minimizes refinancing costs and appraisal costs. An open-end mortgage usually contains more favorable terms than a home improvement loan, which charges a much higher interest rate and must be repaid in a relatively short time. Note that the interest rate on new money under the open-end mortgage may be the current market rate at the time of disbursement. The lender of an open-end mortgage should require a lien search or title update prior to each incremental advance, since intervening recorded liens may have priority over the mortgage. Also called a *mortgage for future advances*, this type of loan is sometimes used by farmers to meet their seasonal operational expenses, much like a line of credit. (*See* FUTURE ADVANCES.)

OPEN HOUSE   The common real estate practice of showing listed homes to the public during established hours. (*See* SIGNS, SITE OFFICE.)

OPEN HOUSING   Housing offered on the market without any discrimination based on race, sex, color, religion, or national origin. Both federal and state antidiscrimination laws are designed to ensure that housing is made available to all who can afford it. (*See* DISCRIMINATION, FEDERAL FAIR HOUSING LAW.)

OPEN HOUSING LAW   (*See* FEDERAL FAIR HOUSING LAW.)

OPEN LISTING   A listing given to any number of brokers who can work simultaneously to sell the owner's property. The first broker who secures a buyer ready, willing, and able to purchase at the terms of the listing is the one who earns the commission. In the case of a sale, the seller is not obligated to notify any of the brokers that the property has been sold. Unlike an exclusive listing, an open listing need not contain a definite termination date. In such a case, the listing terminates after a reasonable time, usually whatever is customary in the community. Either party can, in good faith, terminate the agency at will. Note, however, that some state license laws require all listings to contain definite expiration dates. This type of listing is often used by contractors or builders. Unless stated otherwise, a listing will be treated as an open listing in the form of a unilateral contract. (*See* PROCURING CAUSE.)

OPEN MORTGAGE   A mortgage that may be repaid in full at any time over the life of the loan without levy of a prepayment penalty by the lender.

OPEN SPACE   A certain portion of the landscape which has not been built upon and which is sought either to be reserved in its natural state, or is used for agricultural or recreational purposes, such as parks, squares, and the like. In addition, open space is park land within a subdivision, usually designated as such by a developer as a condition for receiving a building permit from the city or county. HUD provides funds to communities for up to 50 percent of the cost of acquiring, developing, and preserving land for parks, recreation, conservation, science, and historic uses.

OPEN SPACE   The Open Space Act is designed to encourage the
TAXATION LAW   preservation of qualified lands through the application of current use assessment. Certain types of agricultural land, timber land, and just open space or unused lands qualify for a lower assessment, which results in a significant reduction in assessed valuation, which in turn results in lower taxes.

Once the land is classified it must not be applied to any other use. A change of use will result in removal from classification. Upon removal of the land from this classification, an additional tax will be imposed. This additional tax will be the difference in the amount of tax paid as open space and the amount that would have been paid if the land were not classified, plus interest, for a maximum of seven years prior to removal from classification. In addition, there is a penalty of 20 percent of this total amount, which can be avoided if the owner requests removal, in writing, after eight years of classification. This request, which is irrevocable, must be made two years prior to the date of withdrawal. (*See REAL PROPERTY TAXES.*)

OPERATING BUDGET   A itemized statement of income, expenses, net operating income before debt service, and cash flow. Expenses consist of fixed costs, such as employee salaries, taxes, and insurance premiums, and a cash reserve fund for variable expenses, such as repairs, supplies, and replacements. A property manager for an investment property typically is charged with the responsibility of developing an operating budget to give the owner an idea of the cash yield to expect from the property during a fixed period, typically a year. The budget is also helpful as a guide to the manager for the future operation of the property and as a measure of past performance. The budget should incorporate the long-term goals of the owner for the property. The property manager should be conservative in forecasting income for future periods.

OPERATING EXPENSES   Those periodic and necessary expenses which are essential to the continuous operation and maintenance of a property. Operating expenses are generally divided into the following categories: fixed expenses such as real property taxes, building insurance, and so on; variable costs such as utilities, payroll, administration, property management fees; and reserves for replacement. Operating expenses do not include items such as mortgage payments, capital expenditures, and depreciation. (*See MAINTENANCE FEE.*)

OPERATION BREAKTHROUGH   A HUD program, initiated in 1969 to stimulate innovations in housing production in such areas as construction, land-use costs, management, financing, marketing, user satisfaction, appearance, and the overall environment. This is accomplished through research and development activities financed largely by HUD.

OPERATION OF LAW   A term that describes the way in which rights and sometimes duties belong to a person by the mere application to a particular transaction of established rules of law, without any act by the person. For example, a purchaser of land bordering a non-navigable stream has certain riparian rights. These rights are not given by contract, but they pass automatically to the buyer by operation of state law.

OPINION OF TITLE   An opinion by a person competent in examining titles, usually a title attorney, as to the status of the record title of a property. An opinion of title is not a guarantee of title. Examiners only assert that they are competent in examining titles and that they have used care and diligence in examining the abstract of title. (*See ABSTRACT OF TITLE, CERTIFICATE OF TITLE, TITLE INSURANCE.*)

OPTION   An agreement to keep open, for a set period, an offer to sell or lease real property. An option can be used, for example, to give the buyer time to resolve questions of financing, title, zoning, and feasibility before committing the buyer to purchase. Options are frequently used in the land assemblage process. The option must be supported by its actual consideration, separate and independent of the purchase price of the property. A mere recital of consideration alone is not sufficient except in a lease-option in which the provisions of the lease are themselves sufficient consideration to support the option. An option merely creates a contractual right. It does not give the optionee any estate in the property. At the time the option is signed, the owner does not sell nor does the buyer purchase the property. While the owner is obligated to sell if given notice by the buyer, the buyer is not obligated to purchase. An option to buy is also known as a "call"; an option to sell is known as a "put."

An option must contain all of the essential terms of the underlying contract of sale. This means that a binding contract is created immediately upon the optionee's decision to exercise the option. Necessary information includes: the names and addresses of the parties; the date of the option; consideration; words granting the option; the date the option expires; a statement of purchase price, and principal terms. Often a copy of the purchase agreement is attached and incorporated by reference. An option agreement often includes a statement as to the method of notice by which the option is to be exercised; provisions for forfeiture of option money if the option is not exercised; and acknowledged signatures of optionor and optionee (only the optionor *must* sign). Unless prohibited by its terms, the option is usually assignable.

Since an option is usually exercised only when the property has appreciated in value above the option price during the option period, the optionor may feel that, in retrospect, he or she made a bad bargain. In trying to avoid performing under the option, an optionor should have an attorney closely scrutinize the provisions of the option to determine if the option contains all the essential terms of purchase. If the option fails to cover all the material terms and leaves some for future agreement, then the option will not be enforceable. For example, if the option agreement detailed the parties, the property, price and method of payment, but omitted the interest rate on the mortgage, a court would not enforce the contract. Thus, an experienced real estate attorney should be consulted before the parties enter into an option agreement.

If a tenant pays rent with the understanding that the tenant has an option to purchase, and eventually the tenant exercises that option, a certain part of all rents paid may be applied to the purchase price. However, failure to exercise the option will not entitle the tenant to a refund of the portion that would have been applied to the purchase price had the property been purchased.

The option price is set so as to ensure that the optionee is dealing in good faith and that the seller will be covered for any inconvenience and expense for taking the property off the open market while the option is unexercised. Options do create leverage and conserve cash, as options to buy large parcels may be had for a small amount of money.

It is sometimes difficult to distinguish between an option and a contract to buy or sell a property. Since a broker often does not earn a commission on an option until the option is exercised, the distinction has a practical importance. If both parties are obligated to perform, i.e. there is mutuality of obligation, then it is a contract for sale. If just one party is obligated to perform, then it is an option. An option is thus a unilateral contract in which the optionor/offeror agrees to make the offer irrevocable for a certain time in return for the optionee/offeree's performance of payments of the option money. When the optionee gives the appropriate notice of intent to exercise the option, he or she in effect accepts the offer and there is then a bilateral contract for sale with both parties bound to perform. The option money is usually applied toward the purchase price, but the parties should cover this point in the option contract itself.

If the optionee does not exercise the option, most options provide that the optionor keeps the option money and neither party is obligated to perform. Since time is of the essence in an option agreement, the option automatically expires if not exercised prior to the termination date. Death of the optionor or optionee usually does not affect the option. The optionee or heirs can still exercise the right to purchase. The contract is also binding on the optionee's heirs and assigns.

An option should be recorded since the rights of the optionee will relate back to the date of the option and take priority over all intervening rights of third parties with notice of the option. Good title practice requires that a release of option be recorded in the event a recorded option is not exercised. Otherwise, the lapsed option will constitute a cloud on the title. Therefore, many options contain a defeasance clause stating that the recorded option will automatically cease to be a lien on the property upon expiration of the option exercise date.

Some different types of options are the standard fixed option; the step-up option where the purchase price increases during set stages of the option period; and the declining credit option where the percentage of the option price that may be credited toward the purchase price decreases as time passes (opposite of the full-credit option).

An option is not an interest in land and is therefore not acceptable to most lenders as security for a mortgage. Similarly, an optionee will not receive just compensation if the underlying property is taken in a condemnation proceeding. Also, an optionee does not usually have sufficient standing to seek zoning changes.

One who buys and sells options without the exercise thereof must usually obtain a real estate license, except in isolated cases and when not done to evade the licensing requirements. Of course, if the option is exercised, then there is no license required to sell the property since the optionee becomes the owner of the property and owners need not be licensed to sell their own property. The real estate broker should be sure the listing covers the right to and disbursement of a commission upon the broker negotiating an option, rather than an outright sale, during the option period. The listing should also address the issue whether the commission is based on the option consideration (regardless of exercise of the option) or the full purchase price only if exercised.

Some relevant tax features of an option are:

1. The cost of the option (if not applied to the purchase price) is added to the buyer's tax basis of the property when the option is exercised. Thus, an optionee who pays $5,000 for the 3-month right to purchase a farm for $200,000 will have a basis of $205,000 upon exercise of the option assuming the option money is not applied toward the purchase price.

2. The option money is not taxable to the seller upon receipt. When the option is exercised, the money becomes part of the sales price and is given the same tax treatment. If the option is not exercised within the specified time, the option lapses and the option money is taxed as ordinary income in the year the option expires.

3. An option itself is an asset and any profit made on the sale of the option is taxable income. If the underlying property is a capital asset, then the profit may

be taxed at the favorable capital gain rates if held for more than twelve months. Also, the optionee may be able to deduct the cost of the option as a deductible expense if the option is not exercised.

4. The 12-month holding period for the real property for capital gain purposes of the optionee does not commence until the option is exercised. It thus does not include the period of the option.

5. An option may permit the optionor to postpone a sale until after the 12-month capital gain holding period, or to postpone the sale until the next tax year for tax planning purposes. Postponement may also reduce the number of sales in a particular year, thus reducing the investor's risk of being classified by the IRS as a "dealer."

6. On a lease with an option to buy, where the rent or a portion of the rent is applied to the purchase price, and the tenant has the right to purchase the property for a nominal amount at the end of the lease, there is a strong possibility that the Internal Revenue Service will construe this as a disguised real estate contract and assert that it was not a lease with an option, but rather a sale. In such a case, the lease rent payments would not be deductible; they would be treated as installment payments, which the "tenant" must capitalize and for which he or she must take deductions in the form of depreciation deductions. The "landlord" runs the risk of being taxed on the entire gain unless the transaction can qualify for installment reporting. (*See HOLDING PERIOD, LEASE OPTION.*)

OPTION LISTING   A listing in which the broker also retains an option to purchase the property for the broker's own account. Full and fair disclosure must be given to the seller, as there has been much litigation involving breach of fiduciary duties by brokers who conceal offers from buyers until after the broker has exercised the option.

ORAL CONTRACT   A verbal unwritten contract. All real estate contracts must be in writing except leases that are made for a period of one year or less. However, even short-term leases should be in writing to lessen the chances of dispute between lessor and lessee. (*See STATUTE OF FRAUDS.*)

ORDINANCES   The rules, regulations, and codes enacted into law by local governing bodies. Generally, such governing bodies enact ordinances regulating such things as building standards, motor vehicle standards, and subdivision requirements. For example, many areas have enacted ordinances banning the posting of "sold" signs on recently sold real estate. (*See BUILDING CODES, SIGNS.*)

ORDINARY AND NECESSARY BUSINESS EXPENSE   An expense incurred through the normal course of business, such as rent or expenditures for supplies, as opposed to expenses for a specific project or venture. Under federal income tax laws, ordinary and necessary business expenses may be deducted in the year they are incurred, rather than spread over two or more years as with a capital expenditure. (*See CAPITAL EXPENDITURE, REPAIRS.*)

ORDINARY GAIN   A gain or profit for which income tax must be paid at ordinary income rates rather than at the more favorable capital gain rates. Short-term gain, that is, gain resulting from the sale of property held for less than 12 months, and gain from sales of property classified as "inventory" or "dealer property" is taxable as ordinary gain. (See *CAPITAL GAIN, DEALER.*)

ORGANIZATIONAL EXPENSES, PARTNERSHIP   Under the Tax Reform Act of 1976, partnerships and partners can no longer claim deductions under the partnership provisions for amounts paid or incurred to promote the sale (or to sell) partnership interest (called syndication expenditures), or for amounts, except as noted below, incurred to organize a partnership.

Syndication expenditures are those connected with the issuing and marketing of interests in a partnership, such as commissions, professional fees, and printing costs.

However, a partnership may elect to capitalize its organizational expenditures and to amortize and deduct these expenses apportioned over a period of not less than 60 months commencing with the month that the partnership begins business. (See *SYNDICATION.*)

ORIENTATION   Placing a house on its lot with regard to its exposure to sun rays, prevailing winds, privacy from the street and neighbors, and protection from outside noises.

ORIGINATION FEE   The finance fee charged by a lender for making a mortgage. An origination fee covers initial costs, such as preparation of documents and credit, inspection, and appraisal fees. The origination fee is generally computed as a percentage of the face amount on the loan. For example, the lender's fee for originating a $100,000 loan might be two percent, or $2,000. The origination fee is not tax deductible as is interest on borrowed money, but instead is treated as a cost for services rendered and must be capitalized. In VA and FHA transactions involving existing structures, such a fee cannot exceed one percent of the total mortgage amount. Where a lender makes inspections and partial disbursements during construction of a structure, both VA and FHA permit an origination fee in excess of one percent. (See *FINANCE FEE, POINTS.*)

"OR MORE" CLAUSE   A provision in a mortgage, trust deed, or contract for deed, allowing for a larger monthly payment without a prepayment penalty. There may be a limitation, however, on how much may be paid under an "or more" clause. (See *PREPAYMENT PENALTY.*)

OSTENSIBLE AGENCY   An actual agency relationship that arises by the actions of the parties rather than by express agreement. For example, an owner knows a broker is showing the owner's vacant lot to prospective buyers without authority to do so. Unless the owner takes some steps to stop such unauthorized showings, the law will consider that third parties have just cause to believe that the broker is the owner's agent. Thus the owner could become liable for certain acts of the "owner's broker." It is called an ostensible agency because on the surface it appears to exist. Once this type of agency is created, the owner is prevented (by estoppel) to deny its existence. (*See IMPLIED AGENCY.*)

OUTSTANDING BALANCE The amount of a loan that remains to be paid. An outstanding note is one in which there is still a liability.

OVERAGE In retail store leases, the lessee often sets a minimum base rent, with a percentage of the volume of business the store does over a certain amount constituting additional rent. This added rent, or overage, should be treated as excess income by the lessee. (*See PERCENTAGE LEASE.*)

OVERALL RATE The direct percentage ratio between net annual operating income and sales price. The overall rate is calculated by dividing the net income by the price.

OVERFLOW RIGHT The right to flood another person's land. It may be either a temporary or permanent right.

OVERHANG The part of a roof that extends beyond the exterior wall.

OVERIMPROVEMENT An improvement which by reason of excess or cost is not the highest and best use of the site on which it is placed. An example of an overimprovement is a $500,000 home in a neighborhood comprised of mostly $100,000 homes. The term also refers to overimproving an existing property. (*See HIGHEST AND BEST USE.*)

OVERRIDE 1. A provision in a listing agreement that protects a broker's right to a commission for a reasonable time after the agreement expires in the event that the owner sells the property to a prospect with whom the broker negotiated during the time the listing was in effect. (*See EXTENDER CLAUSE.*)

2. A commission paid to managerial personnel, such as the principal broker, on sales made by their subordinates. This is usually calculated as a percentage of the gross sales commissions earned by the salespeople under the manager's supervision.

3. A rental amount paid by a tenant on monies generated by the tenant's business in excess of certain amounts; such as $.01 per gallon of gas sold by a gas station tenant over 50,000 gallons each month.

OVERRIDING ROYALTY A royalty fee retained by a lessee of an oil and gas lease when the property is subleased.

OWELTY Money paid by a favored cotenant to the other members of the tenancy where there is a physical partition of a tenancy into unequal shares. Such payments are usually court-ordered.

OWNER/OCCUPANT   Property owner who physically occupies the property; the opposite of an absentee landlord or owner. An owner/occupant can usually get preferred mortgage rates over an investor/owner.

OWNER'S DUPLICATE CERTIFICATE   When property is registered in the Torrens system, an exact copy of the original certificate of title is recorded with the registrar of titles and a duplicate certificate of title is issued to the owner. The property cannot be transferred without a notation of this transfer being made on the duplicate certificate. An alternative would be to have the owner surrender the duplicate certificate and for the registrar of titles to issue a new certificate. This is also called the "transfer certificate of title," or TCT.

OWNERSHIP, FORM OF   A broker is often asked by his or her buyer clients to advise them on the appropriate form of ownership of real property. The form of ownership is important because:

1. The existing form of ownership determines who must sign the various documents involved in the sale, such as listing, contract of sale, or deed.

2. The form of ownership affects many future rights of the parties. How one takes title to property may have consequences involving income taxes, real property taxes, gift taxes, estate and inheritance taxes, transferability, exposure to creditor's claims, and probate or its avoidance.

A broker should be well versed in the differences between the various methods of owning property, such as joint tenancy, tenancy in common, tenancy by the entirety, tenancy in severalty, community property, partnership, trust, and corporate forms of ownership. Though the broker can discuss these differences with a client, he or she may not recommend a specific form of ownership as that would constitute the practice of law without a license. Rather, the broker should recommend that the client consult experienced tax or legal counsel, especially if there will be multiple owners, to determine the most advantageous form of ownership for the client. For example, when husband and wife are to take title to property, it may be appropriate for them to hold it as tenants by the entirety. However, in certain circumstances, especially if the husband and wife are in a high income bracket, it could be disadvantageous from a tax viewpoint if they take title as tenants by the entirety, because the estate tax on jointly held property might be much higher than if title were held in another form. A broker may therefore be doing a client a disservice by not recommending that the client receive experienced legal or tax counsel as to the method of ownership. (*See ABSENTEE OWNER, GRANTEE, JOINT TENANCY, TENANCY IN COMMON, TENANCY BY THE ENTIRETY, TENANCY IN SEVERALTY, PARTNERSHIP.*)

PACKAGE MORTGAGE A method of financing in which the loan that finances the purchase of a home also finances the purchase of personal items such as a washer, a dryer, a refrigerator, air conditioner, and other specified appliances. The mortgage instrument describes the real property and declares the enumerated home accessories to be fixtures and, thus, part of the mortgaged property. As in a budget mortgage, the monthly payments include principal, interest, and pro rata payments for the appliances. Some lenders feel that the use of a package mortgage results in fewer defaulted loans. This is because a buyer can pay for essential furnishings over an extended period of time without an additional down payment, rather than exhaust his or her resources by buying them outright. The package mortgage is popularly used in the sale of new subdivision homes and in the sale of condominums. Most package mortgages also require the mortgagor to sign and file a financing statement in accordance with the provisions of the Uniform Commercial Code. In a package mortgage, the interest is paid only on the remaining balance and not on the original debt as in the typical consumer installment loan. (*See BUDGET MORTGAGE, FINANCING STATEMENT.*)

PAD The area in a mobile home park allocated for the placement of a mobile home unit.

PANIC PEDDLING The illegal practice of soliciting sales or rental listings by making written or oral statements that create fear or alarm, transmit written or oral warnings or threats, solicit prospective minority renters or buyers, or act in any other manner so as to induce or attempt to induce the sale or lease of residential property, either:

1. through representations regarding the present or prospective entry of one or more minority residents into an area, or

2. through representations that would convey to a reasonable person under the circumstances, whether or not overt reference to minority status is made, that one or more minority residents are or may be entering the area.

The term minority means any group that can be distinguished because of race, sex, religion, color, or national origin. Vigorous solicitation of sellers in a rapidly changing neighborhood is called panic peddling. (*See FEDERAL FAIR HOUSING LAW.*)

PAPER   A business term referring to a mortgage, note, or contract for deed, which is usually taken back from the buyer by a seller when real property is sold. Land developers frequently sell subdivided lots by way of ten-year contracts for deed with down payments as low as five percent. They then sell these contracts, or "paper," at a discount to a lender, or pledge them as security for a loan. (*See CONTRACT FOR DEED, DISCOUNT, MORTGAGE, NOTE.*)

PAR   Average; equal, face value. The accepted method of comparison, such as "this loan is two points above par."

PARAGRAPH 17   Whether a real estate sale of a single-family residence will occur in a tight money market often depends on whether or not there is a due-on-sale clause in the seller's note and underlying mortgage or deed of trust. The clause most frequently encountered that contains a "due on sale clause" is contained in Paragraph 17 of the FNMA/FHLMC Uniform Instrument. (*See DUE-ON-SALE CLAUSE.*)

PARAPET   The part of the wall of a house that rises above the roof line.

PARCEL   A specific portion of a larger tract; a lot.

PARITY CLAUSE   A provision which allows for a mortgage or trust deed to secure more than one note, and which provides that all notes be secured by the same mortgage without any priority or preference.

PARKWAY   A major collector roadway usually containing a medial strip with landscaped setback parklike areas on each side of the right-of-way, generally heavily planted with trees for its entire length.

PAROL EVIDENCE RULE   A rule of evidence designed to achieve a degree of certainty in a transaction and to prevent fraudulent and perjured claims. Although the word "parol" means oral, in this context, it refers to evidence which is extrinsic to or outside and separate from the writing. When the parties to a real estate contract put their agreement into final written form, the Parol Evidence Rule prevents the admission into court of evidence of any prior or contemporaneous oral or written negotiations or agreements which vary or contradict the terms of the written contract. Thus, if the buyer and seller orally agree that the buyer will pay the broker's commission, but the final contract of sale states that the seller will pay, then the written contract prevails and evidence of the prior oral agreement is not admissible. Note that the rule does not prohibit proof of oral contracts entered into subsequent to the formal written contract.

There are many exceptions to the Parol Evidence Rule. For example, parol evidence is always admissible to show that the parties did not in fact intend to create a contract; to show that the contract was illegal in its inception; to show that there were certain conditions precedent to the creation of a contract; or to clarify any ambiguities in the contract. In other words, a party can still challenge the validity of a contract, as opposed to trying to vary, change, or add new terms.

PARQUET FLOOR   A floor made of short pieces of hardwood laid in various patterns; not a strip floor.

PARTIALLY AMORTIZED   Loan repayment schedule that provides for equal payments of principal and interest up to a certain stop-date, at which time the balance of the principal is due in full. (*See BALLOON PAYMENT.*)

PARTIALLY DISCLOSED PRINCIPAL   A situation in which a party to a transaction, such as a seller, knows, or has reason to know, that the agent to the transaction is working on behalf of a principal, but the seller is unable to discern the principal's identity. (*See UNDISCLOSED AGENCY.*)

PARTIAL RECONVEYANCE   An instrument filed when a certain portion of encumbered real property is released from a mortgage or trust deed lien. (*See BLANKET MORT-GAGE, PARTIAL RELEASE CLAUSE.*)

PARTIAL RELEASE CLAUSE   A clause found in a mortgage under which the mortgagee agrees to release certain parcels from the lien of the blanket mortgage upon payment by the mortgagor of a certain sum of money. The clause is frequently found in tract development construction loans. A mortgagee cannot be compelled to release a portion of the realty from the lien of the mortgage unless it is provided for in the mortgage. Thus, in the absence of a partial release clause, a purchaser from a mortgagor/developer cannot compel the mortgagee to release his or her lot from under the lien of the developer's mortgage upon the payment of a proportionate part of the debt. In addition, where the terms of a purchase-money note restrict the purchaser's right to prepay all or part of the amount due thereunder, the purchaser will want the right to obtain releases of portions of the mortgaged property on the substitution of other collateral for the released property. The mortgagee should insist that the mortgagor be free from any default at the time of the release.

Many states require the partial release of condominium units and subdivision parcels from any blanket lien prior to the original conveyance of the unit. (*See BLANKET MORTGAGE, RELEASE CLAUSE.*)

PARTIAL TAKING   In condemnation, when only a part of a privately owned property is taken for public use. Special benefits or damages to the part remaining must be considered in determining the just compensation to be paid for the part taken. (*See BEFORE-AND-AFTER METHOD, CONDEMNATION, SEVERANCE DAMAGES, SPECIAL BENEFIT.*)

PARTICIPATING BROKER   1. A brokerage company or its sales agent who obtains a buyer for a property which is listed with another brokerage company. Usually called a co-operating broker, the participating broker normally splits the commission with the seller's broker in an agreed-upon amount, typically 50 percent. 2. A broker who assists the listing broker on behalf of the seller, whether or not the broker is an agent of the seller, the listing broker, or the buyer. Sometimes a condominium developer lists his or her condominium for sale with several brokerage companies, which are referred to as the participating brokers in the project. (*See COOPERATING BROKER, SUBAGENCY*.)

PARTICIPATION MORTGAGE
1. A mortgage in which the lender participates in the income of the mortgaged property beyond a fixed return, or receives a yield on the loan in addition to the straight interest rate. The lender may share in a percentage of the income of the property and the profits of the mortgagor or can take an equity position in the project. Sometimes called an "equity kicker," lenders generally use participation mortgages in connection with commercial loans as a hedge against inflation and to increase their total yield on the loan. An example of this would be a lender's participation in gross rents over a fixed base of 90 percent. These participations usually occur when an institutional lender, such as a life insurance company, makes loans on commercial properties or multifamily units during periods of high interest rates and tight money. There is some disagreement on the question of whether the lender's participation in the income stream or equity of a project actually constitutes additional interest as related to the state's usury law. (*See KICKERS*.)

2. A loan in which several lenders fund the loan. (*See PIGGYBACK LOAN*.)

PARTICIPATION SALE CERTIFICATE
A mortgage-backed security sold by the Federal Home Loan Mortgage Corporation (FHLMC—"Freddie Mac") to fund its purchases of mortgages in the FHLMC and represent ownership interests in pools of mortgages purchased by FHLMC and serviced by the sellers. The certificates are freely transferable so they may be sold among investors in much the same way as bonds. (*See MORTGAGE-BACKED SECURITIES*.)

PARTITION
1. An interior wall; or 2. The dividing of cotenants' interests in real property. It sometimes happens that one of several owners desires to sell the property while the other owners think it best to retain the investment. If the parties cannot reach an agreement, an action in partition is often the solution. The main purpose of partition is thus to provide a means by which people, finding themselves in an unwanted common relationship, can free themselves of the relationship incidental to such common ownership.

Generally, when two or more persons hold or possess real property as joint tenants or as tenants in common, and one or more of them has an estate in fee, or a life estate in possession, a suit in equity may be brought by any one or more of them, requesting a partition of the property according to the respective rights of the interested parties. If it appears that a partition in kind cannot be made without great prejudice to the owners, the court will order the sale of all or part of the property. The verified petition for partition fully describes the property, and specifically sets forth the rights of all interested parties. The petitioner should immediately file a lis pendens against the property to give constructive notice of the pending action.

The court, in equity, has the power in a partition action to remove any clouds on title (such as an unreleased lien or encumbrance), to vest titles by decree, to cause the property to be divided among the parties as they agree or by the drawing of lots, to divide and allot portions of the premises to some or all of the parties, and order a sale of the remainder, or to sell the whole and use the proceeds to make everyone equal in the general partition. The court can, by decree, vest the purchasers with the title to the property. The court could appoint a commissioner to investigate and advise as to the best course of partition. If directed by the court, the commissioner has power to make deeds of partition or to sell the property.

A joint tenancy may be terminated by an action for partition, but a tenancy by the entirety cannot be terminated by partition. The common elements of a condominium usually cannot be partitioned under most state statutes.

By clear agreement among the parties, the right to partition may be limited or modified. Reasonable restraints upon the right of partition are valid, but must be in writing under the Statute of Frauds. For example, it is not uncommon for joint owners to agree that each has a right of first refusal in the event one wants to transfer his or her interest.

When a partition is decreed, a mortgagee's lien attaches to that portion of the land set apart to the mortgagor, the person who originally took the loan. In some cases, the fact of partition might trigger an acceleration clause in the mortgage.

Because procedures are lengthy, and expensive legal matters, tenants may choose to negotiate the division among themselves or conduct an auction sale of the property. This can be done even if the tenants are the only bidders and a third party acts as auctioneer. (See ACCELERATION CLAUSE, CLOUD ON TITLE, CO-TENANCY, LIS PENDENS, OWELTY.)

PARTNERSHIP   As defined in the Uniform Partnership Act, which is in force in a majority of states, a partnership is "an association of two or more persons who carry on a business for profit as co-owners." Under this act, a partnership can hold title to real property in the name of the partnership, holding by tenancy in partnership. Prior to the act, many partnerships vested the title to property in a trustee of a land trust so as to avoid problems with the spouses of the partners claiming a marital interest in the partnership property. One tax advantage to this form of ownership is that the partnership itself does not pay taxes. It must file a partnership information return showing how much income it distributed to each partner (a Form 1065). But each partner is responsible for paying his or her own tax.

A partnership can maintain a real estate broker's license provided that *all* partners who actively participate in the real estate brokerage business hold their individual real estate broker's licenses. (See CO-OWNERSHIP, DOUBLE TAXATION, JOINT VENTURE, GENERAL PARTNER, LIMITED PARTNERSHIP, TENANCY IN PARTNERSHIP.)

PARTY DRIVEWAY   A driveway located on both sides of a property line and used in common by the owners of each abutting property. It is best for the owners to hold a written agreement detailing the rights and duties of both parties, rather than for them to rely solely on the general law of easements. (See EASEMENTS.)

PARTY TO BE   The person referred to in the Statute of Frauds as
CHARGED   the one against whom the contract is sought to be enforced; the one who is being sued (the defendant) and is thus being charged with the obligations of the contract that person has signed; the one to be bound or held to the contract. (See STATUTE OF FRAUDS.)

PARTY WALL A wall that is located on or at a boundary line between two adjoining parcels and is used, or is intended to be used, by the owners of both properties in the construction or maintenance of improvements on their respective lots. Such a wall is often designed to serve simultaneously as the exterior wall of two adjacent structures. Though it is most often centered, the party wall may be entirely located on one lot. It is often built and maintained under a recorded agreement. The party wall is typically a perimeter wall joining two attached houses giving structural support to both, and is most frequently encountered in row or tract houses in highly developed urban areas where property owners wish to make full use of the width of their lots and to share the building and maintenance costs. The duty to repair a party wall falls equally on both owners, and one owner may not use his or her rights to the wall in such a way as to damage a neighbor.

Each owner holds in severalty that cross-portion of the wall on his or her tract, subject to an easement, called a cross-easement, by the other owner for use of the wall as a perimeter wall of the owner's respective building, and for its support. A party wall may be created by agreement, deed, or implied grant. Since a party wall involves an easement, the agreement should be in writing as required by the Statute of Frauds. The right to a party wall can also arise by prescription, as where a surveyor's error causes a wall to encroach on adjoining land and such encroachment continues for the prescriptive period.

When one property owner decides to build, he or she may enter into a party wall agreement with neighbors. Under a typical agreement, Jones will build first, and then at such time as a neighbor, Smith, decides to build on his or her lot and use the wall, Smith will pay Jones for one-half the cost of the wall. A party wall is also used, for example, in a case where Jones owns two lots and builds a house on each with one wall dividing the two houses and serving as the perimeter wall of each. (See COMMON WALL, PRESCRIPTION.)

PASSIVE INVESTOR An investor who invests only capital and does not take an active role in the packaging, building, or managing of a project; the opposite of an active investor. (See LIMITED PARTNERSHIP.)

PASS-THROUGH 1. Tax advantage of a partnership that permits income, profits, losses, and deductions, especially depreciation, to "pass through" the legal structure of the partnership directly to the individual investors. Also called "flow-through." Also found in REITs. (See LIMITED PARTNERSHIP.)

2. A pass-through security is the type issued by the Government National Mortgage Association (Ginnie Mae) to mortgage investors. With a mortgage-backed security, the timely payment of principal and interest is guaranteed by Ginnie Mae. In 1982, the Federal National Mortgage Association (Fannie Mae) instituted its own mortgage-backed securities program designed to attract billions of dollars into the conventional mortgage market from pension funds and other investors. (See MORTGAGE-BACKED SECURITIES.)

PATENT The instrument that conveys real property from the state or federal government to an individual.

PAVILION A projecting wing or partially connected portion of a building.

PAYEE   The person to whom a debt instrument, such as a check or promissory note, is made payable; the receiver. (*See MAKER.*)

PAYMENT BOND   A surety bond by which a contractor assures an owner that material and labor furnished in the construction of a building will be fully paid for, and that no mechanic's liens will be filed. The payment bond protects subcontractors and materialmen from non-payment by the prime contractor. Also known as a *labor and material payment bond.* (*See COMPLETION BOND, PERFORMANCE BOND.*)

PAYOFF   The payment in full of an existing loan, usually at the time of refinancing or upon the sale or transfer of a secured property. Escrow will contact the mortgagee seeking the "payoff figures."

PEDESTRIAN TRAFFIC COUNT   A systematic study and analysis of the number and kinds of people passing by a particular location which determines the potential buying power in a given area. A pedestrian traffic count is especially important in planning, developing, and leasing shopping centers.

PENALTY   A punishment imposed for violating a law or an agreement. Sometimes a court will not enforce a liquidated damages clause as a penalty for breach of contract if the amount of damages is so excessive that it bears no true relationship to the real damages which are suffered upon the breach.

In such a case, the court will treat the damages clause as a penalty and, therefore, not enforceable. The court will then award the proper measure of damages to the injured party. (*See LIQUIDATED DAMAGES.*)

PENSION FUND   1. An institution holding assets invested in long-term mortgages and high-grade stocks and bonds to accumulate funds with which to provide individuals with retirement income according to a pre-arranged plan. Pension funds are a fertile source of funds for real estate financing. Because pension funds are not taxed on earnings, they can accept a lesser yield on an investment.

2. A popular practice among successful attorneys and real estate brokers is to incorporate individually and set up their own pension and profit-sharing plans because of the very favorable tax treatment given to qualified plans. (*See KEOGH PLAN.*)

PENTHOUSE   A structure on the roof of a building used to store mechanical equipment, or, more commonly, an apartment on the top floor of a building. Generally, when the area of a penthouse used to store mechanical equipment exceeds 20 percent of the area of the roof, or when the penthouse is to be occupied by persons, the penthouse is considered another story.

A penthouse apartment normally sells for a premium above the prices of most other apartments in the building.

PER AUTRE VIE   *See PUR AUTRE VIE.*

PERCENTAGE LEASE   A lease whose rental is based on a percentage of
the monthly or annual gross sales made on the
premises. Percentage leases are common with large retail stores, especially in
shopping centers. An underlying concept of the percentage lease is that both the
landlord and the tenant should share in the locational advantages of the leased
premises. There are many types of percentage leases. Examples are: the straight
percentage of gross income, without minimum, (uncommon); the fixed minimum
rent plus a percentage of the gross; the fixed minimum rent against a percentage of
the gross, whichever is greater; and the fixed minimum rent plus a percentage of
the gross, with a ceiling to the percentage rental.

The Institute of Real Estate Management, the International Council of Shopping
Centers, the Urban Land Institute, and other real estate management organizations
publish percentage lease tables (see sample table that follows), which can be used
as general guides when negotiating lease terms. For example, the percentage range
of bowling lanes might be 8 to 10 percent; for cocktail lounges, 7 to 10 percent; and
movie theaters, 10 to 12 percent.

Most percentage leases are based on a percentage of gross sales, not gross profits,
because of the difficulty in determining what a "profit" is. Utmost care must be
taken to adequately and fully define "gross sales." It is particularly necessary to
differentiate the applicability of the percentage to credit sales, sales made at other
store locations, credit card discounts, mail orders, trade-ins, gift certificates, and
interstore transactions. The definition of gross income usually excludes sales and
excise taxes. A generally acceptable definition of gross sales is "the gross amount
of all sales made in, from, or at the leased premises, whether for cash or on credit,
after deducting the sales price of any returned merchandise where a cash refund is
given."

The landlord should consider protective provisions to cover the following: tenant's obligation to act in good faith; tenant's obligation not to compete by opening
a nearby store; periodic reports of sales volume; landlord's right to inspect books
and records; tax participation clause; landlord's prohibition of assignment or
subletting without consent; and recapture of the premises.

The percentage rent requires detailed auditing procedures which are difficult to
apply to small business operations, difficult to enforce, and do not apply to personal service businesses, such as Realtors® or attorneys. (*See BASE RENT, GROSS
RENT, NET LEASE, NONCOMPETITION CLAUSE, RECAPTURE CLAUSE, SHOP-
PING CENTER.*)

SAMPLE PERCENTAGE LEASE RATES

	%		%
Auto Accessories	3–4	Hardware	5
Books and Stationery	5–7	Leather Goods	5–6
Bowling Lanes	8–9	Motion Picture Theaters	10–11
Cocktail Lounge	8	Office Supply	4–6
Department Stores	3–4	Parking Lots	
Drug Stores (Individual)	4–6	& Garages (Attendant)	40–60
Electrical Appliances	5–6	Photography	7–9
Furniture	5–8	Restaurants	6–7
Gas Stations, cents per gallon	1½–2	Women's Dress Shops	6–7
Grocery Stores (Individual)	3	5 to 10¢ or 25¢–$2 Stores	4–5
Grocery Stores (Chain)	1–2		

PERCOLATION TEST   A hydraulic engineer's test of soil to determine the ability of the ground to absorb and drain water; a perk test. This information helps to determine the suitability of a site for certain kinds of development, and for the installation of septic tanks or injection wells for sewage treatment plants. A subdivider registering his or her subdivision with HUD must include a percolation report in the application.

If water beneath the surface is not confined to a known and well-defined channel or bed, it is called percolating water; if it is so confined, it is termed a subterranean lake or stream.

PERFECTING TITLE   The process of eliminating any claims against a title, such as having a wife execute a quitclaim deed to release any possible dower claim. To "perfect" is to show of record, as in filing a UCC financing statement or recording an affidavit of surviving joint tenant.

PERFORMANCE BOND   A bond, usually posted by one who is to perform work for another, which assures that a project or undertaking will be completed as per agreement or contract. A performance bond is frequently requested of a contractor to guarantee the completion of a project. The bond usually provides that if the contractor fails to complete the contract, the surety company can itself complete the contract, or pay damages up to the limit of the bond. A performance bond is normally combined with a labor and materials bond, which guarantees the owner that all bills for labor and materials contracted for and used by the contractor will be paid by the surety company if the contractor defaults. Thus the performance bond is the best device to protect the owner against mechanics' liens filed by subcontractors. A performance bond typically costs about one percent of the total construction cost. A contractor must have a good record in order to obtain such a bond. (*See COMPLETION BOND, PAYMENT BOND, SURETY.*)

PERIODIC TENANCY   A leasehold estate that continues from period to period, such as month to month or year to year. All conditions and terms of the tenancy are carried over from period to period, and continue for an uncertain time until proper notice of termination is given. The periodic tenancy is thus characterized by this element of continuity. If a yearly rent is reserved, the tenancy is one from year to year regardless of whether the rent is paid monthly or quarterly. This reservation of rent distinguishes a periodic tenancy from a tenancy at will.

A periodic tenancy may arise by express agreement of the parties, but usually arises by implication, in situations in which no definite time of possession has been set but rent has been fixed at a certain amount per week, per month, or per year. (*See MONTH-TO-MONTH TENANCY, NOTICE, TENANCY AT WILL.*)

PERMANENT FINANCING   A long-term loan, as opposed to an interim short-term loan. Certain lenders specialize in lending short-term money to finance the construction of condominiums, shopping centers, or other major projects. Other lenders specialize in lending long-term money to "take out" the interim or construction lender. In the past, permanent loans typically ranged from 20 to 30 years at fixed interest rates. Today a variable interest rate may be used or a rate may be set for an initial period and then renegotiated.

With construction loans, there is often a triparty agreement covering the permanent lender, interim lender, and borrower so that: there is a joint use of documents; the interim lender will agree not to assign the loan to another lender; and the interim loan will be assigned to the permanent lender within a stated time upon completion of construction and satisfaction of specified conditions. (*See TAKEOUT FINANCING.*)

PERMISSIVE WASTE   The failure of a lessee or life tenant to prevent damage to the real property under their control. Also called *negligent or passive waste*. For example, permissive waste occurs when a tenant fails to keep the property adequately protected during winter, resulting in damaged plumbing and improvements. In such a case, the landlord may sue for damages or, in some cases, seek an injunction to prevent further waste. (*See WASTE.*)

PERSON   Statutes vary as to the definition of *person* because a legal person is not always necessarily an individual, but may also be a corporation, a government or governmental agency, a business trust, an estate, a trust, an association, a partnership, a joint venture, two or more persons having a joint or common interest, or any other legal or commercial entity.

PERSONAL LIABILITY   The obligation to satisfy a debt to the extent of one's personal assets. Shareholders in a corporation and limited partners in a limited partnership syndication are usually protected against personal liability for debts of the corporation or syndication. A borrower under a nonrecourse loan also avoids personal liability on the loan (the lender must look solely to the sale of secured property for recovery of amounts owed). A guarantor is personally liable for the default of the borrower. (*See NONRECOURSE.*)

PERSONAL PROPERTY   Things which are tangible and movable; property which is not classified as real property, such as chattels, also called *personalty*. Title to personal property is transferred by way of a bill of sale, as contrasted with a deed for real property.

Items of personal property frequently become the object of dispute between buyer and seller, most often due to whether an item is considered a "fixture" or due to the seller's attempt to substitute a similar item. Some cautious buyers insert a clause in their purchase contracts to the effect that the buyer will get the appliances "as currently installed and used in the premises."

A tree is real property while it is rooted in the ground, but when it is severed, it is transformed into personal property. When lumber is assembled, however, and used as material to construct a house, it once again becomes a fixture, or real property. (*See FIXTURE, REAL PROPERTY, UNIFORM COMMERCIAL CODE.*)

PERSONAL REPRESENTATIVE   The title given to the person designated in a will or appointed by the probate court to settle the estate of a deceased person. Prior to the Uniform Probate Court such a person was called an executor or administrator.

PERSONALTY   Personal property; a chattel.

PER STIRPES   To take a share under the law of descent by right of representation, as opposed to taking *per capita* or in one's individual right. For example, assume Sylvester Lee dies without a will, leaving $60,000. He leaves no wife, but has two children surviving, Pat and Mike, plus two grandchildren by a deceased third child. Pat and Mike take their per capita share of one-third each. The two children of the deceased child would take per stirpes (by right of representation) equally of the deceased child's one-third share. Each grandchild, then, takes a one-sixth share, or $10,000. (*See DESCENT, INTESTATE.*)

PETITION   A formal request or application to an authority, such as a court, seeking specific relief or redress of some wrong. Petitions frequently encountered in real estate include: a petition to a court of equity for partition of real estate; a petition filed in circuit court by a respondent in a state discrimination hearing; a petition to the local zoning board for a zoning change.

PHYSICAL DETERIORATION   A reduction in utility or value resulting from an impairment of physical condition, which deterioration can be divided into either curable or incurable types. A form of depreciation caused by the action of the physical elements, such as wind or snow, or just ordinary wear and tear.

Two common methods of calculating physical depreciation are the observed condition method and the straight-line or age-life method. (*See DEPRECIATION.*)

PHYSICAL LIFE   The actual age or life span of a structure, as opposed to its economic life. (*See ECONOMIC LIFE.*)

PIER   A column, usually of steel reinforced concrete, evenly spaced under a structure to support its weight. In a house, foundation piers are formed by drilling holes in the earth to a prescribed depth and pouring concrete into them. Foundation piers that support some structures, such as bridges, may be above the ground. The term may also refer to the part of a wall between windows or other openings that bear the wall weight.

PIGGYBACK   As it relates to industrial properties, a system in which truck trailers loaded with merchandise are placed aboard rail flat cars to be hauled by railroad between two points.

PIGGYBACK LOAN   A joint loan with two lenders sharing a single mortgage. For example, a bank may originate a loan at 85 percent of the appraised value of the property. Another private lender would supply the top 15 percent. The private lender would most likely obtain private mortgage insurance to cover its loan, and the insurance would continue in effect until the loan was reduced to 70 percent of the appraised value at which point the originating bank would be liable exclusively. The private lender is the piggyback lender and is subordinated to the senior lender. A piggyback loan is distinguishable from a second mortgage in that there is only one mortgage on the property. This distinction is important because many institutional lenders can lend only on first mortgages. (See PARTICIPATION MORTGAGE.)

PILASTER An upright, architectural member or vertical projection from a wall, on either one or both sides, used to strengthen the wall by adding support or preventing buckling.

P.I.T.I. Abbreviation for principal, interest, taxes, and insurance, as commonly found in an all-inclusive mortgage payment.

PLACE A cul-de-sac serving more than three lots and exceeding 125 feet in length.

PLACEMENT FEE A fee charged by a mortgage broker for negotiating a loan between lender and borrower. (See MORTGAGE BROKER.)

PLAIN LANGUAGE LAW A federal or state law which requires certain consumer contracts to be written in a clear and coherent manner, using words with common everyday meanings, and appropriately divided and captioned by its various sections. Some states, such as Hawaii and New York, require real estate rental agreements to be written in plain language.

PLAINTIFF The person who commences a lawsuit; the complainant. (See DEFENDANT.)

PLANNED UNIT DEVELOPMENT (PUD) A relatively recent concept in housing designed to produce a high density of dwellings and maximum utilization of open spaces. This efficient use of land allows greater flexibility for residential land and development. It also usually results in lower-priced homes and minimum maintenance cost. Often, PUDs are specifically provided for in zoning ordinances or are listed as a conditional permitted use.

The developer plans the project and seeks local governmental approval of the proposed PUD zone. To provide for maintenance of the common areas, there is organized a nonprofit community association. The developer records a declaration of covenants and restrictions, and records a subdivision plat reserving common areas to the members of the association but not to the general public.

The PUD concept is really an "overlay" zoning which enables a developer to obtain a higher density (and sometimes a mixed-use for commercial and industrial) than is permitted by the underlying zoning. Because the buildings are usually clustered together, there is more green area left open for parks and recreation. For example, compare the following two illustrations. The first is a rendition of a conventional-design subdivision, containing 368 housing units. Note that it uses 23,200 linear feet of street and leaves only 1.6 acres open for parks. Contrast this with the second figure, the PUD. Both subdivisions are equal in size and terrain.

However, by minimally reducing lot sizes and clustering them around limited access cul-de-sac streets, the number of housing units remains nearly the same—366; the street areas are reduced—17,000 linear feet; and open space is drastically increased—23.5 acres. In addition, using modern building designs, this clustered plan could be modified to comfortably accommodate 550 patio homes or 1,100 townhouses.

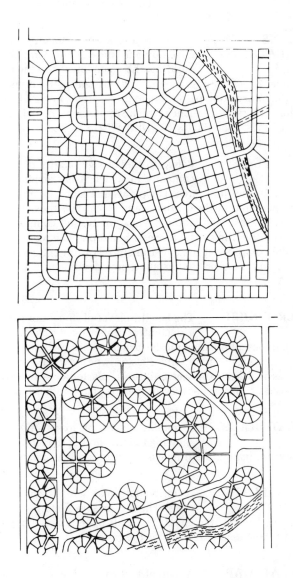

Though similar in some respects, a PUD is quite different from a condominium. In a PUD, the unit is a lot, thus the PUD owners own the land under their houses, there is no direct interest in the common areas, the community association is in corporate form, and the PUD is created by covenants in the deed or master lease. In a condominium, the unit is a space of air, there is a percentage of ownership interest in the common areas, so condo owners do not directly own the land under their units, the association of owners is usually unincorporated, and the condominium is created by recording a declaration pursuant to state condominium laws. PUDs are also used in resort housing and even shopping center projects. (*See* DENSITY ZONING.)

PLANNING COMMISSION An official agency usually organized on the county level, to direct and control the use, design, and development of land.

PLANS AND SPECIFICATIONS Plans include all the drawings pertaining to a development under consideration, such as the building, the mechanical and the electrical drawings, and the like. Specifications include the written instructions to the builder containing all the information pertaining to dimensions, materials, workmanship, style, fabrication, colors, and finishes which supplement the details appearing on the working drawings. (*See* WORKING DRAWINGS.)

PLANT Refers to the storage facility of a title insurance company in which it has accumulated complete title records of properties in its area. The plants also store the original title reports (called *starters*) prepared by the company and sometimes those prepared by other companies as well. Most plants now have sophisticated computer retrieval systems to help speed the title search process. Some plants have computers that are hooked up to the computer at the government recording office, so the title plant has the recording information the instant a new document is entered on record. (*See* TITLE PLANT.)

PLASTER FINISH The last thin layer of fine-grain plaster applied as a decorative finish over several coats of coarse plaster on the lath base. Finishing plaster usually has a high ratio of lime to sand, while coarser plasters have more sand. Plaster is pasty when applied to the wall, but it hardens as it dries. In newer buildings, plasterboard or gypsum board is often used instead of plaster because it does not have to harden.

PLAT BOOK A public record of maps of subdivided land showing the division of the land into blocks, lots, and parcels, and indicating the dimensions of individual parcels.

PLATE A horizontal piece which forms a base for supports. The sill or sole plate rests on the foundation and forms the base for the studs. The wall plate is laid along the top of the wall studs and forms a support base for the rafters.

PLAT MAP A map of a town, section, or subdivision indicating the location and boundaries of individual properties. Generally, a plat illustrates such details as lots, blocks, sections, streets, public easements, and monuments. A plat also includes dates and scales, engineering data such as the location of flood plains, restrictive covenants, elevation, and names of adjoining owners. Plats and platting are generally an important part of subdivision procedures. These procedures often require the subdivider to submit a preliminary plat for consideration. The subdivider later files a final plat after improvements have been completed and approved by the appropriate officials.

PLAZA   A public square or meeting place usually in the center of an area, frequently a shopping complex.

PLEDGE   The transfer or delivery of property to a lender to be held as security for repayment of a debt. An hypothecation, such as a mortgage, differs from a pledge in that hypothecated property is put up as security but possession is not surrendered as in a pledge.

Some savings and loan associations will loan an amount over their authorized limit when the borrower, seller, or some other person pledges sufficient funds to cover such excess amount. The pledge account is like a savings account, although the pledgor cannot withdraw funds except in accordance with the pledge agreement. The lender thus has the benefits of more effective asset management.

A common form of pledge relates to corporate stock certificates delivered to a lender.

PLEDGED ACCOUNT MORTGAGE (PAM)   An alternative mortgage device in which the buyer places down payment funds into an interest-bearing account that is pledged for future payment to the lender. A portion of the interest plus the principal balance is used to supplement the buyer's regular monthly payments in the early years of the loan. (See *FLEXIBLE-PAYMENT MORTGAGE*.)

PLOT PLAN   A plan showing the layout of improvements on a property site, a plot. The plot plan usually includes location, dimensions, parking areas, landscaping, and the like.

PLOTTAGE VALUE   The increased usability and value resulting from the combining or consolidating of adjacent lots into one larger lot. Plottage is also referred to as assemblage although the latter is more often used to describe the process of consolidation. The term is often used in eminent domain matters to designate the added value given to lots that are contiguous. (See *ASSEMBLAGE*.)

POCKET LICENSE CARD   Evidence of real estate licensure, sometimes called a "wallet card," issued by the state real estate licensing agency. This card should be carried by a licensee at all times and should be presented when requested by any person with whom the licensee is dealing with regard to real estate.

POCKET LISTING   A listing which is retained by the listing broker or salesperson, and is not made available to other brokers in the office or to other multiple-listing service members. This practice is strongly discouraged by the profession and is forbidden by many brokers' offices. Under MLS rules, a member *must* generally report any new listing except for commercial listings, which may be optional, within a short time—two or three days after obtaining such a listing. (See *MULTIPLE LISTING*.)

POINT OF BEGINNING   The starting point in a metes and bounds description of property—usually a street intersection or a specific monument. To be complete, a legal description of a property must always return to the point of beginning in order to describe the area accurately. (See *METES AND BOUNDS*.)

POINT OF SWITCH (SWITCHPOINT OR TURNOUT) In the case of one rail track separating from another and diverging (for example, a spur track leaving a drill track), the initial point at which the separation occurs is the point of switch.

POINTS A generic term for a percentage of the principal conventional loan amount; a rate adjustment factor. A lender often charges a borrower some service-charge points for making the loan. Each point is equal to one percent of the loan amount. In the initial stages of a loan application, the lender often does not know what loan amount will be approved, so he or she cannot state the finance charge in dollars and cents. Thus, it is convenient to state the charge as a set percentage of the loan amount, such as five points. Points are sometimes justified to cover lender expenses in originating the loan and to offset any losses when the mortgage is sold in the secondary mortgage market. Points can be used to increase the lender's yield or to "buy down" the rate. In conventional financing, the points may be paid by the buyer or the seller.

With an FHA or VA loan, the buyer by law may only pay the origination fee, and the seller must pay all of the remaining discount charges or discount points. These discount charges have the effect of increasing the yield on the mortgage at the rate of $\frac{1}{8}$ percent for each discount point. A charge of 4 points would thus increase an $11\frac{1}{4}$ percent mortgage to an $11\frac{3}{4}$ percent yield. This rule of thumb formula that one point equals $\frac{1}{8}$ increase in the interest rate takes into account the fact that the present worth of money is economically more valuable than money to be received in the future. Since the discount is a means of raising the effective interest rate, the buyer would be paying a higher interest rate than the law allows on FHA and VA loans if allowed to pay the discount. When a seller pays the discount points, then it really amounts to a discount in the sales price he or she will receive.

An agreement to pay points should be in the sales contract, and should be covered by the broker in the listing agreement. Where a sales contract is silent on the payment of points, a seller cannot be held liable to pay points on a buyer's mortgage. In addition, where a seller pays points, the seller should be made aware that the seller might have to pay more than originally anticipated due to such variables as: an appraisal at a value lower than the seller originally thought; property repairs, as required per FHA, calling for building permit fees and other costs; and market changes that may cause a higher point structure.

Points are a one-time charge paid for the use of money. The federal tax law provides that, where points are paid as compensation for the use of borrowed money (and thus qualify as interest for tax purposes rather than as payment for the lender's services), the points are a substitute for a higher stated annual interest rate. As such, points are similar to a prepayment of interest and are to be treated as paid over the term of the loan for purposes of the prepaid interest rule. This also applies to charges that are similar to points, such as a loan-processing fee or a premium charge. Note, however, that discount charges paid by the seller for an FHA loan are not interest and therefore are not deductible.

The deductibility of points paid on certain home purchase loans and improvement loans paid by a cash-basis taxpayer on any indebtedness incurred in connection with the purchase or improvement of, and secured by, his or her principal residence are deductible in the year of payment if two conditions are met. First, the payment of points must be an established business practice in the area where the loan is incurred. Second, the deduction is allowed only to the extent that the amount of the payment does not exceed the amount generally charged in the area.

Under federal Truth-in-Lending, the borrower's payment of points must be reflected in the annual percentage rate and fully disclosed to the consumer. (*See ANNUAL PERCENTAGE RATE, BUYDOWN, DISCOUNT POINTS, FHA, PREPAID INTEREST.*)

POLICE POWER   The constitutional authority and inherent power of a state to adopt and enforce laws and regulations to promote and support the public health, safety, morals, and general welfare. Such laws must be uniform in operation, nondiscriminatory, and cannot be advantageous to any one particular person or group. In essence, it is a policy power. Police power is derived from individual state constitutions, which also vests the power in counties, cities, and municipalities to adopt and enforce appropriate local ordinances and regulations which are not in conflict with general laws. Some examples of police power are the right to tax, the right to regulate land use through a general plan and zoning, the right to require persons selling real estate to be licensed, the right to regulate pollution, environmental control, and rent control.

Traditional concepts of the police power have been broadened in recent years to include the furtherance of the aesthetic beauty of the community. For example, courts have upheld an ordinance restricting advertising in state parks, and have upheld the regulation of the appearance of a community through design review boards.

Also derived from police power is the right to damage or destroy private property (without compensation to the owner) when such an act is necessary to protect the public interest. This may happen, for example, when a condominium unit is on fire and the fire department must destroy an adjoining unit to extinguish the fire and save the rest of the building. While the government would not be required to compensate an owner for such destruction, a valid claim may be filed against the insurance policy covering the burning unit, or against the owner's own policy. Although police power permits the state to regulate the use of an individual's property in order to protect public health, safety, and welfare, such regulation has its limits. If it goes too far, it will be recognized as a "taking." This requires that the state pay just compensation to the individual affected. (*See CONDEMNATION, EMINENT DOMAIN, ESCHEAT, GENERAL PLAN.*)

PORTE COCHERE   A roofed structure extending from the entrance of a building over an adjacent driveway to shelter those getting into or out of vehicles.

POSSESSION   The act of either actually or constructively possessing or occupying property. Possession imparts constructive notice that the party in possession may have certain rights. Therefore, when someone is in possession of property under a *claim of ownership* and a buyer purchases the property from the *owner of record*, the purchaser for value is *not* protected under the recording laws since possession imparts constructive notice in much the same way as does the recording of a deed. It is said that the purchaser should have inquired into the claims of the person in possession. For this reason, it is sometimes called inquiry notice. Also, possession of a property often cures an indefinite description in deeds, leases, contracts of sale, and the like. The right to possess real property typically passes to the buyer upon the closing of a sales transaction. (*See CONSTRUCTIVE NOTICE, INQUIRY NOTICE, RECORDING, OCCUPANCY AGREEMENT.*)

POSSIBILITY OF REVERTER

A possibility that property granted under a deed may revert back to the grantor if the grantee breaches a condition subject to which the property was granted. For example, Napoleon Baker deeds his farm to Steve Stowe and his heirs, so long as Stowe does not permit the consumption of alcohol on the property. Upon Stowe's breaching the condition by allowing alcoholic beverages on the property, the property would automatically revert back to Baker. The modern view is that a possibility of reverter is an estate in land and can be sold and devised. (See *FEE SIMPLE DEFEASIBLE*.)

POSTDATED CHECK

A check which has on its face a date later than the actual date of signing, and which is therefore not negotiable until the later date arrives, since a bank cannot make payment before the stated date. Such a check is valid provided it was not postdated for an illegal purpose. The person to whom a postdated check is delivered is deemed to acquire title as of the date of delivery, not the date of the check. It is not good practice for a broker to accept a postdated check as a deposit. It is preferable to draw up a promissory note that provides for recovery of costs and attorney fees by the prevailing party if the deposit is not paid on time. When a broker accepts a check or promissory note, the broker must disclose this fact to the principal. Note that an escrow company will not usually accept a postdated check, although they may hold a properly dated check one day before cashing.

POTABLE WATER

Water which is able to be safely and agreeably used for drinking. A public offering statement used in the sale of subdivided land must disclose whether potable water is available.

POWER OF ATTORNEY

A written instrument authorizing a person, the attorney-in-fact, to act as the agent on behalf of another to the extent indicated in the instrument. Also called a warrant of attorney or a letter of attorney. Highlights of pertinent general practice with respect to the use of powers of attorney for the sale or purchase of real estate are:

1. An attorney-in-fact may not require a real estate license to sell the owner's property. An exception to this would occur if the attorney-in-fact is engaged in real estate development or brokerage and is purposely evading the licensing law.

2. Good title practice requires that the power of attorney be recorded; otherwise the document signed by the attorney-in-fact, such as a deed, will not be effective against third parties. The power of attorney must be acknowledged to be recorded. A notice of revocation is needed to revoke a recorded power of attorney.

3. Good title practice also requires that the parties use a "special" or *limited* power of attorney rather than an all-inclusive *general* power of attorney to convey real estate. The power of attorney is strictly construed and thus must specifically authorize the attorney-in-fact to carry out the full transaction. A power to *sell* does not carry with it the power to *convey*.

4. Any instrument signed with a power of attorney should be executed as follows: "John Frank by John Neil his attorney-in-fact." The agent's name should never be signed first. The agent may type in the principal's name.

5. One spouse can be the attorney-in-fact for the other spouse for the purchase of property, but this may interfere with homestead, dower, or curtesy rights in the sale of property. An agent cannot validly act if the agent has an adverse interest in the transaction.

6. Normally, death of either the principal or attorney-in-fact automatically revokes the power of attorney. Most title companies are extremely cautious with power of attorney documents because of the revocation by death rule.

7. Under the equal dignities rule, the power of attorney must be in writing since the real estate documents to be signed under the power of attorney must be in writing.

8. When the transaction is to be closed in escrow, an original and three copies of the power of attorney should be forwarded to escrow. (See ATTORNEY-IN-FACT, EQUAL DIGNITIES RULE, PRACTICE OF LAW.)

POWER OF SALE   A clause in a mortgage authorizing the holder of the mortgage to sell the property in the event of the borrower's default. The proceeds from the public sale are used to pay off the mortgage debt first, and any surplus is paid to the mortgagor. A power of sale clause is also found in trust deeds, giving the trustee authority to sell the trust property under certain circumstances. Powers of sale are not used in all states.

The power of sale is a matter of contract and cannot be validly exercised unless all the terms of the mortgage are complied with.

Generally, when dealing with land registered in the Torrens system, the certificate of title must note that there is a power of sale contained in the mortgage. Otherwise, no subsequent document, such as a deed or assignment of lease executed pursuant to the power of sale will be accepted for registration. (See CERTIFICATE OF TITLE, FORECLOSURE, SOLDIERS AND SAILORS CIVIL RELIEF ACT, TORRENS SYSTEM.)

PRACTICE OF LAW   Rendering services which are peculiar to the law profession, such as preparing legal documents, giving legal advice and counsel, or construing contracts by which legal rights are secured. A broker's license can be suspended or revoked for the practice of law, regardless of whether or not fees are charged. The broker also has an ethical duty to recommend that legal counsel be obtained when the interest of either buyer or seller requires it.

There is universal uncertainty as to whether the broker's use of certain forms constitutes the practice of law. While it is permissible for the broker to help complete certain standard forms, such as a sales contract, the broker has a duty to do so with accuracy and with certainty. Such completion of forms is permissible only where it is incidental to the broker's earning a commission and not where he or she makes a separate charge for filling in the form. In most states the broker cannot prepare documents such as contracts for deed, deeds, options, and certain leases.

Only attorneys and the parties to a transaction are authorized to prepare legal instruments. However, many state Realtor® boards and bar associations have broker-lawyer accords which recognize that the real estate broker must have authority to secure some kind of agreement between buyer and seller, evidence of the transaction, and provisions for payment of the broker's compensation. This usually gives a broker the authority to fill in the blanks of preprinted documents only, and not to draft legal documents or close transactions (as some states recognize these acts as the practice of law). In addition, the National Association of Realtors® considers it both unlawful practice of law and unethical for a Realtor® to draft a power of attorney for a client.

The National Association of Realtors® and the American Bar Association have agreed to a national broker-lawyer accord. Article I of such agreement states that:

> The REALTOR® shall not practice law or give legal advice directly or indirectly; he shall not act as a public conveyancer, nor give advice or opinions as to the legal effect of legal instruments, nor give opinions concerning the validity of title to real estate, and he shall not prevent or discourage any party to a real estate transaction from employing the services of a lawyer.

PRECLOSING   A preliminary meeting preceding the formal closing where documents are prepared, reviewed, and signed, and estimated prorations are made well in advance of the closing date. Preclosings are often used in the conversion of entire apartment buildings to condominiums, as there may be hundreds of separate units to close finally on one day.

PREEMPTION   1. A clause sometimes inserted in a deed of subdivided land, in which the developer either retains the right of first refusal on a resale of the property or that right is given to the owner of an adjacent lot who may exercise the right when the property is offered for sale. Also contained in some condominium documents in which any condo owner has the right of first refusal upon the resale of another unit in the building. (*See RIGHT OF FIRST REFUSAL.*)

2. A legal doctrine in which one law is superior to another. For example, federal lenders make the argument that, under the Supremacy Clause of the U.S. Constitution, the federal laws concerning validity of due-on-sale clauses preempt any state laws or court cases to the contrary. The OCC and the FHLBB have adopted regulations preempting state usury laws under certain conditions.

PREFAB HOUSING   See *COMPONENT BUILDING, MODULAR HOUSING.*

PRELIMINARY COSTS   Those costs which are incurred in conjunction with, but prior to, actual commencement of the main project. An example of such costs would be feasibility studies, soil tests, financing commitments, and preliminary legal matters.

PRELIMINARY REPORT   A title report which is made before a title insurance policy is issued or when escrow is opened. A preliminary report or policy of title insurance reports only on those documents having an effect upon the title and should not be relied upon as being an abstract. An *abstract of title*, on the other hand, reflects all instruments affecting title from the time of the original grant and also includes a memorandum of each instrument, and makes no attempt to determine which of the documents currently affects record title. The "preliminary" is not a binder or commitment that the title company will thereafter insure the title to the property, although this commitment may be obtained at an added cost. (*See ABSTRACT OF TITLE, TITLE REPORT.*)

PREMISES 1. A specific section of a deed which states the names of the parties, the recital of consideration, and the legal description of the property. 2. The subject property, such as the property which is deeded or the unit that is leased. This generally includes the dwelling unit, appurtenances, grounds, facilities held out for the use of tenants, and any other area or facility whose use is promised to the tenant. Premises is sometimes synonymous with land. (*See DEED.*)

PREMIUM 1. The consideration given to invite a loan or a bargain, such as the consideration paid to the assignor by the assignee of a lease or a contract such as an option. In leasing property, sometimes part of the rent is capitalized and this premium is paid in a lump sum at the time the lease is signed. 2. The amount paid for insurance coverage. The unearned premium is that portion which must be returned to the insured upon cancellation of the policy.

PREPAID EXPENSES Expenses which are paid before they are currently due. Most fire insurance premiums are paid three years in advance. Rent is normally paid a month in advance. At closing, the seller is normally credited with prepaid expenses and charged for prepaid income, such as rent received.

PREPAID INTEREST The paying of interest before it is due. Prior to 1975, the prepayment of interest was a tax-saving technique because the IRS allowed a taxpayer to deduct the prepayment of interest under certain circumstances. The Internal Revenue Code, however, now provides that interest cannot be deducted as prepaid. Interest must be deducted over the life of the loan when and as earned. Mortgage service points are also subject to the prepayment rules. However, mortgage service points paid in connection with the financing of a principal residence may be deducted in the year paid, if payment of points is an established business practice in the area, and the amount paid does not exceed the amount generally charged in the area. (*See POINTS.*)

PREPAID ITEMS In setting up a reserve or impound account, as in a VA or FHA loan, the borrower makes one lump sum payment when the loan money is paid out. This payment is often referred to as prepaid items and covers prorated taxes and insurance plus one month's advance payment for taxes and insurance. (*See IMPOUND ACCOUNT.*)

PREPAYMENT PENALTY The amount set by the creditor as a penalty to the debtor for paying off the debt prior to its maturity; an early withdrawal charge. The prepayment penalty is charged by the lender to recoup a portion of interest that the lender had planned to earn when the loan was made. It covers the lender for initial costs to set up the loan, to service it, and to carry it in the early years of high risk. This punitive device also may represent the loss of income to the lender for the time the mortgage is paid off and the funds remain uncommitted. The reason most lenders are willing to allow prepayment *after* five years without penalty is that much of the total note's interest has been paid in by that time.

Typical language concerning prepayment is "additional principal payments may be made with any monthly installment, but prepayments made in any calendar year in excess of 20 percent of the original amount of this note shall be subject to a charge of one percent of such prepayments." Some states limit the prepayment penalties a lender may charge while some prohibit them altogether. Some loans contain a prepayment and coasting clause, under which the buyer can pay before the money is due and then "coast" so long as there is a surplus built up. The amount of the penalty varies, but it is often an amount equal to the interest that would have been paid on the balance for a specified period of, for example, 90 days.

Real estate loans with savings and loan institutions can be prepaid at any time and, by law, the penalty may not exceed an amount greater than one percent of the prepayment amount. The amount of the prepayment penalty is usually specified in the promissory note. The current trend is to treat excessive prepayment penalties as being usurious and thus not enforceable. A reasonable prepayment charge, however, is not considered interest since it is payable only in connection with the borrower's exercise of an option given by the lender.

Some lending institutions will waive the penalty if the borrower refinances with the same lender. Others may waive it provided the source of funds to pay off the loan come from personal means as opposed to refinancing with another lender. On the other hand, some lenders will exercise their penalty provisions even in the event of any involuntary payment such as receipt of condemnation or insurance proceeds.

The regulations of the Federal Home Loan Bank Board provide that there can be no prepayment penalty unless such is mentioned in the loan document. These regulations also set forth limitations on the amount of any prepayment penalty. The trend is toward eliminating the prepayment penalty, as in certain federal credit union rules.

PREPAYMENT PRIVILEGE   The right of the debtor to pay off part or all of a debt without penalty or premium or other fee prior to maturity, such as in a mortgage or agreement of sale. If the debtor prepays part of the loan, the payment is usually applied to the last payments falling due. Thus, if in January the debtor prepays for six months he or she still has to make the February payment and the large payment will be credited against the final six monthly installments of the loan.

No right to prepay exists unless agreed upon, for example, as when monthly payments are in a stated amount "or more" or "not less than," such as "$200 or more per month." Where there is no right to prepay a mortgage, it is called a "closed mortgage." Where there is a right to prepay, it is called an "open mortgage." If there is no right to prepay stated in the contract and the seller won't consent to a prepayment, the buyer cannot force a prepayment by purposely defaulting on several installments, tendering the balance due with interest to the date of payment, and arguing that the default in the mortgage automatically triggered the acceleration clause. Courts have ruled that an acceleration clause is for the benefit of the creditor, and the creditor can elect whether or not to enforce it.

An increasingly popular practice is to have a time period in the first part of the mortgage in which there can be no prepayment. This is generally known as a "lock-in." Note that a lender may not charge a prepayment penalty on any FHA-insured or VA-guaranteed loan. (*See ACCELERATION CLAUSE, INSTALLMENT SALE, LOCK-IN CLAUSE, "OR MORE" CLAUSE*.)

PRE-SALE   A prior-to-construction sales program by a developer. Often a developer is required to pre-sell a certain percentage of units before a lender will commit to finance construction of a condo project. In some states, pre-sales in a condominium project may only be made after the developer obtains a preliminary public report. Such pre-sales are not binding until the purchaser receives the final public report. The more recent marketing trend is away from the pre-sale program and toward selling under a final public report during the construction period, especially if the lender is participating in the profits of the project as a joint venturer.

PRESCRIPTION   Acquiring a right in property, usually in the form of an intangible property right such as an easement or right-of-way, by means of adverse use of property that is continuous and uninterrupted for the prescriptive period established by state statute. Use of land is adverse when it is made under a claim of right. Therefore, there is no adverse use if the owner has granted permission, if the user has paid for the use, or if the user has admitted that the owner has a superior right in the property.

Prescription is often used interchangeably with the term adverse possession, which more strictly refers to the acquiring of *title* to lands. As in adverse possession, the essential elements are that the prescriptive right be adverse, under claim of right, continuous and uninterrupted, open, notorious and exclusive, with the knowledge and acquiesence of the servient owner, and continuing for the full prescriptive period. By continuous is meant that the property is used on a regular basis. There is usually no prescription against the state or against Torrens registered property (*See ADVERSE POSSESSION, EASEMENT*.)

PRESENTMENT   *See NOTICE OF DISHONOR.*

PRESENT VALUE OF   A doctrine which is based on the fact that money
ONE DOLLAR   has a time value. The present worth of a payment to be received at some time in the future is the amount of the payment received in the future less the loss of interest until receipt of the payment. The present value of one dollar receivable one year from now is equal to one dollar less the loss of interest for one year. For example, if interest is six percent a year, then the value of the dollar next year is $.94.

Tables (such as the Inwood tables) have been devised to set forth a list of mathematical factors to be used to discount money to be received in the future at various interest rates over various periods of time. These tables are most frequently used to compute the value of a lessor's reversionary interest especially in long-term lease valuations. They are also used to determine the appropriate conveyance tax on the initial issuance of a ground lease. The present value of one dollar is also used in computations related to the value of a building in determining the present value of the assigned leases. (*See INTERNAL RATE OF RETURN, INWOOD TABLE*.)

PRESERVATION DISTRICT A zoning district established to protect and preserve park land, wilderness areas, open spaces, beach reserves, scenic areas, historic sites, open ranges, watersheds, water supplies, fish, and wildlife, and to promote forestry and grazing.

PRESUMPTION A rule of law which provides that a court will draw a particular inference from a certain fact or evidence unless and until the truth of such inference is disproved or rebutted. For example, the date on a deed is presumed to be the date of delivery, and a transfer to two or more people with no tenancy stated is presumed to be a tenancy in common with equal interests. (*See ADVERSE POSSESSION, DELIVERY, POSSESSION.*)

PREVAILING PARTY The person who wins a lawsuit. Some contracts provide that, in the event of a lawsuit arising under the contract, the prevailing party is entitled to be reimbursed for reasonable attorney fees incurred.

PREVAILING RATE A general term to describe the average interest rate presently being charged by banks and lending institutions on mortgage loans.

PRICE The quantity of a thing which is exchanged for another. The amount of money paid for an item; the consideration; the purchase price. There is a distinction between market price and market value. (*See MARKET VALUE.*)

PRICE FIXING The practice of conspiring to establish fixed fees or prices for services rendered or goods sold. In recent years, the setting of attorney's fees by local bar associations and commission percentages and management fees by local realty associations have been successfully attacked as price fixing and thus violations of the Sherman Antitrust Act. (*See ANTITRUST.*)

PRIMA FACIE EVIDENCE A legal term used to refer to evidence which is good and sufficient on its face ("at first view") to establish a given fact or prove a case. This kind of evidence will prove a case unless it is rebutted or contradicted; presumptive evidence.

PRIMARY MORTGAGE MARKET Refers to the market in which lenders originate loans and make funds available directly to borrowers, bear the risk of long-term financing, and usually service the loan until the debt is discharged. (*See SECONDARY MORTGAGE MARKET.*)

PRIME RATE The minimum interest rate charged by a commercial bank on short-term loans to its largest and strongest clients (those with the highest credit standings). Prime rate is often used as a cost-of-money indicator. Prime rates are determined in part by the rates banks have to pay for the money they lend to their prime rate borrowers. Interest rates obtainable on other types of loans and the return on investments, such as federal government securities, also have considerable influence on the setting of prime rates. The supply of money and the demand for loans causes the prime rate to fluctuate, sometimes on a daily basis. The decisions of the Federal Reserve Bank to increase or decrease the supply of money cause prime rates to increase or decrease, as does the Federal Reserve Bank's rediscount rate.

On many large loans the interest rates float with the prime rate. For example, the interest rate may be stated as three percent (or three "points") above the prime rate of the Bank of Money, determined as of the first banking day of each month. In a very volatile money market, such as where the prime rate changes six or seven times in a month, some lenders structure their loans using the daily prime rate average for the month. Many interim construction loans have the interest rate tied to the prime rate; thus, large increases in the prime rate during construction can have a destructive effect on the profits of a real estate development. (See *FLOAT*.)

PRIME TENANT   A tenant (or related group of tenants) who is the largest single occupant of a building. Such occupancy is usually for 25 percent or more of the building's rental area. The prime tenant may be the principal tenant of a property by virtue of name and reputation. A tenant who occupies the largest amount of floor space leased, or who possibly owns the building it occupies, is also considered a prime tenant. In a sublease situation, the original lessee is sometimes referred to as the prime tenant.

PRINCIPAL   1. One of the main parties to a transaction. For example, the buyer and seller are principals in the purchase of real property.

2. In a fiduciary relationship, the principal is the person who hires a real estate broker to represent him or her in the sale of property. The phrase "principals only," often found in real estate ads, is meant to exclude real estate agents from contacting the owners of the property. (See *FIDUCIARY*.)

3. The capital sum; interest is paid on the principal. An amortized payment includes interest and principal. Note: do not confuse *principal* and *principle*. Principles are rules like codes of behavior or ethics.

PRINCIPAL BROKER   Under some state license laws, the licensed broker directly in charge of and responsible for the real estate operations conducted by a brokerage company. When absent from his or her place of business for more than five calendar days, the principal broker usually must notify the real estate commission and obtain a temporary substitute broker. The principal broker (or "PB") is an employee (usually not an independent contractor) and is often paid a salary and sometimes receives an override on the salespeople's commissions as well. (See *TRUST FUND ACCOUNT*.)

PRINCIPAL MERIDIAN   The prime meridian intersecting the reference marker of a survey which is used as a reference line for numbering ranges. (See *BASE LINE, DESCRIPTION, LEGAL DESCRIPTION, METES AND BOUNDS*.)

PRIOR APPROPRIATION   A theory of water law based on the principle, restated as "first in time is first in right," as regards the right to divert water from a water source. The theory is that if available water were equally divided among all potential users, there would not be an adequate supply to produce anything; but, if the water were concentrated in a few, then at least something would be produced. (*See CORREL-ATIVE WATER RIGHT.*)

PRIORITY   The order of position, time or place. The priority of liens is generally determined by the order in which the lien documents are recorded, except that real property tax liens have priority even over recorded liens. Thus the old adage "prior in time is prior in right." (*See RECORDING.*)

PRIVATE MORTGAGE INSURANCE   A special form of insurance designed to permit lenders to increase their loan-to-market-value ratio, often up to 95 percent of the market value of the property. Many lenders are restricted to 80 percent loans by government regulations, special loss reserve requirements, or internal management policies related to mortgage portfolio mix. A lender may, however, loan up to 95 percent of the property value if the excess of the loan amount over 80 percent of value is insured by a private mortgage guaranty insurer. Mortgages insured by private companies are sometimes called conventional guaranteed mortgages.

If it approves the loan, the mortgage insurance company will issue a commitment to insure the lender under a policy carrying 20 percent of the loan balance. Upon receipt of the Certificate of Insurance, the lender may increase the loan amount to a higher percentage of the value of the property.

The borrower pays the premiums for the insurance. This usually amounts to either 1 percent of the loan at closing and ¼ of 1 percent of the monthly outstanding balance each year until such balance reaches 80 percent of the total value, or one set fee (such as 2½ percent) at the closing. If the loan is prepaid, a portion of the prepaid premium may be rebated to the borrower.

Most policies cover the top 20 percent to 25 percent of the loan, which is viewed to be the risk portion of the higher ratio loan. This enables the mortgage insurance company to charge lower rates than the FHA, which insures 100 percent of the loan. However, unlike the FHA, which requires the insurance be maintained throughout the life of the loan, policies on privately insured loans permit the lender to discontinue insurance coverage when the lender is confident the risk level has been sufficiently reduced. This determination is made on a case-by-case basis. Mortgage insurance is noncancellable in that the mortgage insurance company must always renew the lender's policy on a loan at the rate quoted at issuance unless there has been nonpayment. In the case of a member of the armed forces on active duty, the government may pay the mortgage insurance premium. It should be noted that on 95 percent loans, the Federal Home Loan Bank Board insists that federal savings and loan associations set up a special reserve fund or require insurance for that portion of the loan above 80 percent. This insurance would be private mortgage guaranty insurance. There are special private mortgage insurance programs for commercial properties and for lease guarantees.

Upon default of an insured mortgage loan, the insurer can either buy the property from the lender for the balance due, or it can let the lender foreclose and then pay the lender's losses up to the amount of the insurance. Many insurers elect the first alternative, especially since lenders prefer it. The lender must notify the insurer if the loan is in default for over four months.

Private mortgage insurance has resulted in lessening the appeal of FHA and VA loans, due to the private insurer's lower administration costs and fees and faster processing. There are about 15 private mortgage insurance companies who belong to the trade association, the Mortgage Insurance Companies of America.

Since a private mortgage insurance company cannot insure two mortgages for the same property, many lenders try to structure piggyback loans to create only one mortgage. (*See FHA, MORTGAGE GUARANTY INSURANCE CORPORATION, PIGGYBACK LOAN, VA MORTGAGE.*)

PRIVATE OFFERING

An offering of a real estate security which is exempt from registration with state and/or federal regulatory agencies because it does not involve a public offering. In 1974, the Securities and Exchange Commission adopted guidelines (called Rule 146) in the hopes of bringing more certainty to what constitutes a private offering and thus does not require registration. It is important to note, however, that even though the private offering security may be exempt from the expensive and burdensome registration requirements, it is still subject to the full disclosure and antifraud provisions of the securities laws. (*See ANTIFRAUD PROVISIONS, INTRASTATE EXEMPTION, RULE 146.*)

PRIVITY

The mutual or successive relationship to the same rights of property, as in privity of contract (mortgagor—mortgagee or assignee—assignor) or privity of estate (landlord—sublessee or heir—ancestor). A succession in rights.

PROBATE

The formal judicial proceeding to prove or confirm the validity of a will, to collect the assets of the decedent's estate, to pay the debts and taxes, and to determine the persons to whom the remainder of the estate is to pass. The will is presented to the probate court, and creditors and interested parties are notified to present their claims or to show cause why the provisions of the will should not be enforced by the court (sometimes called Surrogate's Court). A will does not avoid probate. A will does, however, specify the disposition of the testator's property rather than have it pass by intestate succession under the laws of the state where the decedent was domiciled.

Title to any interest in land vests immediately in the heirs or the named devisees. This transfer, however, is not a final sale, as it is subject to some limitations:

1. The title is subject to the personal representative's right to possess the real estate.

2. The title is subject to valid claims against the decedent's estate. If claims are found valid, the property could be sold and proceeds split.

3. The title is subject to the surviving spouse's right to elect against the will.

4. The title is subject to all liens and encumbrances existing as of the date of death.

5. The validity of the will may be attacked.

6. The title is subject to estate and inheritance taxes which attach to all property of the deceased.

Even if the decedent dies without a will, his or her estate is still subject to a probate action. The court determines the rightful heirs, pays legal claims of creditors, and appoints an administrator to distribute the real and personal property according to the court's decree.

To claim an interest in the decedent's estate, a creditor must assert the claim within a specified period of time or be forever barred. An exception to this, however, is that a secured creditor, such as a mortgagee, may foreclose upon the decedent's property held as security even though he or she has not previously filed a claim.

The executor or administrator of an estate (also called the Personal Representative) must file a final accounting in court, showing all income, expenses, and the remaining assets. He or she is discharged upon court approval of the final accounting. When this process has been completed, the real property is fully transferable, free from debts, claims, or taxes of the decedent.

A broker entering into a listing agreement with the executor or administrator of an estate in probate should be aware that the amount of commission is fixed by the court, and that commissions are payable only from the proceeds of the sale. Thus a broker is not entitled to a commission unless the court approves the sale. This is true even if the broker produces a ready, willing, and able buyer. (*See ADMINIS-TRATOR, ESTATE TAX, EXECUTOR, INTESTATE, TESTATOR, WILL.*)

PROCEED ORDER   A written order to a general contractor to proceed with a change in contract requirements, subject to a later equitable adjustment of the contract price and/or completion time as specified in the contract. (*See CHANGE ORDER.*)

PROCEEDS-OF-LOAN ESCROW   An escrow in which loan proceeds are deposited by the lender pending the closing of a real estate transaction. Such a step is particularly important in cases where the loan commitment is due to expire prior to the closing date.

PROCURING CAUSE   That effort which brings about the desired result. Also called the "predominant efficient cause" or the "contributing cause."

Under an open listing, the broker who is the procuring or effective cause of the sale is the one entitled to the commission. A broker can be the procuring cause even though it is only indirectly through his or her efforts that the property is sold. For example, if the broker sent to the owner's home a prospect to whom the owner then sold the property, the broker is considered to have been the procuring cause of the sale.

A commonly used listing is the exclusive right-to-sell contract. With this type of listing the broker is entitled to a commission if the property is sold "by you, by me, or by anyone else," thus eliminating most procuring cause controversies. Procuring cause issues do sometimes arise, however, in disputes between the cooperating broker and the listing broker where both advise the buyer without knowledge of the other's involvement.

Several state Realtor® boards have adopted guidelines by which procuring cause disputes may be settled. Typical guidelines are as follows:

   I. A member who obtains an offer and deposit, and negotiates the close of a transaction, is usually the sole procuring cause. However, the Professional Standards Panel, sitting as arbitrators, after hearing all of the evidence, would be justified in dividing a selling commission between two offices, where each office had made a substantial contribution toward achieving the sale of the property to a particular buyer. If a sale would not have resulted but for the efforts of a member, he may be entitled to a portion of the selling commission, even though another member concluded the transaction and was not guilty of unethical conduct. However, as outlined below, a member must ordinarily have done certain things to entitle him to claim all or a portion of the commission, where he was not the one who obtained the offer and deposit from the buyer, and also, under certain circumstances, rights may be lost, as explained below.

II. A member claiming any portion of the selling commission should establish that he has physically shown the property, diligently followed through, consistently communicated with the buyer, and provided affirmative service, creating a series of events which, without break in continuity, materially contributed to the sale.

III. In the following situations, a commission claim would probably not exist when:

(a) The member refers a prospect to a property or open house, and does not accompany the prospect to the property, has not made an agreement in advance with the member on the property or open house, and the member on the property makes the sale.

(b) The office claiming the commission has never shown the property to the buyer, except in those situations where it clearly appears that it was unnecessary.

(c) The member did not have the right to show the property, either from the owner pursuant to a listing agreement, by way of an agreement to cooperate, or pursuant to the authority conferred by a multiple listing.

(d) The office claiming a commission did not maintain any contact, or "follow-through" with the buyer for a period of 14 days or longer, excepting under extenuating circumstances.

IV. A proper understanding of this policy requires that each member appreciate that the division of a commission cannot be dictated by a buyer or seller. While the expressed wishes of a buyer or a seller should be respected, those wishes should not be the basis to divest a member of his rights to a commission under this policy. The rights of the buyer and seller should never be jeopardized by a procuring cause dispute, since the board believes that through communication or arbitration, the rights of the members can be resolved without harm to the principals. For example, a disputed commission should be held in trust until the dispute is resolved, in order to avoid an adverse effect on a sale.

Conclusion: "Procuring Cause" disputes should, if at all possible, be resolved between the offices involved. It is not the purpose of this policy to reward members for unsuccessful efforts, yet the board recognizes that there are transactions made possible by members who for valid reasons, other than incompetence, do not write the offer. It is hoped that the guidelines set forth in this policy will be helpful in eliminating disputes between members and will encourage respect of the rights of other Realtors.®

PROFIT AND LOSS STATEMENT   A detailed statement of the income and expenses of a business, which reveals the operating position of the business over a certain time. Commonly referred to as a "P & L."

A property manager is charged with the responsibility of preparing "P & L" statements on a regular basis. Most such statements list only the gross receipts rather than itemized sources of income and the total of all operating expenses instead of individual expenditures. (*See BALANCE SHEET.*)

PROFIT A PRENDRE A right to take part of the soil and produce of the land, such as the right to take coal, fruit, or timber. Since a profit is an interest in land, it can only be created by written grant or by prescription, and not by custom or oral agreement. The basic difference between an easement and a profit is that an easement confers only the right to use another's land, whereas a profit confers the right to remove the soil or products thereof. In the event an easement is necessary for the full enjoyment of a profit a prendre, it is called an ancillary easement.

A profit a prendre is different from a natural resource lease in which the owner leases the property to a developer and retains the right to receive a royalty payment, as in an oil or gas lease arrangement with a royalty of one-sixth of the net sales price of the amounts extracted.

PRO FORMA In form only; not necessarily official.

PRO FORMA STATEMENT A projection of future income and expenses or other results. A projected annual operating statement that shows expected income, operating expenses, net operating income, and taxable income and loss. A pro forma statement is frequently found in a prospectus for an offering of a real estate security, such as a limited partnership to own income property. A pro forma statement should be clearly labeled as a projection and distinguished from operating figures, which are based on actual past performance.

PROGRESS PAYMENTS 1. Payments of money scheduled in relation to the completion of portions of a construction project. Progress payments are required of buyers of many new condominium projects, whereby the buyer pays his or her down payment incrementally into escrow, with a certain amount due at the time of purchase, loan approval, completion of the building, and closing.

2. Construction loan funds are usually disbursed as the construction progresses and not in one lump sum at the start of the work. The lender on behalf of the owner normally retains a small percentage of each progress payment to the contractor until satisfied that the work is completed according to specifications. (*See RETAINAGE.*)

PROMISSORY NOTE An unconditional written promise of one person to pay a certain sum of money to another, or order, or bearer, at a future specified time. The words "or order" or "or bearer" are important to make the instrument negotiable since these words enable the instrument to be endorsed and transferred. If negotiable, the maker should be sure to execute and sign only one note and not any copies. The maker usually initials any copies. The Uniform Commercial Code sets the standards for drafting an enforceable and negotiable promissory note.

A broker who accepts a promissory note as a deposit from a prospective purchaser must generally disclose to the seller that the buyer's deposit is in the form of a promissory note. If the broker does not inform the seller his or her license might be suspended or revoked. This requirement stems from the agent's common law duty to inform the principal of all facts relating to the subject matter of the agency that would affect the principal's interest. It is preferable that the broker accept a promissory note rather than a "hold check" (a check which the buyer instructs the broker to hold instead of cashing), or a postdated check. It is good practice to insert a clause in the note to the effect that the prevailing party in any dispute over the note is entitled to costs of collection, including attorney fees.

In real property financing, the promissory note, which is sometimes called the mortgage note, serves as evidence of the debt for which the mortgage on the property is the security. If the security is insufficient to cover the indebtedness, the holder of the note can obtain a deficiency judgment against the debtor for the balance unless the note is labelled a nonrecourse note. (*See NEGOTIABLE INSTRUMENT, NOTE, POSTDATED CHECK.*)

PROPERTY   The rights or interests a person has in the thing he or she owns but not, in the technical sense, the thing itself. These rights include the right to possess, to use, to encumber, to transfer, and to exclude. These are commonly called the bundle of rights. In modern understanding, however, property has come to mean the thing itself to which certain ownership rights are attached. Property is either real or personal. (*See PERSONAL PROPERTY, REAL PROPERTY.*)

PROPERTY   That aspect of the real estate profession devoted
MANAGEMENT   to the leasing, managing, marketing, and overall maintenance of the property of others. The property manager strives to maintain the investment and income in the property and to maintain the physical features of the building. In some states, persons performing such functions for others and for a fee, must either hold real estate licenses or special property manager licenses. This generally excludes janitors or custodians working for only one specific property.

The property manager is a member of a real estate office or property management company which manages several properties for various owners. Among a property manager's primary duties are to secure and keep tenants, to provide financial records and accounts, and to provide upkeep and maintenance of the property. In essence, he or she markets space. The property manager performs three basic functions:

1. fiscal management—financial affairs

2. physical management—structure and grounds

3. administrative management—files and records

The individual building manager may be employed by a property manager or directly by the owner of the building, usually on a straight salary basis, to supervise the daily operations in the building. Condominium resident managers normally reside in one of the apartment units on the premises.

The property manager has a fiduciary responsibility not only to the principal (the owner) but also to the residents of the building. While the owner expects the greatest net return on his or her investment, the residents expect the most efficient functioning of the building. To fulfill these responsibilities, the property manager must possess a working knowledge of property maintenance, leasing, accounting, income tax, insurance, real estate law (especially contracts and agency principles), and human relations.

Property managers' fees are usually based on a percentage of gross income (after deducting for vacancies and other rent losses) without taking into account operating expenses.

Some of the more important provisions found in a properly drafted management agreement are the responsibilities of the management agency, the scope of the manager's authority to rent and operate the premises (e.g., can the manager grant concessions), the length of the agreement, the fee, and the identity of the parties and the property (usually not a legal description).

PROPERTY REPORT   A disclosure document required under the federal Interstate Land Sales Full Disclosure Act where applicable to the interstate sale of subdivided lots. The property report is in the form of questions and answers, and covers such matters as topography, accessibility of public transportation and schools, soil conditions, existence of liens and encumbrances, recreational facilities, whether special assessments will be charged, and other similar information. A prospective purchaser must be given a copy of the property report at least 48 hours before committing to purchase, unless the purchaser acknowledges in writing that he or she has received the report and made an inspection of the property. If a property report is not received at least 48 hours before the purchase, the purchaser has seven calendar days to reconsider and cancel. Failure to provide the purchaser with a copy of the property report gives the purchaser the right to rescind the transaction at any time and have his or her money refunded plus interest. (See *INTERSTATE LAND SALES*.)

PROPERTY RESIDUAL TECHNIQUE   An appraisal technique similar to the building residual technique and the land residual technique of capitalization, except that the net income is considered to be attributable to the total real property. The income is capitalized into an indicated value as a whole, based on the premise that the land and the particular improvements on the land are producing income as an economic unit. Under a different legal land use, the property could produce more or less income and thereby have a different value. (See *BUILDING RESIDUAL TECHNIQUE, LAND RESIDUAL TECHNIQUE*.)

PROPERTY TAX   Tax levied by the government against either real or personal property. Real property has traditionally been a favorite subject of taxation due to its immobility and consequent ease to locate, evaluate, and tax. The right to tax real property in the United States rests exclusively with the state and local governments. The U.S. Constitution prohibits the federal government from taxing land.

The general real estate tax is made up of the taxes levied on real estate by various governmental agencies and municipalities. These include the city, town, village, and county. Other taxing bodies are the school districts or boards. These include local elementary and high schools, junior colleges, and community colleges. Drainage districts, water districts, and sanitary districts are also taxing bodies. Municipal authorities operating recreational preserves such as forest preserves, parks, and others are also authorized by the legislatures of the various states to levy real estate taxes.

General real estate taxes are levied for the general support or operation of the governmental agency authorized to impose the levy. These taxes are known as *ad valorem* taxes because the amount of the tax varies in accordance with the value of the property being taxed. About 45 percent of real estate taxes goes to education, with the balance divided between welfare, highways, and public services (police, fire, hospitals).

Under most state laws, certain real estate is exempt from real estate taxation. Common examples are property owned by the government, religious organizations, educational institutions, and hospitals; provided such property is used for tax-exempt purposes. Other state laws allow special exemptions to reduce the real estate tax for homeowners, veterans, and the elderly. Some states offer reductions to attract businesses or to encourage the use of agricultural land.

PROPOSITION   In some states, it is the instrument used to submit an offer; similar to proposed offer to purchase. (*See OFFER.*)

PROPRIETARY LEASE   A written lease in a cooperative apartment building, between the owner/corporation and the tenant/stockholder, in which the tenant is given the right to occupy a particular unit. It differs from the typical landlord-tenant lease in that the tenant is also a stockholder in the corporation which owns the building.

Unlike a standard rental agreement, there is no fixed rental amount. The tenant pays a proportionate part of the carrying charges of the corporation. When a particular unit is sold, the proprietary lease is assigned to the buyer along with the seller's stock certificate. (*See COOPERATIVE OWNERSHIP.*)

PROPRIETORSHIP   Ownership of a business or income property. A sole or individual proprietorship (as opposed to forms such as corporation or partnership) is a form of business ownership which is easy to organize and flexible to operate. It is frequently used in real estate brokerage. An individual proprietor may run a brokerage company if he or she has a valid broker's license. The proprietor may use his or her own name or a fictitious name previously registered as required by state law.

There is a growing tendency for sole proprietors to incorporate and thus take advantage of certain tax and fringe benefits such as those provided by pension and profit sharing plans.

PRORATE   To divide or distribute proportionately. With the exception of principal payments on a mortgage, most real estate expenses such as rent, insurance—which is frequently prepaid for several years coverage—and the like are paid in advance. Some expenses, however, such as real property taxes and interest on a mortgage are paid in arrears. Upon closing a real estate transaction, these various expenses are prorated between the buyer and the seller to assure that each is responsible for the operating expenses of the property during his or her ownership. For example, a seller normally pays the fire insurance policy for a three-year period, and if the owner were to sell the property after the second year, he or she would be credited with a prorated amount equal to the cost of the remaining year. The buyer, then, is responsible for insuring the property and thus will receive the benefit of the policy for that last year. Expenses are usually prorated as of either the date of closing or the date of possession.

In certain cases, a seller might negotiate a provision into the sales contract to the effect that any buyer credits would be applied against the balance due on a purchase-money mortgage taken back by the seller.

Some of the most common items to be prorated are sewer charges, interest on loans, insurance premiums, rent, mortgage impounds, utilities, and real property taxes. (See CLOSING, ESCROW.)

PROSPECT   A party who may be interested in buying or selling real property; a potential buyer; a customer. The prospect does not become a customer or client until the parties establish a fiduciary relationship, such as upon signing a listing or sales contract.

PROSPECTUS   A printed statement distributed to describe and give advance information on a business, venture, project, or stock issue. If a real estate project is offered as a security, the prospectus must fully disclose all material aspects and investment features of the project which conceivably could affect the investor's decision whether to invest or not. The term is generally limited to a publicly offered security (registered). In a private offering, the disclosure statement is called a private placement memorandum. (See PRIVATE OFFERING, RED HERRING.)

PROTEST   See NOTICE OF DISHONOR.

PROXY   A person temporarily authorized to act or do business in behalf of another. Also, the document giving such person the power to act for another—a power of attorney.

Proxies are frequently used in voting or for quorum purposes in condominium association meetings. The proxy is not an irrevocable commitment, and the submission of a proxy merely ensures that the owner's vote will be cast in the event the owner cannot attend the meeting. (See POWER OF ATTORNEY.)

PUBLIC LAND   Land which is owned by the federal government and is available for purchase by a private citizen when the land is no longer needed for government purposes. Public land is administered by the U.S. Department of the Interior's Bureau of Land Management. The General Services Administration participates in the sale of public land that is already fully developed.

PUBLIC OFFERING STATEMENT   The document prepared by a subdivider in accordance with individual state subdivision laws, which discloses all material facts about a subdivision to be offered for sale to the public. No sale is valid unless the purchaser receives a copy of the current public offering statement, is given a reasonable time in which to examine it, and signs a receipt for it.

A public offering statement is not current unless all amendments are incorporated. Therefore, a subdivider who experiences a material change in the project must stop all sales until the proper regulatory agency accepts the amendment and incorporates it into a new public offering statement.

PUBLIC SALE An auction sale for the public, who has been informed by notice or by invitation, so the public has the opportunity to engage in competitive bidding at a place to which the public has access. (*See DEED OF TRUST, FORECLOSURE, MORTGAGE, TAX DEED, TAX LIEN.*)

PUFFING Exaggerated or superlative comments or opinions not made as representations of fat and thus not a grounds for misrepresentation, such as "this property is a real good buy." One test used is whether a reasonable person would have relied on the statement. A statement such as "the apartment has a fantastic view" is puffing because the prospective buyer can clearly assess the view for himself, whereas a statement such as "the apartment has a fantastic view of the lake," when in fact all its windows face the street, would be misrepresentation. (*See CAVEAT EMPTOR, MISREPRESENTATION.*)

PUNCH LIST A discrepancy list showing defects in construction which need some corrective work to bring the building up to standards set by the plans and specifications. A punch list may be filled out by the property owner and/or by the original architect in a final inspection of the building, listing discrepancies in the building plans and other construction flaws. With a punch list in hand, the building contractor may then proceed to correct the defects.

PUNITIVE DAMAGES Exemplary or vindictive court-awarded damages to an injured party; as opposed to compensatory damages, which are damages awarded to repay an injured person for actual losses suffered. The purpose of punitive damanges is to punish the perpetrator, not to reward the injured party. The general rule is that no money damages are recoverable for purely mental suffering due to breach of a contract. Also, punitive damages may not be awarded unless there has been some actual damage.

A broker may be liable to a defrauded client for punitive damages if he or she retains a salesperson known to have a propensity for defrauding the real estate consumer.

PUR AUTRE VIE For another's life. A life estate pur autre vie is a life estate that is measured by the life of a person other than the grantee. For example, George Primo grants to Harry Brew a life estate in his mansion for the life of Sally Lane.

While an estate pur autre vie is not strictly an estate of inheritance, it is generally considered a freehold estate which can pass to heirs, at least until the death of the measuring life. (*See LIFE ESTATE.*)

PURCHASE-MONEY MORTGAGE A mortgage given as part of the buyer's consideration for the purchase of real property, and delivered at the same time that the real property is transferred as a simultaneous part of the transaction. A purchase-money mortgage is usually used to fill a gap between the buyer's down payment and a new first mortgage or a mortgage assumed, as when the buyer pays 10 percent in cash, gets an 80 percent first mortgage from a bank, and the seller takes back a purchase-money second mortgage for the remaining 10 percent.

A purchase-money mortgage has certain priorities. For example, suppose Fred Wilson buys a farm for $50,000, pays $10,000 down, and gives the seller or lender a $40,000 mortgage. At the same time Wilson has a $10,000 judgment lien outstanding against himself. The judgment lien, even though prior in time, is inferior in right to the security lien of the seller/mortgagee. This is because the mortgagee made it possible for Wilson to own the land against which the judgment creditor now claims a lien. The delivery of the deed and taking back of the purchase-money mortgage is deemed one transaction in which there is no time for any other lien to intervene.

If a person gives a mortgage on one piece of property to raise money to buy another piece, it is not a purchase-money mortgage. Where a developer purchases land and then obtains a construction mortgage loan to build structures, the transaction is not a purchase-money mortgage.

When a seller agrees in a contract of sale to take back a purchase-money mortgage for part of the purchase price, the terms and conditions of the mortgage (such as interest rate, duration) must be set forth in detail; otherwise the contract might not be enforceable due to incompleteness or uncertainty.

Depending on state law, a deficiency judgment may or may not be permitted upon default of a purchase-money mortgage. In some states (e.g., New York), a purchase-money mortgage is exempt from the state's usury ceiling.

Technically speaking, any mortgage on real property executed to secure the purchase money by a purchaser of the property contemporaneously with the acquisition of the legal title thereto is a purchase-money mortgage. Thus, the fact that a mortgage is made to a person other than the seller does not prevent its being a purchase-money mortgage. The only disclosure under the federal Truth-in-Lending law required of a first purchase-money mortgagee on a dwelling is the annual percentage rate. (See *TRUTH-IN-LENDING LAW.*)

PURCHASER'S POLICY   A title insurance policy, also called an *owner's policy*, generally furnished by a seller to a purchaser under a real estate sales contract or contract for deed, insuring the property against defect in record title. (See *TITLE INSURANCE.*)

PYRAMIDING   A process of acquiring additional properties through refinancing properties already owned and then reinvesting the loan proceeds in additional property.

The tax is regressive in nature. There is no relation between the owner's income or ability to pay and the tax rate. Thus low-income families tend to spend a larger share of their income for property taxes.

The general tax rate may be quoted as so many dollars per $100 of assessed valuation or so many mills (one thousandth part of a dollar, $.001) per dollar of assessed value. For example, a property valued at $20,000 with a tax rate of $2.10 per $100 of assessed valuation will be taxed $420, computed as follows:

$$\$20,000 \div \$100 = 200$$
$$200 \times \$2.10 = \$420$$

The same tax quoted at a millage rate is 21 mills per dollar; this is $21 per $1,000 assessed value.

Property is valued or assessed for tax purposes by county and township assessors. The land is usually appraised separately from the building. The building value is usually determined from a manual or set of rules covering unit cost prices and rates of depreciation. Some states require assessments to be a certain percentage of true or market value. State laws may provide for property to be re-assessed periodically. Property owners claiming that errors were made in determining the assessed value of their property may present their objections, usually to the local board of appeal or board of review.

In some jurisdictions, when it is necessary to correct general inequalities in statewide tax assessments, uniformity may be achieved by using an equalization factor. Such a factor may be used in counties or districts where the assessments are to be raised or lowered. When the equalization factor is used, the tax rate is applied to the equalized assessment. For example, to increase the assessed value of a property which has been valued by the assessor at $10,000, an equalization factor of 1.40 for the county in which the property is located is multiplied by the original assessment. With a tax of $3.10 per $100 of equalized value, the tax would be $434, computed as follows:

$$\$10,000 \times 1.40 = \$14,000$$
$$\$14,000 \div \$100 = 140$$
$$140 \times \$3.10 = \$434$$

In most states the general real estate tax becomes a lien on January 1 of the year of the tax. In some states the tax is payable within a month or two after it becomes a lien. One state, for example, levies its tax on January 1 of the year of the tax and it must be paid by February 28 or 29 of that same year. Other states, however, provide that the tax becomes a lien on January 1 of the year of the tax, but the tax is not payable until sometime later in the same or the following year. Many states permit the tax to be paid in two installments.

Some states have adopted the so-called "Pittsburgh Law," an amendment to the real property tax law that requires the tax rate for buildings to be less than that for the land, to encourage proper development and utilization of urban lands. This law establishes a graded tax for different categories: land and improvements for residential, apartment/hotel, commercial, and industrial. The land and improvements for agriculture/conservation are assessed as one.

The taxes for a condominium unit are assessed against each individual unit. It is not necessary to assess and tax the common elements individually since the market value of each unit reflects not only the value of the unit itself, but also the proportionate value of ownership in the common elements.

Real property taxes are deductible items for income tax purposes. However, the deduction does not extend to special assessment taxes for improvement districts.

The following is a quick guide to the deductibility of real property taxes in special situations:

1. Tenancy in Common—a tenant in common can deduct only his or her proportionate share of the tax even if he or she paid the entire amount of the tax bill.

2. Tenancy by the Entirety—either tenant can take the deduction if he or she pays the tax.

3. Joint Tenancy—the one who pays the tax can take the deduction.

4. Mortgagee—a mortgagee cannot deduct property taxes paid for periods prior to acquiring title to the property. If the taxes are paid before foreclosure, they represent an additional loan on the property. If they are paid after foreclosure, they represent an additional cost of the property.

5. Back Taxes Paid by the Buyer—the buyer gets no deduction for any back taxes he or she pays. The sum paid is added to the purchase price.

QUADRANGLE   A tract of land in the U.S. Government Survey System measuring 24 miles on each side of the square. (See CHECK.)

QUALIFICATION   The process of reviewing a prospective borrower's credit and payment capacity prior to approving a loan. Brokers who assist a seller in reviewing a prospective buyer's qualification to purchase a property in which the seller is carrying back financing should be aware of the possible application the the federal Truth-in-Lending and Equal Credit Opportunity Acts.

QUALIFIED ACCEPTANCE   An acceptance, in law, which amounts to a rejection of an offer and is a counteroffer; an acceptance of an offer upon certain named conditions, or one that has the effect of altering or modifying the terms of the offer. The qualified acceptance does not comply with the terms of the offer, and is not an acceptance of the offer. (See COUNTEROFFER.)

QUALIFIED FEE   An estate in fee which is subject to certain limitations imposed by the owner. For example, a grantor may convey his or her farm to a grantee with the stipulation that the grantee not build a liquor store on the premises. In the event that the grantee builds a liquor store on the property, the farm reverts to the grantor. A qualified fee can also be granted in a will where a testator leaves property to a spouse "so long as she (he) does not remarry." Also called a *base fee, defeasible fee,* or a *fee determinable.* In modern practice, a qualified fee includes all types of defeasible fees including a fee simple subject to a condition subsequent.

QUANTITY SURVEY   A method of estimating construction cost or reproduction cost; a highly technical process used in arriving at the cost estimate of new construction and sometimes referred to in the building trade as the price take-off method. A quantity survey involves a detailed estimate of the quantities of raw materials (lumber, plaster, brick, cement) used, as well as the current price of the material and the installation costs, and also includes indirect costs, such as building permit, land survey, and overhead. An example of what such a survey would include would be: 10,000 concrete slabs at $2 per slab, 1,500 doorknobs at $5 each, and so on. These factors are added together to arrive at the total cost of a structure. Quantity survey is a time-consuming method and is most frequently used by contractors and experienced estimators. (See UNIT-IN-PLACE METHOD.)

QUANTUM   A term used in describing the amount or quantity of an estate as measured by its duration and not its quality; for example, an estate for life, or for 55 years, or forever. The quantum of an estate is generally found in the habendum clause. (*See HABENDUM CLAUSE.*)

QUARTER SECTION   A land/area measure used in connection with the government (rectangular) survey of land measurement. A quarter section of land is 160 acres, 2,640 feet by 2,640 feet. Historically, it is the area of land originally granted to a homesteader.

Note that when lands throughout the United States were originally surveyed, lakes, streams, and other features were sometimes encountered which resulted in fractional pieces of land less than a quarter section. These pieces were called *government lots* and were identified by a specific lot number, which became the legal description for that parcel of land. (*See GOVERNMENT SURVEY METHOD.*)

QUASI   Latin for "as if"; similar to; almost like. Commonly used in real estate with such terms as quasi-contract, quasi-judicial, quasi-corporation. A quasi-contract can arise to prevent an unjust enrichment, such as when a landowner mistakenly pays taxes on his or her neighbor's property.

QUICK ASSETS   Assets that are quickly and easily convertible into cash; liquid assets. (*See LIQUIDITY.*)

QUIET ENJOYMENT   The right of an owner or lessee legally in possession of property to uninterrupted use of the property without interference from the former owner, lessor, or any third party claiming superior title. (*See COVENANT.*)

QUIET TITLE ACTION   A court action intended to establish or settle the title to a particular property, especially where there is a cloud on the title. All parties with a possible claim or interest in the property must be joined in the action. A quiet title action is frequently used by an adverse possessor to substantiate the title since having official record title makes it easier to market the property. Once the judgment or decree of the court has been recorded, proper record notice of the claimant's right and interest in the property is established.

A quiet title action can generally be used to extinguish easements; remove any clouds on title; release a homestead, dower, or curtesy interest; transfer title without warranties; clear tax titles; or simply release an interest when the grantor may have some remote claim to the property. The seller who holds a forfeited contract for deed, which the buyer had recorded, sometimes brings a quiet title action to clear the cloud on title produced by the recorded contract for deed, especially where the buyer refuses to release or quitclaim the interest. (*See CLOUD ON TITLE.*)

QUITCLAIM DEED   A deed of conveyance which operates, in effect, as a release of whatever interest the grantor has in the property; sometimes called a *release of a deed*. The quitclaim deed contains similar language to a deed, with the important exception that rather than using the words "grant and release," it contains language such as "remise, release, and quitclaim." Grantors therefore do not warrant title or possession. Grantors only pass whatever interest they may have, if any. In effect, a grantor forever quits whatever claim he or she had, if in fact any existed.

The quitclaim deed transfers only whatever right, title, and interest the grantor had in the land at the time of the execution of the deed and does not pass to the grantee any title or interest subsequently acquired by the grantor. Thus the grantee cannot claim a right to any after-acquired title.

Although a quitclaim deed may not vest any title in the grantee, it is not inferior to the other types of deeds with respect to that which it actually conveys. For example, if a grantor executes and delivers a warranty deed to one person and subsequently executes and delivers a quitclaim deed to the same property to another person, the grantee under the quitclaim deed will prevail over the grantee under the warranty deed, assuming he is first to record the deed.

Depending on local custom, ordinarily a warranty or bargain and sale deed will be used to transfer a fee simple interest. A quitclaim deed is not commonly used to convey a fee, but is usually restricted to releasing or conveying minor interests in real estate for the purpose of clearing title defects or clouds on the title. It may also be used to convey lesser interests such as life estates and to release such interests as a remainder or reversion.

A title searcher will regard a quitclaim deed in the chain of title as a red flag, and most title companies will not guarantee titles derived out of a quitclaim deed—at least not without further explanation.

Quitclaim deeds also are often used between close relatives, such as when one heir is buying out the other, or where a seller is in such poor financial shape that it is inconsequential to the buyer whether he or she is getting any warranties or not. (See *CLOUD ON TITLE, DEED.*)

QUORUM   The minimum legal number of people required to be present before a specified meeting can officially take place or authorized business can be transacted.

R-VALUE   A special rating or method of judging the insulating value of certain insulation products. The Federal Trade Commission requires that sellers of new homes must disclose in their sales contracts certain insulation data such as type, thickness, and R-value. (*See INSULATION.*)

RAFTER   One of a series of sloping beams that extend from the exterior wall to a center ridgeboard and provide the main support for the roof.

RANGE   An open land area for grazing or a series of mountains.

RANGE LINE   A measurement, used in the government (rectangular) survey system, consisting of a strip of land six miles wide, running in a north-south direction. (*See GOVERNMENT SURVEY METHOD, TOWNSHIP.*)

RATE OF RETURN   The relationship (expressed as a percentage) between the annual net income generated by a business and the invested capital (or the appraised value, or the gross income) of the business. The rate of return is the percentage yield to the investor based on the property's production of income. (*See INTERNAL RATE OF RETURN.*)

RATIFICATION   The adoption or confirmation of an act already performed on behalf of a person without prior authorization. In agency law, a principal by his or her actions may ratify the previously unauthorized acts of an agent. Upon reaching legal age, a person can ratify a contract made during his or her minority. (*See SCOPE OF AUTHORITY.*)

RAW LAND   Unimproved land; land in its unused natural state prior to grading, construction, subdividing, or improvements such as streets, lighting, and sewers.

"READY, WILLING, AND ABLE"   A phrase referring to a prospective buyer of property who is legally capable and financially able to consummate the deal. Traditionally, the broker earns a commission upon procuring a "ready, willing, and able" buyer on the listing terms, regardless of whether the seller actually goes through with the sale. The "ready and willing" means, generally, that the broker must in fact produce a buyer who indicates that he or she is prepared to accept the terms of the seller and is willing to enter into a contract for sale. The buyer is not "ready and willing" when he or she enters into an option with the seller; but the buyer is "ready and willing" when the option is exercised. The buyer is not "ready and willing" when the offer is subject to any new conditions, such as making closing date an unreasonably long period, such as one year from the offer. Contracts of sale subject to conditions not contemplated in the listing agreement do not entitle the broker to a commission until the conditions have been satisfied or waived. (See CONTINGENCY, QUALIFIED ACCEPTANCE.)

The "able" requires that the buyer be financially able to comply with the terms of the sale in both initial cash payment and any necessary financing. The broker is not required to show that the purchaser has actual cash or assets to pay off the mortgage. But the broker is required to reveal the identity of the buyer if requested by the seller.

When a seller accepts an offer from a buyer, the seller implicitly approves the buyer as being "able"; if the buyer thereafter defaults by not coming up with the purchase price, the seller normally cannot argue that the broker had failed to produce an "able" buyer. However, there is recent case law to the effect that the broker does have the added responsibility to find out whether or not, in fact, the buyer is "able," and where the buyer turns out to be financially unable the broker is not entitled to a commission. Note also that a corporation not yet formed cannot be a "ready, willing, and able" buyer. (See COMMISSION.)

REAL ESTATE The physical land at, above, and below the earth's surface with all appurtenances, including any structures; any and every interest in land whether corporeal or incorporeal, freehold or nonfreehold; for all practical purposes synonymous with real property. (See LAND, REAL PROPERTY.)

REAL ESTATE COMMISSION A state governmental agency whose primary duties include making rules and regulations to protect the general public involved in real estate transactions, granting licenses to real estate brokers and salespeople, and suspending or revoking licenses for cause.

REAL ESTATE EDUCATION, RESEARCH AND RECOVERY FUND A special state fund, supported either by a portion of the real estate licensing fees or by a special fee, used to encourage real estate education and to provide a source of financial relief for persons injured by the fraudulent practices of a judgment-proof licensee. (See RECOVERY FUND.)

REAL ESTATE INVESTMENT TRUST (REIT) In the 1960s Congress provided favored tax treatment for certain business trusts by exempting from corporate tax certain qualified real estate investment trusts (REIT) which invest at least 75 percent of their assets in real estate and which distribute 95 percent or more of their annual real estate ordinary income to their investors. As an alternative to the partnership or corporate methods of investing in real estate, the REIT offers some of the flow-through tax advantages of a partnership/syndication while retaining many of the attributes and advantages of a corporate operation. The REIT is usually organized as a Massachusetts business trust. Investors purchase certificates of ownership in the trust which, in turn, invests the money in real property and then distributes any profits to the investors free of corporate tax. In many ways, a REIT is similar to a mutual fund, which is treated similarly for tax purposes. As a part owner of real property, the shareholder pays normal income tax on the ordinary income from the trust and receives capital gains treatment for any capital gains distribution. A REIT must meet the following qualifications:

1. It must be a corporation, trust, or association.

2. It must have a minimum of 100 owners and 50 percent or more of the shares cannot be held by five or fewer shareholders.

3. It must have centralized control vested in the trustees, limited liability to the beneficial owners, and free transferability of the certificates.

4. Its income must accrue from passive real estate investment, such as rents and mortgage interest.

Some advantages of the REIT are: avoidance of corporate tax (thus no double taxation), centralized management, continuity of operation, transferability of interests, diversification of investment, and the benefit of skilled real estate advice. Some of the disadvantages are: investments are passive in nature and usually are restricted to very large real estate transactions; any losses cannot be passed through to the investor to offset his or her other income, as is the case with syndications; and usually the trust must be registered with the Securities and Exchange Commission, a burdensome and expensive process.

REAL ESTATE MORTGAGE TRUST (REMT)

REMTs are a type of REIT that buys and sells real estate mortgages (usually short-term junior instruments) rather than real property. Major sources of income for REMTs are mortgage interest, origination fees, and profits earned from buying and selling mortgages.

A related trust is the combination trust, which combines real estate equity investing with mortgage lending, thus earning profits from rental income and capital gains, as well as mortgage interest and placement fees.

REAL ESTATE SETTLEMENT PROCEDURES ACT (RESPA)

This federal law, enacted in 1974 and later revised, ensures that the buyer and seller in a real estate transaction have knowledge of all settlement costs when the purchase of a one- to four-family residential dwelling is financed by a federally related mortgage loan. Federally related loans are broadly defined to include loans made by savings and loan associations or other lenders whose deposits are insured by federal agencies (FDIC or FHLB), insured by the FHA or VA, administered by the Department of Housing and Urban Development, or intended to be sold by the lender to Fannie Mae or a similar federal agency. RESPA effectively covers most institutional loans.

Note that RESPA regulations apply to first mortgage loans only. RESPA requires that loans covered by the act comply with the following items:

1. *Special Information Booklet*—A lender must give every person from whom it receives or for whom it prepares a loan application a copy of the HUD-published booklet, "Settlement Costs and You." The booklet provides the borrower with general information about settlement (closing) costs and explains the various RESPA provisions. It also gives a line-by-line discussion of the uniform settlement statement.

2. *Good Faith Estimate of Settlement Costs*—At the time of, or within three business days of application, the lender must provide the borrower with a good faith estimate of the settlement costs the borrower is likely to incur. This may take the form of a specific figure or a range of costs based upon comparable past transactions in the area. In addition, if the lender requires use of a particular attorney or title company to conduct the closing, the lender must state if any business relationship exists, and give an estimate of that individual's charges. The lender is limited in the amount it may require to be escrowed (impounds) of taxes, insurance premiums, and other charges.

3. *Uniform Settlement Statement*—RESPA provides that loan closing information be prepared on a special HUD form designed to detail all financing particulars of the transaction. The statement must itemize all charges imposed by the lender, as well as all other charges paid out of the closing proceeds. Charges incurred by the buyer and seller, contracted separately and outside the closing, do not have to be disclosed. Items paid for prior to the closing must be clearly marked as such on the statement, and are omitted from the totals. Lenders must retain these statements for two years after the date of closing unless the loan (and its servicing) is sold or otherwise disposed of. Note that the uniform settlement statement may be changed to allow for local custom; that is, certain lines may be deleted if they do not apply in the area. Upon the borrower's request, the settlement agent (usually an attorney) must permit him or her to inspect the settlement statement, to the extent that the figures are available, one business day before closing. Also, lenders may not impose a fee for preparation of the Uniform Settlement Statement or any statement required under the Truth-in-Lending Act.

4. *Prohibition Against Kickbacks*—RESPA explicitly prohibits the paying of kickbacks or unearned fees, such as when an insurance agency pays a kickback to a lender for referring one of the lender's recent customers to the agency. Exempted, however, are payments made pursuant to cooperative brokerage or referral arrangements, or agreements between real estate salespeople and brokers.

RESPA is administered by the Office of the Assistant Secretary for Consumer Affairs and Regulatory Functions at HUD. Respa does not apply to loans secured by mortgaged property larger than 25 acres, to installment land contracts (contracts for deed), and certain construction loans, home improvement loans, and loans on property where the primary purpose of purchasing is future resale.

REAL PROPERTY   The earth's surface, the air above, and the ground below, as well as all appurtenances to the land, including buildings, structures, fixtures, fences, and improvements erected upon or affixed to the same. This excludes growing crops. The term "real property" refers to the interests, benefits, and rights inherent in the ownership of real estate, i.e., the bundle of rights. (*See BUNDLE OF RIGHTS, PROPERTY.*)

That which is not real property is personal property. Because the law treats real property and personal property differently, it is important to distinguish between the two:

1. Instruments affecting *real property* must be in writing and should be recorded, whereas instruments affecting *personal property* may be oral or written, ordinarily they need not be recorded, and they can be transferred merely by delivery.

2. Tax laws make many important distinctions between *real* and *personal* property.

3. The law of the state where the *real property* is located governs the acquisition and transfer of title to land, including important matters such as rules of descent and probate. *Personal property* on the other hand is moveable, and would be governed by the laws of the jurisdiction in which it is located.

4. Under common law principles, leaseholds are treated as *personal property*, commonly referred to as "chattels real," although for some purpose (e.g. taxation, condominium) certain long-term leaseholds have been classified by statute as *real property*.

5. Court-ordered judgment liens may attach to real property only. Usually, personalty must be sold to pay debts before realty can be levied upon.

6. Some of the more typical zoning classifications of real property are: 1. Residential, such as single-family homes, townhouses, multifamily apartments, and condominiums; 2. Commercial, such as retail shopping centers and high-rise office buildings; 3. Industrial, such as warehouses, loft buildings, and industrial parks; and 4. Special purpose, such as hotels, motels, schools, and mobile home parks. (*See LAND, LEASEHOLD, PROPERTY.*)

REAL PROPERTY SECURITIES REGISTRATION The process of disclosure and notification to the proper government agency of an issuer's intended real property security offering. A real estate security is treated the same as any other security for federal and most state regulatory purposes. A security for these purposes is defined as an *investment contract* transaction, or scheme whereby a person invests money in a common enterprise and is led to expect profits from the efforts of a third party. The method by which some real estate is offered for sale may determine whether the offering constitutes a real property security. Thus, for example, the offering of a limited partnership interest in a real estate venture involves the offering of a real property security; as does the sale by a developer of a condominium combined with a mandatory rental pool or hotel operation.

All real property securities, unless exempt, must be registered with the federal Securities and Exchange Commission (SEC) and usually with a securities commission in the states in which the securities will be offered for sale. The two most frequently claimed exemptions are the *intrastate exemption* and the *private offering exemption*. An offering which is directed solely to residents of a single state where the issuer is also a resident and doing business is exempted from registration with the SEC under the intrastate exemption. The offering, nevertheless, must be registered with the state, unless it is also exempt from state registration requirements as a private offering. The private offering exemption rules are designed to exempt from the costly and time-consuming registration process an offering which is of a limited scope and directed to such a selected type of investor that the prospective purchasers do not need the protection afforded by the SEC disclosure requirements. The main thrust of the federal requirements for a private offering exemption is that the offering be made to investors sophisticated and wealthy enough to withstand a loss of invested funds and knowledgeable enough to evaluate fully the risks of the investment. The Securities and Exchange Commission's Rule 146 further defines the limits of this private offering exemption.

If the issuers of real property securities believe that they are exempt from registration, they may proceed to issue the securities without obtaining consent from the SEC or other regulatory agency. Some issuers request a "no action" letter from the SEC, in which the SEC, after reviewing the facts, states that it will not take any action against the issuer if the securities are issued without registration. It should be noted that if the SEC alleges that an exemption is not available, the issuer has the burden of proving the exemption. In this regard, the issuer should be careful to keep detailed records of all offers and sales of the securities. If an issuer who is required to register a security sells a security without having first registered it, all purchasers of that security have the right to rescind the transaction and get their money back plus interest.

Even if exempt from registration, an offering is still subject to disclosure requirements (private placement memorandum or offering circular) and to the antifraud provisions of the federal Securities Exchange Act of 1934, provided there is some contact with interstate commerce (such as the use of United States mails). The act forbids fraudulent and deceptive practices in the offering.

The SEC also regards the offering of condominiums to be real property securities under certain circumstances; that is, when the units are offered with emphasis placed on the economic benefits to be derived from the rental of the units or where there is a rental pool or mandatory rental agreement. The developer who has not registered a condominium offering with the SEC must carefully instruct all salespeople not to make any representation as to rental income that a purchaser may receive, but rather to leave the dissemination of any such information to those rental agents chosen by the purchaser. Sample instructions are as follows:

> "Developer advises that no representations or references will be made to either purchasers or prospective purchasers concerning rental of the apartment, income from the apartment, or any other economic benefit to be derived from the rental of the apartment, including but not limited to, any reference or representation to the effect that developer or the managing agent of the project will provide, directly or indirectly, any services relating to the rental or sale of the apartment, or as to possible advantages from the rental of an apartment under federal or state tax laws. Rental of the apartments, and the provision of management services in connection therewith, is and shall be the sole responsibility of the purchaser."

If the condominium is to be offered for sale in other states, the securities laws of these states (their blue-sky laws) must be reviewed to determine whether registration in those states is necessary. For instance, the California Commissioner of Corporations has ruled that the California offering of Hawaii condominium units coupled with a voluntary rental pool constitutes the offering of a real property security under the laws of California. (See ABSENTEE OWNER, ANTIFRAUD PROVISIONS, INTRASTATE EXEMPTION, INVESTMENT CONTRACT, PRIVATE OFFERING, RED HERRING, RENTAL POOL, RULE 10-B5, RULE 147, UNDERWRITER.)

REALTIST   A member of a national organization, generally composed of black real estate brokers, known as the National Association of Real Estate Brokers. The association was formed in 1947 and has local boards in principal cities throughout the United States. It is the oldest and largest of the minority trade associations serving the nation's housing industry. The Realtists subscribe to a code of ethics and strive to work for better housing in the communities they serve under the theme of "Democracy in Housing." NAREB has approximately 5,000 members.

REALTOR®   A registered tradename which may be used only by members of the state and local real estate boards affiliated with the National Association of Realtors® (about 1,850 local boards). The term "Realtor" designates a professional who subscribes to the strict code of ethics promulgated by the National Association of Realtors® and adopted by individual state associations of Realtors® to govern real estate practices of members of the board. The use of the name Realtor® and the distinctive seal in advertising is strictly governed by the rules and regulations of the national association. There is a trend among local boards to change to the single all-Realtor® concept in which salespeople as well as broker members can use the Realtor® label. Wisconsin, for instance, is an all-Realtor® state. (*See NATIONAL ASSOCIA-TION OF REALTORS®.*)

REALTOR-ASSOCIATE®   A licensed *salesperson* who is a member of the National Association of Realtors® and who subscribes to the high standards of practice set forth in the Realtors® Code of Ethics.

REALTY   Land and everything permanently affixed thereto. (*See LAND, PROPERTY, REAL ESTATE, REAL PROPERTY.*)

REASONABLE TIME   A fair length of time that may be allowed or required for an act to be completed, considering the nature of the act and the surrounding circumstances. It is best to state a definite time for performance of a contract, otherwise the courts will imply a "reasonable time," which could vary considerably from case to case.

If the parties state in their contract a definite time for performance and add that "time is of the essence," then a court would not allow a reasonable time to perform after the expiration of the definite time stated.

A lender's decision to exercise a "due-on-sale" clause must be done within a reasonable time after the event that triggers the clause. (*See OFFER AND ACCEPTANCE.*)

REBATE   1. A reduction or kickback of a stipulated charge. A property manager may not accept any commission, rebate, or profit on expenditures made in behalf of an owner without the owner's knowledge and consent. Practices such as collecting revenues from vending machines, buying at discounts but charging a client retail prices, receiving rebate money or goods from contractors, are prohibited. (*See RESPA.*)

2. In certain cases it is permissible for a broker to rebate a portion of the broker's commission to a principal in the real estate transaction. The rationale is that the

payment is not for the performance of any act for which a real estate license is required since the owner-principal is usually exempt. It is simply a refund or reduced commission. However, full disclosure to the seller is required if the seller's broker is going to rebate part of the commission to the buyer.

3. Also, a return of an unearned finance charge where there has been a prepayment of the debt. (*See RULE OF 78s.*)

Even though excess depreciation may be taxed at ordinary rates when the property is sold, a knowledgeable investor realizes that dollars saved in taxes in the early years of investment can earn substantial income before those same dollars go to pay taxes at the time of the recapture of the excess depreciation. Also, if a tax deferred exchange should take place, the tax on the excess depreciation taken is deferred.

RECAPTURE To tax at the same rate as the previous deduction, i.e. ordinary tax. All depreciation or cost recovery taken on depreciable real property in excess of the amount allowed under the straight-line method is subject to the recapture provisions of the Internal Revenue Code, which have the effect of taxing this excess at ordinary income rates. These provisions are designed to prevent the taxpayer from taking advantage of both accelerated depreciation and capital gain treatment.

Under the federal tax rules, any depreciation taken in excess of straight-line on a residential property is taxed at the ordinary, less favorable income rate at the time of sale. However, when an investor sells commercial property acquired after 1980 that has been depreciated under the accelerated method, *all* depreciation taken is taxed or recaptured as ordinary income (so-called Section 1245 recapture).

Where a lessor is treated as the owner of property under a safe harbor lease election made for qualified leased property, and the lessee-user acquires the leased property after the lease term and subsequently disposes of it, recapture on the later sale is computed by the lessee by including the lessor's recomputed basis adjustments. (*See SAFE HARBOR LEASE ELECTION.*)

Recapture rules now apply to single-purpose agricultural and horticultural structures and storage facilities used in connection with the distribution of petroleum and its primary products. They are treated as a five-year recovery property.

The 1981 Economic Recovery Tax Act also established a new recapture system of investment credit allowed and taken if during any tax year prior to the close of the recapture period (ACRS life) the property is disposed of. The investment credit is recaptured as tax. (*See ACCELERATED DEPRECIATION, CAPITAL GAIN, COST RECOVERY INVESTMENT CREDIT.*)

RECAPTURE CLAUSE A clause usually found in percentage leases, especially in shopping center leases, giving the landlord the right to terminate the lease, and thus recapture the premises, if the tenant does not maintain a specified minimum amount of business. The tenant may try to negotiate a provision that keeps the lease in effect by increasing the minimum rent to the amount the owner would have received had the expected sales volume been achieved.

A recapture clause may also be used to give a ground lessee the right to purchase the fee after a set period of time has elapsed. Or the landlord may have the option to regain the premises in the event the tenant gives notice of its intention to assign or sublet to another or surrender a portion of the lease space or term.

A recapture provision in an office lease gives the lessor the right to recover any space that the tenant is unable to occupy or sublease.

RECAPTURE RATE   An appraisal term describing that rate at which invested capital will be returned over the period of time a prudent investor would expect to recapture his or her investment in a wasting asset. (*See CAPITALIZATION RATE.*)

RECASTING   The process of redesigning existing loans, especially where there is a default. The term of the loan may be extended, with the interest rate adjusted periodically to alleviate the pressure on the borrower. Care must be taken to avoid the risk of intervening liens attaining priority over the recast loan. In some cases, the lender may prefer to go along with a delinquent construction loan until the building is sold because a modification and recasting of the loan might jeopardize lien priorities. (*See FORBEARANCE.*)

RECEIPT   A written acknowledgment of having received something. Many purchase contracts serve as a receipt, in addition to being the offer to purchase and acceptance form. Thus, a broker should not sign the receipt portion of the contract unless he or she has, in fact, received the buyer's deposit. (*See DEPOSIT.*)

RECEIVER   An independent party appointed by a court to impartially receive, preserve, and manage property which is involved in litigation, pending final disposition of the matter before the court. Such a case might be a bankruptcy action, or a case where a subdivider is enjoined from selling his or her unregistered subdivision. In some states, a receiver is appointed during the statutory redemption period after the foreclosure sale. A receiver would not need a real estate license to sell real estate under his or her control, but the sale would require court approval.

RECIPROCAL EASEMENTS   Easements typically arising upon the development of a planned subdivision, in which easements and restrictions are created as covenants limiting the use of the land for the benefit of all the owners in the entire tract.

RECIPROCITY   The practice of mutual exchanges of privileges. Some states have reciprocal arrangements for recognizing and granting licenses to licensed brokers and salespeople from other states.

RECITAL OF CONSIDERATION   A statement of what constitutes the consideration for a particular transaction. While technically a deed does not require consideration to pass title to real property, it is good practice to recite some consideration, especially to support any covenants or promises in the deed. The consideration recited in the deed need not be the actual consideration, and is frequently stated nominally as, "for $10 and other good and valuable consideration." (*See NOMINAL CONSIDERATION.*)

RECLAMATION The process of converting wasted natural resources into productive assets, such as desert
land reclaimed through irrigation or swamp land that is filled in.

RECOGNITION Recognition is a precise tax term meaning that the
transaction is a taxable event. If a gain or loss is
"recognized," the gain is taxable and the loss is deductible. Usually, recognition
occurs at the time of the sale or exchange. Some exceptions are in the sale of a
principal residence, involuntary conversion, and some sales between related parties. (*See RESIDENCE.*)

**RECOGNITION
CLAUSE** A clause found in some blanket mortgages and
contracts for deeds used to purchase a tract of
land for subdivision and development. The
clause provides for protection of the rights of the ultimate buyers of individual lots
in case of default under the blanket mortgage by the developer. It is similar to a
nondisturbance clause in a commercial office building mortgage.

RECONCILIATION 1. The final step in an appraisal process, in which
the appraiser reconciles the estimates of value
received from the market-data, cost, and income approaches to arrive at a final
estimate of market value for the subject property. Also called correlation.

2. The balancing of entries in a double-entry accounting system.

RECONVEYANCE The act of conveying title in property back to the
original owner. Under a deed of trust, the trustor
(borrower/mortgagor) conveys title to a third party trustee as security for a debt.
When the debt is paid off, the property is then reconveyed by the trustee to the
trustor by means of a reconveyance deed. (*See DEED OF TRUST.*)

RECORDING The act of entering into the book of public records
the written instruments affecting the title to real
property, such as deeds, mortgages, contracts for sale, options, and assignments.
There is also a body of public records apart from the real estate recording system
that has a bearing on the quality of title. A title searcher would also check, for
example, public records regarding probate, marriage, taxes, and judgments.

Under the individual state recording acts, all instruments in writing affecting any
estate, right, title, or interest in land must be recorded in the county where the
land is located. The purpose of this is to give to everyone interested in the title to
a parcel of real estate notice of the various interests of all parties. From a practical
point of view, the recording acts give legal priority to those interests that are
recorded first.

Proper recordation imparts constructive notice to the world of the existence of the
recorded document and its contents. It protects both innocent purchasers for
value who act in ignorance of an unrecorded instrument and the grantee in the
event that the deed is altered or lost. Any conveyance *not* properly recorded is
generally *void* as against any subsequent purchaser, lessee, or mortgagee *in good
faith and for a valuable consideration* who, without having actual notice of the
unrecorded conveyance, records his or her subsequent interest in the property.
The act of recordation protects only subsequent purchasers *for value* and not

donees or beneficiaries under a will, nor does it protect against interests that arise by operation of law rather than by recordable document, such as dower, curtesy, and homestead rights, prescriptive and implied easements, and title by adverse possession. (In the case of adverse possession, however, the adverse possessor's physical possession of the property ordinarily would have provided constructive notice to the subsequent purchaser of the possessor's interest in the property and thus he or she would not be in "good faith.") Further, the act of recordation raises a presumption (rebuttable) that the instrument has been validly delivered, and that it is authentic. On the other hand, failure to record a document does not impair its validity as between the parties thereto and all other parties having notice of its existence. Note, however, that if a recorded contract is for some reason void, the mere fact that it is recorded will not make it valid. Under the Torrens system of land registration, however, documents must be properly registered to be effective.

The priority of property tax liens, mechanics' liens, and special assessment liens are not determined by date of recordation, since they are considered to be matters of public record. Other tax liens, such as for income tax and payroll tax, must be recorded to take priority over subsequent recorded interests. Thus, the system of recording creates a hierarchy of claims against a property with priority to be determined by the order in which the claims are recorded. Except for certain governmental tax liens which automatically take first priority, the order of recorded priority will not be disturbed unless there is a subordination or the recordation of a release.

To be eligible for recording, an instrument must be drawn and executed in conformity with the provision of the recording statutes of the state in which the real estate is located. The prerequisites for recording are not uniform. Many states require that the names be typed below the signatures on a document, and that the instrument be acknowledged before a notary public or other officer with the authority to take acknowledgments. In a few states the instrument must also be witnessed. Some states require that the name of the attorney who prepared the document also appear on it.

There are three major types of recording acts: notice; race-notice; and pure race. In a notice jurisdiction, a subsequent purchaser has priority if at the time of becoming a grantee for a valuable consideration he or she had neither actual nor constructive notice of the prior grant. It does not matter that thereafter the prior grantee may record first. In a race-notice jurisdiction, the subsequent purchaser, to be protected, must not only satisfy the requirements of the notice statute, but must also record first. In a pure race jurisdiction, notice is irrelevant. The party who records first is the one who prevails.

Each county has a public recorder's office, known variously as the county recorder's office, county registrar's office, or bureau of conveyances. The person in charge is generally known as either the recorder, registrar, or commissioner of deeds. When a copy of the deed is recorded, the recorder cross-indexes it under the names of both grantor and grantee. Thus, anyone who knows one of these names may learn the other by examining the records. The registrar usually charges a flat fee per document or per page. (See CHAIN OF TITLE, CONSTRUCTIVE NOTICE, CONVEYANCE TAX, GRANTOR-GRANTEE INDEX, NOTARY PUBLIC, PRIORITY, REGISTRAR, SUBORDINATION AGREEMENT, SUBSEQUENT BONA FIDE PURCHASER, TORRENS SYSTEM.)

RECORD OWNER   The owner of property as shown by an examination of the records; the one having record title.

RECORD TITLE   Title as it appears from an examination of the public records. (*See CHAIN OF TITLE, TITLE INSURANCE.*)

RECOURSE NOTE   A debt instrument with which the lender can take action against the borrower or endorser, personally in addition to foreclosure of the property covering the lender's mortgage. (*See DEFICIENCY JUDGMENT.*)

RECOVERY FUND   A state-regulated fund generally defined and described in the state real estate license law used as a source of money to indemnify buyers of real estate who have suffered losses due to a real estate licensee's misrepresentation or fraudulent acts (usually not negligent acts). The recovery fund thus underwrites the payment of otherwise uncollectible court judgments against a real estate licensee.

Generally, to seek money from the recovery fund, an injured person must first obtain a court judgment. After obtaining a judgment, the injured person must usually first attempt to collect the money by discovering and executing upon the licensee's assets. If the licensee is judgment-proof or has insufficient assets to satisfy the judgment, the aggrieved person can file a verified claim in the court in which he or she obtained the judgment and apply to the court for an order directing payment out of the recovery fund. The court may then order the commission to pay out of the recovery fund an amount not to exceed a specified amount per aggrieved person or transaction. Upon payment from the fund, the wrongdoer's license is usually terminated.

It has been held that a real estate licensee is *not* "an aggrieved person" for purposes of recovering from the fund, if the claim is based on an unsatisfied judgment against another licensee in a claim of fraudulent real estate transaction. (*See REAL ESTATE EDUCATION, RESEARCH AND RECOVERY FUND.*)

RECREATIONAL LEASE   A contract in which the lessor (usually a developer) leases recreationally related facilities (tennis courts, gyms, swimming pools) to a tenant for a stipulated time and rent consideration. Recreational leases are found in townhouse developments and subdivisions, but primarily in residential condominium projects. Typically, these leases are long-term, triple-net leases with a rental index increase tied to the consumer price index.

Recreational leases in condominiums have been the subject of much litigation from discontented lessees, especially where rent increases doubled in short periods of time. Many leases were successfully challenged as being unconscionable and both federal and state statutes have been proposed to help curb developer abuses in this area.

RECTANGULAR SURVEY METHOD   *See GOVERNMENT SURVEY METHOD.*

REDDENDUM CLAUSE   A clause in a conveyance that reserves something for the grantor, such as rent payable to a lessor or an interest in a life estate to a remainderman.

**REDEMPTION,
EQUITABLE
RIGHT OF** The right of a mortgagor who has defaulted on the mortgage note to redeem or get back his or her title to the property by paying off the entire mortgage note prior to the foreclosure sale. The equitable right of redemption comes into existence immediately upon execution of the mortgage and continues to exist until the mortgage is either satisfied and discharged by payment or until the right of redemption is cut off by foreclosure sale. After the property has been sold at a foreclosure sale, however, the mortgagor has no right of redemption, unless state law grants a statutory redemption period. (*See* *FORECLOSURE.*)

**REDEMPTION
PERIOD** A period of time established by state law during which a property owner has a right to redeem his or her real estate after a foreclosure or tax sale by paying the sale price, interest, and costs. Note that many states do not have such statutory redemption periods. During the redemption period (which may be one year or longer) the court may appoint a receiver to take charge of the property, collect rents, pay operating expenses, and so on. If the person in default can raise the necessary funds to redeem within the statutory period, the redemption money is paid to the court.

Historically, the right of redemption is inherited from the ancient chancery proceedings in England in which the court sale ended the equitable right of redemption. In many states, a statutory redemption period, which begins after the sale, is provided by state law to give the mortgagor a further opportunity to regain title to his or her land.

REDEVELOPMENT The improvement of cleared or undeveloped land, usually in an urban renewal area.

**REDEVELOPMENT
AGENCY** A quasi-governmental agency whose primary purpose is to develop property or improve housing opportunities in urban renewal areas, and to relocate residents displaced by the redevelopment of the area. The redevelopment agency usually has the power of eminent domain and often condemns smaller parcels and assembles these lots into one large development project. The redevelopment agency might enter into a development agreement with a professional developer and restrict the amount of profit the developer can derive from the project.

RED HERRING A term describing a preliminary prospectus for the sale of a security which is filed with the Securities and Exchange Commission, but the registration of which has not yet become effective. Red herring derives from the red printing along the left-hand margin of the prospectus, which states that a registration statement has been filed but is subject to change, and that the securities covered in this prospectus may not be sold before the registration statement becomes effective.

REDISCOUNT RATE The rate of interest charged by the Federal Reserve Bank for loans to member banks; also called the *discount rate*. The rediscount rate has an indirect effect on the interest rates charged by member banks to the public and the supply of funds for loans.

REDLINING   A practice by some lending institutions which restricts the number of loans or the loan-to-value ratio in certain areas of a community. A redlining policy may be so severe that in effect the lending institution prohibits lending any money in certain areas of a city. The usual justification for redlining is that the lender wants to limit the risks in an area that is deteriorating. The lender discriminates against a whole class of risks rather than distinguishing between individual risks.

A redlining policy based on the fact that a certain area of a community is becoming racially integrated is illegal and is in violation of Title VIII of the Federal Civil Rights Act and the Federal Home Loan Bank Board (FHLBB) antiredlining regulations. For example, it would be illegal redlining for a lending institution to require a higher down payment because the home the borrower is buying is located in a racially mixed area.

The antiredlining regulations are aimed at reversing the trend of abandonment and decay of certain neighborhoods, particularly in urban centers. Under the Home Mortgage Disclosure Act, lenders must disclose information as to how they determine their pattern of making loans in given geographic areas. A related area of concern is insurance redlining, which may be covered under the provision in the Federal Fair Housing law prohibiting conduct which would tend to make housing unavailable.

The Federal Home Loan Bank Board has also issued a regulation prohibiting redlining. It states that refusal to lend in a particular area solely because of the age of the homes or the income level in a neighborhood may be discriminatory in effect, since minority group persons are more likely to purchase used housing and to live in low-income neighborhoods. The racial composition of the neighborhood where the loan is to be made is always an improper underwriting consideration. (*See FEDERAL FAIR HOUSING LAW.*)

REDUCTION CERTIFICATE   An instrument that shows the current amount of the unpaid balance of a mortgage, the rate of interest, and the date of maturity. A reduction certificate is normally required from a mortgagee when a prospective purchaser is to assume or to take title subject to an existing mortgage. The mortgagee, then, cannot later claim that the mortgage amount or terms were different from those stated in the certificate. A reduction certificate is similar to an estoppel certificate except that it is executed by the mortgagee. The reduction certificate is useful since only the original amount of the loan is a matter of public record. Any reduction of principal is known only between the parties. The instrument is usually acknowledged, but need not be recorded. It is also called a statement of condition from the lender, or a beneficiary statement in a deed of trust situation. (*See ESTOPPEL CERTIFICATE.*)

RE-ENTRY   The repossession of real propery in accordance with a legal right reserved when the original possession was transferred. The grantor of a fee simple subject to a condition has the right to re-entry upon the breach of that condition. In essence, it is a power of termination.

The right of re-entry should be distinguished from the right of entry that a landlord possesses to go in and inspect the leased premises.

REFEREE   A disinterested, neutral party appointed by a court to arbitrate, investigate, find facts, or settle some dispute or legal matter. A referee in bankruptcy acts as a temporary administrator of a bankrupt's assets, which may be sold to satisfy the claims of creditors. (*See BANKRUPTCY.*)

REFERRAL   The act of recommending or referring; a sales lead. A referral in real estate is a client who has been obtained through the efforts or recommendation of another person. A broker can usually compensate or split commissions with a person who refers a client only if that person is licensed as a real estate broker. If the person is a licensed salesperson, the referral fee must be paid through the salesperson's supervising broker. While a seller can pay a referral fee to anyone, the person receiving the fee *may* be deemed to be acting as a real estate salesperson and, if that is the case, he or she must have a real estate license. (*See FINDER'S FEE.*)

REFINANCE   To obtain a new loan to pay off an existing loan; to pay off one loan with the proceeds from another. Properties are frequently refinanced when interest rates drop and/or the property has appreciated in value. Sometimes, a buyer will purchase a property by way of a contract for deed with the expectation of either selling the property before the balance under the contract for deed becomes due or refinancing at better terms and interest rates than exist at the time the agreement of sale is entered into.

Income properties are frequently refinanced by investors seeking additional capital with which to purchase other investment properties. Large real estate holdings are often amassed in this manner, a technique known as pyramiding through refinancing.

The Federal National Mortgage Association (Fannie Mae), a federally chartered secondary purchaser of home loans, will refinance a loan it holds for a new purchaser, usually at less than the market rate. A form of wraparound mortgage, this new loan would take the place of a second mortgage sometimes used to cover the difference between a purchase price and an assumable mortgage.

REFORMATION   A legal action necessary to correct or modify a contract or deed which has not accurately reflected the intentions of the parties, due to some mechanical error such as a typographical error in the legal description. If one of the parties will not execute a correction deed, the other party can seek a court order reforming such a deed, also called a reformation deed. A grantor under a general warranty deed usually agrees to perform any necessary act of reformation pursuant to the covenant of further assurance. (*See CORRECTION DEED.*)

REGISTERED LAND   Land which is registered in the Torrens system. (*See TORRENS SYSTEM.*)

REGISTRAR   The person usually having the duty to maintain accurate official records of all deeds, mortgages, contracts for deed, and other instruments relating to real estate titles filed for recordation; often associated with the Torrens system of title registration. (*See RECORDING.*)

REGRESSION   A principle of appraisal which states that, between dissimilar properties, the worth of the better property is adversely affected by the presence of the lesser-quality property. Thus, in a neighborhood where the homes average in the $50,000 range, a better-built structure, which in another neighborhood would be worth at least $60,000, would tend to be valued closer to $50,000. The principle of progression is the opposite; that is, the worth of a lesser object is increased by being located among better objects. (*See OVERIMPROVEMENT.*)

REGULAR SYSTEM   A system of recordation of documents affecting land not registered in the Torrens system; also known as the *unregistered system*. While the recording fees in the regular system are generally greater than in the Torrens system, the requirements for recordation are typically less stringent. (*See RECORDING.*)

REGULATION   A rule or order prescribed for management or government, as in the rules and regulations of the real estate commission. In many states, once the commission's regulations are approved by the governor following a public hearing, they have the force and effect of law.

REGULATION A   A special exemption from standard SEC registration of a security issue where the aggregate amount of the offering is less than $1,500,000. Even if the issue qualifies under Regulation A, the developer still must file a short-form registration with the regional SEC office and provide prospective purchasers with an offering circular containing much of the same information contained in a formal prospectus. Thus, Regulation A is not really an exemption from registration but rather a simpler form of registration. (*See REAL PROPERTY SECURITIES REGISTRATION.*)

REGULATION Q   A federal regulation that allows certain federal agencies to establish different interest rates on savings deposits for commercial banks and thrift (savings and loan) institutions.

REGULATION T   A federal regulation, administered by the Federal Reserve Board, governing the extension of credit arrangements for the extension of credit by securities brokers and dealers. The Federal Reserve Board lists only certain securities upon which security dealers can extend credit, and then restricts the amount of credit which may be extended by means of margin requirements.

The possible application of Regulation T to condominium securities had been the subject of much controversy between developers, the Federal Reserve Board, and the SEC because condominium securities were not approved securities upon which credit could be arranged. This continued interpretation would have had obvious adverse effects upon the financing and sales of condominium securities. However, the Federal Reserve Board has effectively exempted these securities from Regulation T.

REGULATION Z   See TRUTH-IN-LENDING LAWS.

REHABILITATE   To restore to a former or improved condition, such as when buildings are renovated and modernized. Rehabilitation may include new construction, buildings, or additions, but is usually performed without changing the basic plan, form, or style of a structure. In urban renewal projects, rehabilitation is the restoration to good condition of deteriorated structures, neighborhoods, and public facilities. Neighborhood rehabilitation encompasses structural rehabilitation and, in addition, may extend to street improvements and a provision of such amenities as parks and playgrounds.

The Internal Revenue Code provides for certain tax benefits in connection with the rehabilitation of real property. A 15 percent investment tax credit for "qualified rehabilitation" will be given for structures at least 30 years old, 20 percent for structures at least 40 years old, and 25 percent credit for certified historic structures. A "qualified rehabilitation" means any building which has been substantially rehabilitated, which was in use prior to beginning the revitalization, and which retains at least 75 percent of the existing external walls.

REINSTATEMENT   To bring something back to its prior position, as in restoring a lapsed insurance policy or restoring a defaulted loan to paid-up status. A borrower in default under a deed of trust can avoid a foreclosure sale by reinstating the loan prior to foreclosure; afterward, the borrower usually has a one-year statutory right of redemption, but the entire debt would have to be paid, not just the amount in default. (See DEED OF TRUST.)

REINSURANCE   A contract by which the original insurer (the ceding company) obtains insurance from another insurer (the reinsuring company) against loss on the ceding company's original policy. The reinsurance company takes on all the rights, duties, and liabilities of the ceding company under the original policy.

REISSUE RATE   A reduced charge by a title insurance company for a new policy if a previous policy on the same property was recently issued.

RELATED PARTIES   Parties standing in a certain defined relationship to each other; parties may be related by blood, by fiduciary relationships, or by ownership interest in a corporation. Under the Internal Revenue Code, any loss on the sale of property between family relations may be nondeductible. Also, the gain may be treated as ordinary income in the case of a sale or exchange of depreciable property between certain related parties. The sole test is the relationship of the parties and not the fairness of the sales price or rental. (See IMPUTED INTEREST, INSTALLMENT SALE.)

RELATION-BACK DOCTRINE   In a valid escrow, there is an irrevocable deposit of the executed deed, purchase money, and instructions into the escrow pending performance of the escrow conditions. Under the relation-back doctrine, the death of the grantor does not terminate the escrow or revoke the agent's authority to deliver an executed deed. The delivery of the deed to the grantee relates back to the date it was originally deposited with the escrow agent, and it is considered as if the grantor made the delivery to the grantee before the death of the grantor. When the escrow conditions are performed, title passes to the grantee and the deed can be formally delivered to the grantee without any probate court approval. Were this not so, an action for specific performance would have to be brought against the grantor's heirs. In addition, delivery of a deed into escrow will also cut off the rights of any of the seller's attaching creditors and thus pass clear title as of the date of the escrow. (*See DELIVERY, EQUITABLE CONVERSION, ESCROW.*)

RELEASE   The discharge or relinquishment of a right, claim, or privilege. Since a formal release is a contract relieving a person from any further legal obligation, it must contain a valuable consideration. Releases involving real property transactions should be acknowledged and recorded, and should also note the liber and page number of the document released.

RELEASE CLAUSE   1. A provision found in many blanket mortgages enabling the mortgagor to obtain partial releases of specific parcels from the mortgage upon a payment larger than the pro rata portion of the loan. Most mortgagees insert a clause that no partial release will be issued if the mortgagor is in default under the mortgage.

Many transactions involving incremental development of land employ release clauses. As the developer sells off the subdivided lots, a portion of sales proceeds is used to partially satisfy the mortgage. In return, the mortgagee executes and records a release of the particular parcel sold, so that the purchasers can obtain clear title. Usually the release clause contains a formula for the release payments, such as the payment of a sum which is in the proportion that the area of the land to be released bears to the total area of the land under the blanket mortgage, multiplied by 125 percent of the original mortgage amount. For example, if there were five parcels covered under the blanket mortgage, the lender might require the payment of one-fourth of the loan before he or she will release one parcel.

Since the best lots are usually sold first, the release price is pegged higher than the average mortgage value of the undivided lots, thus assuring adequate security for the remaining loan balance. In other words, the release price is higher to compensate for the earlier sale of the best lots. The developer should insert in the release clause a provision to the effect that all payments made on the note for which the developer did not request a release should apply to release payments. Thus, if one parcel can be released upon payment of $20,000 and the developer has already reduced the principal on the note by $8,000, then the $8,000 should be considered part of the release payment so that only an additional $12,000 is required. In addition, some lenders use a very sophisticated "adjacent and contiguous, backward and forward" release clause (forward—borrower pays in advance; backward—borrower pays on time; adjacent—next to; contiguous—in order) to prevent the developer from checkerboarding in the selling and releasing of lots, thus reducing the value of the entire development and perhaps leaving some landlocked parcels. Note that the description of the parcels to be released should be definite enough to avoid the argument that the mortgage is unenforceable for vagueness. (*See BLANKET MORTGAGE, PARTIAL RELEASE CLAUSE.*)

2. Release clause also refers to a contingency provision in a purchase agreement, which allows the seller to continue to market the property and accept other offers. Upon acceptance of an offer from another buyer, the original buyer has a period of time, such as 72 hours, in which to waive the contingency, such as the sale of the buyer's present home, or to release the seller from the agreement so he or she can sell to the second buyer. (*See CONTINGENCY.*)

RELICTION   The gradual recession of water from the usual watermark and, therefore, an increase of the land. Reliction refers to a situation where land that once was covered by water becomes uncovered. The uncovered land is treated as alluvion and the rules of accretion apply to the ownership of this new land. This new land usually belongs to the riparian owner. (*See ACCRETION*.)

RELOCATION CLAUSE   A clause in a lease giving the landlord the right to relocate a tenant. The landlord may want this right when an older building is renovated or, when smaller tenants are relocated, to provide flexibility in accommodating larger tenants' expansion requirements.

RELOCATION COMPANY   A company retained by large corporations to help their employees move from one location to another. A primary function of this service is to purchase the transferee's home so that the transferee will have the funds to locate new housing and not have to worry about the uncertainties of first selling the present home. The employer corporation usually pays all the costs incurred by the relocation company in its buying and reselling of the employee's present home.

The relocation company's offer to purchase is usually based on two or more independent fee appraisals. Since the relocation company has purchased the property, they are concerned in marketing the property with a combination of sales price, carrying costs, closing costs, and costs of repair and improvements as they relate to the estimated cost of their services. Relocation companies frequently select a top broker in a community to handle the sales of all its properties. In addition, the relocation companies insist that their properties be listed in the multiple-listing service to get the maximum exposure.

REMAINDER ESTATE   A future interest in real estate created at the same time and by the same instrument as another estate, and limited to arise immediately upon the termination of the prior estate. For example, Joe Phigg owns a property in fee simple and conveys the property "to Barry Clink and, upon Clink's death, to Cora Quibb and her heirs." Cora Quibb has a remainder estate, which is vested because the estate *automatically* passes to Cora Quibb and her heirs upon the death of Barry Clink. Whereas a reversion is an estate which is retained by the grantor when he or she conveys a lesser estate, a remainder is a future estate created by the grantor in favor of some third party.

A remainder may be either vested or contingent. It is *vested* if the only uncertainty is the actual date of the termination of the prior estate. It is *contingent* when there is some other uncertainty. For example, Harry wills (devises) his farm to his son as a life estate with the remainder going to his son's living children. But if there are no children, then the estate goes to Harry's brother Jim. Jim has a contingent remainder, which ceases if the son dies leaving a child.

A gift of a remainder interest in real property is subject to federal gift tax rules. Since it does not qualify as a "present interest," the remainder interest does not qualify for the $10,000 annual exclusion. The IRS will compute the value of the remainder interest by using tables based upon the life expectancy of the donor, and a discount factor of 6 percent. (*See REVERSION*.)

REMAINDERMAN   One entitled to take an estate in remainder. For example, Armand Lee, seized in fee simple of

Blackacre Acres, grants a life estate in Blackacre Acres to August Kim, remainder to Lawrence Park for life, then to Don Yee in fee. Thus, Mr. Kim has a life estate which passes in fee upon his death to Mr. Yee, who is also a remainderman until Park's death. Although the remainderman has only a future interest, he or she still has some present rights. The remainderman has the right to bring court action against the current possessor for committing waste.

REMISE To give up, to remit. Typical language found in a quitclaim deed.

RENDERING An artist's or architect's interpretation, in perspective, of a completed development, usually done in color or ink.

RENEGOTIABLE RATE MORTGAGE (RRM) A short-term loan secured by a long-term adjustable rate mortgage, with interest renegotiated at the time of established automatic renewal periods. While modeled after the Canadian Rollover Mortgage, there is a big difference: under the Canadian plan, the mortgage itself is renewed rather than short-term interest adjustments of a long-term mortgage.

Under the original plan, as approved by the Federal Home Loan Bank Board (FHLBB), a three-, four-, and five-year renegotiable rate loan would be secured by a long-term mortgage and would be repayable in equal monthly installments. The interest rate would be adjusted at renewal periods and would be computed based on a national mortgage index representing the average interest rate of all conventional mortgages written by savings and loan associations each month (Table 5.5.1 of the FHLBB Journal).

The maximum increase or decrease during the life of the loan would be 5 percentage points with a 0.5 percent change permitted each year. A prepayment without penalty is allowed after the first renewal notice, and a 90-day notice period is required before automatic renewal.

Since the introduction of the adjustable mortgage loan, many of the original restrictions on RRM no longer apply. (See *ADJUSTABLE RATE LOAN.*)

RENEGOTIATION OF LEASE The review of an existing lease after a specified period of time to negotiate the lease terms anew. The most common reason for the renegotiation of a lease is to establish a new annual rent for an additional period based on changed economic conditions. Many leases provide that renegotiated rent is to be based on mutual agreement and, failing that, by an independent appraisal based upon a rate of return to the fee owner equal to some specific rate fixed when the lease is first negotiated. An alternative method uses outside indicators by which the rent is increased at set intervals, e.g., U.S. Labor Department Cost of Living Indicator. In listing a leasehold, a broker should be careful to verify the renegotiation period and terms, if any. (See *GROUND LEASE, LEASEHOLD.*)

RENEWAL OPTION A covenant in a lease which gives the lessee the right to extend the lease term for a certain period, on specified terms, provided the tenant is not in default. The landlord, however, usually cannot enforce an automatic renewal clause against the tenant unless the landlord gives prior notice of the renewal. The covenant should state whether the option to renew is transferable in the event the lease is assigned. (*See EXTENSION.*)

RENT   Fixed periodic payment made by a tenant or occupant of property to the owner for the possession and use thereof, usually by prior agreement of the parties. The common law rule is that rent is not due until the end of the term. Most leases, however, state that rent is due in advance. Unless the lease specifies otherwise, the rent must be paid to the landlord at the leased premises. If the landlord makes an expressed or implied authorization for the rent money to be mailed to him or her, delivery to the post office constitutes payment and the landlord suffers the risk of any subsequent delay or loss.

RENTABLE AREA   As standardized by the Building Owners and Managers Association International, rentable area of an office on a multiple tenancy floor is computed by measuring to the inside finish of permanent outer building walls, or to the glass line if at least 50 percent of the outer building wall is glass, to the office side of corridors and/or permanent partitions, and to the center of partitions that separate the premises from adjoining rentable areas. No deductions can be made for columns and projections necessary to the buildings. (*See USABLE AREA.*)

RENTAL AGENCY   Any person who for compensation or other valuable consideration acts or attempts to act as an intermediary between a person seeking to lease, sublease, or assign a housing accommodation and a person seeking to acquire a lease, sublease, or assignment of a housing accommodation. Such a person may not have to obtain a real estate license but may, under state law, need a special rental agency license.

RENTAL AGREEMENT   An agreement, written or oral, which establishes or modifies the terms, conditions, rules, regulations, or any other provisions concerning the use and occupancy of a dwelling unit and premises; a lease on residential property. Certain states have "plain language" laws requiring rental agreements to be written in clear and understandable, everyday language, appropriately captioned and paragraphed.

RENTAL POOL   A rental arrangement whereby participating owners of rental apartments agree to have their apartment units available for rental as determined by the rental agent, and then share in the profits and losses of all the rental apartments in the pool according to an agreed formula. Some rental pool plans base the payment of the profits on the number of days the unit was available for rental. If a condominium is offered for sale and the offer includes participation in a rental pool arrangement, that condominium offering is considered an "investment contract" and therefore a security. Consequently, the offeror must have the condominium registered with the SEC as a security. After a project has been sold, the owners can form a rental pool without the need for SEC registration. (*See REAL PROPERTY SECURITIES REGISTRATION.*)

RENT CONTROL   Regulation by state or local governmental agencies restricting the amount of rent landlords can
charge their tenants; such regulation has been upheld as a valid exercise of the
state's police power in the jurisdictions that currently employ rent controls.

Two major themes in rent control have emerged nationwide:

1. the use of rent control to regulate the quality of rental dwellings, with controls
   to be implemented only against those units that do not conform to applicable
   building codes, as in the case of New York City.

2. the use of rent control across the board to remedy high rents caused by the gross
   imbalance between supply and demand in housing, such as is seen in Massachusetts and California.

An interesting merger of the two has occurred in New Jersey, where the enabling
statute leans heavily toward quality control, while local jurisdictions have enacted rent control ordinances to cope with emergency housing shortages and in-
flated rents in Fort Lee, N.J., and in other towns close to New York City.

RENT-UP   1. The process of filling a new building with tenants. 2. The requirement of a lender, typically a
leasehold mortgagee, that the mortgagor (developer/owner) achieve the leasing of a
stated amount of space in the building as a prerequisite to a permanent lender
"taking out" the interim construction lender. The developer must present certified
rent rolls which are usually checked by the lender's servicing agent. If the developer does not meet the rent achievement amount, a floor loan for a reduced
amount will have to be disbursed and gap financing sought. (See FLOOR LOAN,
GAP FINANCING.)

REPAIRS   Current expenditures to restore to an original condition; minor alterations made to maintain the
property rather than to extend the useful life of the property. The cost of repairs
normally is tax deductible as a business expense if the property is income-producing property. Substantial repairs, however, are treated as capital expenditures, and
thus increase the basis of the property. Capital expenditures involve changes in
either the form of material of the building or the renewal of any substantial part of
it which results in an increase in the asset's useful life. An example would be a
new addition or a replacement of carpeting or roof. (See CAPITAL EXPENDI-
TURE.)

Unless the lease provides to the contrary, the landlord normally does not have to
make any repairs whatever in the leased premises. Under some states' residential
landlord-tenant codes, however, the landlord has a specific duty to keep the premises in a habitable condition. There is no legal requirement that repairs be made by
the lessee or lessor. The lessee must return the property in the same condition as
it was leased, less reasonable wear and tear. To eliminate disputes, the lease
should specify who is responsible for the various types of repair. A tenant is not,
however, under a duty to make extraordinary repairs unless he or she willfully or
negligently caused the damage.

With respect to the sale of property, the parties should specify in the sales contract, when applicable, the items which the seller should repair before the closing.
Sellers of property to be purchased with a nonconventional VA or FHA loan
should be aware that their net sales proceeds will be reduced by the cost of any
repairs required by VA or FHA.

For tax purposes, the seller of a principal residence can deduct from the selling price the cost of fix-up repairs made within 90 days of the date of sale and paid for within 30 days of closing. Such eleventh-hour expenses are treated as part of the selling cost when the sale of one's personal residence is involved. (*See FIXING-UP EXPENSES; RESIDENCE, SALE OF.*)

REPLACEMENT COST   *See REPRODUCTION COST.*

REPLEVIN   Legal proceedings brought to recover possession of personal property unlawfully taken, as in a case where a landlord has unlawfully taken the personal belongings of the tenant due to the tenant's failure to pay the rent. (*See DISTRAINT.*)

REPRODUCTION COST   The cost, on the basis of current prices, of reproducing a new replica property with the same or fairly similar material. Most appraisers estimate reproduction cost by the comparative cost method, in which estimates are made on the basis of the current cost to construct buildings of similar size, design, and quality. Other methods are the quantity-survey method and the unit-in-place method. Comparisons are usually made on a square-foot or cubic-foot basis.

Reproduction cost is often used synonymously with replacement cost, but the terms are different. Reproduction cost refers to exact duplication; replacement cost refers to a building that has the same functional ability but possibly is of different size, materials, or design. After arriving at the reproduction cost for a new building, the amount of accrued depreciation due to physical, functional, and economic causes must be deducted to complete the appraisal. (*See COST APPROACH.*)

RESCIND   To annul, cancel. (*See RESCISSION.*)

RESCISSION   The legal remedy of cancelling, terminating, or annulling a contract and restoring the parties to their original positions; a return to the status quo. Contracts may be rescinded due to mistake, fraud, or misrepresentation; there is no need to show any money damage. Where a seller seeks to rescind a contract with a defaulting buyer, the seller must return all payments made by the buyer, minus a fair rental for the time the buyer has been in possession. This is not true, however, under a contract for deed. Sellers often insert a forfeiture clause authorizing them to keep all payments in the event of a buyer's default. Courts, however, are reluctant to enforce such a forfeiture clause, especially where it is in the nature of a penalty, and often the court will order rescission instead.

Purchasers are sometimes given a "cooling-off" period after they sign a contract of purchase during which they can rescind the contract for any reason whatsoever. For instance, the purchaser of land, which is registered with HUD, or should have been, is given a rescission period of seven calendar days from the time of receipt of the property report. Also, in VA and FHA financing, the buyer is given a right to cancel should the purchase price exceed the official valuation by an FHA- or VA-approved appraiser. There is also a right of rescission under the federal Truth-in-Lending Law and most state timesharing laws. (*See CONTRACT FOR DEED, FORFEITURE, INTERSTATE LAND SALES, TRUTH-IN-LENDING LAWS.*)

RESCISSION CLAUSE   1. A specific clause occasionally found in a contract for deed, which requires the seller to return all of the buyer's payments, minus the cost and a fair rental value, in the event the buyer defaults. Because such a clause may overly favor the buyer, it is not found in many contracts for deed. 2. A clause in a contract, required by some state subdivided land sales laws, that informs a purchaser of his or her rescission rights as provided by state law.

RESERVATION   The creation, in behalf of the grantor, of a new right issuing from what was granted. A reservation thus is something that did not exist as an independent right before the conveyance. For example, Smith conveys to Jones a 10-acre parcel "reserving to Smith a life estate therein." A right or interest cannot be reserved in favor of a third party.

Title to all property passes to the grantee but a use may be reserved in the grantor. In an *exception*, title to a portion is retained by the grantor. (*See EXCEPTION.*)

RESERVE FOR REPLACEMENTS   A typical entry in an operating statement to provide for the replacement of short-life items, such as air-conditioning units, carpeting, and appliances; an allowance that is necessary in order to maintain a projected level of income.

RESERVE FUND   Monies a lender will often require a borrower to set aside as a cushion of capital for future payment of items such as taxes, insurance, furniture replacement, and deferred maintenance. Sometimes a reserve fund is referred to as an impound account or customer's trust fund. Replacement reserves should be maintained especially when the owner is installing property with a short life expectancy, such as a refrigerator, or furniture and carpeting in a furnished apartment.

RESIDENCE   One's home or place of abode. Residence is defined differently for tax, license, and education qualification purposes. While a person can have several residences, he or she can have only one domicile. A residence would include such things as a trailer, a cooperative, a condominium, or even a houseboat. (*See DOMICILE.*)

RESIDENCE, SALE OF   Under certain circumstances, the taxable gain from the sale and replacement of one's *principal* residence may be recognized only to the extent that the adjusted sales price of the old residence (gross sales price less sales expenses, less fixing-up expenses) equals or exceeds the cost of purchasing (or constructing) a new residence. Thus, gain would be recognized to the extent that the purchase price of the new residence is less than the sale price of the old residence. Assume Mr. Brown sells his principal residence for $50,000 (adjusted), which gives him a profit or gain of $12,000. He then buys a new home for $60,000. For income tax purposes, Brown pays no tax on the $12,000 gain, but the $12,000 gain is deducted from the $60,000, giving Brown a "basis" of $48,000 in the new home. Any sale of the new home in excess of $48,000 would be a taxable gain to Brown unless it too is nonrecognized gain under IRC 1034.

To qualify for nonrecognized status, the home must be the principal residence of the taxpayer. This is a question of fact based on all the facts and circumstances, including the taxpayer's good faith. If the taxpayer has rented the house for significant periods of time, it may not be treated as a principal residence and he or she thus loses the benefits of 1034 status. If part of the house is used for business purposes, for example an office, only the part allocated to personal use can take advantage of this nonrecognition of gain treatment. A principal residence would include a house, a condominium unit, or a cooperative unit. The taxpayer must replace the old principal residence and occupy the new home within a period beginning two years prior to the date of sale and ending two years after the date of sale. For those in active military service the replacement time is longer.

The date of sale is the date the title is transferred or the date that possession and control pass to the buyer under a contract for deed. Where the taxpayer builds the home him or herself or contracts to have it constructed, the construction must begin no later than one year after the date of sale of the old residence and the taxpayer must actually occupy the new residence as his or her principal residence no later than 24 months after the date of sale of the old residence.

The unrecognized gain is, in effect, *deferred* until the taxpayer sells his or her new home. If the taxpayer then buys another principal residence, he or she can keep deferring payment of any capital gains tax. The taxpayer must substantiate the adjusted basis when the final residence is sold and a capital gains tax must be paid. If the taxpayer cannot produce good records substantiating the basis, the IRS might assign an approximate or even a zero basis, thus resulting in a substantial capital gain tax payment. Upon the owner's death, the basis of the property "steps up" to its fair market value and the heirs are not liable for payment of any of the deferred gain (though an estate tax is levied on the property).

If a taxpayer sells his or her residence at a gain but buys more than one home during the two-year replacement period, only the latest purchase will be considered as the replacement residence for tax purposes. Likewise, if a person purchases a new residence but sells it before selling the previous home, the newer residence will not be considered as a replacement residence.

Generally, only one Section 1034 benefit is allowed in each two-year period. However, under the Tax Act, taxpayers may claim more than one sale during a two-year period, if the sales were made for employment reasons, such as job transfer. In this case they may also deduct certain job-related moving expenses from their incomes. Although taxpayers applying for a Section 1034 benefit may be either employees or self-employed, they must meet certain requirements for geographic location and term of employment.

Taxpayers 55 years of age or older may be entitled to a once-in-a-lifetime $125,000 exclusion of the profit made on the sale of a principal residence. (See *BASIS, CAPITAL GAIN, FIXING-UP EXPENSES, SALE OF RESIDENCE BY ELDERLY, VACATION HOME.*)

RESIDENT MANAGER   A salaried agent of the owner employed to manage a single building. Generally, a resident manager need not be licensed under the state real estate license laws, if he or she merely acts as custodian or caretaker. (See *PROPERTY MANAGEMENT.*)

RESIDENTIAL ENERGY CREDIT   The Energy Tax Act of 1978 provides a nonrefundable income tax credit for qualifying solar and wind energy equipment expenditures for installations on the principal residence of a taxpayer. The credit would amount to 30 percent of the first $2,000 and 20 percent of the next $8,000 of qualifying expenditures, for a maximum credit of $2,200. A $10 minimum limit also applies to this credit.

Original use of the property must commence with the taxpayer. In addition, the property must reasonably be expected to remain in operation for at least five years. Further, if administrative regulations are in effect with respect to the property, it must meet those regulatory standards.

The credit may be claimed for expenditures made on or after April 20, 1977, and before January 1, 1986. A credit carryover is provided to the extent that the credit exceeds the taxpayer's tax liability and extends for two years beyond the termination date (through taxable years ending before January 1, 1988).

The credit would apply to both "active" and "passive" solar systems, to equipment using geothermal energy, and to other equipment items which rely upon "renewable energy resources."

RESIDENTIAL INSULATION AND OTHER ENERGY-CONSERVING COMPONENTS The Energy Tax Act also provides an income tax credit for insulation and other energy-conserving component expenditures for installations in or on the principal residence of a taxpayer. Construction of the residence must have been substantially completed before April 20, 1977. The credit is 15 percent of the first $2,000 of qualifying expenditures (maximum credit of $300). To be claimed, the credit must amount to at least $10. This credit is available for expenditures made on or after April 20, 1977, and before January 1, 1986. A credit carryover is provided to the extent that the credit exceeds the taxpayer's tax liability, but such carryover is limited to tax years ending before 1988. Among those eligible for the credit are owners, renters, individuals owning stock in a cooperative housing association, and members of a condominium management association. The residential energy credit is nonrefundable.

The credit applies to qualifying insulation and other energy-conserving components. Insulation is defined as any item specifically and primarily designed to reduce the heat loss or gain of the dwelling or water heater. "Other energy-conserving components" include: (1) a furnace replacement burner which is more energy efficient, (2) a device for modifying flue openings designed to increase efficiency of the heating system, (3) an electrical or mechanical furnace ignition system that replaces a gas pilot light, (4) a storm or thermal window or door, (5) an automatic energy-saving setback thermostat, (6) caulking or weatherstripping of an exterior door or window, (7) energy usage display meters, and (8) other items which are specified by regulation as increasing the energy efficiency of a dwelling. As to both insulation and other energy-conserving components, the original use must begin with the taxpayer, the insulation or component must reasonably be expected to remain in operation for at least three years, and must meet the performance and quality standards (if any) stated by regulations.

RESIDUAL 1. That which is left over, such as the residual value of property after its economic life is completed. 2. Deferred commissions; that is, commissions which are earned but payment of which is put off for a stated period. For example, in a real estate sale, a broker earns a commission when the buyer signs and the seller accepts the purchase agreement. But, by prior arrangement between seller and broker, the commission may possibly be paid in part upon the down payment, and in full, the residual, upon closing which, with a new project under construction, could be as much as 18 months away. It is permissible for a salesperson in certain cases to accept residuals directly from a former employing broker rather than have these pass through his or her new employing broker. (*See DEFERRED COMMISSION.*)

RESIDUAL PROCESS   An appraisal process, used in the income approach, to estimate the value of the land and/or the building, as indicated by the capitalization of the residual net income attributable to it. (*See APPRAISAL, BUILDING RESIDUAL TECHNIQUE, CAPITALIZATION, PROPERTY RESIDUAL TECHNIQUE.*)

RESORT PROPERTY   Property which lends itself to vacationing, recreation, and/or leisure enjoyment because of either its natural resources or beauty (mountains, lakes, or sea) or its manmade improvements (tennis courts, golf courses, manmade ski hills).

RESPA   *See REAL ESTATE SETTLEMENT PROCEDURES ACT.*

RESPONDEAT SUPERIOR   A principle of agency law which states that the employer (principal) is liable in certain cases for the wrongful acts of his or her employee (agent) committed during the course of employment, so long as those acts of the agent were performed within the scope of the agent's authority. (*See SCOPE OF AUTHORITY.*)

RESTRAINT OF TRADE   Contracts or combinations that are designed to eliminate or stifle competition, to create a monopoly, to control prices, or otherwise to hamper or obstruct the normal operation of business. Restraint of trade is generally illegal under federal and state antitrust laws. (*See ANTITRUST LAWS.*)

RESTRAINT ON ALIENATION   A limitation or condition placed on the right to transfer property. Restraints can take the form of conditions and covenants in deeds or restraints on use of the property. Restrictions placed on the vesting of an estate until some remote time are regulated by the rule against perpetuities, which requires the vesting of contingent interests to take place, if at all, within the period of lives-in-being plus 21 years.

One of the bundle of rights in the ownership of real property is the right to convey, therefore the courts will not enforce any unreasonable restrictions placed by the grantor on this right. For example, a condition in a deed that the grantee may sell to tall people only would be an unreasonable restraint on alienation and hence the condition, but not the deed, is void. Restraints based on race, color, religion, sex, and ancestry are void under antidiscrimination laws.

Some state courts have held that the automatic exercise of a *due-on-sale* clause by a mortgagee upon a sale of the property covered by the mortgagee is an illegal restraint on alienation and some courts have refused to enforce the due-on-sale clause. The courts have held that in order to exercise its due-on-sale clause, the lender must show some impairment to its security. (*See RULE AGAINST PERPETUITIES.*)

RESTRICTION   A limitation on the use of property. Private restrictions are created by means of restrictive cove-
nants ("CC&Rs") written into real property instruments, such as deeds and
leases. Well-drafted restrictions have a tendency to stabilize property values, since
property owners can be certain as to the permitted uses of the neighboring properties. Such covenants might restrict the number and size of structures to be placed
on the land, the cost of structures, fence heights, setbacks, the use of the property
for the sale of intoxicating beverages, and the like. Such restrictions can be terminated by a quitclaim deed executed by the necessary parties. It is always best to
consult a title company to determine whose signatures are necessary on the deed.
Restrictive covenants which discriminate by restricting the conveyance to or use
by individuals of a specified race, sex, color, religion, marital status, or ancestry
are void.

Private restrictions can be found in deed restrictions, mortgage restrictions, and/or
declarations of restrictions used in developments such as subdivisions, PUDs,
shopping centers, and industrial parks. Restrictions are usually enforced by means
of court injunction. The restriction language should be precise, as interpretation
differences frequently occur.

Public restrictions are created by means of zoning ordinances. Unlike private restrictions, they must tend to promote the public health, welfare, and safety. Restrictive covenants which tend to create a monopoly on any line of commerce or
whose effect may be to lessen competition are generally illegal. Thus, a restriction
that the grantee cannot conduct any business except a funeral parlor on the
deeded property may be in violation of the law. (*See DECLARATION OF RE-
STRICTIONS, RESTRICTIVE COVENANT.*)

RESTRICTIVE   A private agreement usually contained in a deed
COVENANT   or lease, which restricts the use and occupancy of
real property. This is sometimes called private
zoning. Such a covenant is said to run with the land and binds all subsequent
purchasers, their heirs and assigns. It also normally covers such things as lot size,
building lines, type of architecture, and uses to which the property may be put.

Restrictive covenants may generally be terminated by obtaining quitclaim deeds
from all benefitting owners. However, this may be impractical since the termination must be unanimous, and the consent of the underlying mortgagees may be
required as well. The covenants may also be terminated by acquiescence of repeated violators and by merger of the burdened and benefitting properties. Often,
subdividers specify that deed restrictions will expire after a set length of time or
such expiration may be also specified by state law. This is done to avoid tying up
land use needlessly in the distant future. Restrictive covenants are strictly construed against persons seeking to enforce them. All ambiguities, then, are resolved
against the restriction and in favor of the person seeking the free and unrestricted
use of the property.

RESUBDIVISION   The act of taking an existing subdivision and either replatting it (that is, changing the lots from
the old grid pattern to the more modern irregular lots), or dividing it even further
(that is, taking 20-acre lots and dividing them into five-acre parcels). For purposes
of county subdivision approval, and state and federal land sales registration, a
resubdivision is the same as a new subdivision. (*See SUBDIVISION.*)

RESULTING TRUST   A trust which is implied by law, resulting from the acts or relationships of the parties involved. A situation, for example, in which Buck Davis supplies the money to buy a certain high-rise apartment building, with title taken in Sandy Pincurl's name for convenience, would be a resulting trust in which Pincurl holds the property in trust for Davis.

RETAINAGE   A portion or a percentage of payments made by a landowner to a contractor for construction work completed, which portion is withheld until the construction contract has been satisfactorily completed and the period for filing mechanics' liens has expired (or when the lien has been released by the contractor and subcontractors). Likewise, the contractor holds back a portion of its payments to subcontractors until the subcontractor's work has been completed and a waiver of any mechanics' liens has been obtained.

The amount of retainage is usually 10 percent of each progress payment. In some situations, rather than taking the retainage out of the progress payments, the owner will simply pay the last one or two payments into escrow for release when the lien period has expired. Retainages are also called *holdbacks*.

RETAINING WALL   Any wall erected to hold back or support a bank of earth. A retaining wall is also any enclosing wall built to resist the lateral pressure of internal loads.

RETALIATORY EVICTION   An act whereby a landlord evicts a tenant in response to some complaint made by the tenant. Many state laws, as well as the Uniform Residential Landlord and Tenant Act, provide that if the tenant has complained in good faith to the proper authorities of conditions which constitute a violation of a health law or regulation, or if the authorities have filed a notice or complaint of a health or building code violation resulting from a tenant's complaint, or if the tenant has in good faith requested necessary repairs, then the landlord cannot for these reasons alone evict the tenant, demand an increase in rent, or decrease the services rendered to the tenant. The tenant would generally be entitled to damages for such an eviction.

However, even after a complaint is made by the tenant, a landlord can still evict a tenant for good cause. For example, if the landlord or his or her immediate family wants to occupy the premises, or the landlord is going to take the premises off the rental market, he or she can still evict the tenant. Also, a landlord can still raise the rent if he or she can show that increased taxes and other costs have forced an increase in the rent.

REVERSE ANNUITY MORTGAGE   A form of mortgage which enables elderly homeowners to borrow against the equity in their homes so they can receive monthly payments needed to help meet living costs. Under this plan, the inflow and outflow of funds is in reverse to the standard conventional loan. The homeowner receives periodic payments (not necessarily equal payments) based on accumulated equity; the payments are made directly by the lender or through the purchase of an annuity from an insurance company. The loan comes due either upon a specific date or upon the occurrence of a specific event, such as sale of the property or death of the borrower.

REVERSE LEVERAGE   A situation that arises when financing is too costly—when the total yield on a cash investment is less than the interest rate on borrowed funds. (*See NEGATIVE CASH FLOW.*)

REVERSION   The estate remaining in the grantor, or the estate of a testator, who has conveyed a lesser estate from the original. A future estate in real property created by operation of law when a grantor conveys a lesser estate than he or she has. Because a reversion is created by operation of law, no express words of creation are needed. The residue left in the grantor is called a reversion which commences in possession in the future upon the end of a particular estate granted or devised, whether it be freehold or less than freehold. For example, Adam grants Eve a life estate. Eve in turn grants Junior a 10-year leasehold. Junior would have an estate for years, Eve would have a reversion for life which would transform into a life estate at the termination of the 10-year lease, and Adam would have a reversion in the fee, which would revert to Adam upon Eve's death.

Sometimes a grantor stipulates a condition in a deed which would result in the reversion of the property to the grantor if not complied with. For example, Adam grants Alice the property and in the deed stipulates that Alice shall not use the premises as a restaurant. If she does so use the property, title shall automatically revert to the grantor. Such a condition creates what is called a possibility of reverter in the grantor. In some states, the courts will not enforce a possibility of reverter. They would, however, enjoin Alice from violating the condition and could even award the grantor damages for breach of the condition. In effect, therefore, the courts tend to interpret the condition more like a covenant. (*See COVENANTS AND CONDITIONS, REMAINDER ESTATE.*)

Under common law principles, all improvements placed by the lessee on the leased premises would revert to the lessor upon the expiration of the lease. Some statutes, however, provide that at the termination of any residential lease, or at the expiration of the lease term, the lessee may remove all improvements on the lot which were constructed at the cost of, or otherwise paid for by, the lessee, without having to make any compensation to the lessor so long as he or she does not damage the property in doing so. (*See LEASEHOLD, RENEGOTIATION OF LEASE.*)

REVERSIONARY FACTOR   A mathematical factor found in present-worth tables used to convert a single, lump-sum future payment into present value, given the proper discount rate and time period. Frequently used to determine the value of the lessor's leased fee interest.

REVERSIONARY VALUE   The expected worth of a property at the end of the anticipated holding period. Present worth tables are used to determine the current value of a reversion.

REVOCATION   The act of terminating, cancelling, or annulling, as when a seller *revokes* a broker's agency by cancelling the listing. A broker or salesperson's license can be revoked for cause. It is important to distinguish between the *power* of an agent to revoke and the *right* to revoke an agency contract. Unless the agency is coupled with an interest, the principal always has the power to revoke; but if the principal has no justifiable grounds to revoke, the principal may be liable for money damages.

RIDER An addition, amendment, or endorsement ("special endorsement") annexed to a document and incorporated into the terms of the document. Riders are frequently attached to insurance policies, usually to provide some extended coverage such as a fire liability coverage as a rider to a comprehensive personal liability policy. Buyers under a contract for sale often request that a rider be attached to the seller's insurance policy so that the buyer is also covered (called a contract for sale rider clause). It is usually good practice to have the parties initial a rider addendum to a sales contract, to officially establish its authenticity.

RIDGEBOARD A heavy horizontal board set on edge at the apex of the roof to which the rafters are attached.

RIGHT OF CONTRIBUTION The right of one who has discharged a common liability to recover from another liable party his or her pro rata share. For instance, a right of contribution exists in favor of one cotenant who pays taxes or other liens against the entire property. The cotenant (tenant in common, or joint tenant) is entitled to an equitable lien on the cotenants's shares and the cotenant may enforce this lien by foreclosure on their shares. (*See TENANCY IN COMMON.*)

RIGHT OF FIRST REFUSAL The right of a person to have the first opportunity either to purchase or lease real property. Unlike an option, however, the holder of a right of first refusal has no right to purchase until the owner actually offers the property for sale or entertains an offer to purchase from some third party. In a lease situation, a right of first refusal might give the tenant the right either to purchase the property, if offered for sale, or to renew the lease or to lease adjoining space. This right is clearly more advantageous to the tenant than it is to the landlord. A property burdened with a right of first refusal is less marketable than one without such a right. One purpose of putting a right of first refusal into a lease is to encourage the tenant to make improvements the tenant might otherwise be reluctant to do.

Under an option to purchase, the tenant can decide whether or not to exercise the option at a fixed price during the option period. In a right of first refusal, however, the holder can exercise the right only if the owner has offered to sell or lease the property or has entertained a bona fide offer by a third person to purchase or lease the property. At that point, the holder may match the offer. If the owner first offers the property to the tenant and he or she refuses, then the owner is free to offer to any third party at that price or higher. A key to the difference between an option and a right of first refusal is to determine which party has the right to initiate the sale or lease. In both an option and a right of first refusal, the holder has no interest in the land or equitable estate until the option or right is exercised.

In some condominiums, the association of apartment owners retains the right of first refusal on any sale of a unit. Some state laws give a right of first refusal to a tenant whose apartment is to be converted into a condominium unit. In HUD-FHA regulated condominiums and in condominiums eligible for FNMA financing, however, restrictions such as a right of first refusal are not permitted. Rights of first refusal are common in agreements between partners, shareholders, joint owners (where the ultimate effect is to act as a waiver of the right of partition), land-lords, and tenants. (See *OPTION, PREEMPTION CLAUSE.*)

RIGHT OF RE-ENTRY The future interest left in the transferor of prop-erty who transfers an estate on condition subse-quent. If the condition is broken, the transferor has the right and the power to terminate the estate. Unlike a possibility of reverter, however, the transferor must take affirmative steps to terminate the estate, such as file a court suit; otherwise the condition may be discharged. For example, Adam grants Alice some property on the condition that Alice does not raise pigs on the property. If Alice raises pigs, Adam must actually re-enter and take the premises; that is, there is no automatic reverter. (See *FEE SIMPLE DEFEASIBLE, POSSIBILITY OF REVERTER, REVER-SION.*)

RIGHT OF SURVIVORSHIP The distinctive characteristics of a joint tenancy (also tenancy by entirety) by which the surviving joint tenant(s) succeeds to all right, title, and in-terest of the deceased joint tenant without the need for probate proceedings. (See *JOINT TENANCY, TENANCY BY THE ENTIRETY.*)

RIGHT-OF-WAY 1. The right or privilege, acquired through ac-cepted usage or by contract, to pass over a desig-nated portion of the property of another. A right-of-way may be either private, as in an access easement given a neighbor, or public, as in the right of the public to use the highways or streets, or to have safe access to public beaches. A gas com-pany, for example, might send out one of its right-of-way agents to negotiate the purchase of easements from owners of land to be crossed to gain access to gaslines. 2. Land which is either owned by a railroad or over which it maintains an ease-ment for operating on its trackage in accordance with government safety regula-tions and industry standards. (See *ACCESS.*)

RIGHT, TITLE, AND INTEREST A term often used in conveyancing documents to describe the transfer of all that the grantor or as-signor is capable of transferring. In a quitclaim deed, the grantor transfers all right, title, and interest in a property without making any representations as to the extent of such right, title, and interest, if any.

RIPARIAN Those rights and obligations which are incidental to ownership of land adjacent to or abutting on watercourses such as streams and lakes. Examples of such rights are the right of irrigation, swimming, boating, fishing, and the right to the alluvium deposited by the water. Riparian rights do not attach except where there is a water boundary on one side of the particular tract of land claimed to be riparian. Such a real property right in water is a right of use, or a *usufructuary right*. It is the right held in common with other riparian owners to make reasonable use of the waters that flow past provided such use does not alter the flow of water or contaminate the water. In addition, an owner of land bordering on a non-navigable stream owns the land under the watercourse to the center of the watercourse. If the body of water is in movement, as a stream or river, the abutting owner is called a *riparian owner*. If the water is not flowing, as in the case of a pond, lake, or ocean, the abutting owner is called a *littoral owner*. The word *riparian* literally means "river bank."

RISER   The vertical face of the step that supports the tread. As you walk upstairs, the riser is the part of the step facing you.

RISK CAPITAL   Capital invested in a speculative venture, thus being the least secure, and offering the greatest chance of loss. However, risk capital often yields the greatest rate of return. The concept of risk capital is often discussed in defining whether an offering is a security.

RISK OF LOSS   Responsibility for damages caused to improvements. The Uniform Vendor and Purchaser Risk Act, adopted in many states, covers the standard real estate sales contract situation. Unless the terms of the contract provide otherwise, the vendor cannot enforce the contract and the vendee can recover all monies paid if a material part of the real estate is destroyed without fault of the purchaser or is taken by eminent domain, *provided neither legal title nor possession has passed* to the vendee.

A more difficult question arises upon destruction by fire in the event the buyer decides not to rescind and elects to seek specific performance of the contract; that is, the buyer wants the seller to rebuild the house and sell the property as promised. Most courts will order the seller to transfer title to the destroyed premises and to assign the insurance proceeds to the buyer. They usually do not require the seller to rebuild and absorb all the carrying charges until completion.

As a practical matter, most sales contracts should transfer possession to the buyer upon closing. Where legal title or possession has passed to the vendee, and all or part of the realty is destroyed without fault of the vendor, or is taken by eminent domain, the vendee cannot recover any monies paid in, and he or she is not relieved of the duty to pay the full purchase price. The risk of loss passes to the vendee when either title or possession passes, and the vendee should protect him- or herself by securing proper insurance. If the buyer takes possession before closing and there is no rental agreement, then the buyer may assume the risk of loss. If, however, there is a rental agreement, the buyer would not assume the risk of loss unless the contract so provides. (*See UNIFORM VENDOR AND PURCHASER RISK ACT.*)

ROAD   A collector roadway in the rural district generally without full improvements such as curbs and sidewalks.

ROD   A measure of length containing 5 ½ yards or 16 ½ feet; also, the corresponding square measure.

ROLL-OVER   1. Refers to tax provisions which enable the taxpayer to defer paying taxes in certain situations such as the replacement of a principal residence or involuntary conversion.

2. In a financing sense, it refers to the practice of rewriting a new loan at the termination of a prior loan, such as a three-year mortgage with a roll-over provision to grant a new loan at different terms at the end of the three years using a roll-over note. Popular with adjustable mortgage loans.

ROOF BOARDS Boards nailed to the top of the rafters, usually touching each other, to tie the roof together and form a base for the roofing material. The boards, or roof sheathing, can also be constructed of sheets of plywood.

ROOFING FELT Sheets of felt or other close-woven, heavy material placed on top of the roof boards to insulate and waterproof the roof. Like building paper, roofing felt is treated with bitumen or some other type of tar derivative to increase its water resistance. Roofing felt is applied either with a bonding and sealing compound or with intense heat which softens the tar and causes it to adhere to the roof.

ROOFING SHINGLES Thin, wedge-shaped pieces of wood, asbestos, metal, clay, or other material used as the outer covering for a roof. The tiles are laid in overlapping rows to completely cover the roof surface. Shingles are sometimes used as an outer covering for exterior walls.

ROOF INSPECTION CLAUSE A clause sometimes inserted in a real estate sales contract specifying that the seller must provide the buyer with a certified report of the kind and condition of the building's roof. If the roof is found to be faulty, it must then be repaired at the seller's expense.

ROOMING HOUSE A house where bedrooms, as such, are furnished to paying guests.

ROOT TITLE The conveyance or instrument which starts the chain of land title; the original source of title.

ROW HOUSE One of a series of individual homes having architectural unity and a common wall between units.

ROYALTY 1. The money paid to an owner of realty for the right of depleting the property of its natural resources, such as oil, gas, minerals, stone, builders' sand and gravel, and timber. Usually, the royalty payment is a stated part of the amount extracted, such as: one-sixth or one-eighth of the oil and gas removed, or six cents per ton of sand and gravel taken away, or a given price per cubic yard of material extracted. The royalty payment is a combination of rent and depreciation (depletion charge). 2. Also, a franchise fee.

RULE 10-B5 A rule of the SEC enacted under the antifraud provisions of the Securities Act of 1934. The rule makes it unlawful for any person, in connection with the purchase or sale of any security, to employ any device, scheme, or artifice to defraud; to make any untrue statement of a material fact, or to omit to state a material fact necessary so that the statements made are not misleading; or to engage in any act, practice, or course of business which operates or would operate as a fraud or deceit on any person. It should be noted that even if an offering of securities is exempt from registration under the intrastate or private offering exemptions, the issuer nevertheless is subject to the antifraud provisions of both the federal and state securities laws. In other words, if the issuer fails to state a material fact, this would give a purchaser of the security the right to rescind the transaction and recover all of his or her money plus interest from the date of purchase. (*See* ANTIFRAUD.)

RULE 146

A rule, often called the *private offering or private placement exemption*, adopted by the Securities and Exchange Commission in 1974, which is designed to provide more objective standards for determining when offers or sales of securities are transactions "not involving any public offering" and thus would be exempt from the registration process. With the Securities Act of 1933, Congress intended to create a system which provided full and fair disclosure to the consumer in connection with the offering or sale of securities. Congress recognized, however, that there were certain circumstances in which the consumer would not need the protection afforded by the Act. It was felt that the Act should not apply where there was not a public offering. The important determination is whether or not the consumer needs the protection afforded by the disclosure required under the Securities Act, as evidenced by whether the consumer has access to the same kind of information that registration would disclose, whether the consumer is sophisticated enough to protect him- or herself, and whether the consumer can afford the loss of the investment.

Under the "rich and smart" concept, Rule 146 permits an unlimited number of offers, provided that the issuer knows in advance that offerees are sophisticated enough (smart) in real estate investments to evaluate the risk themselves or are represented by an independent advisor having such experience, and are wealthy enough to bear the risk of loss (rich). The rule places a limit of 35 on the number of sales (not offers) made under $150,000, with no limit on sales above that amount. All purchasers must certify in writing that they are buying for investment only and not for resale. (*See* LEGEND STOCK, PRIVATE OFFERING, REAL PROPERTY SECURITIES REGISTRATION.)

RULE 147

A rule adopted in 1974 by the Securities and Exchange Commission to clarify the intrastate or local offering exemption from registering a security with the SEC. The rule establishes guidelines for determining when one is deemed a resident of a state, especially with regard to legal entities such as corporations and partnerships. In order to fit under the intrastate exemption, the issuer must be both a resident of and doing business within the state in which all offers and sales are made. An issuer is deemed to be doing business within a state if its principal office is located within the state, at least 80 percent of its gross revenues are derived from operations within the state, 80 percent of its assets are located within the state, and it uses 80 percent of the proceeds from the sales of securities within the state. Thus a local issuer seeking to raise money for a local project might not be exempt if it has substantial assets (such as real estate holdings) in another state. The rule also sets forth restrictions on the further transfer of exempt securities to nonresidents of the issuer's state for at least nine months from the date of the last sale by the issuer and receipt of all money of any part of the securities issue ("coming to rest"). (*See* INTRASTATE EXEMPTION, LEGEND STOCK.)

RULE AGAINST PERPETUITIES

A rule of law designed to require the early vesting of a future contingent interest in real property and thus prevent the property from being made inalienable for long periods of time. The effect of the rule is to destroy future interests which impede the vesting of property rights for longer than the prescribed period, which is usually no later than 21 years after some life or lives in being at the creation of the interest. For example, in a conveyance "to George Allen for life, then to his son, Butch Allen, for life, and remainder to Butch's children who reach age 24," the remainder violates the rule since it is possible that the remainder will not vest until after 21 years of some life in being; that is, George and Butch could die when Butch's only child is one year old. The net effect of a violation is to destroy the void interest at the outset but to leave the valid interest intact. The rule applies only to contingent interests.

RULE OF FIVE A rule of thumb used by subdividers to approximate subdivision costs. As a general rule, 1/5 (20 percent) of the final total sales price is allocable to land acquisition cost; 1/5 (20 percent) goes to improvement costs such as engineering, grading, roads, legal fees; 1/5 (20 percent) goes to miscellaneous costs such as interest and carrying charges plus unsold lots; and 2/5 (40 percent) goes to cover administration costs, advertising, sales commissions, and the profit.

RULE OF 72 A rule of thumb in financing which states that the interest rate at which a single sum will double can be found by dividing into the number 72 the years during which the money is growing. For example, if the money is growing during an eight-year period, a financier would figure $72 \div 8 = 9$ percent, or $72 \div 9$ percent $= 8$ years.

RULE OF 78s A method of computing refunds of unearned finance charges on contracts which include precomputed finance charges so that the refund is proportional to the monthly unpaid balances at the time of the refund. Under this rule, on a 12-month contract, the creditor would retain 12/78 of the total finance charge for the first month, 11/78 for the second month, and so on. If the creditor held a 12-month contract for only six months, it would be entitled to 57/78 of the total finance charge ($12 + 11 + 10 + 9 + 8 + 7 = 57$). In turn, the consumer would be entitled to the remaining 21/78 of the finance charge.

Under the truth-in-lending laws, the creditor must identify the method of computing any unearned portion of the finance charge in the event of prepayment of the obligation. Most creditors identify their rebate method as the rule of 78s.

RUN WITH THE LAND Rights or covenants which bind or benefit successive owners of a property are said to run with the land. An example would be a restrictive building covenant in a recorded deed which would affect all future owners of the property. Unlike an easement in gross, an easement appurtenant runs with the land and thus passes to a succeeding owner even if it is not specified in the deed. Note that if, for example, the grantee Sylvia Buckner agrees, as part of the consideration to a transaction, to repair a building located on land owned by grantor Leonard Musslewhite, such a covenant will not run with the land. This is because it merely places a duty upon the grantee Buckner. The promise does not touch and concern the land granted from Musslewhite to Buckner—it is only a personal covenant for the grantor's benefit.

RURAL A land use classification pertaining to the country, as opposed to urban; land devoted to the pursuit of agriculture.

RURBAN Refers to those fringe areas situated outside but adjacent to cities where the land use is in a stage of transition from rural to urban.

SAFE HARBOR
LEASE ELECTION
The Economic Recovery Act of 1981 recognizes that some businesses may not be able to use completely the increased cost recovery allowances and the increased investment credits available for recovery property under the Accelerated Cost Recovery System; the ACRS will provide the greatest benefit to the economy if deductions and investment tax credits are more easily distributed throughout the corporate sector. Under pre-1981 Tax Act law, three party financing leases ("leverage" leases) were widely used to transfer tax benefits to users of property who did not have sufficient tax liability to absorb those benefits. Under pre-1981 Tax Act administrative practice, however, lease characterization was subject to specific IRS guidelines. Moreover, court decisions had not prescribed clear guidelines as to the appropriate tax characterizations of financing leases. (See *ACCELERATED COST RECOVERY SYSTEM.*)

The Economic Recovery Act of 1981 creates a safe harbor that guarantees that a transaction will be characterized as a lease for the purposes of allowing investment credits and capital cost recovery allowances to the nominal lessor. Lessors will be able to receive cost recovery allowances and investment tax credits with respect to qualified leased property. It is expected that lessees will receive a very significant portion of the benefits of these tax advantages through reduced rental charges for the property (in the case of finance leases) or cash payments and/or reduced rental charges in the case of sale-leaseback transactions.

SAFE HARBOR RULE
1. In general terms, it means an area of protection. For example, the IRS has outlined certain standards for a real estate broker to meet in treating its salespeople as independent contractors. As long as the broker meets these criteria, the broker will be in a "safe harbor" and not subject to attack by the IRS for failing to withhold taxes from its employees. (See *INDEPENDENT CONTRACTOR.*)

2. An IRS rule pertaining to taxation of limited partnerships in which the general partner(s) are all corporations. It provides that a corporate general partner must have and maintain a fair market value net worth (without considering its interest in the partnership) equal to the lesser of $250,000 or 15 percent of the amount invested by the limited partners if the amount so invested is $2.5 million or less; or equal to 10 percent of the amount so invested if that amount exceeds $2.5 million. If the general partner maintains the specified net worth, and if the venture meets the other partnership requirements, the IRS will issue an advance private ruling treating the venture as a partnership for tax purposes, rather than as an association taxable as a corporation. (See *NET WORTH, PARTNERSHIP.*)

SAFETY CLAUSE
(LISTING)
See *EXTENDER CLAUSE.*

SALE BY THE ACRE   The sale of land described in the sales contract and instrument of conveyance documents by stating the exact area of land (for example, 269 acres). Under a sale-by-the-acre contract, the buyer does not take the risk of any deficiency nor does the seller take the risk of any excess.

Sometimes large acreage is sold by stating the approximate rather than the exact acreage, such as "269 acres more or less," i.e., a sale in gross. In such a case, neither party would receive any compensation if there were a slight variance in the exact amount of acres actually conveyed. However, if there is an unusually large excess or deficiency, a court could grant equitable relief to the injured party.

A proper legal description is necessary in the real estate sales contract and all subsequent conveyance documents. (See *LEGAL DESCRIPTION, MORE OR LESS.*)

SALE-LEASEBACK   A real estate financing technique whereby a property owner sells the property to an investor or lender and, at the same time, leases it back. This financing arrangement was inaugurated during the 1940s, when the loan-to-value ratios permitted for mortgages were between 50 percent and 66⅔ percent and companies wanted to free their capital tied up in real estate for more speculative ventures. The lease utilized for this method is usually a full net lease that extends over a period of time long enough for the investor-lender to recover his or her funds and to make a fair profit on the investment.

The sale-leaseback approach to real estate finance is generally applied to commercial properties since rents paid by businesses and professional people are fully deductible expenses in the year in which they are incurred. Using this approach, a seller/lessee enjoys many benefits: retaining possession of the property while obtaining the full sales price and, in some cases, keeping the right to repurchase the property at the end of the lease; freeing the capital which was frozen in equity; maintaining an appreciable interest in realty, which can be capitalized upon by subleasing or mortgaging the leasehold; and getting a tax deduction for the full amount of the rent, equivalent to taking depreciation deductions for both the building and the land.

The cash secured from the sale might be utilized for plant expansion, remodeling, or investing in other opportunities. In addition, a lease appears as an indirect liability on a firm's balance sheet, whereas a mortgage shows up as a direct liability and adversely affects the firm's debt ratio in terms of obtaining future financing.

The advantages to the investor/landlord in this type of arrangement include a fair return *on* and *of* investment in the form of rent during the lease term, and ownership of a depreciable asset already occupied by a reliable tenant. In other words, the investor is buying a guaranteed income stream which can probably be sheltered through the proper use of depreciation allowances. When determining the rent to be paid on the lease, the investor can actually manage his or her risk by the amount of rent he or she requires. The rent for a quality tenant, such as Safeway Corporation, a large, fully leveraged company that sells and leases back most of its stores, will be lower than the rent for a high-risk tenant.

When the lease includes an option for the tenant to repurchase the property at the end of the lease term, it is called a *sale-leaseback-buyback.* However, care must be taken to establish the buyback price for the fair market value at the time of sale; otherwise the arrangement is considered a long-term installment mortgage and any income tax benefits that might have been enjoyed during the term of the lease will be disallowed by the Internal Revenue Service.

SALE OF LEASED   An owner of property who has given a lease to
PROPERTY   one person may sell the leased property to another. The buyer, however, takes the property
subject to the existing lease. The deed evidencing the sale usually states that it is
"subject to existing leases and rights of present tenants," and this clause means
that the seller cannot deliver actual possession of the property. Unless the seller
has reserved the lease rents, the buyer does, however, have the right to collect rent
due after the sale and to exercise any right of forfeiture for nonpayment of rent
given under the lease. (*See LEASE, LEASEHOLD, RIGHT OF FIRST REFUSAL.*)

SALE OF PERSONAL   A homeowner age 55 or older who sells his or her
RESIDENCE BY   principal residence may elect to exclude from
ELDERLY   taxation all or part of any gain realized from the
sale, up to a maximum of $125,000, if the home-
owner owned and used the house as a principal residence for three of the five
years preceding the date the property is sold. This may include the time the taxpayer lived in an apartment that was converted to a cooperative or a condominium. It is not necessary that the house be the taxpayer's primary residence on the
date of sale. If the taxpayer is married, only one spouse need be 55 years old on the
day of sale to claim the exclusion, provided that that spouse is on title as joint
tenant or tenant by the entirety. For most cases, the day of sale is the day escrow
closes and title passes. Note, however, that this is literally a once-in-a-lifetime
exclusion; once a person elects to claim it, whether for all or part of the $125,000
limit, the entire exclusion is said to be "used up." If the taxpayer is married when
claiming the exclusion, under the law both spouses forfeit their separate exemptions. This means that neither will be able to claim the tax shelter again, even if
one should remarry a person who has not taken the exemption. If a person over 55
has not used the one-time exemption, and he or she marries someone who has
already used the exemption, then they both have now lost the right to use the
exemption.

The $125,000 exclusion can be used to shelter both profit realized from the sale of
the present home and any gain "carried over" from the sale of previous residences. If the gain is less than $125,000, the difference cannot be carried over for
future gain. (*See RESIDENCE, SALE OF.*)

SALES-ASSESSMENT   The ratio of the assessed value of real property to
RATIO   its selling price.

SALES CONTRACT   Another name for a sales agreement or a purchase
agreement, as opposed to a contract for deed or a
land contract. Also referred to as a contract of sale, bond for deed, purchase agreement, deposit receipt, or article of agreement. (*See CONTRACT OF SALE.*)

SALES KIT   An assortment of information about property to
be sold, selected, and organized to familiarize the
salesperson with the property being presented to a prospect and to help the prospect visualize the property. The kit may be in the form of a small loose-leaf book of
typewritten pages, a large loose-leaf book including maps and pictures, or an elaborate zippered briefcase with photographs, building plans, maps, and other statistical data.

SALESPERSON   Any person who, for a compensation or valuable consideration, is employed either directly or indirectly by a licensed real estate broker to sell, offer to sell, buy, offer to buy, or negotiate the purchase, sale, or exchange of real estate, or to lease, rent, or offer to rent any real estate, or to negotiate leases thereof or improvements thereon.

All 50 states have laws that control the licensing of persons who sell, rent, or manage real estate under the supervision of a real estate broker or other person authorized to supervise real estate salespeople. A salesperson's license is issued on the basis of an applicant's character, integrity, and abilities, which must include a reasonable knowledge of real estate law, customs, and usage. The license laws distinguish between the real estate broker and the salesperson, and they limit the latter's activities. For example, a salesperson cannot act as an agent for another person, nor can he or she list or advertise property under his or her own name. The salesperson can carry out only those responsibilities assigned to him or her by that broker.

Salespersons are engaged by brokers as either employees or independent contractors. The agreement between broker and salesperson should be set down in a written contract that defines the obligations and responsibilities of the relationship. Whether a salesperson is employed by the broker or operates under him or her as an independent contractor will affect the broker's relationship with the salesperson and the broker's liability to pay and withhold taxes from that salesperson's earnings. (*See BROKER, INDEPENDENT CONTRACTOR, LICENSE LAWS.*)

SALVAGE VALUE   1. For pre-1981 property, it is the estimated amount at which an asset can be sold at the end of its useful life. The taxpayer's estimate of the amount, made at the time of acquisition of the property, that will be realized at the time of its disposition. The salvage value of an asset (improvement) limits the total amount of depreciation that may be claimed because it provides a floor below which the improvement cannot be depreciated. Toward the end of the useful life of a building, the question of salvage value may be raised by the Treasury to prevent the deduction of current depreciation allowance. If the salvage value is less than 10 percent of the cost, the IRS usually allows it to be ignored. Under the Economic Recovery Tax Act of 1981, salvage value is disregarded.

2. Also refers to the value of a structure to be relocated to another site. Normally used in highway condemnations where large areas must be cleared. (*See DEPRECIATION, USEFUL LIFE.*)

SANDWICH LEASE   A leasehold estate in which the sandwich party leases the property from the fee owner or another lessee and then sublets to the tenant in possession, thereby maintaining a middle, or "sandwich" position. The sandwich party is the lessee of one party and the lessor of another; thus he or she is neither the fee owner nor the end-user of the property. It is a lease occupying a position within three or more leasehold interests in a property.

SANITARY SEWER SYSTEM   A sewer system that carries only domestic water, usually an underground pipe or tunnel to carry off wastes and effluents.

SATELLITE CITY   A planned city in the natural growth path of a nearby larger city, designed to stop urban sprawl to the suburbs and to supplement and aid the larger city's expansion. A satellite city is designed to be comparatively self-sufficient in regard to labor, industry, housing, churches, schools, shopping areas, and like features. Examples are Reston, Virginia, and Columbia, Maryland. (See *NEW TOWN*.)

SATELLITE TENANT   A smaller tenant in a shopping center who is relatively dependent on the ability of a larger, anchor or prime tenant to attract business into the center; such as a small shoe repair shop in a center containing a major department store.

SATISFACTION   The payment of a debt or obligation such as a judgment. The time when the vendee pays in full under a contract for deed and the vendor transfers legal title is referred to as satisfaction or fulfillment.

SATISFACTION OF MORTGAGE   A certificate issued by the mortgagee when a mortgage is paid in full. It describes the mortgage, recites where it is recorded, and certifies that it has been paid and that the mortgagee consents that it be discharged of record.

Upon payment in full of the debt secured by a mortgage, it is said that the mortgage is "satisfied." Even though payment in full has made on the note and the mortgage may have been returned to the mortgagor, this does not change the fact that the records in the recorder's office show an outstanding mortgage against the property. Clear record title is almost as important as clear actual title, and may be more important in some particular real estate transactions. Therefore, the evidence of the satisfaction must be recorded. This document is called a discharge or release of mortgage, or a satisfaction piece. (See *MARGINAL RELEASE*.)

SAVINGS AND LOAN ASSOCIATIONS   Savings and loan associations are the most active participants in the home loan mortgage market. The principal function of a savings and loan association is to promote thrift and home ownership. Depositors earn interest on their deposits, often at a higher rate than is offered at commercial banks. The savings and loan association invests these deposits mainly in residential mortgage loans, enabling more people to purchase and/or repair their homes.

All savings and loan associations must be chartered, either by the federal government or by the state in which they are located. Associations are regulated on a national level by the Federal Home Loan Bank System (FHLB). The FHLB sets up mandatory guidelines for member associations, determines their reserve requirements and discount rates, and provides depositors with savings insurance through the Federal Savings and Loan Insurance Corporation (FSLIC). FSLIC currently insures deposits in amounts up to $100,000 per account. Federally chartered savings and loan associations may be capital stock institutions although most are mutually owned by their investors. State associations are either organized as private stock companies or mutually owned by their depositors.

Real estate mortgages are the main source of investment for savings and loan associations. Over 80 percent of their assets are thrust annually into the mortgage market. Traditionally, these associations are the most flexible of the lending institutions in regard to their mortgage loan procedures, but federally chartered savings and loans (and most state associations) have a geographic limitation placed on their lending plus a maximum loan-to-value ratio of 95 percent. In addition, associations participate in VA-insured and FHA-guaranteed loans to a limited extent.

Savings and loan associations are primarily local in nature because they are usually mutually owned and locally managed. Some capital stock and mutual associations, however, are large, statewide associations, with billions of dollars in assets and hundreds of offices.

Although savings and loan associations are in the midst of a major transition from a regulated to a deregulated savings market, the primary concern of savings and loan associations continues to be granting loans not only for real estate purposes, but for home repairs, construction, and improvement as well. Recent regulatory changes now allow savings and loan associations to offer a wide variety of new savings accounts and services including consumer loans, trust services, debit and credit cards, and interest-bearing checking accounts.

Most savings and loan associations now offer adjustable mortgage loans, although the conventional fixed-rate, long-term home mortgage will continue to be available. The adjustable mortgage, however, has received a strong marketplace acceptance. Restrictions for these loans vary according to the institution offering the loan. (See *DISINTERMEDIATION*.)

SAVINGS AND LOAN SERVICE CORPORATION

A subsidiary of a federal savings and loan association, whose function is to engage in various ventures, primarily real estate oriented, prohibited to its parent company. For example, as part of a project to develop housing, a service corporation may acquire, hold, and rent unimproved property, engage in housing development, and perform all related maintenance, management, and rental services. A service corporation can also enter into a joint venture to develop property—an attractive feature for a developer seeking equity capital. It may also provide the interim financing. Over 3,000 savings and loan service corporations have been created since the 1964 enabling legislation.

SCARCITY

In appraisal terminology, scarcity refers to increased value caused by a demand for some type of goods, the supply of which cannot be increased.

SCENIC EASEMENT

An easement created to preserve a property in its natural state. For example, the state may acquire (through a condemnation proceeding) a scenic easement over certain choice property to preserve its aesthetic quality and, in effect, to prevent a developer from building on the property. A landowner might purchase a scenic easement over a neighbor's property in order to preserve the view.

Because of drastic increases in assessments and taxes, some owners of large tracts of land that possess some scenic or natural beauty attempt to make a gift of a scenic easement over part of the property to the county or state. If the gift is accepted, the landowner can possibly get a charitable deduction for tax purposes and a reduction in the real estate tax assessment. Under the federal Tax Act, a charitable deduction, for income tax purposes, may be taken for contribution of a scenic easement or other partial interest in real estate to be used for public enjoyment, historical preservation, or the preservation of wild areas. The Federal Highway Beautification Act offers incentives to states to acquire scenic or open-space easements to protect the view of historical sites or unusual scenery. (See *CONDEMNATION, HISTORIC STRUCTURES.*)

SCHEMATICS   Preliminary architectural drawings and sketches often prepared at the planning stages of a project; basic layouts not containing the final details of design. A developer often will have an architect prepare schematics of a proposed building or development and then use those drawings either to convince the owner to sell the land or to persuade an investor or lender to finance the project. The architect will often "spec" his or her time; i.e., not charge the developer for the efforts in the expectation that if the project is approved he or she will be retained to perform the architectural services for the full development.

Schematic drawings may include a site plan, dimensional plan of each typical unit, elevations, typical lobby and floor, mechanical facilities, and commercial use areas.

SCOPE OF   A rule of agency law which holds that a principal
AUTHORITY   is liable to third parties for all wrongful acts of his or her agent committed while transacting the principal's business. It is not necessary that the principal actually authorize the act; it is sufficient if the agent had apparent (ostensible) or implied authority to act on behalf of the principal. Ostensible authority is that which a principal, intentionally or by want of ordinary care, causes or allows a third person to believe the agent to possess. The principal is not liable for acts of the agent committed *outside* the scope of his or her authority, nor can the broker collect for services rendered outside the scope of that authority.

An act is within the scope of authority if it was done primarily to further the principal's interests rather than the agent's interests. A third person who knows he or she is dealing with an agent has a duty to ascertain the scope of the agent's authority.

The seller of real property is liable for the affirmative misrepresentations made by his or her broker in the scope of the agent's authority, even though the seller was unaware that the broker had made them. For example, when the broker has knowledge of a defective condition in the house (e.g., a weak foundation), the innocent seller is usually liable to the buyer if the broker does not disclose the defect to the buyer. This is because the knowledge of the agent is imputed to the seller, who is treated as if he or she knew of it. (See *AGENCY, RESPONDEAT SUPERIOR.*)

SEAL   An embossed impression on paper caused by a metal die used to authenticate a document or attest to a signature, as with a corporate or notary seal. The corporate seal contains the name of the corporation, the date, and the state of incorporation. Sometimes the parties use the initials LS after a signature, which is Latin for *Locus Sigilli*—"under seal" or "in place of seal."

Under early common law, a seal took the place of reciting the consideration in a contract. Except as a means of authentication, the common law effect of this seal has been abolished in most states. Thus, where necessary, a party must still prove that consideration was paid. It is good practice to require the seal of a corporation executing a contract, for it is evidence that the instrument is the act of the corporation, executed by duly authorized officers or agents. Under the Uniform Commercial Code, use of a seal has no effect upon the transaction; it "does not constitute the writing . . . and the law with respect to sealed instruments does not apply."

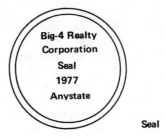

Seal

SEALED AND DELIVERED   A phrase indicating that a transferor has received adequate consideration as evidenced by his or her voluntary delivery. The word *sealed* adds more weight since under old conveyancing law an official seal was used as a substitute for consideration. Today, the term is generally a mere formality and of no legal consequence. (*See* SEAL.)

SEASONED LOAN   A loan borrowed by someone who has a stable and consistent history of payments under the terms of the loan. The term indicates that the mortgage or land contract is not a new one and thus may be a good purchase risk.

SECOND   As used in a metes and bounds legal description, $\frac{1}{60}$ of a degree or $\frac{1}{3600}$ part of a circle. A second is denoted by the symbol ". For example, an angle of 97°25″ would read "ninety-seven degrees, twenty-five seconds." (*See* DEGREE.)

SECONDARY FINANCING   A junior mortgage placed on property to help finance the purchase price, such as a purchase-money second mortgage taken back by the seller to assist a purchaser who has difficulty in paying a large down payment.

Most governmental loan programs (FHA, VA) restrict secondary financing. After the closing of a purchase of property financed through FHA or VA, however, the owner may place a second mortgage on the property.

SECONDARY MORTGAGE MARKET   A market for the purchase and sale of existing mortgages, designed to provide greater liquidity for selling mortgages; also called *secondary money market* and not to be confused with secondary financing. Secondary (or resale) mortgage market lenders or investors buy mortgages as long-term investments as opposed to other types of securities, such as government and corporate bonds.

The Federal National Mortgage Association (FNMA) purchases many existing mortgages, thus freeing more money for mortgagees to lend. The Government National Mortgage Association (GNMA) and the Federal Home Loan Mortgage Corporation (FHLMC) are also active in the secondary mortgage market, especially where federally subsidized projects are involved.

These agencies act as warehouses of money, buying and selling "pools" of mortgages, thus effectively redistributing funds from money-rich areas to money-poor areas. They permit the loan originators an opportunity to roll over their money and remain liquid enough to meet the demand for new mortgage loans.

Mortgage pools are created when lenders place mortgages in a package and sell securities that represent shares in these pooled mortgages. The pooled mortgages are actually removed from the balance sheets of the originators of the pools and the buyers of the securities become the joint owners. The regular mortgage payment and any prepayments are collected by the originators (who usually continue to service the mortgages) and are distributed to the holders of the securities. (*See* *FEDERAL HOME LOAN MORTGAGE CORPORATION, FEDERAL NATIONAL MORTGAGE ASSOCIATION, GOVERNMENT NATIONAL MORTGAGE ASSOCIATION, MAGGIE MAE.*)

SECOND MORTGAGE   A mortgage (or trust deed) that is junior or subordinate to a first mortgage; typically, an additional loan imposed on top of the first mortgage, taken out when the borrower needs more money. Because the risk involved to the lender is greater with the second mortgage, the lender's conditions are usually more stringent, the term is shorter, and the interest rate is higher than for the first mortgage. Second mortgages usually involve separate closing costs for appraisal, title report, credit check, drafting and recording documents, and other procedures. The degree of risk is determined by the margin between the appraisal value and the total prior liens on the property. This is because the second mortgage can be wiped out by the foreclosure of any senior mortgage or lien holder (such as mechanic's lien or tax lien).

Second mortgages may contain a provision stating that they will remain subordinate to any subsequent first mortgage as long as the new mortgage is not made in an amount exceeding the present first mortgage. Such a lifting clause permits the mortgagor to "lift out" the first mortgage and refinance it with another first mortgage without altering the junior position of the second mortgage.

In the event of default under the prior mortgage, the second mortgagee can elect to redeem the first mortgage and foreclose under the second mortgage or add the amount advanced to the second mortgage. The second mortgagee should request that it receive a notice of any default under the first mortgage. If the second mortgage is in default, the first mortgagee can also foreclose on the mortgagor because his or her security has also been threatened. The second mortgagee can thus exert great pressure on the borrower to pay, yet in doing so it takes the risk that the net proceeds of a foreclosure sale will not be enough to repay the second mortgage after extinguishing the first mortgage note.

Before considering a second mortgage, the parties should check state usury provisions and local laws restricting banks and savings and loan associations from granting second mortgages or limiting the amount loaned or the interest that may be charged. (*See JUNIOR MORTGAGE.*)

SECTION   As used in the government survey method, a section of land is an area one square mile, containing 640 acres. It is 1/36th of a township.

SECTION 179   Under tax law prior to the Economic Recovery Act of 1981, a depreciable capital expenditure was allowed to be partially expensed but generally limited to $2,000, commonly referred to as "first-year bonus depreciation." While the concept of Section 179—election to expense certain depreciable business assets—is generally the same, two important differences exist in the law:

1. The $2,000 limit is raised to $10,000 in 1986, after a phase-in.

2. No investment tax credit is allowed on the expensed portion. (*See DEPRECIATION [TAX]*.)

SECTION 1244 CORPORATION   A corporation qualified under Section 1244 of the Internal Revenue Code. To qualify, a corporation must be a "small business corporation," which means it has a paid-in capital of $1 million or less. A shareholder in a Section 1244 corporation may treat any loss on his or her capital stock investment as an ordinary loss rather than a capital loss, an important consideration when the corporate form of ownership is being used in a speculative venture and there is a strong risk of loss.

SECURED PARTY   The person having the security interest such as the mortgagee, the vendee, or the pledgee.

SECURITIES AND EXCHANGE COMMISSION (SEC)   *See REAL PROPERTY SECURITIES REGISTRATION.*

SECURITY   Evidence of obligations to pay money or of rights to participate in earnings and distribution of corporate, trust, or other property. A security is usually found where an investor subjects his or her money to the risks of an enterprise over which he or she exercises no managerial control.

Securities are regulated by both state and federal law. To prevent fraud and to protect the public against unsubstantial schemes, transactions in which promoters go to the public for risk capital are monitored. (*See REAL PROPERTY SECURITIES REGISTRATION.*)

SECURITY AGREEMENT   A security document that creates a lien upon personal property (chattels), including chattels intended to be affixed to land as fixtures; known as a *chattel mortgage* prior to the adoption of the Uniform Commercial Code. Rather than record the security agreement, the Code provides for filing a notice on a short form called a *financing statement* (form UCC-1). In order to perfect a security interest, the financing statement should be recorded. It will therefore appear on a title report as a lien affecting the real property under search. Brokers frequently come in contact with security agreements in the sale of business opportunities. (*See FINANCING STATEMENT, UNIFORM COMMERCIAL CODE.*)

SECURITY DEPOSIT   Money deposited by or for the tenant with the landlord, to be held by the landlord for the following purposes: (1) to remedy tenant defaults for damage to the premises (be it accidental or intentional), for failure to pay rent due, or for failure to return keys at the end of the tenancy; (2) to clean the dwelling so as to place it in as fit a condition as when the tenant commenced possession, considering normal wear and tear; and (3) to compensate for damages caused by a tenant who wrongfully quits the dwelling unit. The security deposit is not regarded as liquidated damages, but rather is a fund held in trust for the tenant which the landlord can use to offset damages caused by the tenant. A security deposit is not taxable to the landlord until applied to remedy any tenant defaults. Likewise, neither can the tenant take the deposit as a tax deduction. Some states require security deposit monies be placed in an interest-bearing account in trust for the lessee.

The tenant's claim to the security deposit monies is superior to all claims of the landlord's creditors, except those of a trustee in bankruptcy.

Under the Uniform Residential Landlord and Tenant Act, the security deposit may not exceed one month's rent. The landlord must return the security deposit, less any authorized retained portion, to the tenant not later than 14 days after the termination of the rental agreement. The landlord must give written notice to the tenant setting forth the grounds for and evidence supporting any claimed retention of any portion of the security deposit. Certain states require landlords to return security deposits to tenants within a specified time period and to account for all claims to any part of the deposits; disputes over security deposits may be handled expeditiously in Small Claims Court. They provide for penalties in the event that a landlord fails to comply with the regulations. Difficulties in the accounting and administration of security deposits have led some authorities to advocate their abolition. Although the Uniform Residential Landlord and Tenant Act preserves the security deposit, it limits the amount (one month's rent) and prescribes penalties for its misuse. The Act does not limit the prepayment of rent, as distinguished from security deposits, nor does it require the landlord to pay interest on the security deposit.

The lease should clearly specify whether a payment is a security deposit or an advance rental. If it is a security deposit, the tenant is not entitled to apply it as discharge of the final month's rent. If it is an advance rental, the landlord will have to pay taxes on it when received. Many state laws specifically state that the security deposit is not to be construed as payment of the last month's rent by the tenant. When the lessor sells the property, the sales contract should cover the appropriate accounting of security deposit monies. (See *NORMAL WEAR AND TEAR, UNIFORM RESIDENTIAL LANDLORD AND TENANT ACT.*)

SEED MONEY   See FRONT MONEY.

SEISIN   Actual possession of property by one who claims rightful ownership of a freehold interest therein.
A person is seized of property when he or she is in rightful possession with the intention of claiming a freehold estate. Seisin is now generally considered to be synonymous with ownership. The concept is derived from feudal times, when individual ownership was not allowed. A medieval English landowner was said to be seized of his estate, for the King was considered the owner of all lands in England. Also called seizen.

A general warranty deed contains the covenant of seisin in which the grantor warrants that he or she has the estate or interest which he or she purports to convey. Both title and possession at the time of the grant are necessary to satisfy the covenant. In the event of a breach, the purchaser may recover his or her expenses up to the amount paid for the property. (See *DELIVERY, DOWER, FREEHOLD.*)

SELF-HELP The nonjudicial remedies an owner employs to regain possession of his or her property. For example, a landlord whose tenant is in default may attempt to cut off the utilities, forcibly enter the premises, or change the locks in order to force the tenant to pay the rent or move out. Most courts disapprove of self-help remedies and require landlords to follow statutory procedures for eviction. (*See EVICTION.*)

SEMIANNUAL Occurring twice a year, as in semiannual tax payments. (*See BIANNUAL.*)

SEMIDETACHED DWELLING A residence that shares one wall with an adjoining building. (*See PARTY WALL.*)

SEPARATE PROPERTY Property held individually, as opposed to community property or property held jointly. (*See COMMUNITY PROPERTY, JOINT TENANCY, TENANCY BY THE ENTIRETY, TENANCY IN COMMON.*)

SEPTIC TANK A sewage settling tank in which part of the sewage is converted into gas and liquids before the remaining waste is discharged by gravity into a leaching bed underground. Many local planning commissions require a developer to provide a sewage disposal system rather than use septic tanks because of the fear of pollution. Unlike cesspools, however, septic tanks are generally acceptable sanitary systems for low-density developments. (*See CESSPOOL, SANITARY SEWER SYSTEM.*)

SEQUESTRATION ORDER A writ authorizing the taking of land, rents, and/or profits owed by a defendant in a pending or concluded suit, for the purpose of forcing the defendant to comply with a court order. For example, to hold rental monies by court order pending the outcome of litigation.

SERVICE LIFE See *ECONOMIC LIFE.*

SERVICE OF PROCESS The legal act of notifying the defendant of an impending lawsuit and the delivery to him or her of the summons and complaint in the action. Service is usually made upon the defendant by the sheriff's delivery of a certified copy of the summons and the plaintiff's petition. Service of process on Sunday is usually void. If the defendant cannot be found within the state, the court may authorize service by certified mail or by publication, usually in a local newspaper, for at least once each week in as few as four successive weeks.

Under many state license laws, an out-of-state broker applying for registration must irrevocably appoint the public official in charge of real estate registration as his or her agent to receive any lawful process in any noncriminal proceeding relating to his or her real estate activities. Some states require that out-of-state subdividers or foreign corporations comply with a similar regulation in order to qualify to do business in that state.

SERVICING   As specified in a servicing agreement, a mortgage banker's duties performed for a fee as loan correspondent. Such duties generally include collecting payments that include interest, principal, insurance, and taxes on a note from the borrower in accordance with the terms of the note. Servicing also includes such operational procedures as accounting, bookkeeping, preparation of insurance and tax records, loan payment follow-up, delinquency follow-up, and loan analysis. The servicing agreement between an investor and a mortgage loan correspondent is generally written and it stipulates the rights and obligations of each party. The servicing fee is generally one-half of one percent of the outstanding loan.

SERVIENT ESTATE   Land on which an easement or other right exists in favor of an adjacent property (called a dominant estate); also referred to as a servient tenement. If property A has a right-of-way across property B, property B is the servient estate.

The servient owner may not use the property in such a way as to interfere with the reasonable use of the dominant owner. (See EASEMENT, SERVITUDE.)

SERVITUDE   A burden or charge upon an estate. A personal servitude (such as a license) attaches to the person for whose benefit it is established and terminates (if properly renewed) with his or her life. A real servitude (such as an easement) benefits the owner of one estate, who enjoys the use of a portion of a neighboring estate. A real servitude runs indefinitely with the land. (See EASEMENT, EQUITABLE SERVITUDE.)

SET-ASIDE LETTER   A financing term in which the lender sends the contractor of a project a letter to the effect that the lender will set aside money for him or her, and thus induce the contractor to finish a troubled project.

SETBACK   Zoning restrictions on the amount of land required surrounding improvements; the amount of space required between the lot line and the building line. These restrictions, called setbacks and sideyard restrictions, may be contained in local zoning regulations or they may be established by restrictive covenants in deeds and under subdivision general plans normally noted on the recorded subdivision plat.

Setback provisions are designed to keep buildings away from streets and to ensure that occupants have more light and air and less noise, smoke, dust, danger of spread of fire, and, in some cases, a better view at street intersections. It is important to clarify what is meant by a "building"; that is, whether or not the provision includes eaves, steps, bay windows, porch, awnings, walls, or fences. (See ZERO LOT LINE.)

SETOFF   The claim a debtor can make against a creditor that reduces or cancels the amount the debtor owes. (See HOLDER IN DUE COURSE.)

SETTLEMENT   1. The act of adjusting and prorating the various credits, charges, and settlement costs to conclude a real estate transaction. Many brokers refer to this process as the *closing* rather than the settlement. (See CLOSING.)

2. The act of compromising in a dispute or a lawsuit. Such an act is usually not an admission of liability. (*See CONCILIATION.*)

SETTLEMENT ACT *See REAL ESTATE SETTLEMENT PROCEDURES ACT.*

SEVERALTY Sole ownership of real property. Most corporations hold title to real property under tenancy in severalty. In this form of ownership, the title to the property is held by one real or artificial person and is severed from anyone else. Property owned in severalty is subject to probate upon death of the owner. (*See TENANCY IN SEVERALTY.*)

SEVERANCE The act of removing something attached to land or of terminating a relationship. When a fence is torn down, there is a severance of the fence from the real property. The fence thus changes from real property (fixture) to personal property.

When one joint tenant transfers his or her interest, there is a severance of the joint tenancy. The other joint tenant and the new transferee are then tenants in common in the property. Only divorce or joint conveyance by husband and wife can sever a tenancy by entirety.

SEVERANCE DAMAGES Where there is a partial taking of property under the state's power of eminent domain, any loss in value of remaining property caused by the partial taking of this real estate is referred to as severance damages. Severance damages are compensable to the property owner if the partial taking lowers the property's highest and best use, or otherwise limits the use of the remainder of the property.

The value of the benefit conferred, if any, on the portion not taken is offset against or deducted from severance damages. But if the benefit is greater than the severance damages, the benefit is not deducted from the value of the portion taken. (*See BEFORE-AND-AFTER METHOD, CONDEMNATION, LARGER PARCEL, SPECIAL BENEFIT.*)

SHAKE SHINGLE Shingle composed of split wood, most frequently used as a roofing or siding material.

SHALL Common statutory language meaning that which is required.

SHARED APPRECIATION Refers to a form of participation mortgage in which the lender shares in the appreciation of a property mortgaged if and when the property is sold. For a reduction in the current market interest rate by up to 40 percent in some cases, the borrower agrees to share with the lender the appreciation in the home's (or commercial property's) value in proportion to the interest reduction. The normal standard is a 10-year limit, with guaranteed long-term financing at the going rate after that, or sharing in proceeds when the house or commercial property is sold. (*See CREATIVE FINANCING, PARTICIPATION MORTGAGE.*)

SHEAR WALL   Permanent structural wall that provides lateral stability.

SHELL LEASE   A lease in which a tenant leases the unfinished shell of a building, as in a new shopping center, and agrees to complete construction by installing ceilings, plumbing, heating and air conditioning systems, and electrical wiring. It is important for landlord and tenant under a shell lease to agree upon who shall pay the real property taxes against the premises. Many shell leases provide that all improvements shall remain the tenant's personal property and that the tenant must pay the taxes assessed against them.

SHERIFF'S DEED   Deed given by a court to effect the sale of property to satisfy a judgment. (*See DEED.*)

SHOE MOLDING   A thin strip of wood placed at the junction of the baseboard and the floor boards to conceal the joint. The shoe molding improves the aesthetics of the room and helps seal out drafts.

SHOPPING   The practice of negotiating a deal and then attempting to shop around for better terms from others.

SHOPPING CENTER   A modern classification of retail stores, characterized by off-street parking and clusters of stores, subject to a uniform development plan, and usually with careful analysis given to the proper merchant mix.

The shift to suburban living after World War II forced retail and consumer service stores to follow their customers. This promoted the development of shopping centers in the once open tracts of suburban land.

Neighborhood Centers usually consist of a supermarket, variety store, service station, and a few smaller specialty shops. They are designed to serve the immediate neighborhood.

Community Centers usually contain supermarkets, department stores, variety stores, drug stores, and apparel shops. They are larger than neighborhood centers and are designed to serve the entire community.

Regional Centers are large planned centers, sometimes enclosed malls, containing many national chains and in some cases 50 or more stores. Easy access, free parking, and large selections have made regional shopping centers a way of life in many suburban areas.

The most common design for a shopping center is the "strip center," with stores built in a line and facing the street or parking area, with an anchor store at each end (such as a supermarket and a large drugstore). These strip neighborhood centers have not proven to be very efficient because they lack flexibility, and many economists believe that the all-purpose large discount store will replace the neighborhood shopping center in the next decade. Due to increased land costs and high taxes, it is predicted that customers may one day have to pay for shopping center parking, heretofore an important attraction of the shopping center concept.

A shopping center lease is a complicated and lengthy document. It is essentially a net lease with the rental determined on a percentage basis. The applicable percentages vary greatly among the types and sizes of retail stores, with the large department stores paying a less per-square-foot minimum rent and a lower percentage than smaller stores. All tenants must belong to a merchants' association that promotes the shopping center itself through institutional advertising. Stores must be operated during established hours, and limited to the use as specified in the lease. The tenant must pay a pro rata share of taxes, maintenance, and insurance, agree to keep his or her books open for audit, and sometimes use a special type of register to assure the landlord that the tenant accurately records the gross sales upon which the percentage ratio is based. The landlord may go as far as employing spot buyers to make sure that sales are properly recorded on the register.

Most shopping center leases contain some form of "radius clause" which might forbid the landlord to rent premises to the tenant's competitors within a specified radius of the shopping center or that might prevent the tenant from opening another store within a specified radius of the center. Recently, however, these noncompetition clauses have been under attack by the Federal Trade Commission as unreasonable restraints of trade, illegal under the Sherman Antitrust Act. (*See PERCENTAGE LEASE, RECAPTURE CLAUSE, TENANT MIX.*)

SHORELINE The dividing line between private land and public beach on beachfront property. The United States Supreme Court has ruled that the "mean high water mark" should determine the shoreline boundary. There are some coastal states, however, which now treat as public land that shoreline property up to the high wash of the waves, as may be evidenced by the vegetation line.

The prudent seller of shoreline property will carefully describe the land area in approximate language (such as "approximately 10,000 square feet," or "10,000 square feet, more or less"); and the prudent buyer will require that the property be resurveyed to ascertain the proper land area in view of these recent court cases.

A cautious seller may insert in a sales contract protective language such as: "Buyer acknowledges that the property being sold is a beachfront lot and accepts the premises subject to the possibility of dispute with regard to exact location of the shoreline boundary of the property. Buyer agrees to make no claim against the seller on account of any such dispute or any decrease in the area of the property resulting from the resolution of any such dispute." (*See ACCESS, BEACH, ENVIRONMENTAL IMPACT STATEMENT.*)

SHORING The use of timbers to prevent the sliding of earth adjoining an excavation. Shoring is also the timbers used as bracing against a wall for temporary support of loads during construction.

SHORT-FORM DOCUMENT A brief document that refers to a contract such as a mortgage (called a "fictitious mortgage"), lease, option, or sales contract and simply recites the fact that a contract has been made between the parties covering certain described premises. This satisfies the requirements of recordation yet keeps secret the essential terms and conditions of the transaction. A short-form lease, for example, might contain language such as: "This lease has been made upon the rents, terms, covenants, and conditions contained in a certain collateral agreement or lease between the parties hereto and bearing even-date herewith."

SHORT RATE   A higher periodic rate charged for a shorter term than that originally contracted. The increased premium charged by an insurance company upon early cancellation of a policy to compensate the insuror for the fact that the original rate charged was calculated on the full period of the policy. This increased charge enters into a buyer's decision whether to assume the seller's existing homeowner's hazard insurance policy or to cancel it and obtain a new policy.

SHORT-TERM CAPITAL GAIN   Gain from the sale or exchange of a capital asset held for not more than one year. Short-term capital gains (net of short-term capital losses) are taxed at ordinary income tax rates. (*See CAPITAL GAIN.*)

SHOULD   Common statutory language meaning that which is recommended but is not required.

SIDING   Boards nailed horizontally to the vertical studs, with or without intervening sheathing, to form the exposed surface of the outside walls of the building. Siding may be made of wood, metal, or masonry sheets.

SIGNATURE   Use of any name, including any trade or fictitious name, upon an instrument, or any word or mark used as and intended to be a written signature. To be valid, a signature may be handwritten, typed, printed, stamped, or made in any manner, including pencil. To be acceptable for recordation, however, a document usually must be signed in black ink and include one's full legal name (i.e., the name used to sign checks). If the party cannot write, he or she can sign by using a mark, such as "John X (his mark) Brown." This mark signature is referred to as "amanuensis." All but the X can be typed, but the X itself must be affixed by the one signing. In some states, signatures on deeds or contracts for deed must be witnessed.

Under the Statute of Frauds, a real estate sales contract must be "in writing and signed by the person to be charged therewith." This signature need not appear at the end of the document, though it customarily does. If a statute requires that a document be *subscribed*, however, it *must* be signed at the end. For example, witnesses to a will (at least two) must generally subscribe their names at the end of the will and in the presence of the testator, who has already signed above their names.

The signature of an attorney-in-fact is not valid on a real estate contract unless his or her authority is by way of a written power of attorney (under the *equal dignities rule*). The power of attorney should also be recorded when the parties intend to record the documents. The proper form of signature is for the attorney-in-fact to sign first the name of the principal, and then his or her own name as attorney-in-fact: John Fred Principal, by John William Agent, his attorney-in-fact."

A listing agreement need be signed only by the party to be charged therewith. Thus a broker who obtains from the husband a listing which the wife does not sign still has an enforceable employment contract against the husband. A sales contract however, must be signed by both husband and wife (as sellers) to be specifically enforceable. When co-owners are selling property, they all must sign the necessary transfer documents though it is not necessary that they all sign one document; that is, they could convey by separate deeds.

For a written lease to be valid, it is necessary that the lessor sign, since he or she is conveying possession. Though it is not necessary that the lessee sign the document if he or she accepts its terms and takes possession of the leased premises, it is preferable that both lessor and lessee read and sign the instrument to prevent disputes from arising between the parties.

When a fiduciary signs a document, he or she should indicate the capacity in which he or she is signing. For example, a guardian should sign as follows: "Angelo Domini, as legal guardian of Charlie Angel, a minor." Likewise, a trust document should be signed: "Angelo Domini, as trustee for the Charlie Angel Trust, and not individually." (See LEGAL NAME, SEAL.)

SIGNS Printed display boards frequently used to indicate the availability of real estate on the market. Many communities expressly prohibit the display of "for sale," "sold," and "for rent" signs in order to prevent blockbusting, protect existing home values, and eliminate the overall impression of too many signs in the area. In a recent case, the U.S. Supreme Court has invalidated at least one local ordinance which totally banned the use of "for sale" signs in the community. This is still, however, a highly controversial legal issue. Generally it is illegal to place signs such as "Brookshire Condo Complex—Turn Right Three Blocks" on public property or a public right-of-way. Signs are a mode of advertising and must therefore comply with all advertising regulations such as Truth-in-Lending. If a buyer becomes interested in a parcel of real estate as a result of seeing a broker's "for sale" sign, that broker will most likely be deemed the procuring cause of the sale.

Article 29 of the Realtors® Code of Ethics provides that signs giving notice of property for sale, rent, lease, or exchange should be placed on property only if authorized by the owner, and signs should be placed by more than one Realtor® only if the property is listed with and authorization given to more than one Realtor®. Under many local boards of Realtors® MLS rules and regulations, "for sale" signs of only the listing broker may be placed on a listed property filed with MLS, except with the consent of the listing broker.

SILENT PARTNER An inactive partner in business. (See LIMITED PARTNER.)

SILL The lowest horizontal member of the house frame, which rests on top of the foundation wall and forms a base for the studs. The term can also refer to the lowest horizontal member in the frame for a window or door.

SIMPLE INTEREST Interest computed on the principal balance only and not on unpaid but previously earned interest. (See ADD-ON INTEREST, COMPOUND INTEREST.)

SINGLE-FAMILY RESIDENCE A structure maintained and used as a single dwelling unit, designed for occupancy by one family, as in a private home; as opposed to a condominium, apartment building, or PUD. According to the typical landlord-tenant code, "Notwithstanding that a dwelling unit shares one or more walls with another dwelling unit, it shall be deemed a single-family residence if it has direct access to a street or thoroughfare and does not share hot water equipment or any other essential facility in service with any other dwelling unit."

A subdivider often restricts use of subdivided lots to single-family residences. It is advisable to further restrict the property to single-family, *detached* residences, if he or she intends to preclude the possibility of someone using the property for a duplex dwelling.

While zoning ordinances can validly limit the number of occupants or restrict occupancy to a single family, the ordinance cannot be arbitrary and discriminatory in its definition of "family." For example, a commercial boarding house situation may be properly excluded from single-family residential zones whereas a communal living situation (several elderly couples sharing housing) may not be declared improper. Some ordinances include as a "family" unmarried people and their children living together as a family unit and small groups living together in extended families.

SINGLE-LOAD CORRIDOR   A building term used to describe a building design in which the apartment units are located on only one side of the corridor, with a wall spanning the other side. The alternative is a double-load situation with apartments on both sides of the corridor, as in many hotels.

SINKING FUND   A fund created to gradually amass enough money to satisfy a debt or to meet a specific requirement; a fund designed to accumulate money to a predetermined amount at the end of a stated period of time such as a fund set up to repay debentures. The sinking fund method of depreciation contemplates periodic investments of equal amounts of money in a compound-interest-bearing account wherein the investment, plus the compound interest, will replace the improvement at the end of its economic life. For example, assume a retail operator enters into a 20-year lease for a store with an option to buy for $100,000 at the end of the lease term. In order to have $100,000 at the end of the term, the operator would have to set aside each year in a sinking fund the principal amount of $3,024, assuming a 5 percent return compounded annually ($100,000 $\times$ .03024, the factor in a sinking fund table for a 20-year, 5 percent compound return). Also called the *reinvestment method*. A condominium association may set up a maintenance reserve fund in this fashion.

The sinking fund method of depreciation for tax purposes is sometimes used by a taxpayer who desires to take less depreciation in the earlier years and increasing amounts in later years. For example, a young doctor might want to save larger depreciation deductions for later years when he or she will probably have more ordinary income to offset. (*See* AMORTIZATION.)

SITE   The position, situation, or location of a piece of land.

SITE OFFICE   A temporary place of realty business other than the principal place of business or branch office, from which real estate activities are conducted which relate to a specific piece of real property (open house), real estate condominium project, or real estate subdivision. The office must be situated on or adjacent to the specific property, condominium project, or subdivision to be considered a site office, and must comply with respective city and county requirements pertaining to temporary land use. Usually a brokerage company does not need a special license to operate a site office nor does it need a broker in charge of the office.

SKY LEASE   A lease of the air rights above a property. (*See AIR RIGHTS.*)

SKYLIGHT   An opening in a roof that is covered with glass and is designed to admit light.

SLAB   A flat, horizontal reinforced concrete area, usually the interior floor of a building but also an exterior or roof area.

SLANDER OF TITLE   A tort or civil wrong in which a person maliciously makes disparaging, untrue statements concerning another's title to property, thus causing injury. The disparaging statement may be oral or written, but must be published to some third person(s). Some statements are privileged, notably a *lis pendens* pleading filed in the appropriate court. Willful failure to remove a satisfied judgment lien may be grounds for a slander of title action.

SLUM CLEARANCE   The clearing of old, decrepit buildings so the land may be put to a better, more productive use. This is most often done to eliminate the existence of substandard and often unsanitary living conditions. HUD is active in slum clearance, replacing dilapidated structures with new, low-income housing. (*See URBAN RENEWAL.*)

SMALL BUSINESS ADMINISTRATION (SBA)   A federal government agency created to take over the small business function of the Reconstruction Finance Corporation. The SBA is supervised by an administrator appointed by the President. Its function is to administer the federal government's program for the preservation and development of small business concerns. Among other things, the SBA is authorized to make loans to small businesses to finance plant construction, conversion, or expansion, including the acquisition of land. These loans may be made either directly or in participation with private lenders. Before the SBA can make a direct loan, it must try to get a private lender to participate in the loan.

SMALL CLAIMS COURT   A division of the district court whose jurisdiction is limited to cases of small claims (for example, not exceeding $1,000 exclusive of interest and costs). The purpose of the small claims court is to provide an inexpensive and speedy forum for the disposition of minor controversies.

If landlord and tenant disagree about the right of the landlord to claim and retain the security deposit or any portion of it, either the landlord or the tenant may usually commence an action in the small claims division of the district court. (*See SECURITY DEPOSIT.*)

SOCIETY OF REAL ESTATE APPRAISERS (SREA) An international organization of professional real estate appraisers. There are three classifications of professional designations, each having separate qualifications and experience levels:

Senior Residential Appraiser (SRA): One who has successfully completed a program of professional training in the appraisal of single-family residential real estate, defined as one to six units.

Senior Real Property Appraiser (SRPA): One who has successfully completed the professional training and development program, and has demonstrated competence to appraise residential and income properties.

Senior Real Estate Analyst (SREA): One who has had extensive technical training, plus long and varied experience, and has demonstrated competence to appraise all types of real estate interests and ownerships.

The Society requires all professionally designated members to complete a minimum of 50 classroom hours of continuing education every five years as a condition of maintaining professional membership. By requiring periodic recertification, the Society provides some assurance that its designated members are maintaining their professional skills and keeping abreast of new appraisal techniques as they develop.

SOFT MONEY 1. The money to be financed under a purchase-money mortgage as a part of the purchase price; 2. tax-deductible items such as carrying charges (interest, real estate taxes, and ground rents) incurred while holding unimproved property or during construction. Soft money does not increase the equity position as would the payment of hard dollars, and it is not subject to recapture of depreciation rules. (*See CARRYING CHARGES.*)

SOIL BANK A program administered by the Commodity Stabilization Service of the federal Department of Agriculture in which farmers contract to divert land from production of unneeded crops to conservation uses. Such individuals receive an annual rent from the government for this land.

SOLAR EASEMENT An easement designed to protect an owner's access to light and the rays of the sun. There is no common law right to light and air onto one's property. Therefore, if an owner's solar heating system was rendered ineffective because of shadows cast by a neighbor's tree or a proposed nearby condominium, the owner would be left with no legal remedy except to try and negotiate a purchase of an easement to restrict blocking out the sun.

Some jurisdictions are attempting to legislate solar easements to encourage property owners to use more efficient energy systems. California has a statute declaring as a "nuisance" vegetation shading a solar collector. Other communities offer incentives to builders who protect solar access in their designs. For example, a builder might receive a density bonus of up to 20 percent for incorporating solar access into plans of streets, lots, and buildings. (*See RESIDENTIAL ENERGY CREDITS.*)

SOLAR HEATING   A natural system of heating using the energy of the sun. To encourage homeowners to utilize such energy-efficient systems, both federal and tax incentives are offered. Passive solar heating is a system that incorporates some solar heating plus central heating as a back-up.

SOLDIERS AND SAILORS CIVIL RELIEF ACT   A federal law designed to protect persons in the military service from loss of property when their ability to meet their obligations has been materially affected by reason of entering military service. If a person who has mortgaged property enters the military service and, as a result of the drastic change in pay scale, can no longer keep his or her loan current, the court has wide discretion to protect the defaulting soldier. For example, the court can order him or her to pay only interest and taxes and can postpone foreclosure until military service ends.

After a mortgagor enters the service, he or she can request that the mortgage bear only 6 percent interest. This is true whether the soldier enlists or is drafted into the service and whether he or she defaults in the original payments or not. As with the postponed principal payments, the soldier will have to make up all deferred payments upon leaving the service.

Foreclosure of a mortgage where a member of the military is the mortgagor must be done by way of court proceeding, regardless of whether there is a power of sale in the mortgage. It is therefore imperative for the mortgagee, before foreclosing under a power of sale, to check whether anyone interested in the land has entered the military service after the mortgage was made. The power-of-sale foreclosure will be invalid if made during the period of such military service or within three months thereafter. A vendee under a contract for deed who enters the military service is likewise protected by this act.

Note that the protections of this law do not apply to career soldiers or to those service personnel who buy or encumber property *after* entering military service.

Members of the military, and those civilians negotiating business transactions with military personnel, are encouraged to discuss the legal ramifications of this act as well as other military law with qualified counsel from the Staff Judge Advocate's Office of the appropriate military base. (*See MILITARY CLAUSE, POWER OF SALE.*)

SOLE PROPRIETORSHIP   A method of owning a business in which one person owns the entire business and reports all profits and losses directly on his or her personal income tax return, as contrasted with corporate, joint, or partnership ownership. (*See PROPRIETORSHIP.*)

SPACE PLAN   Preliminary drawing by an architect, which lays out the floor plan of a leased space to meet the tenant's requirements.

SPECIAL AGENT   One who is authorized by a principal to perform a particular act or transaction, without contemplation of continuity of service as with a general agent. The real estate broker is ordinarily a special agent appointed by the seller to find a ready, willing, and able buyer for a particular property. An attorney-in-fact under a limited power of attorney is a special agent. (*See AGENCY, AGENT, GENERAL AGENT.*)

SPECIAL ASSESSMENT   A tax or levy customarily imposed against only those specific parcels of realty that will benefit from a proposed public improvement, as opposed to a general tax on the entire community. Since the proposed improvement will enhance the value of the affected homes, it is only those affected owners who must pay this special lien. Common examples of special assessments are water, sidewalk, and sewer assessments, or other special improvements such as parks and recreational facilities. Special assessments differ from property taxes in that the latter are levied for the support of the general functions of government, whereas special assessments are levied for the cost of specific local improvements such as streets, sewers, irrigation, and drainage. In some instances special assessments are periodically levied by improvement districts; in other instances they are levied only by the city and county for a particular work or improvement.

Special assessments are usually paid in installments over several years although the owner always has the option of paying the balance in full. In a few states they are prorated at closing; thus the sales contract should specify which party is responsible for payment of assessments, if any, at the time of closing. Typically, however, the seller pays for all improvements substantially completed by the closing date because of the increased property value generally resulting from the improvement. Improvements not substantially completed but authorized or in progress are usually assumed by the buyer. In any event, this matter is open to negotiation between buyer and seller.

Special assessments are generally apportioned according to benefits received, rather than by the value of the land and buildings being assessed. This apportionment is frequently called the *assessment-roll spread*. For example, in a residential subdivision, the assessment for installation of storm drains, curbs, and gutters is made on a front-foot basis. The property owner is charged for each foot of his or her lot that abuts the street being improved.

According to many state condominium laws, each apartment is subject to separate assessment and taxation, including special assessments. A prospective purchaser of a condominium unit should check whether there are any major improvements contemplated, such as installation of automatic elevators or corridor carpeting, since these special assessments will result in increased monthly payments.

For income tax purposes, real estate taxes are currently deductible. Special assessments, however, are *not* directly deductible because they increase the value of the property and thus, like any other capital expenditure, are added to the cost or basis of the property. (The assessment is not eligible for depreciation, however.) In some cases a special assessment is deductible if the investor/taxpayer can prove that all or part of the assessment is made for maintenance, repairs, or interest charges. (*See INSURANCE, PROPERTY TAXES.*)

SPECIAL BENEFIT   The value added to a property as a result of some governmental improvement. In determining the just compensation for a property that is partially taken by condemnation, the court considers the fair market value of the property taken plus severance damages *less* any special benefits. Thus, if the state takes a portion of a property for an improvement and the improvement actually increases the value of the remaining land, then the court in a condemnation proceeding will consider the value of the special benefit and reduce the just compensation accordingly. (*See BEFORE-AND-AFTER METHOD, JUST COMPENSATION, SEVERANCE DAMAGES.*)

SPECIAL CONDITIONS Specific provisions inserted into a real estate sales contract which must be satisfied before the contract is binding. The following are typical:

1. Subject to buyer obtaining a $95,000 first mortgage at an interest rate not to exceed 13 percent to be amortized for no longer than a 29-year period.

2. Buyer shall furnish seller with a satisfactory written credit report within *(number of calender days)* of acceptance of this offer.

3. *(Any repairs or additions)* to be completed as agreed before closing and approved in writing by buyer and approved in writing by buyer and seller by *(date)*.

4. Subject to buyer's acceptance of written inventory of furnishings, plants, etc.

5. All appliances, electrical and plumbing fixtures and systems to be in good working order on closing.

6. Seller shall furnish a certificate of clearance from a reputable termite company, showing no active, visible infestation of termites in improvements. *(See CONTINGENCY, TERMITE INSPECTION.)*

SPECIAL LIEN A lien or charge against a specific parcel of property, such as a mortgage, attachment, or mechanic's lien. A general lien, on the other hand, is a charge against all the property of the debtor. *(See GENERAL LIEN, LIEN.)*

SPECIAL-PURPOSE PROPERTY A combination of land and improvements with only one highest and best use because of some special design, such as church, school, post office, or hospital.

SPECIAL USE PERMIT Permission from the local zoning authority granting a land use that is identified as a special exception in the zoning ordinance. For instance, a zoning ordinance for a residential area might authorize certain special uses for churches, hospitals, or country clubs, provided a permit is first obtained. A special use differs from a *variance* in that the latter is an authorized violation of the zoning ordinance, whereas the special use is a permitted exception. The standards for a variance are much more difficult than those for a special use permit. *(See NONCONFORMING USE, VARIANCE.)*

SPECIAL WARRANTY DEED A deed in which the grantor warrants or guarantees the title only against defects arising during the period of his or her tenure and ownership of the property and not against defects existing before that time. Such a deed is usually identified by the language "by, through, or under the grantor, but not otherwise." A special warranty deed is often used when a fiduciary such as an executor or trustee conveys the property of his or her principal, because the fiduciary usually has no authority to warrant against acts of his or her predecessors in title. This is also used when one spouse conveys property to the other spouse as part of a divorce decree.

SPECIFICATIONS   Written instructions to a building contractor containing all the necessary information regarding the materials, dimensions, colors, and other features of a proposed construction. Specifications supplement the plans and working drawings. (*See PLANS AND SPECIFICATIONS.*)

SPECIFIC PERFORMANCE   An action brought in a court of equity in special cases to compel a party to carry out the terms of a contract. The basis for an equity court's jurisdiction in breach of a real estate contract is the fact that land is unique and mere legal damages would not adequately compensate the buyer for the seller's breach. The courts cannot, however, specifically enforce a contract to perform personal services, such as a broker's agreement to find a buyer, neither an illegal agreement, an ambiguous contract, nor a contract in which there is inadequate consideration.

If a seller refuses to sell to a buyer under a contract of sale, the buyer can request a court specifically to enforce the contract and make the seller deed the property under threat of contempt of court. Similarly, a buyer can have a judge enforce performance of a conveyance by the heirs of a deceased seller under a contract of sale.

In some jurisdictions, a seller can force a defaulting buyer to purchase the property, especially if land values have declined. In most cases, however, a seller would have a difficult time proving that the legal remedy of money damages would not be adequate relief, and he or she *must* show this inadequacy to obtain specific performance relief.

SPECULATOR   1. One who analyzes a real property market and acquires properties with the expectation that prices will greatly increase, at which time he or she can sell at a large profit. Many states have enacted legislation against certain land speculation. Some states impose a land gains tax on the gain derived from the sale or exchange of land held less than a set period of time. The greater the gain and the shorter the time the land is held before the sale, the greater the tax.

2. An owner/builder who constructs homes ("spec homes") in the expectation that he or she will find willing buyers when the homes are *completed* (rather than have a specific buyer ready at the time construction begins). This practice is often called *building on spec.*

SPENDTHRIFT TRUST   A trust created to provide a source of money for the maintenance and support of a designated beneficiary and, at the same time, to secure the property from being wasted or depleted by the beneficiary's improvidence or irresponsibility. Income-producing real property is sometimes the subject of a spendthrift trust containing provisions against alienation of the trust fund by the voluntary act of the beneficiary or by his or her creditors.

SPIN-OFF   The transfer of a company's assets to a recently formed subsidiary. In order to control a specific real estate development, a corporation will sometimes trade part of its assets to a new corporation in exchange for stock in the new corporation, which is then distributed to the stockholders of the parent company.

SPITE FENCE   A fence of such a height or type that is erected to annoy one's neighbor. Some states have spite fence statutes which limit the height of fences to, say, ten feet. There is some dispute as to whether a maliciously erected fence under the statutory height can be abated.

SPLIT-FEE FINANCING   A form of joint venture participation in which the lender actually purchases the fee land under the proposed development project and leases it to the developer. The lender also finances the improvements to be constructed on this leasehold.

SPLIT FINANCING   A financing situation in which the land and the improvements are financed separately. Split financing is often used by developers to obtain greater total permanent financing than would ordinarily be available by typical conventional financing. Also called component financing. (*See INTERIM FINANCING, PERMANENT FINANCING.*)

SPLIT-LEVEL   A house in which two or more floors are usually located directly above one another, and one or more additional floors, adjacent to them, are placed at a different level.

SPLIT-RATE   Capitalization rates applied separately to land and improvements, to determine the value of each.

SPLITTING FEES   The act of sharing compensation. A broker can generally split a commission only with another licensee in the broker's own state or with a broker from another state who did not participate in any negotiations within the first broker's state. Paying any remuneration to an unlicensed person for referring a client is illegal and could result in the suspension or revocation of the broker's license. If the broker wishes to split fees with a licensed salesperson, the money must pass through the salesperson's employing broker. (*See FINDER'S FEE.*)

SPOT LOAN   A loan on a particular property, usually a condominium unit, by a lender who has not previously financed that particular condominium project. Because of the great amount of background work and investigation required to investigate the entire condominium project and to inspect all relevant documents, many lenders are unwilling to lend money for a single unit in a large condominium development. Other lenders will make spot loans if they are reimbursed for their legal and other service fees in analyzing the loan.

SPOT SURVEY   A survey that illustrates the locations, sizes, and shapes of buildings, improvements, and easements located on a property under appraisal, as well as those on any neighboring property that may encroach on the surveyed property. A lender may require a spot survey and a legal description of the land as a prerequisite to financing a project, especially a large development.

SPOT ZONING A change in the local zoning ordinance permitting a particular use inconsistent with the zoning classification of the area; the reclassification of a small area of land in such a manner as to disturb the tenor of the surrounding neighborhood, such as a change to permit one multi-unit structure in an area zoned for single-family residential use; also called a variance. Spot zoning is not favored in the law. If the change affects only a small area and is not in harmony with the comprehensive general plan for that area, such as a chemical factory in a residential neighborhood, spot zoning is open to attack and will not be permitted by the courts. A permissible spot zone might allow a small grocery store or convenience shop to give easy access to the surrounding residential areas. Also called contract zoning.

SPREADING AGREEMENT An agreement to "spread" or extend a mortgage lien to encompass several properties, in order to give the lender additional security on the loan.

SPUR TRACK That segment of rail track, usually privately owned by the industry using it, which leads off a drill track or main line and services an industrial plant or site.

SQUARE In the government (rectangular) survey of land description, an area measuring 24 miles by 24 miles; sometimes referred to as a *check*.

SQUARE-FOOT METHOD A method of estimating a building's construction, reproduction, or replacement costs whereby the structure's square-foot floor area is multiplied by an appropriate square-foot construction cost figure.

SQUATTER'S RIGHT The right of a person in adverse possession of real property. A squatter's possession must generally be actual, open, notorious, exclusive, and continuous for a period of time prescribed by statute. (*See ADVERSE POSSESSION.*)

STAGING A temporary scaffolding to support workers and materials during construction.

STAGING AREA An area, either outside at a construction site or inside a building, usually close to its loading doors, where material, apparatus, equipment, or merchandise is collected or assembled before it is moved to where it will finally be used or stored.

STAKING A method of identifying the boundaries of a parcel of land by placing stakes or pins in the ground or by painting marks on stone walls or rocks.

STANDARD METROPOLITAN STATISTICAL AREA (SMSA) An important designation given by the federal Office of Management and Budget to counties with at least one central city of 50,000 or more residents. In New England, SMSAs consist of groups of cities and townships rather than entire counties. The SMSA designation is often used as a qualifying standard for governmental grants such as the Community Development Block Grant.

Under the Interstate Land Sales Act, there is a special exemption from registration for subdivisions containing fewer than 300 lots if the purchaser's principal residence is within the same SMSA as the subdivision.

STANDARD PARALLEL

In the government (rectangular) survey system of land description, one of a series of lines running east and west, generally spaced 24 miles apart and located north and south of, and parallel to, the base lines. Such parallels establish township boundaries at 24-mile intervals and correct inaccuracies due to the curvature of the earth; also called correction lines.

STANDARDS OF PRACTICE

A set of ethical criteria formulated by the Professional Standards Committee of the National Association of Realtors®. Such standards of practice are interpretations of certain articles of the Realtors® Code of Ethics. In filing a charge of an alleged violation of the Code of Ethics by a Realtor®, the charge should read as an alleged violation of one or more articles of the code. A standard of practice may be cited only in support of the charge.

STANDBY FEE

A substantial sum paid by a borrower at the time of issuance of a standby commitment letter, as a charge for the lender's risk and responsibility in committing to the loan. The standby fee is forfeited if the loan is not closed within a specified time. Most courts uphold the forfeiture of the standby fee as a lawful damage provision and not as an unlawful penalty. (See *STANDBY LOAN.*)

STANDBY LOAN

An arrangement whereby the lender agrees to keep a certain amount of money available to the borrower, usually a developer, for a specified period of time. Thus a standby loan is like an option on a loan since the developer has the right to borrow the money but is not obligated to do so. In fact, the terms of the standby commitment are usually made so onerous as to discourage the developer from exercising the loan, so it amounts to a commitment to make a loan in the future, in the event the borrower cannot get better financing elsewhere. Standby loans are usually made by noninstitutional lenders and are usually short term, from 18 to 24 months. The standby fee is typically 2 to 3 percent of the loan per year. The developer should be careful to specify those conditions which will excuse his or her performance under the terms of the standby loan agreement such as condemnation of a building site or refusal of a building permit.

STANDING LOAN

A commitment by the interim or construction lender to keep the money he or she has already funded in the project for a specified period of time after the expiration of the interim loan, usually until permanent takeout financing is secured. For instance, a lender might agree to provide an interim construction loan for one year and a standing loan for two years from the date of termination of the one-year loan. This usually enables the borrower to build and rent his or her shopping center or office building before obtaining permanent financing, thus improving the chance of obtaining favorable permanent financing.

A standing loan also refers to a straight mortgage, i.e., one that calls for payments of interest only with no amortization during its term and the entire principal becoming due at maturity; i.e. the entire principal "stands" until satisfaction. (*See STRAIGHT NOTE.*)

STARTER 1. Reference to an earlier title report on a particular piece of real property. Many title companies have copies of earlier policies in their title plants; if there is a starter on a property, the title searcher can avoid having to search back to the original source of title again. The searcher need only search all relevant records for items affecting the title from the date of the starter up to the date of the search.

2. A person's first residence or other real estate investment. (*See PYRAMIDING.*)

STARTS A term commonly used to indicate the number of residential units begun within a stated period of time. (*See HOUSING STARTS.*)

STATEMENT OF RECORD A document that must be filed with a HUD registration of subdivided land intended to be sold using any means of interstate commerce. The lengthy and detailed statement of record requires information dealing with the property, the site, and the developer, including such information as the name and address of each person having an interest in the property, a legal description of the property, general terms and conditions of contracts, including prices, descriptions of access to the property and public utilities, and all encumbrances. In addition, copies of the corporation or partnership documents of the developer and other instruments relating to the property are required. In support of the statement of record the developer must also provide financial statements (certified in certain cases). (*See INTERSTATE LAND SALES.*)

STATE REVENUE STAMPS *See TRANSFER TAX.*

STATUTE A law enacted by Congress (federal law) or by a state legislature (state law), as opposed to judicial or common law; statutory law as opposed to case law.

STATUTE OF FRAUDS State law that requires certain contracts to be in writing and signed by the party to be charged (or held) to the agreement in order to be legally *enforceable.* Most state statutes of frauds are based on the original English Statute for Prevention of Frauds and Perjuries (1677). Statutes of frauds generally require that all contracts for the sale of land or any interest therein (and some listings) be written. Oral leases for a period not exceeding one year, however, are generally valid and enforceable. The law does not require a single, formal contract; the writing could consist of a memorandum of the contract or several items of correspondence as long as the material terms agreed upon are stated. In one case, the commission terms were jotted on the back of the broker's business card and initialed by the seller. The writing can even be a subsequent confirmation of an earlier oral contract (". . . this letter is to confirm our prior telephone understanding. . .").

It is generally held that a valid written agreement can be cancelled by a subsequent oral agreement, since the Statute of Frauds deals only with the *making* of a contract.

The parties to an oral real estate contract may have a valid contract (i.e., one containing all the essential elements), but the contract is not enforceable if it is not in writing. The Statute of Frauds relates to the remedy only and not to the inherent validity of the contract. Thus, the parties to a fully executed or performed oral agreement cannot thereafter assert the Statute of Frauds to seek rescission of the contract. The statute may only be pleaded as an affirmative defense to a lawsuit seeking enforcement of the oral contract.

The purpose of the Statute of Frauds is to prevent the perpetration of fraud by one seeking enforcement of an executory contract that was never in fact made; it is not designed to prevent the performance of oral contracts. There are thus exceptions to the Statute of Frauds, mostly where the assertion of the Statute of Frauds as a defense against an oral contract would, in itself, amount to a fraud or result in unjust enrichment or unconscionable injury. In some instances, part performance of an oral agreement will take the case out of the Statute of Frauds. For example, a contract will be "taken out" of the Statute of Frauds if the buyer, in reliance on a seller's oral promise to sell the property, pays part or all of the purchase price, enters into possession, and makes substantial improvements on the property. In such a case of part performance, some courts refuse to allow the seller to assert the Statute of Frauds as a defense against the buyer's action to force the seller to fulfill the terms of the oral agreement to sell.

The Uniform Commercial Code states that contracts for the sale of personal property in excess of $500 must be in writing. If a seller wishes to retain a fixture (regardless if under $500), this fact must be clearly stated in the contract since a fixture is considered to be real estate. (*See ESTOPPEL, PAROL EVIDENCE RULE, UNENFORCEABLE CONTRACT.*)

STATUTE OF LIMITATIONS   That law pertaining to the period of time within which certain actions must be brought to court. The law is intended to protect the vigilant against stale claims by requiring the prompt assertion of claims; thus an action must be brought (i.e., the complaint filed) within a specified time of the occurrence of the cause of action. After the time period expires, the claim is said to be "outlawed," and may not be enforced in court. The theory behind the Statute of Limitations is that there must be some end to the possibility of litigation. It is said that stale witnesses and stale records produce little truth and result in accidental justice, if any.

If a partial payment is made before the time period has expired, then the full period starts running anew. If the payment is made afterwards, then the debt is not revived and remains outlawed or barred. (*See LACHES.*)

STEERING   The illegal practice of channeling homeseekers interested in equivalent properties to particular areas, either to maintain the homogeneity of an area or to change the character of an area in order to create a speculative situation. This practice makes certain homes unavailable to homeseekers on the basis of race or national origin, and on these grounds it is prohibited by the provisions of the federal Fair Housing Act. Steering is often difficult to detect, however, because the steering tactics can be so subtle that the homeseeker is unaware that his or her choice has been limited.

Steering could be the use of a word, phrase, or act by a real estate licensee which is intended to influence the choice of a prospective property buyer on a discriminatory basis. It is estimated that more than 80 percent of the suits filed by the Department of Justice against real estate licensees for violation of the federal Fair Housing Law have involved steering. (*See FEDERAL FAIR HOUSING LAW.*)

STEPPED-UP BASIS   The new basis of property acquired from a decedent, equal to the value as finally determined by the IRS of the property transferred on the date of death, or on an alternate valuation date for federal estate tax purposes (six months after the date of death), or the fair market value where no estate tax return is filed. (*See BASIS; ESTATE TAX, FEDERAL.*)

STEP-UP LEASE   A lease with fixed rent for an initial term and a predetermined rent increase at specified intervals and/or increases based upon periodic appraisals. Because the main purpose of a step-up lease is to hedge against inflation, its term tends to be longer than a fixed lease. It covers increases due to inflation as well as increased taxes, insurance premiums, and maintenance costs (often keyed to federal cost of living indexes). A lease with specified rent *decreases* is a *step-down lease.* (*See GRADUATED RENTAL LEASE.*)

STRAIGHT-LINE METHOD   A method of depreciation, also called the *age-life* method, which is computed by dividing the adjusted basis of a property, less the estimated salvage value, by the number of years of estimated remaining useful life. The cost of the property is thus deducted in equal annual installments. For example, if the depreciable basis of pre-1981 real property (net, after deducting salvage value) is $100,000 and the estimated useful life is 25 years, the annual depreciation deduction is $4,000 for each year during the useful life of the asset. Taxpayers sometimes use a form of accelerated depreciation such as 175 percent of straight line. The IRS has rules to recapture that amount of depreciation which is in excess of the straight-line rate. (*See DEPRECIATION, RECAPTURE OF DEPRECIATION, SALVAGE VALUE.*)

STRAIGHT NOTE   A promissory note evidencing a loan in which payments of interest only are made periodically during the term of the note, with the principal payment due in one lump sum upon maturity. A straight note is usually a nonamortized note made for a short term, such as three to five years, and is renewable at the end of the term. A mortgage that secures a straight note is a *term mortgage* or *straight-term mortgage.*

STRAW MAN   One who purchases property for another in order to conceal the identity of the real purchaser; a dummy purchaser; a nominee; a front.

At one time, it was necessary for an owner who wanted to change a title to joint tenancy from severalty to convey the property to a straw man who would then convey it back to the owner and joint tenant. Many states no longer require that the joint tenancy be created at the same time by one and the same instrument. Thus, an owner can convey to him- or herself and another party as joint tenants, or convey to him- or herself and spouse as tenants by the entirety without using a straw man.

Where several tracts of land are being assembled for development, confidentiality may be very important—hence the desirability of nominees and straw men. However, a federal court has held that if the nominee misrepresents the identity of his or her principal, with knowledge that the seller would not have negotiated if he or she were in possession of the true facts, the seller may set aside the transaction. In addition, if the nominee or straw man exercises any managerial control over the property, he or she may be held to be the real owner for tax purposes.

In a presale of a condominium, a developer normally must attain a certain percentage of purchases before a lender will commit to lend money; straw men are sometimes used to meet this minimum requirement, though this practice is clearly against the lender's policy and would be illegal in connection with VA and FHA loans. (*See JOINT TENANCY.*)

STREET A fully improved through roadway serving local or minor collector traffic.

STRINGER One of the sloping enclosed sides of a staircase that supports the treads and risers. The term can also refer to a horizontal beam which connects the uprights in a frame.

STRUCTURAL ALTERATIONS Any change in the supporting members of a building, such as bearing walls or partitions; columns, beams, or girders; or any structural change in the roof, but not normally including extension or enlargement of the building. (*See NONCONFORMING USE.*)

STRUCTURAL DEFECTS In residential homes, actual damage to the load-bearing portion of a home, which affects its load-bearing function and vitally affects the use of the home for residential purposes. This includes damage from shifting soil from causes other than earthquake or flood.

STRUCTURAL DENSITY The ratio of the total ground floor area of a building to the total land area. The average density for a general purpose industrial building is about one-third.

STRUCTURE Something built or constructed; an improvement. A structure is often defined in local building codes, usually as "anything that is more than 18 inches off the ground and cannot be lifted by a person without mechanical aid," or "any production or piece of work, artificially built up or composed of parts and joined together in some defined manner." As a rule, a structure can be built only after a building permit is obtained.

An interesting question arises from a poorly drafted restriction against building any structure without developer approval—whether the structure is a swimming pool, fence, or tennis court.

STUCCO A cement or plaster wallcovering that is installed wet and dries into a hard surface coating.

STUD   In wall framing, the vertical members to which horizontal pieces are attached. Studs are placed between 16 and 24 inches apart and serve as the main support for the roof and/or the second floor.

STUDIO   An efficiency apartment; a dwelling that consists of a combination living room and bedroom, plus a bathroom and kitchen.

SUBAGENT   An agent of a person who is already acting as an agent for a principal. The original agent can delegate authority to a subagent where such delegation is either expressly authorized or customary in the trade. For example, it is customary for listing brokers to delegate certain functions of a ministerial nature to subagents, such as to show property and solicit buyers.

Many multiple listing services are based on the theory that a listing is an offer of subagency to members and that members who work on such listings do so as subagents of the listing broker.

Where it is clear that the principal has authorized the agent to appoint subagents, the relation of principal and agent exists between the principal and the subagent. Some courts hold that a subagent who is lawfully appointed represents the principal in like manner with the prime agent; and the prime agent is not responsible to third persons for acts of the subagent. (See *AGENCY.*)

SUBAGREEMENT OF SALE   An agreement of sale (contract for deed) between the original vendee of an agreement of sale and a new purchaser. Under such an agreement there is no contractual relationship between the new purchaser (subvendee) and the owner of the property (original vendor).

An *assignment* of agreement of sale is a transfer to the new buyer of the original vendee's right, title, and interest in that agreement. A subagreement of sale, however, is an entirely new contract, strictly between the original vendee and the new buyer. Since the original vendor usually reserves the right to consent to all transfers by the vendee, the subagreement of sale should not contain any provisions prejudicial to the original vendor; otherwise the vendor can withhold his or her consent and delay the closing of the transaction.

Because of the complications that can arise with a subagreement of sale, many attorneys recommend that the new parties enter into an entirely new contract clearly detailing the rights and obligations of *all* parties, and that they set up a collection account to handle all the payments. (See *COLLECTION ACCOUNT, CONTRACT FOR DEED.*)

SUBCHAPTER S CORPORATION   A corporation which has elected to be treated as a partnership for tax purposes. The subchapter S corporation election allows a business to operate in corporate form and yet not pay a corporate tax, thus avoiding the double tax feature of corporate ownership. Each stockholder is taxable on his or her share of the corporation's income, whether or not it is distributed to him or her. Similarly, the stockholder can report his or her share of the corporation's ordinary losses and deduct them on an individual personal tax return. Long-term capital gains also pass through to the stockholders. Though there is no limitation on the amount of corporate income for a subchapter S corporation, there are several important limitations on the number of shareholders and the sources of income.

The Economic Recovery Tax Act of 1981, effective for tax years beginning after 1981, increases from 15 to 25 the maximum number of shareholders that a tax-option corporation may have. In addition, the Act makes changes in the rules governing the eligibility of trusts with shareholder status. This change becomes effective for tax years beginning after 1981.

Under the pre-1982 rule, only grantor trusts, stock voting trusts, and certain testamentary trusts were eligible to be shareholders in a tax option corporation. The post-1981 rule widens the eligible trust shareholder category in two respects:

1. If a person is treated as the complete owner of the trust, the trust may be a shareholder in a tax-option (subchapter S) corporation (but the deemed owner is treated as the shareholder).

2. A "qualified subchapter S trust" is eligible to become a shareholder of a tax-option corporation if the individual beneficiary of the trust, or his or her legal representative, elects to be treated as the owner of the trust.

A husband and wife (or their estate) will be treated as one shareholder.

The corporation cannot make the election if it has gross annual receipts of more than: (1) 20 percent from "passive income," or (2) 80 percent from sources outside the United States. A subchapter S corporation can hold investment property just as individuals can. The 20 percent passive income rule applies only to rents, dividends, interest, annuities, and gains on sales or exchanges of stock or securities but not on the sale of real estate. Thus, several people can form a subchapter S corporation just to hold one piece of investment property.

The election for subchapter S status must be filed with the tax director of the district in which the corporation files its tax return, together with statements consenting to the election by *all* shareholders. The election must be filed on or before the end of the first 75 days of the taxable year, or during the entire preceding month. No extension of time can be given. A new shareholder must affirmatively refuse to consent to subchapter S status within 60 days of the filing in order to terminate the status.

Although subchapter S benefits are not usually available to the real estate investor because such corporations cannot derive more than 20 percent of their income from passive sources such as rentals, real estate management firms and other real estate businesses may often be organized as subchapter S corporations.

SUBCONTRACTOR   A builder or contractor who enters into an agreement with a developer or the prime contractor to perform a special portion of the construction work, such as electrical, plumbing, or air conditioning installation. The subcontractor does not deal directly with the owner; however, if not paid by the prime contractor, the subcontractor can assert a mechanic's lien against the property within a certain time after a notice of completion is published. (*See* CONTRACTOR.)

SUBDIVIDER   An owner whose land is divided into two or more lots and offered for disposition. Under the Uniform Land Sales Practices Act, a subdivider may also be the principal agent of an inactive owner. If the subdivider later puts improvements on the property, he or she becomes a developer.

SUBDIVISION   Defined under many states' laws as any land that
is divided or is proposed to be divided for the
purpose of disposition into two or more lots, parcels, units, or interests. Subdivision refers to any land, whether contiguous or not, if two or more lots, parcels, units, or interests are offered as part of a common promotional plan of advertising and sale. The law would thus apply to the sale of $\frac{1}{125}$ undivided interest in a large parcel of land.

A developer of a subdivision must first comply with the subdivision regulations of the county or municipality in which the property is located. Upon local approval and posting of any required improvement completion bonds, the subdivider usually must then register his or her subdivision with the proper state agency before beginning to sell. In certain cases, the subdivider must also register the subdivision under the federal Interstate Land Sales Act.

SUBDIVISION   Many states have enacted subdivision registration
REGISTRATION LAW laws to protect prospective purchasers from the
deceptive practices and abuses once common in
the unregulated sale of greater numbers of unimproved lots. There are usually many exemptions from registration. For example, if the consumer is adequately protected by other regulations (condominium law, local building codes), or if there are only a small number of purchasers or lots, the law may provide an exemption.

If the subdivision contains less than 100 lots, and if any means of interstate commerce is used to dispose of the lots (such as the United States mail), the subdivider may have to register the subdivision with the federal Department of Housing and Urban Development (HUD). If each of the lots is 20 acres or more in size (inclusive of easements), the subdivision is exempt from the HUD requirements.

To register a subdivision, the subdivider must submit a form application to the proper state regulatory agency containing such things as a legal description of the property; names, occupations, and interests of applicant's officers and directors; current title policy; copies of all proposed documents the prospective purchaser is to sign; a statement of zoning; advertising material; the proposed public offering statement; and a current financial statement.

If the registration is accepted, the subdivider can then sell the lots using a *public offering statement*, which is designed to disclose fully and accurately to a prospective purchaser all material and relevant facts concerning the subdivision. As with any disclosure device, there is a constant interplay between the subdivider, who considers the public offering statement as a marketing tool, and the attorney preparing it, who considers it as an insurance document against later lawsuits for failing to disclose accurate material facts. If the subdivider does not use the current public offering statement, the regulatory agency can issue a cease-and-desist order to stop all selling and revoke the registration. It is generally unlawful for anyone to sell or offer an interest in nonexempted, subdivided lands without first registering the subdivision, delivering a current public offering statement to the prospective purchaser, and giving him or her a reasonable opportunity to examine it and sign a formal receipt for it. An injured purchaser can usually recover the consideration paid plus interest from the date of payment, property taxes paid, costs, and reasonable attorney fees, less any income received. The scope of liability under these laws is very broad and will generally cover not only the subdivider but also all officers, employees, real estate salespeople, and brokers, who are jointly and severally liable unless they can sustain the burden that they did not know the existence of facts by reason of which the liability is alleged to exist. (*See INTERSTATE LAND SALES.*)

SUBFLOORING Boards or plywood sheets nailed directly to the floor joists serving as a base for the finish flooring. Subflooring is usually made of rough boards, although some houses have concrete subflooring.

SUBJACENT SUPPORT The support which the surface of the earth receives from its underlying strata. (*See LATERAL AND SUBJACENT SUPPORT.*)

SUBJECTIVE VALUE Also called personal value, it is the amount a specific person might pay to possess a property. As opposed to objective value, or what a reasonable person might be expected to pay for the same property.

SUBJECT PROPERTY A reference to the real property under discussion, or the real property under appraisal.

"SUBJECT TO" CLAUSE The clause in a contract for sale setting forth any contingencies or special conditions of purchase and sale, such as an offer made and accepted subject to obtaining financing, approving leases, securing certain zoning, and similar requirements. The seller might sell the property subject to existing leases, certain liens, specific restrictions, or other limitations. If exceptions are not noted in the "subject to" clause, any encumbrance will render the title unmarketable and the seller can be forced to clear the encumbrance. (*See CONTINGENCY, SPECIAL CONDITIONS.*)

"SUBJECT TO" MORTGAGE A grantee taking title to a real property "subject to" mortgage is not personally liable to the mortgagee for payment of the mortgage note. In the event that the grantor/mortgagor defaults in paying the note, the grantee could, however, lose the property, and thus his or her equity, in a foreclosure sale.

For example, if Dudley Bonagel owned a farm valued at $75,000 and had an existing $50,000 mortgage with the Bank of Upson, Bonagel could sell the property to Eugene Green for $75,000 subject to the mortgage. Green's payments would be used to meet the mortgage payments. If Green were to default, however, Green would merely lose the property; the bank would not be able to sue Green for any mortgage deficiency. In response to this, most mortgages now contain acceleration clauses giving the mortgagee the options of whether to declare the debt due when the property is sold, to allow assumption (usually with an assumption fee), or to permit the mortgagor to sell subject to the mortgage. This special acceleration clause is often called an "alienation" or "subject to" clause. The purchaser should request an estoppel or reduction certificate from the lender to ensure that no defaults have occurred; that all installments of the loan and interest have been paid; and that the interest rates, terms, and unpaid balance of the loan are as represented by the seller.

In the usual contract for deed or the wraparound mortgage, the sale is also "subject to the mortgage."

Real estate brokers sometimes buy property subject to existing mortgages when they expect to resell the property shortly and don't want to be named parties on too many mortgages. In such cases, brokers must be especially careful to disclose to the sellers all the ramifications of selling subject to the mortgage. (*See AS-SUMPTION OF MORTGAGE, REDUCTION CERTIFICATE.*)

SUBLEASE   A lease given by a lessee for a *portion* of the lease-hold interest, while the lessee retains some reversionary interest. The sublease may be for all or part of the premises, for the whole term or part of it, as long as the lessor retains some interest in the property. Leases normally contain a clause prohibiting subletting without prior consent of the lessor. The lessee remains directly liable to the lessor for the rent, which is usually paid by the sublessee to the lessee and then from the lessee to the lessor. The sublessee does not have a contractual obligation to pay rent to the original lessor.

If the lessee transfers his or her entire interest in the lease, however, this is called an *assignment of lease*. In an assignment the transferee comes into privity of estate with the lessor, which means that each is liable to the other on the covenants in the original lease that run with the land. (*See ASSIGNMENT OF LEASE, SAND-WICH LEASE.*)

SUBMITTAL NOTICE   Written notice by a broker to a seller with whom he or she has a listing agreement, stating that the broker has shown the seller's property and indicating the prospect's name, address, and the selling price quoted. Such a notice registering a prospect is especially important in open listing situations to avoid procuring cause problems.

SUBORDINATED SALE-LEASEBACK   A financing device used by developers of unimproved land which is either being purchased or is already owned by the developer. In order to raise capital, the developer sells the land to an investor who, in turn, leases it back to the developer. The developer then seeks financing for the improvements and the lessor-investor agrees to subordinate the lease to the mortgage.

SUBORDINATION AGREEMENT   An agreement whereby a holder of a prior superior mortgage agrees to subordinate or give up his or her priority position to an existing or anticipated future lien. Subordination agreements are frequently used in development projects where the seller of the land to be developed takes back a purchase-money mortgage and agrees to subordinate the mortgage or become subject to a construction loan, thereby enabling the developer/purchaser to obtain a first mortgage loan to improve the property. The subordination agreement thus alters the normal rule of giving priority to the mortgage that is recorded first. As a result, the construction mortgage, even though recorded after the existing purchase-money mortgage, becomes the first mortgage.

Many interim lenders refuse to lend any money in the absence of a *subordination clause* in all prior loans or other agreements. Thus, most presale purchase contracts for proposed condominium units have a clause subordinating the apartment purchaser's right to buy the apartment (equitable lien) to any future interim construction mortgage given by the developer. Thus, on default, the lender could wipe out the purchase contract if it wanted to do so.

A developer of leasehold property will often try to get the fee owner to subordinate the fee to a construction loan. In this situation, subordinating is really a misnomer since one cannot subordinate the fee to a leasehold mortgage. What the fee owner is really doing is agreeing to encumber the fee. Sometimes a fee owner will partially subordinate the fee, in which case the landlord/owner is saying to the lender that in the event of foreclosure, no ground rent will be due; the owner is not risking the fee, just the ground rent.

Some states have statutes requiring specific forms and certain disclosures of subordination agreements.

SUBORDINATION CLAUSE A clause in which the holder of a mortgage permits a subsequent mortgage to take priority. Subordination is the act of yielding priority. This clause provides that if a prior mortgage is paid off or renewed, the junior mortgage will continue in its subordinate position and will not automatically become a higher or first mortgage. A subordination clause is usually standard in a junior mortgage since the junior mortgagee gets a higher interest rate and is often not concerned about the inferior mortgage position. A sample subordination clause might read: "This mortgage shall be and remain subordinate to the present first mortgage or any renewal thereof, or in event of its payment, to any new mortgage provided the excess, if any, of said mortgage over the amount of the present first mortgage be applied in reduction of the principal of this mortgage."

A broker should take care to point out to his or her client the implications to all parties of any subordination clauses contained in the mortgage documents and to be sure that the preliminary subordination language in the contract of sale between buyer and seller is definite, certain, and not ambiguous. (*See LEASEHOLD MORTGAGE.*)

SUBPOENA A legal process ordering a witness to appear and give testimony under penalty of law. Anyone refusing to obey the court order can be jailed.

SUBPOENA DUCES TECUM A court order to produce books, records, and other documents.

SUBROGATION The substitution of a third person in place of a creditor to whose rights the third person succeeds in relation to the debt. For instance, a title company that pays a loss within the scope of its policy is subrogated to any claim which the buyer has against the seller for a loss. Insurance policies typically contain subrogation clauses. Whenever a payment is made from a state real estate education, research, and recovery fund to satisfy a judgment, the fund is subrogated to the rights of the injured party.

If the Veterans Administration makes advances to the mortgagee due to the default of the veteran-mortgagor, the VA is subrogated to the rights of the mortgagee against the mortgagor to the extent of these advances.

SUBSCRIBE To place one's signature at the end of a document. Most documents do not need to be subscribed. For example, in a promissory note it is sufficient to write "I, George Smith, hereby promise to pay Tash Lee $100,000." Some statutes, however, require subscribing witnesses, i.e., witnesses who sign at the end of the document after the principal's signature. In many states, it is essential to the validity of a will that there be two disinterested subscribing witnesses. (*See SIGNATURE.*)

SUBSCRIPTION   An agreement to buy a new securities issue.

SUBSEQUENT BONA   One who purchases an interest in real property
FIDE PURCHASER   without notice, actual or constructive, of any
other superior rights in the property. The record-
ing laws are designed to protect subsequent purchasers for value when they deal
with the property without notice of prior unrecorded interests. Thus, a conveyance that is not recorded is void as against any subsequent purchaser (lessee,
mortgagee) who, without having actual notice of the unrecorded conveyance,
records another. Possession of property under an unrecorded deed imparts constructive notice to a subsequent purchaser who records his or her deed. The subsequent purchaser would not then be bona fide and is not protected by the recording
act. Also unprotected would be a subsequent donee or a devisee under a will since
neither is a purchaser. (*See CONSTRUCTIVE NOTICE, RECORDING.*)

SUBSIDY   1. Monetary grants by the government or other
entity made to reduce the cost of one or more of
the housing components—land, labor, management, materials—to lower the cost
of housing to the occupant. (*See SUBSIDY RENT.*)

2. In a buyer's market, a seller or developer might offer some subsidy incentives.
(*See BUYDOWN.*)

SUBSIDY RENT   The difference between the developer's cash out-
of-pocket annual costs allocable to a particular
tenant's space and the tenant's minimum rental. Some shopping center developers subsidize the rent of certain specialized tenants, such as banks or post offices,
in the hopes of attracting more customers to the center complex. In reality, both
the developer and the other tenants are subsidizing the rent since the cash deficit
on that tenant must be made up from other tenants before the developer can make
any profit at all. (*See SHOPPING CENTER.*)

Since the mid-1960s, a number of federally subsidized rent programs have been
administered by the FHA. The Housing and Urban Development Act of 1968 and
subsequent amendments, the 1969 Housing Act and the 1970 Emergency Home
Finance Act, contained a number of programs enabling lower-income families to
rent or purchase shelter under subsidized programs. These laws reflect congressional concern with meeting a growing population's needs for housing, setting up
an urban policy, and encouraging and supporting sound real estate development,
including new community and intercity development.

SUBSTANTIAL   As defined by the Internal Revenue Code, it is any
IMPROVEMENT   improvement made to a building at least three
years after the building was placed in service and,
over a two-year period, the amounts added to the capital account of the building
(not repairs) must be at least 25 percent of the adjusted basis of the building as of
the first day of that period. Under the new Accelerated Cost Recovery System, a
substantial improvement added to a building is treated as a separate building and
the taxpayer can elect any of the specified cost recovery periods, regardless of the
method chosen for the building itself. (*See ACCELERATED COST RECOVERY
SYSTEM.*)

SUBSTITUTION An appraisal principle which states that the maximum value of a property tends to be set by the cost of purchasing an equally desirable and valuable substitute property, assuming that no costly delay is encountered in making the substitution.

SUBSTITUTION OF COLLATERAL Provision in a mortgage to permit the mortgagor to obtain a release of the original collateral by replacement with other collateral acceptable to the mortgagee.

SUBSTITUTION OF ELIGIBILITY See CERTIFICATE OF ELIGIBILITY.

SUBSURFACE EASEMENT An easement permitting the use of below-ground space for such purposes as power lines, sewers, tunnels; also called a *subsurface right*.

SUBURB A town or community located near, and economically linked to, a central city.

SUCCESSORS AND ASSIGNS Words of limitation used in deeds to corporations, referring to those who succeed to or to whom the corporation's rights in the property are transferred. (*See* HEIRS AND ASSIGNS.)

SUFFERANCE See TENANCY AT SUFFERANCE.

SUMMARY POSSESSION A legal process, also called *actual eviction*, used by a landlord to regain possession of the leased premises if the tenant has breached the lease or is holding over after the termination of tenancy. Summary possession proceedings are based on the theory that a landlord-tenant relationship existed and that the tenant is wrongfully holding possession of the demised premises after termination of tenancy by reason of forfeiture or termination under conditions or covenants of lease, including proper notice.

Among the usual specified grounds for summary possession are nonpayment of rent, abandonment, holdover tenancy, violation of governmental or landlord use regulations. Generally, for nonpayment of rent, notice and demand for rent must be given before commencing the summary proceeding. (*See* EVICTION.)

SUMMATION APPROACH The value derived at by adding the estimated value of improvements to the estimated value of the site as of the date of the appraisal. (*See* COST APPROACH.)

SUMMONS A legal notice that a lawsuit has been started against a defendant and that unless the defendant answers the complaint within the specified time (usually 20 days) then a default judgment will be entered against the defendant.

SUM-OF-THE-YEARS'-DIGITS METHOD   A method of depreciation designed to provide the greatest depreciation in the early years of ownership, gradually lessening in the later years. The Economic Recovery Tax Act of 1981 eliminated this method as an acceptable method of accelerated depreciation.

Depreciation by the sum-of-the-years'-digits method is computed as follows:

1. Find the total of the digits for the number of years in the asset's useful life. A handy formula to use, especially with a long-life property, is:

$$\frac{\text{Useful Life x } (1 + \text{useful life})}{2} = \text{Sum}$$

Thus, Useful Life for 50 years

$$\frac{50(1 + 50)}{2} = \frac{2,550}{2} = 1275.$$

2. Each year, the depreciation deduction bears the same proportion to the total depreciation cost as the remaining useful life of the asset bears to the sum total of the digits. The factor for the first year's depreciation would thus be $\frac{50}{1275}$; the second year $\frac{49}{1275}$; the third year $\frac{48}{1275}$; and so on. Multiply the factor times the depreciable cost to find the amount of depreciation. (*See* DEPRECIATION.)

SUMP   A pit or reservoir used for collecting and holding water (or some other liquid) which is subsequently disposed of, usually by a pump.

SUPPLY AND DEMAND   An economic valuation principle which states that market value is determined by the interaction of the forces of supply and demand in the appropriate market as of the date of the appraisal.

SUPPORT DEED   A deed used to convey property which specifies that, as consideration, the buyer will support the grantor for the rest of his or her life. If proper support ceases, the courts will disallow the deed.

SURCHARGE   Additional rent charged to tenants who consume utility services (gas, water, electric) in excess of the amounts allowed in the terms of the lease. Also, an additional charge imposed by the Federal Reserve Bank on member banks who borrow money too frequently.

SURETY   One who becomes a guarantor for another. Surety companies typically execute surety agreements in the form of completion and performance bonds on contractors. If the bonded contractor fails to complete the job, the surety of a completion bond will step in and guaranty its satisfactory completion. If the owner, on the other hand, defaults, the surety under a performance bond would have the same defenses as the contractor and might not be compelled to complete the contract.

The surety does not insure against loss, but rather provides an assurance to the owner that the contractor is financially sound and professionally capable, efficient, and reliable; otherwise the surety company would not bond the contractor. Under the bond, the contractor is the principal, the owner is the obligee and the bonding company is the surety. The bond premium is more of a service charge than a build-up fund against loss. Some states require brokers to post surety bonds with the state real estate commission.

In an assumption of mortgage, the grantee of the mortgagor becomes personally and primarily liable to the mortgagee for any deficiency judgment after a foreclosure sale, with the mortgagor standing in the position of a surety. The lessee under an assigned lease is, in essence, a surety. (*See PERFORMANCE BOND, SUBROGATION.*)

SURFACE WATER   Diffused storm water, as contrasted to a concentrated flow within a stream. In most instances, a person has the right to let water flow through his or her yard and onto the lot below as long as it is in sheet form and is not artificially concentrated by him or her onto the party below. Under the common law, the landowner could take any steps (regrading, paving) to protect his or her land even if this construction had an adverse effect on his or her neighbor's land.

SURMORTGAGE   A type of writ used in some states which specifies that a defaulting mortgagor must show cause why the mortgagee should not foreclose in order to prevent such a procedure.

SURRENDER   A premature conveyance of a possessory estate to a person having a future interest, as when a lessee surrenders his or her leasehold interest to the owner of the reversion interest, the lessor, before the normal expiration of the lease; as opposed to an abandonment of the lease.

If the surrender is accepted by the lessor, then the lessee is no longer liable for rent. However, if the tenant abandons the premises without a formal surrender, the landlord can usually collect either the rent due for the entire period of the rental agreement, or the rent for the time it takes to rerent the dwelling unit at a fair rental *plus* the difference between the fair rental and the rent the tenant had been paying, *plus* a fee for rerenting.

Note that an oral surrender agreement is generally valid only if the unexpired rental period is one year or less. If the balance is for longer than one year, an oral agreement is unenforceable. (*See STATUTE OF FRAUDS.*)

If the parties had recorded the lease, they should execute and record a written surrender agreement to clear the title in the event the lease is terminated prior to its normal expiration.

SURVEY   The process by which boundaries are measured and land areas are determined; the on-site measurement of lot lines, dimensions, and position of houses in a lot including the determination of any existing encroachments, easements, party walls, and compliance with setback requirements.

A broker should check the property at the time of the listing to see if survey stakes are visible. If not, the broker should inform the seller that a survey may have to be ordered at the seller's expense. (Occasionally, a buyer will elect to have the property resurveyed at his or her own expense.) The survey may reveal easements and encroachments that the public records do not reveal.

If there is any discrepancy between the new survey and the original survey, the seller should be required both to remedy the discrepancy and to pay for the cost of the survey.

Lenders frequently require an accurate survey before lending money to finance acquisition of or construction on certain properties. Large construction loans require a "date-down" survey as the construction progresses to ensure that the new building does not encroach beyond the building or lot lines.

In interpreting a survey, compass readings are "bearings," linear measurements are "distances," and directions of a line are "courses."

There are three major types of surveys. The geodetic survey measures the shape and size of the earth. Cadastral surveys are used to determine the boundaries of parcels for defining ownership. Topographic surveys measure the features of the earth's surface (hills, valleys) and the location of roads.

SURVIVAL OF DEED   See MERGER.

SURVIVORSHIP   The right of survivorship is that special feature of a joint tenancy whereby all title, right, and interest of a decedent joint tenant in certain property passes to the surviving joint tenants by operation of law, free from claims of heirs and creditors of the decedent. Upon the death of a joint tenant, it is said that the property is released of his or her interest and the remaining joint tenants share equally in the entire property. Under the Uniform Partnership Act, adopted by many states, the surviving partners have certain rights in property held as tenancy in partnership. Upon the death of a tenant in common, however, all his or her right, title, and interest pass according to his or her will or, if he or she dies without a will, to his or her heirs according to the laws of intestacy. (See JOINT TENANCY, PARTNERSHIP, TENANCY BY THE ENTIRETY, TENANCY IN PARTNERSHIP.)

SUSPENSION   A period of enforced inactivity. The real estate commission has the power, after a hearing, to suspend a real estate license for a violation of the licensing law. During the period of the suspension, the licensee is prohibited from engaging in real estate activities for the purpose of earning a commission or fee. A suspended broker may not employ any salespeople during the period of the suspension; the salespeople must switch their licenses to other firms if they wish to continue to practice.

SWEAT EQUITY   A popular expression for equity created in a property by the performance of work or labor by the purchaser or borrower. It directly increases the value of the property.

SWEETHEART CONTRACT   A slang expression to describe a situation where a developer hires a thinly disguised subsidiary company to manage the developer's project. Most state condominium laws regulate the use of sweetheart contracts and make them subject to cancellation by the homeowner's association.

SWING LOAN   A short-term loan used to enable the purchaser of a new property to purchase that property on the strength of the equity from the property the purchaser is now selling. Thus the loan swings on the equity the borrower has in the existing home. (*See BRIDGE LOAN.*)

SYNDICATION   A descriptive term for a group of two or more people united for the purpose of making and operating an investment. A syndication may operate in the form of a REIT, corporation, general partnership, limited partnership or even as tenancy in common. Some of the parties take an active role in the creation and management of the investment, while others assume a passive role, usually limited to supplying capital. A syndication is not a form of legal ownership, but is rather a term used to describe multiple ownership of an investment. It is essentially a combination of money and management and is frequently treated as a real estate security.

Most real estate syndications are organized as limited partnerships with the syndicator acting as general partner and the investors being limited partners. This enables the partnership to act as a conduit to pass through high depreciation deductions directly to the individual investors and thus avoid the double taxation aspects of corporate ownership. Syndication frequently offers the small investor a chance to participate in a real estate investment that will be managed by experienced persons. The 1976 Tax Act provides that amounts paid to organize a partnership or promote the sale of interests are not deductible. (*See LIMITED PART-NERSHIP.*)

TACKING 1. Adding or combining successive periods of continuous occupation of real property by adverse possessors, thus enabling one not in possession for the entire required statutory period to establish a claim of adverse possession. In order to tack one person's possession to that of another, each of the possessions must be continuous and uninterrupted, and the parties must have been successors in interest, such as ancestor and heir, landlord and tenant, or seller and buyer. (*See ADVERSE POSSESSION.*)

2. A carryover of holding periods for tax purposes. For example, in a tax-free exchange or a replacement of principal residences, the holding period of a new replacement property or principal residence includes the holding period of the formerly held property. (*See RESIDENCE.*)

TAKE DOWN To borrow or draw against funds which were committed by a lender earlier, as in a construction loan. (*See PROGRESS PAYMENTS.*)

TAKEOUT FINANCING Long-term permanent financing. In the usual large construction project, the developer obtains two types of financing. The first is the interim loan, a short-term loan to cover construction costs. Before lending any money, however, the interim lender normally requires a commitment by a permanent lender to agree to "take out" the interim lender in which the lender pays off the construction loan and leaves the developer with a permanent long-term loan when the building has been completed. Such a commitment, called a takeout commitment or a takeout letter, typically is the second phase of financing a development. (*See END LOAN, INTERIM FINANCING, PERMANENT FINANCING, STANDBY LOAN.*)

TANDEM PLAN A mortgage assistance program whereby the Federal National Mortgage Association (Fannie Mae) and the Government National Mortgage Association (Ginnie Mae) can join forces in times of tight money and high discount rates. Basically, the tandem plan provides that Fannie Mae can purchase qualified high-risk, low-yield (usually FHA or VA) mortgage loans at full, current market rates, with Ginnie Mae absorbing the difference between their low yield and current market rates. The mortgages are then accumulated and periodically sold at auction either as securities or as whole mortgages. (*See FEDERAL NATIONAL MORTGAGE ASSOCIATION, GOVERNMENT NATIONAL MORTGAGE ASSOCIATION.*)

TAX AND LIEN SEARCH   A title search issued to cover property registered in the Torrens system. Since the Torrens certificate of title does not reflect certain encumbrances such as real property taxes, city and county assessments, and federal tax liens or bankruptcies, the tax and lien search is used to provide this information. The report issued by a title insurance company is sometimes called a lien letter. (*See TORRENS SYSTEM.*)

TAX BASE   1. Refers to the assessed valuation of all real property within an area subject to taxes. This would exclude exempt church- or government-owned property. 2. For income tax purposes, the tax base is the net taxable income.

TAX BRACKET   The rate at which a taxpayer pays tax on income above a set amount. Individual tax rates are structured on a graduated basis. A taxpayer who pays a tax of 50 percent of his or her income on amounts in excess of a specified amount is said to be in the "50-percent tax bracket" because each dollar of income received over the specified amount is taxed at a rate of at least 50 percent (That is, the last dollar of taxable income earned is taxed at a 50 percent rate). The maximum tax bracket is 50 percent.

TAX CLEARANCE   A form required by the state to be filed by a decedent's estate when real property is owned in that state. The form is used to verify that there are no outstanding inheritance tax liens on the property.

TAX DEED   The instrument used to convey legal title to property which is sold by a governmental unit for nonpayment of taxes. The property may be sold at public auction after proper notice if the tax lien has remained unpaid for a set period of time. The defaulting taxpayer usually has a period after the tax sale in which to redeem the property by paying the purchase price and costs plus interest. The tax deed is presumptive evidence of the propriety and validity of the sale, and must generally be recorded. (*See REDEMPTION PERIOD, TAX LIEN.*)

TAX-DEFERRED EXCHANGE   Under Section 1031 of the Internal Revenue Code, some or all of the realized gain from the exchange of one property for another may not have to be immediately recognized for tax purposes. It is not, however, a tax-free transaction; the payment of taxes is simply deferred to a later transfer.

Both the property received and the property given in exchange must be held for productive use in trade or business or for investment (not a principal residence) and both properties must be "of a like kind." (*See DELAYED EXCHANGE, EXCHANGE, LIKE-KIND PROPERTY.*)

TAX LIEN   A statutory lien imposed against real property for nonpayment of taxes. Note that a tax lien remains on the property until the taxes are paid even if the real estate is conveyed to another person. There are federal tax liens and state tax liens. A federal tax lien results from a failure to pay any Internal Revenue tax, including income tax, estate tax, and payroll tax. A federal tax lien is a general lien on all property and rights to property of the person liable, but its priority depends upon the number of liens previously recorded when notice is recorded.

The state tax lien for unpaid real property taxes generally has priority over all other liens on the property, regardless of whether such liens were recorded prior to the recording of the state tax lien.

Owners of out-of-state properties should be careful about keeping current on paying real property taxes. Absentee owners may find that through inattention they have lost title to their property sold at a tax sale. (See FEDERAL TAX LIEN, INHERITANCE TAX, LIEN, TAX DEED.)

TAX MAP A map drawn to scale showing the location of real property, tax keys, size, shape and dimensions, and so on, for convenience of identification, valuation, and assessment. These maps are usually kept in tax map books, prepared and held by local tax departments.

TAX PARTICIPATION CLAUSE A clause in a commercial lease that requires the tenant to pay a pro rata share of any increases in taxes or assessments above an established base year.

TAX PREFERENCE **Assets placed in service prior to 1981.** As a reaction to the growing use of tax shelters, Congress in 1969 and 1976 established a list of items referred to as tax preferences. Initially there was a minimum tax rate of 10 percent over and above the normal tax rate on these tax preference items. In 1976 this was increased to a 15 percent tax. Individuals, estates, and trusts may be subjected to two minimum taxes on certain tax preference items. One minimum tax is known as "add-on minimum tax" and the other is called the "alternate minimum tax." This later tax, however, applies only to the extent that it exceeds the sum of the taxpayer's income tax and the add-on minimum tax (if any).

Individuals, estates, and trusts had to take the following tax preference items into account in determining their add-on minimum tax:

1. Accelerated depreciation on real property. Accelerated depreciation is the amount allowable for the year that is in excess of depreciation that could have been claimed had the straight-line method of depreciation been used for each tax year. (See ACCELERATED DEPRECIATION.) A separate computation of the excess depreciation must be made for each property.

2. Accelerated depreciation on leased personal property.

3. To the extent that rapid amortization (60 months) of certain types of investment properties exceed the depreciation that would otherwise be allowable.

Assets placed in service in 1981 or later. The Economic Recovery Act of 1981 included as a new item in the list of tax preference items the excess of the Accelerated Cost Recovery System (depreciation) deduction for each leased recovery property (other than 15-year real property) over the straight-line depreciation deduction that would have been allowable if it were computed by disregarding salvage value and by using a half-year convention and a recovery period in accord with the following table.

In the case of: The recovery period is:
3-year property .... 5 years
5-year property .... 8 years
10-year property .... 15 years
15-year property .... 22 years

The above excess of the Accelerated Cost Recovery System (ACRS) deduction over the straight-line depreciation is not an item of tax preference for corporations other than an electing tax-option corporation and a personal holding company. The tax preference for the excess of accelerated depreciation over straight-line depreciation for a net lease of personal property continues to apply to property placed in service before 1981. (See *ACCELERATED COST RECOVERY SYSTEM.*)

For 15-year recovery property that is real property, a new item of tax preference is created for the excess of the ACRS deduction over the amount of a deduction that would have been allowed if the deduction had been determined disregarding salvage value and using the straight-line method over a 15-year recovery period. This amount is a tax preference item for all taxpayers. Therefore, real property (improvement minus land value) can be depreciated over a 15-year straight-line depreciation schedule (6.67 percent per year) with no recapture liability. This schedule is audit proof under the 1981 Tax Act. The tax preference for accelerated depreciation on real property continues to apply to property placed in service before 1981. The minimum tax changes apply to property placed in service after 1980 in tax years ending after 1980.

For 1981, minimum tax preferences continue to reduce the amount of personal service income subject to the 50 percent maximum tax. However, the effect of tax preference items on the maximum tax is eliminated for tax years beginning in 1982, when the maximum tax rate on all income becomes 50 percent.

High-income taxpayers utilizing real estate for tax shelters should consult competent tax counsel in considering any of the above-mentioned tax preference items.

TAX RATE   The rate which is applied to the assessed value of a property to arrive at the amount of annual property tax. The tax rate is established according to assessed valuation which varies depending on land use.(See *MILL, NOTICE OF ASSESSMENT, PROPERTY TAX.*)

TAX ROLL   Public records showing all taxable property, tax amounts, assessed valuations, and millage rates.

TAX SALE   The sale of real property by a governmental unit to satisfy unpaid real property tax liens. There is frequently a statutory period of redemption following the tax sale. (See *TAX DEED.*)

TAX SEARCH   A specific part of a title search which determines if there are any unpaid taxes or special assessments that may be a lien against the property under search.

TAX SHELTER   A phrase often used to describe some of the tax advantages of real estate or other investment, such as deductions for cost recovery (depreciation), interest, taxes and postpone-

ment or even elimination of certain taxes. The tax shelter not only may offset the
investor's tax liability relevant to the real estate investment but also may reduce
the investor's other ordinary income, which reduces the investor's overall tax
liability.

It should be noted that because of recent changes in the tax laws many of the tax
benefits gained through accelerated cost recovery may be offset by the recapture of
part or all of that cost recovery depreciation, which is treated as ordinary income
upon the profitable disposition of the property. Thus the primary concern in investing in real estate should be the economic soundness of the property and not
the tax shelter aspects. (See RECAPTURE OF DEPRECIATION, TAX PREFER-
ENCE.)

TAX STOP CLAUSE   A clause in a lease providing that the lessee will
pay any increases in taxes over a base or initial
year's taxes; also referred to as a tax-escalation clause. The lease should state that
this added amount will be deemed additional rent.

TENANCY AT   A tenancy that exists when a tenant wrongfully
SUFFERANCE   holds over after the expiration of a lease without
the landlord's consent, as where the tenant fails to
surrender possession after termination of the lease. A tenancy at sufferance is the
lowest estate in real estate, and no notice of termination may be required from the
landlord to evict the tenant. This kind of tenancy is designed to protect the tenant
from being classified as a trespasser on one hand, and prevent his or her acquisition
of title by adverse possession on the other hand. The relationship exists not by
express consent of the landlord but by implication. The tenant has only naked
possession and no estate which the tenant can transfer.

A tenancy at sufferance differs from a tenancy at will in that, under the tenancy at
sufferance the landlord has not consented to the continuation of the tenant's possession. Even though the tenant at sufferance may be acting wrongfully, he or she
is not considered a trespasser because the tenant originally entered upon the property with the landlord's consent. Upon the consent of the landlord, a tenancy for
years for the same term (usually not for more than one year due to the tenancy at
sufferance) can be converted into a tenancy at will, a periodic tenancy, or a tenancy for years for the same term (usually not for more than one year due to the
Statute of Frauds). (See HOLDOVER TENANT, SUMMARY POSSESSION.)

TENANCY AT WILL   A tenancy in which a person holds or occupies
real estate with the permission of the owner, for a
term of unspecified or uncertain duration; i.e. there is no fixed term to the tenancy.

A tenancy at will could arise during a time when the parties are negotiating a lease
or purchase of the property, or under a void oral lease or contract of sale. The
reason there is no periodic tenancy is due to the absence of an express agreement
as to the nature and amount of rent. The main features of the tenancy are its
uncertainty of duration and its continuing permissive status. The tenancy is not
assignable though it is usually permissible for the tenant to sublet the premises; an
attempted assignment will typically terminate the tenancy. Unlike a tenancy at
sufferance, all the duties and obligations of a landlord-tenant relationship exist in
a tenancy at will, and notice of termination is required by either party.

In common law, either party could terminate at any time. Most modern statutes
now require a specific notice period, such as 30 days. Unlike other leasehold

estates, a tenancy at will is also terminated by the death of either landlord or tenant, or by a sale of the property (since the sale results in conveyance of the reversion).

TENANCY BY **THE ENTIRETY** **(ENTIRETIES)**	A special joint tenancy between a lawfully married husband and wife, which places all title to property (real or personal) into the marital unit, with both spouses having an equal, undivided

interest in the whole property. In essence, each spouse owns the *entire* estate, i.e. each spouse does not own a fractional share, rather the property ownership is an indivisible entirety. Upon the death of one spouse, the survivor succeeds to the entire property to the exclusion of heirs and creditors of the deceased spouse and without the need for probate. This type of tenancy is frequently used in the ownership of a residence since it guarantees that the surviving spouse will continue to have a home regardless of whether a will is drawn or the property is fraudulently sold. Besides being limited to two specific persons, a tenancy by the entirety differs from a joint tenancy in that neither spouse can convey his or her interest or force a partition during the lifetime of the other, without the consent of the other spouse.

The tenancy by the entirety method of property ownership exists in less than one-third of the United States. It was originally based on the common law theory that the husband and wife were one person, but this theory has been abandoned under modern law which gives women rights in property separate from their husbands.

The creditor of one spouse cannot force a sale of one-half of the property held as tenants by the entirety to satisfy a judgment, as could a creditor of one spouse if title were held in joint tenancy. A creditor of *both* spouses, however, could take legal action in an appropriate case to force a sale of the property to satisfy a *joint* obligation, a reason many lenders seek both spouses' signatures on the mortgage document even though only one spouse signs the note. If there is a judgment outstanding against one of the spouses, it would be difficult for both spouses to obtain a mortgage loan against the property. This is because the lender would fear that the judgment debtor might be the surviving spouse, in which case the judgment creditor would take precedence over the mortgage.

Both spouses can also voluntarily convert the tenancy into a tenancy in common or a joint tenancy.

The tenancy by the entirety may be severed only by mutual agreement, divorce, or joint conveyance; it may not be severed by any attempt of one spouse to transfer his or her interest. While an attempted unilateral transfer is ineffective, the transferor may still be liable to the transferee for money damages for breach of contract. Where divorce severs the tenancy by entirety, the parties become tenants in common (even where the entire purchase price was paid by one party). Upon the death of a spouse, the survivor should record an "affadavit of surviving tenant by the entirety" reflecting the fact of death. This is good title practice and will facilitate any future transfer of title to the property.

In some states, one spouse who owns property can reconvey that property to him or herself and the spouse as tenants by the entirety, without violating the common law rule that the joint interests must be created at one and the same time and by the same instrument. Under the Economic Recovery Tax Act, where property is jointly held by husband and wife with rights of survivorship (this includes tenancy by the entirety), the property will be treated as 50 percent belonging to each spouse for estate tax purposes.

The language creating the tenancy by the entirety should provide, in effect, that the property is conveyed "to John Smith and Mary Smith as tenants by the entirety and with the right of survivorship." However, in some states, a conveyance to husband and wife, without anything else stated further, will automatically create a tenancy by the entirety, while in other states it may create a tenancy in common. (See *GIFT TAX, JOINT TENANCY, PROPERTY TAX, SURVIVORSHIP.*)

TENANCY FOR LIFE

A freehold estate of uncertain duration, which is not an estate of inheritance; a life estate. (See *LIFE ESTATE.*)

TENANCY FOR YEARS

A less-than-freehold estate in which the property is leased for a definite, fixed period of time, be it for 60 days, any fraction of a year, a year, or ten years. In most states such a tenancy can be created only by express agreement, which should be written if the tenancy is longer than one year. The tenancy for years must have a definite term, beginning and ending on dates specified in the lease. In absence of a statute or agreement, the tenancy is considered personal property and passes to the tenant's heirs upon his or her death. The tenancy ends on the last day of the term of the lease without the necessity for the parties giving notice of termination. If the tenant continues in possession, he or she is a holdover tenant or a tenant in sufferance. Most ground leases and commercial leases are tenancies for years. (See *LEASEHOLD.*)

TENANCY IN COMMON

A form of concurrent ownership of property between two or more persons, in which each has an undivided interest in the whole property. This form is frequently found when the parties acquire title by descent or by will. Each cotenant is entitled to the undivided possession of the property, according to his or her proportionate share and subject to the rights of possession of the other tenants. No cotenant can exclude another cotenant, or claim ownership of a specific portion of the property. Each cotenant holds an estate in land by separate and distinct titles, but with unity of possession. Their interests may be equal—as in a joint tenancy—or unequal. Where the conveyance document does not specify the extent of interest of each cotenant, there is a rebuttable presumption that the shares are equal. Unlike a joint tenancy, there is no right of survivorship in a tenancy in common. Therefore when one of the cotenants dies, the interest passes to his or her heirs or beneficiaries and not to the surviving tenants in common. The property interest of a tenant in common is thus subject to probate. Also, unlike joint tenancy, dower rights may exist in property held in common.

Any tenant in common can sell his or her interest in the property without the consent of the cotenants, but no cotenant can attempt to transfer the entire property without the consent of all the cotenants. If one of the common owners wishes to sell the entire property and the other cotenants do not, the co-owner can bring an action for partition and seek to have the property divided up in kind or sold at auction with each owner paid his or her share of the proceeds.

There is a legally imposed relationship of trust and confidence among cotenants. Each cotenant has the right to possess all portions of the property and to retain profits from his or her own use of the property, though he or she must share net rents received from third parties. No tenant in common can be charged for use of the land or may charge rent for other cotenants' use of the land. If one of the cotenants pays taxes or assessments due above his or her share, then the cotenant generally has a lien on the interest of each cotenant for the pro rata share.

A potential problem in a long-term contract for deed where the buyers take title as tenants in common is the confusion which arises when one of the cotenants dies before the property has been finally conveyed. If one of the cotenant-buyers has died during the term of the contract for deed, the seller should be cautious and check with the court to determine the rightful heirs of the deceased cotenant to whom the property should be deeded. If one of the cotenant sellers dies, care should likewise be taken in making the money payments under the contract to the appropriate party.

Unless the intention to create a different form of tenancy is manifestly clear, a conveyance to two or more persons is usually deemed to create a tenancy in common. The tenancy in common is appropriately named since it is the *most common* form of co-ownership which will result unless another intent is clearly specified.

As a general rule, a tenant in common's interest is not considered acceptable security by a lender, since the mortgagee has the additional expense in a foreclosure action of forcing a partition proceeding in order to recover on its security interest.

As with joint tenancy, if one cotenant in good faith makes improvements to the real property without the permission of the other, he or she should be compensated for the improvement in a partition action. The standard used is either the percentage of improvement cost attributable to the other cotenant, or the proportionate share of the increased value of the property.

One problem with tenancy in common is the element of uncertainty connected with the fact that the interest of a deceased cotenant is subject to probate. For example, suppose Smith, Jones, and Wallashinski hold lakefront property as an investment. They are tenants in common. Smith, a single person, dies intestate. He had 12 brothers and sisters and both parents living. One sister dies shortly thereafter leaving a husband and six children. In order to sell the property to a developer, the other tenants in common may have to get the signatures of all Smith's brothers and sisters, parents, and guardian for the minors to release every possible interest. This problem could have been avoided by taking title in partnership form or in a trust.

Every tenant in common assumes the risk that his or her interest in the property will be imperiled by the failure of cotenants to pay their share of taxes, debt service, and other carrying charges. In addition, there is a risk of bankruptcy or involuntary sale or partition of the property to enforce a judgment lien or income tax lien against the interest of one cotenant in the property.

Sample language in a deed creating a tenancy in common would be ". . .to John Smith, single, an undivided one-quarter interest and to Pat Specht, unmarried, an undivided three-quarters interest as tenants in common in the following described property. . . ." (*See COTENANCY, GRANTEE, JOINT TENANCY, OWELTY, PARTITION, PROPERTY TAX, TAX LIEN, UNDIVIDED INTEREST.*)

TENANCY IN PARTNERSHIP A partnership is an association of two or more persons to carry on a business as co-owners and to share in the profits and losses. Generally, a partnership is not a legal entity and from a technical, common law standpoint, a partnership cannot own real estate. The title must be vested in the partners as individuals, not in the firm. Most states have adopted the Uniform Partnership Act under which partnership realty may now be held in the partnership name.

The features of a tenancy in partnership as they affect each partner are generally:

1. that a partner has an equal interest in the property and an equal right of possession of the property, but only for partnership purposes

2. that partner's right is not assignable, except in connection with the assignment of the rights of all partners; thus a purchaser can acquire only the whole title

3. that a partner's right is not subject to attachment or execution except on a claim against the partnership itself, and there can be no homestead exemption claim with respect thereto. The entire property, however, can be sold on execution sale to satisfy a partnership creditor. The partner's interest cannot be seized or sold separately by his or her personal creditor, but a partner's share of the profits may be obtained by a personal creditor by an action called a "charging order."

4. that upon the death of a partner, his or her rights in the partnership real estate vest in the surviving partner(s), though the decedent's estate is reimbursed for the value of his or her interest. The partner's interest in the partnership firm is all that passes to the administrator as personal property on his or her death intestate.

   The heirs have a right in the partnership but not in the specific partnership property. If there are no surviving partners, his or her rights in the property vest in a legal representative. The vesting in the surviving partner or partners and in the legal representative of the last surviving partner conveys no greater right on them than to possess the partnership property for a partnership purpose.

5. that a partner's right to specific partnership property is not subject to dower, curtesy, or family allowances.

6. that because this property is owned by the partnership, no tax exemption applicable to an individual partner will be available to the partnership or its property.

7. that the partnership's property and its income or losses is subject to partnership income tax treatment. (*See PARTNERSHIP.*)

TENANCY IN SEVERALTY

Ownership of property vested in one person alone, rather than held jointly with another; also called several tenancy or sole tenancy. The owner's title is thus severed from any other person. When the sole owner dies, the property is probated and passes to his or her heirs or devisees. A corporation, state, or county often holds title and property in severalty.

TENANT

In general, one who exclusively holds or possesses property, such as a life tenant or a tenant for years; commonly used to refer to a lessee under a lease. A tenant's occupancy, although exclusive, is always subordinate to the rights of the owner. Tenant refers to an occupant, not necessarily a renter.

TENANT CONTRIBUTIONS

All costs for which the tenant is responsible over and above the contract rent specified in the lease. Area maintenance would be an example.

TENANT MIX The selection and location of retail tenants so as to maximize the income to the lessor and stimulate business in general. Stores in a shopping center complex should be situated so that pedestrian traffic stimulated by one business benefits the others, and yet competition does not become a detriment.

TENANT UNION A local organization of residential tenants working for their common interests and rights.

TENDER An unconditional offer by one of the parties to a contract to perform his or her part of the bargain. For example, when a seller brings an action seeking enforcement under a sales contract of the buyer's obligation to pay the purchase price, the seller must first make a tender of the deed. In some states this is done by placing it into escrow. This is required because the buyer's duty to pay is a concurrent condition of the seller's duty to tender the deed. Likewise, a tender of performance by the buyer, for example, by depositing the purchase money into escrow, places the seller in default if he or she refuses to accept it and deliver a deed.

Where money is owed, a tender of the amount owed discharges any lien which is security for the debts, releases sureties, and stops debts from accruing interest.

When parties to a contract clearly show an intent not to perform, that is, where there is an anticipatory repudiation or where the seller has already sold the property to a third party, then no tender is necessary since it would be a useless act. The parties may seek appropriate remedies, including recovery of damages for breach of performance. The seller should not try to resell the property until he or she can establish that a valid tender has been made or that the other party has repudiated the contract. (See *BACKUP OFFER, BILATERAL CONTRACT.*)

TENEMENT A common law real estate term describing those real property rights of a permanent nature which relate to the land and pass with a conveyance of the land, such as buildings and improvements; those things affixed to the land. Tenements include not only land but corporeal and incorporeal rights in real property. In more modern usage, the term refers to apartment buildings, especially the more run-down, old buildings in urban areas. (See *HEREDITAMENT.*)

TENURE A common law term indicating the manner in which land is held, such as a fee simple or leasehold. The manner or system of holding lands or tenements in subordination to some superior right, which in feudal times was the primary characteristic of real property ownership.

TERM 1. A length of time. For example, a mortgage term is the length of time (as set forth in the mortgage) in which the mortgage loan must be paid off. A lease term is the length of time (as set forth in the lease) in which the tenant can rightfully occupy the premises—for example, 60 days, 10 years, life. An option term is the time stipulated in the option agreement for the optionee to exercise his or her rights under the agreement. 2. A provision or condition in a contract.

TERMINATION OF   The cancellation of a broker-principal employ-
LISTING   ment contract. If a listing contains no specific termination date, it is terminated after a reasonable
time. The seller can revoke this type of listing at any time prior to the broker's
producing a ready, willing, and able buyer on the listing terms. If, however, the
listing does contain a specific termination date (usually required of all exclusive
listings), the seller cannot revoke the listing prior to said date without liability for
the broker's expenses (advertising the property, and so on) incurred in marketing
the property. Courts do not look favorably upon provisions for automatic extension of the listing period; that is, "thirty days and continuing thereafter indefinitely until written cancellation is given."

A listing is basically an agency contract and can be terminated under general
agency and contract principles as follows:

1. death or insanity of principal or agent

2. expiration of listing period

3. mutual agreement

4. sufficient written notice

5. completion of performance under the agreement; thus, under an open listing
   the sale by one broker would terminate the agency for all brokers.

6. condemnation or destruction of the subject property

7. bankruptcy of either party

8. abandonment of the agency by the broker (broker might be liable for damages)

9. revocation by the principal (broker may recover damages)

10. a change in law which prohibits the current use of the property
    (See EXTENDER CLAUSE, LISTING.)

TERMINATION   A document recorded to cancel a financing state-
STATEMENT   ment filed under the provisions of the Uniform
Commercial Code.

TERMITE   A visible check of the premises for the presence of
INSPECTION   termites, usually performed by a licensed exter-
minator. Because termite infestation is so com-
mon in many areas, buyers may insert a special condition in the sales contract to
require the seller to furnish a satisfactory termite inspection report, also called a
pest control report, or clearance letter, from a reputable firm chosen by or approved by the buyer, showing the improvements to be free and clear of any live,
visible infestation. VA, FHA, and FmHA all require a termite inspection be made
as a condition to their loan transactions.

The report usually carries a guarantee of 30 days; thus, the seller's broker normally does not order the report until 10 days before closing so the guarantee will
still be in effect when the buyer takes possession. If the seller were required to

warrant the "premises" (rather than just the improvements) to be free and clear, he or she could run into the potential problem of having to go to enormous expense to correct infestation in items on the property such as the grounds and trees. The parties should also address the problem of what responsibility, if any, the seller has to correct existing termite damage to the structure.

The Internal Revenue Service takes the position that termite damage does not ordinarily qualify as a casualty loss.

TERMITE SHIELD   A metal sheet laid into the exterior walls of a house near ground level, usually under the sill, to prevent termites from entering the house. Termite shields should be affixed to all exterior wood in the house and around pipes entering the building. Shields are generally constructed with an overhanging lip to allow for water run off.

TERRE TENANT   One who has actual possession of the land.

TESTATOR   A person who makes a last will and testament; one who dies leaving a will and is said to have died testate. If the testator leaves real property to certain people (devisees), they take title to the property *subject to* any liens in favor of the creditors of the estate. Thus, if the testator dies leaving behind many debts, it is possible that, after exhausting all personal property in the estate, it might be necessary for the personal representative to sell the real property and give the devisees the balance of the proceeds, if any, after satisfying the debts. (*See PROBATE, WILL.*)

TESTIMONIUM CLAUSE   A clause found in a legal document beginning "In Witness Whereof. . ." and then citing the act and date of execution of the document.

THIN CAPITALIZATION   Excessively high ratio of debt to equity in a corporation's capital structure resulting in Internal Revenue Service's treatment of at least some of the debt capitalization as equity and the consequent loss of the tax benefits of debt.

THIRD PARTY   A person who is not party to a contract but who may be affected by it; one who is not a principal to the transaction such as the broker or escrow agent.

TIDEWATER LAND   Land beneath the ocean from low tide mark to a state's outer territorial limits.

TIE-IN CONTRACT   A contract in which one transaction is dependent on another. For example, a developer might agree to sell a choice property only if the buyer also agrees to buy a less desirable property from the developer or agrees to list the property for sale with the developer's brokerage company. Such tie-in arrangements may violate laws and state and federal antitrust regulations. (*See ANTITRUST.*)

TIER   A row of townships extending east and west. (*See GOVERNMENT SURVEY METHOD.*)

TIGHT MONEY MARKET   An economic situation in which the supply of money is limited and the demand for money is high, as evidenced by high interest rates.

"TIME IS OF THE ESSENCE"   The clause in a contract which emphasizes that punctual performance is an essential requirement of the contract. Thus, if any party to the instrument does not perform within the specified time period (the "drop-dead" date), that party is in default provided the nondefaulting party has made a valid tender of performance. If no tender is made, then the clause may be waived. The clause may also be waived by the subsequent acts of the parties such as accepting tardy payments or signing escrow instructions that allow for extensions of time in which to perform.

In equity, time is not regarded as of the essence to a contract unless there appears a clear intention to make it so. The concept cuts both ways—the purchaser is expected to make prompt payments, while the seller must also take timely steps to enforce the seller's rights if the purchaser defaults. Time is of the essence in option contracts; that is, the option is no longer valid if not exercised by the option date. (*See TENDER, WAIVER.*)

TIME-PRICE DIFFERENTIAL   The difference between a property's purchase price and the higher total price the same property would cost if purchased on an installment basis (including finance charges). Under the truth-in-lending laws, a lender must disclose the time-price differential as well as all finance charges of any kind in an installment contract.

TIMESHARE OWNERSHIP PLAN (TSO)   A form of timesharing in which a number of individuals hold legal title to a particular condominium unit or other real estate as tenants in common, entitling them to the use of the property for a specified time each year. There is usually a "separate use agreement" among the tenants in common which details the rights and obligations of each of the owners including any privileges to exchange units in other resort areas.

Under the "interval ownership" concept, ownership is for a specified number of years, after which time all timeshare owners become tenants in common and are free to enter into a new interval agreement, sublet the property, or sell it.

TIMESHARING   A modern approach to communal ownership and use of real estate which permits multiple purchasers to buy undivided interests in real property (usually in a resort condominium or hotel) with a right to use the facility for a fixed or variable time period. Under timesharing forms of ownership, potential purchasers of property buy fixed or floating time periods for use of a specific apartment within a project. Common expenses are prorated among the owners. For example, under one approach twelve individuals could own equal, undivided interests in one vacation home condominium unit and agree that each individual would be entitled to use the premises for one month (fixed or floating) out of each year. Sometimes, timesharing programs have a reservation system or a rotation-of-unit system in which the tenant in common can occupy his or her unit at different times of the year in different years. Other timesharing programs sell specific time periods of each year. Some timesharing programs are based on the purchase or lease of the property ("ownership" programs); others are based on mere licenses to use the property ("right-to-use" or license contracts). (*See RENTAL POOL.*)

In recent years, legislatures have begun to regulate the timesharing industry by requiring special disclosure reports, escrow accounts, licensing of agents, review of promotional material, and complete disclosure of the details of any exchange program in which time share units can be exchanged for other properties. Among the tough questions have been the procedures for billing real property taxes, tax delinquencies, and the assessment valuation problem, i.e. whether the building is valued at the same figure as a similar building that is not timeshare, or at an amount determined by the cost and number of timeshare interests.

The Federal Home Loan Bank Board has granted the authority to federally chartered savings and loan associations and mutual savings banks to provide financing to timesharing purchasers, including both ownership and right-to-use timesharing arrangements.

The Uniform Real Estate Timeshare Act covers all aspects of timesharing and has already been adopted in several states.

TIME VALUE OF MONEY An economic principle that the worth of a dollar received today is greater than the worth of a dollar received in the future.

TIPPING POINT Refers to the point at which sufficient numbers of minorities have moved into a community so that large numbers of majority groups can be expected to move out leaving the project or area a segregated one.

TITLE The right to or ownership of land. Also, the evidence of the right to an estate. Title to property encompasses all that bundle of rights an owner possesses; the totality of rights and property possessed by a person. Title may be held individually, jointly, in trust, or in corporate or partnership form. Title is a common term used to denote the facts which, if proved, would enable a person to recover or retain possession of something.

If one owns real property outright, he or she is said to have title to it. Titles are either original or derivative. Original title can be vested only in the state. This means a title gained through discovery, occupancy, conquest, or cession to the state. All other titles are derivative and these are vested in individuals. Such titles may be divided into titles by descent (no will) and titles by purchase (deed, land contract, will).

TITLE INSURANCE A comprehensive indemnity contract under which a title insurance company warrants to make good a loss arising through defects in title to real estate or any liens or encumbrances thereon. Unlike other types of insurance which protect a policyholder against loss from some *future* occurrence (such as a fire or auto accident), title insurance, in effect, protects a policyholder against loss from some occurrence *that has already happened*, such as a forged deed somewhere in the chain of title.

Needless to say, a title company will not insure a bad title any more than a fire insurance company would insure a burning building. However, if upon investigation of the public records and all other material facts, the title company feels that it has an insurable title, it will issue a policy. Generally, a title insurance policy will protect the insured against losses arising from such title defects ("hidden risks") as:

1. forged documents, such as deeds, releases of dower, mortgages

2. undisclosed heirs; lack of capacity (minors)

3. mistaken legal interpretation of wills

4. misfiled documents, unauthorized acknowledgments

5. confusion arising from similarity of names

6. incorrectly given marital status; mental incompetence

In addition, and most important, the title company will also agree to defend the policyholder's title in court against any lawsuits which may arise from defects covered in the policy.

A title insurance policy generally consists of three sections:

1. the agreement to insure the title and indemnify against loss

2. a description of the estate and property being insured

3. a list of conditions of and exclusions to coverage

These uninsured exclusions generally include such title defects as:

1. rights of parties in possession, not shown in the public records, including unrecorded easements

2. any state of facts that an accurate survey would reveal (e.g. encroachments)

3. taxes and assessments not yet due or payable

4. zoning and governmental restrictions

5. unpatented mining claims

6. certain water rights

Title indemnity is made as of a specific date. Except with certain policies, a one-time premium is paid, and coverage continues until the property is conveyed to a new owner, (including a conveyance to an insured's wholly owned corporation). It does not run with the land. Coverage is thus limited to the tenure of the named insured, and certain of the insured's successors by operation of law. Most policies provide, however, that the coverage does not terminate "so long as an insured retains an estate or interest in the land, or owns an indebtedness secured by a purchase money mortgage given by a purchaser from such insured, or so long as such insured shall have liability by reason of covenants of warranty made by such insured in any transfer of conveyance of such estate or interest. . . ."

There are two major types of title insurance, the owner's policy and the mortgagee's or lender's policy. An owner's policy is issued for the benefit of the owner, the owner's heirs and devisees, or, in the case of a corporation, its successors by dissolution, merger, or consolidation; but the policy is not assignable. For an added premium, title companies will issue an extended coverage owner's policy for certain properties to cover possible title defects excluded from standard coverage. Such title defects may include the rights of parties in possession, questions of survey, and unrecorded liens.

A *lender's policy* is issued for the benefit of a mortgage lender and any future holder of the loan. It protects the lender against the same defects as an owner under an owner's policy, but the insurer's liability is limited to the mortgage loan balance as of the date of the claim. In other words, liability under a lender's policy reduces with each mortgage payment, and is voided when the loan is completely paid off and released. Because of this reduced liability, a lender's policy usually costs less than an owner's policy. Under a mortgagee policy, the loss payable is automatically transferred to the holder of the mortgage. Upon foreclosure and purchase by the mortgagee, the policy automatically becomes an owner's policy, insuring the mortgagee against loss or damage arising out of matters existing prior to the effective date of the policy. In addition to these policies, title companies also issue policies to cover the leasehold interests of a lessee, a lender under a leasehold mortgage, or a vendee under a contract for deed.

In the event of loss under a mortgagee's policy, the insurer pays the mortgagee the balance due on the loan and the owner is thereby relieved from making further payments. However, the owner still stands to lose the property and the investment. For this reason, it is generally sound practice to obtain an owner's policy where the lender is already requiring a mortgagee's policy; there is usually only a slight additional premium to issue both policies simultaneously. Some areas, by custom, require that both policies be purchased. Local practice and custom usually dictate which party to a transaction buys what type of policy. As an example, a seller may pay for the owner's policy, guaranteeing the title; while the buyer may pay for a lender's policy, protecting the mortgagee's interest in the real estate. Title insurance may be required by custom, even where title is registered in the Torrens system, to protect against items not shown on the transfer certificate of title (unrecorded liens, such as federal tax liens). The Federal National Mortgage Association and Federal Home Loan Mortgage Corporation also recognize the importance of title insurance and they require it on every loan they buy.

Title insurance premiums vary throughout the country, but their costs generally reflect the two basic title insurance considerations—cost of title examination and cost of insuring the risk. The average cost is approximately 0.5 percent of the cost of property. It generally takes a week for the policy to be issued; much less than the time it would take to prepare an abstract of title. If the same title company has recently issued a policy on the same property, then they may give a discount called a "reissue rate."

Note that, if an insured property appreciates in value (as when an expensive improvement is made), it is good practice to increase the amount of title insurance to cover possible increased losses. Newer policies have an "inflation guard" endorsement to cover appreciation.

Many (nearly 2,000) title companies belong to the American Land Title Association (ALTA), and use standardized ALTA title insurance policies. (*See AMERI-CAN LAND TITLE ASSOCIATION, CERTIFICATE OF TITLE, EXTENDED COVER-AGE, HIDDEN RISK, LEASEHOLD MORTGAGE, REISSUE RATE, TORRENS SYSTEM.*)

TITLE PARAMOUNT   A superior title.

TITLE PLANT   A place for the storage of title documents. Many of the larger title insurance companies maintain their own title plants, or record rooms, containing copies of all recorded instruments. These title plants often file hundreds of newly recorded documents per day and many have developed effective computerized systems of indexing by parcel of land. This reduces some of the difficulties found in searching title in grantor-grantee indexes, especially with parties having common surnames.

TITLE REPORT   A preliminary report of the current record title to a property. Unlike an abstract of title, a title report shows only the current state of the title along with the recorded objections to clear title such as unpaid mortgages and easements. The title insurance policy is issued based on the title report. The insurer incurs no liability under a preliminary report. (*See CERTIFICATE OF TITLE, TITLE INSURANCE.*)

TITLE SEARCH   An examination of the public records to determine what, if any, defects there are in the chain of title. The title search is usually performed by an experienced title company or abstractor. A title search is not normally ordered until major contingencies in the sales contract have been cleared, such as financing (that is, securing a loan commitment) and the like. Similarly, before an institutional lender will loan money secured by real estate, it will order a title search at the expense of the borrower to assure itself that there are no liens superior to its mortgage on the property.

The title searcher begins the examination with the original source of title, which often dates from a government patent grant or award of title or 40–60 years earlier depending on local custom. After examining the original source of title, the searcher then "runs the title" in the recorder's office, and searches the records in other governmental offices such as the tax offices and assessment offices (for sewer or street assessments that may be in effect). Title searchers are often confronted with spelling differences in similarly sounding names. In this regard, there is the legal "rule of *Idem Sonans*" which allows the rebuttable presumption that names which sound alike refer to the same person despite minor inconsistencies in spelling.

After conducting its title search, a title company will issue either a title abstract, a preliminary report, a certificate of title, a continuation certificate of title, or a title insurance policy. Some of these various documents give title opinions, while others merely state the facts disclosed by the search. (*See ABSTRACT OF TITLE, CERTIFICATE OF TITLE, CHAIN OF TITLE, FEDERAL TAX LIEN, GRANTOR-GRANTEE INDEX, TITLE INSURANCE.*)

TITLE-THEORY STATES   States in which the law considers the mortgagee to have legal title to the mortgaged property (usually in the form of a trust deed) and the mortgagor to have equitable title. Title-theory states, also called conveyance or transfer theory states, follow the common law approach that a mortgage is a conveyance defeasible upon a condition subsequent. The condition to the defeasance is the payment of the mortgage debt when it becomes due. Thus, in receiving a mortgage, the creditor takes title to the property; the debtor regains ownership when the debt is repaid. Under title theory, a mortgagee has the right to possession and rents of the mortgaged property upon default. A mortgagee in a lien-theory state must foreclose to assert the same rights. (See *LIEN-THEORY STATES*.)

TOLLING   Refers to the suspension or interruption of the running of the statute of limitations period. For example, the running of the statute of limitations regarding adverse possession may be suspended during the time the record owner is mentally incompetent.

TONGUE AND GROOVE   A method of joining two pieces of board wherein one has a tongue cut in the edge and the other board has a groove cut to receive the corresponding tongue. The method is used to modify any material prepared for joining in this fashion, as tongue and groove lumber.

TOPOGRAPHY   The nature of the surface of the land; the contour.

TOPPING-OFF   The highest point in a building's construction. This is sometimes signified by securing a tree branch to the topmost point in the project.

TORRENS SYSTEM   A legal system for the registration of land, used to verify the ownership and encumbrances (except tax liens), without the necessity of an additional search of the public records. The purpose of the Torrens Act pertaining to registration of title to land is to conclusively establish an indefeasible title to the end that anyone may deal with such property with the assurance that the only rights or claims of which he or she need take notice are those so registered. The Torrens system of registration is the title itself; it differs from a title insurance policy which is only evidence of title. In other words, a person does not acquire title to Torrens registered real property unless that person registers the title.

The distinctive feature of registered property is that title does not pass, and encumbrances (such as mortgages) are not effective against the property until such encumbrances or conveyances are noted on the registered certificate of title. A party who suffers loss through an error made by the governmental registrar can recover damages from the state through an assurance fund. The registrar, however, will not personally defend against litigation or reimburse the landowner for litigation expenses, which is one reason why most mortgagees require title insurance even for Torrens-registered titles.

Under the Torrens system, the landowner initially petitions a state court to register his or her property, giving notice to all interested parties. After a search of title is filed with the court, there is generally a hearing to determine the status of the title and the court's determination is made in the form of a court decree. The procedure is similar to a quiet title suit. The initial use of the Torrens system is optional. But once property is registered, all subsequent transfers must follow the registration procedures.

The system was developed in 1857 by an Australian, Sir Robert Torrens, who took the idea from the system of registering title to shipping vessels. Approximately 10 states have adopted the Torrens system. It is also popular in Canada, Australia, and Great Britain. In some states, Torrens-registered property is not subject to a general judgment lien nor can title be lost through adverse possession. (*See TAX AND LIEN SEARCH, TRANSFER CERTIFICATE OF TITLE.*)

TORT A negligent or intentional wrongful act arising from breach of duty created by law and not contract; violation of a legal right; a civil wrong such as negligence, libel, nuisance, trespass, slander of title, false imprisonment. For example, an escrow agent who negligently or intentionally fails to comply with the escrow instructions may be liable in a tort action for the damages caused by its negligence. The escrow agent may also be liable for breach of its contract for failure to perform according to its agency.

TOWN HOUSE A type of dwelling unit normally having two floors, with the living area and kitchen on the base floor and the bedrooms located on the second floor. Town houses, or row houses, are very popular in cluster housing, and often employ the use of party walls and shared common grounds. Town house developments are often planned unit developments (PUDs), with each individual owner possessing fee title to the structure and the land underlying the structure; many are organized in the condominium form of ownership. The surrounding land, including sidewalks, open spaces, and recreational facilities, is normally owned in common with others. The town house concept is a hybrid of the single-family home and the apartment, and is sometimes used in areas which have height restrictions preventing highrises. (*See PLANNED UNIT DEVELOPMENT.*)

TOWNSHIP A division of territory, used in the government (rectangular) survey system of land description, which is 6 miles square, and contains 36 sections, each of which is 1 mile square and consists of 23,040 acres. A township also refers to a strip of township running east and west. (*See GOVERNMENT SURVEY METHOD.*)

TRACK RECORD 1. The previous operating results of a sponsor (or developer) or a real estate project. In making a credit check, the creditor looks at the debtor's track record or past history of paying other creditors. 2. Also refers to the past history of a real estate syndicator and is required to be disclosed in a public or private placement offering.

TRACT A lot or parcel of land; a certain development. Generally refers to a large area of land.

TRACT HOUSE A house mass-produced according to the plans of the builder, as one of many residences in a subdivision, which are very similar in style, materials, and price. It is distinguished from a custom home, which is built to the specifications of the homeowner.

TRACT INDEX An index of records of title according to the description of the property conveyed, mortgaged, or otherwise encumbered or disposed of. (*See CHAIN OF TITLE.*)

TRADE FIXTURE   An article of personal property annexed or affixed to leased premises by the tenant as a necessary part of the tenant's trade or business. At the termination of a lease, a tenant must leave most fixtures in the premises; however, trade fixtures are removable by the tenant before expiration of the lease and the tenant is responsible for any damages caused by their removal. However, a tenant cannot usually remove replacement fixtures, that is, improvements installed to replace worn-out ones. If a tenant, for instance, installs a new bar to replace an old bar in a tavern the tenant leases, the tenant cannot remove the bar upon termination of the lease. If the tenant fails to remove trade fixtures within a reasonable time of the expiration of the lease, the fixtures will be considered abandoned and will become the property of the landlord. (See FIXTURE.)

TRADE-IN   An agreement by a developer or broker to accept from a buyer a designated piece of real property as a part of the purchase price of another property. The usual scenario is this: a homeowner agrees to purchase another home and the builder of the other home or the selling broker agrees to purchase the owner's present home at a specified price if the home has not sold for that price or more within a certain time. This arrangement guarantees that the owner will have the necessary financial resources to purchase the new home.

Under FHA trade-in regulations, a nonoccupant borrower may accept a property in trade provided he or she and the lender agree to do so before the mortgage is insured and at least 15 percent of the mortgage proceeds are placed in escrow. If the property is sold within 18 months to a qualified owner/occupant, the 15 percent will be released. (See GUARANTEED SALE PROGRAM.)

TRADE USAGE   A uniform course of conduct followed in a particular trade, calling, occupation, or business. Any practice or method of dealing having such regularity of observance in a place, vocation, or trade as to justify an expectation that it will be observed with respect to the transaction in question.

TRADING ON THE EQUITY   The practice of agreeing to buy real estate and then assigning the purchase agreement to another buyer before closing takes place; thus turning a profit by "selling the paper."

TRADING UP   Buying or exchanging for something more expensive than what is currently owned. By trading up with one's personal residence, the taxpayer can defer any taxable gain on the sale. (See RESIDENCE.)

TRAILER PARK   A developed site having facilities for permanent and/or semipermanent mobile homes. The trailer park contains all utilities, streets, parking, and amenities. (See MOBILE HOME.)

TRANSFER CERTIFICATE OF TITLE (TCT)   A duplicate Torrens system certificate of title. Under the Torrens system of registration of title to property, the court issues an original certificate of title in the owner's name once the owner has established rightful title to the property. The certificate is issued in duplicate and shows the owner's name, the date of registration, the Torrens documentation number, and all encumbrances on the title. The original certificate is then recorded and a duplicate copy is given to the owner (or it is sometimes held by the mortgagee). When the original owner sells the property, the owner delivers a typical deed along with a transfer certificate of title. The original certificate and owner's duplicate are then cancelled and the registrar issues the grantee a new transfer certificate of title. (See CERTIFICATE OF TITLE, TORRENS SYSTEM.)

TRANSFER OF DEVELOPMENT RIGHTS (TDR)   A newly evolving concept of land use planning which looks at land development rights as being a part of the bundle of individual rights of land ownership. Under this concept any one of these bundle of rights may be separated from the rest and transferred to someone else, leaving the original owner with all other remaining rights of ownership. By viewing development rights as a separable economic entity, communities have considerable power to direct growth, preserve landmarks or unique environmental features, and maintain adequate amounts of open space. All of this is done without placing undue financial burden on the community or on the owners of the lands which will remain undevelopable in the community interest. TDR may be implemented in a variety of ways, but the end result is that the owner of the development rights will be reimbursed by the person acquiring the rights for the rights that are given up.

Although still in its infancy, TDR has been proposed or adopted in some fashion to promote various community values in several areas of the country. New York and Chicago have used it to preserve landmarks. It was proposed to preserve the ecologically fragile Phosphorescent Bay in Puerto Rico. Southampton, New York, has adopted TDR to encourage construction of moderate and low-income housing. The state of New Jersey and counties in Virginia and California are developing proposals to use TDR as a primary system of land use regulation and preservation of open space.

TRANSFER TAX   Tax stamps required to be affixed to a deed by state or local law. The federal Revenue Tax on conveyances of real estate, which had been in effect for many years, was repealed effective December 31, 1967. Following the repeal of the federal tax, most states have passed laws providing for revenue stamps to be affixed to deeds and conveyances.

Each state which has enacted a real estate transfer tax has established the amount of its tax, the procedures used to determine the taxable consideration, and those deeds or transactions which are exempt from the transfer tax. The transfer tax is usually paid by the seller. A tax rate of 50 or 55 cents for each $500 or fraction thereof of taxable consideration is common in many states. Generally, when the real estate is transferred subject to the unpaid balance of an existing mortgage made by the seller before the time of transfer and being assumed by the buyer, the amount of the assumed mortgage may be deducted from the full consideration to determine the taxable consideration. However, this is not true in all states. The tax usually is payable at the time of the recording of the deed by purchase of stamps from the county recorder of the county in which the deed is to be recorded. In many states a transfer declaration form must be signed by both buyer and seller or their agents. Often this form must provide information such as the legal description of the property conveyed, the address, the date and type of deed, the type of improvement, and whether the transfer is between relatives or is a compulsory transaction in pursuance of a court order.

Certain deeds may be exempted from the tax, such as: gift deeds; correction deeds; conveyances to or from or between governmental bodies; deeds of easement; deeds by charitable, religious, or educational institutions; deeds securing debts or releasing property as security for a debt; partition deeds; tax deeds; and deeds pursuant to mergers of corporations and those from subsidiary to parent corporations for cancellation of stock. (*See CONVEYANCE TAX, FEDERAL REVENUE STAMP.*)

TREAD   The horizontal surface of a stair step resting on the riser. The tread is the part you step on.

TREBLE DAMAGES   Damages provided for by statute in certain cases, as in an antitrust suit; the actual damages may be tripled. For example, a court may have the power to treble damages when a landlord wrongfully and willfully retains all or part of a tenant's security deposit.

TRESPASS   Any wrongful, forceful invasion of land ownership by a person having no lawful right or title to enter on the property. Trespass can occur on the land, below the surface, or even in the air space. Certain trespasses are privileged, such as trespasses to prevent waste, to serve legal process, and to use reasonable airspace for flights by aircraft.

The unauthorized possession of real property is a mere trespass and cannot ripen into ownership, unless all the elements of adverse possession are present. Since a tenant is entitled to the exclusive possession of the leased premises, not only against third parties but the landlord as well, any unauthorized entry by either the landlord or a third party would constitute trespass.

Generally, a landowner is not liable for injuries suffered by a trespasser whose presence is not known. When the landlord knows of the trespass, however, the landlord must not create conditions or do anything which may imperil the trespasser. (*See ADVERSE POSSESSION, ATTRACTIVE NUISANCE, NUISANCE, SELF-HELP*).

TRIM   Wood or metal interior finishing pieces such as door and window casings, moldings, and hardware.

TRIPLE "A" TENANT   A commercial tenant with a top credit rating, especially desirable as an anchor tenant in a shopping center.

TRIPLE NET LEASE   A net-net-net lease, where in addition to the stipulated rent, the lessee assumes payment of all expenses associated with the operation of the property. This includes both fixed expenses, such as taxes and insurance, and all operating expenses, including costs of maintenance and repair. In some cases the triple net tenant even pays the interest payments on the lessor's mortgage on the property.

Strictly speaking, a triple net lease is a redundant term since a net lease is enough to describe the situation. Rather than to rely on labels, however, it is important to examine the provisions of the lease to discover the extent of the tenant's responsibilities.

TRIPLEX   A building comprised of three dwelling units, each having a front and rear (or side) door and yard; similar to row houses. (*See ROW HOUSE.*)

TRUCK WELL   A depressed area abutting a loading dock (either inside or outside a building) sufficient in depth to permit direct loading from the floor of the building onto the bed of a truck which has backed into the well.

TRUE ESCROW   *See HOLDING ESCROW.*

TRUSS   A type of roof construction employing a rigid framework of beams or members, which supports the roof load and usually achieves relatively wide spans between its supports.

TRUST   An arrangement whereby legal title to property is transferred by the grantor (or trustor) to a person called a trustee, to be held and managed by that person for the benefit of another, called a beneficiary. The grantor and trustee initially may be the same person as in a "declaration of trust." The beneficiary holds equitable title. Trusts may be created by express agreement or by operation of law, and may be actual or constructive. For purposes of estate planning, there are *inter vivos* (or *living*) *trusts* and *testamentary trusts*. (*See INTER VIVOS TRUST, LAND TRUST.*)

TRUST BENEFICIARY   The person for whom a trust is created. The beneficiary is the party who receives the benefits or proceeds of the trust and it may be the same person as the grantor.

TRUST DEED   *See DEED OF TRUST.*

TRUSTEE   1. One who holds property in trust for another as a fiduciary, and is charged with the duty to protect, to preserve, and to enhance the value and the highest and best use of the trust property. Great care should be taken to set forth in the trust agreement the powers and responsibilities of the trustee. 2. One who holds property in trust for another to secure the performance of an obligation.

In those states using trust deeds as security devices, the trustee holds bare legal title to the property pending the borrower/trustor paying off the underlying debt or promissory note. The trustee is usually a lending institution, trust company, or title insurance company. Some states employ a public trustee to hold title in trust for the lender. The two main functions of a trustee in a trust deed are to sell the property at public auction if requested by the beneficiary when the debt is not paid and when the trust deed contains a power of sale, and to execute a reconveyance (release) when requested to do so by the beneficiary when the debt has been paid off. Many financial institutions have set up an auxiliary corporation to act as trustee in a deed of trust situation. In such a case the corporation is more a common agent than a true trustee.

TRUSTEE IN BANKRUPTCY   One who is appointed by the court to preserve and manage the assets of a party in bankruptcy.

TRUST FUND ACCOUNT   An account set up by a broker, attorney, or other agent at a bank or other recognized depository, into which the broker deposits all funds entrusted to the agent by the principal or others; also called an earnest money or escrow account. The trust fund for a brokerage firm account must designate the principal broker as trustee, and must provide for withdrawal of the funds upon demand. A principal broker may generally permit a broker-in-charge of a branch office to have custody and control of trust funds on behalf of the principal broker on transactions transpiring at said branch office. The principal broker and broker-in-charge are usually held jointly responsible for any trust funds the principal broker authorizes the broker-in-charge to handle. Note that since a broker is liable for the acts of his or her salespersons, the broker is liable to a buyer if one of the salespersons embezzles earnest money deposited in a trust fund account. Note also that if a broker deposits earnest money in the broker's own personal bank account or spends it, the broker may be guilty of commingling, a violation of most state license laws. Most license laws, however, allow a broker to keep a small amount of personal funds in a client trust account in order to keep the account open. The broker cannot use trust fund monies to offset even a valid debt owed by the client to the broker. (See *CLIENT TRUST ACCOUNT, COMMINGLING.*)

TRUTH-IN-LENDING LAWS   A federal law effective July 1969 as part of the Consumer Credit Protection Act, and implemented by the Federal Reserve Board's *Regulation Z*. It was amended in 1982 by the Truth-in-Lending Simplification and Reform Act. The main purpose of this law is to assure that borrowers and customers in need of consumer credit are given meaningful information with respect to the cost of credit. In this way consumers can more readily compare the various credit terms available to them and thus avoid the uninformed use of credit. This law creates a disclosure device only, and does *not* establish any set maximum or minimum interest rates or require any charges for credit. In addition, some states have adopted their own truth-in-lending laws.

All real estate credit is covered by Federal Reserve Regulation Z when it is extended to a natural person (the customer) and is not to be used for business, commercial, or agricultural purposes. Personal property credit transactions over $25,000 are exempt from Regulation Z, as is the extension of credit to the owner of a dwelling containing more than four-family housing units or a construction loan to a builder (this is considered a business purpose). However, if the extension of credit is secured by real property or by personal property used or expected to be used as the principal dwelling of the consumer (mobile home), then the transaction is covered by Regulation Z.

The credit offered must either involve a finance charge or, by written agreement, be payable in more than four installments.

Finance Charge

The finance charge and the annual percentage rate are the two most important disclosures required. These disclosures provide a quick reference for customers, informing them how much they are paying for credit and its relative cost in percentage terms. Note that there is a cushion or tolerance given of $5 if the transaction is less than $1,000 and $10 if it is more than $1,000. The finance charge is the total of all costs which the customer must pay, directly or indirectly, for obtaining credit, and includes such costs as interest, loan fee, loan-finder's fee, time-price differential, discount points, service fee, and premium for credit life insurance if it is made a condition for granting credit. Real estate purchase costs which would be paid regardless of whether or not credit is extended, such as legal fees to prepare deeds, taxes not included in the cash price, survey fees, recording fees, title insurance premiums, investigation, or credit report fees are *not* included in the finance charge, provided these fees are bona fide, reasonable in amount, and are not excluded for the purpose of circumvention or evasion of the law.

Annual Percentage Rate

The annual percentage rate as it is used in Regulation Z is not interest, though interest is figured in along with the other finance charges in computing the annual percentage rate. This rate is the relationship of the total finance charge to the total amount to be financed and must be computed to the nearest one-eighth of one percent. Note, however, that many real estate mortgages call for interest based on a simple annual rate, which is lower than the annual percentage rate because certain elements in addition to interest (for example, points or other fees) which must be included in the total finance charge are not included in the calculation of the simple annual interest rate.

Disclosure Statement

The disclosure statement for real estate transactions must contain the following information:

1. the total dollar amount of the "finance charge," using that term, and a brief description such as the "dollar amount the credit will cost you"

2. the "annual percentage rate," using that term and a brief description such as "the cost of your credit as a yearly rate"

3. the number, amounts, and timing of payments

4. the "total of payments," using that term, and a descriptive explanation such as "the amount you will have paid when you have made all scheduled payments"

5. the amount charged or method of computation for any late payment other than a deferred or extension charge

6. the fact that the creditor has or will acquire a security interest in the property being purchased

7. whether you have to pay a prepayment penalty and whether the debtor will be entitled to a refund of part of the finance charge

8. an identification of the method used to compute any finance-charge rebate which might arise in the case of prepayment of contracts involving precomputed finance charges

9. the total amount of credit which will be made available to the borrower, including all charges (individually itemized) which are included in "amount financed"

10. amounts that are deducted as prepaid finance charges (for example, points) and required deposit balances, such as tax reserves

11. in the case of contract for deed, the cash price (purchase price), total down

payment, the unpaid balance of the case price, and the deferred payment price (which is the total of the cash price, finance and all other charges). The deferred payment price, however, does not apply to the sale of a residential dwelling.

Right to Rescind

The customer has a limited right to rescind or cancel a credit transaction. This rescission is intended to protect the homeowner from losing his or her home to unscrupulous sellers of home improvements, appliances, or furniture, who secure the credit advance by taking a second mortgage on the purchaser's home. If a creditor extends credit and receives a security interest (nonpurchase money mortgage or contract for deed, mechanic's lien) in any real property which is used or expected to be used as the principal residence of the borrower, the creditor must give the borrower the prescribed notice of right of rescission. The borrower then has the right to cancel the transaction (in writing) by midnight of the third *business* day (including Saturdays) following the date of consummation of the transaction delivery of the notice of right to rescind, or delivery of all material disclosures, whichever is *later*. A transaction is considered to be consummated at the time a contractual relationship is created between a creditor and a customer, irrespective of the time of performance of either party. Further, the disclosures are now required to be made *before* the transaction has been consummated. Disclosures involving real property must be made at the time the creditor makes a firm loan commitment with respect to the transaction.

Note that the right to rescind does not apply to a "residential mortgage transaction," defined as a transaction in which a mortgage, deed of trust, purchase money security interest arising under an installment sales contract, or equivalent consensual security interest is created or retained in the consumer's principal dwelling to finance the acquisition or initial construction of that dwelling.

But all loans, secured or otherwise, to finance the acquisition of building lots or raw acreage where the buyer expects to use the lot as a principal residence must disclose the total payments and the finance charge, and give notice of the three-day right of rescission. In this regard, a purchaser of unimproved land may have a basis to rescind his or her real estate purchase since many subdividers who sell under a contract for deed do not give the purchaser a notice of the right of rescission. The prudent developer might have the prospective purchaser execute a statement to the effect that he or she purchased the lot for investment and resale and does not intend ever to use the lot to build his or her principal residence.

Without such a written declaration or other exemption, the developer must give the purchaser notice of the right to cancel by giving him or her two copies of a notice of rescission in the form prescribed by Regulation Z. One of these may be used to cancel the transaction. The customer may waive his or her right to cancel a credit agreement only if the credit is needed to meet a bona fide personal financial emergency, such as emergency repair work (for example, a flooded basement). The use of printed waiver forms for this purpose is prohibited.

If the required disclosures were not made or a notice of rescission was not given to a borrower, the borrower's right to rescind continues for a period of three years after the date of consummation of the transaction or upon sale of the property, whichever occurs earlier. When a customer exercises the right to rescind under the federal Truth-in-Lending Law, he or she must tender any property received to the creditor provided the creditor first returns the customer's payments. The tender must be made at the location of the property or at the residence of a customer, at the customer's option. If the creditor does not take possession of the property within 20 days after tender by the customer, ownership of the property rests in the customer without obligation on his or her part to pay for it. Upon rescission, the borrower is not liable for any charges. Also, the creditor must return all money within 20 days after the notice of rescission is received.

A first mortgage on a home, given to a contractor for home improvements, would be subject to both the finance charge and the notice of rescission requirements. In such case, the contractor should not commence work until the expiration of the cancellation period, three business days. Many contractors are unaware that they are deemed to be creditors and subject to the law where they permit payment in more than four installments.

Creditors

This law requires compliance by all creditors who regularly extend, or arrange for the extension of, credit. A person "regularly extends" credit only if the person extended credit more than 25 times (or more than 5 times for transactions secured by a dwelling) in the preceding calendar year. Thus, the owner/occupant of a single-family home ordinarily does not have to comply with the disclosure requirements of Regulation Z even when selling under a contract for deed payable in more than four installments. However, if such owner/occupant were to prearrange to discount the contract for deed immediately to a lender, he or she may be deemed to be a mere straw man for the lender and thus lose the exemption. A broker who assists a buyer in preparing a credit application may be an arranger of credit and subject to the law. A broker who is an operative builder, a subdivider, a broker selling property on his or her own account (except for the sale of his or her own permanent dwelling), or a broker taking a second mortgage as a commission, may be deemed to be a creditor and thus must comply with the law.

Advertising

Regulation Z also affects all advertising to aid or promote any extension of consumer credit, regardless of who the advertiser may be. All types of advertising are covered, including window displays, fliers, billboards, multiple-listing cards if shown to the public, and direct mail literature. The ad is subject to the full disclosure requirements if it includes:

1. the amount or percentage of down payment (for example, 5 percent down)

2. the amount of any installment payment

3. the dollar amount of any finance charge

4. the number of installments or the period of repayment, or that there is no charge for credit

If any of these items are included, the ad must disclose the amount or percentage of down payment, the terms of prepayment, the annual percentage rate, and if the rate may be increased after consummation, that fact. General terms such as "small down payment ok," "FHA financing available," or "compare our reasonable rates," are not within the scope of Regulation Z. When advertising an assumption of mortgage, the ad can state the rate of finance charge without any other disclosure. The finance charge, however, must be stated as an annual percentage rate, using that term and stating whether increase is possible. For example, "assume 8 percent mortgage" is improper, whereas "assume 8½ percent annual percentage rate mortgage" is permissible. The interest rate can be stated in advertisements in conjunction with, but not more conspicuously than, the annual percentage rate.

Also, the annual percentage rate should be spelled out and not reduced to "A.P.R." or otherwise abbreviated. Bait advertising is prohibited; thus, an advertisement offering new homes at "$1,000 down" is improper if the seller normally does not accept this amount as a down payment, even if all the other required credit terms are disclosed in the ad.

Certain credit terms, when mentioned in an ad, trigger the required disclosure of other items. The purpose of this requirement is to give the prospective purchaser a complete and accurate picture of the transaction being offered. The trigger terms and required disclosures are:

Column A Trigger Terms	Column B Required Disclosures
Appearance of any of these items in Column A requires inclusion of everything in Column B	
• the amount or percentage of down payment	• the amount or percentage of down payment
• the amount of any installment	• the terms of repayment
• the finance charge in dollars or that there is no charge for credit	• the terms of repayment
• the number of installments	• the annual percentage rate and if increase is possible
• the period of repayment	

Any advertisement that mentions an interest rate, but omits the annual percentage rate or omits the words "annual percentage rate" is in violation. Any advertisement which includes any trigger term (Column A) without all of the required disclosures (everything in Column B) is in violation.

Creditors should keep records of all compliance with the disclosure requirements of the federal Truth-in-Lending Law for at least two years after the date disclosures are required to be made or action is required to be taken. Truth-in-Lending requires advance disclosure of any variable rate clause in a credit contract that may result in an increase in the cost of credit to the customer.

Where joint ownership is involved, the right to receive disclosures and notice of the right of rescission, the right to rescind, and the need to sign a waiver of such right, applies to each consumer whose ownership interest is subject to the security interest.

Penalties

The penalty for violation of Regulation Z is twice the amount of the finance charge or a minimum of $100, up to a maximum of $1,000, plus court costs, attorney's fees, and any actual damages. Willful violation is a misdemeanor punishable by a fine up to $5,000 or one year imprisonment, or both. The federal agency in charge of enforcing Regulation Z is the Federal Trade Commission. (See ANNUAL PERCENTAGE RATE, FINANCE CHARGE, RULE OF 78s.)

TSUNAMI DAMAGE   Damage caused by tidal wave action. Owners of property located in flood zones must obtain insurance to cover flood and tsunami damage, as the federal government no longer compensates fully for this type of damage. Lending institutions now require flood insurance in order to complete a mortgage loan transaction involving any building or its apartments located in a designated flood or tsunami zone. Thus, an owner attempting to sell a beachfront resort condominium might run into a problem when reselling the unit, unless the condominium association takes out sufficient insurance to conform with the new federal requirements. (*See FLOOD INSUR-ANCE.*)

TURN-KEY PROJECT   A development term meaning the complete construction package from ground breaking to the completion of the building. All that is left undone is to turn over the keys to the buyer. Some governmental housing projects are turn-key projects with a private developer completing a housing development which is then totally purchased by a governmental agency for use as low-income family housing. A turn-key job is different from a "package deal," which typically includes the financing as well.

A turn-key lease is one in which the landlord agrees to give the leased premises to the tenant in a ready-to-occupy condition. (*See BUILD TO SUIT.*)

TURNOVER   Refers to the frequency with which real property in a given area is sold and resold.

ULTRA VIRES   Acts of a corporation that are beyond its legal powers as set forth in its articles of incorporation.

UNBALANCED IMPROVEMENT   An appraisal term describing an improvement which is not the highest and best use for the site. It may be either an overimprovement or an underimprovement.

UNCONSCIONABILITY   A legal doctrine whereby a court will refuse to enforce a contract which was grossly unfair or unscrupulous at the time it was made; a contract offensive to the public conscience. The Uniform Residential Landlord and Tenant Act expressly provides that courts may refuse to enforce an unconscionable rental agreement either in whole or in part. Under the Uniform Commercial Code, unconscionable contracts are also expressly rendered unenforceable.

UNDER-FLOOR DUCTS   Floor channels which provide for the placement of telephone and electrical lines required for the floor; this placement allows flexibility in space planning and furniture arrangement in commercial office buildings.

UNDERIMPROVEMENT   An improvement which, because of its deficiency in size or cost, is not the highest and best use of the site. Usually, a structure which is of lesser cost, quality, and size than typical neighborhood properties. For example, a single-family home in an area zoned to allow six-unit dwellings. (See OVERIMPROVEMENT.)

UNDERLYING FINANCING   A mortgage or deed of trust which takes precedence over subsequent liens, such as contracts for deed or mortgages on the same property. In taking a listing, a broker should check the terms of any underlying financing documents affecting the property.

UNDERSIGNED   The person whose name is signed at the end of a document; the subscriber.

UNDERTENANT   One who holds property under one who is already a tenant, as in a sublease; a subtenant.

UNDERWRITER   1. As an insurance term, it refers to a person who selects risks to be solicited and then rates the acceptability of the risks solicited. In this sense, a mortgagee is an underwriter. For example, a local title company usually buys insurance from a larger title company (the underwriter) for all or part of the liability of the policies that it originates.

2. As the term applies to real property securities, an underwriter is a person who has purchased securities from the issuer with the intention to offer, or actually does sell or distribute, the securities for the issuer. For example, if a syndicator retains a securities firm to sell its limited partnership units, that firm is an underwriter. An underwriter may have to be registered in his or her state and/or with the Securities and Exchange Commission as an underwriter or broker/dealer.

3. Underwriting a loan is the analysis of the extent of risk assumed in connection with a loan. It includes the entire process of preparing the conditions of the loan, determining the borrower's ability to repay, and the subsequent decision whether to give loan approval.

UNDISCLOSED AGENCY   A situation where an agent deals with a third person without notifying that person of the agency. In some cases, the broker is instructed not to reveal the name of the client. Where the agent signs his or her own name to any contract without disclosing the agency, the agent becomes fully liable for any breach or failure to perform on the contract. In order to avoid liability, the broker must declare the agency on the contract so it is clear that all parties intended to bind the principal and not just the agent.

The seller has the right to know the identity of the purchaser. If the broker refuses to disclose the true identity of the buyer, the seller has the right to decline the offer and the broker cannot then assert a claim for commission based on procuring a ready, willing, and able buyer.

UNDISTRIBUTED TAXABLE INCOME   Income received by a subchapter S corporation which has not been distributed to the shareholders but is nonetheless taxed as part of the shareholders' income. (See SUBCHAPTER S CORPORATION.)

UNDIVIDED INTEREST   That interest a co-owner has in property, which carries with it a right to possession of the whole property along with the co-owners. The undivided interests may be equal, as in a joint tenancy, or unequal, as sometimes in a tenancy in common. No owner has the right to any specific part of the whole. Thus, each owns a fractional share of the entire parcel, not a specified piece of it.

To acquire a right to a specific part of a property, a co-owner must petition the court for a petition or division of the property. For example, if Julie Tempo owned a $9/10$ undivided interest of a 10-acre parcel of land, she would not own nine acres—all owners with undivided interests have the right to complete possession. In other words, there is no physical division of the land between the co-owners. Thus, one cotenant cannot convey or encumber a specific part of the property.

Condominium owners have a specified undivided interest in the common areas according to their percentage of common interest. There is no limit to the number of persons who may own an undivided interest in real property.

Each of the co-owners has a separate economic right in a property. Thus, if part of the parcel is arid and part is fertile, it would be unlikely, in a partition action, for a court to partition the property into equal geographic areas.

The sale of undivided interests is specifically covered under the Uniform Land Sales Practices Act, which regulates the mass marketing of undivided interests in land; for example, if a developer sells a $1/175$ tenancy in common interest in a large parcel of land this may be taken as an attempt to evade the subdivision registration law. (See TENANCY [all forms], UNIFORM LAND SALES PRACTICE ACT.)

UNDUE INFLUENCE Strong enough persuasion to completely over-power the free will of another and prevent him or her from acting intelligently and voluntarily, as in a case where a broker guilty of blockbusting has induced someone to sell in fear of a change in the racial character of the community. Undue influence usually requires a close or confidential relationship like parent-child, broker-seller, attorney-client, or trustee-beneficiary. Where a person has been unduly influenced to sign a contract, that person can void the contract.

UNEARNED INCOME Income derived from sources other than personal services. Rents, dividends, and royalties would fit into this tax category whereas wages, tips, and commission money would not.

Prior to 1982 the maximum tax upon unearned income was 70 percent, while the maximum tax on "earned " or "personal service" income was 50 percent. Certain tax preference items reduced the amount of income eligible for this 50 percent "maxi-tax."

The Economic Recovery Tax Act of 1981 abolished this distinction. The maximum tax rate on all income is 50 percent.

UNEARNED INCREMENT An increase in value to real property which comes about from forces outside the influence and control of the property owner, such as a favorable rezoning or a favorable shift of population in the neighborhood.

UNENCUMBERED PROPERTY A property that is free and clear of liens and other encumbrances; a "free and clear" property.

UNENFORCEABLE CONTRACT A contract which was valid when made but either cannot be proved or will not be enforced by a court. An unenforceable contract is not merely one which is void or illegal. A contract may be unenforceable because it is not in writing, as may be required under the state statutes of frauds, or because the statute of limitations period has elapsed. The contract is nevertheless valid for certain purposes, such as evidence of a pre-existing debt. Also, certain government contracts may not be enforceable against the government; that is, they are enforceable to the extent the government permits it. (See STATUTE OF FRAUDS.)

UNETHICAL Lacking in moral principles; failing to conform to an accepted code of behavior. Real estate agents can lose their licenses for not abiding by a code of conduct as set forth in most states' licensing laws. (See CODE OF ETHICS.)

UNFAIR AND DECEPTIVE PRACTICES Sales practices which do not involve deception but are still illegal under the regulations of the Federal Trade Commission. A sales practice is unfair if: 1. the practice offends public policy; 2. it is immoral, unethical, oppressive, or unscrupulous; or 3. it causes injury to consumers. This concept applies to practices such as inducing purchases by intimidation and scare tactics; substitution of products; wrongful refusal to return deposits or refunds; or use of two-way radios and other high-pressure sales gimmicks.

Under the Federal Trade Commission regulations, the Commission can enjoin unfair and deceptive practices, issue complaints and prosecute, issue cease-and-desist orders, and impose fines.

UNFINISHED OFFICE SPACE Space in a "shell" condition excluding dividing walls, ceiling, lighting, air-conditioning, floor covering, and the like. In leasing unfinished office space, the landlord often provides the building with standard items and/or a construction allowance.

UNIFORM AND MODEL ACTS Laws proposed for adoption in the individual states. Such uniform laws are approved by the National Conference of Commissioners on Uniform State Laws and many have been adopted in one or more states. Some examples are the Uniform Commercial Code, Uniform Condominium Act, Uniform Consumer Credit Code, Uniform Fraudulent Conveyances Act, Uniform Land Sales Practices Act, Uniform Land Transactions Act, Uniform Partnership Act, Uniform Real Estate Timeshare Act, and the Uniform Residential Landlord and Tenant Act.

UNIFORM BUILDING CODE A national code published by the International Conference of Building Officials and used mostly in the western states. It has been adopted in part by over 1,000 municipalities throughout the United States.

UNIFORM COMMERCIAL CODE (UCC) A body of law which attempts to codify and make uniform throughout the country all law relating to commercial transactions, such as conditional sales contracts, pledges, and chattel mortgages. The UCC also covers personal property transactions, including negotiable securities and commercial paper.

The main relevance of the UCC to real property is in the area of fixtures, as covered in Section 9 of the Code. Where a chattel is purchased on credit or is pledged as security, a security interest is created in the chattel by the execution of a security agreement. Rather than recording the agreement, the creditor would file a financing statement in the recorder's office. If the financing statement has been properly filed, the creditor, upon default, can repossess the chattel and remove it from the property. (See *BULK TRANSFER, FINANCING STATEMENT, SECURITY AGREEMENT.*)

UNIFORMITY An appraisal term used in tax assessment practice to describe assessed values that have the same relationship to market value and thus imply the equalization of the tax burden.

UNIFORM LAND SALES PRACTICES ACT   *See INTERSTATE LAND SALES.*

UNIFORM LAND TRANSACTIONS ACT   A uniform model law proposed by the National Conference of Commissioners on Uniform State Laws, which covers a wide range of real estate transactions, including sales, conveyances, mortgages, and leases. The law has not yet gained wide support.

One of the more important financing proposals urges the elimination of the present distinctions among mortgages, deeds of trust, and contracts for deed.

UNIFORM LIMITED PARTNERSHIP ACT   A model act, adopted in whole or in part by many states, which establishes the legality of the limited partnership form of ownership and provides that realty may be held in the name of the limited partnership. (*See LIMITED PARTNERSHIP.*)

UNIFORM PARTNERSHIP ACT   A model act, adopted in whole or in part by most states, which establishes the legality of the partnership form of ownership and provides that real estate may be held in the partnership's name. (*See PARTNERSHIP.*)

UNIFORM RESIDENTIAL LANDLORD AND TENANT ACT   A number of states have adopted all or parts of the Uniform Residential Landlord and Tenant Act, or have enacted similar legislation. Generally, the act is intended to provide some uniformity in regulating the relationship of landlord and tenant in residential leases.

Rental Agreements

Unless otherwise specified in a lease or rental agreement, the act considers a tenant to have a periodic tenancy. The term of the tenancy is held to be week-to-week in the case of a roomer who pays weekly rent, and month-to-month in all other cases. If either the landlord or the tenant signs and delivers a written rental agreement, it is considered accepted by the other party, even without his or her signature, if the other party either pays rent or accepts rent without objecting to the agreement. If no specific amount of rent is agreed upon, the rent due is considered to be the fair rental value of the unit. In the case of a legal suit between the lessor and lessee, the fair amount of rent would be determined by the court. The rental agreement may not contain certain provisions: the tenant does not have to agree to forego rights or remedies under the act, to authorize any person to confess judgment on a claim arising from the rental agreement, or to pay the landlord's attorney's fees. A rental agreement may limit the landlord's liability for fire, theft, or breakage with respect to common areas, but the tenant does not have to agree to otherwise limit the landlord's liability. In the case of a legal dispute between a landlord and a tenant, the court may refuse to enforce an agreement, or any portion thereof, which it finds to be unconscionable, that is, grossly unfair as to violate the public conscience.

Condition of the Premises

Within five days after the tenant takes possession of the premises, the lessor and lessee must make a joint inventory detailing the condition of the premises and any of the furnishings or appliances supplied by the landlord. A fully signed copy of this document must be given to each party.

Security Deposits

The maximum security deposit the landlord may receive is one month's rent on an unfurnished unit, and one and one-half month's rent on a furnished unit. If the landlord allows pets, he or she may require an additional half month's rent on either furnished or unfurnished units. When the tenancy ends, the landlord may apply the deposit against any accrued rent or damages to the premises. An itemized list of damages must be given to the tenant and any balance remaining must be returned to the tenant within the time specified in the act. If the landlord fails to return the deposit, the tenant has the right to recover the money due him or her, together with damages in an amount equal to one and one-half times the amount wrongfully withheld, plus reasonable attorney's fees. A tenant is prohibited from deducting any portion of the security deposit from his or her final month's rent. If a tenant does so, the landlord is entitled to recover the rent as though the security deposit had not been deducted.

Use of the Property

The landlord may establish rules concerning the use and occupancy of the property, if such rules are reasonably related to preserving the property and promoting the safety and welfare of the tenants, and are equally applicable to all tenants. The rules must be clearly written so that the tenant understands what he or she must do to comply. At the time the tenant enters into the rental agreement, the landlord must give notice of any such rules. Any later rule which substantially modifies the rental agreement is enforceable against the tenant only if signed by him or her. Unless otherwise agreed, the tenant may use the premises only as a dwelling unit. The tenant may not unreasonably withhold his or her consent from the landlord for entry to the premises.

Landlord's Obligations

After giving reasonable notice, the landlord may enter the premises at reasonable hours to inspect the unit, make necessary repairs or improvements, supply services, or show the unit to prospective buyers or tenants. Only in cases of extreme emergency may the landlord enter without prior permission from the tenant.

At or before the commencement of the tenancy, the landlord must disclose in writing the name and address of the person authorized to manage the property, and of the person who is to receive service of process or other legal notices for the landlord. This information must be kept current.

It is the landlord's obligation to make all repairs necessary to keep the premises fit for habitation. The landlord must comply with local building and housing codes in providing and maintaining in good operating condition all electrical, heating, plumbing and similar systems, and other facilities and appliances, such as elevators, which are supplied by him or her. The landlord must also provide for the upkeep of the common areas, and for trash and garbage receptacles. Running water, a reasonable amount of hot water, and heat during the required months must be supplied by the landlord unless the building is not required by law to be equipped for these purposes, or unless the tenant has exclusive control over the installations supplying water and heat. The tenant may agree in writing, however, to pay for any or all utility services.

These duties of the landlord do not apply if compliance is prevented by conditions beyond the landlord's control. If the property is sold, the landlord is relieved of liability as of the date of sale, with the exception of the duty to return security deposits. The previous landlord's duties and liabilities are thus assigned to and assumed by the new owner.

Tenants' Obligations

The tenant must comply with local building and housing code provisions affecting health and safety, such as keeping the unit clean and safe for habitation and disposing of trash and garbage. All plumbing fixtures, elevators, and other facilities provided by the landlord, as well as electrical, plumbing, heating, and air conditioning systems, must be used in a reasonable manner by the tenant. The tenant also must not willfully destroy or damage the premises, or allow others to do so, and must not disturb his or her neighbor's quiet enjoyment of the premises.

Termination of the Tenancy

If the tenant is guilty of a significant failure to comply with the terms of the rental agreement in maintaining the premises, the landlord may deliver written notice to the tenant specifying the nature of the breach and stating that the rental agreement will terminate in 30 days, if the tenant does not begin a good faith effort to repair the breach within the time specified in the notice.

If, however, the tenant's noncompliance consists of failure to pay rent, the landlord may terminate the lease within three days after giving notice, if the tenant still has not paid. If the tenant's noncompliance can be remedied by the repair or replacement of damaged items, and the tenant does not make such repairs within a reasonable time after the written notice is given, the landlord may enter the unit and have the necessary work performed. An itemized bill for the actual and reasonable cost of the work is then presented to the tenant as due with the next periodic rent payment. However, if the landlord chooses to terminate the rental agreement, the itemized bill is presented to the tenant for immediate payment. In either case, if the rental agreement is terminated, the landlord has a claim for possession and rent owing, and a separate claim for actual damages and reasonable attorney's fees. The landlord does not have the right to a lien on the tenant's household goods, however.

If the tenant abandons the unit, the landlord must make a reasonable effort to rerent the unit at a fair rental price. The tenant's obligation for rent continues until either the rental agreement expires or the unit is rerented, whichever occurs first. However, if the landlord does not try to rerent the unit, or if he or she accepts the abandonment as surrender of the premises, the rental agreement is terminated when the landlord has notice of the abandonment.

If the landlord is guilty of significant failure to perform his or her duties, the tenant may also terminate the rental agreement by giving the landlord 30 days notice of contract breach. The landlord can stop termination, however, by beginning a good faith effort to remedy the breach within the time specified by the notice. In addition to termination of the rental agreement, the tenant also has the right to sue for damages and obtain a court injunction directing the landlord to correct the breach. If the landlord's noncompliance is willful, the tenant may also recover reasonable attorney's fees. Whenever a rental agreement is terminated through noncompliance on the landlord's part, the tenant is always entitled to recover the security deposit and any prepaid rent.

If the landlord willfully fails to deliver possession of the unit, the tenant's obligation to pay rent stops until possession is delivered. The tenant may either terminate the rental agreement or sue for performance, and obtain possession, reasonable damages and attorney's fees.

If the landlord negligently fails to supply heat, running water, or some other essential service, the tenant may give written notice of the contract breach to the landlord, and the tenant may then take appropriate measures to obtain the services and deduct the cost from rent payments (the so-called rent and deduct statutes), sue for damages based upon the decrease in the fair rental value of the unit or procure substitute housing until the breach is remedied. If substitute housing is obtained, the tenant's obligation for rent ceases during the landlord's period of noncompliance. The cost of such housing may be recovered, not to exceed the amount of periodic rent, along with reasonable attorney's fees, if the tenant files suit against the landlord. When the cost of the necessary repairs is small, and the landlord fails to comply within a reasonable time after written notice has been given, the tenant may have the work performed, present an itemized bill to the landlord and deduct the cost of repairs from his or her next rent payment.

If the dwelling unit is damaged or destroyed by fire or other casualty to such an extent that enjoyment of the premises is impaired, the tenant may immediately vacate the premises and notify the landlord in writing of his or her intention to terminate the rental agreement as of the day of vacating. In cases where portions of the dwelling are still habitable, the tenant may vacate the damaged part of the dwelling, and his or her liability for rent is reduced in proportion to the decrease in the fair rental value of the unit.

If the landlord illegally excludes the tenant from the premises or willfully diminishes services to the tenant, the tenant has the right to either recover possession or terminate the rental agreement. The tenant may also recover reasonable damages and attorney's fees.

A landlord is prohibited from increasing the rent or decreasing the services of a tenant who has made a complaint to the landlord or to a governmental agency, or who has joined a tenant's union.

Exemptions

The Uniform Residential Landlord and Tenant Act would not, however, usually apply in the following situations:

1. a person occupying property under a contract for deed

2. residence at a public or private institution for the purpose of receiving education, counseling, health care, or a similar service

3. occupancy by a member of a fraternal organization in a structure operated for the benefit of the organization

4. transient occupancy in a hotel or motel

5. occupancy by an employee of the landlord, when the employee's right to occupy is conditional upon his or her employment

6. occupancy by an owner of a condominium unit or holder of a proprietary lease in a cooperative

7. agricultural leases

8. rental of mobile-home lots, unless the landlord also furnishes the mobile home
   (*See HOUSE RULES, LEASE, REPAIRS, SECURITY DEPOSIT, SURRENDER.*)

UNIFORM SETTLEMENT STATEMENT The standard HUD Form 1 required to be given to the borrower, lender, and the seller at or prior to settlement by the settlement agent in a transaction covered under the Real Estate Settlement Procedures Act. The lender must retain its copy for at least two years.

UNIFORM SIMULTANEOUS DEATH ACT A statute adopted in most states designed to cover the situation where two joint tenants are killed in a common disaster. In essence, the statute provides that the parties died as tenants in common with equal shares. Typical language is:

> Where there is no sufficient evidence that two joint tenants died otherwise than simultaneously, the property so held shall be distributed one-half as if one had survived and one-half as if the other had survived. If there are more than two joint tenants and all of them have so died the property thus distributed shall be in the proportion that one bears to the whole number of joint tenants.

Naturally, if there are several joint tenants and all but one die in a common disaster, the statute does not apply and the surviving joint tenant continues to own the entire property, now as tenant in severalty. (*See JOINT TENANCY.*)

UNIFORM VENDOR AND PURCHASER RISK ACT A law adopted in many states to determine which party bears the risk of loss in the event the property is damaged or destroyed prior to legal title passing to the vendee under a contract for sale. Unless the purchase agreement provides otherwise, the risk of loss does not pass from vendor to vendee until either legal title or possession has passed to the vendee. Once title or possession passes to the vendee, the vendee must pay the full purchase price if all or part of the property is destroyed without fault of the vendor or is taken by eminent domain. Unfortunately, the act does not address the question of what the parties do after loss when the vendee elects not to rescind but, rather, insists on the vendor rebuilding and specifically performing the contract obligations. (*See RISK OF LOSS.*)

UNILATERAL CONTRACT A contract in which one party makes an obligation to perform without receiving in return any express promise of performance from the other party. One party gives a promise in exchange for an act; that party is not obligated to perform on that promise unless the other party decides to act. An example would be an open listing contract, where the seller agrees to pay a commission to the first broker who brings a ready, willing, and able buyer. The contract actually is created by the performance of the act requested of the promisee, not by the mere promise to perform. Note that a *uni*lateral contract contains a promise on *one* side, whereas a *bi*lateral contract contains promises on *two* sides.

Before the act is performed, the promise of the promisor is a mere unilateral offer. When the act is performed, this unilateral offer and the performed act give rise to a unilateral contract. The broker makes no promise to perform or to do any acts such as advertising. He or she can accept the contract and thus bind the seller only by actual performance, that is, by producing such a buyer. (Many standard exclusive-right-to-sell listings are now written as bilateral contracts wherein the broker agrees to use reasonable efforts to locate a buyer and the seller agrees to pay a commission if the property is sold by the broker, the seller, or by anyone else.)

The classic example of a unilateral contract is a newspaper notice offering a reward for the return of a lost dog. The offeree is under no obligation to look for the dog, but if he or she does in fact return the dog, then the offeror owes him or her the reward money.

Another example would be a brokerage company that promises to pay a $1000 bonus to the salesperson who sells the most units in a specific condominium project. An option in which the seller agrees to sell for a certain period of time at set terms provided the buyer performs by paying the specified option price is also a unilateral contract. (*See BILATERAL CONTRACT.*)

UNIMPROVED PROPERTY Land without buildings, improvements, streets, and so on. The fact that property is unimproved must be clearly stated in all disclosure statements in promoting subdivided land. (*See RAW LAND, SUBDIVISION.*)

UNINCORPORATED ASSOCIATION An assembly of people associated for some religious, scientific, fraternal, or recreational purpose. Members of such associations are not personally liable for debts incurred in the acquisition or leasing of real property used by the association, unless they specifically assume liability in writing. The association itself normally does not hold title to property. Any title is held through a trustee. It is therefore important when dealing with unincorporated associations, such as churches, that the broker check to see whether the person representing the association has actual authority to convey title to the property. A majority of condominium owners' associations are unincorporated.

The Internal Revenue Code allows two types of housing associations to elect to be treated as tax-exempt organizations—condominium management associations and residential real estate management associations. But this tax-exempt status will protect the association from tax only on its exempt-function income, such as membership dues, fees, and assessments received from member/owners of residential units in the particular condominium or subdivision involved. For example, on any net income that is not exempt-function income, the association is taxed at corporate rates but is not permitted the corporate surtax exemption granted to regular domestic corporations. It may, however, use the alternative tax on its net long-term capital gain. (*See CONDOMINIUM OWNERS' ASSOCIATION, COOPERATIVE OWNERSHIP.*)

UNIT A part of the property intended for any type of independent use and with an exit to a public street or corridor. Unit commonly refers to the individual apartment units in a condominium, exclusive of the common areas. A unit normally consists of the walls and partitions, which are not load-bearing, within a condominium's perimeter walls, the inner decorated or furnished surfaces of all walls, floors and ceilings, doors, windows, or panels along the perimeters, and all original fixtures. The particular condominium declaration should be consulted for the exact definition of the unit.

UNIT-IN-PLACE METHOD An appraisal method of computing replacement cost, also called the segregated cost method, which uses prices for various building components, as installed, based on specific units of use such as square footage or cubic footage. These cost figures include the cost of labor, overhead, and profit. For example, insulation may cost $.07 per square foot, dry wall $1.50 per square yard, painting $.08 per square foot, and so on. The total in-place cost of each unit (unit value) is multiplied by the number of such units in the building to determine the total replacement cost for the entire building. Sample building components are roof, floor, concrete, electrical, plumbing, and parking area. (See *QUANTITY SURVEY.*)

UNIT VALUE   Value or price related to a unit of measurements, for example, $20 per square foot, $200 per front foot, and so on.

UNITY (JOINT TENANCY)   A concurrence of certain requirements. Under common law rules, there are four unities essential to the creation of a joint tenancy: unity of interest, title, time, and possession. That is, the tenants must have one and the same equal interest; the interests must arise from the same conveyance instrument from the same grantor; they must commence at one and the same time; and the property must be held by one and the same undivided possession.

By statute in many states, however, an owner of property can convey to him- or herself and another as joint tenants, thus altering the common law rule requiring *unity of title*. In a tenancy in common, the only unity is that of possession. (See *JOINT TENANCY.*)

UNJUST ENRICHMENT   The circumstances in which a person has received and retains money or goods which in fairness and justice belong to another. A lawsuit may be necessary to recover such money or goods. (See *QUASI.*)

UNLAWFUL DETAINER ACTION   A legal action which provides a method of evicting a tenant who is in default under the terms of the lease; a summary proceeding to recover possession of property. (See *SUMMARY POSSESSION.*)

UNMARKETABLE TITLE   A title to property, which contains substantial defects such as undisclosed encroachments, building code violations, easements, or outstanding dower. A title acquired by adverse possession is usually not marketable until a quiet title suit is brought. (See *MARKETABLE TITLE.*)

In some cases a title insurance company might insure a title even though there are some remote claims to the title. The title is then insurable though not marketable. This can cause problems should a subsequent title examiner object to the title and effectively prevent a resale of the property. Since no actual loss has occurred, the coverage under the original title insurance policy is not applicable.

UNREASONABLY WITHHELD CONSENT   Many legal documents, such as leases and contracts for deed, contain a transfer clause which states, in effect, that the property may be transferred only with the owner's consent, "which consent shall not be unreasonably withheld." There is no acceptable definition of what is unreasonable. For example, it would be reasonable for a lessor to refuse to transfer a lease to a new tenant whose business would directly compete with another tenant in the same shopping center complex (i.e. poor tenant mix).

In a contract for deed situation, it would generally be unreasonable for the vendor to refuse an assignment or to demand a share in the profits where the assignee is as good a credit risk, if not better, as the assignor-vendee.

To avoid lawsuits, it would be best to set forth some criteria for reasonable consent in the transfer clause itself. (*See ASSIGNMENT.*)

UNRECORDED DEED A deed which has not been recorded. An unrecorded deed is valid between grantor and grantee, and anyone with notice of the ownership of the property. An unrecorded deed is different from a wild deed, which is one not properly recorded. (*See WILD DEED.*)

UNSECURED A debt instrument, such as a debenture, which is backed only by the debtor's promise to pay. (*See DEBENTURE, NONRECOURSE.*)

UPGRADES Changes in design or improvements to property after the purchase but before the closing date, such as added appliances, carpeting, or reconstructed roof. The purchaser would absorb the costs for such improvements.

UP-LEG The replacement property purchased in a Section 1031, tax-deferred exchange; typically, the taxpayer trades up in an exchange. (*See EXCHANGE.*)

UP-RAMP An inclined or sloping roadway or walk leading from one level to another, often employed to gain access from ground level to the floor level of a dock-high building for either personnel or vehicles.

UPSET DATE A date stipulated in a contract which specifies when a building must be ready for occupancy or when the buyer has the option to rescind the agreement.

UPSET PRICE A minimum price set by a court in a judicial foreclosure, below which the property may not be sold by a court-appointed commissioner at public auction; the minimum price which can be accepted for the property after the court has had the property appraised. The upset price should not exceed the reasonable market value of the property at the time of foreclosure. It sometimes happens that the upset price is so high that there are no bidders and the entire process leading up to the public auction must be repeated. The resulting time delay and expense are reasons why many attorneys provide for nonjudicial foreclosure proceedings under a power of sale provided in the mortgage instrument. (*See FORECLOSURE.*)

UPZONING A change in zoning classification from a lower to a higher use. (*See DOWNZONING.*)

URBAN ENTERPRISE   A relatively new approach to urban renewal pat-
ZONE   terned after a British model. An enterprise zone is
a depressed neighborhood, usually within an
urban area, in which business enterprises are given tax incentives (reduced property taxes) and exemptions from many governmental restrictions (no rent control)
in an attempt to stimulate new business activity, provide jobs, and revitalize the
area. The emphasis is on removing government financial burdens rather than providing direct government subsidies.

URBAN LAND   An independent, nonprofit research and educa-
INSTITUTE   tional organization incorporated in 1936 to improve the quality and standards of land use and
development. The Institute conducts practical research into the various fields of
real estate knowledge, identifies and interprets land use trends in relation to
changing needs, and disseminates information from over 100 books to promote
orderly and efficient land use.

URBAN RENEWAL   A process of upgrading deteriorated neighborhoods through clearance and redevelopment, re-
habilitation, and the installation of new public improvements, or modernization
of existing ones. Urban renewal activities may be funded with a combination of
federal and local funds, or strictly with private monies.

For example, the FHA 229(d)(3) program insures mortgages for rent-subsidized
housing projects in approved urban renewal areas and subsidizes mortgage interest for qualified housing sponsors. (See NEW TOWN, SLUM CLEARANCE.)

URBAN SPRAWL   The unplanned expansion of a municipality over
a large geographical area.

USABLE AREA   On a multitenancy floor, usable area is the gross
area minus core space. Core space includes the
square footage used for public corridors, stairwells, washrooms, elevators, electrical and janitorial closets, and fan rooms. On a single tenant floor, the usable area is
the gross square footage excluding building lobby and all penetrating shafts (that
is, ducts, stairwells, and elevators).

USEFUL LIFE   That period of time over which an asset, such as a
building, is expected to remain economically fea-
sible to the owner. Since the annual amount of tax depreciation results from an
apportionment of the investment in the building over its useful life, it has traditionally been important to ascertain correctly the proper useful life. The shorter
the life, the more the annual deductions.

Under the Economic Recovery Tax Act of 1981, the concept of useful life based on
actual economic life was replaced with an arbitrary "cost recovery period." As a
result, the former battles between the taxpayer and the IRS over the useful life law
have been eliminated. With real estate, the cost recovery period is normally 15
years, although optional periods of 35 or 45 years may be used (for personal property, it is 3, 5, or 10 years). (See ACCELERATED COST RECOVERY SYSTEM,
DEPRECIATION [TAX], SALVAGE VALUE.)

USE TAX   A tax imposed on the purchaser or importer of tangible, personal property for resale, use, or consumption.

USE VALUE   The subjective value of a special purpose property, designed to fit the particular requirements of the owner, but which would have little or no use to another owner. Also called value-in-use, it includes the valuation of amenities attaching to a property.

U.S. GEOLOGICAL SURVEY   An agency within the U.S. Department of the Interior with responsibility for conservation, geological surveys, and mapping of lands within U.S. boundaries (See BENCHMARK.)

U.S. LEAGUE OF SAVINGS ASSOCIATIONS   The national trade association for savings and loan associations and cooperative banks.

USUFRUCTUARY RIGHT   The right to the use, enjoyment, and profits of property belonging to another, such as an easement or profit a prendre. (See EASEMENT.)

USURY   The act of charging a rate of interest in excess of that permitted by law. Some states have set a specific interest limit, charging more than which would be usury, while others have what is known as a floating interest rate, usually pegged each month at a certain percent above a fluctuating economic indicator, such as the interest rate on long-term Treasury notes or Federal Reserve discount rates. A lending contract which charges a usurious interest rate may be void or voidable in certain states. Deliberately charging or receiving usurious interest rates on loans is known as loan sharking, a crime which may be considered either a misdemeanor or a felony. In some states, the penalty for usury is that the lender is not entitled to any interest and must apply all interest collected to reduce the principal balance of the loan.

Certain transactions are exempt from state usury laws, such as VA and FHA transactions. Under the federal Depository Institutions Deregulation and Monetary Control Act of 1980, the federal government preempted state usury ceilings for federally related conventional residential first mortgage loans unless a state enacts overruling legislation by April 1, 1983. (See INTEREST.)

UTILITIES   The basic service system required by a developed area such as telephone, electricity, water, and gas. Utility easements are usually gross easements running on, over, or under the property.

UTILITY ROOM   A room, often located on the ground floor, that is designed for use as a laundry or service room.

UTILITY VALUE   The value in use to an owner-user, which includes a value of amenities attaching to a property; also known as subjective value.

VACANCY FACTOR An allowance or discount for estimated vacancies (unrented units) in a rental project. The vacancy and loss in rent factor is important in assembling an investment income analysis of a property, such as an apartment building. The vacancy rate is the ratio between the number of vacant units and the total number of units in a specified project or area.

Current statistics on vacancy factors can be obtained from the U.S. Census Bureau, regional housing reports published by the Department of Commence, and local utility companies.

VACATE To give up occupancy or surrender possession.

VACATION HOME A residence, usually in a resort or vacation area, used as a second home for recreational purposes. Many taxpayers owning such property attempt to rent it during periods when they are not occupying it. Federal tax laws limit the business-type deductions an owner may claim relating to rental of a second home if the owner's personal use exceeds the 14 days or 10 percent of the number of days it is actually rented, whichever is greater. If the personal use limitation is exceeded, deductions for cost recovery, maintenance, and utilities can be deducted only for the rental portion of the year, and then only to the extent that rental income exceeds interest and real property taxes. However, if the vacation home is rented for less than 15 days, the owner need not report the income, nor may the owner deduct any business expenses on his or her tax return for that year. (See ABSENTEE OWNER, RENTAL POOL.)

VALID Legally sufficient or effective, such as a valid contract—a contract which must in all respects comply with the provisions of the contract law. A valid contract should be executed with proper formalities, should satisfy legal requirements, should have sufficient legal force to stand against attack, and should be for a legal purpose.

VALUABLE CONSIDERATION The granting of some beneficial right, interest, or profit, or the suffering of some legal detriment or default by one party in return for the performance of another, usually as an inducement for a contract. Valuable consideration is different from good consideration, which is love and affection with no pecuniary measure of value, such as a father might use as consideration to grant an estate to his son or daughter.

Valuable consideration is always sufficient to support a contract, whereas good consideration may in some cases be insufficient. For example, a father might agree to transfer title to real property to his son in consideration for the son's abstention from smoking, drinking, and going out with women of questionable moral character before the age of 21. If the son does agree to forbear, at the age of 21 the son can enforce the contract because he has provided valuable consideration; that is, he gave up a right in return for his father's promise.

However, if the father had agreed to convey title to the property in consideration of the love and affection that the son has for him, the son would not be able to force the father to transfer the property to him. Although it would be sufficient to pass title if stated in the deed; it is not enough to support the contract because the son has not given up any rights or made any promises. (See CONSIDERATION, LOVE AND AFFECTION, SPECIFIC PERFORMANCE.)

VALUE The power of a good or service to command other goods in exchange for the present worth to typical users and investors of future benefits arising out of ownership of a property; the amount of money deemed to be the equivalent in worth of the subject property. The four essential elements of value are utility, scarcity, demand, and transferability. Cost does not equal value, nor does equity. There are various types of value, such as market value, tax assessed value, book value, insurance value, use value, par value, rental value, and replacement value. By far, the type of value used for the largest number of real estate transactions is fair market value.

In addition, there are many factors which influence the value of a particular property. It is generally agreed that of them all, location is most important. Other factors are size and shape, utility, access, and exposure. For example, the south and west sides of business streets are usually more valuable because pedestrians seek the shady side of the street and display merchandise is not damaged by the sun.

VARIABLE INTEREST RATE A modern approach to financing in which the lender is permitted to alter the interest rate under a loan, with a certain period of advance notice, based upon an agreed basic index. Monthly mortgage payments can then be increased, decreased, or maturity extended, depending on how the base index varies. For example: "The sum of $50,000 payable in monthly installments of $400 each, including interest on the unpaid balance at the rate of 8½ percent per year or two percent higher than the prime interest rate in effect at the Bank of Primo, whichever is greater (such rate to be established once each year on the first banking day of each calendar year), provided that the interest rate shall not exceed the maximum rate permitted by law."

A variation of this concept was recently introduced with 1-year maturity/20-year amortization mortgage loans. At the end of one year the loan is renegotiated at the then current interest rate and the remaining principal balance and new interest payments are spread over a 19-year period. This process continues every year the loan is outstanding.

VARIABLE PAYMENT PLAN A mortgage repayment plan which allows a person to make small payments early in the loan term, increasing in future years, presumably as the mortgagor's income increases. This is also called the *flexible rate mortgage*, the design of which is to help borrowers qualify for loans by basing repayment schedules on salary expectations.

The variable index may be external (interest rate on government bonds) or internal (tied to the rate paid on the lender's savings deposits).

VARIABLE RATE MORTGAGE (VRM)   A mortgage used prior to 1982 in which the interest rate will vary in accordance with an agreed-upon base index, thus resulting in a change in the borrower's installment payments. Many lending institutions use the cost-of-funds index at the Federal Home Loan Bank Board (FHLBB) as the base index.

If the interest rate is increased, the borrower has the option of increasing the monthly payment, keeping the payment constant but extending the term of the loan, or refinancing without penalty.

The VRM has been replaced in the 1980s by various types of adjustable mortgage loans. (*See ADJUSTABLE RATE LOAN.*)

VARIANCE   Permission obtained from governmental zoning authorities to build a structure or conduct a use which is expressly prohibited by the current zoning laws; an exception from the zoning laws. A variance gives some measure of elasticity to the zoning game.

To eliminate land speculation, many variances are granted conditioned upon the commencement of construction within a certain time period (for example, twelve months). There are use variances such as for apartment use in a single-family residential area. There is also an area or building variance where the owner attempts to get permission to build a structure larger than permitted.

The applicant usually must describe how the applicant would be deprived of the reasonable use of the land or building if it were used only for the purpose allowed in that zone; how the request is due to unique circumstances and not the general conditions in the neighborhood; and how the use sought will not alter the essential character of the locality nor be contrary to the intent and purpose of the zoning code. (*See NONCONFORMING USE.*)

VENDEE   The purchaser of realty; the buyer. The buyer under contract for deed.

VENDOR   The seller of realty. The seller under contract for deed. In some cases, the vendor may not be the owner—he or she might be the holder of an option.

VENDOR'S LIEN   The equitable lien of the grantor upon the land conveyed, in the amount of the unpaid purchase price. Unlike a mortgage, it is not an absolute interest in the property, but is only an equitable right to rely on in case all of the purchase money is not paid.

VENEER   A layer of material covering a base of another substance, such as mahogany veneer on other less valuable wood, or brick exterior finish over wood framing.

VENT   A small opening to allow the passage of air through any space in a building, as for ventilation of an attic or the unexcavated area under a first-floor construction.

VENTURE CAPITAL   Unsecured money directed toward an investment. Because of the risks involved, it usually commands the highest rate of return for its investment.

VENUE   From the Latin word meaning "to come," it refers to the place where the cause of action arose, or the place where the jury is selected and the trial is brought. An acknowledgment contains a statement of the county and state where the acknowledgment is taken and where the officer taking the acknowledgment is appointed—his or her venue.

VERIFY   To confirm or substantiate by oath. Claims made to small claims court must be verified. (See AFFIRMATION.)

VESTED INTEREST   A present right, interest, or title to realty, such as a vested remainder, which carries with it the existing right to convey, even though use of possession is postponed to some uncertain time in the future. For example, when Phil Black grants John Park a life estate in his ranch, the property reverts to Black upon the death of Park. The reversion is a vested interest.

VESTIBULE   A small entrance hall to a building or to a room.

VETERANS ADMINISTRATION (VA)

History and Eligibility

Under the Serviceman's Readjustment Act of 1944, as amended by the Korea GI Bill of 1952, the Veterans Housing Act of 1974 and 1978, and the Veterans Disability compensation and Housing Benefits Amendments of 1980, eligible veterans and unremarried widows or widowers of veterans who died in service or from service-connected causes may obtain partially guaranteed loans for the purchase or construction of a house or to refinance existing mortgage debt. An eligible veteran is one who served a minimum of 181 days active duty between September 16, 1940, and September 7, 1981. During specifically designated wartime periods, the minimum requirement is 90 days of active duty. Any enlisted member of the Armed Forces who began service after September 7, 1981 or any commissioned officer who began active service after October 16, 1981, must complete a total of two years active service to be eligible for a VA-guaranteed home loan. There is a special provision allowing active duty personnel with less than two years service to obtain a VA-guaranteed home loan after 181 days so long as they are still on active duty. Eligibility can be determined by contacting any Veterans Administration Regional Office or through most VA-approved lending institutions.

The main purpose of the GI loan is to assist veterans in financing the purchase of reasonably priced homes, including condominium units and mobile homes, with little or no down payment, relatively easy qualification criteria, and a comparatively low rate of interest. The VA program encourages private lending institutions to make what are often very high loan-to-value mortgages by guaranteeing part of the loan in event of default.

Entitlement and Loan Guaranty

From time to time Congress has increased the amount of entitlement all veterans receive for use in the home loan guaranty program. As of this writing, the amount of entitlement available to all eligible veterans regardless of when they served in the Armed Forces is $27,500 for home and condominium purchases and $20,000 for mobile home purchases. Only in certain rural areas where home financing is not reasonably available does VA lend money itself. Usually the veteran makes application with a VA-approved lending institution of his or her choice, which will consider the veteran's application knowing the loan will be at least partially guaranteed against loss by VA. VA will guarantee the lender against loss up to 60 percent of the initial loan amount or $27,500, whichever is less. This is the maximum amount VA will pay the lender after foreclosure in case there is a deficiency upon the sale of the property.

Interest Rate and Loan Limits

The maximum interest rate permitted on VA loans is set by the Veterans Administration Administrator. For many years this rate has been identical with the FHA interest rate as set by the Secretary of Housing and Urban Development. The length of the loan can be for any number of years up to a maximum term of 30 years. Two factors limiting the length of the mortgage are: 1. the term of the loan cannot exceed the dwelling's remaining useful economic life as determined by a VA appraisal; and 2. the term of the loan can be only for the remaining fixed rental period on a ground lease property.

VA sets no maximum loan amount. In effect the "maximum VA loan limit" is established by the highest dollar amount of VA loans which the secondary markets (FNMA and GNMA) are willing to purchase. Loans are made in increments of $50. The maximum loan amount available on a specific property is based on the purchase price or the VA-appraised value, whichever is less. (It should be noted that VA recognizes FHA appraisals, but not conventional appraisals.) VA requires that the real estate sales contract on a property include a provision (usually in the form of an addendum) that should the property appraise for less than the sales price, the seller agrees to refund the buyer's good faith deposit and cancel the contract if the veteran does not wish to complete the purchase of the property.

Under certain conditions, secondary financing is permited at the time a VA-guaranteed loan is made. Basically VA requires that: 1. the second mortgage document be as protective of the veteran's rights in a default situation as is the VA first mortgage; and 2. that the second mortgage be fully amortized with no balloon payment. An exception to the latter requirement may be made if the veteran can demonstrate at the time of the loan application that he or she already has the funds available with which to meet the balloon payment when it comes due. The borrower must be prepared to pay cash for all closing costs (it is permissible for the seller to pay closing costs) and for the difference between the sales price and the maximum loan amount (which the seller cannot pay or otherwise credit the veteran). In fact, the borrower must provide evidence of the needed funds before VA will make its commitment to guarantee the loan. There is no prohibition against placing secondary financing on the property after the VA mortgage is closed and VA has issued the VA guarantee to the lender.

Loan Fees and Discount Points

A VA loan applicant is allowed to pay a loan origination fee of not more than one percent of the amount borrowed. The buyer is *not* permitted to pay any loan discount points except in the case of refinancing or builder-mortgagors. The lender normally finds it necessary to charge loan discount points to increase the yield on the loan from the set VA interest rate to a level reflective of the cost of funds in the financial marketplace. One point equals one percent of the total mortgage loan amount. During periods when credit is difficult to obtain, VA discount points have run as high as 10 or 12 points. While this is not the usual situation, the discount paid by a seller on a $50,000 loan could amount to as much as $5,000 or $6,000. A more normal range for discount points would be from two to five points.

Programs

VA-guaranteed home loans are granted for construction or purchase of a home. They may also be obtained to refinance existing mortgage debt. In all cases, however, VA requires the veteran to certify that he or she occupies or intends to occupy the property as his or her home. This certification must be given at time of loan application, and again at closing. The veteran is subject to criminal prosecution for making false certifications, although after fulfilling the owner/occupancy requirement the veteran would be allowed to rent the home or sell it while retaining the VA loan.

There are two types of VA loans—level payment mortgages and graduated payment mortgages. The level payment or "traditional" VA loan has for some years had a maximum loan-to-value ratio of 100 percent for properties where the sales price or the appraisal (whichever is less) does not exceed four times the amount of entitlement the veteran has available. For any sales price of appraisal value exceeding four times a veteran's available entitlement, the loan-to-value ration is 75 percent on that portion greater than four times the entitlement figure. These loan-to-value ratios are not set by VA, but are requirements set by the secondary market purchasers of VA loans (FNMA and GNMA).

In late 1981, VA introduced a graduated payment mortgage program to permit lower monthly payments in the early years of the mortgage through negative amortization. The structure of the program is virtually identical with the FHA-245 loan program. As with the FHA graduated mortgage, the VA GPM requires a higher down payment than the level payment loan and is designed for the young homebuyer starting out to be able to qualify to buy a home sooner than if the veteran had to earn the income necessary to qualify for a higher payment level loan.

Assumptions

At this writing VA loans remain fully assumable with no escalation of interest rates or modifications or changes to the underlying loan. A veteran may sell a home purchased with a VA-guaranteed loan to anyone including a nonveteran. The veteran can choose to remain liable for the VA loan or may seek a release of liability on the loan if the person assuming the loan is financially qualified to make the mortgage payments. Further, if the person assuming the loan is an eligible veteran, he or she can substitute the entitlement for that of the seller. Upon substitution, which also requires the veteran-purchaser to qualify to release the veteran-seller of liability, the veteran seller then has his entitlement reinstated to allow the use of a VA loan privilege in a future home purchase.

VETO CLAUSE   A clause in a shopping center lease, which gives the tenant, usually an anchor tenant, the right to bar any lease between the landlord and another tenant. Such clauses are generally held invalid under modern antitrust interpretation.

VIOLATION   An act, deed, or condition contrary to the law or permissible use of real property.

VISUAL RIGHTS   The right to prevent a structure from being erected where it would obstruct a scenic view (e.g., billboards) or interfere with clear vision at a traffic intersection.

VOCATION   One's regular calling or business. The work in which a person is regularly employed. In most states, one can be a real estate broker or salesperson as a part-time vocation.

VOID   Having no legal force or binding effect; a nullity; not enforceable. A void agreement is no contract at all. A void contract need not be disaffirmed nor can it be ratified. A contract for an illegal purpose (for example, gambling) is void. Under many state and local discrimination laws, any restrictive covenant which discriminates on the basis of race, sex, color, religion, marital status, or ancestry may be void (although the nondiscriminating portions of the document in which it is contained may still remain valid). (See *UNENFORCEABLE CONTRACT.*)

VOIDABLE   A contract which appears valid and enforceable on its face, but is subject to rescission by one of the parties who acted under a disability. This would include such disabilities as being a minor or being under duress or undue influence; that which may be avoided or adjudged void but which is not, in itself, void. A voidable contract is one that is *able* to be *voided*. Voidable implies a valid act which may be rejected by an act of disaffirmance, rather than an invalid act which may be confirmed. For example, assume that a minor contracts to buy a diamond ring, the contract can be avoided by the minor because of his or her lack of sufficient age. If, however, the minor elects to enforce the contract, the contract is valid and the other party cannot assert the minor's lack of age as a defense.

In cases of fraud against the buyer or real estate, the buyer may affirm or disaffirm the contract within a reasonable time after the truth is discovered. For the duration of a license suspension, a broker's listings are voidable because of his or her inability to perform contractual obligations. (See *MINOR, VOID.*)

VOUCHER SYSTEM   In construction lending, a system of giving subcontractors a voucher that they may redeem with the construction lender in lieu of cash. The voucher system is the opposite of a fixed disbursement schedule under which the lender forwards certain amounts of capital under a fixed schedule to subcontractors.

WAINSCOTING   Wood lining of an interior wall. Wainscoting is also the lower part of a wall when finished differently from the wall above.

WAIVER   To give up or surrender a right voluntarily. Since the waiver is a frequently used defense to a breach of contract suit, it is good practice to insert a clause into every contract which stipulates that no waiver, modification, or amendment of any provision in the document will be valid unless it is in writing and signed by the party against whom the enforcement is sought. In some cases, the law prohibits a person from waiving certain rights granted by statute. For example, a provision in a contract is generally void if it purports to bind any prospective purchaser of subdivided lands to waive compliance with the protections afforded under state subdivision registration laws. Also void may be agreements to waive rights provided under a landlord and tenant code.

In building construction situations, the general contractor usually retains a portion of the final payment to his or her subcontractors until they present waivers of their mechanics' lien rights. This is called a waiver of lien.

The general rule is that a contingency placed in a contract for one person's benefit can be waived by that person for any reason. For example, a buyer who agrees to buy a farm contingent on favorable soil tests can decide to waive the contingency and purchase the farm even if the soil tests are negative.

WALK-UP   An apartment in a building in which there are several levels and no elevator.

WALLBOARD   A board used as the finishing covering for an interior wall or ceiling. Wallboard can be made of plastic laminated plywood, asbestos/cement sheeting, plywood, molded gypsum, plasterboard, or other materials. Wallboard is applied in thin sheets over the insulation. It is often used today as a substitute for plaster walls but can also serve as a base for plaster.

WALL SHEATHING   Sheets of plywood, gypsum board, or other material nailed to the outside face of the wall studs to form a base for the exterior siding.

WALL STUD   *See STUD.*

WALL-TO-WALL   Carpeting which fully covers the floor area in a
CARPETING   room. When a seller lists property to include
wall-to-wall carpeting, the broker should take
care to verify that there is, in fact, wall-to-wall carpeting. This may avoid the not
too uncommon problem which occurs when the seller removes the furniture, and
the buyer discovers that there are gaps in the carpeting. In most cases, wall-to-wall
carpeting is treated as a fixture, but to avoid disputes the buyer and seller should
specify in their sales contract whether or not the wall-to-wall carpeting will pass
to the buyer.

Wall-to-wall carpeting meeting minimum FHA standards is now accepted as finished flooring in proposed or existing homes and multifamily properties, and as
such is considered part of the real property.

WAREHOUSE   A building used to store merchandise and other
materials or equipment. As an investment, a
warehouse is considered low risk, has a relatively low rate of return, and is usually operated under a net lease. Such properties are usually classified as industrial. (*See MINIWAREHOUSE.*)

WAREHOUSING   A term used in financing to describe the process
employed by loan correspondents to assemble
into one package a number of mortgage loans, which the correspondent has originated and which he or she sells in the secondary mortgage market. The sale of
these mortgages provides added capital with which to make more loans, which
can then be packaged and sold, thus repeating the cycle. Lenders frequently accumulate FHA loans to process in a group package.

A mortgage banker will often borrow short-term money to initially fund mortgage
loans. The banker will then warehouse a number of such loans (much as a whole-
saler will warehouse clothing or furniture) to be sold at a later date to a large
financial institution. When the loans are sold, the mortgage banker will generally
receive the value of the warehoused mortgage loans, plus a 1 percent origination
charge and a commitment for approximately ½ of 1 percent servicing fee over the
life of the loan.

WARRANTY   A promise that certain stated facts are true. A
guaranty by the seller, covering the title as well as
the physical condition of the property. A warranty is different from a representation in that a representation is a statement made in the course of negotiations
leading up to the sale, but not incorporated into the contract. A warranty, on the
other hand, would be a statement *in the contract* asserting the truth of certain
things about the property. In order to prove a breach of warranty, a buyer must
prove that the situation in violation of the warranty was in effect as of the date of
closing (such as when the seller asserts that there is adequate water available for
drinking purposes when in fact there is not). A breach of warranty action can only
result in damages being awarded by the court, not rescission as with a misrepresentation.

In contract law, a warranty is basically a written or oral undertaking or stipulation
that a certain fact in relation to the subject matter of the contract is or will be as it
is stated or promised to be. A warranty differs from a representation in that a

warranty must always be given contemporaneously with, and as a part of, the contract, while a representation precedes and induces the contract. While that is their difference in nature, their difference in consequence or effect is this: upon the breach of a warranty, the contract remains binding, and only damages are recoverable for their breach. Upon a false representation by the seller, the purchaser may elect to avoid the contract and recover the entire price paid.

There is a current trend in the courts to enforce an implied warranty of fitness and merchantability against builders and sellers of new homes, including condominium units. This rejection of the common-law caveat emptor doctrine has not yet been applied to the resale of older homes. (See *CAVEAT EMPTOR, IMPLIED WARRANTY OF HABITABILITY.*)

The Magnusen-Moss Warranty Act is a federal law requiring the full and fair disclosures of any warranty on any consumer product in the home, whether the manufacturer's or the seller's. The law covers separate items of equipment attached to real property, such as air-conditioners, furnaces, and water heaters. The Act is administered by the Federal Trade Commission.

WARRANTY DEED   A deed in which the grantor fully warrants good clear title to the premises. Also called a general warranty deed. The usual covenants of title are: covenant of seisin, covenant of quiet enjoyment, covenant against encumbrances, covenant of warranty forever, and covenant of further assurance. A warranty deed warrants the title, not the fitness or quality of construction of the real property. A warranty deed is used in most real estate deed transfers and offers the greatest protection of any deed. (See *DEED.*)

WASTE   An improper use or abuse of property by one in possession of land, who holds less than the fee ownership, such as a tenant, life tenant, mortgagor, or vendee. Such waste thus impairs the value of the land or the interest of the one holding the title or the reversion (for example the lessor). The term "waste" includes *ameliorating waste,* which is the unauthorized alteration by the occupant of improvements on the land, even though such changes in fact increase the value of the property. While the tenant is usually not liable for ameliorating waste (since it increases the worth of the future interest), the owner of the future interest does not have to pay for the improvement.

Waste could occur through failure to pay property taxes, insurance, or mortgage payments, as well as by making material changes to the original use of the property, such as converting from residential to heavy industrial. In essence, any act on the land which substantially impairs the security value of the real estate is considered waste. Other examples of affirmative or voluntary waste would be cutting timber, removing minerals, or destroying buildings.

WASTELAND   Land which is deemed to be unfit for cultivation; unproductive, unimproved, barren land such as lava land. An owner may be able to apply to the local tax agency to classify his or her property as wasteland for real property tax purposes.

WASTE LINE   A pipe that carries waste from a bathtub, shower, basin, or any fixture or appliance, except a toilet.

WASTING ASSET   Property such as timber, an oil well, a quarry, or a mine, the substance of which is depleted through drilling and exploitation. Also refers to rights such as patent rights and franchises for a fixed term. (See DEPLETION.)

WATER   In its natural state, water is real property. When it is severed from the realty and reduced to possession by putting it in containers, it becomes personal property.

There are three classifications of water. *Surface water* is water diffused over the land surface, or contained in depressions therein, resulting from rain, snow, or that which rises to the surface from springs. It is thus distinguishable from water flowing in a fixed channel, so as to constitute a *watercourse,* or water collected in an identifiable body, such as a river or lake. The extraordinary overflow of rivers and streams is known as *flood water.* (See CORRELATIVE WATER RIGHT, RIPARIAN.)

WATERCOURSE   A running stream of water following a regular course or channel and possessing a bed and banks.

WATERFRONT PROPERTY   Real estate (improved or unimproved) abutting on a body of water such as a canal, lake, or ocean.

WATERSHED   The drainage area contributing to the water found in the abutting stream; the drainage basin. Many municipalities restrict owners from filling in or otherwise disrupting water flow in a watershed area.

WATER TABLE   The natural level at which water will be located, be it above or below the surface of the ground.

WAY   A street, alley, or other thoroughfare or easement permanently established for passage of persons or vehicles.

WEAR AND TEAR   The gradual physical deterioration of property, resulting from use, passage of time, and weather. Only property subject to wear and tear is eligible for cost recovery. Generally, a tenant must return the leased premises to the landlord in good condition, ordinary wear and tear excepted. (See NORMAL WEAR AND TEAR.)

WEEP HOLE   One of several small holes left in a wall to permit surplus water to drain; as used in a retaining wall or foundation.

WET COLUMN   A column containing plumbing lines facilitating the installation of sinks, drinking fountains, and like things.

WETLANDS   Land areas where ground water is at or near the surface of the ground for enough of each year so as to produce a wetland plant community, such as swamps, floodplains, and marshes. Since these areas are so susceptible to flooding, they are subject to many federal, state, and local controls, including environmental protection and zoning for special preservation and conservation.

WIDOW'S QUARANTINE   That period of time after the husband's death that a widow may remain in the house of her deceased husband without being charged for rent therefore. In the meantime, she is entitled to her reasonable sustenance out of his estate. (*See DOWER.*)

WILD DEED   A deed appearing in the chain of title in which the first party (grantor) has no recorded interest in the subject property. If the grantor is a stranger to the chain of title, the deed does not give constructive notice of its existence. However, actual knowledge of its existence puts one on notice that this first party may have had a legitimate interest in the subject property under an unrecorded instrument. (*See CHAIN OF TITLE; NAME, CHANGE OF.*)

WILL   A written instrument disposing of probate property (tenancy in severalty or tenancy in common) upon the death of the maker (the testator). A will takes effect only upon the testator's death, not during his or her life, and thus can be revoked or amended at any time during the testator's life. The testator must generally be of sound mind, of adult age, and must declare the writing to be his or her *last will and testament* and sign it, usually in the presence of two or more credible persons who subscribe their names as witnesses to the will. A witness must generally be a person other than a beneficiary under the will. The testator often designates an executor or personal representative and where there are minor children, he or she usually nominates a guardian. No one should attempt to write a will without first consulting an attorney. When a person dies either without a will or with a defectively executed will, his or her property passes to the heirs according to the laws of intestacy. A surviving spouse may be able, by law, to elect to take a one-third life estate as dower or curtesy, an elective share, or some other survivorship portion given by statute in lieu of his or her share provided in the will, if any. (*See DESCENT, HOLOGRAPHIC WILL, INTESTATE, PROBATE, TESTATOR.*)

WINDOW JAMB TRIM   A thin vertical strip of molding covering the junction of the vertical members of the window frame and the jamb.

WINDOW SASH   The movable frame that holds the window glass. Sash windows move vertically; they may be either a single in which only the lower half of the window opens or a double in which both the upper and lower portions are movable.

WITHOUT RECOURSE   A form of qualified endorsement relieving the maker of personal liability. In a promissory note secured by a mortgage on real property, a *without* *recourse* note means that the mortgagee can only satisfy the claim against the property; that is, the mortgagee cannot sue the defaulting mortgagor for a deficiency judgment.

WITNESS To sign one's name to a contract, deed, will, or other document for the purpose of attesting to its authenticity and proving its execution by testifying, if required.

As a general rule, witnesses are not necessary to the validity of a real estate contract. A will, however, must usually be witnessed by at least two disinterested third persons. (*See SUBSCRIBE.*)

WOMEN'S COUNCIL OF REALTORS® An organization within the National Association of REALTORS® whose purpose is to expand its members' knowledge of the real estate business and provide an opportunity for sharing experiences and exchanging information.

WORKERS' COMPENSATION LAW A state law requiring all employers to provide insurance coverage for their employees. This law may apply to real estate brokers, regardless of whether or not the broker considers his or her salespeople to be employees or independent contractors. If a salesperson is thus injured on the job, he or she will be covered for specified medical expenses and lost wages. If a broker does not carry the requisite insurance, the broker may be subject to civil penalties, including suspension or revocation of the broker's real estate license. (*See INDEPENDENT CONTRACTOR.*)

WORKING CAPITAL Liquid assets available for the conduct of daily business.

WORKING DRAWINGS The final-stage drawings by an architect that shows the lighting layout, electrical plugs, telephone outlets, and similar items and details the precise method of construction. (*See BLUEPRINT, PLANS AND SPECIFICATIONS.*)

WORK LETTER A detailed addition to a lease defining all improvement work to be done by the landlord for the tenant and specifying what work the tenant will perform at his or her own expense.

WORK-OUT PLAN An attempt by a mortgagee to assist a mortgagor in default to workout a payment plan rather than proceed directly with a foreclosure. Some possible work-out plans could include extending the loan term, accruing interest, or reducing the interest rate. (*See FOREBEARANCE.*)

WORTHIER TITLE DOCTRINE A common law doctrine which held that where a testator devised to an heir exactly the same interest in land as such that the heir would take by the laws of descent, then the latter was regarded as worthier and the heir took his or her title by descent rather than by devise.

WRAPAROUND A method of financing in which the new mortgage
MORTGAGE   is placed in a secondary or subordinate position;
               the new mortgage includes both the unpaid prin-
cipal balance of the first mortgage and whatever additional sums are advanced by
the lender. Sometimes called an all-inclusive loan, an overriding loan, or an overlapping loan. In essence, it is an additional mortgage in which another lender
refinances a borrower by lending an amount over the existing first mortgage
amount, without cashing out or disturbing the existence of the first mortgage. The
entire loan is treated as a single obligation (like a "consolidated loan") and the
wrap, or secondary, mortgagee pays the obligations of the first mortgage from the
total payments received. The difference between the interest of the two mortgage
notes is called the arbitrage. While the wraparound lender makes the debt service
payments on the first mortgage, the lender does not assume liability for this first
lien. A default on the wraparound mortgage would usually result in a default on
the underlying mortgage.

For example, assume property is worth $300,000 and there is an existing first
mortgage in the amount of $100,000 at 9 percent interest with 15 years remaining
on the term. The owner desires to raise an additional $100,000 in capital. Under
conventional financing, the owner would have to refinance the building for
$200,000, probably at a higher interest rate, say 15 percent, and use $100,000 to
pay off the existing first mortgage and the balance for the new needs. By using a
wraparound mortgage, he or she can obtain a lower interest rate, say 11 percent.
The actual amount advanced to the borrower under the wraparound mortgage is
$100,000 and the new lender makes the payments on the underlying $100,000 first
mortgage at 9 percent and receives payments from the owner on the newly negotiated 11 percent $200,000 wraparound or overriding mortgage.

It is essential that the first mortgage not contain an alienation clause ("due-on-
encumbrance") since this could effectively preclude the use of the wraparound
mortgage. Since VA and FHA loans cannot be called, (i.e. no due-on-sale clause),
these loans are popular in wrap transactions. The wraparound mortgage is attractive in condominium conversions where the existing mortgage usually has a
lower-than-current market interest rate.

Because the usury ceiling laws in many states apply to second liens but not to
residential first liens, many state laws have been amended to define wraparound
loans as first liens following the definition created by the Federal Home Loan
Bank Board. Thus institutional lenders can make wraparound loans. (See *ALL-
INCLUSIVE DEED OF TRUST, ARBITRAGE.*)

WRITE-OFF 1. To clear an asset off the accounting books, as
               with an uncollectible debt. 2. A tax deduction.
               (See *TAX SHELTER.*)

WRIT OF EXECUTION A court order authorizing and directing an officer
                       of the court to levy upon and sell property of the
defendant to satisfy a judgment. The officer (sheriff, police officer) may be required to give prior notice of the sale and first attempt to sell enough personal
property to pay the judgment before executing upon the defendant's real property.
Generally, the title of a purchaser at an execution sale relates back to the date of
judgment and is free from any lien created after the attachment.

When there is insufficient property within the district in which the judgment was
rendered, the plaintiff can obtain a writ of execution from a higher court covering
all property of the defendant, wherever situated in the state. (See *ATTACHMENT,
LEVY.*)

X An individual who cannot write his or her name can indicate the intention to sign by marking an X in the place for signature. A witness would then write the name of the signator alongside the X. When a person appearing before a notary cannot sign his or her name, the notary must first satisfy him-herself as to the identity of the person by requiring some proof of identification. The notary would then have the person place an X on the document, after which the notary would indicate that it is the mark of the person. For example, X (mark of Charlie Smith).

Also found on some maps in the form: X marks the spot where . . . ." (*See SIGNATURE.*)

X-BRACING Cross bracing in a partition.

YARD 1. A unit of measurement equalling three feet.
2. The open, unoccupied space on the plot between the property line and the front, rear, or side wall of the building. There are three main types of yard:

Front Yard: The yard across the full width of the plot facing the street extending from the front line of the building to the front property line. On a corner lot, both yards facing a street are considered front yards.

Back Yard: The yard across the full width of the plot opposite the front yard, extending from the rear line of the building to the rear property line.

Side Yard: The yard between the side line of building and the adjacent side property line, extending from the front yard to the rear yard. (*See SETBACK.*)

YEAR-TO-YEAR TENANCY A periodic tenancy in which the rent is reserved from year-to-year. Sufficient notice (if not specified in the contract, then a reasonable time) must be given to terminate this tenancy. Where the tenant holds over after the first year, he or she normally creates another year-to-year tenancy. (*See PERIODIC TENANCY.*)

YIELD The return on an investment or the amount of profit, stated as a percentage of the amount invested; the rate of return. In real estate, yield refers to the effective annual amount of income which is being accrued on an investment. The yield on income property is the ratio of the annual net income from the property to the cost or market value of the property. The yield, or profit, to a lender is the spread or differential between the cost of acquiring the funds lent and the interest rate charged.

YIELD TO MATURITY   A method of financing repayment in which a borrower pays a certain percentage of actual funds borrowed each year (such as interest only) and pays the loan off in full at the end of its maturity.

ZERO LOT LINE   A term generally used to describe the positioning of a structure on a lot so that one side rests directly on the lot's boundary line. Such construction is generally prohibited in many areas by setback ordinances unless, of course, it is a part of a special space-conserving project. (See PARTY WALL, PLANNED UNIT DEVELOPMENT.)

ZONE CONDEMNATION   The demolition and clearance of entire areas to make way for new construction, especially in slum clearance projects.

ZONING   The regulation of structures and uses of property within designated districts or zones. Zoning regulates and affects such things as use of the land, lot sizes, types of structure permitted, building heights, setbacks, and density (the ratio of land area to improvement area).

Zoning laws are enacted in the exercise of police power and are upheld as long as they may reasonably protect the public health, safety, morals, and general welfare of an area. Counties and/or municipalities generally enact their own zoning ordinances pursuant to an enabling act of the state.

Requests for rezoning may have to be directed toward a special zoning appeals board or other administrative body, since the change can usually be accomplished only by passage of a special ordinance.

Purchasers of property must be aware of the zoning requirements; that is, zoning regulations do not render the title unmarketable where they differ from what the purchaser thought they were. Consequently, the broker has an obligation to ascertain whether the contemplated use of the property conforms to existing zoning. However, *violations* of zoning regulations *do* render the title unmarketable. Where the zoning permits single-family dwellings only and the seller has a duplex, the title is therefore rendered unmarketable unless the buyer agrees to accept title under those conditions. Also, where either the seller or the broker misrepresents the actual permitted zoning use, the buyer can rescind the transaction on the basis of the misrepresentation.

Where the downzoning (for example, from urban to conservation) of an area results in the lessening of property values, the state is not responsible to make just-compensation payments to the owners (as it is when property is condemned under the power of eminent domain). Some special types of zoning are:

Bulk Zoning: Controls density and avoids overcrowding, such as restrictions on setback, building height, and percentage of open area, as its primary purpose.

Aesthetic Zoning: Requires that new buildings conform to specific types of architecture.

Incentive Zoning: Requires that street floors of office buildings be used for retail establishments.

Directive Zoning: Encourages zoning as a planning tool to use land for its highest and best use.

Zoning laws are generally enforced through the requirement that a building permit must first be obtained in order for one to build on his or her land. A permit will not be issued unless the proposed structure conforms to the permitted zoning, among other things.

Often the purpose of zoning is to implement the master plan. Zoning codes determine such things as the type and intensity of use, the density of living or business population, height regulations, accessory buildings, and essential facilities such as recreation and parking standards, including off-street parking and loading. Where zoning and private restrictions conflict, whichever is the most restrictive must be followed. (*See BUFFER ZONE, COMMINGLING, GENERAL PLAN, NONCONFORMING USE, SPOT ZONING, URBAN ENTERPRISE ZONE, VARIANCE.*)

ZONING ESTOPPEL   A rule which bars the government from enforcing a new downzoning ordinance against a landowner who had incurred substantial costs in reliance on the government's assurances that the landowner had met all the zoning requirements before the new down-zoning took place.

appendix a: abbreviations

BOMA	Building Owners and Managers Association
BOMI	Building Owners and Managers Institute
BTU	British thermal unit

C

CAE	Certified Assessment Evaluator
CAE	Certified Association Executive
CAI	Community Associations Institute
CAM	Certified Apartment Manager
CBD	Central business district
CBS	Concrete block and stucco
CCIM	Certified Commercial Investment Member
CC&Rs	Covenants, conditions, and restrictions
CD	Certificate of deposit
CDO	Capital district ordinance
CDUA	Conservation district use application
CE	Certified Exchanger
CERT.	Certificate of Title (Torrens)
CID	Commercial investment division
CJ	Certificate of Judgment
CLIC	Commercial Leasehold Insurance Corporation
CMB	Certified Mortgage Banker
Co.	Company
CO	Certificate of occupancy
COB	Close of business
CON	Connected (sewer)
CPA	Certified Public Accountant
CPE	Certified Personalty Evaluator
CPI	Consumer Price Index
CPM	Certified Property Manager
CRA	Certified Review Appraiser
CRB	Certified Residential Broker
CRE	Counselor of Real Estate
CREA	Canadian Real Estate Association
CRS	Certified Residential Specialist
CRV	Certificate of reasonable value
CSM	Certified Shopping Center Manager

CT	Conveyance tax
CTF	Customer trust fund
CTL	Cash-to-loan ratio
CUNA	Credit Union National Association
CZC	Comprehensive zoning code
CZMA	Coastal Zone Management Act

D

DCF	Discounted cash flow
dba	"Doing business as"
dbh	Diameter-Breast-High
DCRR	Discounted Rate of Return
DLIR	Department of Labor and Industrial Relations
DLUM	Detailed land-use map
DP	Down payment
DPC	Debt previously contracted
DPP	Direct Participation Principals License
DPR	Direct Participation Representative License
DRM	Direct Reduction Mortgage
DT	Depth table

E

EC	Extended coverage
ECOA	Equal Credit Opportunity Act
EIS	Environmental impact statement
EM	Earnest money deposit
EMAC	Enclosed Mall Air Conditioned
E & O	Errors & Omissions Insurance
EPA	Environmental Protection Agency
ESOP	Employee stock ownership plan

F

FAR	Floor area ratio
FCA	Farm Credit Administration
FCRA	Fair Credit Reporting Act

FDIC	Federal Deposit Insurance Corporation	**GNMA**	Government National Mortgage Association (Ginnie Mae)
FEA	Federal Energy Administration	**GP**	General plan
FH	Flood hazard	**GRI**	Graduate, Realtors® Institute
FHA	Federal Housing Administration	**GRM**	Gross rent multiplier
		GSA	General Services Administration
FHLB	Federal Home Loan Bank	**GSP**	Guaranteed Sales Program
FHLMC	Federal Home Loan Mortgage Corporation (Freddie Mac)		
FICA	Federal Income Contributions Act		

H

FICB	Federal intermediate credit banks	**HOA**	Homeowners Association
FIDA	Federal Institution Deregulation Act	**HOW**	Homeowners Warranty Program
FIFO	First in, first out (accounting)	**HUD**	U.S. Department of Housing and Urban Development
FIG	International Federation of Surveyors		
FIRPA	Foreign Investment Real Property Act		

I

FL	Fort land		
FLB	Federal Land Bank	**IAAO**	International Association of Assessing Officers
FLBA	Federal Land Bank Association	**ICSC**	International Council of Shopping Centers
FLI	Farm and Land Institute	**IFA**	Independent Fee Appraiser
FLIP	Flexible Loan Insurance Program	**Inc.**	Incorporated
FmHA	Farmers Home Administration	**INTEREX**	International Exchangers Association
FMV	Fair market value	**IRC**	Internal Revenue Code
FNMA	Federal National Mortgage Association (Fannie Mae)	**IREF**	International Real Estate Federation
FP	File plan	**IREM**	Institute of Real Estate Management
FRM	Fixed Rate Mortgage	**IRS**	Internal Revenue Service
FRS	Federal Reserve System		
FS	Fee simple		
FSBO	For Sale by Owner		
FSLIC	Federal Savings and Loan Insurance Corporation		

J

FTC	Federal Trade Commission		
FUTA	Federal Unemployment Tax Act	**J/T**	Joint tenant

G

L

GAO	General Accounting Office	**L**	Leasehold
GCR	Guest-car ratio	**L#**	Liber number (book number)
GIT	Gross income tax	**LAL**	Limit on artificial accounting losses
GLA	Gross leasable area		

LDD	Local Development District	**NACORE**	National Association of Corporate Real Estate Executives
LH	Leasehold		
LHA	Local Housing Authority	**NAHB**	National Association of Home Builders
LIFO	Last in, first out		
LIR	Land-use intensity rating	**NAHC**	National Association of Housing Cooperatives
Lis/P	Lis pendens		
L.P.	Land patent	**NAIFA**	National Association of Independent Fee Appraisers
LS	Locus sigilli (Latin—"place of seal")	**NAIOP**	National Association of Industrial & Office Parks
LSR	Livability space ratio		
Ltd.	Limited	**NAMSB**	National Association of Mutual Savings Banks
LUI	Land-use intensity		
LUL	Land-use law	**NAPRM**	National Association of Professional Resident Managers
LUMS	Land utilization marketing study		
		NAR	National Association of REALTORS®
L/V	Loan-to-value ratio		
		NAREB (NAR)	National Association of Real Estate Boards (now NAR)
		NAREB	National Association of Real Estate Brokers
M		**NAREE**	National Association of Real Estate Editors
MAGIC	Mortgage Guaranty Insurance Corporation (also MGIC)	**NARELLO**	National Association of Real Estate Licensing Law Officials
MAI	Member Appraisal Institute		
MBA	Mortgage Bankers Association of America	**NASD**	National Association of Securities Dealers
MC	Model Cities Program	**NC**	Not connected (sewer)
MF	Multifamily	**NCHP**	National Corporation for Housing Partnerships
MGIC	Mortgage Guaranty Insurance Corporation		
MGRM	Monthly gross rent multiplier	**NCUA**	National Credit Union Association
MICA	Mortgage Insurance Companies of America	**NEPA**	National Environmental Policy Act
MIP	Mortgage insurance premium	**NFCA**	National Federation of Condominium Associations
MIRM	Member Institute of Residential Marketing		
MLS	Multiple listing service	**NHP**	National Housing Partnerships
MPR	Minimum property requirement	**NIFLB**	National Institute of Farm and Land Brokers
		NIREB	National Institute of Real Estate Brokers
		NLA	Net leasable area
N		**NOI**	Net operating income
		NOW	Negotiable Order of Withdrawal
n/A	Not available or not applicable	**NSMA**	National Second Mortgage Association
NAA	National Apartment Association		
		NSPE	National Society of Professional Engineers
NAAO	National Association of Assessing Officers	**NPA**	National Parking Association

NRV	Net realizable value		**R**	
NSF	Not sufficient funds			
NTC	National Timesharing Council		R	REALTOR®
NTO	National Tenants Organization		RA	REALTOR-ASSOCIATE®
			RAM	Reverse Annuity Mortgage
			REA	Reciprocal Easement Agreement
			REC	Real estate commission
	O		REEA	Real Estate Educators Association
			REG.	Regular system (recording)
OAR	Overall rate		REIT	Real estate investment trust
OCC	Office of Comptroller of Currency		REPAC	Real Estate Political Action Committee
OEO	Office of Economic Opportunity		RESPA	Real Estate Settlement Procedures Act
OEQC	Office of Environmental Quality Control		RESSI	Real Estate Securities and Syndication Institute
OE&T	Operating expenses and taxes		RM	Residential Member
OILSR	Office of Interstate Land Sales Registration		RNMI	REALTORS® National Marketing Institute
OIR	Official interpretation rulings		ROI	Return on investment
OL&T	Owner's, landlord's, and tenant's public liability insurance		RP	Royal patent
			RPA	Real property administrator
			RRA	Registered Review Appraiser
ORE	Owned Real Estate		RS	Revenue stamp
OTC	Over the counter		RV	Recreational vehicle
			R/W	Right-of-way
	P			
PAM	Pledged Account Mortgage			
PB	Principal broker			**S**
PC	Participation Sales Certificate			
PDH	Planned development housing		S	Salesperson
PE	Professional engineer		S	Section
PHA	Public Housing Administration		SARA	Society of American Registered Architects
P&I	Principal and interest		SBA	Small Business Administration
PITI	Principal, interest, taxes, and insurance (monthly payments)		SBLN	Setback Line
			SEC	Securities and Exchange Commission
PMI	Private mortgage insurance			
PMM	Purchase Money Mortgage		SIR	Society of Industrial REALTORS®
POB	Point of beginning			
POC	Paid Outside Closing		S&L	Savings and loan association
PRD	Planned residential development		SMSA	Standard metropolitan statistical area
PRM	Permanent Reference Marker		SOYD	Sum of the years' digits
PSC	Participation sale certificate		SRA	Senior Realty Appraiser
PUD	Planned unit development		SRA	Senior Residential Appraiser

SREA	Senior Real Estate Analyst	**UPA**	Uniform Partnership Act
SREA	Society of Real Estate Appraisers	**URA**	Urban Renewal Administration
SRPA	Senior Real Property Appraisers	**URETSA**	Uniform Real Estate Timeshare Act
SS	Scilicet (Latin—"namely")	**URLTA**	Uniform Residential Landlord and Tenant Act
SSCRA	Soldiers and Sailors Civil Relief Act	**USGS**	United States Geological Survey

T

T/C	Tenant in common
TCT	Transfer Certificate of Title
TDI	Temporary disability insurance
TDR	Transfer of Development Rights
T/E	Tenancy by entirety
TSO	Timeshare ownership

V

VA	Veterans Administration
VRM	Variable Rate Mortgage
Vs	Versus

W

WCR	Women's Council of REALTORS®
WROS	With right of survivorship
W/W	Wall to wall

U

UCC	Uniform Commercial Code
ULI	Urban Land Institute
ULSPA	Uniform Land Sales Practices Act
ULTA	Uniform Land Transactions Act

Z

Z	Zone

appendix b: realtor® code of ethics

Revised and approved by the delegate body of the association at its 67th annual convention November 14, 1974

Preamble . . .

Under all is the land. Upon its wise utilization and widely allocated ownership depend the survival and growth of free institutions and of our civilization. The REALTOR® should recognize that the interests of the nation and its citizens require the highest and best use of the land and the widest distribution of land ownership. They require the creation of adequate housing, the building of functioning cities, the development of productive industries and farms, and the preservation of a healthful environment.

Such interests impose obligations beyond those of ordinary commerce. They impose grave social responsibility and a patriotic duty to which the REALTOR® should dedicate himself, and for which he should be diligent in preparing himself. The REALTOR®, therefore, is zealous to maintain and improve the standards of his calling and shares with his fellow REALTORS® a common responsibility for its integrity and honor. The term REALTOR® has come to connote competency, fairness, and high integrity resulting from adherence to a lofty ideal of moral conduct in business relations. No inducement of profit and no instruction from clients ever can justify departure from this ideal.

In the interpretation of this obligation, a REALTOR® can take no safer guide than that which has been handed down through the centuries, embodied in the Golden Rule, "Whatsoever ye would that men should do to you, do ye even so to them."

Accepting this standard as his own, every REALTOR® pledges himself to observe its spirit in all of his activities and to conduct his business in accordance with the tenets set forth below.

Article 1

The REALTOR® should keep himself informed on matters affecting real estate in his community, the state, and nation so that he may be able to contribute responsibly to public thinking on such matters.

Article 2

In justice to those who place their interests in his care, the REALTOR® should endeavor always to be informed regarding laws, proposed legislation, governmental regulations, public policies, and current market conditions in order to be in a position to advise his clients properly.

Article 3

It is the duty of the REALTOR® to protect the public against fraud, misrepresentation, and unethical practices in real estate transactions. He should endeavor to eliminate in his community any practices which could be damaging to the public or bring discredit to the real estate profession. The REALTOR® should assist the governmental agency charged with regulating the practices of brokers and salesmen in his state.

Article 4

The REALTOR® should seek no unfair advantage over other REALTORS® and should conduct his business so as to avoid controversies with other REALTORS®.

Article 5

In the best interests of society, of his associates, and his own business, the REALTOR® should willingly share with other REALTORS® the lessons of his experience and study for the benefit of the public, and should be loyal to the Board of REALTORS® of his community and active in its work.

Article 6

To prevent dissension and misunderstanding and to assure better service to the owner, the REALTOR® should urge the exclusive listing of property unless contrary to the best interest of the owner.

Article 7

In accepting employment as an agent, the REALTOR® pledges himself to protect and promote the interests of the client. This obligation of absolute fidelity to the client's interests is primary, but it does not relieve the REALTOR® of the obligation to treat fairly all parties to the transaction.

Article 8

The REALTOR® shall not accept compensation from more than one party, even if permitted by law, without the full knowledge of all parties to the transaction.

Article 9

The REALTOR® shall avoid exaggeration, misrepresentation, or concealment of pertinent facts. He has an affirmative obligation to discover adverse factors that a reasonably competent and diligent investigation would disclose.

Article 10

The REALTOR® shall not deny equal professional services to any person for reasons of race, creed, sex, or country of national origin. The REALTOR® shall not be party to any plan or agreement to discriminate against a person or persons on the basis of race, creed, sex, or country of national origin.

Article 11

A REALTOR® is expected to provide a level of competent service in keeping with the standards of practice in those fields in which the REALTOR® customarily engages.

The REALTOR® shall not undertake to provide specialized professional services concerning a type of property or service that is outside his field of competence unless he engages the assistance of one who is competent on such types of property or service, or unless the facts are fully disclosed to the client. Any person engaged to provide such assistance shall be so identified to the client and his contribution to the assignment should be set forth.

The REALTOR® shall refer to the Standards of Practice of the National Association as to the degree of competence that a client has a right to expect the REALTOR® to possess, taking into consideration the complexity of the problem, the availability of expert assistance, and the opportunities for experience available to the REALTOR®.

Article 12

The REALTOR® shall not undertake to provide professional services concerning a property or its value where he has a present or contemplated interest unless such interest is specifically disclosed to all affected parties.

Article 13

The REALTOR® shall not acquire an interest in or buy for himself, any member of his immediate family, his firm or any member thereof, or any entity in which he has a substantial ownership interest, property listed with him, without making the true position known to the listing owner. In selling property owned by himself, or in which he has any interest, the REALTOR® shall reveal the facts of his ownership or interest to the purchaser.

Article 14

In the event of a controversy between REALTORS® associated with different firms, arising out of their relationship as REALTORS®, the REALTORS® shall submit the dispute to arbitration in accordance with the regulation of their board or boards rather than litigate the matter.

Article 15

If a REALTOR® is charged with unethical practice or is asked to present evidence in any disiplinary proceeding or investigation, he shall place all pertinent facts before the proper tribunal of the member board or affiliated institute, society, or council of which he is a member.

Article 16

When acting as agent, the REALTOR® shall not accept any commission, rebate, or profit on expenditures made for his principal-owner, without the principal's knowledge and consent.

Article 17

The REALTOR® shall not engage in activities that constitute the unauthorized practice of law and shall recommend that legal counsel be obtained when the interest of any party to the transaction requires it.

Article 18

The REALTOR® shall keep in a special account in an appropriate financial institution, separated from his own funds, monies coming into his possession in trust for other persons, such as escrows, trust funds, clients' monies, and other like items.

Article 19

The REALTOR® shall be careful at all times to present a true picture in his advertising and representations to the public. He shall neither advertise without disclosing his name nor permit any person associated with him to use individual names or telephone numbers, unless such person's connection with the REALTOR® is obvious in the advertisement.

Article 20

The REALTOR®, for the protection of all parties, shall see that financial obligations and commitments regarding real estate transactions are in writing, expressing the exact agreement of the parties. A copy of each agreement shall be furnished to each party upon his signing such agreement.

Article 21
The REALTOR® shall not engage in any practice or take any action inconsistent with the agency of another REALTOR®.

Article 22
In the sale of property which is exclusively listed with a REALTOR®, the REALTOR® shall utilize the services of other brokers upon mutually agreed upon terms when it is in the best interests of the client.
Negotiations concerning property which is listed exclusively shall be carried on with the listing broker, not with the owner, except with the consent of the listing broker.

Article 23
The REALTOR® shall not publicly disparage the business practice of a competitor nor volunteer an opinion of a competitor's transaction. If his opinion is sought and if the REALTOR® deems it appropriate to respond, such opinion shall be rendered with strict professional integrity and courtesy.

Article 24
The REALTOR® shall not directly or indirectly solicit the services or affiliation of an employee or independent contractor in the organization of another REALTOR® without prior notice to said REALTOR®.

Where the word REALTOR® is used in this Code and Preamble, it shall be deemed to include REALTOR-ASSOCIATE®. Pronouns shall be considered to include REALTORS® and REALTOR-ASSOCIATES® of both genders.

The Code of Ethics was adopted in 1913. Amended at the Annual Convention in 1924, 1928, 1950, 1951, 1952, 1955, 1956, 1961, 1962, and 1974.

Standards of Practice Relating to Articles of the Code of Ethics (Adopted through November 17, 1981)

The Standards of Practice relating to the Code of Ethics are "interpretations" of various Articles of the Code of Ethics and are not a part of the Code itself. The proper relationship between the Standards of Practice and the Code of Ethics is set forth in the following advisory opinion by the Professional Standards Committee, which was approved by the Board of Directors of the National Association:
"In filing a charge of an alleged violation of the Code of Ethics by a REALTOR®, the charge shall read as an alleged violation of one or more Articles of the Code. A Standard of Practice may only be cited in support of the charge."
The Standards of Practice are supplementary to, and do not replace, the "numbered cases" found in *Interpretations of the Code of Ethics.* A Standard of Practice is a statement of general principle related to an Article of the Code of Ethics to guide REALTORS® and REALTOR-ASSOCIATE®s as to the professional conduct required in the specific situation described by the Standard of Practice, whereas each of the "numbered cases" in *Interpretations of the Code of Ethics* presents a set of particular facts alleging a violation of the Code of Ethics, and describes the conclusion determined on merit by the Professional Standards Committee as related to the particular facts of the case.
As additional Standards of Practice are adopted, Member Boards and Board Members will be advised of their adoption.

Standard of Practice 4-1
"The REALTOR® shall not misrepresent the availability of access to show or inspect a listed property."

Standard of Practice 7-1
"The REALTOR® shall receive and shall transmit all offers on a specified property to the owner for his decision, whether such offers are received from a prospective purchaser or another broker."

Standard of Practice 7-2
"The REALTOR® acting as listing broker shall submit all offers to the seller as quickly as possible."

Standard of Practice 7-3
"The REALTOR®, in attempting to secure a listing, shall not deliberately mislead the owner as to market value."

Standard of Practice 7-4
(Refer to Standard of Practice 22-1, which also relates to Article 7, Code of Ethics.)

Standard of Practice 7-5
(Refer to Standard of Practice 22-2, which also relates to Article 7, Code of Ethics.)

Standard of Practice 7-6
The REALTOR®, when acting as a principal in a real estate transaction, cannot avoid his responsibilities under the Code of Ethics.

Standard of Practice 9-1
"The REALTOR® shall not be a party to the naming of a false consideration in any document, unless it be the naming of an obviously nominal consideration."

Standard of Practice 9-2
"The REALTOR®, when asked by another REALTOR®, shall disclose the nature of his listing, i.e., an exclusive right to sell, an exclusive agency, open listing, or other form of contractual agreement between the REALTOR® and his client."

Standard of Practice 9-3
(Refer to Standard of Practice 7-3, which also relates to Article 9, Code of Ethics.)

Standard of Practice 9-4
"The REALTOR® shall not offer a service described as 'free of charge' when the rendering of a service is contingent on the obtaining of a benefit such as a listing or commission."

Standard of Practice 9-5
"The REALTOR® shall, with respect to the subagency of another REALTOR®, timely communicate any change of compensation for subagency services to the other REALTOR® prior to the time such REALTOR® produces a prospective buyer who has signed an offer to purchase the property for which the subagency has been offered through MLS or otherwise by the listing agency."

Standard of Practice 9-6
REALTORS® shall disclose their REALTOR® status when seeking information from another REALTOR® concerning real property for which the other REALTOR® is an agent or subagent.

Standard of Practice 11-1
"Whenever a REALTOR® submits an oral or written opinion of the value of real property for a fee, his opinion shall be supported by a memorandum in his file or an appraisal report, either of which shall include as a minimum the following:
1. Limiting conditions
2. Any existing or contemplated interest
3. Defined value
4. Date applicable
5. The estate appraised
6. A description of the property
7. The basis of the reasoning including applicable market data and/or capitalization computation

"This report or memorandum shall be available to the Professional Standards Committee for a period or at least two years (beginning subsequent to final determination of the court if the appraisal is involved in litigation) to ensure compliance with Article 11 of the Code of Ethics of the NATIONAL ASSOCIATION OF REALTORS®."

Standard of Practice 11-2
"The REALTOR® shall not undertake to make an appraisal when his employment or fee is contingent upon the amount of appraisal."

Standard of Practice 11-3
"REALTORS® engaged in real estate securities and syndications transactions are engaged in an activity subject to regulations beyond those governing real estate transactions generally, and therefore have the affirmative obligation to be informed of applicable federal and state laws, and rules and regulations regarding these types of transactions."

Standard of Practice 12-1
(Refer to Standard of Practice 9-4, which also relates to Article 12, Code of Ethics.)

Standard of Practice 15-1
"The REALTOR® shall not be subject to disciplinary proceedings in more than one Board of REALTORS® with respect to alleged violations of the Code of Ethics relating to the same transaction."

Standard of Practice 16-1
"The REALTOR® shall not recommend or suggest to a principal or a customer the use of services of another organization or business entity in which he has a direct interest without disclosing such interest at the time of the recommendation or suggestion."

Standard of Practice 19-1
"The REALTOR® shall not submit or advertise property without authority, and in any offering, the price quoted shall not be other than that agreed upon with the owners."

Standard of Practice 19-2
(Refer to Standard of Practice 9-4, which also relates to Article 19, Code of Ethics.)

Standard of Practice 21-1
"Signs giving notice of property for sale, rent, lease, or exchange shall not be placed on property without the consent of the owner."

Standard of Practice 21-2
"The REALTOR® obtaining information from a

listing broker about a specific property shall not convey this information to, nor invite the cooperation of a third party broker without the consent of the listing broker.''

Standard of Practice 21-3
''The REALTOR® shall not solicit a listing which is currently listed exclusively with another broker unless the listing broker, when asked by the REALTOR®, refuses to disclose the nature and current status of such listing; i.e., an exclusive right to sell, an exclusive agency, open listing, or other form of contractual agreement between the REALTOR® and his client.''

Standard of Practice 21-4
''The REALTOR® shall not use information obtained by him from the listing broker, through offers to cooperate received through Multiple Listing Services or other sources authorized by the listing broker, for the purpose of creating a referral prospect to a third broker, or for creating a buyer prospect unless such use is authorized by the listing broker.''

Standard of Practice 21-5
''The fact that a property has been listed exclusively with a REALTOR® shall not preclude or inhibit any other REALTOR® from soliciting such listing after its expiration.''

Standard of Practice 21-6
''The fact that a property owner has retained a REALTOR® as his exclusive agent in respect of one or more past transactions creates no interest or agency which precludes or inhibits other REALTORS® from seeking such owner's future business.''

Standard of Practice 21-7
''The REALTOR® shall be free to solicit a listing in respect to any property which is 'open listed' at any time.''

Standard of Practice 21-8
''Unless otherwise precluded by law, the REALTOR® may discuss with an owner of a property which is exclusively listed with another REALTOR® the terms upon which he would accept a future listing upon the expiration of the present listing provided the owner initiates the discus-

sion and provided the REALTOR® has not directly or indirectly solicited such discussion.''

Standard of Practice 21-9
''In cooperative transactions a REALTOR® shall compensate the cooperating REALTOR® (principal broker) and shall not compensate nor offer to compensate, directly or indirectly, any of the sales licensees employed by or affiliated with another REALTOR® without the prior express knowledge and consent of the cooperating broker.''

Standard of Practice 22-1
''It is the obligation of the selling broker as subagent of the listing broker to disclose immediately all pertinent facts to the listing broker prior to as well as after the contract is executed.''

Standard of Practice 22-2
''The REALTOR®, when submitting offers to the seller, shall present each in an objective and unbiased manner.''

Standard of Practice 24-1
''The purpose of Article 24 is to discourage salespersons from breaching their agreements with the REALTORS® by whom they are employed or with whom they are affiliated. Its further purpose is to prevent REALTORS® from inducing salespersons to breach such agreements.
''Article 24 must not be contrued as precluding a REALTOR® from making an offer of employment or affiliation to the salesperson of another REALTOR® at any time or on any terms he deems appropriate. Any use of Article 24 to limit the opportunities for employment or affiliation available to salespersons is improper and a violation of Article 24.
''Article 24 is infringed only in the case where a REALTOR® solicits the services of a specific employee or independent contractor salesperson of another REALTOR® who is under a written agreement. A general announcement by a REALTOR® that he is interested in expanding his staff and invites qualified persons to call or write him is not a solicitation violative of Article 24. Nor would a REALTOR® be required by Article 24 to notify the REALTOR® with whom salespersons responding to such general announcement are associated.''

appendix c: sample closing problem

INTRODUCTION

The following information is based on a typical real estate transaction. All computations have been made and the proper information has been entered on two different common closing statement forms—the two-part statement used in many areas, and a RESPA disclosure/settlement statement (*See RESPA*). The expenses for this transaction have also been entered on a settlement statement worksheet for your information. Worksheets of this kind are frequently used to double check all computations and entries, and are particularly useful because they allow quick examination of all credits and debits. Remember, however, this form is *not a closing statement. It is only a worksheet.* All computations have been carried out to three decimal places, except for the final figures, which have been carried out to two places. All prorations have been made based on a 30-day (statutory) month.

Information Describing the Transaction

Donald and Rhonda Hennesey are selling their brick colonial house located at 1101 West Hester Street, Clifton, Stateside, 00010, to Irving and Celia Splatt, also of Clifton. The property includes a two-car detached brick garage. Above the garage is a studio apartment which the Henneseys rent out for $160 per month. The rent is due on the first day of each month. The property's legal description is, "Lot 6, Block A, Hillfarm Acres."

The Splatts have agreed to pay $68,800 for the property, and an additional $700 for the Henneseys' wall-to-wall carpeting, gas stove, and electric refrigerator. The Splatts are obtaining a $55,000 first mortgage loan from the First National Savings and Loan of Wembley (loan number 316612). The couple received a loan commitment from the lender on June 5, 1978. The Henneseys are paying off the remaining mortgage balance of $8,200 on their property from the proceeds of this sale. The Splatts have deposited $7,000 earnest money with Herman Holesley, the broker who negotiated the transaction. Holesley will receive a 6½ percent commission for his services. The Splatts received an advance disclosure statement of closing costs on June 5. The transaction will be closed on June 20, 1978 at the Wembley Title Company, 1000 Beeker Street, Wembley, Stateside, 00010.

The expenses involved in the transaction include the following:

- The Splatts will assume the Henneseys' one-year fire and hazard insurance policy with a premium of $103. The policy will expire on September 1, 1978.

- The Henneseys will pay the $185 charge for the title abstract done by the Wembley Title Company.

- The Splatts will pay the $130 expense for the survey performed by the Jiffy Survey Company. The survey was required by the mortgage lender.

- The Henneseys will pay the state transfer tax of $1.75 per $500 (or fraction thereof) of the total purchase price.

- The Splatts will pay for the recording and notary fees (E.P. White, notary public)—$6.00 and $3.00 respectively.

- The Splatts will also pay a loan origination fee of $175, and have agreed to pay $115 to cover the cost of a lender's title insurance policy, obtained through the Wembley Title Company.

- The parties have agreed to prorate the combined city and county real estate taxes of $714.65. Taxes are due and are payable in arrears on January 1.

COMPUTATIONS

Rent: Rent on the studio apartment is $160.00 per month. Before settlement, 20 days of the 30-day month have expired.

        30-day month
      − 20 days expired before settlement
        10 days credit to buyer

        $160 ÷ 30 = $5.333 rent per day

        $5.333 x 10 = *$53.33* credit to buyer, debit to seller

Insurance: The Splatts, the buyers, will assume the fire and hazard insurance policy at the closing. Computed here are the number of days left on the policy and the cost of the assumed policy to the Splatts.

                8.583 per month
      12) $103.000 policy

                .286 per day
      30) $ 8.583

        2 months, 10 days remaining on policy as of settlement date
        $8.583 x 2 months = $17.166
        $ .286 x 10 days   = $ 2.860
                            $20.026 = $20.03, debit to buyer, credit to seller.

Taxes: Since taxes are paid in arrears, the buyer will be paying 1978 taxes on January 1, 1979. The sellers, then, must pay the buyers the portion of taxes owed from January 1, 1978, to the date of closing, June 20, 1978. To compute this the salesperson must compute the amount owed per month and per day for the year, and multiply by the number of months and days between January 1, 1978 and the closing, June 20, 1978.

$$12 \overline{)\,\$714.65} \quad \text{taxes} \qquad 59.554 \text{ per month}$$

$$30 \overline{)\,\$59.554} \qquad 1.985 \text{ per day}$$

2 months, 10 days remaining on policy as of settlement date

59.554×5 months = \$297.770 1.985×20 days = \$39.700

$297.770 + 39.700 = \$337.47,$ debit to seller, credit to buyer

Broker's commission: Commission is computed by multiplying the selling price by an agreed upon percentage of the selling price—in this case, 6½ percent.

$68,800 \times .065 = \$4,472.00,$ debit to seller.

Transfer tax: The sellers pay the transfer tax which is computed by dividing the selling price by \$500.00 (remember, any fraction of \$500 is computed as if it were a full \$500) and multiplying by the transfer tax rate.

$$\$500 \overline{)\,\$68,800} \qquad 137.6 = 138$$

$138 \times \$1.75 = \$241.50,$ debit to seller

SETTLEMENT STATEMENT WORKSHEET

	BUYER'S STATEMENT		SELLER'S STATEMENT	
	DEBIT	CREDIT	DEBIT	CREDIT
PURCHASE PRICE	$68,800.00			$68,800.00
EARNEST MONEY		7,000.00		
HENNESYS' MORTGAGE			8,200.00	
SPLATTS' MORTGAGE LOAN		55,000.00		
BROKER'S COMMISSION			4,472.00	
REAL ESTATE TAX		337.47	337.47	
HAZARD INSURANCE	20.03			20.03
RENTS		53.33	53.33	
TITLE SEARCH			185.00	
LENDER'S TITLE INSURANCE	115.00			
SURVEY	130.00			
TRANSFER TAX			241.50	
RECORDING FEE	6.00			
NOTARY FEE	3.00			
LOAN ORIGINATION FEE	175.00			
TOTAL DEBITS + CREDITS	69,249.03	62,390.80	13,489.30	68,820.03
DUE FROM BUYER AT CLOSING		6,858.23	55,330.73	
DUE TO SELLER AT CLOSING				
	$69,249.03	$69,249.03	$68,820.03	$68,820.03

CLOSING STATEMENT

BUYER'S CLOSING STATEMENT

FORM No. 781
Stevens-Ness Law Pub. Co.
Portland, Oregon —KA

Property of _Donald AND Rhonda Hennesey_
Sold to _Irving AND Celia Splatt_
By _Herman Holesley_ , Broker
Description: _Lot 6, Block A, Hillfarm Acres_
City of _Clifton_ , County of _Corn_
State of _Stateside_ , Settlement date _June 20_ , 19 _78_

	DEBIT	CREDIT
PURCHASE PRICE	$ 68,800.00	
EARNEST MONEY PAID		$ 7,000.00
CONVEYED SUBJECT TO: 1st Mtg. bal., plus int.		55,000.00
2nd Mortgage balance, plus interest		
Contract balance, plus interest		
Chattel Mortgage balance, plus interest		
MTG. given seller as part of purchase price		
CONTRACT given as part of purchase price		
TAXES: Paid in advance by seller		
Assumed by buyer, plus interest		337.47
INSURANCE: Fire—unearned premium	20.03	
Liability—unearned premium		
MUNICIPAL LIENS: Paid in advance by seller		
Assumed by buyer, plus interest		
RENTS: Paid in advance to seller		53.33
Due at settlement—adjusted		
WATER CHARGES: Paid in advance by seller		
Assumed by buyer, plus interest		
LOAN ORIGINATION FEE	175.00	
NOTARY FEE	3.00	
LENDER'S TITLE INS.	115.00	
SURVEY	130.00	
RECORDING FEE	6.00	
CASH PAID BY BUYER ON CLOSING		6,851.23
TOTALS (Debit and Cr. columns must balance)	$ 69,249.03	$ 69,249.03

Did broker advance fee for recording buyer's deed? _NO_
If so, did he collect payment back in addition to "Cash Paid on Closing"?
Has all insurance been transferred? Yes _X_ No
Will buyer let broker handle insurance at expiration? Yes _X_ No
The foregoing statement is hereby certified to be correct.

H. Holesley Broker

MANUAL DELIVERY: Received a true copy of above statement, certified to be correct.

Irving Splatt
Celia Splatt

Date _June 20_ 19 _78_ Buyer
MAIL DELIVERY: Copy of above statement sent U.S. Registered Mail; registry return receipt card to be attached.
Date _____ , 19 ___ Broker

SELLER'S CLOSING STATEMENT

FORM No. 781
Stevens-Ness Law Pub. Co.
Portland, Oregon —KA

Property of _Donald AND Rhonda Hennesey_
Sold to _Irving AND Celia Splatt_
By _Herman Holesley_ , Broker
Description: _Lot 6, Block A, Hillfarm Acres_
City of _Clifton_ , County of _Corn_
State of _Stateside_ , Settlement date _June 20_ , 19 _78_

	DEBIT	CREDIT
PURCHASE PRICE		$ 68,800.00
CONVEYED SUBJECT TO: 1st Mtg. bal., plus int. $		
2nd Mortgage balance, plus interest		
Contract balance, plus interest		
Chattel Mortgage balance, plus interest		
PAID BY BROKER FOR SELLER AT CLOSING: 1st Mortgage balance, plus interest	8,200.00	
2nd Mortgage balance, plus interest		
Contract balance, plus interest		
Chattel Mortgage balance, plus interest		
Taxes due to _12/31_ , 19 _78_	337.47	
Municipal liens		
Water charges		
MTG. given seller as part of purchase price		
CONTRACT given as part of purchase price		
TAXES: Paid in advance by seller		
Assumed by buyer, plus interest		
INSURANCE: Fire—unearned premium		20.03
Liability—unearned premium		
MUNICIPAL LIENS: Paid in advance by seller		
Assumed by buyer, plus interest		
RENTS: Paid in advance to seller	53.33	
Due at settlement—adjusted		
WATER CHARGES: Paid in advance by seller		
Assumed by buyer, plus interest		
TITLE INSURANCE or Abstract	185.00	
REVENUE STAMPS	241.50	
RECORDING FEES—Paid by seller		
BROKER'S COMMISSION @ 6½%	4,472.00	
BALANCE DUE SELLER BY BROKER		55,330.73
TOTALS (Debit and Cr. columns must balance)	$ 68,820.03	$ 68,820.03

The foregoing statement is hereby certified to be correct.
H. Holesley Broker

MANUAL DELIVERY: Received a true copy of above; also broker's check for balance due seller as shown above; the above statement hereby is certified to be correct.

Donald Hennesey
Rhonda Hennesey

Date _June 20_ , 19 _78_ Seller
MAIL DELIVERY: Copy of above statement sent by U.S. Registered Mail with check for balance due seller as shown above; registry return receipt cards to be attached.
Date _____ , 19 ___ Broker

CLOSING STATEMENT (cont.)

➡ **ALL REMAINING INFORMATION IS FOR BROKER'S FILE**

Property of ....

Sold to ....

DISTRIBUTION OF COMMISSION BY BROKER	DEBIT	CREDIT
Total commission on deal		$
Salesman's share	$	
Listing commission		
Office share		
....		
....		
....		
TOTALS (Debit and Cr. columns must balance) . $		$

Has information on insurance renewal been filed? Yes .... No ....

Abstract ( ) Title Insurance ( ) ....

....

....

....

Delivered to ....

Title insured by .... Policy No. ....

FORM No. 781
Stevens-Ness Law Pub. Co.
Portland, Oregon   —KA

STATEMENT SHOWING ONLY CASH RECEIVED AND DISBURSED BY BROKER

	DEBIT	CREDIT
EARNEST MONEY RECEIVED		$ 7,000.00
CASH PAID BY BUYER ON CLOSING $6,858.73 *MORT.*		55,000.00
PAID OUT FOR SELLER:		
1st Mtg.— Prin. $ 8,200.00 Int. $		$ 8,200.00
2nd Mtg.— Prin. $ .... Int. $		
Contract— Prin. $ .... Int. $		
Chat. Mtg.— Prin. $ .... Int. $		
Taxes		
~~Municipal liens~~ *Loan Orig.*		175.00
~~Water charges~~ *Survey*		130.00
Title Insurance or Abstract		185.00
Revenue stamps		241.50
Recording fees		6.00
Broker's commission		4,472.00
Lender's Title Policy		115.00
Notary Fee		3.00
Balance paid seller by broker		55,330.73
TOTALS (Debit and Cr. columns must balance) $ 68,858.23		$ 68,858.23

FORM No. 781
Stevens-Ness Law Pub. Co.
Portland, Oregon   —KA

RESPA SETTLEMENT STATEMENT

Form Approved OMB NO. 63-R-1501

A. U.S. DEPARTMENT OF HOUSING AND URBAN DEVELOPMENT SETTLEMENT STATEMENT	B. TYPE OF LOAN
	1. ☐ FHA 2. ☐ FMHA 3. ☒ CONV. UNINS. 4. ☐ VA 5. ☐ CONV. INS. 6. FILE NUMBER: 7. LOAN NUMBER: 316612 8. MORT. INS. CASE NO.:

C. NOTE: This form is furnished to give you a statement of actual settlement costs. Amounts paid to and by the settlement agent are shown. Items marked "(p.o.c.)" were paid outside the closing; they are shown here for informational purposes and are not included in the totals.

D. NAME OF BORROWER:	E. NAME OF SELLER:	F. NAME OF LENDER:

G. PROPERTY LOCATION: 1101 W. Hester St. Clifton, Stateside, 00010	H. SETTLEMENT AGENT: Wembley Title Co. PLACE OF SETTLEMENT: 1000 Beeker St. Wembley, Stateside, 00010	I. SETTLEMENT DATE: 6/20/78

J. SUMMARY OF BORROWER'S TRANSACTION:		K. SUMMARY OF SELLER'S TRANSACTION:	
100. **GROSS AMOUNT DUE FROM BORROWER**		400. **GROSS AMOUNT DUE TO SELLER**	
101. Contract sales price	**$68,800.00**	401. Contract sales price	**$68,800.00**
102. Personal property	700.00	402. Personal property	700.00
103. Settlement charges to borrower (line 1400)	449.03	403.	
104.		404.	
105.		405.	
Adjustments for items paid by seller in advance		*Adjustments for items paid by seller in advance*	
106. City/town taxes to		406. City/town taxes to	
107. County taxes to		407. County taxes to	
108. Assessments to		408. Assessments to	
109.		409. HAZARD INSURANCE to 9/1/78	20.03
110.		410.	
111.		411.	
112.		412.	
120. **GROSS AMOUNT DUE FROM BORROWER**	$69,249.03	420. **GROSS AMOUNT DUE TO SELLER**	$68,820.03
200. **AMOUNTS PAID BY OR IN BEHALF OF BORROWER**		500. **REDUCTIONS IN AMOUNT DUE TO SELLER**	
201. Deposit or earnest money	$ 7,000.00	501. Excess deposit (see instructions)	
202. Principal amount of new loan(s)	55,000.00	502. Settlement charges to seller (line 1400)	$ 4,898.50
203. Existing loan(s) taken subject to		503. Existing loan(s) taken subject to	
204.		504. Payoff of first mortgage loan	$ 8,200.00
205.		505. Payoff of second mortgage loan	
206.		506.	
207.		507.	
208.		508.	
209. Rents	53.33	509.	
Adjustments for items unpaid by seller		*Adjustments for items unpaid by seller*	
210. City/town taxes to 12/31/78		510. City/town taxes to 12/31/78	
211. County taxes to 12/31/78	337.47	511. County taxes to 12/31/78	337.47
212. Assessments to		512. Assessments to	
213.		513. Rents	53.33
214.		514.	
215.		515.	
216.		516.	
217.		517.	
218.		518.	
219.		519.	
220. **TOTAL PAID BY/FOR BORROWER**	$62,390.80	520. **TOTAL REDUCTION AMOUNT DUE SELLER**	$13,489.30
300. **CASH AT SETTLEMENT FROM OR TO BORROWER**		600. **CASH AT SETTLEMENT TO OR FROM SELLER**	
301. Gross amount due from borrower (line 120)	$69,249.03	601. Gross amount due to seller (line 420)	$68,820.03
302. Less amounts paid by/for borrower (line 220)	(62,390.80)	602. Less reduction amount due seller (line 520)	(13,489.30)
303. **CASH (☒ FROM) (☐ TO) BORROWER**	$ 6,858.23	603. **CASH (☒ TO) (☐ FROM) SELLER**	$55,330.73

HUD 1A REV. 5/76 AS & AS (1323)   SELLER'S COPY

RESPA SETTLEMENT STATEMENT (cont.)

U.S. DEPARTMENT OF HOUSING AND URBAN DEVELOPMENT
SETTLEMENT STATEMENT
PAGE 2

L. SETTLEMENT CHARGES	PAID FROM BORROWER'S FUNDS AT SETTLEMENT	PAID FROM SELLER'S FUNDS AT SETTLEMENT
700. TOTAL SALES/BROKER'S COMMISSION based on price $ 68,800.00 @ 6½ % =		
Division of commission (line 700) as follows:		
701. $ to		
702. $ 4,472.00 to Herman Holesley, selling/listing broker		
703. Commission paid at Settlement		
704.		
800. ITEMS PAYABLE IN CONNECTION WITH LOAN		
801. Loan Origination Fee %	$175.00	
802. Loan Discount %		
803. Appraisal Fee to		
804. Credit Report to		
805. Lender's Inspection Fee		
806. Mortgage Insurance Application Fee to		
807. Assumption Fee		
808.		
809.		
810.		
811.		
900. ITEMS REQUIRED BY LENDER TO BE PAID IN ADVANCE		
901. Interest from to @ $ /day		
902. Mortgage Insurance Premium for mo. to		
903. Hazard Insurance Premium for yrs. to		
904. 2 mo., 10 days yrs. to 9/1/78	20.03	
905.		
1000. RESERVES DEPOSITED WITH LENDER FOR		
1001. Hazard insurance mo. @ $ /mo.		
1002. Mortgage insurance mo. @ $ /mo.		
1003. City property taxes mo. @ $ /mo.		
1004. County property taxes mo. @ $ /mo.		
1005. Annual assessments mo. @ $ /mo.		
1006. mo. @ $ /mo.		
1007. mo. @ $ /mo.		
1008. mo. @ $ /mo.		
1100. TITLE CHARGES		
1101. Settlement or closing fee to		
1102. Abstract or title search to Wembley Title Co.		$185.00
1103. Title examination to		
1104. Title insurance binder to Wembley Title Co. — Lender's Policy	115.00	
1105. Document preparation to		
1106. Notary fees to E. P. White, Notary Public	3.00	
1107. Attorney's fees to		
(includes above items No.:)		
1108. Title insurance to		
(includes above items No.:)		
1109. Lender's coverage $		
1110. Owner's coverage $		
1111.		
1112.		
1113.		
1200. GOVERNMENT RECORDING AND TRANSFER CHARGES		
1201. Recording fees: Deed $ 6.00 ; Mortgage $; Releases $	6.00	
1202. City/county tax/stamps: Deed $; Mortgage $		
1203. State tax/stamps: Deed $ 241.50 ; Mortgage $		241.50
1204.		
1205.		
1300. ADDITIONAL SETTLEMENT CHARGES		
1301. Survey to Jiffy Surveyor's, Inc.	130.00	
1302. Pest inspection to		
1303.		
1304.		
1305.		
1400. TOTAL SETTLEMENT CHARGES (enter on lines 103 and 502, Sections J and K)	$449.03	$4,898.50

The Undersigned Acknowledges Receipt of This Settlement Statement and Agrees to the Correctness Thereof.

_____ _____
Buyer Seller

about the author

John W. Reilly is a graduate of Hamilton College and Fordham Law School in New York. A former U.S. Army legal officer, he is a member of the New York, California, Hawaii, and Federal Bars, as well as a REALTOR® and a licensed real estate broker in both Hawaii and California. Mr. Reilly is currently practicing law in Honolulu, Hawaii, with the law firm of Robbins, Reilly & Hisaka. He is a lecturer on real estate law and is a licensed real estate instructor for both salesperson and broker classes. Mr. Reilly has served as Educational Consultant to Hawaii's Real Estate Commission. He is co-author of the book **Questions and Answers to Help You Pass the Real Estate Exam.**